MW00635564

ALSO BY WILLIAM HOGELAND

The Whiskey Rebellion

Declaration

Autumn of the Black Snake

Founding Finance

Inventing American History

THE HAMILTON SCHEME

The *Hamilton* SCHEME

AN EPIC TALE OF
MONEY AND POWER IN
THE AMERICAN FOUNDING

WILLIAM HOGELAND

FARRAR, STRAUS AND GIROUX
NEW YORK

Farrar, Straus and Giroux
120 Broadway, New York 10271

Copyright © 2024 by William Hogeland
All rights reserved
Printed in the United States of America
First edition, 2024

ILLUSTRATION CREDITS
Page 11: Gouverneur Morris and Robert Morris. Charles Willson Peale, 1783.
(Philadelphia Academy of Fine Arts)
Page 67: Tarring and feathering a tax collector. Artist unknown.
(Glasshouse Images / Alamy Stock Photo)
Page 173: Alexander Hamilton monument at the U.S. Treasury Building. James Fraser,
dedicated 1923. (Dan Vera / Wikimedia Commons)
Page 249: *The End of Pain*. Anonymous, 1794 (from a print by Thomas Overton).
(Prints and Photographs Division, Library of Congress)
Page 329: TOP: Albert Gallatin. Rembrandt Peale, 1805.
(Wikimedia Commons)
BOTTOM: Albert Gallatin. Mathew Brady, date unknown.
(Prints and Photographs Division, Library of Congress)

Library of Congress Control Number: 2023050752
ISBN: 978-0-374-16783-7

Designed by Patrice Sheridan

Our books may be purchased in bulk for promotional, educational, or business use. Please
contact your local bookseller or the Macmillan Corporate and Premium Sales Department at
1-800-221-7945, extension 5442, or by email at MacmillanSpecialMarkets@macmillan.com.

www.fsgbooks.com
Follow us on social media at @fsgbooks

1 3 5 7 9 10 8 6 4 2

To Gail again

I must Create a System. or be enslav'd by another Mans
I will not Reason & Compare: my business is to Create

So Los, in fury & strength: in indignation and burning wrath
Shuddring the Spectre howls. his howlings terrify the night
—William Blake, *Jerusalem: The Emanation of
the Giant Albion*, Plate 10 (1804–1820)

CONTENTS

Introduction: Their Fights, Our Fights   3

PART I
THE HATCHING

1. Meet Alexander Hamilton   13
2. Founding Fatcat   29
3. Exchanging Eye-rolls   45
4. In Which We Are Introduced to the Public Debt
   of the United States   55

PART II
THE FIRST GREAT AMERICAN CLASS WAR

5. Man in Black   69
6. Nothing Commonsensical   90
7. Never Waste a Crisis   113
8. Peacetime   133
9. The New Jerusalem   139
10. Washington's County   148
11. To Annihilate All Debts   164

PART III

THE SCHEME AND THE SYSTEM

12. The Hamilton Constitution   175
13. Ta-da!   195
14. Breakup   211
15. Industry and Rye   227
16. Six Greek Columns and a Roman Pediment   238

PART IV

TO EXTREMES

17. The Husband Scheme   251
18. Reason   263
19. Enemies Everywhere   270
20. Too Big to Fail   279
21. Uprising, Crackdown   292
22. Biblical   308

PART V

A SCHEME SUPERSEDED?

23. Albert Optimiste   331
24. The Jesuit   344
25. Triumvirate   358
26. Albert Agonistes   374

Epilogue: From the Jackson Era to the New Deal
to the Great White Way   395

Notes   431
Sources   491
Acknowledgments   505
Index   507

THE HAMILTON SCHEME

INTRODUCTION

Their Fights, Our Fights

WE'RE OFTEN REMINDED THAT the American founders weren't larger than life. Remarkable, it more or less goes without saying, but real human beings, with flaws.

Yet Alexander Hamilton and others who drive this story's action do seem larger than life—at least to themselves. They feel charged with a duty to fulfill the highest purposes. Their success seems to them critical to national, global, in some cases even cosmic outcomes, their failures cataclysmic. They call their opponents not just flat-out wrong but toxic to the very meaning and purpose of America. Certain traits commonly accepted as flaws may be what make these people tick.

Put it another way: they're a lot of drama. Nearly everybody in the political conflicts that develop here will sooner or later stop pretending to persuade via reasoned debate. They'll resort to spin, propaganda, and the smoke-filled room, some to armed violence. This version of our national founding may feel strange. Or strangely familiar.

The word "scheme" is loaded, of course. In this book's title, it refers to Hamilton's vision of American economics and governance. "Scheme" can mean simply a plan or design, but it can also mean a secret plan or design for nefarious ends. It depends on where you sit. Where he and his allies sit, Hamilton is providing the United States with an expert method for driving the country forward as a rich, strong, imperial competitor. To his enemies—in conflict with one another, not just with him—his design is a system of political corruption that enriches government insiders at the expense of everybody else. Fiercely held differences over the purposes and effects of the Hamilton Scheme sparked the roughest disputes in the U.S. founding period.

Lately they've been renewed. Populism versus elitism. Democracy versus oligarchy. The working class versus the professional-managerial class. Wall Street versus Main Street. Party radicals versus party leadership. Wealth concentration, free markets, income inequality, monopoly power, corporate personhood. Bank crashes, financial crises, government bailouts, mass foreclosure. Inflation. Recession. Taxation. Regulation . . . Passionate political conflicts over the relationship between American government and American money first came to life in the founding fight over the Hamilton Scheme.

Strange, then, that the best-known presentations of Hamilton's career largely avoid the nuts-and-bolts reality of the machine he invented, his near-maniacally committed efforts on its behalf, and his enemies' equally over-the-top dedication to dismantling it or just smashing it to bits. The creative verve, cultural power, and sheer fun that exploded, in 2015, in *Hamilton: An American Musical* gained force from coming seemingly out of nowhere. But while unpredictable indeed, the explosion was ignited by a long chain of biographies, op-eds, documentaries, museum exhibits, and other efforts that, beginning in the 1990s, sought to rehabilitate Hamilton in the public mind by blurring out the very elements most critical to his and his enemies' and friends' fights, the real drama. Once called the forgotten founder, Hamilton remains forgotten because he's become so well remembered for traits, friendships and rivalries, a marriage, an extramarital affair, death by pistol shot. In aid of that kind of memory, highly knowledgeable biographers, opinion writers, and other public intellectuals across a liberal-conservative spectrum have bundled an impressive command of fact into what remains a pretty general, even vague sense of their man as a stone genius at public credit, central banking, and capital markets, hence an avatar of national greatness, even supposedly an enabler of American upward mobility, thus of American democracy itself. The effect has been to misconstrue the impulses that got Hamilton up in the morning and out the door and the action that made him so critically important to the nation's founding.

Consider the career of the Public Debt of the United States (in this book, the Debt becomes a kind of character, hence the title case). Quite easy to grasp in its broad outlines, of great excitement to Hamilton himself, the financial obligation spawned by the War of Independence has been so routinely mischaracterized in so many authoritative sources that attentive readers have a perfect right to their mistaken impressions of the Debt as, first, largely foreign, and then as a daunting challenge that Hamilton, as the nation's first treasury secretary, had to do his level best to face up to, wrestle down, beat into some kind of submission.

That's pretty much the opposite of how the homegrown prima donna called the Debt looked to Hamilton and how it operates in this story. The Debt's feeding and care and the loving encouragement of its stability play into the most heroic errand of all, to Hamilton: authoring great concentrations of monetary, industrial, and military power for the purpose of launching an American empire.

Given such aims, he's unafraid to go to adventurous lengths. Some of them may seem unsettling at best. Maybe it's really not so strange that the people who are the most eager to invoke Hamilton's legacy today—they include members of recent U.S. presidential administrations, across party lines—haven't wanted to get down in the trenches and find out what, to Hamilton, constituted the real drama.

In this book, a knockdown, drag-out fight, sometimes physical and even literally warlike, over founding the United States as a national economy becomes the prime mover in founding the national government of the United States as a whole. Here, that is, the Constitution of the United States is Hamiltonian.

Naturally, Hamilton takes the struggle for national government as a struggle for Hamiltonianism; people on his side have plenty of reason to see the Constitution as fundamentally dedicated to enabling the Hamilton Scheme. His enemies in the governing elite, facing a more challenging interpretive task, begin by condemning the Constitution for its manifest Hamiltonianism. Then they decide the Constitution's essence prohibits Hamiltonianism. From that reversal flows a host of problems we live with today.

Despite Hamilton's centrality to the big events in this story, though, there's no danger here of Dreaded Monocausality—that tendency to ascribe all effects, particularly in the founding of the United States, to a single impending force. This is a real fight. It comes replete with garbled inputs, near misses, accidents, unintended consequences, weird upendings. What professional historians call contingency can trigger political romp, sometimes mayhem, sometimes slapstick.

Nor is the story by any means Hamilton's alone. In the first act, the adventures of the flamboyant war profiteer Robert Morris, Hamilton's most important mentor—barely mentioned in Hamiltoniana, though without him the United States probably wouldn't exist—put together the entrepreneurial and governmental platform upon which Hamilton will build his system. In the third act, Albert Gallatin, a brilliant Genevan émigré, treasury secretary to two presidents, wears his abstemious soul down to a nub in the fetid summers of barely built Washington, D.C., trying to discover the antidote to Hamiltonianism. That task puts him and the country through some surprising changes.

Morris—Hamilton—Gallatin. That's an important part of the story, the official story of founding the economic United States. To all three, "the economic United States" was redundant; it just meant the United States.

Yet it's a guiding precept for this book that the official story can't be truly appreciated without bringing into focus the opposing story of an unofficial conflict to which Hamilton himself gave particularly intense attention. It's a conflict between the famous founders and a movement on behalf of ordinary American workers—on behalf, that is, of free labor, the group often called the white working class today.

That's right. As introduced in Chapter 5, a flat-out class war, sometimes involving actual warfare, drives the plot.

This organized mobilization of the working class, with deep roots in the colonial period, occurs in a barely-starting-to-industrialize United States and embraces subsistence farming families, tenant families working on manors and plantations, small artisans, urban mechanics, dockworkers, seamen, landless rural and urban day laborers, and a growing number of factory workers, mainly still women and children. It also embraces their allies at higher yet modest and precarious levels of farming and artisanship.

The movement was thus on behalf of the overwhelming majority of free people in the founding generation. Its nation-making advance against the small, upscale class represented by the famous founders and that class's nation-making reaction have been neglected in popular nonfiction about the founding. General readers of U.S. history have gotten used to defining the essential American conflict in terms of two opposed forces, broadly represented by Hamilton and Jefferson. Stressing this third force—"the Democracy," the founders sometimes called it, with a shudder—doesn't just complicate the famous Hamilton versus Jefferson binary. It raises questions about that binary's long-standing primacy in common understandings of U.S. founding politics.

Broad acceptance of a stark division between Hamilton and Jefferson as the primal national archetype has relied in part on associating Hamilton with opposition to the founding American institution of racial chattel slavery, and it's been easy to do far more than merely associate Jefferson with perpetuating the institution. While the two men's attitudes about and degrees of involvement with slavery do count as sharp differences between them, scholars' recent explorations of Hamilton's ownership of people may have begun dimming one of the brightest lines so often drawn between them.

Hamilton and Jefferson did also have divergent ideas of what American prosperity would look like. As we'll see, Hamilton's purpose was to consolidate public and private high finance, via a powerful administrative state, to promote national industrialization and make both manufactured and agricultural goods domestically, at a big scale, thus building out the United States as a global force; that's why his fans call him the inventor of modern America. Jefferson did prefer a less centralized and—at least at first, and philosophically, anyway—a more agrarian society, driven at scale in the South mainly by the forced labor of the enslaved, along with the labor of the tenanted and the hired, though Jefferson preferred to link his values philosophically with a smallholding yeomanry. Like Hamilton, Jefferson wanted to foster a major economy, but his interest, at least at first, was mainly in agricultural products.

So certain key differences between the Jeffersonian and Hamiltonian philosophies more or less hold up. Within the governing class of the founding generation, the differences became existential, zero sum. Hamilton and James Madison, especially, went through a painful breakup over the fundamental meaning of American government.

But take for a moment the point of view of the free-laboring many and the Hamilton and Jefferson groups, so deafening in mutual vituperation, collapse into a small hegemony forever bickering over how best to exploit the free majority, as well as the enslaved, and control and distribute the fruits of labor. As this story develops, activists for the majority—they have plenty of drama too—seek to smash the hegemony, seize the fruits, and distribute them differently. In the 1780s, violence ensues. Hamilton, mentored by Morris, births his scheme. In the 1790s and early 1800s, the conflict comes to a series of heads, with more violence. In that process, thanks in part to Madison and especially to Gallatin, relations between the Jeffersonians and the white working class grow fraught, in ways that have baffled our history and civics down through the centuries.

It should be noted that most of the action taken here by the force known as the Democracy isn't on behalf of what many people today—and the people excluded then—would call equality. The white working class is just that, white, and it's led—on the record, anyway—largely by men. While the actions the movement takes can be connected to related actions taken by black people, indigenous people, and women throughout what scholars call the Atlantic and Caribbean worlds, the labor leadership operating on the ground in this story seeks political and economic equality for white men, regardless of contributions to the movement by others. Most important to this story: disabling that particular effort is what most concerns Hamilton.

At moments, white agitators' and insurgents' attitudes toward enslaved black people can become complex, even mysterious, as can elite attitudes, in a few cases even truly abolitionist. But that's about as far as things get in this story. Regarding the Shawnee, Delaware, and other woodland nations, white people across all social classes are most often flat-out bloodthirsty, at best brutally patronizing. The eighteenth-century working-class movement and the political establishments it opposed had some things in common.

This book's reviving the day-to-day action of the Morris-Hamilton-Gallatin arc, in the process of restoring the all-important impact of the Democracy, represents an effort to achieve a narrative realism not often found in books on the national founding for general readers—and not always found in scholarship. The effort ushers in some characters rarely seen in the Hamilton context. Thomas Paine takes a tragicomic trip here; others, less well remembered, take trips too. A quiet math teacher named James Cannon organizes a working-class revolution that triggers American independence. An Irish émigré worker-turned-lawyer named William Findley assails Hamilton in the U.S. House of Representatives.

Regarding one character, a mild spoiler. Hamilton will try to get both Findley, his antagonist in the House of Representatives, and Gallatin, who will become a successor at the Treasury, arrested and hanged on trumped-up charges. Obviously he'll fail with Gallatin, but in fact he'll fail with both. Findley, born an outsider, lives to become the longest-serving member of the House and will die at home at the age of eighty.

The man Hamilton moves heaven and earth to arrest, and succeeds in arresting, is Herman Husband. Though reaching number one on the Washington administration's enemies list for 1794, his name will be forgotten almost as soon as the arrest is made. He was living high in the mountains. He was seeing visions. He was preaching them, writing them down, publishing them. Much later, without knowing anything about them, we would refract Herman Husband's visions into phenomena as varied as the Emancipation Proclamation, the Fourteenth Amendment, the Industrial Workers of the World, the Equal Rights Party, the New Deal, the Securities and Exchange Commission, the Bretton Woods System, the Progressive Party, *Griswold v. Connecticut*, the Great Society, Modern Monetary Theory. A pacifist and abolitionist, a dissenter in religion, an objector to the conquest of indigenous North Americans' land, a defender of liberty, a critic of the gold standard, a dreamer about birth control, Husband was so highly regarded by ordinary people in the remote western regions where he lived that he was elected to office multiple times and ranked by Hamilton as a danger above all others to the Hamilton Scheme.

Some just called him crazy. To make prophecies like Herman Husband's in the eighteenth century, maybe you'd have to be. This story isn't about people with flaws. It's about people who exercise creative power, for good or ill, depending on where you sit, in a struggle to create and build out the first iteration of American nationhood—and for all of them, wherever they sat, the struggle was quite explicitly over the relationship between money and political power. That's why the fight at the core of this origin story remains one of our most dire fights today.

PART I

THE HATCHING

1

MEET ALEXANDER HAMILTON

JOHN ADAMS ONCE MOCKED Alexander Hamilton's birthplace as a remote speck on the map. That was preposterous. When Hamilton was born on the island of Nevis, a continuous movement of cargo to and from Europe's ports made Britain's Caribbean colonies more important than all of the Atlantic thirteen put together. The roar of commerce enveloped him even before he could think.

He was born a colonial citizen of the British Empire because, just for one thing, the leaves of the tea plant fed caffeine addiction in Europe and its colonies. The British had introduced tea, indigenous to China, into India at great scale and made drinking it a British Isles ritual. The nice, hot cup might be enhanced by sweetening it with lumps cut from cones of sugar refined from a cane plant, indigenous to the eastern tropics, introduced by Europeans into the western tropics, and raised and processed in the Caribbean, also at great scale. Everywhere in the world Britain called British, the lumps were stirred into steaming cupfuls of tea, West meeting East, East meeting West, sip after sip soaking billions of taste buds in the global reach of empire.

So sugar moved a lot of people. Among them was James Hamilton, a younger son of a Scottish noble line. He was drawn to Britain's Leeward Islands colony in 1741 by the chance to get rich quick. It might have looked easy. Fashionable Europe was already reacting to tea's commonness by seeking new buzzes in bitter drinks that really wanted sugar: coffee from Java and Mocha, Caribbean cocoa. Then there was molasses, the Indies' black cane syrup beloved in the Atlantic colonies. From molasses came rum, distilled best in New England, doled out in rations to thousands of able seamen and hapless soldiers all over the world whose hard, often forced, labor, disciplined with punishment, transported and guarded the empire's cargoes, some of it human and subject to more awful punishment. British colonials in the Caribbean, making more and more money exporting more and more sugar, could afford to import more and more products of British industry, increasing the wealth of industrialists and stockholders who invested profits in the Bank of England, which extended the Crown loans that enabled the global expansion, and that was a boom. When James Hamilton arrived in St. Kitts, the bigger Leeward island, the colony was on its way to becoming Britain's richest. He was one of many hoping for a taste.

But he didn't get rich quick. He didn't get rich at all.

It wasn't as easy as it might have looked. This trade was by no means a free trade. Free labor didn't plant, chop, pack, and boil the cane. The boom depended on the arrival in the Caribbean of ships with lower holds crammed with men, women, and children taken from Africa, made chattel—enslaved for life, and heritable—and subjected first to the horrors of the ocean passage and then to the toil and brutality of the shimmering fields and the boiling facilities, raising and processing cane until they died. By the time James Hamilton began his career in the Leeward Islands, the original inhabitants were all but eradicated, only a tenth of the population was white, and the whole operation was peaking on a sugar high fueled by the toil of enslaved black people.

Capital wasn't free either. Enslaved people and some raw and semiprocessed product could be shipped directly from one colony to another, but much of the product had to go back to Britain to be processed or finished there, marked up and sold to middlemen, and then sold to retailers and wholesalers in markets at home and abroad. "Abroad" was key. A purpose of empire was to maintain far-flung markets for home goods. Because British colonials were by and large forced by law to sell to Britain and buy British, they had to import even products made from the raw materials they exported home. Growers, shippers, and investors had to analyze, comply with, and find ways of eluding various acts of Parliament that incentivized, disincentivized, and outright restricted commercial decision-making.

Sugar men faced existential challenges too. With its twelve-month growing season, the Caribbean might at first have seemed to Europeans a new Eden, but now it was a sweltering, always-on industrial hellscape, running on the mass violence inextricable from forced labor. Adventurers like James Hamilton naturally hoped to make their piles fast and get out. Cut off from home norms, pursuing a commerce grounded in brutality, many lived alcoholic, self-immolating lives and died young right there.

James Hamilton may not have had what it took to get rich in sugar. But he didn't get out and didn't die young. In St. Kitts, Rachel Hamilton gave birth to James Hamilton, Jr.

She and James Sr. weren't married, but people called her Mrs. Hamilton anyway. Out-of-wedlock families lived openly and without stigma, not only in the Caribbean but throughout the British colonies and in Britain itself. The family's real trouble was money. James held an administrative job at the St. Kitts port and maintained some solvency with handouts from relatives back home, but to dodge prosecution for debt, after their son was born the Hamiltons moved from St. Kitts to St. Eustatius, a Dutch colony. Then they moved back to the British colony, where Rachel had inherited a house in Charlestown, the port of the smaller Leeward island, Nevis, which had lagged behind the big island economically but was rebounding in the boom. There, in 1754, Rachel gave birth to Alexander Hamilton.

Soon the family moved back to St. Eustatius. Dutch and Danish empires placed fewer restrictions on trade; British subjects pursued commerce in those colonies, and in St. Eustatius the Hamiltons conformed to the hyper-British ways that British colonials far from home often adopted, worshipping in the Anglican Communion and socializing with other British colonials. Still their troubles mounted. James worked for a time as head clerk for a tobacco-shipping business but remained in financial straits. When the boys were seven and five, Rachel's wedlock husband sued her for divorce. She'd left him in the Dutch colony of St. Croix, with their son; the divorce complaint excoriated her sexual conduct. In 1765, the family moved yet again, this time to St. Croix, and from there, the boys' father took off.

In St. Croix, Rachel was known by her maiden name and sometimes by her former husband's. The Hamilton brothers entered adolescence having lost their father and becoming conscious of their mother's precarious situation, but she worked hard to prevent any descent into squalor and depression and did quite well, opening a store in Christiansted, the port town. The family home above the store, neatly kept, featured trappings of solidity: a feather bed, silver spoons, porcelain plates, books. Having inherited enslaved laborers, she hired out the adults and used their children as house servants for her sons. Rachel, it turned out, was the enterprising Hamilton parent.

But less than two years after James left, she died, and while the boys would have inherited her inventory, enslaved people, and household items, her former husband sued to disinherit her children by James Hamilton, calling them obscene. After a year of probate, their half brother by the former husband was awarded everything they would have had. Effectively parentless, the Hamilton boys were assigned a guardian, but he soon killed himself.

There was no choice. They had to get jobs.

James was apprenticed to a carpenter, by no means the worst business to get into, and Alexander did better. At fifteen, he moved in with a rich Christiansted merchant and was hired as a clerk for a firm owned by David Beekman and Nicholas Cruger, recently arrived from the up-and-coming port of the British Atlantic colony New York; both of their families had long been in the trade there. At Beekman and Cruger, the adolescent Alexander Hamilton began learning by doing.

Bright, diligent, placed in hour-by-hour intimacy with the merchant firms' pivotal place in a busy imperial endeavor, he did a lot, so he learned a lot. The British Crown entrusted overall operations to a few big companies, intermingling them with government by royal charters that made it a crime to compete with them. The most famous, the British East India Company, had staggering scope, with a monopoly on all imports from the East; by now that meant not only India but China too. A group of London merchants had a similar monopoly on all imports from the Caribbean.

Yet as Hamilton quickly grasped, the multitude of smaller firms like Beekman and Cruger, operating as agents for the big monopolies and one another, conducted the day-to-day buying and selling, the carrying and warehousing, the advertising and marketing, the borrowing and lending that enabled the imperial giant to import and export Caribbean sugar, tobacco, and coffee; Indian raw cotton and cotton textiles, opium, and tea; Chinese tea, rice, silk, and porcelain; Atlantic fur, lumber, rice, indigo, tobacco, wheat, and rum; and African people. From Christiansted to Boston, from Bristol to Delhi, on wharves and at auctions, in taverns, coffeehouses, warehouses, and countinghouses, the merchants and their employees made promises and extended credit, issued and took out insurance policies, gave breaks to steady customers, charged premiums to the less trustworthy, reinvested profits big or small, and sustained losses ranging from the manageable to the disastrous. Merchants had to be wary yet form tight alliances, cautious yet bold at the right moment. They had to be creative yet punctilious.

Hamilton showed the qualities necessary for success in the trade. He crossed every *t* and dotted every *i* in the never-ending flurry of contracts, manifests, invoices, and bills of lading that drove the business. By the dawn of the 1770s he'd become a surprisingly clear commercial thinker, even a demanding boss in the making. At seventeen, left briefly in charge of the shop, he strode right into the supervisory mode that would mark his later career, writing a stern letter to a ship's captain and advising his bosses' partners on measures he deemed indispensable to ensuring the safety of cargo. If the self-confidence was a bit startling, the judgment was good.

But while his job was demanding, its day-to-day limitations insulted his dreams. Restless, a close reader of classics and military strategy and a writer of poetry, young Hamilton pined for romance and action and especially for the glory to be gained in armed combat. Rising to merchant status wouldn't have been impossible. His potential seemed to him and others to be of another order.

And so a path to more exciting things was rolled out for him. His bosses and other adults saw the clerk as a bright and capable young man likely to benefit from the formal education not easily gained amid the Caribbean's all-work harshness. While the best education might be had in Britain, Beekman and Cruger were well-connected in their native city, and in the course of business Hamilton had gotten to know some New York merchants. A fund was started to send him to college there. In 1774, he sailed for Boston to travel to New Jersey and ultimately New York.

He wouldn't be a merchant. But it was the merchants who made him, and by the time he went in search of higher learning, he'd already had his hands deep in the guts of a commerce fueled by government and operating on the grandest scale. He would always say that his time at Beekman and Cruger gave him the most useful part of his education.

Hamilton fit right into New York and started moving up fast. His gifts were evident, his ambition and focus intense, and the barriers, for the likes of him, low. Caribbean origins only meant he'd come from one of the trade's hottest spots to a hustling competitor port. His out-of-wedlock birth, if known or rumored, posed no impediment to progress in the colonial American elite, which had seen that before. In the Dutch and Danish colonies, he'd been living as a kind of immigrant; now this son of a British subject, born in a British colony, of noble lineage at that, was back in a British colony, as much a citizen of empire as anybody else in town and, as a gentleman with the wherewithal to go to school and spend freely, living a far easier life than the overwhelming majority of those born there.

He was a bit too old to prep for college. Already nothing if not de- cisive, he made that problem go away by changing his birthdate to 1757, shedding three of his twenty years and becoming something of a wunderkind. In 1774, he entered New York's King's College. The institution was governed by the city's biggest operators in sugar, tobacco, and slavery. Good-looking and brimming with ambition and self-confidence, he naturally attracted well-connected friends there.

Then came a great stroke of luck. Thirteen of Britain's Atlantic colonies were joining in a confrontation with the mother country. At issue were parliamentary restrictions on the colonies' trade, and many of the New York merchants, Hamilton's kind of people, were joining in the resistance. Jumping on the emerging crisis with all of his pent-up desire for adventure, Hamilton began by publishing some political pamphlets. They showed notable facility in the established modes of orotundity and snark, and his passing for only eighteen made the mastery all the more impressive.

Far more important for his future, his martial dreams came true. With classmates, he crammed the basics of soldiery and artillery and formed a volunteer drill company. New York, improvising wildly under the pressure of a probable British invasion, issued him a captain's commission for an artillery company, and in July 1776, even as American independence was adopted in Philadelphia, by a delegated body calling itself the Continental Congress, making Hamilton's home no longer a province but an independent state, the British invaded. New York City was where they landed.

The opportunity was priceless. Hamilton had no military experience. Neither did many of the other lower officers in the state's forces. Even many high officers in what was known as the Continental Army were just armchair strategists playing catch-up against one of the most fearsome military machines ever. Things didn't go well for the United States, but they went well for Hamilton. His unit took a minor part in the American defeat in the Battle of New York and then, under General George Washington, the Continental Army's commander, a more important part in the more disastrous defeat at Harlem Heights. With Washington's troops fleeing across New Jersey, the British occupied New York City.

The general in retreat was by no means the august figure he would soon become. A big Virginia operator in the slavery-driven production of agricultural product for the imperial trade, George Washington was first and foremost a politically well-connected businessman. He'd been early to identify and relentless in trying to monopolize a vast financial speculation in white development of the fertile woodlands west of the Blue Ridge Mountain, lands used and inhabited by Shawnee, Miami, Delaware, and other nations. He'd always had military leanings; he'd coveted a commission as a British army officer. But when Britain started restricting Americans' freelance efforts to buy the western nations' territory, Washington joined the interstate resistance to British policies in America.

His military experience was thus strictly limited. In 1754, having led a militia to the Ohio headwaters to scare the French out of the region, the young Washington had become notorious in Britain for a series of blunders that started the global conflict known as the Seven Years' War, the first true world war. During that war, also near the Ohio headwaters, he led troops in the retreat of the British general Edward Braddock, routed by the French and Shawnee. Washington was commanding the Continental Army now thanks mainly to authoritative physical presence in uniform, a notable regard for his own integrity, and the lack of any feasible alternative. Some of the British officers disdained him as a mere Virginia "land-jobber"—a hustler in real estate—whose leadership pretensions were absurd. And by late 1776, the general's prospects against the British army did look grim.

After the flight from New York across New Jersey, Hamilton got his biggest break yet when Washington, headquartered at Morristown, invited him to serve on his staff. Hamilton joined the Continental Army in March of 1777 with the rank of lieutenant colonel and got busy doing what he knew how to do. To military administration, he brought the attention to detail, the powers of analysis, and the comfort with supervising others that he'd learned so young at Beekman and Cruger. Over the next three years, as the army began to have success in the field, Washington came to depend on Hamilton as an administrative right hand. If the young man wasn't the staff's de facto chief, he was unabashed about acting like it.

In April 1780, he hit another benchmark of manly achievement: getting engaged to marry up. If the best part of Hamilton's education came at Beekman and Cruger, his entry into New York's upper class, via engagement to Elizabeth Schuyler, honed that education to exciting new purposes.

His in-laws-to-be, Philip and Catherine Van Rensselaer Schuyler, came from old colonial families in the Dutch-descended landlord class of New York's Hudson Valley, where millions of acres had long produced tobacco and grain for the imperial trade. The Schuyler couple was fabulously rich and getting richer; they were also showy. Big agriculture for export involved fierce competition. Displaying success was critical to maintaining success. Landlords lived large and pursued dynasty. Schuylers and Van Rensselaers had been intermarrying for years.

Still, like his son-in-law-to-be, Philip Schuyler had married notably well. When he and Catherine began courting, Philip was more or less comfortably landed, with a couple of thousand acres; her family had some 150,000 and would end up with about a million. It was an abrupt lift for his fortunes when, one day, serving in western New York in the Seven Years' War, he was ordered home on a leave he hadn't applied for and then ordered, on arrival, by Catherine's father, to prepare for marriage. Five months after their wedding, she bore their first child.

The couple built a mansion in Albany. The house featured not only the biggest room in the city but also the second-biggest, with wallpaper in the entrance hall imported from England and costing thirteen times the average annual rent paid by the tenant families who labored on the Schuylers' great acreages. The grounds had formal gardens. The fields rolled down to the Hudson. There were Madeira wines, fine clothing, beautiful color schemes, hundreds of books. There were enslaved black people in bright livery: the Schulyers were among the biggest enslavers in Albany, and Elizabeth would bring slaves to her marriage. Hamilton was already starting to have big ideas about the future of an independent

United States that would make him an opponent of the institution. Later, he would join an anti-slavery organization. But he owned and dealt in people too.

By the time Hamilton began moving in their orbit and noting the priorities of their type, the Schuylers had become at least as relentless as George Washington and everybody else in the colonial, now revolutionary, elite in pursuing and defending personal interests. That quality informed ideas that Hamilton was quickly developing about the country as a whole.

The relentlessness could amount to ruthlessness. When the Schuylers' second son, John, sexually assaulted a woman named Mary Carpenter, Philip paid her a lifetime annuity on condition she decline to testify, relocate to Quebec, and never come back. In the 1760s and '70s, when new British laws started giving New York's tenant farmers protections from abuses by judges appointed by the landlords, Schuyler joined others throughout the colonies in protesting what they called illegal mother-country interference in American commerce. As those tensions mounted toward civil war, many New York tenants and other poorer people saw a better bet in sticking with the British than with their landlords. Schuyler built spy networks with sophisticated ciphering systems, identified loyalists and defectors, drew up lists, and started surveilling, arresting, and interrogating them. When civil war became the War of Independence, he got inside, no-bid supply deals, submitting to the Continental Army after-the-fact invoices for gigantic purchases he'd made, as a general, of his own oysters and ferry services.

Ruthlessness extended to military strategy. As power broker for the colony, Schuyler had gained the trust of the Six Nations of the Iroquois as a good-faith negotiator. In 1779, he proposed to Washington a total-war program for burning the towns and food supplies of the five British-allied Iroquois nations, advising Washington that once the nations had gathered their whole strength for attack, their villages would "be left with only their old men, women and children . . . Should we be so fortunate as to take a considerable number of the women and children of the Indians, I conceive that we should then have the means of preventing them hereafter from acting hostilely against us." Washington took the advice, ordering "the total destruction and devastation of their settlements and the capture of as many prisoners of every age and sex as possible."

Both men were thinking about victory in the war—and about their long game in land speculation. Burned out, the enemy's soil would have a deeply depressed value. Claimed personally by men who had officially ordered it destroyed and depopulated, it would recover naturally over time and gain high value in what would become, with victory in the war, a land-investment bubble. When Elizabeth Schuyler accepted Alexander Hamilton's proposal, her father was one of the richest, wiliest, and most powerful and aggressive men in revolutionary New York, with much to show the younger man about the ways of the class he typified.

Thus affianced, Hamilton began attracting the approval of New York high society in general. Handsome and unusually trim, if not tall, with a somewhat swashbuckling air and in good moods a charmer, he was known as a fluid and creative problem-solver who could accommodate rafts of facts, break down intricate concepts, turn data to persuasive purposes, cross every *t*, dot every *i*. Mental agility and punctiliousness went hand in hand with impatience with others not so gifted, even when they agreed with him, and pretty frank disdain for anyone who disagreed with or tried to obstruct him.

Personal touchiness was common, even stylish, in men of his type. Yet Hamilton seemed at once gifted and cursed with an unusually stubborn confidence in the rightness of his own judgment and the necessity of being free to act on it. Arrogance and defensiveness were perhaps to be expected in one wafted so quickly and easily up from clerkdom, but while he would get better at the politics—somewhat, sometimes—he wouldn't age out of the attitude.

It worried his father-in-law. Nobody appreciated better than Schuyler the importance of curating friendly connections with the right people. Attitude had begun to roil Hamilton's relationship with the most important connection of all, Washington, by now the one person in the United States it might have seemed fatally foolish to offend. Hamilton evinced no concern about being at odds with his mighty boss. Overwhelmingly concerned, like others of his kind, with his own honor, the lieutenant colonel considered it necessary to his honor to command troops in the field. The general, overwhelmingly concerned with winning the war, took no interest in what people under him considered necessary to their honor. Hamilton had gone out of his way to make himself an indispensable administrator. Field command would take him away from the staff. He couldn't be spared. Discussion over.

Or so the general might have thought. The frustrated subordinate kept bringing it up.

Hamilton faced frustration on another front too. He'd begun turning his early knack for commerce and operations into a deep self-education in the British banking system and the advanced work of European economists and finance officials. He didn't just understand these matters. He was developing a fully informed point of view on the intricate relationships between government and money and imagining a thrilling future for the United States of America.

He was excited by Enlightenment-inspired writings on economics by the Scottish philosopher David Hume. He was in awe of Robert Walpole, prime minister of Britain from 1721 to 1742, who had established borrowing by the Crown as a means of financing war and other expensive imperial projects.

But he was especially taken by the work of Jacques Necker, a Swiss banker, serving in the 1780s as director general of Louis XVI's Royal Treasury of France. Necker not only gave detailed, technical explanations of the fiscal, finance, and banking policies that make great nations, but also painted a gripping picture of the crusading finance minister, to Necker the most important person in any government, the true author of national greatness. Combining selfless dedication to country with the special fitness that makes contravening his will tantamount to a crime against nature, Necker's finance hero achieves secular immortality, a kind of godhood. Hamilton, devouring both the technicalities and the heroism, was coming up with a national idea of America at once so arcane and so vaulting that few around him could grasp it well enough to encourage or criticize it.

He'd become, for one thing, a confirmed Continentalist. In that, he was by no means alone. Washington and Schuyler were Continentalists. So were other influential men, from various states. The term referred to a desire for consolidation of American government. The Continentalists believed there was no happy future for an independent United States where each state government continued to enjoy sole lawmaking power over its citizens and no single government had the power to legislate for all of the people throughout all of the states on any matter. To their ongoing frustration, the Continental Congress was required to operate on the basis of its mutually agreed-on Articles of Confederation, which, though they wouldn't be finally signed until 1781, made the Congress only that, a congress, meaning a delegated meeting of sovereign entities, confederated in this case for fighting a war and totally dependent on its member states. Delegates to the Congress represented the separate governments that sent them. They debated and passed measures to organize those governments in the collaborative operations of war and related diplomacy. Hence the body's other name, from "confederation": "the federal government."

The Articles thus gave the Congress no lawmaking power, no power to govern citizens. Only the separate states' representative legislatures, elected by qualified voters, could do that. Even when the Congress passed uniform, countrywide measures in support of the war, it had to frame those measures as instructions to the states—requests, in practice, since it had no realistic power to compel them—to pass the laws separately, in each of thirteen legislatures, and then enforce them, each state in its own way. A mess in practice, this strict limitation on the Congress's reach undermined the war effort, the Continentalists believed, and boded ill for the future of the country.

They wanted a radical change: power in the Congress to pass its own laws, effective countrywide, and to enforce those laws directly on the citizenry throughout the states. They wanted the United States to have, that is, a national government. Without such an overhaul, they believed, the country faced what Hamilton would soon be calling a catastrophe: likely defeat in the war or, with victory, a failure of unity among the states.

The Continentalists' desire to gain the Congress lawmaking power of a national kind faced opposition both in the Congress and in the state legislatures. Strict limitations on the Congress's power were not only good, in the view of many powerful American leaders, but absolutely critical. Britain had encroached unconstitutionally on the states' sovereign lawmaking powers. The war was being fought, according to State Sovereigntists, to rescue those very powers; by no means should the Congress be allowed to encroach on them. The State Sovereigntists envisioned their own looming catastrophe—a catastrophe for liberty—ensuing from any expansion of federal power, and they included a lot of influential men: Elbridge Gerry of Massachusetts, Patrick Henry and Richard Henry Lee of Virginia, David Howell of Rhode Island, George Clinton of New York, others.

A fundamental conflict thus prevailed, within the American governing elite, over the very purpose of the War of Independence and the future of the United States. But Hamilton's frustration wasn't only with his State Sovereigntist opponents, though he did consider them small-minded, ignorant, knee-jerk, backward-looking.

Elder Continentalists frustrated him too. They moved incrementally, diplomatically, even timidly. Individually, they remained intensely committed to their own personal and dynastic gain, as did the State Sovereigntists. Such was the nature, Hamilton was learning, of the revolutionary elite. Yet most Continentalists were missing the nation-making capabilities that their own drive to accumulate wealth pointed to.

Evidently it was up to him to put them in the picture. Beginning in 1779, and then with serious concentration in September 1780, stationed with Washington in New Jersey, Hamilton sat with his books and wrote, and soon here it all was, a comprehensive, detailed scheme for redesigning government in America, taking key powers away from the states and giving the Congress exclusive legislative control, throughout the country, over the big three areas of public power: trade, war, and finance, that last term embracing everything money-related: banking, coining, printing currency, taxing. Hamilton intended the plan to start the Congress on the path to becoming a national government fostering commercial prosperity.

By now he'd gotten the generous attention of some big men. The brash manner might raise eyebrows, but Hamilton could be charming, and he was both Schuyler-connected and impressive in his own right. A well-regarded New York delegate to the Congress, James Duane, had expressed interest in the young man's views. Hamilton sent Duane his scheme and waited for him to present it to the Congress, the Continentalists to push it, and the body to adopt it in full, altering in one fell swoop the basis of government in America.

James Duane was a veteran politician. He was looking at a document in which a young general staffer, on his own and in his spare time, had worked up a program for throwing away the whole agreed-upon wartime political structure of the country and giving the Congress, overnight, legislative power over citizens throughout the states. The tone seemed to reflect preemptive scorn for any dissent, even for any input. It was as if in the face of such dazzling technical perfection, all opposition must simply collapse.

Duane cautioned Hamilton politely that, for the moment anyway, his ideas were totally infeasible.

Frustrated again, Hamilton had reason to think he'd been quite politic with Duane. His real plans for the country were even more extensive than what he'd written. He wanted to extinguish the states as governments altogether. He envisioned a single American government—like Britain's, to him the best in the world—where the states might become regional departments of a national government, might even have some delegated powers for efficient administration, but would by no means retain any independent lawmaking power. Even Hamilton had known not to bring that idea up, even to a Continentalist ally like Duane.

Then the fraying bond with Washington snapped. One day at headquarters, the general passed Hamilton on the stairs and said he needed to speak to him. Hamilton said he'd be right up, continued downstairs, delivered a note, and spoke with a fellow staffer. When he did go up, Washington met him at the top of the stairs and accused him, in front of others, of disrespect. Hamilton replied that if Washington really felt that way, they must part. Washington said fine. Hamilton said fine. Both stalked off. When the general sent Hamilton a message apologizing for his temper and asking Hamilton to come speak to him, Hamilton sent back a message to say that he saw no purpose in such a conversation.

That was according to Hamilton, narrating the exchange to Schuyler with a mixture of aggrievement and preening. Working for the so-called great man had been horrible, Hamilton confided: the general always wanted greater personal closeness than he did; he'd had to take steps to keep their relationship military and professional. Anyway, he told Schuyler, Washington's generalship wasn't as great as everybody had recently started saying it was. Schuyler was unaware that his son-in-law had once disparaged his generalship too, in just such terms. He advised Hamilton to patch things up with Washington and stay on the staff, but Hamilton was in no mood to be advised. He quit. Remaining on active duty, looking out for a more fulfilling assignment, he kept wheedling an increasingly irritated Washington, by letter, at length, and with attitude, for field command.

His great goal remained: rescue the United States from imminent catastrophe. To reach that goal, he would need a Continentalist ally more simpatico than George Washington, bolder than James Duane, more imaginative than Philip Schuyler.

In the spring of 1781, he found him. And then some. Robert Morris, the most powerful American revolutionary—to his contemporaries, the most controversial—would become Hamilton's only mentor in developing a scheme for national greatness and taking on all comers to bring it about. Without Morris, both Alexander Hamilton and the United States of America might have barely rated a footnote.

2

FOUNDING FATCAT

GREGARIOUS, FABULOUSLY CORPULENT, REPUTEDLY the richest man in English-speaking North America, Robert Morris was a lavish host and an inveterate risk-taker. Though a reluctant revolutionary at first, by the time he and Hamilton picked each other out of the Continentalist crowd and began a collaboration that would forever change the United States, Morris was devoting every bit of his prodigious wealth and enthusiasm to the war effort, and he held immense sway over the Congress.

He also faced powerful opposition, both in the Congress and in his home state, Pennsylvania. He needed good help.

Morris's rise to power involved a series of untoward events. He was born in 1734, in the port city of Liverpool, England, where his father, also Robert Morris, worked as a clerk and then as a broker for a shipping company. When the London merchants, advantaged by operating at the seat of imperial power, received their famous Crown monopoly on exporting goods from the Caribbean, the Liverpool merchants showed their competitive ingenuity, developing direct connections to West Africa and more or less inventing the transatlantic triangular trade, with its infamous middle passage for transporting a violated human cargo. Characteristically Liverpudlian, the elder Robert Morris wanted to quit working for the shipping company, open his own shop, and start innovating for his own competitive advantage.

He wasn't married to his son's mother, and she soon left the family for points unknown—young Robert wouldn't remember her—and the father left too, crossing the Atlantic to the Maryland shore for new opportunities and leaving his son to be cared for by the maternal grandmother. European addiction to nicotine had made tobacco the Atlantic colonies' most lucrative export. The elder Morris went into tobacco shipping, and when young Robert turned thirteen, his father sent for him. The son arrived in Maryland in 1747, with the father a success now, an innovator not just in tobacco but in trade of many kinds, including the trade in people. He had a big house, well-staffed by slaves, on the main street of Oxford, a small Chesapeake Bay port town.

Young Robert was privately tutored, mainly in math. Every bit as eager for commerce as his father, he showed himself even more talented. Oxford was clearly too small for him, so his father sent him, at fifteen, to Philadelphia, where he was taken on as an apprentice to the shipping and trading firm of Charles Willing.

For anybody in the British Atlantic colonies with the bounding commercial ambitions of young Robert Morris, Philadelphia was the place to be. Sheltered well upriver from Delaware Bay, the port was the colonies' busiest. When Morris arrived, two miles of more than sixty piers were a scene of what would have looked like sheer chaos to anyone outside the trade. Ships loaded and unloaded, casting off and tying up amid noises and smells emitted by horses, mules, drivers, tarmakers, ropemakers, wagonmasters, sailors, stevedores, and other menial laborers free, indentured, and enslaved. Shouting and chat came in every English dialect, and in German.

The merchants themselves were right down in the middle of it. Shedding their coats, they joined in rolling barrels to and from vessels, wagons, warehouses. They inspected everything from manifests to seaworthiness. They hectored captains on the exact and proper routes. In dockside countinghouses they put in long days of paperwork and dealmaking. In smoky taverns and coffeehouses they met with middlemen, partners, and competitors and ended long nights drinking the French brandy they imported and singing boisterous songs and tear-jerking ballads.

The city that ran briefly westward from that riverside bustle was laid out on a grid of broad streets, originally drawn by the city's Quaker founder William Penn, at once a utopian and, like many Quakers of the seventeenth century, a slaveholder. By the 1750s, when Morris came to know it, Philadelphia was by no means either utopian or fully Quaker, and while many Quakers now rejected the institution of slavery on moral grounds, the city still numbered many enslaved Africans. Because most of the city's slaveholders held only one or two people, daily life could seem less engaged in the practice than the towns and plantations of the southern Atlantic and Caribbean colonies—less even than Delaware, or New York. But slavery contributed mightily to Philadelphia's prosperity. Many of the merchants eagerly took part in both the Atlantic slave trade and the trade within the colonies, and a slave auction went on at the London Coffee House, at the corner of Front and High Streets. Free-laboring families too, black and white, put in long days of hard physical work and often suffered fetid, miserable living and employment conditions.

Well-off Philadelphians considered their city the second most sophisticated in the empire. Their houses were elegant and restrained, made of brick, designed in the symmetrical Georgian style. Pennsylvania's State House, on the western outskirts, was super-symmetrical, with a sky-piercing bell tower ornamented with clocks, the most substantial and graceful public building in British America. Intellectual institutions included the Library Company of Philadelphia and the American Philosophical Society Held at Philadelphia for Promoting Useful Knowledge. Both were founded by Benjamin Franklin, famous in Europe for scientific discovery, who had risen from apprenticeship and artisanship to become one of the city's richest citizens. There were bookstores, print shops, newspapers. Upscale dining clubs did good works. West of town, on the Schuylkill River, an upscale fishing club offered leisure to the well-off.

Just as the young Hamilton would, young Morris took on big responsibilities at an early age. Unlike Hamilton, Morris found himself exactly where he wanted to be. The Willing firm had its own wharf and ships and a dockside warehouse, store, and countinghouse, and Morris relished everything about the trade. At first he only stocked the warehouse and took inventory, but soon he was spending long days and nights at the countinghouse, bent over a desk reading and writing ledgers, lists, orders, and letters. Soon he took a ship to the Caribbean, where in the suffocating heat he stood on the wharves and oversaw sales and purchases of raw and finished products and of black people.

Back at his desk in Philadelphia, he sorted out empires' and companies' various exchange rates for paper currencies and notes against real money, known to merchants as "hard money": gold and silver coins, which, since the Atlantic colonies had no precious metals, came from France, Portugal, and Spain. The Spanish silver dollar, favored in the Atlantic colonies and indeed around the world, had a highly recognizable design and was "milled" to make its edge ridged, obstructing forgery and any shaving of slivers. It could be cut and used in pieces known as "bits," legally up to eight of them; its silver weight was highly consistent.

But hard money could become scarce and was always heavy to carry in purses, crates, bags. And it had to be vigilantly protected. To ease trade, merchant firms, banks, and colonial and imperial governments issued various paper instruments, and Morris became his firm's expert in balancing their values in relation both to metal and to one another. He had the discipline and the math brain.

For him, though, the real thrill lay in taking big risks. So rife with uncertainty was the trade that merchants were really professional gamblers, living and dying on their bets. The men pacing around wharves shouting orders didn't really have much control or even much good information. Ships' captains took unapproved routes, and even well-piloted ships could sink, sending cargoes and gold and silver to the bottom. Pirates, freelancing or working for competing empires, waylaid captains, carried off everything of value, and burned or took the vessels. Letters and accounts might travel more quickly than the product itself, but never quickly enough. Unknown agents might control irresistibly attractive opportunities and turn treacherous. Creditors with no pity for the daily ups and downs banged ceaselessly on home and office doors.

So the trade tended to select for a certain personality type. You couldn't afford to show fear.

Robert Morris seemed to not even know fear. In his quest to scoop up advantage for the company by dominating markets, he showed not tolerance for risk but delight in it. Early in his time with Willing, having learned from one of his personal contacts about a rise in flour prices in foreign markets, he decided—on his own, the boss was away—to bet a lot of the firm's ready cash in buying up all local flour, thus cutting out competitors and monopolizing the price advantage for Willing. It paid off. The key to commercial domination was inside intelligence, developed via personal relationships, and in a gregarious business, Morris soon became the most gregarious in the business, with loyal contacts at every level of the trade and in every part of the empire where the firm had interests. A fount of new ideas, he made skirting disaster in pursuit of monopoly his specialty.

In 1754, he became a partner in the firm, henceforth known as Willing and Morris, and in twenty ensuing years of ceaseless hustle, Morris got the company so far ahead of its competitors that it became the most successful merchant firm in Britain's Atlantic colonies, owning nine ships and holding shares in dozens of others. He married Mary White, a daughter of one of Philadelphia's wealthiest, best-respected Anglican families. The Morrises had an elegant town house and a summer mansion and farm up the Schuylkill, with beautiful gardens and groves, both households well-staffed by slaves; they would soon buy yet another, even better summer place, near the falls of the Delaware River, and name it Summerseat.

Mixing business with pleasure amplified both. Known as a witty and generous entertainer, a conspicuous consumer and provider of all that he imported, Morris was friends with Benjamin Franklin and the other city leaders. Nobody in North America had better reason for satisfaction with the basic structure of the imperial trade.

So he found himself in an awkward position when, in the 1760s and the early '70s, tension and then crisis arose between the North American colonies and the mother country. The issues devolved hardest on his own profession—acts of Parliament were reining in and drawing new revenue from the American colonies' commerce—but Morris wasn't political. Though ruthless in seeking commercial dominance, he was at heart a clubman, a schmoozer. He'd never even stood for elective office. In this rising crisis, he preferred to stick to business.

But he soon found that protests against the Stamp Act and other parliamentary obstructions of trade were bringing together the commercial leaders of all the port cities, from Boston to New York, from Philadelphia to Charleston. If only as a clubman, a schmoozer, Morris wouldn't have wanted to oppose any mood prevailing in his profession. Too, he was committed to Pennsylvania's interests, and possibly because of his British origins, he looked beyond his own locale: when most colonists called their colony their country, he was calling himself an American.

Then the Atlantic colonies violated, as a group, a fundamental rule of the imperial system. To punish Parliament for its innovations, they refused to serve as a captive market for British products and collectively stopped importing British goods. Under the rules of the trade, there was no legal way to buy most goods from other countries, so this boycott involved serious privation for America, and Morris considered it at least as much of a pain as the restrictions it protested.

Still, he joined his fellow merchants up and down the coast in ceasing to import. He made his first foray into office-holding, serving on the ad hoc, extralegal committees in Philadelphia that enforced the nonimportation agreement. When the Continental Congress first convened, in the fall of 1774, its wealth and strategic location made Philadelphia a natural meeting place. The most influential planters and merchants came to town as delegates sent by their colonial legislatures. Robert Morris wasn't about to be left out of that.

The first Congress took over Carpenters' Hall, the artisans' headquarters on Chestnut Street, beautifully engineered but not large; when the body reconvened in the spring of 1775, it borrowed the Pennsylvania assembly's tall-windowed, light-filled room on the ground floor of the most impressive public building in British America, on the outskirts of the city farther west on Chestnut: the Pennsylvania State House. Though high-ceilinged, the space was intimate, even domestic, a true political meeting room with desks and chairs and no public galleries. Not big enough to accommodate all of the states' attendees without some closeness, the room was pungently imbued with human sweat fumes in summer, expectorations in winter, constant tobacco consumption, mainly by nose, and foul moods, with causes ranging from perennial suffering of the ill and otherwise afflicted men present to the social and intellectual challenges that came from having to push full-on attacks through labyrinthine channels of politeness. Still, some men, though forever emphasizing an onerous obligation to duty, seemed to live for the game.

Morris brought to the game his characteristic gregariousness, serving both as a delegate to the Congress from the host province and as a host of the delegates, treating them to feasts at his town house. He hit it off especially well with another dedicated pursuer of commercial advantage, George Washington, then serving as a delegate from Virginia.

But while Washington and his cadre in Virginia government were taking an increasingly uncompromising position regarding American rights, Morris still hoped for moderation. What he wanted out of the meetings of the Congress, out of the protests and boycotts—what he wanted even out of a shooting war between British troops and local militias, which broke out in Lexington and Concord, Massachusetts, in April 1775—was to bring the home government to its senses, arrive at a negotiated reconciliation, reinstate imperial neglect of the Atlantic colonies, and go on getting rich.

In taking this reconciliationist position Morris was by no means alone. John Dickinson, the most powerful politician in all-powerful Pennsylvania, led the protests and the boycotts, pursued expulsion of loyalists, and countenanced outright warfare against British troops, yet Dickinson too believed that declaring the colonies independent would represent a violation of the framework of British rights that the colonists were fighting to rectify. Dickinson, Morris, and others also feared that independence might threaten America's social and economic hierarchies. Unsettling working-class agitation was already being felt in the host state itself.

Yet the crisis kept mounting, so Morris kept doing what he'd always been good at: innovating for advantage. After Lexington and Concord, a British invasion looked likely. Parliament had banned exports of military supplies to North America. There was a desperate need for gunpowder for the military defense of Pennsylvania in the event of invasion. Morris, as usual, saw opportunity.

He placed a network of top merchants under him and invented a whole new form of the trade. Trashing the long-standing British restrictions against direct American commerce with other empires, he commissioned dozens of ships, loaded them with American product, and put them out to sea, bound for European ports to trade for arms. This high-risk, illegal operation was just his sort of thing. He created fake companies and forged manifests to bamboozle British customs at European ports. He chose unlikely routes in hopes of avoiding capture by sea patrols. Key to success were the long odds against perfect British enforcement and his own deep experience in exchanging a lot of small losses for a few big gains. Many of his ships were captured and lost.

But many brought back gunpowder and other military supplies, bought in the nations, especially France, that competed with Britain. Morris's success as an illegal arms dealer changed the game for the military defense of his city and province.

It also changed the game for his commercial operations. By breaking imperial trade restrictions, he unleashed something new. He'd always sought market dominance. Parliament had violated its own authority; no government had any legitimate power to restrict his efforts. Trade, Morris now insisted, should be "as free as the air." The Congress, as desperate for gunpowder as Pennsylvania, came to him, and soon wagonloads of his European ammunition were rolling into New York and New Jersey, where the Continental Army, commanded by his friend Washington, was readying itself for the possible British invasion. On the strength of those orders, Morris bought new ships, hired new captains, and quickly built out his merchant network into a veritable arms-dealing fleet.

American merchants in other port cities smuggled arms from Europe too. Nobody came close to the sheer volume of Morris's operation. In wresting himself free of the web of imperial strictures and becoming the biggest military contractor in America, he discovered a whole new scope for monopolization. He did keep taking losses as well as making gains. The priceless thing was what he'd always sought above all: advantage.

When the Congress, still trying to pressure the mother country to negotiate, added a nonexportation rule to the nonimportation boycott, no American product could go out to Britain or the British Caribbean; and ships bobbed at the docks while big investments collapsed. Morris and his handpicked partners, however, critical to the gunpowder trade, were already buying and selling directly in European markets in violation of imperial law. Their operation didn't have to be limited, Morris saw, to military supply; commercial product too could be shipped home from non-British ports. He and his partners started bringing in the basics that were becoming painfully scarce—woolens, linens, pins and needles— and selling them throughout the Atlantic colonies for what he'd rightly predicted would be immense profits. The way he saw it, his own gain was the country's gain.

The Congress gave official responsibility for making arms deals to its Secret Committee of Trade, so Morris joined the committee and took an official hand in awarding contracts to himself and his partners. He was by no means the only merchant on the committee who did business with it, but he was by far the most energetic and creative, and by early 1776 he'd become its effective head, writing contracts for hundreds of thousands of dollars in public money that flowed through him to his private networks. Because secrecy was essential to eluding British intelligence, most of his fellow delegates didn't know, at first, about Morris's dual role as the Congress's chief awarder of contracts and the Congress's chief contractor.

Business had transformed him into a political leader. Political leadership was transforming his business.

He was reconciliationist to the end. In May 1776, Morris and Dickinson were serving in both the Pennsylvania assembly, which had moved to a committee room upstairs, and the Congress meeting in the assembly's regular ground-floor room. They went up and down the wide staircase at the State House to wield their province's sway in preventing the Congress from making America independent, but in a rapid series of events, which even Morris found impossible to track perfectly, the assembly began succumbing to pressure from pro-independence forces in the Congress and organized agitation from the street. By June, Pennsylvania's decisive power switched. On July 4, the Congress declared independence, even as the British were invading New York Harbor. What had begun as a defensive war for reconciliation became the War of Independence.

Morris swallowed hard. New opportunities might balance the new risks. John Dickinson never signed the Declaration of Independence—he led his militia battalion to New Jersey to resist the invasion—but Morris took a different approach. That August, when delegates to the Congress began putting their names to the document, he put his at the top of the Pennsylvania delegation's. He was on the record as the top revolutionary from the top state.

The British invasion made the military situation desperate. Morris's innovations got bolder and more profitable. Cornering the market on tobacco, the American product most in demand in Europe, he got it past British patrols by shipping it from the Outer Banks of North Carolina via agents who had accounts both with the Secret Committee and with him personally. The same agents got American indigo and rice to the Caribbean. They loaded both public and private cargo on the same ships, brought back military supplies from both Europe and the Caribbean, and profited themselves and Morris.

Franklin and Morris soon had the Secret Committee so well in hand that nobody else bothered to spend any time on it. Franklin sailed to ask the French Crown for direct financial aid in the form of a secret loan. John Hancock, president of the Congress, sent along a document giving Morris and Franklin, together, sole authority to act on behalf of the United States in all matters with France. The merchant once too intent on business even to stand for office had become a high official of the revolutionary United States, with wide-ranging powers at home and abroad.

So novel was the free trade that Morris had inaugurated that hundreds of adventurers, from many parts of the world, came rushing into this space where international diplomacy, public commissions, and personal gain combined. It wasn't just that Morris's private agents and partners were also agents of the Congress, and agents of the Congress were also his private agents and partners. In New Orleans, in Martinique, in Paris, and even through cutouts in enemy Britain itself, he was networking the most advanced financial speculators, the biggest merchants, and the highest imperial diplomats. At echelons official and unofficial, in marble-floored chambers and plank-floored coffeehouses, men made interlocking deals for money and treaties based on complicated logics that spawned further deals, side pots, skims. The American Revolution and big commerce, loosely and vigorously organized under Robert Morris, were one.

The war itself, though, was going badly for the United States. In 1777, the British occupied Philadelphia, and both the Congress and the state assembly had to evacuate, first to Baltimore, Maryland, and then to interior Pennsylvania towns to meet in county courthouses. Morris, as a delegate, moved with the Congress; his partner Willing stayed in the occupied city to pursue their firm's business. In some quarters of the American governing class, a feeling was growing that Morris's now pretty obvious dual role as the top war contractor and the top awarder of war contracts violated the integrity in government that Americans saw themselves fighting to defend. Soon a move was on to restrain him.

Especially eager to prove Morris corrupt and shut down his operation were the brothers Arthur and William Lee, delegates to the Congress and members of a famous Virginia family that had been early in supporting American independence. The Lee brothers focused their attention on the operations of one Silas Deane, a Connecticut partner of Morris, a merchant in the slave and other trades, a war contractor, and a sometime delegate to the Congress. Deane was now serving as Morris's and Franklin's secret agent in France on fake papers as a businessman from Bermuda, and he gave the Lees an easy target, having enmeshed himself in a set of schemes so complicated that they would never be comprehensively accounted for. A partial list of what came to light in the Lees' investigation included secret meetings at Versailles; millions of livres from the French Crown for arming America; the political and commercial recklessness of Pierre Beaumarchais, the author of *The Barber of Seville*; the drunkenness and incompetence of Robert Morris's half brother, Thomas; a multitude of shell companies; Deane's personal wartime speculations in the British stock market; top-secret documents leaked to the press; and the burgeoning personal wealth of Deane and Morris themselves. When the anti-Morris faction in the Congress lodged corruption charges against Deane, the Congress recalled him from France and threatened a formal investigation of Morris himself.

And yet after months of mutual invective, the Deane investigation collapsed. Related efforts to discredit Morris also inspired passionate speechmaking on both sides and went nowhere.

It wasn't so easy, it turned out, to distinguish corruption from noncorruption. The old colonial export market to Britain had evaporated with the war, and with regional and state economies depressed, self-dealing looked rampant. Military procurement was full of speculators pilfering budgets and awarding big contracts on the friends-and-family plan. Army hospital officials were suspected of selling medical supplies for personal profit.

Too, Morris's enemies' assertions of high principle could look as compromised as Morris's notion that whatever benefited him benefited the country. The Lee brothers' animus toward Deane and Morris was at least as personal as it was principled. Despite a familial posture of disdain for what some land-rich Virginians saw as grubby commerce, William Lee was a merchant himself. He'd done business and even held office in London. He resented Morris's and Deane's European deals largely because they cut him out.

The most rhetorically intense attack on Morris's character came from Henry Laurens, a delegate to the Congress from South Carolina, the archetype of those who saw land wealth as incorruptible and commercial and monetary wealth as sleaze. Laurens announced that the difference between his own views and Morris's was the difference between virtue and Mammon. That was as stark a distinction as could be made.

On Laurens's lands, enslaved black people of all ages produced rice for export, one of the deadliest crops for those who toiled in the slippery, reptile-infested ditches; Laurens also made a fortune in the slave trade. He did oppose the institution that made him rich. His son John, a friend of Alexander Hamilton, was even more fervently committed than his father to ending slavery. Still, the distinction that Henry Laurens drew so easily between virtue and Mammon wouldn't have been obvious to everybody.

Anyway, Morris knew the war effort needed him more than it needed anyone else, with the possible exception of Washington. He was fronting the Congress big, frequent infusions of his own cash and credit. Without him, army supply would topple overnight. He had the grateful approval of army officers, including Schuyler and Hamilton, and of Washington himself. In the end, the Congress officially cleared him of all charges.

In 1778, Morris left the Congress—temporarily, it would turn out—to stand for election to return to the Pennsylvania assembly for the 1779 session. But even then he continued to finance the Revolution, and be financed by it, and build his wealth to staggering scale, and early in 1781, the Congress pleaded with him to come back. Having run out of the paper money it had been issuing, called Continental currency, the body was broke. It wanted Morris to serve not as a delegate now but as the appointee to a new administrative office: superintendent of finance.

This office was his own idea. He'd long been urging the Congress to shut down the cumbersome standing committees of delegates and give sweeping executive power to appointed solo heads of departments staffed by employees. Lately the idea had gained traction. Ongoing failure in the war effort had demoralized many Americans, but in some influential circles failure was a spur for action. Even those most deeply wary of Continentalism were calling for more consolidated federal measures, if only to win the war.

As always, Morris saw opportunity. He accepted the new job on conditions that would make his administrative power nearly absolute. The new solo superintendencies weren't to be equal; he was to rule the whole system as a kind of super-superintendent. In some ways, that seemed natural enough. As Jacques Necker had pointed out, European governments had long made the head of finance the premier administrative position; in the British cabinet, the minister known as the First Lord of the Treasury had been called "prime" long before the office of prime minister formally existed. Morris's conditions for accepting the job gave him power not only to hire everyone in his own department but also to fire anyone anywhere in the congressional administration and the military who handled public money. He was thus empowered to have his allies appointed superintendents of other departments and to take full control of international diplomacy.

He had one more condition. There was to be no more carping about his mingling private and public business and private and public funds. A majority in the Congress voted, at first, against giving him such carte blanche, but Morris wouldn't budge, and a feeling was growing that without him, there might soon be no Congress at all. Even his worst enemies openly admitted that Robert Morris had them at his mercy. With all conditions met, the apostle of what he called free trade enjoyed dictatorial control over the U.S. federal administration, civil and military, and a personal monopoly on commerce.

From that height, he got a long-range view of a possible American future. Even amid the desperate state of warfare, the merchant once so leery of declaring American independence had become the leading enthusiast of the potential—the national potential—of an independent United States.

It was war indeed that clarified Morris's national vision. He was looking forward to a peacetime America consolidated on the wartime model that he was even then in the process of creating. Strong executive power—the power he now held—might direct the power of great wealth—his and others'—into peacetime projects equivalent to war. America might grow by leaps and bounds through private investment in industrialized forms of agriculture, both southern and northern, powered by both slave and free labor; investment in development of the vast woodlands, now held by the woodland nations and speculated in by George Washington and others; construction of canals and bridges for moving western produce eastward; even manufacturing. American national greatness would ensue from fulfilling its own needs for manufactured goods, each region selling to others. Pursuing grand public-private and interstate ambitions, merchants and growers alike would be enriched, and so would the whole country.

Little tangible evidence existed, in 1781, for the great American economic future Morris was projecting. What, even, were the country's basic economic conditions? Informed people in various industries might estimate what percentages of the overall British American economy their industries accounted for, but in the absence of the kind of national government the Continentalists wanted, it was hard for even the most expert observer to assess what would later be thought of as a whole country's economic health. In 1781, nobody knew even how many people lived in the United States.

The interstate nature of the war, though, offered a blurry snapshot, and Morris was studying it. The war enriched men like him while depressing everyday economies, yet his vision of dynamic American growth drew on an inveterate confidence that deploying public policy to enrich men like him would organize and concentrate American wealth, centralize domestic and foreign commerce, and lift the whole country. That was the key to national greatness: a consolidation of wealth and government.

Or the Money Connection. That's what Morris called the new American phenomenon for growing wealth through government, and centralizing government in wealth, that he was first to identify and pursue. Just as he began using his new powers as super-superintendent to start building out the Money Connection, he was surprised to receive a thick envelope from Alexander Hamilton of New York.

3

EXCHANGING EYE-ROLLS

HAMILTON WAS EXCITED ABOUT Morris's appointment as superintendent. The Congress and the states seemed to be turning their backs on the suffering army; the great merchant, using his own cash and credit to supply it, was lauded by a grateful Washington, Schuyler, and others in Hamilton's circles. Hamilton had suggested to his elder ally James Duane a restructuring of the Congress under executive superintendents, and Duane had urged the move on the Congress, so Hamilton gave himself credit for having at least accomplished something on that front; he'd even recommended Morris for the finance job.

Presuming he was in a position to make such a recommendation might have seemed just his trademark brashness. But by now, Hamilton's book-learning on finance was becoming better known. His own name had come up, if briefly, as a possible nominee for the job.

So with reason to see himself as the one man in the country with the expertise to help Morris out, in April 1781 he worked up a set of detailed guidelines for the superintendent's next moves. The year before, he'd tried to show Duane that any feasible Continentalist plan would have to rely on some form of centralized banking. Now, for Morris's edification, Hamilton thoroughly built out, on paper, that one feature: a national-style bank for the United States. That's what got pulled from its envelope, unfolded, and laid on a desk in Morris's Office of Finance on Front Street in Phila-delphia in early May 1781.

The document, totally unsolicited, came from somebody Morris knew only as a son-in-law to his political and commercial ally Philip Schuyler and a staffer of another ally, General Washington. And it looked less like a letter than a technical manual.

Unlike Duane, however, Morris had a sense of humor. He called Hamilton's document a performance.

The author actually began quite modestly. He said he was sending only some ideas and apologized for their being crude, inchoate. Then he stopped being modest and stopped apologizing and rolled it all out, at nearly incredible length and detail, and Morris couldn't help being impressed. Hamilton explicitly modeled his proposed bank on the Bank of England, and Morris had to like that; the institution was admired by high-finance people everywhere. Founded in 1694 for the immediate purpose of making a loan to the British government—£1.2 million, at 8 percent interest, to pay for a war with France—and privately owned by its subscribed stockholders—that's who profited from the interest payments—the Bank of England operated on a charter granted by the Crown. The monarch, as one of the subscribers, held stock personally, and the charter made the bank what was called a corporation, a com-pany created by specific legislative action, in this case making it the only corporation with a right to conduct banking operations in England. The bank thereby integrated the public force of imperial government with the private wealth of the country's richest investors and depositors, including government itself.

Important to Morris and—he could see from the young man's communication—to Hamilton was the Bank of England's history of eas-ing large-scale commercial enterprise by issuing high-denomination notes, intricately engraved pieces of high-quality paper. Challenging to forge, each note promised to pay its bearer the bank's gold and silver coin—"hard money," the only real money—in the amount printed on the note's face and therefore known as face value. Paper notes were also issued by merchant firms and by other governments, but Bank of England notes, considered as good as gold, were accepted especially eagerly in payment of debts and invoices and circulated widely in high-end trade throughout the empire; the bank also cashed IOUs and other institutions' notes, for a cut of the face value.

It was also clear to Morris that Hamilton shared his view that Britain's success in the current war was largely due to the overwhelming financial advantages conferred on the British national government by Bank of England innovations. If the United States had something similar, it would not only aid the war effort but also tend to nationalize the country by centralizing finance. And yet Hamilton's plan for a U.S. bank called for an initial capitalization of $10 million in gold and silver. That took the superintendent aback. There was simply no way to raise anything like it. The young man's ambition burst the dams of political and financial reality.

Still, the letter had irresistible appeal. Much energy and brainpower, combined with the punctilio, that characteristic crossing of t's and dotting of i's, had been applied to shaping a mass of deeply informed detail for purposes close to Morris's heart. When he got back to Hamilton to thank him for the performance, Morris wasn't just humorous but warm, respectful, encouraging.

And now they had something a bit more practical to discuss. So simpatico were these two that when he received Hamilton's bank plan, Morris had been working on a bank plan of his own—not as grandiose as Hamilton's, but with all the Morris flair.

The superintendent named his proposed institution the Bank of North America, after the whole continent, to brand it a consolidating force like the Continental Army. He proposed to locate it across the street from the Pennsylvania State House, where the Congress met, suggesting quasi-national prominence for both bank and Congress. As a private enterprise, owned by Robert Morris and other stockholders, the Bank of North America would attract, he hoped, an initial investment of $400,000 in gold and silver—paltry only if you'd seen Hamilton's plan— and operate as the organizing hub for the Money Connection by holding the Congress's cash, extending the Congress short-term loans, making advances on the Congress's behalf to the army-contracting network, and issuing the large-denomination notes, backed by the bank's coin, that would facilitate the large-scale war trade conducted by Morris and other contractors.

To that end, Morris asked the Congress to issue the charter that would make his bank a corporation, with an effective monopoly on government banking. The charter would subject the institution to federal oversight, and as the Congress's superintendent of finance, Morris himself would carry out that oversight, even while serving as the bank's chief stockholder and a member of the board of directors: private money and public effort, integrated at the federal level, in the person of Morris. He and the bank's other investors would thrive, the war effort recover—yet another benefit shared by him and the public.

One problem. It wasn't clear that the Congress had any power, under its Articles of Confederation, to charter a bank. State Sovereigntists, now seeing how far Morris wanted to extend the Congress's reach, asserted that the body had no such power, so Morris worked hard to make the bank look more like an emergency war measure than the permanent American institution he really wanted it to become and the bank charter did pass the Congress, barely; the institution was also chartered in the state of Pennsylvania, where it was physically located. Morris wrote to rich men throughout the states to invite them to become his fellow investors. He attracted some big subscribers, including delegates to the Congress. He made his old partner Thomas Willing the bank's president. He packed the board with merchant allies.

He'd been right, though, about the challenge of raising funds. By no means did enough investors have enough confidence. The subscription fell short, but he used his executive power as superintendent to funnel French money, sent to support the war, into the bank.

So the United States of America, though only a confederation, and without anything like a national government, had a kind of national bank—a force, in Morris and Hamilton's shared view, from which actual nationhood might begin to develop by consolidating wealth across state lines and connecting it, by charter, to the federal government. In his letter back to Hamilton, Morris agreed that the $400,000 capitalization wasn't nearly enough. He assured his new protégé that he expected the investment to grow.

For Morris and Hamilton, the bank was only the beginning. When they next connected, nearly a year later, so much had changed, both for each man and for the country, that a collaboration seemed ripe.

Hamilton had been having a busy time. He'd gone on hocking Washington for a field command and at last had been given a light-infantry brigade. In the fall of 1782, at the Battle of Yorktown, Virginia, after further pleading on the spot—he saw his last chance slipping away—Washington sent the battalion on a bayonet charge, and Hamilton finally checked the glory box. Then he sent the general a sniffy letter, asking permission to retain his rank when out of active service, scorning to request a pension, and alluding, under thin cover of strained politeness, to Washington's unfairness in denying earlier requests. The tone was such that there was no underlying sense of any expected further communication.

Hamilton didn't seem concerned about being more or less estranged from the man now widely hailed as the greatest in the world. He was moving on. U.S. victory at Yorktown seemed to presage U.S. victory in the war. Hamilton wrote a series of newspaper essays, notable for their Continentalist blatancy, calling for expanding the Congress's powers and praising Robert Morris's work as superintendent. He also moved into the Schuyler mansion in Albany to study law. He didn't want to be a lawyer, particularly; he had bigger things in mind. But he expected to master the entire curriculum in six months, on his own, with no teacher.

Morris crashed into those studies.

Hamilton would indeed complete his self-taught course in six months and be certified to practice law in New York. And he would practice. He needed the income. The Schuyler connection, though overwhelmingly advantageous, didn't make him rich. Elizabeth Hamilton wouldn't inherit for years. Her mother kept diluting inheritances by bearing more children. Hamilton would be a lawyer.

But Morris invited him into public life for the first time. He asked the young man to serve as his receiver of the Congress's revenue in New York. He was offering Hamilton a practical, active focus for what had heretofore been only extraordinarily ambitious and impressively well-thought-out ideas.

For Morris had been busy too. With the Bank of North America up and running, the Congress had access to the bank's large-denomination notes, backed by Morris's and the other investors' gold and silver. But another big-time currency now existed too. Morris had started personally issuing a large-denomination paper backed by his own coffers of gold and silver; known as "Mr. Morris's notes," they were circulating widely in government-merchant commerce. Further pulling together his public and private roles, further linking big commerce to federal government, the notes were signed by Morris yet watermarked "United States."

He was doing something else, which the Congress had never even tried before: cracking down on the states for money. All of the states had tax-collection systems, widely varying and deeply rooted in the colonial period. Morris sent a testy circular letter directly to governors, demanding that they pressure their legislatures to tax citizens for the war requisitions that had been agreed to, early in the war, in amounts proportional to states' overall real-estate wealth. The states had never come close to complying. In 1781, Congress had asked for $3 million in requisitions and received less than $40,000. Now Morris upbraided the states for weakness and lack of patriotism in failing to pass and enforce taxes and demanded gold and silver, nothing in-kind, like army supplies.

That's why he was getting in touch now, he explained to Hamilton. He'd just persuaded the Congress to pass a whole new requisition in coin, proportioned among the states, and for the first time, a federal officer was to be embedded within each state to collect the gold and silver personally. This newly pervasive system would get the superintendent's fingers, or at least their tips, into all of the states' separate and chaotic systems for taxing citizens. Morris wanted Hamilton, his brightest acolyte in Continentalism and the Money Connection, to serve as the New York officer.

Tax collectors normally received a percentage of whatever they could collect, incentivizing as much collection as possible. But Morris told Hamilton that he was paying his new tax officers, instead, a percentage of the total quota demanded of each state, regardless of how much they could actually collect.

Under those conditions, Hamilton accepted the offer. He also took Morris's somewhat counterintuitive point. Had the superintendent been offering to pay the usual percentage of actual funds collected, nobody would have taken the job. Morris knew that despite the toughness of his oratory when rousting the state governors, his federal receivers would find it impossible to enforce anything like full compliance with the new requisition.

That the plan could only fail became clear during Hamilton's frustrating experience as federal receiver. In the spring and summer of 1782, he made official trips to the state capital in Poughkeepsie, at Morris's behest, to receive funds for the Congress. Collecting the requisition anything like in full proved impossible. For one thing, Morris was refusing to accept for requisition payments the states' paper currencies. He wanted hard money, and there wasn't much of that around.

This strong position against government paper became critical to Hamilton's understanding of the nationalizing power of the Money Connection. Gold and silver, the raw materials for coining money, had never been found and mined in Britain's Atlantic colonies. Coin thus remained scarce in the American economy—not just in wartime but at the best of times—and so the various colonies, now states, sometimes issued small-denomination paper currencies to ease trade: government notes. Printed on the notes' faces were the equivalent values in metal, usually at length and in multiple fonts, to make forgery more difficult: "This Bill of *One Ninth of a Dollar* shall entitle the bearer to receive *GOLD* or *SILVER*, at the rate of Four Shillings and Six-pence Sterling per DOLLAR for the said Bill, according to a *RESOLVE* of the CONVENTION of . . ." and naming the issuing government.

For Morris, however, this government paper wouldn't do—especially for paying states' requisitions to the Congress. Merchants, relying on notes issued by well-capitalized private firms like Morris's, now including the Bank of North America, had come to despise state governments' paper as weak, unreliable, even a kind of robbery. The states sometimes made their currencies "legal tender." That meant lenders had to accept the paper for interest payments, and because the states often ran low on gold and silver, their notes weren't as reliably backed by hard money as the bank's notes or Mr. Morris's notes. That made the paper's value unstable. When sellers of goods and services feared that a government might not have enough metal to back its paper—if everybody holding the paper went to the government all at once to exchange it for hard money and found the government unable to pay in full—sellers would provide buyers with fewer goods and services in exchange for paper than for the same amount in metal, making it more expensive to buy with paper than with coin, thus informally setting the real-world trading value of paper lower than its printed face value: depreciating it. Informal depreciations, varying from place to place, and especially volatile across state lines, tended to further reduce confidence in a state's currency and trigger deeper depreciations. A government might at last be forced to devalue its currency officially.

So lenders forced by law to take a crashing paper for interest payments hated both the law and the paper, because they were losing value on their loans. That's why merchants didn't like state currencies, and that's why the only paper Morris would accept from the states for war requisitions were Bank of North America notes or Mr. Morris's notes. To comply with his demand for gold and silver, the states had to levy taxes payable in coin, whose scarceness made the taxes hard to collect.

Hamilton also faced a particular problem trying to collect in New York. The State Sovereigntist governor, George Clinton— really more of a New York sovereigntist—liked to view his state as first among equals. Increasingly at odds with New York's Continentalist faction, led by Philip Schuyler, Clinton was busy with plans for keeping public wealth out of money pits like the army, the Congress, and Robert Morris. Anyway, New York and other states were already taxing their citizens for state purposes. There was only so much taxation people could take.

As Hamilton reported to Morris one failure after another by New

York to raise the requisition money, the superintendent and his employee exchanged eye-rolls over all states' weak, byzantine tax-collection processes and encouraged each other in slamming what they called the fundamental defects of the whole state-by-state system: "the epitome of the follies that prevail," as Morris put it. They were failing to work a system that they saw as unworkable in its essence.

Such was Alexander Hamilton's full matriculation at the Robert Morris school of money and politics, where his education would reach its climax. At Beekman and Cruger, he'd learned the logistics of big commerce. He'd observed the priorities of the commercial class, up close, in his relationships with Washington, the Schuylers, and their circles. From Necker and other writers he'd gleaned the theory of public finance and thrilled to its romance. In 1780 he'd pushed on James Duane a Continentalism based largely on government's relationship to money.

But only now, working for Morris, did Hamilton start putting all of the elements together.

The current confederation system wasn't just courting catastrophe; it was the catastrophe. Unsustainable already, it must collapse. Ameliorative measures—the appointment of federal receivers—only perpetuated and thus continuously exposed what Morris and Hamilton agreed was a systemic disaster that had to be reversed. Massive amounts of public money would always be needed. Even after Yorktown, a large army was in the field, moving about the country, fighting mop-up battles and voraciously consuming food, clothing, fodder, maintenance, ammunition, and much else, all day, every day. Nor would the end of war reduce the need. Morris's vision of great American nationhood involved taking up big federal projects equivalent to war, but as long as the Congress had no way to get money of its own, no power to tax citizens itself, uniformly and directly throughout the states, the body would remain forever dependent on each state's raising funds through its own wayward process, or raising some funds, or no funds at all. Morris's most aggressive measures at repair of the requisition system only dramatized the crying need for an end to the system.

And looking at the issue that way, it turned out that there really was a mechanism for fundamentally altering the nature of the Congress as a government and consolidating American wealth and American political power in dynamic nationhood—a mechanism for building Continentalism on the Money Connection. Morris had identified the mechanism. He already had one piece in place: the Bank of North America.

But that institution lacked the great driving wheel that had made the Bank of England a hub for accelerating the British Empire. The driving wheel did exist in the United States, but only in component parts, lying around useless. Morris knew the parts. Hamilton began learning how, when shaped, buffed, polished, and interconnected, they might be hooked up to the bank and other financial machinery and get the whole thing pumping to found a great nation.

That driving wheel was the Public Debt of the United States.

4

IN WHICH WE ARE INTRODUCED TO THE PUBLIC DEBT OF THE UNITED STATES

THE PUBLIC DEBT OF the United States. The very term suggested to many then, and would suggest to many later, nothing but a big problem. That's the opposite of how Robert Morris saw the Public Debt, the opposite of how Hamilton got to know it. Care and feeding of the Public Debt would come to define his hopes and plans for the country.

He already had a strong general understanding of the workings of a public debt in building advanced nations. He'd made heroes of men who had both theorized about the subject and actually pulled it off: Necker in France, Walpole in Britain. It impressed Hamilton, as it decidedly didn't impress his State Sovereigntist opponents, that far from weakening a nation, as the land-rich, anti-money types always insisted, public borrowing enabled governments to finance big projects otherwise beyond reach without having to gut their coffers or tax their citizens at impossible rates. The British Empire, fighting wars in Europe and colonizing large parts of the world, didn't use a pay-as-you-go, one-huge-budget-at-a-time approach, funded by heavy taxes earmarked for each budget. The government paid regular interest to those who loaned the Crown big money on an ongoing basis. Rich people bought interest-bearing government bonds in large

numbers and made money on their money by funding the country's imperial efforts. Taxes were earmarked not for project budgets but for paying
interest on the bonds.

Hamilton was up on all that. But now it was time to get specific. This
wasn't imperial Europe. A very different, very fractious situation prevailed in the supposedly united states. There were thirteen governments.
There were competing visions of the aims of American independence
and the future and even the existential purpose of the country. So how
might a public debt be deployed, here, to reduce the power of the state
governments and realize the Continentalist idea of a thriving, consolidated, national government?

Hamilton had always been a quick study, but the answer wasn't really
hard to grasp. The Public Debt of the United States was the star player
in a fairly simple if quite dramatic story, its beginnings embedded in the
beginning of the American Revolution itself.

Robert Morris knew the story intimately. He'd been there. He was in
many ways the story's author.

In July 1776, the Continental Congress of the United States of America turned an insurrection against Great Britain into the War of Independence and found itself with a desperate need not only for arms, which
Robert Morris was already supplying, but also for funds with which to
pay suppliers like him and cover all the other expenses of war. Given the
country's confederation structure, the states were supposed to generate the
funds, via separate tax laws, and send those requisitions to the Congress,
at rates apportioned and managed by that body under its agreed-upon
war-making authority, which sounded good at the time, but as Hamilton
learned later, when working for Morris, the system foundered because
the states didn't pay. As early as the end of 1776, it was clear that to get
sufficient funds for fighting a war, the Congress would have to borrow.

There were two places to look for loans. One was Europe, and Morris's
and Franklin's diplomacy did secure loans from France and Spain, empires
more than willing to help fund an American war against Britain, as well
as from private lenders in Holland, Europe's finance center. But those
foreign sources yielded little money—only $2 million in the first five years

of war—and served mainly as starter engines for the dynamic power that Morris identified in the second source.

That was money not foreign but homegrown. It was borrowed by the Congress, and by each state government on its own, from individual citizens throughout the states; it would grow to about $63 million by 1790. At the hot, glowing core of that domestic part of the Public Debt of the United States was some money that a very small, very upscale group, composed largely of American merchants and led by Robert Morris himself, loaned to the Congress as a business venture.

Lending money as a business venture was in itself nothing new in America. The big merchants and some of the big landlords, operating in global networks for buying and selling in the imperial trade, got their hands on large amounts of the gold and silver so scarce in the American economy and made money on their money by lending it to their less fortunate neighbors at staggering interest rates. Britain had long since banned banking operations in its colonies, but the American rich formed an ad hoc lending industry anyway. When the War of Independence began, it was therefore presumed that, given their experience as private creditors, and given what was presumed to be their patriotism, even merchants and landlords who, like Morris, had originally opposed declaring independence would jump at the chance of becoming creditors of the United States—public creditors—by investing in war.

Late in 1776, therefore, via a system first invented by Robert Walpole and the Bank of England, the Congress issued for sale a total of $5 million in war bonds. These were instruments intricately engraved on high-quality paper, bearing 4 percent annual interest, with maturity dates stating when, with the war presumably won, they'd be paid back.

But the lending class didn't bite. Achieving victory over Britain placed a pretty stiff condition on payback. And while getting paid back was indeed essential to the proposition, it wasn't the real purpose of lending. The real purpose was to profit, via annual interest payments, and that's where the Congress's bonds really looked ugly. The Congress was offering to pay the interest not in gold or silver coin but in the paper money it began printing in 1775, known as Continental currency. No government paper looked likelier to depreciate than the Congress's currency. When colonial legislatures issued paper, they fought depreciation, sometimes successfully, by avoiding printing too many bills and levying taxes payable in those bills, withdrawing the currency to bolster public confidence that the government would always hold enough hard money to back the paper in circulation. But the Congress wasn't a legislature. It couldn't levy taxes on citizens, and paying mounting war expenses would clearly require printing more and more of the paper. American investors of 1776 correctly predicted the ultimate crash of the Congress's currency and had no desire to support the War of Independence by purchasing federal bonds bearing only 4 percent interest payable in that paper.

The Congress improved the offer, upping the interest to 6 percent, but what really made the difference, for a small class of particularly well-connected investors—what really launched the domestic part of the Public Debt—was Benjamin Franklin's getting that secret French grant: 2 million livres, to be repeated annually, with no deadline for repayment. Morris and Franklin agreed that the money wasn't to be used for buying supplies and paying soldiers but secretly earmarked for paying 6 percent interest to American war-bond investors, if not literally in gold and silver, then in the equivalent: paper notes issued by European governments and banking houses, called "bills of exchange," fully backed by those institutions' large supplies of coin. Such bills traded readily, at full face value, in every port on the Atlantic coast.

Anyone in the know about this secret foreign loan to the Congress—their number included some of the delegates to the Congress—could now count on getting 6 percent per year in the equivalent of hard money. Federal bonds began to look a lot more attractive.

Best of all, the Congress was accepting its own weak Continental currency for purchasing the bonds. The currency's depreciation had already begun. By 1777 and 1778, its real buying power in trade would diminish by about 80 percent. Yet in selling bonds, the Congress accepted the paper at face value: a $1,000 federal bond could be bought with Continental notes really worth only $200 in trade. Four annual interest payments of 6 percent would more than recoup the real purchase price; after that, the interest income was gravy. And that was net. Nobody had ever heard of a tax on interest income.

Given this deal, the most elite members of the American investing class saw their way to lending the Congress money to pay for the War of Independence and quickly bought up $2.5 million in federal bonds. Those bonds soon became very special, because the Congress rethought its offer. For all bonds sold after March 1778, it withdrew the coin-interest deal and paid interest only in Continental currency. The first-round bonds, paying in the equivalent of gold and silver, thus came to represent the preferred tier of the Federal Debt, gained on the cheap and inside by a small group made up of the country's richest and most influential investors, the class crucially important, in Morris's view, to the country's future: his own class.

So the best slice of the Debt, held in a few hands, remained relatively small. Yet public expenses on the scale of the War of Independence hadn't been known in America before, and while the bonds that the Congress offered after March 1778 provoked little investor enthusiasm, thanks to the interest paid in badly depreciating paper, they infiltrated the upscale sector of the economy anyway, in huge numbers, because the Congress, going broke, started using them in lieu of payment on its invoices. Merchants, in their role not as investors but as military contractors, found themselves forced to accept these weaker bonds: it was that or wait a long time to get paid, maybe forever.

Then, in 1779, the Congress gave up and stopped even printing its currency. People holding the bonds that paid interest in that currency saw their interest going out of existence, and all classes of bondholders knew that the Congress was failing to collect any hard money from state requisitions. In late 1781, after the battle of Yorktown, a prospect of victory in the war came on the horizon. Peace would dry up foreign loans too.

Where was the Congress supposed to get money to pay interest on any of its bonds? Would the body even survive victory? How would the principal ever be paid back? People once skeptical about investing in the war had become giddy with financial opportunities the war had unlocked, queasy at the prospect of peace. Some wanted out. Some still wanted in. Some forever changed their minds.

Secondary markets therefore sprang up. Impromptu exchanges taking over offices, coffeehouses, taverns, and street corners all over the country became scenes of sheer speculative wildness. Soon the bulk of the domestic part of the Public Debt was in the hands of secondary holders who now made up, with the original holders, a small but very busy trading class. The most preferred bonds, the first round, paying interest in the equivalent of metal, were hard to get—original holders tended to hang on to them, if with rising anxiety—and nobody knew what the less-preferred bonds were really worth. They traded far below face value and might still be trading way too high. If the interest on any tier would be paid by somebody, somehow, someday, maybe at face value or near it, you'd be the biggest loser in the world if you sold them cheap. Six percent annual interest, paid on the face value of an instrument bought for a tenth of that value, would get you an interest payment of 60 percent on your real outlay. You couldn't have too many of such bonds and would buy as many as anybody wanted to sell.

But what if the interest was never paid? Then the bonds' value was on the verge of collapse, and you'd be the world's biggest loser if you failed to cut your losses and dump as many as possible, as fast as possible, for almost anything you could get from the suckers deluding themselves that interest would be paid. These violently opposed positions, inspired by baseless analysis and yielding ever-changing predictions that really came down to rumor, vied for dominance on any given day or hour, sometimes in the minds of individual investors.

And there you had it: the domestic part of the Federal Debt, circa 1782, as Alexander Hamilton came to know it under the aegis of Robert Morris. Jittery financial speculation in war had become intertwined with the long-range ambitions of a key sector of the small class that dominated American politics and business. The Debt was big, unreliable, potentially fabulously enriching, just as potentially ruining. Its powers and vulnerabilities, thrilling and terrifying investors throughout the states, held a privileged group in an emotional turmoil caused by a combination of high risk and total uncertainty.

Robert Morris knew all about risk and uncertainty. He was counting on emotional turmoil to concentrate minds.

Then there was the States' Debt. This subset of the domestic part of the Public Debt of the United States played an especially important role, if a somewhat counterintuitive one, in Morris's and Hamilton's thinking about how to found a national government on the Money Connection.

The States' Debt was made up of money borrowed, also for fighting the war, not by the Congress but by each of the thirteen state governments, on each state's separate responsibility for fulfilling its own obligation. Some of the legislatures sold securities, which, like federal bonds, bore annual 6 percent interest, payable in metal by some states and in state paper currency by others, with varying payoff schedules. Some holders and traders of federal bonds stayed away from the state bonds; others bought and traded both types. Widespread uncertainty about reliability made state bonds' value, too, fluctuate wildly in the markets, also well below face value.

But all of the states took on a whole other kind of obligation. This was a strange one, because the states' responsibility for paying on it merged at times with a responsibility of the federal government. Strange, too, because this segment of the Debt wasn't originally intended as an investment opportunity. In the fervid atmosphere of wartime investing, it morphed.

Throughout the war, ordinary Americans provided huge amounts of food, animals, fodder, clothing, horseshoes, wagons, and a multitude of other military necessities both to their states' forces and to the Continental Army. This wasn't formal military contracting, carried out on a grand scale by profit-seeking merchants like Robert Morris. This was sheer impressment: the traditional power of wartime government to take military supplies and services from the people by force. The Congress passed a resolution asking the states to pass laws enabling impressment; under those laws both the state governments and the Continental

Army issued farmers and artisans written promises, in the form of chits, to pay later for supplies taken now. The terms of these coerced loans, made by ordinary people to their states and the army, were dictated by military officers, sometimes literally at gunpoint. Simple IOUs, the chits were at first handwritten, later printed and filled in by hand. They bore no interest.

In some states, people came to hold maybe $20 million in this part of the Debt. The countrywide total may have reached as much as $95 million—at face value, as documented on the chits, but here face value became especially vague. The only actual value of any chit depended on people's faith in a state's or the Congress's willingness to someday make good on it.

That faith simply didn't exist, for good reason. Farmers and artisans seeking to have their IOUs honored during the war were sent away empty-handed from both state and federal loan offices. After 1780, some states did accept the chits in payment of taxes, but tenants, small farmers, and artisans were crushed by personal debts of their own to the creditor class of merchants and landlords and forever threatened with loss, foreclosure, and eviction; now they were struggling in a wartime depression. People naturally started using their supply-impressment chits in everyday trade for basic necessities, sometimes at pennies on the dollar.

At first glance, this weakest, murkiest part of the Debt might have seemed an unlikely object of sophisticated financial speculation. It had little proven value. It was scattered all over the country in bushels of depreciated paper chits. It bore no interest. It wasn't even always clear whom the IOUs obligated.

But American investors were by now so deeply enmeshed in fierce, full-on competition for any financial advantage spawned by war that the chits' very weakness, outsize issuance, and holders' desperate need for money gave them appeal. Networks of agents fanned out to find this paper, because many holders turned out to be eager to part with it in exchange for metal, or even for Continental or state currencies, at infinitesimal fractions of face value. Investors grabbing the chits up in bulk were betting on their being paid off, someday, by one government or another, if not at face value, then at a nice margin above the rock-bottom price of purchase. The investing class's veering hopes and fears had securitized and financialized even this least reliable class of the Debt.

One last promise, also made by the states and the federal government to ordinary citizens, created a similar investment opportunity. Officers and soldiers alike had been going largely unpaid, so both the army and the states began issuing soldiers another kind of chit, supposed to be exchanged for pay in coin later on. This army-pay paper did bear interest; some was added to the States' Debt, some to the Federal Debt. But the great majority of soldiers, the privates, were drawn from that smallholding, artisan, tenant, and day-laboring class that needed money now, not pieces of paper that might or might not draw interest later. Like the army-supply chits, the army-pay chits sold throughout the country, at very low rates and in great numbers, to organized investors betting on handing them in someday, at or somewhere near face value, and reaping the reward.

And that's all any ambitious young Continentalist, or anyone else, ever needed to know about the domestic part of the Public Debt of the United States, the important part, the driving wheel for founding an American nation on the Money Connection. Late in the war, the domestic part of the federal obligation, later reckoned at about $40 million, and the state obligation, harder to reckon but at least $20 million, were lying in various tranches in investor portfolios and both causing mounting hope and mounting anxiety.

But what *about* the domestic part of the Debt made it the driving wheel for American nationhood? How would sustaining that Debt tend to consolidate money and government and unleash the country's dynamic potential?

From his reading of Necker and Walpole and others, Hamilton had a keen understanding of a general answer. Morris had an answer peculiar to the United States.

It was all about the hope and anxiety. What the Debt had wrought was the consolidation of a small group of rich Americans from every state, a class now known as the public creditors. The class was desperate for assurances of regular interest payments on both federal and state bonds, desperate to trade those bonds in less uncertain markets, desperate to realize margins on chits they'd bought cheap. The creditors had become reliant on somebody's, anybody's, devising some plan, any plan, for saving them from ruin and enriching them over the long term by paying the agreed-upon interest on war bonds for many years to come. Many in the agrarian elite, loving land wealth and hating the moneymen, clung to the belief that the only legitimate thing to do with a public debt is pay it off as fast as possible, but neither Morris nor the public creditors wanted fast paydowns of principal. Morris wanted government to spend funds on public operating expenses and projects; the creditors wanted regular interest coming in for generations. They also wanted opportunities even better than war, for achieving even greater wealth, by lending for the projects that Morris envisioned for the country.

So what the Congress had to do now, Morris said, was commit with renewed intensity—meaning with newly credible ways and means—to reliably paying the federal bondholders regular interest over a long term. He'd earmarked the recent war requisitions on the states for paying investors before paying soldiers and suppliers, but it had been proved that state requisitions could never be reliably collected. A different, credible means of collection would make the Congress, and the Congress alone, indispensable to the richest, most influential people throughout the country. That would bring about the consolidated government the Continentalists had always wanted, because to live up to a commitment to reliably pay those people their interest, the Congress would have to assume the crucial thing it had always lacked and the Continentalists had so long wanted: direct lawmaking power over citizens throughout all of the states. The Congress had to draw gold and silver coin not indirectly and unreliably, from requisitions on the state governments, but directly from the whole people, via federal taxation: the Congress's own money, levied via the Congress's own laws, collected by an interstate federal administration, totally independent of the states, with police powers everywhere in the country. The money collected would be deposited in the Congress's Money Connection hub, the Bank of North America, earmarked for paying the bondholders interest, and paid to them either in metal or in banknotes fully backed by metal. An interstate federal collection power, consolidating public finance and energizing the Money Connection, would naturally lead to further federal lawmaking in trade, in finance, and in other areas, transforming the existing Congress, step by step, into a national government for the United States.

Morris knew that to fully achieve that goal, an even greater change was required. He didn't just want to put the Congress in a position to pay regular interest on its own obligation, via federal taxes earmarked for investors. He did want that, but his longer-range plan involved a counterintuitive insight into the nature of the states' bonds too, as well as the huge number of IOU chits. While at times Morris concurred in the orthodox, even reflexive notion that the Federal Debt was already too big, the main thrust of his policy was to make it, at any size, the dominant form of public obligation. What kept him up at night was the fact that some state legislatures were already undermining the Debt's nationalizing force. States planned to pay their own public creditors off quickly, raising the money through state taxes. Each state's going its own way like that, a drastically deconsolidating project both economically and politically, would defeat the nation-making potential. Morris wanted these state-oriented quick-payoff plans stopped in their tracks.

So the big win would be to get the Congress to assume all of the states' separate obligations in the Federal Debt, thereby wiping out the States' Debt and swelling the Federal Debt to huge proportions. The single-payer structure would also simplify responsibility for the IOU chits. With literally all of American public finance consolidated in the Congress, the federal government would become the exclusive site of public interest payments and public investment, drowning the states' economic power in federal economic power and yoking every hope of the small financial elite throughout all states to federal, not state, government. It was federal assumption of the States' Debt, ultimately, that would usher in the amazing national future of the United States.

All of Alexander Hamilton's efforts to date, so brilliant, so fully informed, had proved inchoate and infeasible. He'd tried to push the country into Continentalism all at once, by sheer force of will, and gotten nowhere. Employed by Morris, his talents were now organized in a practical scheme. Morris had his own brand of incrementalism, by no means a function of Duane-like political caution. With his long experience in risk, with his intimate knowledge of money's power, the superintendent was pointing the way to a transformation of the confederation Congress into a true national government founded on the Money Connection.

First crawl. Then walk. Then run. When Hamilton began engaging with the power of the Debt under Morris's influence, their long-range wish to assume the States' Debt in the Federal Debt remained just that, a long-range wish. What simply had to be gotten through the Congress right away, according to Morris, was a single federal tax with revenues earmarked for investors in the Federal Debt. That would get the Congress on the hook before peace demolished the weak American unity fostered by war. Once the Congress, the states, and the people faced up to this novel concept of one federal tax, collected uniformly throughout the states by agents of the Congress, then more federal taxes would follow, he explained, ultimately a whole slate.

The first federal tax was thus to be a wedge. It would pry open a door through which would rush federal taxes on domestic products, the kind known as excise; federal flat fees paid by each individual, known as poll taxes; federal land taxes. Assumption of the States' Debt in the Federal Debt should follow too, but in 1782, Morris's immediate objective was the wedge. He had to get the Congress to pass one federal tax and earmark it for the federal bondholders' interest payments. "The political existence of the United States," Morris said, "depends on the accomplishment of this plan."

Pass one federal tax. Hamilton committed his prodigious energy and relentless self-confidence to achieving that objective. He would face powerful opposition. He would take startling risks. He would begin to make his name.

PART II

THE
FIRST GREAT
AMERICAN
CLASS WAR

5

MAN IN BLACK

IN 1782, WHEN MORRIS and Hamilton began a national transformation built on the Money Connection, the man who would one day face greater danger than anyone else for opposing their efforts was living in the steep, twisty remoteness of the Allegheny Mountains. His name was Herman Husband.

Or Harmon Husband. Or Harman, or Husbands, and those were just variations on a birth name; he had true aliases and pseudonyms too. A sometime fugitive from hanging for treason, a preacher to the backcountry poor, and a radical political activist, Husband withdrew behind masks in his writings and sometimes in his life, disappearing into projections of himself as the Old Quaker, Hutrim Hutrim, Lycurgus, and the dead-giveaway in-joke Tuscape Death.

In both fiction and fact, Husband saw visions and read biblical prophecy and applied them to his ideas about contemporary politics and economics. Having visions was of course unusual, even strange, but biblical interpretation, violating no known boundary between science and religion, was a common practice of sophisticated Enlightenment-era people. The great physicist Isaac Newton wrote a famous treatise making detailed predictions based on close reading of the Books of Daniel and Revelation. Herman Husband himself wasn't just a visionary evangelical but a self-taught naturalist, an expert in geology, with refined surveying and mapmaking skills. He also engaged in the pragmatics of electoral politics. In multiple legislative bodies, he represented people whose interests were normally ignored.

Sometimes he went much further than that on his constituents' behalf. He could disappear, but he could reappear too, sometimes when least expected.

The inveterate resistance to received authority that would ultimately pit him against Alexander Hamilton became evident in Husband before Hamilton was born. Husband was born in 1724, and, unlike the constituency he spoke for, he was born rich. The Husband family had arrived in the Atlantic colonies as indentured laborers; by the time he appeared, they'd managed to rise to the second tier of a tobacco aristocracy that thrived, via enslaved labor, on the Maryland banks of Chesapeake Bay. The boy's overwhelming sense of moral imperative kicked in when he was sent, at the age of seven, to live for a time with his maternal grandfather, who operated on what he himself defined as the strictest religious principles: unlike Husband's parents, he owned no people and grew tobacco without relying on slavery. Evenings, the boy bunked with the indentured workers and hired hands in their quarters, listening as the old man read Bible passages aloud and the workers recited prayers by heart. Back home, he still heard his grandfather's deep voice and felt the evil in his family's reliance on evil systems that sustained him in luxury.

At twelve, he began having experiences of his own sinfulness, which plunged him into anguish, and of divine forgiveness, which gave him great relief and joy. At that age, the sins had mainly to do with showing off, and he vowed to give up jumping and wrestling. As a teenager, he was a good dancer and card player, yet he disdained the waste, greed, and sheer vapidity he saw everywhere in the leisured, partying plantation life he was being raised to take up.

For him, these spiritual conflicts took embodied form. He was really in the Temple with the money changers when Jesus came in with the many-corded whip. When he cried out in regret, he saw, in reality, the anger on the face of God melt away in pleasure and love. His parents' Anglicanism—the Church of England was legally established in

Maryland—seemed to offer no path for exploring the intensity of these experiences. Anglicanism felt deadly to his spirit, and at seventeen, amid a joyful experience of what was called New Birth, he left the established church and joined the Calvinists in dissenting Presbyterianism.

Not so long ago, wars had been fought over those conflicting theologies. Making a religious break, Herman Husband scandalized his family and the whole world he came from.

He wasn't alone. He was being drawn away from his family and its plans for him by a youth and working-class movement that came rolling through the Atlantic colonies in the 1730s and '40s, outraging traditional religionists and bewildering liberal rationalists. The movement's participants criticized religious formalities, favoring an individual's inner feeling of divine presence. They castigated the ordained clergy for obstructing the spirit's growth. Holding spontaneous services in the fields and streets, they succumbed to the delight of a loving holiness inherent in Creation and called their mass movement a Great Awakening. To them, not dull practice but direct perception and living emotion offered the only way to the Millennium, the biblically prophesied rule of Christ returned to Earth.

This insistence on interior, personal experiences seemed in some ways a revival of older theologies. At this scale, though, it was new. The Awakening unified enthusiasts throughout British America in breaking a lot of rules.

To young Herman Husband, it was thrilling. The Awakening reflected back to him, en masse, powerful religious intimations he experienced in solitude. Old Christian teachings conflicted regarding the Millennium. Some traditions predicted a time of horrible global tribulation under an Antichrist, the Beast of the Book of Revelation; some saw a final showdown, a titanic war ending all life on Earth, with the faithful ascending to eternal bliss in Heaven, the infidels damned to eternal torture in Hell. But some Awakening preachers were suggesting that the Millennium might be imminent in this generation, without any tribulation. The rule of Christ might prevail eternally here on an Earth blissfully and peacefully transformed. Christ was the consciousness of divine love and forgiveness within each person, a consciousness occurring at first in America—as evidenced by the Awakening itself—and soon to spread around the world.

For Husband, these ideas about a loving and forgiving earthly transformation enlivened not just his mystical calling but also his opposition to what he experienced as brutality in human affairs. The Awakening was introducing him to a whole community that made connections like his, connections between intense religious experience and opposition to political and economic oppression. For generations, agitation for equality had perennially gone on in the British Atlantic countryside and port cities, a movement aiming to undo combinations of wealth and government and equalize access to political power. It embraced the sailors toiling under violent discipline on the merchant and slaving ships, the tenants who worked the great landlords' fields, the day-laborers who made farms bustle and produce, and the small landowners and artisans, crushed by debt and threatened with foreclosure, who by the 1770s would be selling government chits cheap to rich investors. The great majority of free people, that is, living in the colonies that nobody yet knew would become the United States.

These American conflicts between labor and wealth played into the Great Awakening, and they would have a decisive impact on the American Revolution, but they went back to Britain. In 1649, Charles I was executed during the English Civil War. In the turmoil leading up to and away from that event, Puritan leaders denied a divine right to rule and established Britain as what they called a commonwealth. Even more radical religious groups defied not just monarchy but all hierarchies of British society. Workers' petitions calling government spiritually and politically corrupt demanded political and economic equality. The group known as Diggers, living in a state of spiritual communism, occupied land enclosed by the aristocracy, farmed it, and refused to leave. Sects known as Levellers, Familists, Fifth Monarchy Men, and Muggletonians also lived to varying degrees communally, embodying in their own lives the reign of Christ on Earth. Ranters ranted; Quakers quaked; all were pushing back against what they saw as satanic oppressions perpetrated by the spiritually, morally, and politically dead who lived in tyrannical idleness on the labor of others.

Foreshadowing a tone later taken by Herman Husband himself, the Diggers' declaration of 1649 denounced British government as "subtle selfish councils . . . by open and violent force . . . to uphold civil propriety of honour, dominion and riches one over another." Demanding liberty for the poorest people, the petitioners addressed "thou Powers of England" this way:

> Though thou hast promised to make this people a free people, yet thou hast so handled the matter, through thy self-seeking humour, that thou has wrapped us up more in bondage, and oppression lies heavier upon us; not only bringing thy fellow creatures, the commoners, to a morsel of bread, but by confounding all sorts of people by thy government of doing and undoing.

The petition promised defiance: "If you do oppose us," the workers warned, ". . . you shall be left without excuse."

The best-known radical group, the Levellers, were common soldiers in the anti-Royalist Puritan army led by Oliver Cromwell, which deposed the king. They wanted the right to vote for all adult male citizens. England's deeply rooted traditions of representative government, going back at least to the Magna Carta in 1215, acknowledged no such right. Because liberty and rights were equated with protecting property from taking by the sovereign without consent given by elected representatives, the right to vote was conditioned on owning a certain amount of property, the right to stand for representative office on owning even more. To the Levellers, both reason and Scripture seemed to point to a redeemed world where all people not only are created equal but also enjoy equal political participation and economic opportunity, because they're equal in the sight of God. At famous debates in 1647 at a church on the Thames in Putney, just southwest of London, Levellers argued eloquently that in a nonmonarchical system, ordinary men too should be allowed to vote for members of Parliament and other offices.

Cromwell, soon to make himself a dictator, didn't see it that way. The Leveller dream died at Putney. Working-class radicalism went on, though. And it crossed the ocean.

Few radical leaders in America or Britain were explicitly attuned to the liberation of anyone other than white men. Some were, sometimes. Some were capable of seeing the historic position of women as an unacceptable subjugation; more frightening to the upscale were actions carried out by women themselves when forming crowds and confronting, even outright attacking, price-gouging food merchants and retailers. Some pirate crews included women in egalitarian oceangoing communities performing famous feats of robbery. The movement could cross lines between free and chattel labor. Some beat-down white seamen and dockworkers, horrified by the traffic in human beings they took part in, organized to help the enslaved resist and escape. Black people in rebellion sometimes opposed the terrible physical discipline inflicted on white workers in ports and at sea, whose labor seemed, to Olaudah Equiano, an enslaved West African abolitionist and sailor, just slavery of another kind. Equiano envisioned an insurrection carried out by all of the oppressed together, black and white.

Still, the rebellions that Herman Husband would take up in colonial and Revolutionary America were led largely, on the record, by white men. The stated goal was to gain access to political power for white men regardless of property ownership and start legislating to restrain the power of wealth and promote equality for free working people.

Husband didn't embrace this radical political tradition all at once. Like other young men of his class, he was being trained as a businessman, planter, and investor. Yet the Great Awakening, shaking up processes and hierarchies relied on by the great merchants and landlords, led not just Husband but many other young, idealistic children of privilege to question established authority and make common cause with the lower classes. The sense of transformative potential equally alive within every individual inspired calls for abolishing slavery, encouraged churches led by black ministers, fostered demands for political participation by the working class, and aided women in making surprisingly independent decisions. Awakening preachers castigated the greed and luxury of the rich far more than they castigated sexual pleasure. Laborers filled with the spirit left their jobs to pray at odd hours. Churches split into old-light and new-light factions, old lights defending traditional worship routines, new lights joyfully improvising in the immediate presence of godhead. Husband, caught up in a flowering counterculture, broke with the old-light Presbyterians and joined the new-light Presbyterians.

But then he broke with them too. He'd discovered the Society of Friends, known as Quakers.

Even the new-light Calvinists retained a lot of formal structure and imposed insight through prescribed practice that fostered hierarchy. Husband found in Quaker theology a relentless focus on inner light and the movement of the spirit within. While that theology's roots were squarely in the old confrontational traditions of the Levellers, Ranters, Diggers, Familists, and others, by the eighteenth century the Quaker Meeting had largely shed the histrionic style. Though still widely discriminated against, by the time Husband joined them the Quakers were often successful businessmen and other respectable citizens, their church systems highly organized yet dedicated to inner light and equal participation. To Husband, the meeting's encouragement of freedom of conscience, greater equality of women, strict code of nonviolence, and the beginnings of a turn against slavery seemed closest to the divinity he was experiencing on his own.

His joining the meeting further shocked the world he came from, but he fully adopted its ways. He seemed to have finally found both God and himself.

And yet one day, after many years as a leading member of the Quaker community, a successful planter and investor with a growing family, the mature Herman Husband felt moved by the spirit to break the shared silence of meeting for worship and speak in condemnation of Quaker discipline itself. He announced that it had become impossible for him to comply with that discipline while also following the spirit's promptings of his free conscience.

This was in 1764. Husband and his family were living in the back-country of North Carolina. Throughout his long spiritual journey, despite restless moral and political probing, he'd been having a busy and financially successful time. When still in Maryland, he'd married, had children, bought a plantation, become part-owner of two copper mines and a smelting business. He was a diversified planter and businessman, like his father—though, like his grandfather, he never enslaved anybody.

He'd first come to western North Carolina in the 1750s, on business. A fad was under way among upscale British Atlantic colonials for specu-lating in western land; he'd come on a buying expedition for a Maryland consortium. The region was little settled by white people then, and Hus-band soon owned more than 10,000 acres of his own along the Sandy Creek and the Deep River. Western land, vast and fertile, had high value, at least as a speculation, but another appeal of the backcountry, for him, came from a sense that traditional social oppressions might be sloughed off here. Husband was immersed in reading and interpreting the pro-phetic books of the Bible, especially the Book of Daniel. He had a feeling the American western country had potential as a new promised land, a literal manifestation of the biblical land of Canaan.

The exact nature of his 1764 conflict with the Quaker Meeting of Cane Creek in backcountry North Carolina was poorly documented and would never be perfectly understood, but to Husband it involved freedom of conscience. He'd committed to the Quakers in part because they en-abled unusually equal status for women. Yet the confrontation emerged from his displeasure with the community's decision to certify one Ra-chel Wright, a minister in the church, as a member of good standing. She'd gotten in trouble with the meeting, openly criticizing it for its assessment of an allegation of rape brought by her daughter Charity: the meeting blamed both the rapist and Charity; Rachel found shar-ing the blame outrageous. Then she apologized for her criticism and asked for the "good standing" certificate. She wanted to move away from the region while continuing in the church. The meeting decided to grant her request. Then it named Herman Husband as a ringleader of a group that, having wanted to deny the certificate, dissented from the decision to grant it.

It was true that Husband had no desire to support Wright. There was some poorly recorded bad blood between them. But when he inveighed during the meeting against Quaker discipline, his point was that the organization was trying to scapegoat and silence him. The whole point of this church, Husband insisted to the congregation, was to hold sacred the free expression of individual conscience. For that rant, the meeting expelled him.

Every church does this in the end, he thought—denies a member the right to voice revelations of the spirit when those revelations conflict with procedures of the church. He was forty now. For the first time since his youth, he had no religious community. Caught up in intimations of the sacred, immersed in studying the prophetic books, Herman Husband, no longer seeking a spiritual home, was on his own.

He'd meanwhile been pursuing hopes both spiritual and political for the western country. Back in the East, he'd seen the worst of the situation of free labor up close. Few people there were able to do what the Husband family had done: rise up from servitude and become independent, even prosperous. Two-thirds of white arrivals in the Atlantic colonies came as laborers for others, either indentured or, worse for the laborers, contract-free and working only at will. Everybody's goal was to save money from wages and become small landowners, but most of the good land was held in huge parcels by a small number of old colonial families who pursued dynasties that Husband called "Babylonish," setting their descendants up to avoid work and live in dazzling splendor for generations to come.

Anyway, indentured labor killed many of the laborers before their contracts ended. Various infringements could end up extending servitude more or less indefinitely. For many who outlived their contracts and entered a growing workforce, all hopes for independence were stifled by systems made and managed by those who lived off their work in what Husband had learned from the Bible to condemn as luxury and idleness. Many who produced that wealth by working the land, making the goods, and providing the services became tenants at best, landless day laborers at worst. Many who did become smallholders lived in constant fear of ruin.

Husband could see clearly that this state of oppression emerged from practical structures deliberately built into colonial seaboard governments from the beginning of British settlement. The tenants working landlords' properties paid rent in money or crops or both. Any shortfall became a debt to the landlord; tenants falling further and further behind lost the chance to save hard money and get out. Owners of small farms and shops were stymied by revolving debts to the class of landlords and merchants who would, in 1776, become investors in the Public Debt of the United States. Poor farmers and artisans needed money to sustain and improve their businesses, and only merchants and landlords had it, so loan terms were set by the lenders at interest rates at times reaching as high as 12 percent per month, payable only in the same hard-to-find coin. Debtors went into downward spirals that turned their hard work into pure debt service.

And when they defaulted, creditors foreclosed and took furniture, farms, shops, livestock, and tools, turning families out, monopolizing more and more land, and making former owners tenants and laborers or making them vagrants, subject to arrest. With the tenant class getting dug in, smallholders trapped by predatory lending feared falling into tenancy, or day labor, or prison. The rich, in the process, got richer.

It was all by design, and Husband, inspired by his reading and his experience, saw the chief designer as the Beast in the Book of Revelation, the design itself as the rule of the Antichrist. The key feature of the system was extreme political inequality. The whole purpose of colonial governments in the seaboard capitals seemed to be to deny ordinary people legal recourse for their oppression and keep them eternally under wealth's boot.

The right to vote in the colonies, as in Britain, had always been conditioned on owning a certain amount of property—protecting property remained the avowed purpose of representative government—but the electoral inequality went further than that. Small farmers and master artisans who did qualify to vote suffered systemic disadvantage. More prosperous counties held more of the seats in colonial legislatures. Port cities, where merchants held sway, had legislative seats of their own. Legislatures refused to establish rural counties where population size justified them. Polling places, conveniently located for the well-off, forced smaller players to take precious time to travel on bad roads just to cast a vote. Taxes passed by the gentry in the legislatures gave no breaks to poor and ordinary people, and the taxes were regressive, often taking the form of labor. People were required to work on roads and other public projects, which were designed for the convenience of big growers and merchants; the rich bought themselves out of performing the labor and won, from legislator cronies, lucrative no-bid contracts for managing the projects.

Law existed to enforce the inequality. Judges appointed by governors were themselves landlords, merchants, and creditors and eagerly punished poor debtors and tax delinquents. Government administrators were gentry too, appointed by friends and family. One well-connected person could hold so many positions at once that the appointments were passed down in rich families as assets. Town commissioners thrived on salaries funded by the taxes they collected; they also took cuts of the taxes and were themselves often exempt from taxation. Sheriffs seized tax delinquents' and debtors' property, also for a cut, at many times the rate of what was owed. Registrars and notaries did little but charge high fees, often set by whim, for stamps and signatures required by law mainly for their own enrichment. The legal establishment of religion required people of all faiths and varying churches to pay onerous tithes and church fees to the established clergy.

All that's what ordinary people meant by corruption: political, moral, spiritual. American government was rife with it.

But when Husband first arrived as a buyer in western North Carolina, the backcountry had few roads coming from the East. The big spaces, the high, deep, uncut timber, the sparser administrative systems: opportunities seemed to exist for starting over, manifesting his political and religious ideas, building Canaan in a new American form.

The backcountry wasn't by any means uninhabited. People had long been living there. Husband was keenly aware of the fact that white people moving into the region went to war with the original inhabitants; awful violence was committed by both the encroachers and the defenders. Some settlers also brought with them what Husband saw as the evil of African slavery. As he assessed the situation, white people stole land from what he called American Natives and stole what he called African Natives' labor to work that land, a system that left poor white backcountry settlers in poverty, already starting to face the problems they'd left the East to escape. Fulsome false advertising by big speculators drew poor white people to western North Carolina, on tracks called the Great Indian Trading Path and the Great Wagon Road; many found on arrival that corrupt local administration prevented them from getting clear title to tracts they thought they'd bought. They were required to pay extra, or pay rent, or go into debt. Many effectively became instantaneous tenants, even while paying the usual high fees for required government services.

At first, Husband believed such violations could be reversed by persuasion. In 1756, when still only contemplating a permanent move to the backcountry, he'd written to Lord Granville, the proprietor, via a Crown charter, of the region where Husband had bought his land. He asked Granville to make a fair peace with the Native people and called for outlawing slavery in the western backcountry.

"However trifling this may seem," he warned the proprietor, "[slavery] will one time or other be the exercise of the whole nation either in timely stopping such growing evil, or when time is past in lamenting that which cannot be recalled." He also urged Granville to allow no religion to be legally established in the backcountry, stifling freedom of conscience. He suggested that the legislature take active measures to prevent administra-

tors and landlords from issuing fraudulent warrants and charging exorbitant rents and random fees; legislation should instead actively aid the
smaller western farmers, artisans, and laborers, those without Husband's
kind of acreages, in prospering independently.

He sent the letter to Granville in London. Granville didn't respond.
By 1764, when he was thrown out of the Quaker Meeting, Husband had
already faced the fact that in contradiction of his hopes for the West,
North Carolina's endemic corruption was flowing westward. In 1766,
when a local movement began forming to take direct action against government, on behalf of the oppressed and disadvantaged, people looked
to him for leadership, and he wanted to take a stand. He and the Quakers were done. The Great Awakening, too, had petered out. For many
young people of means, the movement had been a kind of fad; in the
1760s, maturity directed them back to more respectable worship. But not
Husband—and not the working class, where evangelical fervor still connected with protest against social and political inequality.

He had big responsibilities now. His family spanned almost a generation. Two wives had died; his third wife, Emy, like his eldest son, John,
was in her twenties, and her education was more advanced than that of
most backcountry settlers. Husband had met Emy in the Quaker meeting; after he was expelled, she was warned by the church not to marry
him, but she came from notably independent, even confrontational people. Her brother had been expelled from the meeting for out-of-wedlock
sexual activity with two women. When Emy did marry Husband, and the
meeting prohibited members from attending the wedding, her mother led
a group of women in a walkout, went to the ceremony, and celebrated her
daughter's marriage. Then they were expelled.

Emy bore him more children, and Husband engaged in what he knew
was some dangerous thinking. The way he felt, the first stage of sexual
attraction between a man and a woman represents the crown of creation
biblically evoked by the Song of Songs. Asceticism had it wrong: uncon-
summated desire, he thought, is the highest creative state of the spirit,
an image of Christ's love for his church. The penalty for consummation,

though, is marriage, and marriage, he'd come to think, fosters not just repetition, jealousy, and exclusivity but the production of too many children. Husband loved Emy and his children. But if people were allowed to consider both the realities of nature and their consciences, he thought, they'd find some reliable way of controlling their own reproduction. "I shall not say all I can say," he added when writing those ideas down.

He certainly hadn't been able to control his own reproduction. His family's support would be critical to what he sensed was a new purpose in his life. If the poor farmers of backcountry North Carolina wanted leadership by the better-educated and better-off, it wasn't just Husband who had the right qualities. Emy and the older children were ready to make a stand.

As he began what was to become his most dramatic resistance to authority so far, his spiritual life began changing too. Having spent his life studying the prophetic books, he was reading them in a new way. The authors of Daniel, Ezekiel, Nehemiah, and Revelation had been talking all along, Husband saw now, about the pragmatics of bringing about what he was beginning to call good government in contrast to the corrupt, satanic government that thrived on economic oppression of the many. The old prophecies and narratives, intricately detailed with coded imagery, showed in simple, practical terms exactly how the tyranny advancing daily in the American backcountry worked and how it might be overcome. The whole purport of biblical prophecy was radical political economy in America.

Ezekiel 41:7 describes the restored Temple of the New Jerusalem. To Husband, that passage now demonstrated the proper structure of good government: a building resting on a broad, representational foundation, with side chambers winding upward, creating a tapering effect to indicate increasing purity at the higher levels. Daniel 11:31 condemns "the abomination that maketh desolate," glossed by Matthew 24:15 as "the abomination of desolation": the destruction of the Temple of Jerusalem, the ruination of the sacred city, the captivity of a lamenting people, the end of good government, and the theft of labor by those who want to live in idle luxury.

Certain particularly American conflicts were also clarified. In Ezekiel 47:22–23, the prophet is given the exact boundaries of Israel and learns that the land must be allotted to immigrants as well as descendants. The passage revealed to Husband that the land being stolen from the original people of the West would be a "prize worth all the kingdoms of Europe," he wrote, ". . . if [the Native people and the colonial settlers] were united and able to defend ourselves in the peaceable possession thereof . . . Could we but hit on a plan . . . to enjoy it in peace among ourselves and secure it under a true and free republican government to our posterity, free to emigrants from all parts of the world who will come and join us in the union."

The fifth chapter of Nehemiah enjoins rulers from subjecting the people to bondage via food scarcities. It told Husband that the North Carolina government must be forced to pass laws restraining the big land speculators and protecting the rights of those who do the physical labor that improves the land. "Nothing is more hurtful to the common wealth," he told his neighbors, citing scriptural authority, "than for individuals to hold unreasonable quantities of lands and rent them out to the poor."

He read Genesis 49 in a new light too. There Jacob criticizes his grown son Issachar—who prefigures one of the tribes of Israel—by likening him to a strong ass, bearing two burdens, who sits on the ground and becomes passive, paying tribute despite his strength. Husband took the ass to be a symbol for the unfortunate people who assent to their own oppression under dual burdens—crushing civil taxation and religious tithes and fees—"rather than exert themselves," he said, "to maintain their liberties . . . neutrals," he called them, who by degrees become "despicable slaves."

His mission now was to arouse the people to use their strength. If Issachar only knew it, he could rise and shake the burdens off.

The kind of bottom-up action Husband began leading in the North Carolina backcountry in the mid-1760s was known as a regulation, its proponents regulators. The term, like the action, went back to Britain's old traditions of labor agitation. Ordinary American colonials demanded that the provincial legislatures regulate the power of wealth. Break up landlord and merchant monopolies on land and credit. Make judges accountable to the majority. Prohibit the cronyism in official appointments. Free the debtor class from predatory lending by establishing public banks, known as land banks, for small, easy-term loans to farmers and artisans. Lower the barriers to voting by enfranchising poor white men.

Regulators often demanded, too, that government issue low-denomination paper currencies and make them legal tender, requiring merchants and landlords to accept them for payment of interest on debts. The British government never liked the colonial government's paper currencies—by the time Husband got involved with regulation in North Carolina, Parliament was moving to prohibit the colonies from issuing them—and the American investing class soon to be led by Robert Morris would come to loathe being forced to accept depreciating paper at its face value for interest payments and loan payoffs.

But that's exactly why regulators embraced government paper as the people's money. It wasn't just that paper eased small-scale trade in the ordinary coin-starved economy. It did, but depreciation itself was a boon to strapped debtors. Paper's value diminishing below face value over time built a form of debt relief right into money. To the most radical regulators, interest and principal payments ought to be reduced all the way down, an effective debt cancellation, as in the Bible days of Jubilee.

Husband endorsed those aims. Joseph advises Pharaoh to keep a surplus in good times to be drawn on in lean times, advice Husband read as a guide to elevating government paper currency and reducing reliance on metal. In his view, clinging to gold and silver, as the merchants did, perpetually shifted Joseph's surplus away from the workers who create it, locking it in the coffers of the idle few and impoverishing the countryside. By 1766, he was more than ready to help lead a direct effort, politically and biblically ordained, to end corruption in government and free the people.

But he faced a fundamental problem of conscience. Denied fair access to voting, regulators sought to force government to comply with the will of the majority by engaging in what was known as riot, with two related goals: making it impossible to enforce oppressive laws and intimidating a legislature into changing the laws. That was regulation: direct attack on the perpetrators of corrupt systems. Husband remained a pacifist. Though no longer a Quaker, he remained committed to the teaching that violence, in its essence, spawns violence: transformative, lasting change comes only from confronting evil nonviolently.

And riot was flat-out violence. Communal, festive, theatrical, rough, terrorizing, an integral part of the long movement on behalf of labor, crowd action had gone on for generations in Britain and then in its Atlantic colonies. Smash-and-grab food rioters attacked the stores of price-gouging merchants and owners. Men with blackened faces, dressed in women's clothes or as fantastical renditions of Native people, seized debt courts and disrupted prosecutions. Gangs broke into jails, rescued debt prisoners, enforced boycotts of foreclosure auctions, and cut down trees to block sheriffs' entry to their regions. Often the targets of riot weren't just officials and businesspeople but those seen as collaborators with official oppression, who might be tarred and feathered or forced to ride backward on horses or rails.

Such actions could be impressive. Colonial legislatures could be made wary of enforcing certain laws. Sometimes they even passed the economic-relief laws the people demanded.

But Husband made clear to his comrades in regulation that he refused on principle to engage in any act of violence, even in self-defense, even against what he condemned as satanic abomination. He could organize. He could publish pamphlets calling on Issachar the strong ass to shake off its burdens. "Should we now through fear or favor act as we have done, contrary to duty and Interest?" Husband asked the people of western North Carolina:

> So far as we do this, we contribute to all the mischief consequent upon it. Where then is that moving principle self-preservation? Will you, can you, voluntarily submit yourselves to ignominy and want?

These will aggrandize themselves and swim in opulence. Have they not monopolized your properties; and what is wanting but time to draw from you the last farthing? Who that has the spirit of a man could endure this? Who that has the least spark of love to his country or to himself would bear the delusion?

He could also represent the regulation through legitimate channels. In 1769, neighbors middling enough to have the wherewithal to vote elected him to the provincial legislature, the assembly that met in New Bern, on the eastern shore. Emy, at home, was to organize communication between him and the regulators as he argued their case in the legislature.

Serving in the assembly was what really changed Herman Husband's life. Immediately he came at odds with the body he'd been elected to serve, and while that body was powerful, he was fearless. His style alone made him an outsider. In Quaker black, he was already becoming gray- and wild-haired, with the presence of an older man, even an ancient from another time and place. Demands he made on the assembly brought him, for the first time, into direct conflict with the law. Spiritually inspired by the freedom of his own conscience, he was speaking in the assembly against the assembly. That was sedition.

Husband was arrested and jailed repeatedly, sometimes in New Bern, sometimes near home. At one point, a jury refused to indict him. Another time, hundreds of regulators massed and threatened to free him; the government, frightened, let him go. In one assembly debate, he warned the body that if he were arrested while speaking there, men would march on the provincial capital itself. For that, he was stripped of his legislative powers, expelled from the assembly, and arrested yet again. But when the regulators did march, the court acquitted him.

Under these circumstances, Husband was finding it impossible to fully dissociate himself from violence. He was a folk hero now, subject of song and rumor. "Who would have thought Harmon, that humdrum old fox, / Who looks so bemeaning with his tousled locks, / Would have had resolution to stand the tack . . . ," went an agitprop regulation song by Rednap Howell, an itinerant teacher from New Jersey living in the North Carolina backcountry and soon to be declared an outlaw.

Husband didn't want fame any more than he wanted violence. Yet his pamphlets and speeches were assailing authorities in uncompromising terms, and in September 1770, the violence they inspired went to extremes in the court-and-market town of Hillsborough, where the richest people in the region lived. Regulators entered the courthouse and handed the judge a petition. It included Husband's citations of biblical prophecy condemning regressive taxes, official fees, devious lawyers, and the lazy merchants and landlords who harmed hardworking laborers and small producers. The regulators demanded the court stop persecuting poor debtors and instead try the corrupt officials.

That was only a warning. Two days later, a crowd of about 150 men came whooping and jeering into Hillsborough. Husband was among those in front. They entered the courthouse and shut it down. Husband's disapproval of violence couldn't stop his colleagues from beating up lawyers and whipping justices of the peace. They dragged the most notoriously corrupt local official by his heels over the cobbled street, whipped him, chased him out of town with rocks and dogs, and dismantled his fancy house brick by brick. Occupying the town for two days, they held their own trial, putting a black prisoner at the lawyers' desk and shit in the judge's chair and convicting a list of officials of corruption.

For taking part in that riot, Husband was finally expelled from the assembly. The colony was in crisis, and so was he. On biblical principles, he'd been urging the people to resist. On biblical principles, he couldn't countenance the violence inherent in his comrades' resistance.

The government was meanwhile resorting to violence too. The North Carolina proprietorships had been bought out by the Crown and replaced with a royal government, and now the royal governor, Lord William Tryon, found himself dealing with trouble from two angles. The assembly, elected mainly by upscale eastern colonists, was even then coming into conflict with Parliament's new trade acts; North Carolina was joining others in the intercolonial resistance to royal government. The backcountry regulators identified those self-described patriots, now protesting British taxation without representation, as the same speculators, absentee landlords, administrators, and legislators whose corruption and unfair taxation they'd been seeking to overturn. The assembly escalated, passing a riot act that made participating in the regulation punishable by death. The regulators escalated back, announcing they would attack anyone in the western part of the province who sought the legal protection of the government. That was outright western secession, and the easterners had major land interests in the western country. Governor Tryon had hoped to quell the regulation by a tough negotiated settlement, but now he readied the provincial militia to move against the regulators.

Husband, inspired not only by principles of nonviolence but also by his realistic calculation of the result of an outright war between the regulators and the government, urged his comrades to moderate their stand and avoid armed combat. But in March 1771, when Tryon led the militia westward under his own command, the regulators armed up to meet it. On a field in the county of Alamance, Husband took part in last-minute negotiations with the governor's people. He knew he'd be hanged for treason no matter the result. He did what he could to achieve a nonviolent solution.

Negotiations broke down. Battle lines formed. Husband mounted up, eluded the troops, and escaped on the gallop.

His direst predictions were borne out when, after two hours of fighting, in what became known as the Battle of Alamance, many of his comrades had fled, with up to twenty-seven killed and sixty-one wounded. Of those taken prisoner, one was summarily hanged on the spot; six were tried and then hanged. Within months, six thousand regulators had signed loyalty oaths and received an amnesty for any past crimes.

Husband kept riding. He was going as fast and far as possible into parts unknown, a fugitive from royal justice wanted on a capital charge, his community shattered, his friends hanged, his farm seized by troops.

Emy, pregnant again, was following at a distance with her young children and older stepchildren and trying to avoid surveillance.

They were all heading northward to disappear. For Herman Husband to reappear, certain long-standing American conditions would have to change fundamentally.

6

NOTHING COMMONSENSICAL

TO ROBERT MORRIS, ALEXANDER Hamilton, and almost all of the other American Revolution leaders whose names would go down in history, what happened to the North Carolina regulators was exactly what should happen. Continentalists and State Sovereigntists alike stood firm in a belief that their struggle for freedom from British tyranny was not to be confused with a struggle for political participation by the unpropertied and legislation for the benefit of labor.

The upscale even had a name, shared across partisan lines, for the long tradition of direct action on behalf of labor. They called it "the Democracy." The term could refer to mob rule, attacks on both order and liberty, a resurgence of what they called the "levelling" ways of the spiritual communists of England in the previous century. It could also refer to representative legislatures that, while not of course filled with members of the laboring class, were overly susceptible to pressure from the levelling mob.

And yet given the sheer numbers necessary to success, the American Revolution depended on the support of ordinary working people. For the governing elite, that fact presented a puzzle. How to keep the masses focused on opposition to British tyranny, not opposition to American wealth?

For the Democracy, the same fact made liberating the majority of people essential to the Revolution's meaning. Workers had new hopes now. Independence from Britain might make America truly revolutionary and bring on at long last the egalitarian future.

A critical episode in the Democracy's crucial relationship to American independence occurred only a few years after Husband's escape from the regulators' defeat at the Battle of Alamance and brought the fight straight to Robert Morris himself, on his home turf in Philadelphia, where the radical movement scored an astonishing, even world-changing victory. To the Democracy's adherents, this episode demonstrated their centrality to the purpose of the American Revolution, making the War of Independence worth fighting. To Robert Morris, it revealed the Democracy as his most significant obstacle, more stubborn than State Sovereigntism, to founding an American nation on the Money Connection. The episode and its lessons would shape the course of Alexander Hamilton's career.

In Philadelphia in the mid-1770s, there lived a group of down-at-the-heels, radical political outsiders. They were about to have a decisive impact on the world-changing events of their day. Yet only one of their number would enjoy lasting fame, and that would be for all the wrong reasons.

He was Thomas Paine. In 1774, he showed up in Philadelphia and became the most obscure outsider in a group of obscure outsiders. Born in Thetford, England, in 1737, a working-class product of the imperial homeland, he'd been apprenticed in his father's trade as a maker of stays for corsets and sailed at sixteen on a privateer, probably the most degrading work available to white men of empire, also a site of rowdy, collective opposition to authority. Back on land, he scrounged a low-level job as a tax collector. He was fired. He got the job back. He was fired again. His wife died. They'd had no children. He kept going, but by the early 1770s, when he reached his late thirties, nothing looked likely to go well for Thomas Paine.

And yet through those hard years, he treasured an inner life so intense that it spilled over into a kind of elated worship of reason, free-thinking, science, liberty—of humanity's astounding potential for change and growth. He devoured the French Enlightenment philosophers in translation. He studied physics, chemistry, and engineering in depth. Never formally educated, with no Latin or Ancient Greek and no modern language but English, Paine was an intellectual anyway. And for all of his aimlessness, dishevelment, and learning, he was easy to talk to, penetrating, persuasive.

In 1774 he somehow got into a dinner at the Society of Honest Whigs, a fancy London dining club for discussing science, philosophy, and politics, organized by Benjamin Franklin, then living in London while serving as agent to Parliament on behalf of Pennsylvania and other colonies. Paine chatted Franklin up on their shared passion for experimental science, and when he mentioned possibly emigrating to one of the North American colonies, Franklin suggested his own, where even in absentia he remained the most powerful politician. Writing Paine a general letter of recommendation, Franklin suggested that the bearer might be employed as a clerk or an assistant tutor or surveyor.

Paine had married again and separated from his second wife under obscure circumstances. The separation somehow brought him a settlement of £35, and he spent part of it on a first-class ticket to Philadelphia. He caught typhus at sea and was carried in a blanket off the ship onto those noisy wharves, knowing nobody on the continent. He recovered, and thanks to Franklin's recommendation and his own irrepressible personality, he started making friends. Soon the owner of a Philadelphia bookstore made him the editor of a startup magazine.

Being an editor meant producing a lot of the content. Approaching middle age, Thomas Paine started doing something he'd never done before. Well-educated people in the Atlantic colonies often wrote for the public by imitating ham-fisted Latin translation and indulging in bombast and bathos, but Paine's English was colloquial and unpretentious, at once startling and absorbing. Before any other writer in America sounded especially American, this Englishman did, and it wasn't just the freshness of the voice. He attacked the institution of African slavery. He evoked sufferings at imperial hands of original inhabitants of both the

Americas and India. He showed an awareness of the social and economic plight of women.

His burst of creative and intellectual power didn't come out of nowhere. Paine had fallen in with the crew of radical outsiders. They wanted to put his talents to work, and they had personalities as creative and idiosyncratic as his.

One was Thomas Young, forty-four in 1775, an atheist and reader of Voltaire. He'd grown up on a subsistence farm in the foothills of the Berkshire Mountains, a child prodigy self-taught in multiple languages and on the violin. By apprenticeship, not schooling, Young had become a medical doctor—not an upscale profession. Like Paine, he had a romance with both reason and liberty, and Young could get pretty loud about it. A proponent of inoculation, he publicly called skeptical, better-established doctors blockheads. He was threatened with expulsion from Dutchess County, New York, for calling Jesus Christ a knave and a fool. Always poor, he had a growing family and an ailing wife, and his patients among the Dutchess tenant and laboring families were poor too. In the 1760s, like the North Carolina regulators, they began rioting for better working conditions and an end to the dominance of the region's landlords, the Schuylers and Van Rensselaers and others. Young advised and supported the rioters.

He arrived in Philadelphia by way of Boston, where he'd stood out for espousing class-war ideas that the upscale Boston Sons of Liberty found novel and dangerous. Not only should the American colonies rebel against Britain, Young urged, but also American working people should rebel against the American rich, and the American government should start favoring labor, small farming, and artisanship over wealth. Samuel Adams, the leading Boston organizer, disdained such ideas, but he had a more strategic approach than others in the middle and upper classes and saw in this energetic doctor a useful force. By the time Young got to Philadelphia, still poor, still accompanied by his wife and family, he'd ridden all over Massachusetts under Adams's aegis to integrate the town meetings into a single shadow government in opposition to the Crown. In Pennsylvania, he was ready to go further than that.

Another important member of the radical Philadelphia crew was James Cannon, Young's temperamental opposite. Born in Scotland, he was thirty-four, a quiet math teacher who liked to stay in the background, but his acuity as an organizer and his ambitions on behalf of laboring people were as strong as Young's. Cannon and Young worked especially closely with Timothy Matlack and Christopher Marshall, both longtime Philadelphians, both lapsed Quakers. Though known as a brawler and hard drinker, Matlack, thirty-nine, a brewer and bottler, seemed to get along with everybody and moved easily in circles both down- and up-scale. Marshall, sixty-eight, was a druggist; his profession seemed both scientifically advanced and weirdly suspect, even alchemical. Marshall also had universalist religious convictions that put him at odds with Thomas Young's high-volume atheism.

The group included another medical doctor: Benjamin Rush, thirty, the upwardly mobile son of a master artisan. Rush was torn. A fervent Presbyterian with advanced ideas about public health, the abolition of slavery, the plight of the poor, and the oppression of women, he had dreams of a genteel life and liked knowing famous people. He wasn't sure about some of the more radical aims of his group. There were others too: this group was loose, and it made common cause, when it could, with sympathetic members of the better-connected.

When Paine started drinking a lot of coffee with these men at Christopher Marshall's pharmacy, James Cannon's rooms, and Philadelphia's busy London Coffee House, they'd already begun using the emergency of the imperial crisis to bring about a startling social and economic revolution in Pennsylvania—a revolution far more radical than independence from Britain. Philadelphia had many scenes of squalor and neglect. Most of the better-off citizens chose to view poverty as a moral failing, their own prosperity as well-deserved. The only institution for relief of the poor was known as the Bettering House, where indigent families were sent to be morally "bettered" by Quakers, who took them in, segregated them by sex in dorms, and set them to spinning, weaving, and dyeing textiles for the profit of the house while being lectured on virtue.

The math teacher Cannon and the pharmacist Marshall decided to launch a venture in competition with the Bettering House. They called it the United Company of Philadelphia for Promoting American Manufactures, or the American Manufactory. In this system, women spun at home, on their own time. They brought the spun product to the Manufactory for dyeing and weaving by men. Families stayed together. There was no "bettering." Workers sat on the company's board, giving it a cooperative quality.

In output, the venture began bettering the Bettering House. The the radical group met and drank coffee there too, making their company an informal school of working-class politics. To the irritation of merchants such as Robert Morris, the city's workers demanded political participation in the new, ad hoc governing bodies that were emerging in resistance to Britain. In June 1774, more than a thousand artisans and laborers marched to the Pennsylvania State House and forced their way into an upscale meeting in solidarity with Boston's resistance. The crowd taunted the attendees. This wasn't a city committee, they said, but a merchants' committee. They demanded inclusion.

The patriot merchants' resistance, needing the crowd action that artisans, farmers, and laborers could provide, wanted to keep working-class agitation focused on harassing British government and its supporters, not rich Americans in general. As the ad hoc committees' social composition began going downscale fast, the upscale began pulling out of the committees and locating protest against Britain in the official Pennsylvania assembly. But that only made the city committees more working-class. And given the crisis, the committees were gaining, in some areas, more day-to-day power than the assembly. A class conflict thus prevailed within the most powerful colony's resistance to Britain.

Then, in April 1775, up in Massachusetts, shooting broke out between the British Army and local militias. Some delegates to the Congress, meeting in the assembly's ground floor room at the State House in Philadelphia, wanted to declare the colonies independent of Britain, but the body held fast to the position that what had now become an outright war was still being fought to bring the mother country to the negotiating table and arrive at a reconciliation that would keep the colonies within the empire. Declaring American independence would require unanimity among the the states. It remained off the table.

This reconciliationist position was led by the Pennsylvania assembly, which controlled the whole middle-colony bloc; it had moved to a committee room upstairs in the State House, where the Congress met downstairs. Reconciliation's firmest adherents included Robert Morris, then serving in the assembly, and the assembly's majority leader, John Dickinson. The body, though weakened, retained sole power to appoint and instruct Pennsylvania's delegates to the Congress; Morris and Dickinson themselves were among those delegates. With Pennsylvania withholding approval upstairs, there was no way to declare independence downstairs.

But the ad hoc committees, outside the assembly, more and more working class, more and more favored breaking with the mother country in order to bring about a social revolution at home. When militias started drilling in Pennsylvania in response to the possibility of a British invasion, James Cannon saw a way of taking control of the province's resistance to Britain and getting the Congress to declare independence.

In more than thirty new companies of city militia and more than fifty battalions across the countryside, the biggest class in every company held the rank of private. The mass of men with too little property to vote, that is, had suddenly become essential to Pennsylvania's survival, and the militia system did involve some degree of democracy. Musters saw drink, debate, caucus, and electioneering. Officers from colonels down were chosen by the militiamen themselves, who were allowed to vote in this case regardless of property ownership. Organizing all privates, across every militia unit, into a single committee that embraced the whole province would make them an irresistible armed force.

Thomas Young had experience from Massachusetts in riding far and wide to foster networks. Soon Cannon's idea was a reality. Pennsylvania's poorest white men were represented by a province-wide organization called the Committee of Privates, which served as yet another school of radical politics. With the province's security now dependent on organized labor, the privates saw themselves as a revival of Oliver Cromwell's New

Model Army, which had defeated monarchy in England in the previous century and spawned the Levellers. Robert Morris was then arming Pennsylvania, gaining new political power and monopolizing new commercial opportunities in the process. The province's poorest men, armed by him, were looking to end monopolies on both power and commerce. The country's strongest colony, host to the Congress, was in crisis over the very purpose of fighting a war with Britain.

In the winter and spring of 1776, Pennsylvania's internal division made something clear to the Massachusetts second cousins John and Samuel Adams, Richard Henry Lee of Virginia, and certain others in the Congress who, like the local radicals, wanted the war to lead not to reconciliation with Britain but to a collective resolution for American independence. Reconciliationists had been holding sway in the Congress because they were led by the all-powerful Pennsylvania delegation, instructed by the assembly upstairs. The Adams-Lee group now saw traditionally unenfranchised laboring people of Pennsylvania getting into a position to take down the host state's duly elected government and replace it with a legislature that would reverse current policy and shift Pennsylvania's great sway to supporting a break with Britain.

As much as anyone else in the patriot elite, the Adams-Lee group despised the Democracy. But neither Virginians nor New Englanders felt any special concern for the immediate fate of government in Pennsylvania. Samuel Adams had made use of Thomas Young's talents before. John Adams was friendly with Benjamin Rush. The gregarious Timothy Matlack got along with all classes and was serving as secretary to the Congress. In May and June, Samuel Adams convened a series of secret, strange-bedfellow meetings between his upscale independence faction in the Congress and Young, Cannon, Marshall, Paine, and their outsider crew from the street.

From there, even Robert Morris couldn't follow all the head-spinning things that started happening to his province and the country. On May

15, the Adams-Lee faction got a resolution through the Congress with a preamble that roped the other colonies' delegations, largely unwittingly, into calling Pennsylvania's duly elected assembly illegitimate. Paine coordinated with that effort, quick-publishing stirring pamphlets that linked the position of the Adams-Lee resolution with the position of the Philadelphia street and countryside. As secretary to the Congress, Matlack violated his oath of secrecy and helped the outsiders time their actions to coincide with the Adams-Lee efforts inside. On May 20, the radical crew called a crowd to the yard outside the State House. There, the people shouted away the elected assembly and adopted, by acclamation, resolutions to create a new government. On June 10, Philadelphia's militia battalions mustered. The privates acclaimed aloud, battalion by battalion, an end to the elected assembly; the officers followed the men. Via hard, long-distance riding by Young and others, that news was circulated to privates throughout the province, who took the same stand.

The Committee of Privates sent formal notice to the Pennsylvania assembly. Because they couldn't vote in assembly elections, the privates said, and were therefore not represented in that house, they would no longer follow its orders.

That bloodless military coup, carried out by the state's armed working class, self-organized on behalf of the Democracy, via efforts by Cannon and Young and the radical Philadelphia outsiders, toppled not just the assembly but the whole government of Pennsylvania that William Penn had founded in 1681. Less- and unenfranchised men—the majority of men—had taken control. They were looking to American freedom from Britain to cement their new power, and just as the Adams-Lee group had planned, the position of the mightiest province did now shift. On July 2, Dickinson and Morris, yielding to the collapse of their government, abstained, and the majority in the Pennsylvania delegation voted in favor of a resolution, introduced in the Congress by Richard Henry Lee, for making the American colonies independent of Britain. The resolution passed with only one state, New York, abstaining—close enough to call unanimity. The Declaration of Independence, explaining the resolution to the world, passed on July 4.

Drafted by Thomas Jefferson, a Virginia delegate, the Declaration would become famous for invoking equality. The word meant different things to different people. Neither Jefferson nor the other signers by any means believed that centralized government policy should regulate commerce to foster equality, socially and economically, throughout the United States, but the Declaration was issued by the Congress that July 4 only because people who believed in exactly that kind of equality pulled off a coup in Pennsylvania. The critical part played by radical populists in bringing about the country's independence would be expunged, ironically enough, from the most popular renderings of the Fourth of July story. At the time, the Democracy thought it had good reason for placing itself at the center of the American Revolution.

In September, with independence declared and the War of Independence under way, the radicals of Pennsylvania wrote a state constitution that fulfilled democratic dreams stymied since the time of the Levellers. The Congress continued to meet in the assembly's regular room, so the state constitutional convention met in the courtroom across the hall, letting the upscale men of the Congress take note, with amazement, of what was going on. Even the procedures for sending men to the convention were shocking to the American patriot elite that had adopted the Declaration. The convention delegates had been elected without regard for property.

Benjamin Franklin presided over the state convention and was later sometimes credited with having written the resulting document. A situationist not always as wily as he tried to be, never in any way politically consistent, Franklin was hoping, as always, to land on what he guessed might be the winning side of history, and he did edit and provide input for an early draft of the new state constitution and supported many of its measures. Still, it wasn't clear to some observers that he was paying much attention to the proceedings. In the chair, he dozed. Just as often he crossed the hall to work on his real interest, the Congress's diplomacy with France. Soon he would be back in his beloved Paris, the American revolutionary toast of the town.

Writing the new Pennsylvania constitution was led most notably by the teacher James Cannon, with help and some mutual dissent among the activist Thomas Young, the brewer Timothy Matlack, and the druggist Christopher Marshall, and they based the document directly on their comrade Thomas Paine's famous pamphlet "Common Sense." That publishing phenomenon of January 1776 had made its author abruptly and internationally famous by calling for American independence and castigating the king. But it called for and castigated far bigger things than that. While Benjamin Rush had persuaded Paine to give the pamphlet a nonthreatening title, there was nothing commonsensical about "Common Sense."

Paine set out an ambitious blueprint for creating an egalitarian national government of the United States. Young, Cannon, Matlack, and Marshall used that blueprint to build out a new, constitutionally democratic Pennsylvania. The most radical element in "Common Sense," which the convention delegates put into practice in Pennsylvania, was Paine's blunt rejection of the American merchant and landlord class's justification for war on Britain: defending supposedly ancient rights, supposedly inherent in property. Paine wasn't saying outright that he wanted to remove property qualifications for voting in an independent America, but that's what he meant, and his imagined national legislature, gathering in a huge house, was to be hyperrepresentative, filled via a multitude of tiny election districts and passing laws unchecked by any upper house. Paine's national government also had no monarch, only an executive body elected by the representative legislature. Thus the executive was made dependent on the legislature, with no veto power over laws. And judges were to be directly elected by the people.

These proposals were shocking. Upscale American revolutionaries revered aspects of what they called the true and "ancient" British constitution; they hymned its fabled checks and balances, which protected an individual right of property via representation of the propertied. To them, the American Revolution was a moral response to Britain's having violated, in that precise regard, its own supreme law: government had taken property, via taxation, without representation, plus related tyrannical outrages.

By rude contrast, "Common Sense" derided the British constitution as no constitution at all, its so-called checks and balances only an out-of-balance check against the people. In a free United States, which Paine wanted to see ruled more representatively than any nation had ever been, all people—he meant, at first, all free male adults—were to enjoy equality via an underlying right, not of property, but of national citizenship.

This radical program for the whole nation was piloted in the new Pennsylvania constitution. The document's authors removed property qualifications not only for voting but also for holding office. They gave ordinary Pennsylvanians power, not just in a big, one-chamber assembly but diffused throughout town meetings and committees, with farmers, artisans, tenants, and landless laborers carrying out direct political oversight beyond election time. Cannon and Young even proposed giving the new legislature a power to cap how much property any one citizen could own—even to confiscate the excess.

That didn't fly, but the emerging government was a full-fledged legal mechanism for ending the elite monopoly on politics and thereby curbing concomitant monopolies on commerce. When the convention finished its work, Pennsylvania had the first government anywhere in Europe and its colonies to disconnect liberty from ownership. The new constitution didn't abolish slavery. But in 1780, an assembly operating under it would also make Pennsylvania the first government anywhere in Europe or its colonies to pass an act for gradual abolition, freeing by law those born in slavery.

The opening day of the first assembly elected under the new state constitution saw not only some traditionally upscale elected officials coming down the State House hall, but also farmers, artisans, and laborers, most of them having never served in government before. They passed the assembly room where the Congress met and went up the stairs to a committee room to start legislating. "Good God!" said John Adams. He was reacting to the new Pennsylvania constitution. In his last-ditch, backroom quest for American independence, he'd secretly helped bring about a radically democratic Pennsylvania, and he had plans to make sure nothing like that happened in Massachusetts. He predicted that under this kind of government, the people of Pennsylvania would soon want King George back. Other signers of the Declaration naturally agreed.

The people of Pennsylvania didn't seem to feel that way. Sixteen months later, a gray and tousled man in black, representing a remote western part of the state, appeared in the assembly to take his seat. It was Herman Husband.

Back in March 1771, when negotiations with the royal governor of North Carolina broke down before the Battle of Alamance, Husband had ridden away, a fugitive from hanging, and kept moving, riding at last all the way up into the rugged mountainous terrain of a barely settled part of Pennsylvania known as the Glades, whose one tiny village, when he got there, was Bedford, with a steep dirt road and a tiny fort on the banks of the Juniata River. The Glades lay about one hundred miles east of the village of Pittsburgh at the headwaters of the Ohio River. Yet, the combination of altitude and loneliness made the place seem even more western and remote.

The mountains were hard to pass over. The country shot upward and downward, full of boulders, huge trees, steep cliffs. Bottomlands grew bluegrass as tall as a person. Human settlement was scarce. The area had mainly seen hunting parties, both Native and white, taking bear, deer, and beaver for the skin trade and camping while packs of wolves bayed at night.

An ideal hideout. Yet Husband couldn't seem to keep his head down. Some of the white men's hunting camps were becoming semipermanent, even quasi-settlements. Husband introduced himself to the hunters as "the old Quaker." He wouldn't shoot game, but he helped out around the camps, and the hunters protected him. Soon he started claiming Glades property, long considered too wild to farm, and registering it under a more revealing alias, Tuscape Death.

With only his horse and basic tools, he cleared land and built a cabin and shed and sent Emy news of his whereabouts. She'd given birth to a son and was awaiting word in Hagerstown, in western Maryland, with the children. When the farm was ready, Husband took the risk of traveling, in disguise and under aliases, to meet them. He led them up to the place where few people, Native or European, had ever tried to live.

The Husband family was used to backcountry life. Still, when traveling into the mountains with packhorses, his grown sons bucked their father's refusal to bear arms. They walked with guns loaded.

The region turned out to be fertile. Before long, the Husbands were prosperous, growing rye in abundance, with two stables, a threshing floor, a commercial sawmill, a nice house, and a library of ultimately more than eight hundred books and pamphlets. Though still in hiding, Husband explored the most forbidding parts of the Alleghenies, looking for easier east-west passes to help develop the region. Hauling surveying rods and chains, he and his horse wore suits of thick hide to fight their way through and around laurel and thorns, fallen timber, huge rocks.

He brought his love of scientific precision to studying the complexity of the flora and fauna. He identified and catalogued multiple mineral types. He drew elegant maps, perfectly scaled on grids, plotting longitudinal and latitudinal degrees and integrating neatly handwritten annotations. He revived his hopes for a better world in a remote western backcountry.

Partly as a result of his efforts, however, there was an influx of new settlers, sparking the interest of the usual speculators and absentee landlords. A political ring, tied to eastern officialdom in Philadelphia, formed at the courthouse in Bedford and promoted creditor and landlord interests via the usual lucrative public offices. To Husband, the Bedford ring represented the further progress of the Antichrist, and yet the world-changing events of 1776 filled him with excitement. Many former North Carolina regulators, mistrusting the upscale patriots they'd been trying to regulate, had stayed loyal, but Husband had a more hopeful experience. When first reading the eastern merchants' and lawyers' petitions and articles against British trade laws, he'd gotten the sense that the authors were moved, if possibly unknowingly, by the same Millennial spirit of good government that was moving him. The American Revolution, he now believed, would bring about what he'd wanted from the regulation. The Bible clearly prophesied American victory over British tyranny.

His pacifism thus again involved him in a contradiction. He abhorred war. He saw the War of Independence as a spiritual force for drastic cosmic change, General Washington leading the army prophesied to win the last battle for permanent good government on Earth. While it was clear that the agents of the Antichrist were alive and well, in Bedford's courthouse ring and elsewhere, Husband believed the independent United States, as prophesied, would destroy the rings of corruption and establish a new, national government, along radically democratic lines.

So when the Declaration of Independence nullified the old royal charges against him, Husband was ready to resume his quest for good government, for the Millennial America. And under the new democratic state constitution, his poor neighbors in the mountains had both the vote and equal representation for a remote county. Hence his election, in late 1777, to the wartime Pennsylvania assembly.

Taking his seat in Lancaster—during Philadelphia's British occupation, both the assembly and the Congress were meeting there—Husband entered a political maelstrom.

The state had become a scene of class conflict at a pitch never seen in elected government before. The traditional elite hadn't been purged. Robert Morris, for one, was a delegate to the Congress. The shift was that the anti-elites had come in. So while Pennsylvania still had the country's biggest and most dynamic commercial economy, with the Morris-led merchant conglomerates getting richer in wartime contracting, it also had the most democratic government in not only the country but pretty much anywhere: ordinary people dedicated to using their new power to level the economic playing field, not just via access to the vote but by serving on committees, outside the assembly, with ongoing regulatory powers.

Husband and the forces that he saw as the Antichrist were thus locked in a war within Pennsylvania's government. The war was over government's relationship to the practical economic matters that, for Husband, were the true subject of biblical prophecy.

And thanks to drastic inflation, practical economic matters in 1778 Pennsylvania were disastrous. The merchants' and investors' businesses were suffering; ordinary families were literally hungry. Food prices were quintupling in a year. The political division was over what to do about it. Times of privation had seen food riots, often led by women, but now the Democracy held a majority, in a legitimate legislature, with regulatory powers far superior to riot. The merchants, though, feared any government intrusion on their wealth. Each side blamed the other for the economic straits.

To this first stress test for the first radically democratic government, Husband brought, as usual, his own ideas. They differed sharply from the ideas of the merchant class. They also differed somewhat from the ideas of his colleagues in the Democracy.

Before his arrival, the democratic majority had voted to issue a small-denomination paper currency, unsupported by taxes or any other means of ensuring stability, and to make it legal tender. The merchants forever excoriated government paper's depreciation as confiscatory: government's taking value away from their investments and giving it to their debtors as a form of relief. They also asserted that this new currency would only drive prices further up. The people accused the merchants of price-gouging, deliberately slowing, even breaking, supply chains and withholding desperately needed staples, especially flour and wheat, to time the market for the highest return. In April 1778, the majority in the assembly introduced a system of regulation curbing such practices. There was even talk, especially outrageous to the merchants, of fixing prices by law. Trade, the merchants argued from the Morris position, should be as free as the air.

Husband supported the regulation system, as well as legal measures to break up merchant monopolies, but he presented the assembly with a bigger idea, a long-term solution. During his fugitive years, he'd been developing his biblically inspired vision of the fundamental nature of money. To him, the investing and merchant class, with its horror of any and all depreciation, was lost in superstition: they really believed stability was magically intrinsic to precious metals. But he saw the people, understandably desperate for relief from usurious rates, relying on currency depreciations that only contributed to the inflation that crushed them. It seemed to him that if paper fluctuated in value because of anxiety about its value against coin, the main problem wasn't that paper lost value, though it did, but that gold and silver, being scarce, were persistently overvalued. The whole paper-versus-metal monetary system, that is, which the two sides kept fighting over, fundamentally couldn't work.

So unpeg paper currency from metal, Husband now urged the assembly. Go off the hard-money standard.

To the bewilderment of both sides, he presented a full-scale plan for a currency-only system disconnected from coin and created and managed by government fiat. If some degree of currency depreciation were accepted as a balsam of life to a nation, as Husband put it—a natural tax, effectively, on the waste and superfluity that the rich draw from the excess production of laborers—then both inflation and depreciation might be steadied, regulated, by a centralized policy for depreciating paper on a slow, predictable schedule, with the rates printed on the bills. One good effect of this scheme, he said, if adopted throughout the states, or by the Congress itself, would be to free the whole United States from dependence on scarce foreign coin.

Another good effect would be to keep merchants from hoarding money. For in Husband's finance scheme, the rich would pay tax on both land and money in what would later be called graduated form: the richer paying progressively higher proportions, the poorer lower. "Money," he announced, "should be taxed, equal with property." And tax revenues should be earmarked not for interest payments to investors in public securities— such payments would cease—but for pulling each depreciating emission of paper out of circulation and issuing a new round at the new value, as well as to aid war widows and orphans and others who were suffering.

That was Herman Husband's monetary plan for bringing about good government on biblical principles. And by now, Robert Morris had just about had it.

These efforts in his state's government to regulate and equalize the economy by what Morris saw as ill-advised programs of government regulation, put forth by obscure, inexperienced people, for the direct benefit of their own kind and at the direct expense of his, to the detriment of what he saw as the state's overall economic health, which was inextricable from the health of the country: all that had to be pushed back hard. This was when, having served as a delegate to the Congress, Morris left the body—it would turn out temporarily—and was elected back to his state assembly for the 1779 session. He had a project to carry out there. It put him eyeball-to-eyeball with the Democracy for the first time.

When Morris reentered the Pennsylvania assembly as a minority member, leading a cadre representing the embattled elite, the mood in Philadelphia was tense. Because France had entered the war in support of the United States, partly thanks to the decisive 1777 American victory at the Battle of Saratoga, New York, British strategy required a massive defense of New York Harbor against the French fleet, so the British Army evacuated Philadelphia and marched north. Both the state assembly and the Congress returned from Lancaster to the State House in a city full of nervous suspicion.

Seeming British collaborators faced hostility and violence. Men were tried for treason. When loyalists' property was seized, the small, rich merchant group—those who caused and benefited from staples shortages and speculated in the Debt—defended loyalists' property rights. That made the rich seem, to ordinary citizens, literally traitorous, enemies to the people of the state, to the Democracy's aims for American independence, to the United States as a whole. People remained hungry while the merchants, despite their own complaints about the economy, were doing so ostentatiously well that courtiers at the French court of Versailles, hardly known for republican simplicity, spoke with disdain of "the rapid progress of luxury at Philadelphia" in the midst of a war. Rich people weren't serving army tours of duty. Some upscale Philadelphians had attended extravagant balls and shows put on by the British occupiers, and the city's Continental Army commander, General Benedict Arnold, was sponsoring the same kind of event and riding around town in a fancy coach, while both the public and the army rank and file suffered. Those known to have originally opposed independence, like Morris himself, came under especially intense scrutiny.

In the assembly, Morris's minority was trying to undo the democratic state government. They had an assembly committee writing a new constitution with an upper house, to put a check back on representation, and a powerful solo executive. They repeatedly demanded that the assembly call a referendum on the new-constitution question and tried to cripple the democratic majority by staying home to deny the assembly a quorum.

Tension started becoming unbearable in the spring of 1779. Responding to renewed street protests by sailors and other citizens, the assembly majority passed the kind of law Morris detested, further restricting monopoly, price gouging, and staples withholding. In keeping with the democratic constitution, enforcement of the new regulations was to be carried out by citizen committees, both in the city and throughout the state. The merchants, feeling harassed and cramped, responded by getting together with big farmers in refusing to accept paper money for sales of flour. The allied French fleet was coming into port with silver and gold, hard money—much preferred. But paper was all the money the people had, and they needed bread.

In May, furious citizens gathered in a mass meeting to do the one thing that Morris had inveighed most passionately against: instituting price controls by law and enforcing acceptance of paper money. Presided over by the universalist druggist Christopher Marshall, late of the radical crew behind the state constitution, the people elected new citizen committees to enforce compliance, investigate merchants and retailers who exceeded price ceilings, and distribute bread and flour to the poor. The fight was getting physical. As the committee and the militia began showing up at dockside warehouses and storefront streets to drag merchants and retailers off to jail, merchants and retailers resisted arrest.

Morris was naturally a chief subject of the committee's investigations. And yet there always seemed to be more evidence of chicanery against other merchants than against the man at the top of the merchant networks. He remained unabashed in organizing opposition to price-fixing rules and pursuing a revision of the state constitution. Others opposing price controls included some democratic leaders unsure of controls' efficacy and afraid poor farmers would get hurt; some upscale people, on the other hand, actually considered controls necessary, just as a wartime measure. In the end, the controls more or less failed on practical grounds and the committee dissolved, but hunger kept getting worse. By fall, Philadelphia's firewood prices were beyond reach, foretelling a deadly winter.

People expected the assembly to act to combat hunger and inflation, but that body, always less fully radical than the committees, chose not to act. In October, a reenergized Committee of Privates called another rowdy mass meeting. This time, the militiamen went all the way. They issued a proclamation identifying certain "disaffected persons" now living in the city.

That meant, that is, the Morris cadre. The militia mustered and announced an operation to seize all such people and exile them from the city. The assembly, the state's executive council, and even the city committee had begun to think things were going too far. But the privates were a committee too, and the militia—the city's whole male citizenry, armed—had rights and powers of its own. They were ready to march.

The merchants, as fed up as the militia, gathered in a three-story house on the corner of Walnut and Third. It was owned by James Wilson, a rich central-Pennsylvania lawyer, a friend of Morris, and a fellow speculator in the Debt and western land. Slight, bespectacled, brainy, Wilson had fortified his place against attack months before. Naming the house Fort Wilson, the merchants armed up and called for the support of an upscale group of officers known as the silk-stocking brigade. They prepared to defend Fort Wilson.

The militiamen arrived by drumbeat, parading four captive merchants they'd already nabbed. Later, some claimed they were passing the house when they were fired upon; either way, the militiamen quickly set up artillery and stormed the door. On gaining entrance, they set fire to the first floor and shot and killed one of the defenders, but gunfire beat them back, and now the silk-stocking brigade showed up, led by the president of the state's executive council, Joseph Reed. Though condemned by the merchant lobby as a rank appeaser and arouser of the people, Reed considered the attack on the house outside the law. He hoped to restore order.

In the ensuing fight, most of the casualties were on the city militia side, with four or five killed, including a black man, and around seventeen wounded, some badly. In the Battle of Fort Wilson, the merchants and investors held off the Democracy. The American class war, however, wrapped into and around the war against Britain, had taken on qualities never seen before. In the colonial period, riot by the Democracy had gone on intermittently against government and the rich, as had crackdowns by government on behalf of the rich—even the full-scale battle at Alamance that ended the North Carolina regulation. The Battle of Fort Wilson was something else again. Elements of constitutional government cracked down on the rich, the rich shot back at those elements of government, and moderates were caught in a crossfire both political and literal. Revolutionary Pennsylvania looked like a world turned upside down.

Even the elite's thrill of victory was short-lived. As Joseph Reed and the assembly scrambled to achieve some degree of compromise, Robert Morris was swept out of office in a landslide. The merchants' effort to bring back an antidemocratic constitution only seemed to place government ever more firmly in the hands of the people.

So when Morris returned to the Congress in 1781 and took up his job as the super-superintendent, and when he and Alexander Hamilton joined forces in failing to collect state requisitions in 1782, the ongoing situation in Pennsylvania had made clear to both of them the most disastrous effects of the state legislatures' jealous insistence on autonomy. It was true that Pennsylvania's assembly and executive council had disavowed, in the end, and even actively opposed, the militia attack on Wilson's house. But the council then pardoned all of the attackers. The assembly approved a city-administered flour-distribution program with special attention to militia families. As council president, Reed even issued a stern warning to the merchants: they couldn't expect to live in peace and luxury while the majority around them went hungry. Outraging the merchant and lending class, Reed was invoking a government power to require the cooperation of business on behalf of a greater good, even a regulation of private commerce by state law, if the merchants made that necessary.

It was also clear to Morris and Hamilton that these radically democratic economic policies weren't meant to stay in Pennsylvania. Both the national government that Paine proposed in "Common Sense" and Husband's monetary proposals reflected the movement's sense of itself as a kind of alt-Continentalism, in which legislating equality, not forging the Money Connection, was to be the nationally unifying force. Pennsylvanian ideas and tactics could already be seen creeping. Morris and Hamilton looked with dismay at many states where the upper classes did retain traditional powers, yet the legislatures remained lame in suppressing popular agitation. They bent to pressure, opening land banks, emitting paper money, passing legal-tender laws, breaking up monopolies, regulating prices, failing to collect taxes for requisitions dedicated to interest payments on federal bonds: a "detestable tribe," as Morris put it, of restrictions and obstructions of trade and commerce.

Not that most State Sovereigntists were by any means social radicals. They were weak, in the Morris-Hamilton view, scared, susceptible, sentimentally agrarian, outdated. If such trends were allowed to continue, the whole lending class's invested wealth, both private and public—notably the domestic part of the Public Debt of the United States, the dynamic, nation-making part—would wash away in a ruthless tide of pulp, the Money Connection would rust and break, all hope for national consolidation through high finance would die.

Pass one federal tax.

That remained Morris's first step in reversing course. One federal tax, its proceeds earmarked for the federal bondholders, would begin to sustain the Debt and consolidate financial power in the Congress, with two related effects: erode State Sovereigntism and suppress the Democracy. Suppress the Democracy financially, by taking all fiscal and monetary power away from the too-susceptible separate states and placing that power in the Congress. Suppress it legally, by gaining the Congress the power to pass and enforce uniform laws obligating the citizens of all states. Suppress it militarily, by unleashing the physical might that would compel compliance with federal law. By 1782, Morris and Hamilton knew what they had to do.

As for Herman Husband, he'd disappeared again. Abandoning the gold standard had proved too outlandish even for his radically democratic colleagues in the assembly's majority; they admired his ideas but remained leery of the centralized governing power that his plans required. In 1779, after only one session, he rode westward, just missing the Battle of Fort Wilson. He climbed the rugged, flat-topped mountain chain, made his brief descent on the western side, and rejoined his family on the farm near Bedford to wait out the war. The Glades region was suffering deepening poverty. Fear of attack by the British-allied Shawnee and other woodland nations had people fleeing to forts. There was a forty-day blizzard.

Husband's hopes stayed high. The greatest events in the history of creation were unfolding. The Antichrist was on the run. Husband predicted imminent American victory in the Revolution and the adoption, in the end, of his biblically prophesied nuts-and-bolts approach to good government. He'd withdrawn to the mountains, but he'd be back.

7

NEVER WASTE A CRISIS

IN THE SUMMER AND fall of 1782, no treaty was yet under way, but peace with Britain was visible on the horizon. For people on all political sides everywhere in the country, the prospect of American independence after seven years of war excited new hope and heightened old conflicts.

For Robert Morris, serving in Philadelphia as the Congress's super-superintendent, with the immediate goal of passing one federal tax earmarked for investors in the Federal Debt, the coming end of war added urgency, even emergency, to achieving that goal. Hamilton, working for Morris in New York, had fully bought into his boss's plan: the Congress's passing that tax was to trigger a chain reaction for eroding State Sovereigntism, suppressing the Democracy, and renovating economic and political life in America. Morris and Hamilton hoped to see further federal taxes and other lawmaking transform the Congress, step by step and willy-nilly, into a national government with legislative power over citizens throughout the states, thus realizing national greatness. Ambitious countrywide programs helping the rich get richer would turn the United States into a commercial empire to rival Britain.

But they had to act fast. Ending the war would cause unity among the states, already weak, to expire, the Congress to grow inert, the Debt to lose its nationalizing power in a host of deconsolidating quick-payoff plans by the states. Before hostilities formally ceased, the Congress had to be put firmly on the hook, on behalf of the public creditors, via one federal tax.

The tax Morris and Hamilton wanted the Congress to pass was a 5 percent duty on all imported products, to be collected at all ports by a body of federal officials created by the Congress and deployed throughout the states. Such taxes were called imposts. This proposed federal impost was to be charged to merchant importers and paid to customs officials, in coin or well-backed bills of exchange, in advance of the product's being legally certified to go to market. Yet while merchants might complain, they knew where their interests lay and were all for the measure. They would just pass the tax on. When the price of imposted goods went up all at once, consumers would really be paying a tax whose proceeds would be dedicated to enriching the merchants in their role as bondholders, who as a bloc naturally supported passage of a federal tax earmarked for their interest payments.

Outright opposition to a federal impost, as well as some less than outright foot-dragging, could be expected to come from some state legislatures, partly on principle—taxing power is a sovereign power—and partly because some of the states were already gaining revenue from their own imposts on foreign goods coming through their ports. A federal impost might undermine the states' ability to sustain their imposts; there was only so much tax an importer could pay. Effectively consolidating the separate imposts into one federal impost would rob the states not only of their exclusive power to tax their citizens but also of hard money, which would flow to the Congress instead. The fight over passing the impost was going to get rough.

Morris was ready for that. With Hamilton operating in New York, the superintendent had a strong team of supporters working with him in Philadelphia, starting with his assistant superintendent, Gouverneur Morris, no relation, first name pronounced "governeer," a scion of the upper echelon of New York's landlord class, twenty-nine when his boss first started pushing the federal impost. Gouverneur was a wit, a sybarite, a staunch Continentalist, and, to a degree unusual in his class, a vocal opponent of the institution of slavery. He also had even more than the normal disdain for the Democracy as a movement and for ordinary working people in general. Educated, like Hamilton, at King's College, Gouverneur lent Robert cachet and had helped work up the plan for the Bank of North America. A recent carriage accident had left him with only one leg, but his wooden prosthetic seemed to be slowing him down not at all.

Another key member of the Morris team: James Wilson, of Fort Wilson fame. A Pennsylvania delegate, thirty-nine, born in Scotland, Wilson ran a central-Pennsylvania legal practice that had made him rich. He was a partner with Morris in the bank, at least as obsessed a speculator, especially in land, and a learned, deep-thinking legal scholar who could serve as a powerful intellectual advocate for Morris's programs. The militia attack on his house had given him personal experience of the damage that the Democracy, when empowered by the law, could do to the entrepreneurial aims of men like him, as well as to his conception of order and stability.

The team had yet another penetrating legal mind in James Madison, thirty, a delegate from Virginia with little knowledge of the bustling, urban, mercantile world of Robert Morris. Madison, too, wanted to create a pervasive authority in the Congress, the beginning of a true American nationhood. Short, slight, studious, not notably charismatic, he came from great Virginia tobacco wealth fueled by slave labor. Yet he'd attended the intellectually advanced College of New Jersey instead of his own colony's College of William and Mary and was always digging into history, philosophy, politics, and government.

In his alliances and positions, Madison could be cagey, even mysterious. Already a keen navigator of political relationships, he was by no means the only Continentalist Virginian; the top Continentalist, George Washington, was also the top Virginian. Still, Madison could take an ambivalent, agrarian-influenced attitude toward some of Morris's plans, even while collaborating in them. He'd voted, for example, against chartering the Bank of North America. Many upscale Virginians thought the bank threatened their traditional role as private lenders and centralized too much economic power in the North.

But Madison did see the nationalizing capabilities of a federal impost. He supported its passage wholeheartedly.

The team had to scramble if it expected to get the impost passed and its revenues earmarked for the bondholders' interest before peace broke out and spoiled the opportunity. Morris had tried before. He'd first pushed the federal-impost idea as early as the spring of 1781, in conjunction with his bank plan, hoping to breeze it through the Congress as just another emergency of war, not even bringing up federal bondholders as the tax's intended beneficiaries. His dearest hope, he'd claimed then, was just to get the Congress enough of its own money to make foreign governments confident about lending to the United States.

But his first-draft resolution slipped in language that made the taxing power permanent, by no means limited the purpose to getting foreign loans, and left open the possibility of further federal taxes. That made it clear to many delegates that the impost wasn't really just another war-emergency measure. Morris did what he could to underreport and hide the money he was getting from foreign sources, but foreign loans obviously weren't in jeopardy.

So now, with the advent of peace amping the time pressure, the Morris team had what looked like a major obstacle to surmount. The Articles of Confederation had finally been signed by all of the state delegations and ratified by the state legislatures. The Articles required the federal requisitions to be apportioned among the states, and this proposed federal tax, to be paid by individual importers, didn't fit the requisition state-apportionment model, so it couldn't be adopted by the Congress until every state legislature had ratified it.

For all of his power as superintendent, Morris couldn't fight that. Job one for his team in the Congress and allies in the states was to push the legislatures to agree to an amendment.

As it turned out, many states seemed more or less fine with this plan. There was a benefit to avoiding the Articles' state-by-state tax-apportionment requirement, which in fact was touchy. Whenever it came up, states' population sizes came up, which meant the subject of slavery came up. Everybody preferred to avoid that subject. Some states also felt bullied by other states' imposts. Imported goods crossing from Rhode Island to Connecticut, for example, were marked up to accommodate the former's impost. Connecticut didn't like that.

There was thus some practical interest in federalizing the process, and Morris kept the pressure on. In New York, Hamilton wrote pro-impost resolutions; at a special session of the assembly at Poughkeepsie, Philip Schuyler read them into the record. Soon, despite Governor Clinton's New York sovereigntism, there was a good chance of that state's legislature's agreeing to amend the Articles to allow the tax.

Morris didn't let up. To foster as much anxiety as possible about the Congress's financial plight and frame the impost as salvation, he'd been canceling all debts, other than federal bonds, incurred by the Congress before his tenure as superintendent, including all contractor invoices, aside from those owed to some of his friends. He canceled army pay too, already unreliable enough. If the states wouldn't pay full requisitions, Morris said, then he couldn't pay officers or soldiers, and he told the states making meager efforts to pay their own soldiers that he wouldn't credit them for such payments in the final postwar accounting of what the state and federal governments owed each other.

But the main thing was to scare his fellow bondholders into getting their states to support a federal impost amendment. Morris therefore asked France to stop lending for the purpose of paying interest on federal bonds; all such paying should be done, Morris said, by the Congress, via the impost; foreign credit would be all the stronger in the end. He'd already stopped making interest payments on the second tier of federal bonds. Now he announced that until there was a federal tax to support it, he couldn't pay interest on the first tier either, the preferred tier, bearing interest in coin and held by a tight circle of the savviest.

Just as he'd predicted, a gaggle of panicky bondholders crowded into his Office of Finance.

He gave them the unhappy news. There was no way to get them paid but a federal tax. It was up to them to pressure their states to get the Articles amended to allow the impost.

But he also took this opportunity to pitch the bondholders on the life-changing benefits, to them, of a federal government with powers far beyond impost—powers even beyond taxation, powers quelling the states' powers. He urged them to demand that the Congress pass federal legislation striking down the states' legal-tender laws, price-control regulations, antimonopoly rules, all of the inroads being made by the Democracy on the economy. Frame the effort high-mindedly, he coached them: widows, orphans, love of country. He was organizing the investing class as a lobby for transforming the Congress into a national government with power to override the states and thus crush the democratic finance.

The bondholders took his advice—in part. They did pressure their state legislatures to amend the Articles to allow a federal impost. But they just wanted to get paid, so they also pressured their states to take over interest payments on their federal bonds. That idea spelled disaster for consolidating public finance in the Congress, and Morris dispatched Hamilton in a rush to a bondholder meeting in Albany. Philip Schuyler, who held federal bonds in large numbers, presided over the meeting; on behalf of Superintendent Morris, Hamilton urged the lobby not to seek redress from the states. Their only hope, he insisted, was the federal impost. Nobody would get paid anything, by anyone, unless the Congress passed that one tax.

That was the Morris team's inflexible line. And it was working. New York listened to Hamilton and voted to allow the impost. Pennsylvania, center of the Democracy, and Virginia, protector of the planter class's liberties, did too. Overexcited now, the Morris team got a committee of the Congress to advise the body to pass other federal taxes too, right away: land taxes, poll taxes, an excise on whiskey. Wildly premature, that didn't fly, but most states looked close to agreeing to the impost.

Nothing could happen, though, without perfect unanimity, and Rhode Island was a holdout. David Howell, recently sent to the Congress on an updraft of anti-Continentalism among that state's elite, was thirty-five, a lawyer, a judge, and a professor of science, math, and languages, with an eloquent, dramatic style and a grand sense of his small state's importance. Howell wanted to preserve Rhode Island's lucrative impost. He rose in debate to insist on the principle that even one federal tax, collected within the states by the Congress, would make the Congress sovereign over the people within the states. Since that really was Morris's goal, the point was hard to refute. The Rhode Island legislature put off voting on the impost amendment. The Morris team in the Congress, feeling the time pressure of new rumors of treaty-making with Britain, responded by flat-out demanding that Rhode Island's delegates get their state to take a clear position. That only seemed to confirm Rhode Island's worst fears. Wasn't this exactly how a too-strong Congress would act: threatening the sovereign independence of any one state, especially a tiny, outnumbered one?

So David Howell did take a clear position on the impost. Casting Rhode Island as a David defending liberty against a federal Goliath, he condemned the federal impost as a permanent measure and a wedge for further taxes, a "yoke of tyranny fixed on all the states, and the chains riveted."

The image resonated. When the Rhode Island legislature finally held a vote on ratifying the impost amendment, it chose not to relinquish its exclusive right to tax its citizens and voted the impost down. When Virginians learned of Rhode Island's refusal, their assembly—led in part by Morris's enemies in the Lee family—pulled out too.

With unanimity fractured, there was no prospect of an amendment to enable the federal impost before the end of the war. The Morris team, suddenly desperate, resorted to a last-ditch move. Robert Morris's assistant, Gouverneur Morris, said he believed that nothing but absolute monarchy was likely to hold the wayward states and people together. But at least, he said, the country still enjoyed what he called "that great friend to sovereign authority, a foreign war." If the war could be continued, the people would have to "entrust proper powers to the American sovereign," meaning the Congress. Only going on fighting would hold the country together long enough, and be expensive enough, to give the states no choice but to submit to federal taxation.

Robert Morris wrote to Washington. The general was a strong Continentalist. "War is more likely than peace," the superintendent urged him, "to produce funds for the public debts, increase of authority to Congress, and vigor to the administration as well of the union as of its component parts." The only hope for nationhood was to continue the war, in support of the unifying power of the Debt incurred by the war.

But Washington didn't reply, at least not on the record, and on November 30, 1782, a preliminary treaty-in-principle was struck between the United States and Great Britain. The Morris team was at its wit's end.

That's when Alexander Hamilton arrived in Philadelphia. Earlier that month, the New York legislature had elected him, at the ostensible age of twenty-five, to serve as its only delegate to the Congress that year who wasn't a returning incumbent. In late November, he checked into a boardinghouse near Morris's Office of Finance and only a few minutes' walk from the State House where the Congress met. No longer employed by Morris as a tax receiver, he was ready to make his mark as a delegate to the Congress and a member of the Morris team in Philadelphia.

When he took that walk for the first time, went through the big doorway, turned left, and entered the ground-floor assembly room where the Congress had declared independence in 1776, Hamilton was by no means overawed by any sense of admission to a council of greats. Quite the contrary. Locating the appropriate desks, exchanging polite remarks with his colleagues, absorbing the close-quarters atmosphere of a deliberative body drawn from all over the country, the clashing regional accents, the individual quirks of dress, hygiene, health, and habits of consumption, he remained certain that the overall quality of these delegates was uneven at best. Such was the unfortunate nature of the American situation, he thought, that the best men stayed home to serve in their supposedly august legislatures and sent second- and third-raters to Philadelphia.

He wasn't yet widely known outside New York, but just as in college and amid the officer class and his state's governing class, nothing about his background gave cause for raised eyebrows in the Congress. A lot of people didn't like Robert Morris. Nobody cared that Hamilton's parents hadn't been married, and the fact that he had overcome some genuine early adversity only placed him in good company. Washington's chief artillery officer, Henry Knox, Washington himself, Benjamin Franklin, and other well-known American revolutionaries had overcome family and social disadvantages. It wasn't his background but his commitment to Morris's plans that was about to set Hamilton at odds with some of the most powerful forces in the country.

As the newest member of the Morris team in the Congress, he hit the ground, as always, running. Hamilton and Madison hadn't met before. Now the two young lawyers began working together to save the impost from what looked like almost certain death. Amending the Articles had failed, so they sought a way for the Congress to impose a tax anyway. To Madison, deep precedents in the emergency of war made the Congress sovereign over the states in certain areas. Anything a body is empowered to do, he said, implies unenumerated powers necessary to getting that thing done. Robert Morris's legal theory—he wasn't a lawyer—had it that if a measure is "neither wrong nor forbidden," and if you can get it passed, and if it's complied with, the measure becomes de facto constitutional. People get used to things. Influence leads to authority. And authority, Morris said, would "open the purses of the people."

Yet neither Madison's shrewd legal calculation nor Morris's realpolitik was getting the federal impost anywhere, and Hamilton could hardly believe his new degree of frustration. He'd hit the ground running into a brick wall. The war was effectively over, the first-step federal tax was dying, and with it all hopes for a Continentalist United States. Taking extreme positions might only cause backlash, he believed, yet the catastrophe he'd long predicted was looming, and there was nothing for him to do in the Congress but seethe.

He knew his passion was at odds with his reason. He couldn't help almost wishing there was some way to literally force the wayward country to move toward nationhood.

In January 1783, a major general and two colonels of the Continental Army appeared in Philadelphia. They'd traveled from Newburgh, New York, on the hills above the Hudson River, where General Washington was making his latest headquarters and holding the main part of his army pending completion of a peace treaty. The three officers had a petition to deliver to the Congress. It was signed by the entire officer class at Newburgh, aside from the commander. It regarded army pay.

Many delegates were startled by this visitation, but the uniformed emissaries were hardly arriving unannounced. Henry Knox, Washington's artillery commander and most trusted immediate subordinate, had overseen the petition's drafting and sent a letter to the Congress's secretary at war to prepare him for its arrival. Washington himself had written to a Virginia delegate in the Congress to notify him that the petition was coming and warn that it should be met with a soothing attitude. The commander didn't say explicitly that he'd vetted it. To those in the know, however, his sponsorship was plain.

The army pay situation was atrocious. Partly thanks to Morris's policy of paying bondholders before anybody else, neither the officers nor the men had been remunerated in any consistent way for years. Regarding officer pay in particular—that was the officer petitioners' only real concern—in 1780 the Congress had promised that when the war was over, officers would receive, in lieu of full pay for the duration of their service, half pay for life, a major pension. That had sounded good at the time, but now a peace treaty was in the offing, and the Congress had no money of its own and no way of getting any. The officers couldn't see how their pensions were to be honored once the army disbanded. In the petition, they were demanding their payoff right now.

In other words, the entire officer class of the Continental Army was a public creditor of the United States. A gigantic one. Armed.

That's how Robert Morris, with a surge of hope, took the arrival of the three officer emissaries and the nature of their demand. He had reason to think the officers took it that way too: within a day of their arrival, they brought their petition to his office. Morris welcomed them with his usual bonhomie, and he and the officers quickly clarified their relationship.

The Congress's plan had been to disband the army, with everybody going docilely home. But what if the army refused to disband? Like the investing class, the officer class was large, organized, motivated, and owed a lot of money. Unlike the investing class, it numbered 550 veterans in command of almost 10,000 enlisted men hardened by seven years of warfare. If the interstate military officers saw a federal impost as the only reliable means of funding their pay, and if they refused to lay down their arms and submit to civil authority without such funding—effectively a threat of military coup—the Congress would have a hard time not passing the impost.

The officers' most pressing demand was that the half-pay-for-life deal be rolled over into a single lump-sum payment, to be made now. They were expecting to get the Congress to oversee a plan to that end, by which the separate legislatures would pay each state's officers, but to Morris, that idea squandered an amazing opportunity. Instead, he suggested, the officers should demand their lump-sum pensions in something high-value and long-term profitable, the preferred instrument of professional investors: federal bonds bearing 6 percent annual interest.

The potential benefits to the officers were clear. With both the interest payments and the bonds' underlying value supported by a Congress empowered to levy a countrywide tax earmarked for funding them, officers' money would make money and create legacies for descendants. Their families would occupy the pantheon of those called upon to invest in and manage future public projects, building the country, getting richer. They'd be not only members of the Money Connection but as patriot warriors for their country's independence, especially honored members.

But it wouldn't work, Morris also made clear, unless the officers demanded that the Congress get its own taxing power and use that power not to pay the officers off for good, in a onetime deal, but to make them holders of long-term interest-bearing federal securities, reliably funded by the Congress. If the officers wouldn't agree to his plan, he said, they'd end up with nothing. He wanted them to see the Congress as their only hope. By the same token, he wanted the Congress and the states to see passing the impost, for the benefit of both the officers and all other federal bondholders, as the only hope for avoiding a military takeover by the Continental Army.

The Morris team began pushing concerns about a military coup on other delegates in the Congress, and there was plenty to push. If the ungrateful states wouldn't submit to the impost as a means of paying the army, why shouldn't these long-abused officers impose a countrywide tax and start collecting it themselves, the old-fashioned way? Arthur Lee, Morris's nemesis from the Deane affair, could sniff the purpose of the scare: "Every engine is at work here," he wrote to Samuel Adams, "to obtain permanent taxes and the appointment of collectors by Congress in the states. The terror of a mutinying army is played off with considerable efficacy."

The officer emissaries met officially with a committee of the Congress and explicitly brought up mutiny as the probable if unfortunate outcome of their demands' not being met. They moved into the city, making it clear that they weren't going anywhere without a favorable response. Delegates' fears were further amplified by rumors of possibly mutinous moves up at Newburgh, against Washington himself. The commander's long-standing enemy General Horatio Gates was said to be considering a takeover of the army there, with officer-pay grievances again the inciting issue.

Amid the terror rising in the Congress over a coup and military dictatorship, delegates who hadn't known Hamilton knew him now. Carrying the Morris team's ball along with James Wilson, the young New York delegate rose again and again to weld officer grievances to bondholder grievances and get the impost passed. He shot down all proposed alternatives: passing an impost to pay off the officers but not to fund the bonds, or leaving the whole issue to the states. He insisted that the officers be paid, and paid only in the Congress's bonds, and that all such bonds must be fully funded, for all holders, via the federal impost. It was that or live in fear, or worse.

The brashness that Hamilton was exposing on the floor worried his close-to-the-vest partner Madison. The Virginian blanched when one day in debate, Hamilton conjured a thrilling future for a United States nationally unified via the deployment throughout the country of a force of federal tax collectors. Painting such a clear picture was "imprudent and injurious to the cause which it was meant to serve," Madison wrote in his private notes. His New York partner had "let out the secret."

Hamilton himself was considering all options. Reason alone suggested that collaborating with a real coup attempt would be ill-advised. Not only Washington but also Knox, Schuyler, and Hamilton himself disrespected General Gates above all others. Still, any moral distinction between threatening a military takeover, to scare the states into taxing the country, and the army's actually taking over and taxing the country might seem fairly subtle. Hamilton wrote to Governor Clinton and suggested the governor ask the legislature to reserve a lot of land and offer tracts, on liberal terms, to any officer or soldier who would agree to become a citizen of New York. He wanted more than anything, he told Clinton, for the union to stand. But disunion looked eminently possible too, and drawing a large part of the army into New York would foster security in any ensuing civil conflict.

Other members of the Morris team in the Congress were busy contacting various officers at Newburgh. Gouverneur Morris wrote to General Nathanael Greene to say that if the officer class demanded a federal tax, the states would have no choice but to agree to it. He wrote to Knox more than once: after the generals had taken the post, Gouverneur urged Knox metaphorically, the public creditors would garrison it. Knox didn't respond.

At the end of January Robert Morris made a histrionic move, resigning as superintendent of finance, effective November 1, and went so far as to publish his resignation in the papers in February, with an outright attack on the Congress for irresponsibility and incompetence, a public statement of no confidence in the body he was appointed to serve. That tactic pushed to the utmost the fears of the officers, the bondholders, the congressional delegates, and the state legislators and placed the whole country in total financial uncertainty.

Hamilton meanwhile appointed himself to sound out the most important person at Newburgh—really, in the country. In a meeting with

Madison at the home of their ally Thomas Fitzsimons, a delegate from Philadelphia, he suggested that, as a former staffer, he was in the best position to divine what Washington was really thinking about the crisis and guide the general in the right direction.

In fact, he and Washington hadn't communicated since their snippy exchange when Hamilton was leaving the army. Hamilton nevertheless evinced not the slightest hesitation in taking what might easily be viewed as an astonishing risk. Sedition seemed in the air both at Newburgh and in Philadelphia. Nobody showed greater sensitivity than Washington to his own reputation for honor, integrity, and virtue. Approaching him with any solicitation, even with any question that might strike him as faintly improper, had a good chance of backfiring hard.

But events were moving too quickly for excess of caution. This last chance for passing the impost had the Morris team at once desperate and eager. Washington, a firm Continentalist, was fed up almost beyond patience by what he saw as the states' failure to support his suffering army through seven years of war. As a speculator and big businessman, he shared the Morris team's national vision, and he and Morris had long been both personally friendly and politically aligned. On February 13, Hamilton wrote to Washington.

In the letter, he did his best to employ degrees of innuendo and indirection that came not at all naturally to him. He began by framing this out-of-the-blue communication as nothing more than a friendly offer to the general of an inside report on the overall state of the Congress—plus, should Washington ever feel the need, a back-channel means of communicating with that body, with Hamilton as go-between. Time pressure was such, though, that he had to plunge straight from his opening into the unsolicited so-called report itself, which was that the Congress was out of money, and sadly, Hamilton told Washington, the troops really would be justified in staying armed.

Having set the issue up as best he could, he now alluded, delicately but without missing his chance, to what he really wanted to know. Giving the general some polite, even fawning coaching, he only feared, he said, that Washington's admirable scruples against exploiting his own great power might possibly be viewed, by the general's own officers, as a barrier to getting them paid. Rumors had reached Philadelphia of mutinous plans at Newburgh, Hamilton reported. The great need of the Congress was of course to get its own funds, and the army, properly directed, might have a strong influence on bringing that outcome about. If dangerous unrest over officer pay really was in the offing, mightn't it be better if General Washington himself—here Hamilton couldn't help but underline—*took direction of* the effort at redress?

However artfully Hamilton might have thought he'd couched it, the stage-whispered prompting was unnecessary. The commander had already taken direction of the situation. The mood in Newburgh did seem dangerous to him: that's why he'd sponsored delivering the petition and why his closest subordinate, Knox, had written it. Washington was in that sense the real author not only of the petition's demands but also of the officer emissaries' assertive tactics. First and foremost, he wanted his officers paid.

But he also wanted federal taxes passed for funding the public creditors. Washington shared Morris's national vision and had reason to sniff, on Hamilton's letter, what the Morris team had been up to in contacting his officers, coaching his emissaries, now coaching even him. In their eagerness, they were threatening his own efforts at a resolution that might satisfy the needs of the officers, retain political stability, and realize Continentalist ambitions for the country via the impost. By playing with the army, Washington believed, the Morris team might be blowing its best chance of getting the Congress its own money.

From Newburgh, the general went into action. Giving Hamilton's ill-concealed nudges no place to land, he wrote back to say that he fully endorsed the goal of national taxation and strong federal government— without that, he said, all that he and the country had suffered would be for nothing—and that things seemed calm at Newburgh, that rational elements of the army would no doubt prevail. He thereby shut the door Hamilton had tried to open, but Morris was meanwhile going harder, faster, and wider, with increasing abandon. In the face of Knox's silence by letter, he finally dispatched one of the three petitioning officers up to Newburgh to ask Knox face-to-face to support a refusal to disband the army if the impost weren't passed.

Thus forced to speak, Knox said no: threatening the states would be highly improper. Gates and a group of other disgruntled officers then got word from Philadelphia that the bondholding class was eager to connect its interests with theirs. A letter began circulating in camp, calling the officers to an army-pay-grievance meeting, to be chaired by Gates.

So Washington confronted the Congress himself. Accepting the offer to serve as a go-between, the general asked Hamilton to make urgently clear to that body and to the states that if the worst should happen, it would be their fault they'd failed to address the desperate needs of his army. To the Morris team, this represented progress. With the most important man in America implicating the Congress in responsibility for possible mutiny, it might be only a short hop for the body to absolve itself by passing the impost and earmarking it for funding both the officers and the bondholders.

Washington also moved to defuse any mutinous impulses that really might be brewing at Newburgh. First he said he couldn't make the meeting Gates was chairing. Then, with the officers gathered, he showed up after all. Gates relinquished the chair, and the commander gave his abashed subordinates a lecture on the moral imperatives of loyalty to civil authority, driving his point home with a dramatic enactment of his own sacrifices to honor. He started to read aloud a letter from the Congress on officer pay, but then he stopped. He reached for his glasses. Apologizing as he settled them on his nose, he remarked that having gone gray in the service of his country, he seemed to have gone blind too.

The performance brought some in the audience to tears. When Washington strode out, Knox and others, at the ready, prepared resolutions of officer loyalty to the Congress. They were unanimously adopted.

That scene positioned Washington to make his final move. It had already been suggested that he write to the Congress himself on behalf of the officers, and now he did.

He reported that he'd just personally averted the civic nightmare of an officer mutiny. The news might have stilled all fears that the Morris team had been ginning up in the Congress, but Washington went further. While at the moment he had his officers largely under control, he said, their grievances remained painful, the situation dangerous. In that context, he advised the Congress to give satisfaction to their demands. The Congress complied instantly.

A deal was framed by Morris and written up in a committee by Hamilton. The officer class was offered five years' full pay "in money or securities on interest at six per cent, as Congress shall find most convenient . . . the said securities to be such as shall be given to other creditors of the United States." If they thought they could get paid in one form or another by their states, the officers of any state were free to apply— collectively, and only collectively, and only before a set deadline—to that state's legislature.

No contest. The entire officer class gave up on their states and opted for the federal pension. Each general received $10,000, about fifty times average annual income; lower officers received successively lower amounts. This deal added about $5 million to the Federal Debt, a big chunk held by a particularly influential group of interstate creditors. That was a huge win for Morris's and Hamilton's effort to build Continentalism on a federally supported consolidation of wealth, and by mid-April, the Congress seemed to be moving at last toward passing the impost to fund interest for all federal bondholders. Washington, who never took bonds or pay of any kind, had brought about what Morris had wanted for so long, even while containing and resolving the dangers Morris was courting.

The bonds weren't to start paying interest until the completion of a postwar financial settlement between each state and the Congress, flattening who owed what to whom. So while the officers had been added to the holders of the Federal Debt, payoffs did remain speculative. Knox led the officers in setting up a centralized organization with a chapter in each state, whose stated purposes didn't explicitly include watchdog-ging the payoff situation; the officers would soon make clear that such a purpose was critical to its mission. They named it the Society of the Cincinnati, after the Ancient Roman general Lucius Quinctius Cincin-natus, admired by all liberty-loving people. Made dictator in a military emergency, the familiar story went, Cincinnatus could have held on to that power and started an imperial-military dynasty, but instead, after saving the Roman republic on the field of battle, he relinquished his posi-tion, returned power to the civic authority, and went back to his farm, a model of disinterested republican virtue.

In the story, Cincinnatus doesn't arouse fears that he'll stay armed unless the civic authority hands him and his descendants a nice payoff. Still, with their demands on the Congress met, and fear of a military take-over thereby dissolved, those officers of the Continental Army who had served at least three years or until the end of the war became latter-day Cincinnati. Their eldest male descendants would be Cincinnati, down through the ages. Consolidating the interstate officer families with fed-eral authority, the society combined a heroic ethos of self-sacrifice with the speculative wealth of the Money Connection and the Continental-ist ethos of centralization. Prescribed rules and rituals created by Knox made the Cincinnati quasi-national, with state-chapter meetings to be held annually, on July Fourth, and a big celebratory and administrative meeting of all chapters in Philadelphia every three years in May; meet-ings were to involve grand processions by companies on horse and foot, dinners, toasts, orations. Framing itself as a noble force for the ongoing support of the country, the society naturally made General Washington its nominal head.

Just as naturally, controversy broke out. The hereditary-membership feature seemed to weave a Continentalist-aligned power into the American future, a financially interested, professional, interstate military class, anathema to State Sovereigntist philosophy. In response to that criticism, Washington insisted the society lose its hereditary function. But while his officers would never stop lionizing Washington oratorically, they flatly rejected the one demand he ever made on them. They retained hereditary membership. Washington came to find the Cincinnati an irritating embarrassment.

Others loved it, especially Knox. The society was soon inducting upscale noncombatants as honorary members, including Robert Morris. Hamilton hoped to take things even further than that, transforming the Cincinnati into an officially certified military arm of the American elite, fully organized, chaptered, and officiated and legally integrated with government. Later in the decade, in an outright military conflict with the Democracy, elements of that idea would come to unexpected fruition.

Hamilton also began strengthening his reconnection to Washington. Keeping up their revived correspondence, thrashing out the recent crisis, they arrived at a new understanding. Washington told Hamilton point-blank that he believed the public creditors had been manipulating his army and risking civic disaster, and he blamed Morris. In defending Morris, Hamilton noted that the man's judgment could at times be clouded. Washington clarified. He'd been blaming Gouverneur, not Robert.

Responding to a letter in which Washington warned him that an army is a dangerous instrument to play with, Hamilton crossed out an admission that the Morris team had helped foster a threat of coup. But even in the final draft, he admitted they'd deliberately blended creditor and officer interest, and he said he'd do it again. While he'd always placed the army's interest, he swore, first and foremost, securing the creditor class's payoffs remained critical to all national aims. What else could the team have done?

Again Washington clarified. Even before receiving Hamilton's reply, he'd written again to say that when he'd called the army a dangerous plaything, he'd been tired. He'd really only meant that an army is so volatile that manipulating it might have ended with the State Sovereigntists winning the day and all funding for the public creditors lost. He was, he repeated, fully committed to the Morris team's goals.

They were learning how to talk to and around each other in pursuit of overlapping aims. Having taken astonishing risks, Hamilton emerged from his first major episode in politics a Continentalist leader in the Congress, with Washington no longer his boss, and no longer estranged, but an aegis in the politics of founding American nationhood on the Money Connection.

8

PEACETIME

AND YET CONTINENTALISM FAILED—after all that. Despite the remarkable efforts of Hamilton, Washington, Morris, and their cohort,
by the beginning of 1784 any hope for transforming the Congress into
a national government became manifestly absurd. The body seemed, to
the Continentalists, actively suicidal.

What the Congress passed, after all that, was a resolution recom-
mending that the states adopt a federal impost nothing like a true federal
impost. Hamilton was revolted. The resolution limited the impost to
twenty-five years and created no federal officers for collection. Enforcement was fully dependent on the same state-focused systems that Morris
and Hamilton had been trying, via the impost, to end. The proposal even
asked for a new requisition, to be funded by the same old state taxes.

Hamilton voted against it—after all that—in disgusted protest at its
powerlessness, and the Morris team, for the moment still trying, reverted
to the original effort that Rhode Island had derailed the year before:
get the states to ratify an amendment to the Articles of Confederation
to allow a true federal impost with federal enforcement and no sunset
date. For tanking the earlier effort, Rhode Island was now being widely
excoriated by Continentalists as a "perverse sister" and "a little detestable
corner of the continent," so this time, the state went along with the idea
of amending the Articles.

And this time, to Hamilton's ultimate disgust, his own state became the holdout. The port of New York was growing fast. Governor Clinton wanted tax revenue collected there to stay in what he was starting to call the "Empire State." Thanks to New York now, no unanimity prevailed among the states for amending the Articles, and it was clear to Hamilton that if his state's error were ever to be corrected, it would never be done from the Congress. He was fed up.

Hamilton and Washington did launch one last-ditch effort to salvage some kind of unity via the federal government before everything federal fell apart. With the Continental Army about to disband, they saw a chance of getting the Congress to create a professional, regular, centralized military establishment. Their new work dynamic came into play for the first time when Hamilton got the Congress to appoint a committee, chaired by him, to address the question of military preparedness in a postwar world, got the committee to officially invite the soon-to-be-retired general to provide input, and privately sent Washington a list of things the general might want to advise the committee to do. Washington reviewed the list and saw that it had everything he wanted: a large, professional, regular army, operating solely under the Congress's control, with uniform supply and soldier training—even a federal academy for uniform officer training. The force could be deployed in conquering the western woodland nations, defending against invasion, and suppressing domestic insurrections. To Washington, this was just what the country needed.

Yet he was also painfully aware that many Americans viewed professional, full-time soldiery as a tool of tyranny like Britain's. Because citizen-soldiery, exercised through required participation in the states' militias, was widely considered the only appropriate armed force for a free people, many took it as given that responsibility for postwar defense would now lapse to militia, which really meant lapse to the separate state legislatures, which controlled the state militias. In harsh contrast to that view, Hamilton's list of recommendations was based on his, Washington's, Knox's, and other officers' experience of militias' poor performance in the field during the war.

So Washington toned Hamilton's recommendations way down and

incorporated them in an adroitly politic document of his own. Making comforting noises about militias as the best defense of freedom, he suggested that a peacetime army might serve as a sort of adjunct to the militias—just a small force, nothing to worry about. What he called small was actually large, and what he wanted was something larger. This was what he thought he could get away with for now. Submitting the more palatable version back to Hamilton's committee, the general framed it as just some friendly advice from a soon-to-be-private citizen. In fact, his input lent both the recommendations and the committee itself overwhelming prestige. That gave Hamilton a chance of taking at least the first step toward what they really wanted.

But Hamilton hadn't learned to work this way. He reincorporated Washington's less threatening ideas under his blunt original findings and presented the whole thing to the Congress with the equally blunt title "Report on a Military Peace Establishment." The regular army he proposed was larger than Washington's. His report made no reference to the supposed virtues of militias but openly gutted citizen-soldiery; even local defense was to be carried out by an elite corps of volunteers, overseen not by the states but by the federal government. The report explicitly centralized everything military in the Congress and took everything military away from the states.

Not surprisingly, many delegates saw their worst fears of top-down Continentalism borne out on paper. With taxing authority, military authority was the key sovereign power, and the states had no desire to transfer any of it to the Congress. In debate, David Howell of Rhode Island was excoriating in linking Hamilton's desire for a countrywide tax with his desire for a standing army with the means to collect it. Even Washington's sway couldn't save Hamilton's report from itself. The delegates refused even to debate a peacetime army.

But then events gave Hamilton and Washington new hope. In the summer of 1783, the Congress faced a mutiny—not a threat this time, but the real thing, an armed attack on the Congress, the issue again army pay, but raised now by the men, not the officers. Common soldiers had received only $200–$300 each in federal bonds, a minor contingency of the officers' big payoff. That payment was postponed, so they were paid three months' salary in a special run of Mr. Morris's notes, watermarked "National Debt," a one-off parting gift. Morris did have six thousand notes quick-printed—he sat and signed each one, backed by his own money—but as the soldiers waited to receive them, army contractors sold them necessities on credit and took the notes, when they arrived, at 40 and 50 percent markdowns. Some never got the notes at all and would go home empty-handed after seven years of war.

Now the troops stationed in Philadelphia to defend the Congress sent the body a petition demanding back pay and making an explicit threat of mutiny. When the Congress didn't respond, about eighty men stationed at Lancaster marched to Philadelphia in support of the petitioners. That put a total of about five hundred troops in control of a lot of materiel. Hundreds of them arrived at the State House on the march, guns on shoulders, and put the building under siege, trapping the delegates inside.

Hamilton, assigned to negotiate with the mutineers, promised them that if they let the Congress adjourn, the body would address their demands. Temporarily, the soldiers stood down. Delegates left the building to the soldiers' jeers.

Hamilton had no intention of addressing their demands. Instead, he met secretly with the executive council of Pennsylvania and asked the state to deploy its militia to disperse the mutineers. The democratic majority in Pennsylvania was loath to grant this request. Even John Dickinson, Morris's old comrade in reconciliationism, now serving as president of the executive council and by no means a democrat, objected to the plan. Dickinson presumed the militia would only side with the rebellious soldiers.

For Hamilton, that said it all—about Pennsylvania, the militia, the Democracy, the states, and the Congress. He advised the delegates to retreat to Princeton, New Jersey, for their own safety. As the Congress yet again evacuated the city, this time fleeing armed Americans, he held out hope that this utter embarrassment would lend weight to his plan for establishing a federal army with the power to crush insurrections.

He followed the Congress to Princeton. There he wrote a blazing set of resolutions. He went all the way and said a lot of what he'd always really meant. He even proposed a convention to revise the Articles of Confederation wholesale in favor of a full-scale national government with powers to collect taxes and field an army in peacetime.

But he didn't even put those resolutions on the record for debate. The Congress was already becoming what the Continentalists thought of as inert. On June 24, Washington sent 1,500 troops to Philadelphia and ended the mutiny. In August, he came to Princeton, established a headquarters nearby, and recommitted his influence to the peacetime-army proposal, but debate on the measure was postponed, and on October 31, when the few remaining delegates got word that a treaty had been signed in Paris between Britain and the United States, the Congress barely had a quorum. In November, Washington left Princeton to oversee the British evacuation of New York City and disband the army. The Congress meanwhile voted not to return to Philadelphia. Debate on a permanent home bogged down. In the end, the body was to become permanently itinerant.

The Morris team was already dispersing. Madison, having not even served out his term, was in the Virginia assembly. Gouverneur Morris, having started doing business with Robert Morris while working as his assistant, became his partner and agent in a proliferation of new commercial ventures. James Wilson, too, had big private endeavors under way, including one with Robert Morris: the Illinois-Wabash Company for developing western land, with between 600,000 and a million acres registered in Wilson's own name.

Hamilton left the Congress at the end of 1783. He planned to practice law in New York City. He still wanted to push New York to reverse its refusal to amend the Articles to allow a federal impost, but he didn't have much hope for that. Continentalism everywhere was in retreat. Robert Morris, seeing his whole system falling apart, stopped even trying to run the finance office and stepped down on June 26, 1784.

The super-superintendent and his team had in fact set up some quasi-national systems that survived their exit. The officer payoff created a powerfully influential lobby, organized across state lines via the Society of the Cincinnati and eager to start getting paid regular interest—as was the whole bondholding class. The Bank of North America existed too, chartered both by the Congress and by Pennsylvania.

Still, in 1784 no Continentalist, and certainly not Hamilton, was celebrating any tendency toward consolidation. With the war over and the states going their own ways, the Democracy could be expected to further exploit the separate legislatures' weaknesses to get paper-money and other laws passed, obstruct the consolidation of wealth, and undermine the Money Connection as a nationalizing force. Hamilton declined to stand either for election to his state assembly or for reelection by that assembly as a delegate to the Congress. He might have looked done with public life.

He wasn't. "It is to be hoped," he wrote to a New York ally, John Jay, who was in Paris negotiating peace with Britain, "when prejudice and folly have run themselves out of breath we may return to reason and correct our errors." Before the country could get, in Hamilton's terms, any better, first it would have to get even worse.

9

THE NEW JERUSALEM

BY THE COUNTRY'S GETTING worse, Hamilton meant the Democracy's prevailing throughout the country, and that's just what happened. With American victory over Britain, ordinary people made moves to secure and expand the gains they'd made during the war. Old and new ideas about economic and political equality would soon be spreading so fast that America fell into a condition that Hamilton called a "popular frenzy." But ordinary people didn't see it as a frenzy.

The conflicts between the Democracy and elites that would mark the 1780s looked different from the conflicts of the 1770s. During seven years of fighting, radical leadership, never by any means an official group, had undergone big changes. The group of Philadelphia outsiders that included Thomas Young, James Cannon, Benjamin Rush, Timothy Matlack, Christopher Marshall, and Thomas Paine had succeeded almost beyond belief in creating a democratic government for Pennsylvania; in that sense, they'd become the insiders of a new politics. But tension had always prevailed within that group. Fighting the establishment kept the tensions down. Becoming an establishment brought them out almost overnight.

Even as their democratic constitution was written and passed, in late 1776, the Philadelphia crew was breaking up. Rush, always torn, became close to John Adams and quickly deradicalized. A reformer now, he no longer sought economic equality via government; he even joined Robert Morris's effort to overturn the state constitution he'd helped bring about, calling democracy in Pennsylvania "mobocracy." Marshall, though a universalist, wanted a religious oath constitutionally required for serving office in the state; Young and Cannon opposed all religious tests and lost a bitter fight with their former comrade on that issue. Cannon, having conceived the Committee of Privates that put an end to the old Pennsylvania assembly, never did anything so dramatic again, though he did serve as a justice of the peace under the new constitution; he died in early 1782. Young died in 1777 of a viral infection while serving as an army surgeon, leaving an ill wife and a number of children in penury. Matlack was elected secretary to the state's Supreme Executive Council under the new constitution and would stay involved in Pennsylvania politics into the next century. By the end of the war, the radical crew didn't exist.

As for Paine, by the time peace with Britain became official, he'd made a series of moves that would complicate not just his own life but the whole of the Democracy's postwar advance against the Money Connection. Paine had a very unusual war. When the Declaration of Independence was signed and the British invaded, "Common Sense" had made him famous. Yet he didn't even attend the Pennsylvania constitutional convention where his radical ideas about government became law. He took no role in Pennsylvania's radical government. Instead, he enlisted as a common soldier and left town on the march.

Soon he was stationed in northern New Jersey. Serving on the staff of General Nathanael Greene, Paine met and befriended George Washington.

The friendship changed both men's fortunes. Early in the war, Paine saw two things in the general that nobody else saw. One nobody else saw because it wasn't there. To Paine, Washington was commander in chief of an army fighting not for American independence alone, but for a coming epoch of economic and social liberation everywhere, for all people, a kind of global democracy of freedom. To Paine, that's what the American Revolution meant. It followed that Washington was leading the vanguard for a world where the mass of ordinary people would take a direct part in government.

People who knew Washington better would have been surprised to hear it. Few had less sympathy for the aspirations of ordinary people than the Virginia land speculator and developer and agricultural producer who commanded the Continental Army. His circle embraced the landlords like Schuyler and the moneymen like Morris—the type whose power over wealth and politics Paine was dedicated to ending. Washington was leading the army to achieve, with American independence, an end to British restrictions he'd come to see as tyrannical, not to overturn the long-standing hierarchies in which he'd made his way.

Paine was stubborn in his enthusiasms. If anyone ever tried to talk him out of casting Washington in the role of global liberator, he didn't hear it.

The other thing Paine saw in Washington was military genius. That, too, was a distinctly minority assessment early in the war. In November 1776, with hope for the United States sinking, Paine and Greene looked eastward across the Hudson River from Fort Lee, in New Jersey, and watched the British seize Fort Washington, on the upper end of Manhattan island. The British started crossing the river. Washington ordered the evacuation of Fort Lee. The Continental Army turned and began its flight toward the Delaware River. Failure in New York and retreat across New Jersey caused many, in and out of the army, to criticize Washington as a poor choice of commander, even a coward.

Paine, as usual, had other ideas. On the retreat with Washington and Greene, he started writing a series of articles, *The American Crisis*. In December, he left the frigid emergency camp on the Pennsylvania side of the Delaware and headed for Philadelphia on foot. He arrived in the city for the first time since July to discover a state of panic. With British occupation imminent, the citizens and the Congress alike were packing up to evacuate. To most, the situation looked desperate. Not to Paine. He found the only printing press still running and published "Crisis One" as a pamphlet.

It began with the line "These are the times that try men's souls" and went on to call General Washington firm and his firmness a public blessing. Some would later say, no doubt fancifully, that during Washington's successful attack across the Delaware days after the pamphlet's publication, the American soldiers who defeated the German mercenaries in Trenton were shouting, "These are the times that try men's souls!" In real life, Paine quickly followed up on Washington's first victory by filing a newspaper story in which he reframed the controversial retreat from the Hudson. He compared Washington with Quinctius Fabius, the Ancient Roman general whose defensive strategy bested Carthage.

Paine thus invented the "Great General" before the general achieved anything great. And Washington looked after Paine. While each man in his way was a striver, their differences were more striking than their similarities. Washington had more than made up for certain disadvantages of birth by cultivating a dignified remoteness. Fastidiously turned out, tall and austere, tied financially and emotionally to the development of land, the interests of Virginia, and Robert Morris's consolidating vision for the whole country's economic future, the general wasn't a thinker but a man of action. Paine was a man of action too, but he was a constant thinker-aloud, shortish, wide open in his admirations and hatreds, a European urbanite, a careless dresser. He and his commander made a couple more than odd.

Their views diverged widely too, of course. But where a Benjamin Rush, influenced by friendship with Adams, changed his political views, friendship with Washington inspired Paine to change, in his mind, Washington's. In 1778, employed as the Congress's secretary through Washington's patronage, Paine became so outraged by the operations of Robert Morris that, during the Lee brothers' effort to have Silas Deane recalled and Morris censured, he gave the press a lot of highly classified information implicating Deane. The Congress fired Paine, and in print, Paine went on to excoriate not only Deane but also both Morrises, Gouverneur and Robert, for corruption. Yet Washington remained his hero of global democracy.

Washington, for his part, was by no means unaware of Paine's role in bringing to Pennsylvania exactly the kind of government directly opposed by Hamilton, the Morrises, Washington himself, and almost every other upscale person in America. Paine even served on a Philadelphia price-control investigation committee. Yet the comradeship thrived.

By the time peace was in the offing, Paine was hurting for cash. Both "Common Sense" and *The American Crisis* had huge sales, but he'd placed the works in the public domain and donated any royalties he did receive to supplying the army. Dismissed by the Congress as a leaker, he had no job, so he asked Washington to lobby the Congress to give him a pension, a reward for his decisive work on behalf of American independence. Washington got Paine some money, but it wasn't much, and Washington had another idea anyway. He knew a man with a job to offer.

It was Robert Morris.

No record would survive of Paine's or Morris's first reactions to Washington's proposing to connect those seeming sworn enemies. But Morris wrote to Paine, and in February 1782, George Washington, Thomas Paine, and Robert Morris sat down to dinner. This was when the Morris team was struggling to get the federal impost through the Congress. Morris told Paine they had to persuade not just the delegates and the legislatures but also the public, and for that he needed a writer, and not just any writer but the man who could bring the magic. The pay would be lavish, the relationship undisclosed.

Paine took the job. As the Morris Continentalists' writer-for-hire, he started meeting for brainstorming sessions with both Morris and Washington and cranking out not just pro-federal-tax articles but other pieces rallying the people to strengthen the Congress's powers. Gouverneur Morris sometimes dropped by too. Had the arrangement become known, Paine's friends in the Democracy would have thought their brilliant, world-famous comrade had turned against the cause and sold out his class, or just lost his mind, or both. They would soon come to think so anyway.

But Paine wasn't like them. He hadn't, like Rush, deradicalized; he objected to what he saw as some radicals' departure from reason. He believed big projects and national government could have widespread benefits for ordinary people. He feared dissolution of the country's potential in the varying efforts of wayward states. He viewed paper currencies as undermining struggling people's solvency; he'd even invested in an earlier, state-chartered version of Morris's bank. He'd spoken out against the attack on Fort Wilson. He also made Morris agree that he wouldn't have to write, even anonymously, anything he disagreed with.

This job kept Paine close to Washington amid ongoing, climactic events that the writer saw as globally transformative. In the fall of 1783, after the Congress had moved to Princeton, the two spent time relaxing at the headquarters nearby. They rowed a scow into a creek famous for being flammable and performed a science experiment, tossing gunpowder-charged paper into the water to prove that a gas was the cause of the phenomenon. Washington promised to speak to the Congress again about Paine's financial plight, and when a servant stole Paine's only coat, Washington gave him one of his.

In November 1783, with peace agreed to, British troops finally evacuated New York. A tradition would develop that on November 25, when Washington entered the city with a cadre of the Continental Army, Paine rode beside him at the head of the triumphal parade, a freelance writer and a victorious general paired in the greatest adventure in history. If the tradition was grounded in fantasy, it was thoroughly Paineian.

The postwar moment had begun. Paine saw the success of the American Revolution as a chance to "begin the world again," as he put it, on principles in line with his idiosyncratic idea of democracy built on the transforming power of human reason. This transformation must prevail, he believed, not just in the United States but throughout the whole world. He'd always been fascinated by bridge design and was becoming immersed in the study of advanced engineering. In the face of expert opinion to the contrary, he thought that all-iron structures might be used to span wide rivers, revolutionizing communication across natural and political boundaries. A re-designer of both government and infrastructure, Paine thought the 1780s would be the greatest decade in world history.

*   *   *

Herman Husband, too, harbored great hopes for the 1780s. When the war was still going on, he had a vision more profound and enveloping than any of his earlier revelations, a full-scale prophecy of democratic government in peacetime America. As postwar conflict mounted between the Democracy and the powerful, Husband's new vision would send him back into both preaching and politics, with dramatic results.

When the vision came to him, it was June 1779, and he was busy with an ambitious mapping project. After his brief term in the Pennsylvania assembly, he'd returned to the Glades and continued exploring, surveying, and documenting the vertiginous Alleghenies, seeking passes for accommodating an east-west road to link Philadelphia with the village of Pittsburgh at the headwaters of the Ohio River. Many others were also hoping to create ways across the Appalachians to take settlers westward and bring produce eastward. Entrepreneurs like George Washington formed speculative road and canal companies, but Husband thought private projects like that, involving kickbacks and other corruption, ended up cumbersome, costly, and wasteful—in his terms, impractical.

He was looking for a more natural highway, an infrastructure incorporating the existing mountain passes. By now he was deeply educated in the geology of the mountains. In his hand-drawn, to-scale maps and diagrams, he was plotting a route that, unrealized in his lifetime, would become part of a system opened to public use more than 125 years later.

Surveying one of those passes, he was interrupted by the vision. All at once he saw that the Alleghenies formed the eastern wall of a great city: the New Jerusalem, the redeemed, twelve-gated city of God described in the Books of Daniel, Ezekiel, and Revelation, as well as in the Apocryphal Book of Enoch. By creating the city symbolically, in books, the Bible prophesied a place that literally existed, Husband now saw, at massive scale on the North American continent, a far greater West than British America had ever known.

He was standing, an infinitesimal human form, on the city's massive eastern wall. The most famous gates to the city, the four described by Enoch, must refer to specific mountain passes. If he began following the eastern wall southward, surveying all the way, he would sooner or later arrive at an intersection with the southern wall, which might stretch all the way to the Pacific Ocean. Ultimately all four walls, as well as the gigantic interior, could be surveyed and mapped. Knowing and securing this redeemed city, where all were prophesied to live in happiness: here was the true fruit of the American Revolution, the last battle for good government, the Millennium on Earth.

So his life changed again. For the next five years and more, as the war went on and then ended in the American victory he'd always predicted, Husband traveled by horse and on foot, sometimes bushwhacking, sometimes using existing roads. His cartographical ambitions and biblical interpretations sought new levels. Ezekiel provided the city's blueprint: when his dimensions for fields, walls, and gates were transposed into modern units and scaled up to the mountains' size, they matched the results of Husband's surveying. Daniel's climactic symbol of a glorious mountain represented the whole upthrust Allegheny area. John said the eastern wall was made up of twelve kinds of precious stone, and Husband had already identified, in Appalachian geology, sandstone, limestone, marble, salt, coal, and iron ore. One winter, when raids by the Shawnee and others sent Glades settlers to safety at Fort Cumberland, Maryland, he went back to North Carolina, where two of his grown sons had returned to live; on that trip, he took notes on Virginia's mountains. On another, he wound up in Canada. He covered hundreds of miles, studying, drawing, taking samples and notes.

The great map that slowly emerged showed the eastern wall stretching southward from the Hudson Bay to the southern end of the Appalachians. A southern wall then ran westward, from Georgia all the way to the foot of a north-south range running parallel to the Pacific Ocean and meeting a northern wall, which ran from the upper end of the Pacific range back to the Hudson Bay. This map didn't just confirm Husband's special feeling, at once spiritual and political, for the American West. It projected his hopes into a new dimension. When news came of the signing of the peace treaty with Britain, formalizing the victory over Britain he saw as biblically prophesied, it had become clear that the whole great western region of the continent was specially blessed, not just as a region but as a living force for unleashing the cosmically redemptive power of the Revolution. American independence, now achieved, was jump-starting the Millennium. The American West was ordained ground zero for the final explosion of equality and good government on Earth.

So in the mid-1780s, he returned to preaching and publishing. His aim was to clarify for westerners locally and for far-off easterners the political meaning of his vision and study. As in the regulator days he used the pamphlet form, often calling his works sermons, sending the manuscripts off to be published by a Philadelphia printer. He signed some of them "Hutrim Hutrim." Sometimes he ascribed his ideas to the "Philosopher of the Allegheny," depicted as an elderly wilderness prophet, tall and skinny, with piercing eyes and long white hair and beard, who lived in a cave, studied the stars, and interpreted dreams. In real life, visitors to his prosperous, 4,000-acre farm and busy sawmill found Husband often barefoot and in old clothes. He showed them his great map of the New Jerusalem and explained it with reference to Scripture. Upscale locals and visitors from elsewhere started thinking of him as the Pennsylvania madman. Some were baffled that a woman as seemingly well-educated and practical as Emy Husband could be persuaded by such strange ideas and predictions.

But nothing about the ideas and predictions seemed mad to most of his ordinary neighbors. When Husband stood for elected office again, they voted for him. By returning to public service, he meant to take his part in the prophesied onrush of universal human freedom, protected by a national, democratic American government, sanctified by the holy city that was the American West, and very near at hand.

10

WASHINGTON'S COUNTY

IN 1784, GEORGE WASHINGTON, admired by Herman Husband as the hero who had defeated the forces of the Antichrist, got into a confrontation with some of Husband's western-Pennsylvania neighbors who took quite another view of the general. Their attitude told Washington that if things had to get worse, in Hamilton's terms, before they could get better, getting worse was well under way.

Husband was by no means the only person focused on the American West as the site of great American change. George Washington and others in his circles were too. The region meant different things, conflicting things, to different people; even the term "the West" had varying meanings. It could refer to what the states called their backlands: the Berkshires of Massachusetts, the Ohio headwaters of Pennsylvania, backcountry North Carolina, Virginia's Kentucky County. It could refer to farther-flung boundary lands, more fully inhabited by the woodland nations than by white people and long fought over among the imperial powers and former colonies. Now, with the end of the war, every category of western land was giving eastern speculators and their cronies in the West new reason for excitement about the commercial potential of development.

The excitement itself was nothing new. George Washington, Philip Schuyler, and James Wilson were only among the most conspicuous of the financial adventurers who had long been making western claims. Herman Husband, too, had discovered the West's potential during waves of speculation that had begun in the 1750s. Before the war created the Public Debt of the United States as an object of speculation, the investing class had speculated in western land, and for two generations now, those who could afford to had been claiming land by hook or by crook, though few of these freewheeling investors—Washington was an exception—had ever been there.

A big bet had thus already been placed on the West when, in 1783, peace with Britain boosted the region's monetary potential overnight. All commercial eyes were on 300,000 square miles lying north and west of the Ohio River, an astonishing resource of woodland running all the way out to the Mississippi and all the way up to the Great Lakes. In 1763, Britain had won that gigantic stretch of unmatched fertility from France. During the imperial crisis that led to the American Revolution, control over it had become a bone of contention between upscale Americans, who presumed they were free to pursue their happiness by acquiring and developing that land at will, and British authority, which reserved the land for the woodland nations as partners in the imperial fur trade. Because many of those nations, seeing Americans' intent, allied with the British in the war, fighting had raged through the states' backlands and the farther-west region, and in the treaty ending the war, Britain didn't just give up its thirteen rebellious colonies. It ceded to the United States the whole great woodland lying to the states' west.

That cession created a never-before-seen financial opportunity— especially for the entrepreneurs who had been earliest and boldest in making claims in the region, with Washington only the most adroit. Some early investors now hoped to sell dear. Others wanted to buy more land, farther west. New investors wanted in too. Eastern-backed western operators, like the Bedford Courthouse ring that Husband disdained as the Antichrist, hoped to manage things on the ground. Plans for developing the great new U.S. domain were spread out for discussion on desks and tables in eastern capitals.

The Congress's pivotal role in realizing this great opportunity drew the Continentalists and the State Sovereigntists together. Because the western woodland had been ceded, not in pieces to the separate states it bordered, but as a single entity to the United States, it was the Congress that was sitting on the potential. And it wasn't just the Continentalists Schuyler, Wilson, Washington and others in their circles who had an interest. State Sovereigntists were land speculators too. Both the state governments and the Congress hoped to pay officers in deeds to western land. Morris and Hamilton expected to use western land to help fund the Debt and pay creditors. Everybody in the American commercial and governing elite had public and private interests in a suddenly expanded American West.

So in this area, the Congress showed itself by no means inert. In April 1784, having moved from Princeton, now sitting in Annapolis, Maryland, the body officially created a public domain of the United States, naming it the Territory North and West of the River Ohio—the Northwest Territory, for short—and a team was organized to enter the region and begin surveying it, with a purpose very different from Herman Husband's. The plan was to make big grants of land to startup companies, formed by Congress-connected Money Connection types, for establishing and administering new western settlements. The ultimate goal was to entice hundreds of thousands of renters and buyers, American and European, via fulsome advertising, to surveyed western tracts. Emigrants' labor would clear the huge timbers and improve the land. Harvests at a whole new scale would start to flow eastward, via canals and roads invested in by eastern landlords and merchants. This projected industrialization of agriculture would swell the country in stages toward the Great Lakes and the Mississippi. The owners would rake in returns as their titles' value soared.

There was a major obstruction to realizing the bonanza. A host of nations, including the Shawnee, Miami, Delaware, Wyandot, Kickapoo, Potawatomie, and Wabash, lived, hunted, and did business in what the United States called its Northwest Territory. They began confederating to resist white expansion.

Another obstruction was in some ways more disconcerting to the commercial powers of the East: American settlers already living in the boundary lands. The West, an unparalleled commercial opportunity for the investing class, had become the hottest bed of what Hamilton called things getting worse. With a thirty-year depression pulling remote areas down—ordinary people in the countryside after the war had no money and no credit—the Democracy's dissent had shifted westward along with the speculators' excitement. From the Berkshires to the Alleghenies to Kentucky and beyond, exhausted veterans came home to penury. For owners of small western plots and tenants of absentee landlords, things were even worse after the Revolution than they'd been when Herman Husband first moved to the North Carolina backcountry in the 1750s. The usual corrupt local administration, scarce money, predatory lending, and high taxes combined with the rigorous labor of subsistence family farming to keep tenants stuck in the usual crushing cycles. Many who had recently been small landholders, losing property at accelerating rates to lenders and monopolizers, were now forced to work as tenants and day laborers for the eastern landlords and local cronies of eastern government, who increasingly dominated both farming and local manufacturing of brick, charcoal, iron, pottery, flour, and other necessities. Corruption and depression were making rich westerners far fewer and much richer. By the mid-1780s, the county sheriffs who repossessed foreclosed property had entered the richest top tenth.

Ordinary westerners had ideas about how to solve these problems. Herman Husband was prophesying a democratic American unity, centered on the West and redeeming the East, but many of the people who listened to, respected, and voted for him were leaning the other way. They didn't want to redeem the East. They imagined a western breakaway on behalf of their own economic liberation and self-determination. The state legislatures and the Congress, filled with land speculators, were refusing to negotiate for a permanent deal with Spain that would allow western product to go down the tributaries and into the Mississippi, thence to New Orleans and foreign markets. That policy seemed to shackle westerners to the East, force the fruits of their labor to flow toward the seaboard, and stifle their economic growth. But now, with

American independence, what was to stop western settlers from making their own river-access deals with Spain?

What was to stop them from solving all of their own problems? Eastern governments couldn't control the woodland people, better and better organized for resistance, who kept attacking white settlements. The settlers, crack shots comfortable with violence, had shown themselves capable of taking action against the people they condemned as vicious savages. Given long neglect by both their state legislatures and the Congress, they saw no reason to leave Indian policy, or any other policy, to eastern powers. It was even occurring to some settlers that they might mount a military defense against any eastern government that might try to come west across the mountains, enforce the laws, and throw people off land. If thirteen colonies could declare themselves independent and secede from Britain, why couldn't a western region declare itself independent and secede from a state?

This secessionist mentality, infused by and infusing the long-standing hopes of the Democracy, posed an immediate danger to the land speculators' bounding hopes, to the states' sovereignty, and to the Congress's control over the Northwest Territory. Absentee landlords claiming western tracts, failing to collect rents so far away, knew their land was already being squatted on by people who were impossible to police at such a distance. If western settlers got organized en masse to outright defy the east, the bonanza would be impossible to realize.

George Washington had important, long-standing land claims at the busiest site of growing defiance, from the western slopes of the Alleghenies down to the headwaters of the great west-flowing Ohio River: Herman Husband's part of Pennsylvania. The victorious general also knew all too well, from his earliest speculation and military efforts, the region's special propensity for defiance, a long history of at-will land use and resistance to authority. A quieter kind of secessionism had been brewing there when the British Army built and later abandoned Fort Pitt, at the point where the Ohio formed. Families around the Ohio headwaters moved onto plots claimed by absentee speculators and farmed without paying rent, ignoring not only the titles but also the laws of Pennsylvania and Virginia, which both claimed the area at the time. Shortly before the Revolution, some settlers took local self-determination all the way, gathered the western parts of Pennsylvania, Virginia, and Maryland into a single, self-created entity, named it Westsylvania, and when the war broke out, wrote a Westsylvania constitution and petitioned the Congress to admit the region as a new state. That would have removed valuable territory from three existing states and voided speculators' claims. The Congress ignored the petition.

Now, in the postwar moment, Westsylvanians were no longer talking about statehood. Economic problems for ordinary people were at their worst around the Ohio headwaters; some leaders there were calling for outright independence—both from their states and from the United States. Washington could easily see the threat to his interests and the country's. Westerners might take control of the entrance to the all-important, west-flowing Ohio, tributary of the Mississippi. They might connect their region to Britain, which held the huge area north of the lakes, known as Canada, and still occupied forts on the lakes in ceded U.S. territory; or to Spain, which held the huge region west of the Mississippi. While Kentucky, Virginia's backland county down the Ohio, wanted statehood, some Kentuckians were talking to Spain and making common cause with the Westsylvanians.

An East-West divide was thus becoming stark. It wasn't just Washington. Easterners of every class were calling westerners "white Indians." Filth was a theme, reported back from the West by visitors there: the people were "a pack of abandoned wretches," one observer had it, "living like so many pigs in a sty." "The scum of nature," remarked another. A nicer visitor described a remote cabin as "a dozen logs upon one another . . . the people were very kind but amazingly dirty."

Other stories focused on westerners' supposedly constant inebriation, loose sexual ways, including with Indians, and grotesque feats of violence, habits supposedly inherent to their ethnicity, which was widely and inaccurately taken to be 100 percent Scots-Irish. The takeaway, heavily promoted in the East: ordinary westerners, cut off from civilization, had become deplorably lazy, degraded, and wild. They seemed barely fully human.

The westerners saw themselves not as filthy squatters but as a hard-working people facing special economic problems, improving the land that corrupt, government-connected, far-off easterners wanted only for investment, brutally constrained by worsening conditions imposed on them by those lazy rich, who not only caused foreclosure and other miseries but also caricatured them as animals. It was true that their ruggedness could be powerful. Westerners were proud of their ability to survive and resist. Despite the economic and political conditions they suffered from, they had hope for the future.

Washington decided it was high time to travel right into the heart of what some people there called Westsylvania. His many western claims, illegal under British law, having been legitimized by his leading the United States to victory, he was resuming the busy commercial pursuits that had drawn him into war in the first place. Along with much land elsewhere, he owned 60,000 choice acres across the Appalachians, some in western Pennsylvania, some down the Ohio River. Nowhere near the massiveness of the acreages Robert Morris and James Wilson speculated in, Washington's lands were carefully and personally selected for enormous potential, and in the fall of 1784, he was ready to put an end to their illegal exploitation by unruly western squatters. Before the war, he'd gotten ahead by breaking and ducking the law. Now he meant to see the law enforced.

He had an advantage over many of his colleagues and competitors in western speculation. Unlike most of them, he knew those forests well, and he was confident that he knew the people. He'd never thought highly of white westerners' hygiene, work ethic, or intelligence. Keenly aware that absentee speculators were despised and ignored in the region, he'd had dummy buildings erected on his western properties to bamboozle the locals into thinking they were locally inhabited. Yet somehow they always saw through that ruse because, Washington believed, an incorrigible eagerness to avoid doing the hard work of getting their own land made them perversely wily.

So in early September 1784, the easterner least likely to be intimidated by anything, let alone western travel—beloved by cheering crowds, respected above all by those whose respect he desired, widely known as the greatest man in the world—took his first trip in more than seven years to the distant regions where, as a youngster, he'd had his first experience of warfare and started building his speculative pile in western land. The journey involved three enslaved servants; six horses, three of them carrying baggage, with further horses to be rented along the way; and occasional ride-alongs by friends and family. The equipage left tidewater Virginia and made its way northwest, the route familiar to Washington from his earliest exploratory and military efforts.

One reason to go west now was to inspect certain waterways on behalf of the Potomac Canal Company. Washington was its president and a top investor. The proposed canal was to direct the flow of future western produce toward the Virginia tidewater, creating a distribution monopoly where he made his home and based his commercial operations. On the way west, he had some formal meetings on that project and quizzed random locals about the navigation of various waters. He also stopped at many of his working landholdings, reacquainting himself with their topography and assessing the current value of land, mills, and other operations. He took his usual obsessive notes on the potential for development of every terrain he encountered and everyone's property where he slept.

His trip's main purpose, though, was to confront people living without authorization on his western lands and cow them into getting out or, in some cases, to start paying him regular rent. He had an especially baleful eye on a group of Scottish émigrés who, fifteen years earlier, had started farming a few hundred of his acres along a stream called Millers Run, near the Ohio headwaters, in the poorest and remotest county in Pennsylvania, recently named Washington County in his honor. He'd gotten hold of that plot in the early 1770s, via a business connection with the former colonial governor of Virginia, and had made many efforts over the years to get the Millers Run crew evicted by local agents. The squatters just kept coming back. Now he would bring his imposing personal presence and immense moral authority to pushing them off himself.

After the tortuous passage over the mountains, he entered the head-waters region in late September and revisited the meadow where, as a green youth, he'd established a fort and accidentally kicked off the Seven Years' War. Nowadays he owned the meadow. He passed through the village of Pittsburgh, on the once-wilderness point where the Allegheny and Monongahela Rivers met to form the Ohio. Before Fort Pitt had been built there, let alone Pittsburgh, he'd been one of the few English-speaking people to see the point.

At last he arrived at his Millers Run property. He began by riding around and inspecting the situation. The place turned out to be a kind of compound. Evidently thirteen or so families, on separate lots of varying sizes, some lying within his claim, others not, were deeply settled into living and farming here. They'd built many barns and houses. Harvest-time was beginning. In his diary, Washington noted, as he always did, the condition of the fencing, which was good. At one of their houses, he announced his presence and made an appointment to speak to them. A few days later, accompanied by the high sheriff and three local gentry, he convened fifteen of the Millers Run men and took their names. It was time to lay down the law.

The men seemed surprisingly little cowed by the sudden appearance of the greatest man in the world. Perfectly ready for a free and frank exchange of views, they appointed two of their number to act as spokes-men. Washington made his position clear. Unless the families vacated his land now, he would take them to county court for trespassing and have them evicted by force.

The mere threat of going to law, he'd calculated, should do the trick with a bunch like this, but again they surprised him. The spokesmen explained the economic challenges the group was facing, as well as its history. They were Seceders, a sect that had broken with the Church of Scotland over its practice of allowing great landlords to appoint minis-ters. Their roots in Washington County ran deep; some had served as militia officers in the war.

Then they delivered their own bottom line. They would stand, po-litely enough but without any qualification, on their moral right to live on lands they were improving by their own labor, which had also been their home for fifteen years. In that context, they countered, might the general be interested in selling them the land?

Washington, increasingly irritated, offered them a hard choice. They could either sign a ninety-nine-year lease, as tenants, at ten pounds a year; or make a purchase, at 25 shillings an acre, to be paid in full in only three years, with Washington holding a mortgage for that period at the usual high rate of interest on loans. The men huddled and came back. Noting the scarcity of money and their own relative poverty, the spokesmen agreed on the group's behalf to pay Washington's price—but only on condition that the payment period was lengthened and the interest removed. Otherwise, they were ready to fight eviction in county court.

He could hardly believe he was really going to have to pursue a lawsuit to remove these people. Worst of all, they'd be able to go on using his land while the eviction case went on. To probe for weakness, he polled each of the fifteen men individually. Nobody defected from the shared position.

The meeting was clearly over. Immensely annoyed, giving them the full effect of his hauteur and height, Washington pulled out a red handkerchief and held it by a corner. "Gentlemen," he said, "I will have this land just as surely as I now have this handkerchief." He punctuated the assertion with some profanity. Public swearing was against the law. One of the men, a justice of the peace, fined the general on the spot.

Having handed over his fine, Washington rode into the chilly mountains, ruminating. This encounter with men he considered nothing but lazy and shiftless, characteristic of their kind, wasn't just a one-off frustration. The scene encapsulated for him a larger situation, a grave threat to his and others' business operations, an underlying American political problem. Westsylvania and other self-created entities, widespread squatter farming, putting out feelers to foreign powers—all that had to be stopped if the value of the West was to be secured and the power of government respected.

Washington's view of the real nature of the problem was confirmed in October. Having arrived home, he was advised by a central Pennsylvania lawyer, a colleague of James Wilson, that his Millers Run adversaries' staunchness was grounded in the support of many settlers in Washington County. With people in the county losing land even faster than elsewhere in the headwaters region, the Millers Run matter was turning into a rallying point against speculators and related interests. In cases like this, the lawyer cautioned the general, Washington County's juries—and even some judges—were getting defendant-friendly. The plaintiff would be advised to pursue his suit in state court instead.

It took two years, but the Millers Run crew finally would be forced by the state court to abandon their farms on Washington's property. Still, nobody around the Ohio headwaters was likely to be subdued by seeing such people turned out by judicial process on behalf of one of the biggest of the big-time easterners. Quite the contrary. The urge for freedom and self-determination in the West was only swelling.

Then, in 1785, straight out of the suffering, democratic West, flew a projectile that crashed into the center of the eastern Money Connection and took out a key part of its apparatus. This wasn't western secession. This was western assault—what Hamilton called a popular frenzy and ordinary people called exercising their rights—and it made upscale Americans throughout the states and across the political spectrum think that consolidation of power would be a good thing.

That year poor and middling citizens in the struggling western part of Pennsylvania took advantage of the state's unusually democratic voting franchise to elect two of their class to the assembly in Philadelphia: Robert Whitehill, a middling farmer, and William Findley, born in Ireland, originally an artisan weaver and now a self-taught lawyer. They were elected on a platform for ending a disaster. The postwar depression in the western countryside had led to a terrible foreclosure crisis. Even families working properties they'd legitimately bought were being turned out, like the Millers Run squatters, for not paying taxes and interest on loans, their land taken by creditors, their tools, possessions, and livestock seized and auctioned by sheriffs. The people wanted relief from the legislature.

Whitehill was from Cumberland County—near-backcountry but not the frontier. Findley came all the way from Westmoreland County, just north and west of Herman Husband's Bedford County and not far from the Millers Run situation in Washington County—the Ohio headwaters, where conditions were worst, resistance to government and commercial exploitation strongest. Both men wanted to use the assembly's lawmaking power to destroy the systems they believed fostered these extremes of economic inequality.

With the Congress having left Philadelphia, never to return, the Pennsylvania assembly had moved back at last into its own ground-floor meeting room at the State House. Six years earlier, political battles had blown up in a real battle at Fort Wilson; those same battles were now ongoing in the assembly, with seesawing power swings. The Robert Morris group had been making headway in its efforts to gain a legislative majority and revise the state constitution. The radicals, invigorated by the West, were committed to stopping them.

On arrival, Whitehill and Findley and another western radical, John Smilie, went straight after Morris's great interstate money hub, the Bank of North America. To them, the institution was a mechanism not of great economic potential but of vicious economic destruction, and it operated not only on the quasi-national charter issued by the Congress but also on the state charter issued by the Pennsylvania assembly, so Findley and Whitehill urged the assembly to withdraw the bank charter, shut down the operation, and replace it with a land bank, offering easy-term credit to smallholders and artisans; and to issue a new paper currency and make it legal tender, thus easing commerce among ordinary people and freeing debtors from the predatory private lenders who also ran the bank. This program would give regulators' old economic demands the force of law.

Part of what made an attack on the bank so riveting for people within and beyond Pennsylvania was that Robert Morris and James Wilson, the bank's chief operators, were serving in the assembly too. This debate was pitting representatives of the Democracy against the authors of the Money Connection in real time: an outright class war, not in the street but in the august if sweaty and tobacco-stained assembly room of the Keystone State. Newspapers on both sides of the fight added to the heat.

Findley drew a lot of attention in debate. He had a notable Irish accent, and his speaking style wasn't orotund or dramatic in the familiar ways but hard-nosed, relentless. Some called him a yammering, unlearned demagogue, but he was hard to refute. He asserted that almost a third of the families in his county had already been foreclosed. He blamed the bank's hoarding of gold and silver and refusing to give loans to farmers and artisans; instead, Morris and other directors approved big, barely secured loans to one another and their friends for the purpose of pouring borrowed money into speculating in both state and federal bond markets and millions of acres of western woodland. As a bank director, James Wilson himself had borrowed $100,000 from the bank and sunk it in gigantic parcels of land. Undermining the health of the ordinary economy and risking its own collapse, the bank was no more than a private gambling den, Findley and Whitehill argued.

Findley explained the worst effect. The bank's directors and other high rollers were also delegates to the Congress, members of state legislatures, public officials—with an overwhelming private incentive to secure their own payoffs through heavy taxation of the people and private-public control over acreages, which caused endemic high rents, inflated prices, evictions, foreclosures. The assembly was supposed to be representing the majority, but the majority ended up the losers, and here, said Findley, lay the fundamental evil in what were known as corporations. When a legislature passed a law chartering a private company, such as the bank, thereby making the company a corporation, it became hard and sometimes even illegal to compete with that company. Creating monopolies and near-monopolies, Findley said, the incorporation process enabled government to aid private interest, keep outsiders out, and establish hierarchies by law. The effect of the corruption, even in democratic Pennsylvania, was to destroy democracy.

Anti-corporatism wasn't in itself new. Upscale agrarians, though they

were landlords and creditors, had sometimes also promoted an anti-corpo-
rate ethos as protective of the less-well-off. But Findley wasn't a rich man
presuming to identify his interests with working people's. He was a former
artisan, a member of the working class he spoke for, an outright partisan
for broad democracy giving fresh force to criticizing corporate monopoly.

Morris and Wilson vigorously defended their bank against the on-
slaught. They waved away complaints of unfair discrimination. They dismissed as mere fantasy a pervasive economic depression in the western
countryside. They claimed that anyone with good connections in the
city could easily open an account. They accused their attackers of irratio-
nal bias: Morris said that if an angel from heaven told Whitehill that the
bank was a good thing, the farmer would still disagree. Whitehill replied
that any such angel would have to be a fallen one.

Thomas Paine entered the fight—to somewhat strange effect. He'd
been living on a confiscated loyalist's farm in New Rochelle, New York,
granted to him by the Congress, as well as on a property he'd bought in
Bordentown, New Jersey. No longer in Morris's pay, an independent jour-
nalist again, Paine now published a series of articles against withdrawing
the bank charter. That put his divergence from the Democracy's ortho-
doxies in the open. To Paine, the bank as a chartered corporation—the
connection of finance to government—wasn't in itself the problem. He
thought that such a bank, properly managed, might still be made to serve
the needs of the whole people.

His pro-bank articles drew letters to the papers by members of the
Democracy castigating their former spokesman as a turncoat and a
drunk. But Paine remained inspired by a radicalism all his own. By now
he'd come up with a complete set of drawings for a bridge fully made
of iron. It wouldn't be the very first of its kind, but iron was thought to
impose strict limits on bridges' length and height; Paine had figured out
a way around them. He hoped to span New York's Harlem River with
an all-iron bridge, and his theory, based what would later be called an
algorithm with universal application, fostered adaptability to literally any
width and topography. Many experts scoffed at the idea that the material
would ever be affordable at such scale, so Paine planned to build a physi-

cal model. His former comrades in radicalism couldn't see it, but as events would soon show, his ambitions for democratic government were becoming as revolutionary as his ambitions for infrastructure.

Findley and Whitehill won. The assembly passed legislation taking away the bank's charter. The explosion was felt all over the country. The bank had been centralizing private high finance, just as Morris wanted. Shutting it down removed not only its shareholders' and directors' profit center but also the whole interstate investing class's go-to spot for taking big loans, depositing gold and silver, and using high-denomination notes. Morris accused the assembly of confiscating his property. Whitehill reminded him that the bank charter was the property of the people of Pennsylvania.

All that was scary enough for the class whose ventures depended on the bank, but the Pennsylvania radicals had another plan too. To build on their victory in the bank fight, they launched an attack from the assembly on the whole of the Debt as a speculation. They meant to demolish the great basis of the Money Connection.

To that end, they made their immediate target the speculative value of Pennsylvania's bonds. Like other states, Pennsylvania had issued the securities as a means of funding the war, and in the market they'd fallen to a fraction of face value. Speculators not just in Pennsylvania had therefore bought them at the deeply depreciated price and were pressuring the Pennsylvania assembly to pay the interest on them at face, not market value—an astonishing return for those who had bought so low, more like 20 percent on the investment than the original 6 percent. This payoff was to be funded by taxes imposed on the state's whole citizenry, many of whom, especially in the West, were already suffering economic disaster.

So the radicals pressed the assembly to go another way. Officially depreciate the state's bonds, they proposed, to the value at which the speculators had bought them in the market; then make the bonds legal tender for paying public fees of all kinds, thus transforming the bonds into a currency, easing commerce and relieving tax and debt burdens all at once. The assembly would never have to pay off the bonds: they'd be reabsorbed by government through tax, fee, and mortgage payments to a public land bank. The state's war debt would be extinguished, the investor class incorporated into the ranks of ordinary citizens.

The plan had enthusiastic public support. But to investors expecting huge payoffs, this epitome of democratic finance policy amounted to flat-out robbery and offered a good look at what the Democracy had in mind for economic life in all of postwar America. The plan didn't pass the assembly. That let down the radicals, but the assembly did make a big paper-money emission and allowed paying taxes in it. That let down the investing class. Both Robert Morris and William Findley came away disgusted.

Meanwhile, the Democracy's policies for popular finance were spreading beyond democratic Pennsylvania and beyond the West. Rhode Island had no backland and hadn't given political power to ordinary people. Its coastal State Sovereigntist values had been embodied, until very recently, in the aristocratic, lawyerly anti-Hamiltonianism of David Howell, who had led opposition to passing the federal impost. Still, in 1785, middling voters in that traditionalist state elected an assembly that passed a big paper-money emission and started considering steps for equalizing access to credit. And Rhode Island was only going to get more economically democratic.

By late 1785, that is, things had gotten, in Hamilton's terms, much, much worse. Alarm was resounding among the small, powerful set of Americans who traditionally pursued wealth and served in government. What was going on in Pennsylvania, and now in Rhode Island and other states, looked like legislated confiscation, wearing away investors' stakes in the Debt and gains as private lenders. When it came to western land, the other great bet of the investing class, the alarm was just as high. Continentalists and State Sovereigntists alike were convinced that squatting, rent- and debt-delinquency, and schemes for regional self-determination by wild "white Indian" "scum" were doing as much damage to speculation—and to the legitimacy of state boundaries—as the real Indians' confederated military opposition.

The popular frenzy, as Hamilton called it, had the upscale in a frenzy of their own. That's what he'd been waiting for.

11

TO ANNIHILATE ALL DEBTS

IN 1783, THE CONTINENTALISTS, bruised and exasperated, might have seemed defeated. Now, as 1785 came to an end, panic surging through the upper class made attempting to consolidate government look worthwhile again.

In early 1786, Hamilton, Madison, and Washington discussed widening the scope of—maybe actually hijacking—a convention already called for that fall, at Annapolis, Maryland, by some contiguous states to settle waterway-navigation issues, including Virginia's. The Congress, having moved from Annapolis to Trenton, New Jersey, and then to New York City, had just made clear, yet again, that it wouldn't even seriously debate a federal taxing power. The Continentalists thought a convention held outside that body might do better, so Madison got Virginia to invite other states to send delegates to Annapolis. The plan was to reintroduce the federal impost and get the Articles amended to allow it.

To Hamilton, the results of the Annapolis convention were, as usual, far from satisfactory. He, Madison, Robert Morris, and Gouverneur Morris led the revived Continentalist effort there, aided by Edmund Randolph of Virginia—he was a close ally of Washington—but only five states sent delegates. Still, the convention did acknowledge that facing up to some limited issues of interstate commerce would require a broader look at the Articles as a whole.

The Continentalists seized on that and proposed a general call to the states for a more thoroughgoing convention to meet in Philadelphia. In writing the call, Hamilton used his pen to eviscerate, with relish, the current system's idiocy. But of course he was talked down. Randolph said that what Hamilton had written might have been designed to kill the Philadelphia convention: with the real agenda exposed, Virginia wouldn't play. Madison advised Hamilton to listen to Randolph. Cooler heads prevailed, and Hamilton was forced, yet again, to wait. The final draft sent to the states backed off any outright assertions of what had now become the Continentalists' purpose for the Philadelphia convention: dispense with the Articles, establish a national government, and end the Congress.

As if to prove Hamilton's point, though, events now took a startling turn. Even while the weak Annapolis convention was under way, a movement coming out of the Berkshire Mountains of western Massachusetts started raising the class war's stakes to the highest degree yet. Armed men were shutting down the state's debt courts.

The action had begun in the western part of the state, unsurprisingly, but it was spreading quickly into the east. The men called themselves by the familiar name of regulators, and regulating government's relationship to the economy remained their aim, but they were making it stunningly clear that the War of Independence had changed everything.

These rebels weren't just trying to stop debt trials. Invoking the fundamental moral violation that the American Revolution had called tyranny—taxation without representation—they were out to overturn their state's constitution, written in 1780, largely by John Adams in recoil from the democratic Pennsylvania constitution he'd secretly helped bring about. Because the new constitution placed even higher property qualifications on voting and standing for office than had prevailed before American independence, ordinary people had even less electoral impact than they'd had before the war they'd just served in. The tyranny that Berkshires people saw as written into their constitution took an intolerable form that inspired rebellion when Massachusetts made some big, sudden moves in the ongoing drama of the Debt.

The fiscal situation was much like Pennsylvania's. Massachusetts's bonds had long since crashed far below face value, attracting the usual interstate speculators betting on government's valuing them higher than the market price. By 1785, the bonds were trading, just as a currency in ordinary commerce, at 2 cents on the dollar, but under the usual speculator pressure, the Massachusetts assembly decided to pay interest on the bonds at 25 cents on the dollar, in hard money. That would hand a huge profit to people who had acquired the bonds for so little, and the only way to fund the bonds at such a rate was to levy the usual high tax, payable only in scarce coin, on the whole citizenry and earmark revenue for the few.

But there was a critical difference between the situations in Massachusetts and Pennsylvania. In Massachusetts, the conflict couldn't be debated in the legislature, because in Massachusetts, working people were barred from equal representation. Then, in 1786, the Massachusetts legislature decided not to just pay interest on its state bonds at the high rate; it decided to pay off the whole principal, all at once—not only its own obligation, but the whole principal of its bondholding citizens' stake in the Federal Debt too. This even more gigantic payoff to the richest few naturally required even further taxation. While some of the 1786 taxes were payable in various kinds of paper, many people couldn't pay at all. Poor men had come home from war unpaid. In the mountains especially, many were sunk in the usual revolving debt to landlords and lenders. Families already struggling to revive farms and artisan shops now found themselves smacked down by these laws designed to benefit those same landlords and lenders in their role as state and federal bondholders. Foreclosure, arrest, poverty, and imprisonment boomed. The court system was jammed with debt prosecutions.

To the Berkshires people, the War of Independence, in the form of the Debt that paid for it, was being weaponized against the mass of laboring families who had fought and otherwise sacrificed for victory in that war. They wrote petitions. The assembly ignored them. That's what they meant by taxation without representation, and by tyranny. That's why, in the ongoing spirit of the Revolution, they were taking military action.

Military action—not riot. That was the scariest thing. These Berkshiremen were veterans, rank and file with a few lower officers. Experienced in regular army operations and organized across townships, they marched against the courts without the usual festive disguises of riot, in formation, following orders. Their aim wasn't obstruction and intimidation of government but insurgency. They would complete the American Revolution by toppling the anti-democratic state constitution and undoing oppressive tax policies.

Upscale people called the Massachusetts rebels Shaysites, because the leader was said to be one Daniel Shays, a veteran captain of the Continental Army, supposed to be a desperate debtor and even an escapee of debtors' prison. Word of mouth lent him monstrous qualities: Shays, the cornered rat with nothing left to lose; Shays, the charismatic demagogue who stole from the rich and gave to the poor. In real life, though a leader of the rebellion, Daniel Shays was far from the only one, and he hadn't been to debtors' prison. So little was known about him that much of what was ascribed to Shays by those who feared him most was pure fantasy. What the upscale wanted to imagine even less than a people led astray by one demagogic desperado was a people organizing itself in opposition to long traditions of economic and political oppression.

Especially unnerving: the government of Massachusetts had no way of defending its court system. There was the state militia. But many of the men who served there seemed to be more or less in sympathy with the rebels—in some ways indistinguishable from them—and word had it that unpaid rank-and-file veterans from out of state might be coming to join the rebellion too. The Massachusetts man Henry Knox, now serving as the Congress's secretary at war, wrote to George Washington to report that the Democracy's plan was clearly to seize all property in America; abolish all social, political, and pecuniary differences; share all goods in common; and "annihilate all debts public and private." The people seemed to believe, Knox noted, that as the war had been fought by all, the benefits of independence should be enjoyed by all. Somehow, this trend had to be firmly opposed.

Washington agreed. "The moment is, indeed, important!" he replied. "If government shrinks, or is unable to enforce its laws, fresh maneuvers will be displayed by the insurgents—anarchy and confusion must prevail—and everything will be turned topsy-turvy in that state, where it is not probable the mischiefs will terminate." He knew from experience with his western properties that the mischiefs were already widespread.

In January 1787, the Shaysites went beyond shutting down courts; 1,500 men marched on the federal arsenal in Springfield to seize its arms.

This was an assault not on a state institution but on a facility belonging to the Congress. But that body could do no more to protect its armory than Massachusetts could to protect its courts. Knox had to tell officials in his home state that under the Articles of Confederation he had no legal way of intervening to defend either their courts or the Congress's military stores. Even illegal ways were hard to come by. With the Continental Army disbanded, a skeleton military crew had been sent by the Congress to Fort Pitt at the Ohio headwaters to police the West and provide security for surveying teams in the Northwest Territory. Knox did manage to recruit 500 new troops to fight the Shaysite rebels, but because that violated limits on the confederation's powers under the Articles, the Congress had to pretend it was sending them out to the Ohio. Then the body failed to pass the necessary funding, and no federal force was sent after all.

The whole confederation seemed to have entered a state of paralysis that put both government and property in immediate danger. In September 1786, another armed uprising, this one in Exeter, New Hampshire, sought to force the state to issue a paper currency. That effort was quickly suppressed by the state militia, but in the absence of any might in the Congress, routing the Shaysites required the private vigor of the Society of the Cincinnati. Knox called out the society's Massachusetts chapter, and in a state of visible elation, veteran officers from all over New England, privately funded by Boston merchants, announced that they would never back down. They didn't just mean they'd never back down from the rebels. They would never rest, the Cincinnati said, until public faith and private credit were held sacred by government.

Thus the society clarified its watchdog role. In holding government financially accountable to the investing class, it took up the military

defense of the Debt its members held and the sovereignty of the governments that the Debt obligated, and in February 1787, the Cincinnati did
quell the Shaysites, though mop-up went on into the middle of the year.
Knox wrote to Washington, who found the society irritating, to point out
that it had served an excellent purpose in this case. Samuel Adams, now
serving as lieutenant governor of Massachusetts, suggested that debtors
learn more frugal and industrious ways and called for the death penalty
for the Shaysite rebels.

But the Massachusetts assembly meanwhile panicked. Under pressure of the rebellion, it repealed the taxes it had earmarked for the big
investor payoff and suspended its program for funding and paying off
the Debt. In that sense, the Cincinnati failed. The Debt, malnourished
by a fake federal impost and unenforceable state-tax policies, was dying.
In Massachusetts, where the Democracy was shut out, it was battered
by illegal uprising. In Pennsylvania, where the Democracy held office, it
was battered by legislative process. The West looked shakier than ever
too. In response to a circular letter coming out of western Pennsylvania,
Kentuckians hosted a convention that called on all settlers to unify in
resisting domination by eastern creditors and politicians.

Hamilton had reason to hope that these explosions of popular will
on behalf of democratic finance, legal and illegal alike, had finally proved
the truth of everything he'd been saying about the states' uselessness in
managing economies, the importance of a serious federal military force,
and the crying need for a national government. The most important
states were now among the most culpable. His own New York had tanked
the Congress's weak attempt to revive the federal impost. No hotbed of
egalitarianism, the state just seemed to see itself as a separatist empire.
Massachusetts, for its part, veering between agrarian horrors of public
debt and demands by public creditors, had tried not to fund the Debt but
to pay it off fast, not just its own obligation but also its citizens' part of
the Federal Debt. State-oriented payoff policies were anathema to Morris's and Hamilton's hopes anyway; then Massachusetts validated popular
violence by repealing its taxes. Pennsylvania, of course, remained largely
in the hands of the tyranny of the many who had confiscated the bank's

charter. Widespread fear among the well-off boded well, from the Continentalist point of view, for the planned Philadelphia convention, but the convention hadn't yet been approved by the Congress, and Hamilton decided to make yet another push.

In February 1787, while the Cincinnati were putting down the Shaysites, he rose and spoke in the New York assembly. Recently elected, he'd been trying, yet again and with great frustration, to get his state to reverse its position and agree to a federal impost. New York had actually agreed, in the abstract—but with so many state-oriented conditions that agreement, as Hamilton saw it, amounted to rejection.

So he was timing his assembly speech to reach both local and countrywide audiences. The Congress, having recently moved to New York, was meeting in the building on Wall Street, once the city hall, where the state assembly met too. The speech would get attention, and its subtext was the unscheduled Philadelphia convention.

"If these states are not united under a federal government," Hamilton told his audience, "they will infallibly have wars with each other; and their divisions will subject them to all the mischiefs of foreign influence and intrigue." Noting the contested condition of the West, he said that in the East, too, state sovereignty was at risk, civil war even within states possible. New York was divided by the readily navigable Hudson River. If people in the western part of the state became disaffected, he said, New York City itself might be vulnerable to literal invasion by rowdy upstate settlers.

"Can our national character be preserved without paying our debts?" he asked. "Can the union subsist without revenue? Have we realized the consequences which would attend its dissolution?" His overt plea was still only for the salvation of the union—not for outright replacement of the confederation—but the implication was growing clearer.

Governor Clinton's majority in the state assembly, however, remained unmoved. The body refused even to debate Hamilton's pitch for the federal impost.

*   *   *

So it was that in New York, in 1787, Robert Morris's long-standing first step for igniting a transformation of the country—*pass one federal tax*—died the last of its many deaths under the confederation system. In that sense, the confederation died too. By no means everybody knew it yet—but Hamilton did. The impost, he would later say, in a note-to-self, "begat convention." He meant the impost's failure had fostered a new susceptibility in the country's political elite to considering very serious corrective measures.

The Congress now did approve the proposed Philadelphia convention and scheduled it for May. "That a thorough reform of the present system is indispensable," Washington wrote to Madison in anticipation, "none who have capacities to judge will deny." He was being urged by Madison, Knox, and Randolph to lend the upcoming event the great weight of his personal presence, but the general was concerned that if he attended at all, he'd obviously be presiding, and that might not be a good look. Then again, he fretted, not attending might make him look bad too.

Knox took advantage of the general's ambivalence to make a strong and prescient pitch. He told Washington that if the convention did nothing but amend the Articles of Confederation, his reputation might indeed suffer somewhat, but, "Were an energetic and judicious system to be proposed with your signature, it would be a circumstance highly honorable to your fame, in the judgement of the present and future ages, and doubly entitle you to the glorious republican epithet—The Father of Your Country."

Washington decided to attend. By April, it was clear that every state but the perennial holdout Rhode Island would be sending delegates. While not all of them would like what the Continentalists planned to spring on them, the Democracy's successes had brought together upscale forces with nothing in common but an urgent need to shut down the Democracy.

Hamilton knew exactly what he hoped to get out of the Philadelphia convention.

His American education was complete. From Schuyler, Washington, and others in their circles he'd learned what the most ambitious sectors of the American commercial class wanted and how far they'd go to get it. From Morris, the farthest-seeing member of that class, he'd learned the nation-making potential of linking those financial desires and anxieties, across state lines, to a centralized political power committed to paying interest on the Debt. If Hamilton himself could get the right job in a new, pervasively powerful, national government—and he had good reason to think he could—it would be up to him to create a fully integrated scheme for exercising those powers to bring about the consolidation of wealth and government that, in Morris's vision, would unleash national greatness. Hamilton would be the one to author the United States as a rich, military, commercial, even industrial new force.

What had begun as Robert Morris's vision was now a blueprint for the Hamilton Scheme. He only needed the new national government to possess certain critical features.

PART III

THE SCHEME
AND THE SYSTEM

12

THE HAMILTON CONSTITUTION

IT WAS THE MORNING of June 18, 1787, and Alexander Hamilton, referring to a set of handwritten notes, was about an hour and a half into what would turn out to be more than five hours of disgorging, at last, every idea he'd ever had for overhauling government in America. Restrained by cooler heads no more, he stood yet again in that ground-floor room of the Pennsylvania State House where the Congress had adopted the Declaration of Independence and where, as a member of the Congress, he'd made his name by speaking in favor of the federal impost. The room had then seen the fight in the Pennsylvania assembly between the radicals Findley and Whitehill and the bankers Morris and Wilson over withdrawing the bank charter. Now Hamilton was speaking in the convention that had been called in response to democratic finance measures like curtailing the bank; finance-policy rebellions like the Shaysites'; egalitarian secessionism in the West; and the final failure to pass a federal impost for paying interest to federal bondholders. This was the Continentalists' big chance.

In the chair was Nathaniel Gorham, of Massachusetts, presiding over a committee of the whole in a body officially chaired by George Washington. Delegated by twelve of the states, with Rhode Island as usual the holdout, the body had ostensibly convened to consider improving the confederation by making some limited improvements to the Articles, but the announced purpose had quickly been superseded by the real purpose, kept secret from everyone outside this room: throwing out the Articles altogether, forming some kind of full-scale national government, and disbanding the Congress for good.

With stakes so high, things had grown tense. Streets outside were getting scorching and steamy, flies plentiful. The atmosphere inside was at least as oppressive, the normal olfactory and social challenges of serving in such close quarters enhanced by a heavy stillness. The agenda was so secret that the delegates had voted not only to publish no records but also to keep the door and windows shut tight. Sweat never stopped springing. Nobody would be foolish enough to be first to doff his coat. And now this speech from Hamilton. And he was going on and on.

At first, he'd kept surprisingly quiet. Like most of the other delegates, Hamilton hadn't even made it to Philadelphia by May 14, the convention's scheduled opening day. So slow were the delegates to arrive that the opening had to be pushed back, enabling Madison, who had made a point of arriving early, to caucus secretly and at length with Robert Morris, Gouverneur Morris, James Wilson, Benjamin Franklin, Edmund Randolph, and George Washington. State Sovereigntists had become so desperate to regain elite control over the country that they'd agreed to attend, but many prospective delegates would have been shocked if they'd known of the extremity of the proposal that the Continentalists were about to spring on them. Madison and the caucus planned to expose, early in the proceedings, their secret agenda—sidelining the separate, weak, too-susceptible state legislatures to the nth degree politically feasible, thus ending the Democracy's recent inroads on public and private wealth—and then move aggressively to bring it off. Arriving on May 18, Hamilton was so well aligned with Madison and the rest of the old Morris team, as well as with Randolph and, of course, Washington, that he didn't need the confab, but in his own delegation he was odd man out. Robert Yates and John Lansing were Clinton men, New York Sovereigntists. They could be expected to balk as soon as the agenda was revealed.

Hamilton stayed quiet on opening day, May 29, when, with the delegates in the room at last and sworn to secrecy, the victorious general authoritatively in the chair, and the windows shut, Edmund Randolph kicked things off by stating what had brought them all there. "Our chief danger," Randolph bluntly declared, "arises from the democratic parts of our constitutions." None of the states, he said, had established "sufficient checks against the Democracy."

He laid it all out. There was the collapse of the federal obligation to support the public creditors; many in the room were members of that group. There was the scourge of paper currencies and other popular finance measures deleterious to the portfolios of the wealthy. There was of course the abject failure of the legislatures and the Congress to suppress debtor insurrection and prevent other popular outrages committed on behalf of democratic finance. Such was the nature of what Randolph called the "imbecilities" of the existing system.

Everybody in the room, Continentalist and State Sovereigntist alike, knew what kind of wealth was at stake. It helped that Randolph was saying it—a scion of the Virginia planter class, not a northern, urban moneyman like Robert Morris.

Then he went all the way. Given the states' failures, he asserted, there was no way to achieve the shared goal of checking the Democracy without ending the Articles and forming a truly national government, with jurisdiction throughout the country.

And it was amazing. This manifest attack on the states' exclusive sovereignty shocked plenty of delegates from all regions, but real discussion ensued. Beginning with Randolph, who segued into a plan that had been developed largely by Madison in the pre-convention caucus, various ways of forming a true national government were advanced and debated. As recently as 1783, such a development looked utterly remote. Hamilton, in his chair at the New York desk, in the back row, near the shut and guarded door, might have been relieved and pleased to see these handpicked men of twelve states finally getting down to the business he'd been pushing them to get down to since 1780.

He wasn't relieved. He wasn't pleased. The proposals the delegates advanced in those early days seemed to him typically mealymouthed and weak: half-measures at best.

At least they all seemed to agree, Hamilton admitted to himself, that the goal was to rescue stability, order, and property from attack by the Democracy. Considering that, he started scribbling notes. The means they kept proposing just seemed absurdly . . . democratic. He kept scribbling. There was all this talk about a nationally elected lawmaking body. Hamilton agreed that establishing such a body would of course be necessary to passing laws obligating citizens throughout all states, just as he, Morris, and others had always wanted. Even the suggestion that this new legislature should be elected by a majority of qualified voters throughout the country made great sense. Britain's House of Commons was elected by a majority of the suitably well-propertied to represent their interests; an American version could be expected to vitiate the exclusive lawmaking power that state legislatures had enjoyed during the confederation, and by keeping national election districts pretty big, and the elected house thus relatively small, any tendency toward overrepresentation— the ever-present democratic threat—would be stymied. All that was good, as far as it went.

But here came a nasty snag. An elected house, even one fairly unrepresentative, should of course be subjected to an unelected check on its outcomes. Such was the function of Britain's House of Lords: a hereditary upper house, beyond the reach of popular pressures, limiting the scope of what the lower house did. So could Hamilton really understand some of his fellow delegates—including Madison—to be suggesting that in a national American government, this check on an elected house might take the form of an upper house that was also elected? Possibly elected by the lower house itself? And in that sense also representative, if somewhat indirectly? How was that a check on representation?

But it got worse. One proposal actually had it that in the national legislature, each state would get one vote, just as in the confederation Congress. That would make it not a national government at all. And when listening to the various ideas for creating a national executive, Hamilton could only mentally smack his head and go on scribbling.

Hence the depth of the silence, on June 18, when he stopped being quiet, stood beside the New York desk, and revealed his low opinion of everything he'd been hearing for nearly three weeks and everything he wanted to see instead. He delved deeply into the history and science of government. That's part of what made the speech so long. But behind all his history and argument lay what Hamilton saw as the simple fact that, as he told the chair, any national government as representative as those proposed—so similar to the state governments, which everyone here agreed, at least tacitly, were failing to obstruct the Democracy—could only fail too.

Many of his own proposals, he admitted to the convention, were shocking on their face. He wanted to copy the British constitution, so when it came to the executive, he wanted not just a strong, solo official but a monarch. Not a hereditary monarch. But a monarch nonetheless, elected for life and enjoying the broad powers enjoyed by the British Crown in its relationship to the representative, legislative power of Parliament. The American executive should wield, for one thing, an absolute veto on all legislative bills, with no recourse for the legislature.

This appeal to monarchism was indeed shocking. Yet regarding the relationship between the states and the new national government, Hamilton went even further.

He wanted to eradicate the states altogether. He admitted it. He wanted to eradicate them as governments. He wouldn't, he said, actually propose such a measure, because he knew it was too shocking to get anywhere, but that was the only reason he wouldn't propose it, because nothing real was to be gained and much lost, he said, by maintaining the states as anything but regional administrative departments of a national government run by governors appointed by the national executive. In any event, the new national government certainly ought to have the power—as already proposed by Madison—to strike down state laws.

It was a painfully long speech, but the main things that would attach themselves to Hamilton's name for all time were his hymning the British constitution, his call for an elected monarch, and his desire to shut down the states and turn them into, at most, regional departments. It was the middle of the afternoon when he finished speaking and sat. There was no debate. His allies and opponents alike had settled into a silence so deep that a chair leg's creak would resound, any throat-clearing or sniff of a pinch be amplified. The steaming body sought relief from physical and mental torment by collecting its thoughts and lumbering toward the next order of business: a motion, readily seconded, to adjourn for the day.

Hamilton's lips had been moving. Sounds had been coming out of his mouth. Evidently he hadn't said anything. The speech that would remain the convention's longest was widely viewed as an embarrassing faux pas, leaving only a blank.

Yet the speech made something plain. The kind of national government Hamilton had sketched was simply not to be considered. Hamilton's allies did of course want things just like that. To a man like Henry Knox, who was not a delegate, it went almost without saying that the existence of the state governments was "an insuperable evil in a national point of view." Madison, a leading delegate, wanted a strong, solo executive with independent powers; at all costs, he wanted the states, since he knew they really couldn't be eradicated—Hamilton did too—suppressed as far as humanly possible, for all the obvious reasons, going back to his and Hamilton's time together in the Congress. Hamilton, the delegate from beyond the pale, had forced the convention to glance over a precipice and take a look at the abyss the State Sovereigntists most feared, and Madison had experience in working with and around Hamilton's unsettling tendency to say the quiet part out loud. Indeed, the two knew how to work together. To delegates like the New Yorkers Yates and Lansing, everything Randolph had rolled out on day one already tended toward an eradication of states' power; their fellow New Yorker Hamilton seemed so extreme on the issue that nobody could even acknowledge his views. His speech, shocking the convention into a blank, had the counterintuitive effect of soothing fears by framing Madison as the saner alternative.

As for Hamilton himself, he retained hope for a new government that would give him enough of the power he needed to bring about enough of the great change he wanted to make. Whatever happened now, it was clear that both the states and the new national government would have to enjoy sovereignty. The problem was that, according to all political theory known to the delegates, sovereignty is indivisible.

Even before Hamilton's speech, Madison had been striving to de-emphasize the crushing losses for the states that would inevitably arise from the sovereignty of a national government. As Hamilton relapsed to relative quiet, his Virginia partner, along with James Wilson and others, playing a guiding role in debating, drafting, and revising what was shaping up to be a national constitution, would seek more covertly to realize the ends that Hamilton had stunned the body by calling for overtly.

Hamilton did speak again, however, and speak all too frankly, on what overall form the new government should take. The convention was converging on establishing some kind of republic: a system where a representative body, not a single person, has a lot of control over lawmaking. The colonial governments had always had republican aspects: legislatures elected by the propertied, operating under the aegis of, and at times in opposition to, royal elements with executive power. When the provinces had become independent states, they'd dumped the royal elements and kept the representative ones.

Still, republicanism on the national scale now contemplated by the convention had long been an aspiration more literary than political. That made the convention's project fresh and exciting yet reassuringly conservative too. An elected representation of the well-propertied seemed the optimal way of preventing both a tyrannical monarch and a tyranny of the many, fostering a state of balance among all social and economic classes—"balance" as defined by the convention delegates, who saw the Democracy's recent efforts as throwing everything wildly off-balance. What they took to be ironclad lessons of history taught them that efforts at enforcing social and economic equality lead inevitably to the emergence of a strongman and the end of liberty. Republicanism, with all of its risks, hedged against such an outcome.

Hamilton didn't see it that way. On June 26, he admitted to his fellow delegates that he didn't like the idea of forming a republic. By now he seemed to accept that his remarks wouldn't land, but if his colleagues really insisted on going for a republican government, he advised them to "tone it as high as possible." He meant that, given the role of representation in republics, they should build in strong measures for ameliorating the all-too-representative weaknesses that had made the states so catastrophically incompetent in fending off the Democracy.

This, coming from the man who had just publicly embraced monarchy, could be expected to offend many delegates. Elbridge Gerry, of Massachusetts, was one. An inveterate resister of heavy-handed authority, prickly in a long New England anti-Crown tradition, Gerry was a wartime shipper who had moved arms and other supplies from France and Spain and sponsored privateering expeditions against the British—but, unlike Robert Morris, he wasn't a profiteer. Gerry opposed merchant traditions of price gouging. He even favored price controls. He owned no people. Above all, he had a fervent commitment to what many New Englanders had long cherished as the providentially ordained autonomy of their states and their region. He wasn't inclined to give any of it up.

Hamilton and Gerry might thus have represented the farthest poles on the convention's Continentalist–State Sovereigntist spectrum. What was emerging in debate, however—what Madison and Wilson and others had to work with—was the stubborn fact that while Hamilton and Gerry might be in opposition politically, even in a sense existentially, they agreed on the underlying purpose of the convention itself. At one point, Gerry confessed a change of heart he'd undergone. He'd once believed, he said, that a large representation of the propertied in the state legislatures would provide more than enough government to protect rights in America. Then the Shaysites Rebellion made his beloved New England a scene of evil, flowing from what he now saw as the excesses of democracy that state governments seemed powerless to prevent and sometimes even encouraged: "the levelling spirit," as he put it. Shaysites weren't the type, Gerry believed, to be self-motivated, and they didn't lack virtue. Their tragic degradation could be explained only by inflammations fostered by a desperate demagogue like Daniel Shays and unwittingly encouraged by a lack of strength in government. He'd learned his lesson, Gerry said. He was ready to compromise with the formation of a higher, more pervasive authority.

As the subcommittees began drafting, and as the committee of the whole debated and revised a host of measures for creating a real national republic in a legally binding document, Madison kept trying to create multiple points of entry for men like Gerry, those worried equally about the assault by the Democracy and about losing states' autonomy. To that end, he did his best to mask certain aggressive advances he was making on behalf of the old Morris team's brand of Continentalism and against the states' powers. At one point, he revived his idea, passed over earlier, of giving the national government what Robert Morris had coached the bondholder lobby to demand back in 1782: a power to strike down democratic finance laws passed by the states. Before the convention, Madison had assured Washington, whose main concern was what he called "justice to the Public Creditors," that a veto by the federal government *"in all cases whatsoever* on the legislative acts of the states, as heretofore exercised by the kingly prerogative, appears to me to be absolutely necessary." Such a power would stifle what Madison thought of as the Democracy's "improper and wicked project[s]" for undermining both the Debt and private property generally: issuing paper money, abolishing outstanding loans, dividing property equally. It also would effectively bring about what Hamilton had called for: removing the states' power to legislate independently.

The federal veto didn't get anywhere. Madison harbored a hope of slipping it in somewhere later.

And even if the states' power to legislate couldn't be taken fully away, in certain key areas it might be limited, even superseded. In the drafting debates, two key powers of government therefore became especially touchy: taxing power and control over the military.

Regarding the military, it was obvious to the convention delegates that there could be no national government lacking an exclusive power to make war. A fundamental principle even of simple union had always been that the separate states weren't allowed to field armies against foreign powers or one another. Military policy—the confederation's original basis—had always been consolidated in the Congress.

But the states had militias. They identified their sovereignty with their exclusive control over those militias; too, many State Sovereigntists and some Continentalists remained committed to a fear of professional armies and a faith in citizen soldiery. So it was controversial enough when Madison and others proposed giving the national government a power to create the professional army and navy that Hamilton and Washington had been calling for, but when they proposed placing the states' militias under national control in the event of war or insurrection—a power critical to the old Morris team's dreams of suppressing democratic resistance to tax collection—Gerry reacted hard. His reaction exposed a bind that many of the delegates had gotten themselves into.

On the one hand, the Shaysite rebels had turned Gerry into a kind of grudging Continentalist. The appeal of forming a national government lay in the sheer force that such a government would have in preventing uprisings where state militias notably failed. Yet faced with what that would mean in practice, Gerry recoiled from giving up states' control. He rose to assert that had the federal government stepped in to quell the Shaysites, things would have gotten even worse. A federal militia power, he went on with mounting emotion, would remove the legislatures as commanders of their own forces—reducing the states to mere drill sergeants, passing along orders from higher-ups to the troops. Because that was indeed the purpose, Madison had to go to great lengths trying to persuade Gerry that no such thing would ever happen.

Taxing power, the other key element of sovereignty, remained the one thing critical to Hamilton's and Morris's plans for the national future. "Impost," as Hamilton wrote in his note-to-self, "begat convention": the Congress's failure to get the states to agree to a truly federal tax and earmark its proceeds for the bondholding class had brought these delegates together. Extinguishing the states, as Hamilton wanted, would have placed all taxing power in the national government, and that would have kept things simple, but it was totally out of the question. On the other hand, discussions going on as early as the convention's opening days had more or less presupposed creating a national taxing power, and if the states were to continue to exist, and clearly they were, then they would

THE HAMILTON CONSTITUTION

have to have taxing power too; otherwise, they wouldn't be states at all. The national taxing power couldn't be exclusive.

The power's mere existence, however, would take away from thirteen separate entities the exclusivity of their power to tax their citizens, a tectonic shift that would make the United States no longer a confederation but a nation. Just on a practical level, federal taxes would hamper states' ability to tax: there was only so much taxation people could take. But at the highest level, national taxation would create a new class of people, subject to law across state lines: the citizens of the United States.

Citizens of a republic can't be taxed without their consent, given through representation. Much debate and drafting therefore came down to the dicey question of how to represent the new national citizenry in the new national government. And in that context, the delegates couldn't help but run up against slavery.

It was a subject they didn't feel like talking about. Some, including Hamilton, had strong feelings against the institution. Some slaveholders could be fulsome in deploring the immorality of a practice they perpetuated daily. Yet slavery's rank immorality would by no means become central to the convention debate, partly because a massive public violation of moral principle is an embarrassing thing to discuss publicly, but largely because the issue didn't divide the delegates along political lines. The critical divisions and alliances were over other matters; they crossed the moral divide. Some southern slaveholders objected to certain proposals made by Madison, a fellow southern slaveholder, and joined in certain objections made by Gerry, a northern anti-slavery man. Gerry opposed some of Hamilton's ideas about the future of the country, wanted just as eagerly as Hamilton to shut down the Democracy, and openly opposed slavery, as Hamilton did, but, unlike Hamilton, Gerry had never held anyone in slavery. Hamilton's and Madison's notable differences regarding slavery never caused their partnership any trouble at all. They would be at odds later—but not over that.

An exception was Gouverneur Morris. The man whose disdain for ordinary people was among the most explicit, and whose aristocratic pretensions were especially pronounced, spoke up passionately against

the continued existence of slavery in the United States. His speech had
no direct impact on the convention's outcome.

The delegates avoided as far as possible the question of whether slavery should exist and got down to sorting out—at times fighting over—
how the institution's effects on political power should be managed in the
new national context. The real slavery questions therefore had to do,
again, with the national taxing power. Would the importation of enslaved
African people be made subject, like other imports, to national import
duties—to a federal impost? Such duties might bring in significant national revenue. Some anti-slavery proponents thought high duties might
even slow or stop the Atlantic trade, but Madison didn't want to call
people property in a national constitution, and the delegates as a whole
didn't like to refer to enslaved people at all, so a compromise measure was
quickly drafted and adopted, prohibiting any ban on the Atlantic trade
until 1808 and allowing no more than ten dollars for any import duty,
as the delegates chose to put it, "on such persons as the several states . . .
shall think proper to admit." That number was low enough to keep the
trade viable and high enough to bring in some money. But in fact a duty
on the trade would never be levied.

A related measure involved an agreement that anyone enslaved, indentured, or apprenticed, having fled to a free state, must be extradited
by the free state on the demand of the person who claimed the escapee's
labor. Delegates' objections to this one focused solely on the expense to
the free state and distinctions that might be made between an escaping
person and, say, a runaway horse, and were easily overcome.

The major issue involving slavery flowed from national representation: how to best represent the nationally taxed interstate citizenry in the
national government? How, that is, should the government count states'
populations to properly apportion representatives in the legislature?
Also, if the states' governments were to be represented in the national
legislature—against ongoing efforts by Madison, Wilson, Gouverneur
Morris, and others—should their representation be based on the relative
proportion of states' populations or be arrived at some other way? And
how should a solo national executive be elected—again, with the relative

proportions of states' populations possibly playing a role? That all had to do with how to count the population for the purposes of representation.

In the long summer of drafting, debating, and redrafting, those and other questions were subjected to compromises later celebrated as grand, annoying to everybody at the time. When the delegates, having invented a form of sovereignty divisible between the nation and the states, emerged at the end of the summer with the Constitution of the United States, all sides felt they'd given up too much and gained too little.

Some of the delegates refused to sign the document. They included Gerry and in the end even Randolph, on the basis of a too-great loss for state sovereignty. Gouverneur Morris went the other way. He thought the states retained far too much power, the southern states especially, and threatened to vote against the document on that basis. But he was talked around—by Hamilton, among others.

For Hamilton was the cooler head now. The creation of a real national government was a triumphant achievement for the old Morris team. By working with, around, and even occasionally against one another, supported tacitly and firmly by the silent authority of George Washington and aided, if only at first, by Edmund Randolph, they'd gotten the republic toned very high, just as Hamilton openly advised and Madison, Wilson, and both Morrises wanted. They'd achieved national goals to a degree that would change the country fundamentally.

The states did still exist—with no federal veto on their laws. That was highly regrettable to Hamilton and others, but they'd known all along that getting rid of states was impossible. Knox, writing to Washington with his impressions of the final document, put it this way: "I do not well see how in this stage of the business [the states] could be annihilated—and perhaps while they continue, the frame of government could not with propriety be much higher toned than the one proposed." The thing to celebrate was the creation of the new, consolidated citizenry known as the people of the United States of America, uniformly subject to a national taxing power because they enjoyed representation in a consolidated governing body. The national government was empowered explicitly to regulate interstate commerce and generally to do anything "necessary and proper," as the document put it, to carry out explicit powers. Hamilton had reason to be sure that if he had the right job, he could finally get done what he'd long believed had to be done.

His long-obstructed goals were achieved by the Constitution on a number of levels. At the highest, the document placed strict limits on representation. That was in direct opposition to the national plans of Paine and his cohort, as piloted in the government of Pennsylvania. Where Paine had called for an abundance of representatives in a unicameral national legislature, fostering unchecked, highly localized representation, the real national legislative branch was bicameral: a representative chamber with only sixty-five members, to be chosen by the qualified electorate throughout all states; and a small upper house, not elected, whose job was to check any tendency on the part of the representative house to pander to the policies perennially demanded by the Democracy. That was good for the purpose Hamilton had so long pursued: stifling egalitarian finance policy.

And yet for Hamilton and the whole North, the means of counting population for apportioning that limited representation, via federal congressional districts, rankled and would go on rankling. States with large numbers of enslaved laborers had wanted the enslaved fully counted in their populations, for the purposes of various forms of representation. That would give the South a lot more representation than counting only free people. But because the enslaved were of course by no means citizens, and in that sense weren't represented, the North, whose economy depended far less on the institution of slavery—many northern states were beginning to ban it altogether—wanted enslaved people counted at zero. In debate, Gerry got off a bitter crack about southerners' wanting to count as people what they actually considered their property; Hamilton proposed, again bluntly, that representation be based on counting only free inhabitants.

In the end, though, the delegates arrived at what was in fact an older compromise for counting the enslaved—in that sense a fairly predictable outcome. Back in 1783, under the Articles of Confederation, the Congress had considered shifting apportioning the basis of states' requisitions from relative overall real-estate values to relative population sizes, counting the enslaved at only three-fifths of a person: two-fifths less than the South wanted, three-fifths more than the North did. That discussion had foundered, but now, for the purpose of national representation, the delegates adopted the three-fifths standard, giving the South less representation than it wanted and more than the North thought it should have. A bitter pill for Hamilton and his allies.

Another one: the procedure for choosing members of the legislature's unelected upper chamber, to be known as the Senate. It hadn't been created solely as a check on the lower chamber, known as the House of Representatives, a function Hamilton naturally endorsed. Against all of Madison's and Wilson's efforts, the Senate was also to serve as an institution where the state legislatures were represented in the national government, and represented equally, each legislature sending two appointees regardless of a state's population size.

This equality of states' representation—the only provision made perpetually unamendable—had the effect of lodging in the national government exactly what Hamilton, Madison, and other Continentalists saw as the old, backward-looking, state-focused, confederation structure they'd come to Philadelphia to destroy. It also made no sense. The chamber meant to check too-popular overreach by the representative chamber was also to represent the state legislatures that had proved so susceptible to pandering to demands for popular economics and finance.

But there was another big victory for Hamilton, just at this high level of governmental structure. Instead of some weak executive committee chosen by the representative branch, the Constitution established an independent solo executive. All-important to Hamilton's goals, that office didn't rise to the level of monarchy, but it beat creating a weak force beholden to the legislature.

Even here the victory was mixed. The strong solo executive was not to be elected directly by all qualified citizens throughout the country. James Wilson had urged direct election, as it would utterly sideline the states, but instead the executive was to be chosen by a group of electors named by the state legislatures in numbers proportional to states' populations, as defined under the three-fifths compromise. Wilson, Hamilton, and their allies had hoped to keep the states completely out of choosing the executive. But at least the executive so chosen would be solo and strong and have broad powers.

Hamilton could celebrate one more important victory written into the Constitution's structure. The document created a national judicial branch and made it independent of both the executive and the legislature. Unlike the elected judiciary of democratic Pennsylvania, that is, federal judges would be appointed by the executive, with the advice and consent of the upper house, lacking any direct electoral support at all, thus subject to no popular pressure. Serving for life, removable only by impeachment and conviction in the national legislature, they would provide another sharp check on representation, even beyond the check provided by the upper house. Hamilton could envision judges setting aside any Democracy-appeasing fiscal, property, and debt-relief laws that either the national or state legislatures might pass.

Such were the structural components that made the Constitution, if imperfectly Hamiltonian, Hamiltonian enough for Hamilton's aims. Three granular measures, however, sometimes taken for granted later, made the Constitution truly Hamiltonian. They created national powers that would enable him, if he had the right job, to consolidate and grow the country economically while putting an end to the egalitarian economics of the Democracy—a finance-minister hero in the Jacques Necker mode, the single-handed author of great nationhood.

One measure was the grand prize: national taxation itself. Because the new government was granted an unlimited power to tax the whole people uniformly, within and throughout the states, the old Morris slate of imposts, excises, poll taxes, and land taxes had finally been made feasible. True, the process for imposing federal poll and land taxes—what the Constitution now called "direct taxation"—was cumbersome, its design haunted by ghosts of the old state requisition system that had impeded collection. The unlimited nature of the power nevertheless represented a critical victory. Back in May, some delegates couldn't have imagined that in August they'd be signing off on anything like an unlimited national taxing power, but to Hamilton, impost begat convention; creating that power had been the whole point of calling the convention and writing the Constitution. The bondholding class, for whose ongoing benefit national taxes would now be collected, saw the Constitution that way too.

The second granular Hamiltonian measure was closely related to the national taxing power. The Constitution prohibited the states from printing paper currencies, issuing bonds, and making anything but gold and silver legal tender, ending in one blow the states' long-standing capacity for knuckling under to egalitarian finance policies. By the same token, the investing class now had nowhere but the national government to look to for new issues of bonds and other public financial opportunities. The Money Connection was written inextricably into the law of the land.

Finally, to put teeth in the other two measures along with a power to create the professional, regular army that Hamilton and Washington had long been calling for, the national government had the power to call out the state militias to enforce its laws and to exercise sole control over them when doing so. National taxation for the benefit of bondholders would be enforced. State forces would no longer be able to take rioters' sides. Insurgencies by the Democracy could be put down.

Those three legal powers and prohibitions were still only that: powers and prohibitions. They would have to be exercised by the national legislature and enforced by the solo executive. If he could get into a position to get that process going, Hamilton could expect a strenuous reaction. Still, the Constitution of the United States enabled the key financial and monetary institutions that Hamilton and Morris had been urging for so long, building those institutions into national government and national government into those institutions.

The old Morris team was already in full-on selling mode. In the process laid out for making the Constitution law, each state was to hold a delegated convention to debate the question of ratifying the document; when only nine states ratified, the national government would have jurisdiction over the people in all states. If that was pretty strong-arm, the process was too. Though arrived at in secret, the document was to be ratified or rejected by each state convention as written, no proposed changes allowed.

With Gouverneur Morris serving as copy lead, his team built the pitch right into the product. They began with "We, the People of the United States," crediting the whole interstate people newly created by the document as the document's author; it stood to reason that the people would ratify their own effort "to form a more perfect union," as the preamble had it. The word "perfect" meant "complete," so the expression "more perfect," which would sound awkward in later years, suggested that the original union of states was only being made stronger, not gut-renovated.

Nomenclature did some selling too. The national legislature was to be called the United States Congress, as if it were replacing the old Congress, though the new body wasn't a congress at all, in the original sense of a meeting of independent states, and it was defined by having lawmaking powers that the former body had been defined, precisely, by lacking. The executive was to be known as the president. In the convention debates, most of the delegates had referred to the office as the executive magistrate. But as the old Congress had been presided over by an officer elected by the body and officially powerless, the new title evaded the fact that the new office, far from doing any presiding, was to operate independently of the legislature and enjoy its own powers.

And the new government as a whole was called federal, as if it followed in the footsteps of the confederation instead of replacing it. Proponents of the Constitution even called themselves Federalists. In reaction, those who wanted to keep things truly federal, and opposed the Constitution on that ground, called themselves Antifederalists.

To further aid ratification, Hamilton, Madison, and a highly placed pro-Constitution diplomat and legislator from New York, John Jay, wrote a series of newspaper essays under the collaborative pen name Publius, urging the New York ratifying convention to accept the Constitution.

Hamilton wrote most of them. In the first, he called the proposed national government a chance to start governing, for the first time ever, rationally and coolly, by what he called "reflection and choice," but he knew that getting the Constitution ratified would really depend on how effectively the Federalists appealed to what Hamilton and others called passions and interests. In the essays later collected as *The Federalist*, he appealed to elites' worst fears and framed ratifying the Constitution as the only safe harbor.

Hamilton and his co-authors were hoping their essays would influence the whole country. But while their work would have a long life as a resource on the supposed meaning of the Constitution, it had no impact on ratification even in New York. Enough states ratified while the New York convention met that the national government became technically a fait accompli. Practically speaking, though, New York really had to come along too. At the state convention, held in Poughkeepsie, the Antifederalists led by Governor Clinton outnumbered the Federalists 46 to 19. Hamilton spoke at length to no evident effect. Some said he and Jay finally confirmed a rumor that if the state refused to ratify the Constitution, New York City would secede and join the United States on its own, but in any event, despite Clinton's bluster, the prospect of mounting a civil war against the rest of the states, and possibly within one, wasn't realistic, and the possibility of getting later constitutional amendments was. New York finally ratified the Constitution by three votes.

It was in Pennsylvania, headquarters of both the Democracy and the Money Connection, where ratification really set off an explosion. Things had been changing in Pennsylvania's government. In the assembly, the cadre led by Morris and Wilson—Federalists now—had been advancing. They still hoped to rewrite the state constitution to restore traditional hierarchies, and they'd set back the radicals by persuading a new majority to recharter the Bank of North America. That majority naturally also favored ratifying the Constitution.

James Wilson led the case for ratifying his own work. His old enemies from the bank-charter fight, western leaders of the Democracy, including William Findley and Robert Whitehill, took the case against, but they were on the back foot now. As price-fixers, Debt-depreciators, anti-monopolists, and land-bank and paper-money proponents, they were better able than many upscale Antifederalists to discern the Hamiltonian finance purposes embedded in the Constitution. Their success in removing the bank charter—achieved, like the Constitution itself, in this assembly room—had been a key factor in the interstate elites' decision to convene and write the document the radicals now hoped to resist.

So, like the bank-charter conflict, but now with the highest possible stakes, the ratification dispute got hot. Whitehill, arguing in the assembly against a motion even to call a ratifying convention, noted that the Federalists' haste to ratify suggested that haste would be especially ill-advised. He pointed with special derision at "We, the people." Not one in twenty people in Pennsylvania, he said, even knew the Constitution existed. The majority moved to schedule the ratifying convention anyway. To quell some powerful published criticism of the Constitution, Wilson made a pro-ratifying-convention speech to the public, in the State House yard, where in 1776 the crowd had shouted away the elected government; the 1787 crowd seemed pretty pro-Constitution. Feeling bullied and pushed, the anti-ratification minority resorted to the oldest trick in the book and stayed away from the chamber to paralyze the majority by denying it a quorum.

Radicalism had grown in the West, but Philadelphia's working class had become more conservative since the Battle of Fort Wilson. The Federalists called out a group that only a few years earlier James Wilson would have disdained as a mob and sent them to break into minority members' homes, shove, drag, and frog-march them over to the State House and force them into the chamber, so the motion to call a convention could go through. It wasn't rationally and coolly that Pennsylvania, the site of the Democracy's triumph in 1776, scheduled ratification of the national document dedicated to crushing the Democracy.

13

TA-DA!

WITH THE CONSTITUTION RATIFIED, everybody understood that without George Washington as the first president of the United States, the whole thing would be a bust. Hamilton, given his revived closeness with the retired general, had reason to expect an important position in a Washington administration; he hoped, of course, to run the new nation's treasury. So while Washington had virtually no chance of not being unanimously elected, Hamilton didn't want virtually no chance. He wanted literally no chance. The first presidential election seemed to call for crossing some *t*'s and dotting some *i*'s: his forte.

In one of the Publius essays, he'd called the presidential election system airtight, but he knew otherwise. Each elector was to cast two votes: the candidate with the most votes would be president; the candidate with the second most, vice president. It was obvious that every elector would vote for Washington. It was also obvious that while some of the secondary votes would be scattered among various candidates, for favorite-son, runner-up bragging rights, most of them would go to John Adams, the presumptive vice-presidential candidate, and Hamilton viewed Adams as the type to want a huge number of those votes and not be above lobbying to get them. He also viewed the electors as likely to include some incompetents who wouldn't understand how to fill out their ballots and some Antifederalists and other enemies just messing with the system. In

Hamilton's worst nightmare, Adams snuck ahead of Washington. In a somewhat less outlandish scenario, the vote for Washington wasn't quite unanimous, suggesting division at the outset of the nation's existence.

So Hamilton contacted certain electors likely to vote not only for Washington, as everybody would, but also for Adams, and urged James Wilson to contact others, advising them to award their second vote to somebody else, thus hedging the Adams vote and reducing the infinitesimal likelihood of any unwelcome outcome. The electors had every reason to assume this was a tacit request of Washington himself and performed as instructed. Washington got one of each elector's votes, making the choice unanimous. That result wasn't likely to have been caused by Hamilton's effort to fix it, but the secondary votes were more scattered than expected, and while Adams received the second most votes, Hamilton had read his ambitions right. The showing was less impressive than the stung, infuriated vice president–elect considered his due. Later, Adams would get wind of the probable reason. His mutual enmity with Hamilton would one day cause a dangerous rift in their political faction.

Hamilton moved right along. Washington now held the position most closely equivalent, to Hamilton, of a monarch—not for life, as he'd wished, but still—and the new president did ask him to serve as head of finance, the equivalent, to Hamilton, of prime minister. Washington had first asked Robert Morris. The former superintendent, now representing Pennsylvania in the first U.S. Senate, was deeply enmeshed in his business ventures and naturally recommended his former protégé. Hamilton planned to realize the basics of Morris's vision through the logistics of a more sophisticated scheme of his own.

His new position didn't exist. The Constitution hadn't created any executive departments; it was up to the first U.S. Congress to do that. Conveniently for Hamilton, the federal government was setting up in his hometown. When the U.S. Congress met for the first time in what now became known as Federal Hall—the former City Hall on Wall Street where the old Congress, now defunct, had concluded its business—creating his office sparked heated debate in the House of Representatives.

After Robert Morris had resigned his position as superintendent of finance in the old Congress in 1782, the finance job lapsed to a supervisory board. Many of the old Continentalists, increasingly called Federalists because of their support for the Constitution—Hamilton's allies, with a strong majority in the U.S. Congress—wanted to create a solo treasury secretary, a role something like Morris's had been, appointed to provide advice to Congress and propose finance and economic policy. The minority opposition, though, drawn largely but not exclusively from the old State Sovereigntists, wanted to preserve a board. They feared vesting too much power in any one man; they also feared that giving the finance office any input beyond bean-counting and reporting would threaten the separation of powers, threaten republican government itself. Elbridge Gerry was one of them. In the end, he'd refused to sign the Constitution; in the end after the end, he'd supported ratification in his state, Massachusetts. Now, joined in debate by John Page of Virginia, Gerry conjured a vision in which the House just folded up for good in the face of a treasury secretary's presenting any policy ideas at all.

Hamilton's allies in the House majority included, with Madison, Fisher Ames of Massachusetts, no admirer of his fellow caucus member Gerry and a staunch believer in the highest-toned republicanism; and Thomas Fitzsimons and Thomas Scott of Pennsylvania, also strong Federalists. In debate, they took the lead in poking holes in this notion that just because Congress solicited a secretary's expertise, the country would crumble into lawmaking by executive fiat. The majority held. The law creating the Treasury Department made the head a solo executive, called the secretary of the treasury, and gave the office plenty of latitude.

On September 11, 1789, the Senate confirmed Alexander Hamilton's appointment as the Jacques Necker demigod: crusading finance minister, creator of great nationhood. He'd been trying for ten years to get where he was right now.

Hamilton opened the first office of the U.S. Treasury at his home on Wall Street, near Broadway, and got it going fast. The Federalist majority in the first Congress had already exercised its hard-won national taxing

power, as provided by the Constitution, and imposed a duty on all foreign imports, with special taxes on selected items. This was the federal
impost, its proceeds earmarked for paying interest to federal bondholders,
but this time it was real, for in a separate act Congress created a cadre
of federal customs officers, now under Secretary Hamilton's aegis, to collect the money, unhampered by state lines or state laws, with powers
including search and seizure. Interstate consolidation, as Hamilton and
Morris had once envisioned it, was becoming a reality. The impost wasn't
enough—Morris had always seen it as only a beginning—but it really
was a beginning.

Enforcing the impost meant creating a vigorous national customs
system. From his days at Beekman and Cruger, Hamilton knew a lot
about customs: cargo typically listed on manifests, secure warehousing,
even lighthouse operations. Hiring deputies and assistants, he launched
his office with thirty-nine full-time employees, the most in any executive
department, and that staff would grow quickly.

This bustle represented a new kind of work not only for Hamilton
but also for the United States. He started sending detailed questionnaires
out to his customs officers and others who had economic and commercial
information. Soon the federal treasury was receiving piles of data, input
for building a model of the whole country's economic conditions and enabling projections for the dynamic national growth Hamilton intended
to foster.

One of the biggest tasks, in terms of literal volume, was an accounting matter called *final settlement*. Some states claimed to have made war
expenditures on behalf of what were supposed to be the old Congress's
responsibilities and wanted to get paid back by the U.S. Congress. The
old Congress had been forced to spend money that the states should have
provided, by requisition; the U.S. Congress wanted that money paid to it.
The federal government was therefore charged with scrutinizing all state
and federal claims and completing a final accounting to flatten who owed
what to whom. Robert Morris and the board succeeding him had begun
a process requiring all-important punctilio but no great imagination, as-

sessing states' complaints and complicated prevarications and crossing lots of t's and dotting lots of i's.

The much more exciting project, for Hamilton, was to unleash at long last the nationally consolidating power of the domestic part of the Public Debt of the United States: that multitude of obligations the federal and state governments owed, not to each other, as in final settlement, but to the nervous, avid, individual investors known as the Public Creditors, now formed up as a powerful lobby. Federally funding the bonds and other obligations over the long term—the project that had drawn Hamilton into public life in the first place—would make the Debt the national driving wheel that Morris had identified, the most important thing the U.S. Congress could do, in Hamilton's view, to begin establishing itself as a national governing force and the United States of America as a dynamic nation.

But maintaining any public debt at all was bound to strike a lot of members of Congress as strange, some of them as flat-out dangerous. Hamilton knew what to tell Congress to do. He'd been thinking about that for a long time. Now he had to figure out how to get Congress to go ahead and do it, and that would take politics, both on the floor and in back rooms.

The political situation looked pretty good for his purposes. His strongest leverage lay in the hopes and fears of the investing lobby addicted to buying and selling public securities. Adding up only the domestic, nationally dynamic part of the Federal Debt, leaving aside the smaller, foreign aspect, Hamilton arrived at an impressive $40,414,085.94, and regarding that obligation, the House was in receipt of a blunt petition from the leading federal bondholders of Pennsylvania. More or less channeling Hamilton, they demanded that the U.S. Congress preserve the sanctity of their investments, pilloried the now-defunct confederation, lamented the ruinousness of paper currencies, and pointed to the grand national potential in paying interest on the Debt over a long haul. Most to the point, they praised the Constitution of the United States as dedicated, in its very essence, to binding up the creditors' wounds.

The majority in both houses of Congress agreed with that constitutional interpretation. Many members were bondholders; the petition spoke not only to them but also for them. Federalists, more or less by definition, including President Washington, believed in the nationalizing force of servicing the domestic part of the Debt.

In late September, therefore, the House passed a resolution calling on Secretary Hamilton to submit a report on the status of the public credit of the United States and a plan for addressing it. The investing class had good reason to expect to get from Hamilton what Morris had always projected: a full slate of federal taxes, collected throughout the country by federal officers, with proceeds earmarked for paying federal bondholders 6 percent annual interest on full face value.

But that's not how Hamilton did it.

By the end of September, Congress had written amendments to the Constitution, established the executive departments, set up a federal judicial system, and wrangled over where to locate a permanent national capital. That was a lot. The body went into recess and left Federal Hall. The president left for Virginia.

Hamilton lived in New York and didn't take a break. He had what he'd always wanted: a directive to produce a report on the state of public credit, with his plan for doing justice to holders of the Federal Debt. That fall, painting a masterpiece more than a decade in preparation, he worked in a white heat, yet exactingly, getting everything right. He'd be ready as soon as the federal government came back to town in January to show Congress something that nobody else could have created.

He did seek input. Businesspeople consulted on industry minutiae and modes of taxation. Philip Schuyler helped with the math. Hamilton wrote to Madison, who was spending the break at home in Virginia, for ideas on appropriate taxation, and Madison responded with some thoughts, as well as expressing, for the first time, some misgivings about any long continuance of national indebtedness. He qualified those doubts in a somewhat surprising profession of general vagueness on the whole subject. He'd also been leading a charge in the House, unwisely in Hamilton's view, to single out British ships in U.S. ports for high use charges, know as tonnage duties. Hamilton had even felt called upon to let a British official know privately that Madison, while a good man, had little knowledge of how the world really worked. Still, he incorporated Madison's ideas in his report and kept going.

New York, as the nation's temporary capital, was also now the capital of the interstate American investing class's thrills and chills. Speculating in the Debt had never stopped, but now everybody knew what Hamilton was working on in his Wall Street office. Big payoffs might be about to emerge from Congress's funding the Debt via federal taxes. Robert Morris was serving in the Senate; his Philadelphia operations were of course heavily involved in the action, and networks of Morris's colleagues and competitors from Boston to New York and beyond were working hard too.

One of Morris's most frequent partners was the New York merchant William Constable, born in Ireland. With a mansion on Broadway, well-known as a global financier, Constable was in the process of buying up a third of the state of New York and five hundred thousand acres farther west; opening the New York–China trade in collaboration with Gouverneur Morris; and investing in a canal project to link Albany to Lake Erie. He also speculated in the Debt, buying and selling with a Boston partner, Andrew Craigie, who had parlayed serving as apothecary general in the Continental Army into a fortune in drugs and bought and sold land, both in the Boston area and in the West.

Constable and Craigie were now at the top of the small group busy figuring out what parts of the Debt to buy and sell in advance of Hamilton's report. New York's taverns, coffeehouses, homes, and offices had become exchanges where businessmen on higher and lower rungs bought and sold and debated some urgent questions:

Was Hamilton really going to persuade the U.S. Congress to pay interest on federal bonds over the long term? That one wasn't too tough. The answer was very likely yes. *But were the bonds to be funded at their face value?* They'd been trading far below that rate; if the secretary was about to advise Congress to pay on them at face value, they were well worth buying and holding, but then again, *Would the bonds' original 6 percent interest rate hold up?* If you'd bought bonds at a fourth of face value, and they ended up paying at or near 6 percent on even close to half that value, your interest margin would be huge, your bonds highly valued in the market. Then again, Hamilton might devalue the bonds.

Was the States' Debt to be assumed in the Federal Debt, as Robert Morris always wanted? That would change everything. Overnight, state legislatures would be out of the business of weakly trying to shore up and pay off their bonds; all of those bonds, turned federal, would become as solid as the original federal bonds were hoped to become—but if not, not.

A very peculiar class of paper sparked the biggest questions and caused the highest excitement. These were bills called indents. Back in 1783, when Robert Morris resigned as superintendent, they were printed by the Congress and given to investors to document their unpaid interest on federal bonds. The idea was that the states would pass taxes, payable in the indents, to fund a new requisition to the Congress, but that never happened, so really all the Congress had done was create a new class of paper, held by the investing class and supposedly documenting interest owed. Passed around in commerce as yet another deeply depreciated currency, indents traded at less than a third of face value.

But now: *Was Hamilton about to raise indents to face value, treat them as a kind of bond, and pay interest on them—interest on the deferred interest?* If the answer was yes, better snap up as many indents as possible at a low price from those who hadn't guessed the answer.

These questions were so urgent because the speculation spike was driven by borrowing. Investors were taking loans at high interest rates from one another and European lenders to buy federal and state bonds, indents, IOU chits, and even the defunct Continental currency. They were also borrowing the instruments themselves, from one another, some betting on the paper's value going up, maybe all the way to face value, others betting on its falling below the rate when borrowed and thus profiting the lender via the payback price: shorting the market. It was taken as a given that in this market, the outsider was doomed, and the difference between bliss and misery lay in every decision Hamilton was privately making. Hence the desperate search for good information.

Why not just ask Hamilton? Some old friends figured there was no harm in trying. Henry Lee of Virginia, nicknamed "Light-Horse Harry" for horsemanship in the war, an old comrade-in-arms now serving in his state's assembly, wrote to the secretary:

> From your situation you must be able to form with some certainty an opinion concerning the domestic debt. Will it speedily rise, will the interest accruing command [hard money] or anything nearly as valuable, what will become of the indents already issued?
>
> These queries are asked for my private information, perhaps they may be improper, I do not think them so, or I would not propound them—of this you will decide and act accordingly. Nothing can induce me to be instrumental in submitting my friend to an impropriety.

On what was to become the record, Hamilton managed both to say no . . .

> I am sure you are sincere when you say you would not subject me to an impropriety . . . But you remember the saying with regard to Caesar's Wife. I think the spirit of it applicable to every man concerned in the administration of the finances of a country. With respect to the conduct of such men, suspicion is ever eagle-eyed, and the most innocent things are apt to be misinterpreted.

. . . and to pretend he was turning down Lee's obviously improper solicitation only to avoid unfair accusations of impropriety.

Still, Morris and Schuyler were speculators in the Debt. Hamilton's long relationships with them made it silly to try to find any bright line there. Morris was the first architect of a cruder form of the very program that Hamilton was now bringing to fruition; his networks were operating all the time every day, and having spent a career working with inside information, he was bound to let selected others in on what he thought he knew. Schuyler, too, was in the Senate, and he held the equivalent, 230 years later, of about $1.8 million in the Debt. He was working directly on Hamilton's report, and had a lot of friends. Through them, Hamilton also knew the New York financier Constable, who now told his Boston partner Craigie that he had critical information, straight from Hamilton over dinner in New York, that indents would indeed be fully funded. Constable could quote the secretary's table talk only in pretty general terms. Nor did he have information on the rate at which indents would be funded. Still, his supposedly hot tip sent indent prices shooting up.

To Hamilton, all this was to be expected. He'd long since learned from the Schuyler family and other Hudson Valley growers, from Robert Morris and the Philadelphia merchants, and from Washington's laser focus on planting and land-speculating operations, which the new president was carrying on while in office, that there was no known limit to the unabashed pursuit of gain upon gain upon gain, carried out all day and every day, by the small interstate class that had taken him in so early and so warmly. That's just what his mentors did, how they were wired, their discipline, their preoccupation, their art form. In the 1760s, British restrictions on their pursuits had put them on a path of resistance that led to a war for American independence. Protecting their gains from the Democracy had inspired them to create the national government.

So Hamilton, too, was betting—for stakes far higher than those the speculators played for. They wanted to get fabulously rich for generations to come. He wanted to author a rich, powerful nation, an empire. The bet was on his own ability to channel, direct, and leverage the Money Connection's bottomless greed to the purpose of creating the economic United States—to him, the United States itself—and make it a global player.

That wasn't necessarily his longest-term strategy. Maybe he'd be in a position one day to connect national wealth to the country's growth on bases less volatile than the day-to-day wheeling and dealing of the small class of wheelers and dealers he knew so well. Still, he had reason to think his immediate use of private pecuniary interest would pay off. He only needed the kind of people he knew to go on behaving as he'd always known them to behave.

His confidence in this strategy was exemplified that fall, while he was working on the report, by a major hire, William Duer, whom Hamilton appointed assistant secretary of the treasury. They'd been friendly for years. Duer, too, had come to the Atlantic colonies from the Caribbean; was a protégé of Morris, Schuyler, and Washington; married a Schuyler relation; and possessed a lot of dash and charm. A kind of Hamilton-on-the-flip-side, he lacked even a shred of his mentors' interest in the future of the United States or in anything but achieving unprecedented degrees of personal wealth. A charismatic enthusiast of money and nothing but money, Duer knew Constable and Craigie and every other player in the New York, Boston, and Philadelphia financial markets and had become a master at deploying sophisticated systems for leveraging inside information, and sometimes misrepresenting it, to make his bets pay off at the expense of the less-well-connected. He seemed unable to lose. Everybody wanted to invest with this money-whisperer who, if he liked you, could make you a fresh fortune overnight.

Duer took to extremes the personal qualities Hamilton was betting on leveraging and channeling for the benefit of the national economy. Nobody who knew the man expected propriety. With the report under way, and speculation raging, nobody was more active than the new assistant treasury secretary in relaying privileged information and making his own moves in the bond and indent market. To Hamilton, that was a feature and a bug.

In January 1790, Hamilton was ready for his ta-da moment. What had emerged from three months of intensive work was a gigantic, multifaceted program whose outsize audacity was supported by characteristically

maniacal attention to close research, precise descriptions, logical procedure, and relentless accounting. More than ready, he was eager. He wrote
to the House and proposed to come over to Federal Hall and present the
report personally. He'd make explanatory comments, do some Q&A . . .

He had a lot to learn. Members acutely sensitive to unchecked executive power had recoiled from putting a solo person in charge of the
treasury and allowing the office legislative initiative. Did the secretary
presume he'd now be welcomed in the sacred groves of representation
to give them a lecture in economics and dictate a law? Even Hamilton's
majority knew their man hadn't put his best foot forward here. The offer
was declined, the report requested in writing. When it arrived, it was
ordered printed so members could study it. The official "opening" was
postponed until February 8.

Unveiled in preparation for debate, the report was staggering. It
added up to more than fifty small-print pages, in part because Hamilton
had anticipated being barred from explaining it in person and embedded
a lot of explanation in the document. To members opposing him, this
process still reeked of British-style effrontery and corruption. William
Maclay, a Pennsylvania senator deeply libertarian and agrarian, had his
back especially up. A kind of prime minister had sent down a bill, as
Maclay saw it, expecting a compliant House to pretend to debate it and
then pass it. To Maclay and his kind, support for any public debt, which
the report was clearly promoting, signaled nothing but the old British
royalist trick of concentrating mercantile wealth in the capital of government. In this philosophy, everybody around the court was on the take,
so the real agenda seemed obvious: maneuver New York City—Maclay
called it "Hamiltonople"—into becoming the permanent U.S. capital,
enriching the city and, Maclay assumed, Hamilton himself at the expense of all others. It was all simple enough to Maclay.

Others could see that the report wasn't simple. But what was it? The
document seemed in some ways an impenetrable monolith, in other ways
a blizzard of infinitesimal detail: multiple tables, charts, schedules, row
after row of figures, the main body followed by Appendices A through K
listing all imaginable government expenditures and revenue sources in a

barrage of numbers. Everything at every level was nailed down so tightly that to propose any change, where would you start? How could you gauge the effect, on the whole thing, of moving even one piece?

And yet, as each member tried to puzzle it out in the days before debate, it wasn't all that hard to see, in very broad outline, that the report was built on three major elements for dealing with the domestic part of the Public Debt of the United States. It was also clear that each element was political dynamite.

The first of the three gave instantaneous relief to the speculating class. Instead of slashing the valuation of the Federal Debt to market value and paying it all off quickly, Hamilton was asking Congress to commit to funding the bonds at face value, not current market value, paying ongoing interest on them in hard money for a very long time to come. There was no set maturity date. Congress could technically pay down chunks of principal at will, but Hamilton put a limit on the total percentage of principal the government could retire in any given year. He was signaling to the bondholding-and-trading community that he intended to avoid early payoffs, sustain investor profits over ensuing decades, and make the secondary markets less volatile. In a big win for some, he was also proposing to pay interest on the indents, just as William Constable had predicted.

All this might have seemed thrilling news for federal bondholders and holders of indents. But the national commitment to their ongoing profit came at a less than thrilling cost. Hamilton proposed to start paying interest on some bonds now and some later, under a formulation that worked out to an average rate of around 4 percent, not the original 6. He did compensate for the rate reduction with a variety of appealing payment options, including payment in western land, and he predicted that a rise in the bonds' market value over ten years, thanks to their being so well-supported, would give the holder an appreciation equivalent to 6 percent interest over that same period. It was all a lot better than paying the whole thing off fast. Still, the interest reductions got some bondholders grumbling.

Given such a long life for the Debt, lest anyone think national indebtedness was to become permanent, or that there was no means for ever paying off its principal, Hamilton was following Prime Minister Walpole's and Finance Minister Necker's creation of a fund dedicated to "sinking," or paying down, the principal slowly and in small amounts, for a long time. He proposed building the sinking fund on the proceeds of the U.S. Post Office and establishing a board for managing it, to include the members of the president's cabinet and others. While Walpole's original fund hadn't significantly reduced much of the national debt of Britain—many called the mechanism nothing but a sop to anti-debt sensibilities—Necker and other high-finance experts held that even when a sinking fund couldn't pay off much principal, it encouraged public confidence in a nation's ability to manage its debt. If the whole basis of credit is confidence, a sop that works is more than a sop.

Such was the first of the scheme's three elements. It was known as the funding program. Bailing out federal bondholders and welding their future to that of the national government, the plan was plenty controversial on its own. Agrarians didn't like sustaining a public debt over a long term. Bondholders didn't like the reduction in interest.

But the second element caused sheer amazement in many of the members. Others had been made aware of this element, either through inside information or good guesswork—they included Constable and Craigie—and were betting on it.

Along with sustaining the domestic part of the Federal Debt, Hamilton was proposing to balloon it. He wanted Congress to commit to paying the interest—and ultimately, way down the road, paying off the principal—not only on its own bonds but also on the whole of the States' Debt.

Morris had always seen assumption of the States' Debt in the Federal Debt as the ultimately nationalizing step, a flowering of the interstate Money Connection. Hamilton now proposed to make that dream come true. All investors, in all forms of the Debt, were to turn in their state and federal bonds, IOUs, army certificates, even any Continental currency they held, which would be paid at 40:1—buyers at 500:1 were among the big winners—and receive a clean, new issue of federal bonds, making the Federal Debt, with its domestic part grown by nearly $25 million overnight, the only viable form of the domestic Public Debt of the United States.

This second element became known as the assumption plan, and as shocking as it was, to those not in the know, it wasn't really secondary. To Hamilton and the few others who understood it, assumption was rolled into the nationalizing purpose of funding the Debt at all. Taking on an obligation at such scale would redefine not only the size but also the structure of what the federal government was agreeing to fund and require expanding federal taxation beyond the current impost, altering not just on paper, as in the Constitution, but in the day-to-day logistics that gave constitutional provisions force, fundamental dynamics between the state governments and the federal government. With states out of the public-finance business, with federal economics swamping state economics, with federal officials operating in every state to collect federal money, federal power would trump state power. Giving real-world force to the losses that the Antifederalists had objected to in the Constitution, the assumption plan could be expected to cause major controversy.

The third and final element of the scheme was, if anything, even more politically problematic. Linchpin of funding and assumption, it provided the practical means by which paying bondholders' regular interest on a substantially swollen Federal Debt was to be accomplished. The reduction in the bonds' valuation was critical: lower interest made money available to pay interest at the new scale. And Hamilton proposed to add new duties on foreign wine and spirits to the existing federal impost, improving what was called the external revenue.

But he also wanted internal revenue. He was therefore proposing something new: a federal tax on an American product.

Morris had always seen the federal impost on foreign goods as a wedge for a full slate of federal domestic taxes. The surprising thing about Hamilton's use of the hard-won federal taxing power was his proposing just one tax on just one product: distilled spirits of alcohol—whiskey—made in the United States from American-grown grain. Such taxes were known as excises. Levied on a consumer good, collected from the manufacturer at the point of production before the product was legally certified to go to market, excises had a long history in Britain; American colonial and state governments had used them too. In both Britain and America, excises were unpopular. Their enforcement had often come with summary powers, including denial of jury trials. Hamilton's tax was to be collected in cash from distillers countrywide by internal revenue officers appointed by the Treasury Department. The revenue was to be earmarked, like the proceeds of the customs duties, for paying interest to federal bondholders.

That third and final element was known as the revenue plan, and sometimes by its most controversial element, the excise. It, too, wasn't separate from the other elements. "Revenue" meant the money to support the whole plan; the scheme couldn't begin to work without it. So critical was the excise, in fact, that Hamilton had taken the liberty of writing the House a long, detailed bill for establishing all of the many complicated mechanisms he had in mind for charging, administering, and enforcing a whiskey tax throughout the country.

He included his excise bill in the main body of the report. He was hoping to do Congress's work for it. There was no need, the whole document seemed to suggest, for the House to take up each part separately; the three were interdependent; the expedient thing was just to pass the whole scheme, right away, funding, assumption, and excise, and let the secretary get to work putting it into action.

Nothing like that was going to happen. The pro-Hamilton majority could see the minefields, and the opposition had feared just this: the executive branch's presuming to do the legislative branch's work for it. On the morning of February 8, 1790, the House gallery in New York's Federal Hall was packed with spectators—including Hamilton—as the chamber formed itself as a committee of the whole. When the committee officially opened the secretary's report, the whole body knew it was about to have the fight of its founding sessions.

14

BREAKUP

BACK IN THE CONFEDERATION Congress in Philadelphia, Hamilton had fired off his own arguments. In New York, as an officer of the executive branch, he couldn't engage in debate. He could sit in the public galleries. He could waylay people going in and out of Federal Hall for meetings in committee rooms and rented digs. But to carry out his mission on the floor of the House, to defend his report, he had to rely on allies, with no coaching from the stands.

Taking the field for Hamilton in debate in the House: the Federalists. The term was coming to refer to the majority faction in Congress that supported the Washington administration's policies. Notable members included Thomas Fitzsimons and Elias Boudinot, of Pennsylvania; William Smith, of South Carolina; and Fisher Ames and Theodore Sedgwick, of Massachusetts. As veteran state legislators, they were experienced in jumping on opponents' arguments with barrages of facts, theories, expertise, logic. Hamilton's solo voice might be enriched and amplified through these multiple brains and throats. Yet having to speak through them was also bound to complicate matters. Each man had his own interests and alliances.

At first, though, there was no speaking at all. When the report was officially opened that morning, a long silence ensued. Then Hamilton broke the silence, first through William Smith, then through Elias Boudinot and Thomas Fitzsimons. They told the members in detail and at length exactly how Hamilton wanted them to understand the report.

John Page, of Virginia, now a full-on opponent, countered by moving to have the whole document read aloud. He wanted to let the members absorb it, independently, he said, free of any heavy-handed guidance by the secretary's allies. So there went that day.

The next day, opposition to the Hamilton Scheme began in earnest. Frustrating Hamilton's aims right away, the committee of the whole House chose not to debate the scheme as the three-covalent-part entity he'd presented. Unsurprisingly to veteran pols, the committee took up the least politically unpalatable part first: just funding the Federal Debt at all, without even considering the controversial proposal to assume the States' Debt in it, or the proposed ways and means by which such funding might be paid for. Funding any public debt of any size, and by any means, was controversial enough.

James Jackson of Georgia took the loudest lead for the opposition. Born in England, he was a voluble brawler, a participant in many duels, an old-school agrarian rooted in English anti-court and anti-city traditions, a proponent of the rights of his state and of the states in general, and unabashed about making noise. He began by railing against what he cast as the ill effects of any public debt, which turns a republican government, he asserted, into a servant of the moneymen; his implication, common among land-wealth-owning types like him, was that moneymen are nothing but hucksters. As for the sinking fund, to be maintained for paying down principal and managed by a board, Jackson was taking the classic position that the sinking fund's inventor, Robert Walpole, had faced too: it was a well-known royalist fraud, Jackson said, always raided in emergencies, leaving public debt permanent, which in his view was the secret intention of such systems anyway. Just reduce the Debt to market value and pay it all off—interest and principal in one fell swoop—via a onetime general tax on everybody, possibly payable in paper: this was James Jackson's advice. His approach to debate was such that at one point, the members of the Senate, meeting upstairs, closed their windows to avoid hearing him. He concluded by roundly rejecting

Secretary Hamilton's report as a moral disaster and moved to adjourn the committee of the whole and end the entire discussion.

In this assault, Jackson was joined more quietly by Michael Jenifer Stone, of Maryland. Rising to underscore the source of the Debt in the recent war, Stone pointed to the tendency of public debt in Britain to encourage wars—those monuments to the folly and vice of mankind, as he put it—by making it cheap to go adventuring with hired soldiers.

The funding plan's most direct opponents were thus old-school agrarians, reviving aspects of colonial oratory against British royal government. They were also in the minority. Their motions to end debate and reject the report wholesale were voted down.

Then James Jackson came roaring back with a new angle. Accepting funding, which he'd cast as morally criminal only days earlier, he brought to light a new crime. Hamilton was proposing to pay all holders of the Debt equally. This, Jackson said, must be prevented at all costs.

It was hardly a new issue. When Hamilton was writing the report, one of the questions causing suspense was whether his payoff would discriminate between those who had bought or been issued the instruments directly, from the old Congress and the states, and those who had bought them in secondary markets. Some believed on principle that people classified as original holders—especially ordinary people who had been issued chits for goods and services and army pay—were entitled to rewards as patriots, but commercial speculators weren't.

Aedanus Burke, of South Carolina, now introduced a resolution in support of Jackson's tirade. It accepted funding, but slashed to the low market value all bonds and other paper bought in secondary markets; only original holders would get interest payments at the rates Hamilton had proposed. Opposition members rose to wax poetic on the original holders' patriotic virtues. Jackson jumped back in to proclaim, eyes rolled upward, arms outstretched, that the honest soldier was being called upon by Hamilton to reward the speculator tenfold. That soldier could be rescued, he insisted, only by discrimination.

It was getting emotional. The idea had a certain obvious moral aura, even a seeming appeal to the values of the Democracy. Burke and Jackson and other upscale agrarians, though by no means egalitarian, sometimes framed their opposition to consolidated government as protecting the poor.

But the idea also made no sense. In his report, Hamilton had openly rejected discriminating between types of holder; now Fisher Ames had no trouble shooting discrimination down in debate. Key to the proposed finance plan was sustaining a viable, credible market for government bonds. The first, small, blue-chip slice of the federal part of the Debt hadn't moved much, but the bulk, in all of its forms, from bonds to chits, federal and state, was now in the hands of the organized speculating class critical to the success of Hamilton's plan and already unhappy about a proposed reduction in the interest rate on federal bonds. Drastically further reducing value for the larger class of creditor, by retroactive fiat, would make government a flaky, even dishonest borrower and further muddle the market, just when Hamilton was trying to shore up government credit and stabilize the market.

Ames's barrage in the House debate was so intense that Burke withdrew the discrimination amendment he'd introduced and said he hadn't planned on voting for it anyway. The minority, stymied again, let go of its latest ploy.

But no. James Madison rose to speak.

He was turning against Hamilton.

Many observers wouldn't have seen this coming—Madison's opposing his old partner by bringing the discrimination idea back from the dead. As the Virginian began speaking, he framed a discrimination amendment of his own as a virtuous alternative to corruptions supposedly inherent in Hamilton-Morris policy, positioning himself as both an advocate for the rights of the states and a protector of poor farmers and soldiers. Jackson and Burke had been making gestures common among agrarian State Sovereigntists, casting themselves oratorically as protectors of the less-well-off, but Madison's expressing solicitude for the states and the hopes of ordinary people was startling. He'd been disappointed in the

Constitution because it hadn't done enough to vitiate the sovereignty of the states or establish federal power as supreme. He'd always bluntly excoriated egalitarian finance measures. And when it came to discrimination, in 1783 he'd declared that discriminating among original and secondary bondholders would be wrong, that government must of course treat its obligations equally.

So this was a drastic reversal—but Hamilton had been waiting for it. Before revealing his funding plan to Congress, he'd naturally discussed it with his partner in Continentalism and had come away shaken. Expressing revulsion at the surge in speculation, Madison told Hamilton pointblank that he was going to oppose the plan in the House. If many in the chamber and the gallery had reason to be surprised by Madison's move, Hamilton had at least been given time to absorb his own disappointment.

Still, as a guiding force behind the Constitution, Madison was lending gravitas to the original-holders versus speculators notion; worse, he didn't, as Ames said of Jackson, simply re-bellow his points but spoke with his usual quiet precision, weaving such intellectual nuance into the song of the average farmer and soldier that sniffles and blown noses could be heard in the chamber and the gallery. Where once he'd modulated Hamiltonian extremes in order to bring about Hamiltonian results, now he was staking out territory seemingly less extreme than Jackson's in aid of Jackson's attacks on Hamilton. His beautifully discursive, tear-inducing pitch for discrimination was followed by more bombastic speechifying from both Page and Jackson.

Yet in this new game, Madison faltered. It wasn't just Hamilton's proxies' pointing out, yet again, the absurdities of discrimination. Senator Maclay, too, though utterly opposed to Hamilton, found the original-holder idea off-point. Lecturing Madison dyspeptically after the House speech, Maclay asserted that the only republican thing to do about public debt was to reduce its value and pay it off, all of it, at once, in paper, with no new taxes levied for funding: discriminating between classes of creditors only muddied the waters and wasted time. The senator didn't know that muddying the waters and wasting time were Madison's tactics.

The majority remained Hamiltonian. On February 22, Madison's discrimination amendment, lacking even the full support of his new allies in the opposition, went down in flames in the committee of the whole, 36 to 13. Hamilton could breathe. The House had effectively agreed to fund the Federal Debt by paying interest over the very long term, with no discrimination among types of holders. The first part of the Hamilton Scheme was more or less accomplished.

He remained stung. Madison had so far only implied, but would soon begin asserting, a revision of all their work together. It was as if the Virginian had suddenly seen venal purposes underlying his former ally's efforts, but for Hamilton, it was Madison who was now showing his true colors. The secretary told friends that if he'd known he wouldn't have Madison's support, he would have thought twice about taking the job.

In this abruptly altered political climate, with funding the Federal Debt agreed to and a contest opened between Hamilton and Madison, the House turned to the second element in the plan, with its even more explosive question: Should the States' Debt be assumed in the Federal Debt?

The measure was critical to the Hamilton Scheme as a whole. And now the scheme got in real trouble.

The James Jackson wing began with the usual motions to end debate. Assumption of the States' Debt was just too risky and expensive, they said, and must be rejected wholesale. Hamilton responded, this time through William Stone, by noting that his report clarified exactly how to make assumption both manageable and affordable.

Madison took a more nuanced approach. His strategy seemed to be to appear to accept certain big ideas in principle and then propose supposedly fairer ways—complicated ways, often totally unrealistic ways, time-consuming to explain and rebut—of achieving the secretary's stated goals. He muddied and dabbled and ran what passed for a clock, declining to object to assumption outright. He argued instead that assumption might be a fine idea, but the less-indebted states, and those that had already paid off a lot of their debts—such as Virginia—would be robbed if the federal government took on the obligations of the more-indebted states. If he was expected to support assumption, Madison wanted the federal government to make compensatory payments to states like his. Especially his.

As with discrimination, this idea made no sense to Hamilton. It reflected such an elementary misunderstanding of his report that it was hard to tell whether Madison meant it or was only advancing another agenda: maybe he hoped to load so many amendments onto an assumption bill that it would become infeasible, or get a payoff for Virginia as the price of support. Madison was demanding that any assumption bill include a clause linking assumption to the separate process known as final settlement, that flattening of what states and Congress owed not to the public creditors but to each other. He wanted Congress to give cash premiums to states that had already paid off all or most of their debts and postpone assumption until final settlement was complete.

But to Hamilton, no state, regardless of its current indebtedness, could lose or gain anything from assumption of the States' Debt into the Federal Debt. When a state was relieved of an obligation, thanks to the federal government's assuming that obligation, the amount would be charged against the state and paid by the state to the federal treasury in the final settlement. By the same token, any state that had already paid all or part of its obligations, such as Virginia, wouldn't be so charged. Discrepancies among the states would thus even out, with the U.S. Treasury serving as clearinghouse. There was no good reason to give certain states up-front money as a price of assumption—and certainly no reason to postpone assumption until after final settlement. Skeptical Federalists read Madison's threat to vote against assumption as a ploy to get his state's final-settlement claims against Congress, which were hefty, paid in full without scrutiny, in exchange for his support.

However sincere or baseless, though, the attack by Virginia on immediate assumption was now joined by other states, also clamoring for compensation. The assumption element of the Hamilton Scheme was causing divisions in the House its author hadn't anticipated. Some state delegations, powerful Massachusetts most notably, pressed for immediate assumption, along Hamilton's lines. Pennsylvania now looked like the swing state, and Hamilton might have had reason to expect the new Federalist majority in Pennsylvania, the Money Connection state, to lend him powerful support. But now its delegation, too, started giving him headaches over assumption, for other reasons. Some federal bondholders, especially members of the powerful Philadelphia lobby, had stayed out of the States' Debt markets and didn't like the proposed reduction in the federal bonds' interest, which Hamilton presented as a cost of assuming the States' Debt. They also feared that paying interest on the States' Debt would undermine the government's ability to pay on their federal bonds. They'd been nagging their representatives in Congress: *Could Hamilton's plan really accommodate paying interest on both the Federal and the States' Debt? Did federal bonds' interest really have to be reduced?*

The answer, to an increasingly exasperated Hamilton, was an obvious yes. He'd explained it in astonishing detail and shown his work. The reduction in federal bonds' value helped make paying interest on assumption feasible, and the third component of his plan, the revenue bill with the excise tax—so far nobody in the House wanted to touch that—provided for enough money to pay interest payments on all of it. His whole plan, if adopted, would benefit the whole investing class mightily in the long run, certainly including federal bondholders in Philadelphia. As the Pennsylvania Federalist and federal bondholder Thomas Fitzsimons put it, regarding his own cadre: "Avarice often disappoints itself." The self-interest that Hamilton's support depended upon was being exposed as shortsighted at best.

Pennsylvania was meanwhile caught up in another issue, which, though unrelated, further dented its all-important support for assumption: where to locate the permanent national capital of the United States.

Having the federal government in your city or region conferred obvious benefits. New Yorkers wanted to keep it where it was. Pennsylvanians wanted it in Philadelphia or maybe somewhere on their stretch of the Susquehanna. Robert Morris thought Philadelphia should serve as a temporary capital while a permanent capital was built next to some highly productive property he owned at the falls of the Delaware. Long before becoming president of the United States, or even commander of the Continental Army, George Washington had seen the Potomac estuary, near his own business operations, as a hub for receiving produce from a settled West of the future and moving goods out to sea in trade; with his canal company dedicated to monopolizing that process, he naturally wanted the capital sited nearby the estuary, and Madison was involved with Henry Lee in a financial speculation for building a commercial center there too. New Yorkers might hold out hope—and they did—but the big competition over the permanent capital was coming down to the Potomac estuary versus somewhere in Pennsylvania.

So as early as Congress's first session, Pennsylvanians had floated a backroom capital deal with Virginian and other southern congressmen. If the South would support making Philadelphia a temporary capital for ten years, Pennsylvania would support a permanent capital at the Potomac. Privately, the Philadelphians were confident that once the capital was established in a civilized location, nobody would want to move to a wasteland, and Philadelphia would become permanent by default. The Virginians were just as sure they could pull off the move to the Potomac. The most powerful man in the country was commercially interested in developing a capital site there.

Hamilton wanted the capital to stay in New York, but he had more important goals. For him, the real problem with all this wangling by Virginia and Pennsylvania was that any capital deal they made might require Pennsylvania to ally with Virginia in blocking assumption. He had reason to worry. His finance plan, intended to unify the country, was getting snarled in state, regional, and personal interests he hadn't predicted as impediments and found absurdly off-point. Outside Federal Hall, rising uncertainty about assumption's passage was roiling the finance markets; boats left the New York docks, heading down the coast in search of state paper. Inside the hall, opposition members excoriated the display of speculative greed and blamed Hamilton, now a constant presence in the gallery and at the door, a bustling executive-branch officer nervously buttonholing allies for backroom chats and offending the opposition's hyperrepublican sensibilities. The press on both sides amped the conflict. House debate bogged down in dilatory opposition tactics: demands for new and pointless finance information from the secretary, long speeches reviewing old questions. Momentum was lost. Assumption's support began to slip. The mood on the floor got rough.

Then the bottom fell out. On April 12, the committee of the whole voted, and assumption lost, 32 to 29. A committee vote wasn't a final vote, but the majority's turning against Hamilton by only a few members was enough to doom assumption, and dooming assumption doomed the Hamilton Scheme. Speculators going all-in on state securities faced likely ruin. Bitter in defeat, Sedgwick of Massachusetts made an emotional speech accusing Virginia of causing his state an injury that would force it to tax its citizens to pay its obligations, as before the Shaysites Rebellion, and those taxes, he said, would make it hard for Massachusetts to accept federal taxation of any kind. Madison pretended to think Sedgwick was threatening secession, and he piled on, suddenly bringing up the excise bill that nobody had wanted to talk about. In Hamilton's plan, Madison pointed out, assumption depended on passing an excise on whiskey, and excises, he reminded the House, were known to be unpopular. That gave Hamilton reason to really grind his teeth. Back in November, Madison had privately suggested an excise. On whiskey.

On April 27, the House assigned a committee to write a bill for funding the Federal Debt without assuming the States' Debt in it. Funding with no assumption: the Hamilton Scheme, three covalent, equally important parts, dead as such in the House.

This was only the first U.S. Congress. But it was already the U.S. Congress, and something was up. Or some things.

But what?

Nobody would ever know all of it. Assumption did end up passing, but the process that led to the first U.S. Congress's most important domestic legislation became so opaque that even the most advanced scholars in future generations couldn't fully agree on what had happened.

A good bit of the confusion was caused by Thomas Jefferson's arrival, in late March 1790, from Paris, by way of Virginia, to start his job as secretary of state of the United States. Red-haired, tall like Washington yet studiously unassuming in dress and manner, a former governor of Virginia, Jefferson had an imagination of the American future as ambitious and passionately held as Hamilton's, less codified, even mercurial, creatively so. He'd been serving as the old Congress's minister to Versailles.

Now, taking up his cabinet post in New York, he began following the House debates on the funding plan and involving himself in the conflict over assumption. Later, enmeshed in an existential war against all things Hamilton, Jefferson would write accounts of what he thought had gone on in 1790—gone terribly wrong, in his opinion—and those accounts would sometimes be treated as fact.

In a story that became famous, Jefferson claimed that when he was still just trying to help, unaware that he was being, as he came to see it, hoodwinked into aiding a system of corruption, he personally brokered a deal for assumption between Hamilton and Madison over dinner at a house he was renting on Maiden Lane. In Jefferson's telling, New York and Pennsylvania, under Hamilton's guidance, were to support a permanent Potomac capital, with Philadelphia the ten-year temporary site; Virginia and the rest of the South, under Madison's guidance, were to come up with enough votes to pass assumption in the House.

Jefferson didn't know—maybe by the time he wrote his two recollections of the event, three years later, then twenty-five years after that, he'd gotten so furiously at odds with the Hamilton Scheme that he didn't care—that any agreement made in any such meeting would have been a formality at the very most. The real wrangling, which lasted from late March into July, was so chaotic yet well hidden, so subject to the vagaries of conflicting eyewitness testimony, so impossible for anyone involved to gestalt, that the faulty simplifications Jefferson made for his own purposes would serve history as a form of relief.

Others on the scene had explanations of their own—like Jefferson's, all too clear, all too simple. William Maclay, for one, could only imagine Hamilton sitting in a back room cold-bloodedly orchestrating the location of the capital and the passage of assumption in one masterful set of secret transactions: every outcome prearranged. In real life, increasingly frantic, dancing as fast as he could to save assumption, Hamilton could see, from his back rooms, only fragments of what was going on in other back rooms. In February, he'd made Congress agree not to go into recess before adopting a comprehensive plan for the Debt; he'd thought it might take weeks at most. Now came the hot New York summer, with chaos and contradictions mounting and everybody wired and fried at once. The congressional reporters even stopped reporting on the debate. Only later would some of that summer's hidden moves come into semi-focus—but only some—and even then only in strangely cropped glimpses, fuzzy with intrigues and failed gambits, with no order of cause and effect ever perfectly knowable:

A *peek into a back room.* Staring down assumption's corpse, Hamilton and his allies come to the conclusion that they should give up on the chamber where the measure died. Maybe the Senate, with a stronger pro-Hamilton majority led by Robert Morris and Philip Schuyler, could just shove assumption back into the funding bill that the House is sending up. This move actually works—at least partially. In June, a Senate committee does write an assumption clause into the House bill. Still, full Senate debate can't begin until July. And even if assumption passes, the two chambers will have to negotiate a final version that can pass the House.

Another peek. Hamilton's men have decided they need to get the leery Philadelphia federal-only bondholders' attention by smacking them in the head with a two-by-four. The method they devise is totally counterintuitive. Seemingly out of nowhere, the day after assumption dies in the House, the majority calls for a vote on the third major element of the finance plan: the revenue measure with the whiskey excise, which the chamber has been so studiously ignoring. Fitzsimons is assigned to head a committee to write a revenue bill—as if Hamilton hasn't already presented an astonishingly detailed one—and he comes right back in with a bill that's exactly Hamilton's.

The House has had reasons for ignoring this issue. They include excise's origins in British royalist circles; the association with the father of moneymen, Prime Minister Walpole; summary police powers associated with enforcement. Jackson-type agrarians have always disparaged such taxes as tools of tyranny. Ordinary people have resisted them by noncompliance and attacks on collectors, the old tools of regulation. As might have been predicted, Hamilton's House opponents attack Fitzsimons's revenue bill on traditional anti-excise grounds.

But then, as could never have been predicted, some of Hamilton's allies join the opposition and vote the bill down in committee, decisively, 35 to 23, not just the excise section but the entire revenue part of the Hamilton Scheme. No assumption of the States' Debt—and now no revenue for funding even the federal part of the Debt.

That's the smack in the head. If the federal-only bondholders want their bonds funded, they'd best accept the whole Hamilton Scheme: funding, excise, and, yes, assumption. Otherwise, Hamilton's allies are saying, there will be no revenue, so no interest payments at all.

Backroom moves failing. All spring and then into the summer, Hamilton keeps offering Pennsylvania various capital-site deals of his own in exchange for support for assumption. The problem is that he has nothing to give. At one point, his new assistant Tench Coxe, a Pennsylvania partisan, tells Pennsylvanians in the House, including Fitzsimons, that if they'll support assumption, Congress will make a site in Pennsylvania, to be named later, not some ten-year temporary capital but the true, permanent capital. That deal would be easy for Fitzsimons and Pennsylvanians to like, but because Hamilton has no way of getting it done, the proposal dissolves in chatter, and Hamilton, plunged back in suspense about what Virginia and Pennsylvania might be cooking up, keeps cooking up ideas of his own.

One truly desperate gambit. Hamilton sends Tench Coxe to talk to Pennsylvania senator Maclay, of all senators. If the national capital were to adjoin his properties on the Susquehanna River, might Maclay deliver enough Pennsylvania votes to pass assumption? Finding even Hamilton's personal manner annoyingly "boyish, giddy," Maclay, a fountain of agrarian rectitude, "constrain[s] his indignation at this proposal with much difficulty within the bounds of decency," he tells his diary, and gives Coxe "such looks and answers as put an end to this business." Hamilton never could have delivered anyway.

Et tu? The Pennsylvania bondholders were supposed to be terrified into submission by the tactical defeat of the revenue bill. But Robert Morris and Philip Schuyler, recognizing their importance to assumption's passing the Senate, suddenly join the Pennsylvanians in complaining about the proposed reduction in the valuation of their federal bonds. Now even Hamilton's mentors threaten to tank assumption unless the interest is raised.

Assumption was Morris's idea, maybe his biggest. Hamilton's father-in-law has worked on the report and knows the math, knows the reduction is critical to paying interest on a Federal Debt swollen by assumption. This is the nationalizing force they've worked toward for so long.

But Morris isn't only a theorist of the investing class; he's also a member, and so is Schuyler. It's only business. Hamilton knows well the class whose ruthless pursuits he's trying to leverage. They know him well. It's unclear who's leveraging whom.

On the sod. During their morning strolls, Hamilton and Morris meet at the flat, grassy Battery at the lower end of Manhattan, as if by accident but in fact by appointment, and "on the sod," as Morris puts it, secretly game out deal scenarios. A national capital at Germantown, Pennsylvania? Or near Morris's place at the Delaware falls? If Hamilton can get New York to give up all hope for the permanent capital, will Morris put together enough votes to pass assumption in the Senate?

Neither man has any way of making good on any of it. And so, as the summer heats up, the moves and countermoves go on and on . . .

Then one day at the end of June, the Pennsylvanians and the Virginians simply concluded their backroom negotiations. Nearly five months after debate on the Hamilton Scheme began, they arrived at an agreement on the capital location that lapsed back to the original: a temporary ten-year capital at Philadelphia, a permanent capital at the Potomac estuary. Jefferson wasn't in the room where it happened. Neither was Hamilton. Fitzsimons nailed down the transaction.

The capital-location issue itself lapsed back to having nothing to do with the assumption issue. Soon after making the deal, Pennsylvania found itself with no further incentive to obstruct assumption, either on behalf of Virginia or on behalf of the Philadelphia bondholder lobby, because Madison and Virginia, at one political extreme, and Schuyler, Morris, and the federal bondholders at the other, withdrew their opposition, and here, anyway, cause and effect were plain. Hamilton addressed the various sides' money issues. Based on the notion—misconceived at best, to Hamilton—that Virginia would suffer from assumption, certain states were now to have compensation, with Virginia getting $500,000, far more than most others, though North Carolina got the most: $800,000. And by the same token, to quash Morris's and Schuyler's complaints Hamilton tweaked the bonds' interest rates upward. With all instruments to be handed in for a clean, new federal issue, some of the newly issued bonds were now to draw 6 percent, some—representing the former indents—3 percent, and some 6 percent but with payments not to start for ten years.

Everybody who had to get paid off got paid off. Leaders in the House came under pressure from the Senate to accept its version of the funding bill. Madison even lined up so much support for assumption that he could maintain his cover by voting against it. James Jackson, nothing if not consistent, went down bellowing against the entire Hamilton Scheme, but on August 4, 1790, the funding and assumption bills, having passed both houses of Congress, went to President Washington to be signed.

15

INDUSTRY AND RYE

A GREAT VICTORY: two parts of the three-part Hamilton Scheme were federal law. While changes had been made, funding and assumption were in place nearly as Hamilton had originally proposed them in January.

Yet the revenue bill—linchpin of the whole thing, voted down tactically in the House in order to wake up the Philadelphia bondholders—had never been revived. That meant the gigantic new funding plan lacked funding, and on August 12, the exhausted members of Congress, as if complying with Hamilton's demand that they complete business before recessing, went home. They wouldn't be returning to New York. The new session would begin in December, in the temporary national capital, Philadelphia.

Hamilton stayed surprisingly cool. While the lack of money to support his scheme might have seemed to render the whole long, hard effort to pass funding and assumption pointless, he'd learned some important things from that long, hard effort—about the U.S. Congress, and maybe about politics and politicians in general. Now he planned to get to Philadelphia well ahead of Congress and follow up his victory with a revenue measure that the members couldn't help passing. He had something else to spring on them too.

But he really had to get that excise passed. A tax on domestic whis-key would do far more to achieve Hamilton's ultimate purposes than many in Congress were likely to understand.

The old impost had been intended by Morris as a wedge, opening the way for excises and other domestic taxes. National government equated for Hamilton with the consolidating tendency of federal taxes directly collected, not just at ports but throughout the country, and earmarked to fund the investing class's interest payments on the Debt. A domestic tax would help pay for federal assumption. But just as important, the ballooning federal expense resulting from assumption justified a domestic tax. Both were means, both ends.

Many leading Federalists by and large understood at least part of the equation. Washington himself had said, when contemplating the process of amending the Constitution, that should the unlimited taxing power of the federal government be amended away, and justice to the public credi-tors therefore couldn't be done, the whole constitutional effort would have been for nothing. The public creditors identified the Constitution's origin and purpose with paying them their interest, as they'd made crystal clear in their petition to Congress the year before, and they formed a sizable chunk of the governing elite. It was plain to the majority party that fed-eral taxation was elemental to American nationhood.

Amid the nuts and bolts where Hamilton lived, though, the excise he'd proposed had specific properties for transforming the whole Ameri-can economy. They operated on a number of levels. At the most basic, a transformative potential lay in the very nature of a tax on a domestic product. The impost, drawing revenue from the American merchants in their role as importers, was a tax on external products. The truly dy-namic power of the Money Connection was predicated on what Morris had once called opening the purses of the people: drawing money, by law, from the interstate many to profit the interstate few who would sup-port and invest in the government that wrote such laws. Unifying the country via concentrated wealth required drawing money from classes of Americans other than merchants, creating an internal revenue with proceeds dedicated to the profit of the highest-end, most competent economic actors, led by merchants themselves: a small pool of lenders eager to earn interest by funding big projects driving national growth.

But that was Money Connection 101. As a student of Necker, Walpole, Hume, and Morris, Hamilton had long since digested the uses of government power in opening the purses of the people. Now he was thinking more closely than Morris ever had about what kind of U.S. economy might emerge from sophisticated exercises of public-private high finance. The big idea wasn't just to set up the Money Connection. The big idea was what the Money Connection was set up to do for the country. Morris had imagined great things emerging from national finance: interstate infrastructure, industrial-scale agriculture and manufacturing. Hamilton, bearing down on process, had to figure out the logistics of making those things real.

Hence his somewhat counterintuitive choice of an excise specifically on domestic whiskey. He'd studied up, of course. It was clear that major changes were taking place in American drinking habits: rum, made mainly from imported Caribbean cane, was less and less popular; consumption of whiskey made from domestic grain, mainly rye, was rising fast. That shift made distilling American grain a major U.S. industry, and Hamilton identified in certain peculiarities of that industry's operations a remarkable opportunity for using federal power to accelerate his integrated purposes all at once: consolidate American wealth, disable the Democracy's efforts at blocking such consolidation, and foster the creation of an industrial economy owned and managed by the commercial and investing class.

That's because the Democracy, too, saw potential in whiskey. In the distilling boom, subsistence farming families were turning their rye into spirits, especially in the West, and making money where money was scarcest. People in the port cities liked to think of western settlers as habitual drunks, and westerners did like whiskey, women and children included. But with coin scarcer the farther you got from the ports, it wasn't western enjoyment of the product that made whiskey the one feasible cash crop for so many poor families. The important customer was eastern.

It was all about markets, costs, and margins. The Mississippi's closure placed easier-access markets off-limits, forcing westerners to look eastward for sales of agricultural product. Trucking eight bushels of milled rye over the mountains to eastern markets required two fully loaded pack animals and might generate gross revenues of only about four dollars: the fixed cost of the trucking could eradicate profits. Two eight-gallon kegs of whiskey, though, distilled from only about five of those bushels, could be loaded onto just one animal, not just reducing trucking costs but also adding whopping value to the product trucked. In the western regions that produced the most in-demand whiskey, a gallon might sell for 25 cents; in the East, that gallon could bring a dollar. In the form of eight kegs, that is, the five bushels could gross up to sixteen dollars.

And while distilling had costs too, they weren't high or fixed. By making the product at home, occasionally and around demands of other work, on a cheap, homemade rig known as a pot still, a subsistence-level smallholder who wanted to grow a farming business could get the money to do so without borrowing from landlords and lenders at the ruinous interest rates that led to mass foreclosures, tenancy, and day labor. Somebody somewhere was always going to pay hard money for whiskey.

So by 1790, when Hamilton was pushing his finance plan through Congress, the benefits of small-scale distilling were rippling through remote communities. With the states now constitutionally prohibited from succumbing to pressure for familiar forms of democratic finance, artisanal distilling fostered new kinds of democratic finance. State paper money was outlawed—but whiskey was a people's currency. Tenants paid part of their rent with part of the grain they harvested, sometimes at exorbitant rates, but such was whiskey's market value that landlords would happily accept it in lieu of crops or cash. Landless laborers often got paid in grain and had to accept bad exchange rates for turning it into coin, but converting a grain salary to whiskey created both value and fungibility in laborers' pay.

Hence a kind of cooperative micro-industrialization. Farmers kept stills running straight through the rye harvest, and people without stills brought grain in and took away whiskey, paying for the service with a portion of the product: a backcountry version of James Cannon's and Christopher Marshall's American Manufactory in Philadelphia, which had beaten the Bettering House in production. Small-batch distilling, confirming western ideas about regional independence, gave poor settlers a way of holding on to land, farms, and tools and growing their enterprises independently of creditors and landlords.

And that's exactly the opposite of what Hamilton wanted for the distilling industry and the country. He was looking at a vast picture and a long future. America's colonial period had involved so little manufacturing that the United States, though independent politically, remained dependent economically on exporting raw materials and importing finished goods. Meanwhile, the British export economy, far ahead of the United States', was rapidly mechanizing. To Hamilton, the ultimate purpose of the financial scheme whose first two parts had been passed into law was to seize this world-changing moment—the factory moment. He wanted to use the speed and scale of industrialization to catch up and challenge Britain as a manufacturer.

So he had no use for small, artisanal, localized, community ventures. The future was all disruption, innovation, mechanization, scale. He'd personally invested in a New York City woolen factory powered by water and was closely following a recent proliferation in Rhode Island of river-powered textile factories. He wanted to foster an industrialized economy for the whole country, in wool and flax, ultimately in paper, shoes, hats, beer, a host of goods. He'd even come up with an idea for building an entire government-chartered factory town, powered by water, living proof that America could make high-quality goods and reduce dependence on imports. Tench Coxe, his assistant, was organizing the industrial espionage and snagging machines, techniques, and expertise from Britain. Congress was already making its huge land grants down the Ohio River to federally chartered companies run by well-connected insiders for developing the Northwest Territory. Land interests were investing in startups to build connective infrastructure: canals, bridges, roads. Federal encouragement would link a boom in southern and western harvesting to a boom in northeastern processing. Industrialization, a nationally unifying force, would build agriculture and manufacturing at once and create an American empire.

Hence the proposed whiskey excise. This particular domestic tax didn't just enable funding and assumption. It interlinked the finance phase of Hamilton's plans to the capstone phase he was working on with Coxe: national industrialization. The challenge for Hamilton's industrialization phase was labor. Work now diffused on small family farms and artisanal shops must be encouraged—spurred, really, and ultimately forced by federal policies creating new circumstances—to become concentrated over time in ventures owned and operated by the entrepreneurial class carrying out large-scale commercial farming and production of goods. Where industrial agriculture in the South depended on forced labor, industrial manufacturing in the North would depend on paid labor. No investment in new machinery would succeed unless people were spending long shifts working the machines, and so many people were working on farms that factory labor tended to be priced, in Hamilton's view, high, but he was sure that with American manufacturing up and running, "competent numbers of European workmen will transplant themselves," "obviating the scarcity of hands" and ultimately lowering wages.

Until then, factory work was most likely to be done mainly by the wives and children of men who worked on farms as smallholders, tenants, and landless hired hands. In existing American factories, a largely women-and-children workforce was already putting in fourteen-hour days, six days a week, a routine borrowed from Britain, whose cotton mills, Hamilton noted approvingly, drew more than half their workers from women and children, mostly children, "many of them of a very tender age"; he meant seven and even younger. Washington, the great agriculturist, concurred. He owned mills and other works and was a student of the factory moment. He "would not force the introduction of manufactures . . . ," Washington said, but "much might be done in that way by woman [sic], children, and others without taking one really necessary hand from tilling the earth."

But Hamilton had a longer view, and the whiskey excise was a factor. The women-and-children workforce could be enhanced, not only by
recent immigrants too poor or for other reasons unable to become smallholders, but also by men of longer standing in the country, drawn away
from farms. The Rhode Island factory innovator Samuel Slater had begun with a workforce made up of seven-to-twelve-year-olds; he'd recently
begun advertising that he was now hiring whole families. Children's labor was more easily managed directly by parents. Working families could
make more pay. Single and married men working as day laborers on farms
might expect to do better as factory workers. Whether in cities and mill
towns or on big, diversified, commercial farms, it was clear to Hamilton
that it would be best for everyone if the great majority of Americans were
working in increasingly mechanized industries.

The excise tax was to serve as the leading edge of that great national
change. The distilling business had already reached industrial scale. In
his study, Hamilton had learned that diversified commercial farms were
growing rye at great scale and operating efficient, modern stills—a far cry
from the homemade pot stills that yielded modest batches. Big operators
"bought up the grain in great quantities," according to an industry observer, and they didn't mind paying high prices, because, unlike the small
western producers who distilled when they had time, seasonally and occasionally and seeking narrow margins, the big operators used hired labor
and could dedicate resources to steady distilling for long hours, months at
a time, making big profits while experimenting for ever-greater efficiency,
running "their stills from twelve to fourteen times in twenty four hours,"
the observer reported, and "sav[ing] wood by it," where the small distillers
"run theirs but three or four times." Constantly seeking patents for their
inventions, big distillers improved methods and equipment and continu-
ally boosted production and reduced costs.

That's how Hamilton wanted the whole national economy to work.
The market should reward scaled-up, innovative, consolidating enterprises seeking efficiency and driving growth.

But the whiskey market wasn't cooperating. The small, seasonal approach was competing with the big industrial approach. The western

artisanal product was good. It had a reputation. It found ready markets in the East and was known even in New Orleans. Ordinary farmers had every reason to continue to pursue success on their own terms through cash-crop distilling at modest scale. Just as the West resisted state and federal authority, the whiskey industry resisted consolidation.

Hamilton's solution: excise. He'd studied, again, Britain, where big distillers connected to government actively favored excises on spirits; their lobbyists wrote the tax laws, and Hamilton had consulted with American commercial distillers in writing his excise. The British public-private partnership was leading to the total elimination from the British Isles of small, seasonal producers. Hamilton wrote his excise bill to give big producers overwhelming competitive advantages over small producers.

Certain mechanisms in the proposed tax had effects that wouldn't be clear to most members of Congress. Hamilton said his target for the internal revenue of the United States was about 9 cents per gallon on all American whiskey distilled from American grain. Distillers were therefore to pay an annual flat tax of $60 per still, a figure based on the hundred-gallon capacity of an up-to-date still; smaller stills would be charged proportionally less, but the trick was to peg the fee to capacity, not actual gallons produced, because Hamilton was taking care to base his predictions of gallons produced on the practices of the biggest, most modern, and fully commercialized operations.

That hundred-gallon commercial still, for example, running steadily for four months, would produce a total of about 710 gallons per year; the $60 annual fee would bring in the target 9 cents per gallon nearly exactly. That might seem a notable tax for a product whose price per gallon, in the best markets, was about a dollar, but the savvy big distillers were all for it. Small producers, distilling for much shorter periods, not working as steadily, rarely producing at full capacity, made many fewer gallons than the number on which Hamilton's calculations were based, so in paying the same flat fee on capacity, their tax per gallon produced would be far higher than the 9 cent target. At the same time, with distilling technology developing and commercial distillers investing capital in innovation, big distilleries would produce many more gallons than the number on which the fee was based and substantially lower their per-actual-gallon tax, ultimately to mere fractions of what small producers paid and even, it was later said, "to about three fifths of a cent per gallon."

Hamilton wanted the federal government to encourage that kind of innovation in all American industries. In his report, he'd assured Congress that while excises are indeed collected at the point of production, and while that might seem a hardship for less solvent operators, excises aren't really paid by the producers. They just pass the tax on to consumers in the price: what's really taxed is the purchase; the real payers are drinkers, the excise an innocuous tax on a luxury item. What he didn't explore for Congress were the real-world ramifications for industry consolidation. Given the big hit they'd be taking from the tax, artisanal producers would have to raise prices. Big producers, benefiting from the tax break, would lower prices, underselling small competitors and driving them out of business.

That effect was shored up by further features deleveling the playing field and subjecting small farmers and artisans to the likelihoods of market failure, foreclosure, forfeiture, even arrest. The tax had to be paid before the product left the still for market. Given coin scarcity, many small farmers had no money until after they'd sold their product, and failure to pay up front would make the product legally unconveyable. Noncompliance, too, would be costly. Failure to register a still was punishable by a fine payable only in scarce coin and set at $150, far more than most people's annual income. While Hamilton's report assured Congress that alleged violators would be entitled to jury trials, he didn't call attention to the fact that those trials, held in federal court in Philadelphia, would pull alleged violators off the job and slow all farm production for long periods.

The excise thus accomplished a lot in one law. It would draw small players off their properties, cause further consolidation of arable land, shift labor to day employment, and put an end to both the democratic finance solutions and the ethos of self-reliance and defiance that had been making the West, in particular, so hard to manage for so long. All revenue drawn from the tax would be dedicated to paying interest, in coin—and tax-free, as it was income—to the merchants, landlords, manufacturers, and former military officers who were invested in the Debt, including the settlers' landlords and creditors, and including the big distillers themselves, who would benefit from the tax two ways: commercially, from the tax's structure; and financially, from interest payments on their government bonds, funded by the tax. Every component of Hamilton's finance and industrialization system was integrated in the whiskey excise, linchpin for funding and assumption.

The challenge, given recent history, might seem to be enforcement. Ordinary westerners were well known for resisting any policy that seemed corrupt, unfair, or just eastern. Economic unrest and popular finance policies had inspired the convention in Philadelphia, but the Constitution that came out of that convention wasn't self-executing; nor was the whiskey tax. Hamilton knew that excises imposed by the states had gone largely unpaid. There had been noncompliance, sometimes violence against inspectors and collectors. Such were the historic tools of the Democracy.

Now, though, a national enforcement system would operate out of his own office in Philadelphia. Internal revenue officers would show up unannounced to inspect every distilling operation, however remote. They would register the still on a uniform federal form. They'd be back to check each cask's alcohol content with a uniform, federally issued hydrometer. Having collected the tax, the officers would federally certify every cask with attached paperwork. The system put the federal government's fingerprints, literally, on homes and businesses in every region, certainly including the far-off, defiant West. The skeleton army at dilapidated Fort Pitt, commanding the point where the Ohio River began, wasn't what Hamilton wanted by way of a national military force, but it was located right there at the headwaters where the most prized whiskey was made and the sharpest resistance to eastern officialdom was concentrated. If some people in the West thought they lived in Westsylvania, enforcement of the whiskey tax would remind them, in the most practical manner, that they lived in the United States.

But the tax hadn't passed.

There was a reason Hamilton was staying so cool. On the day the House ended its session, with funding and assumption accomplished, the chamber had asked for a report explaining how he expected Congress to pay the interest on all this new debt it had taken on. The members were still pretending not to notice the revenue bill he'd sent with his original report. He might have suggested they pull out the bill he'd taken such pains to create for them more than a year earlier and pass it, but he didn't. He was learning.

16

SIX GREEK COLUMNS AND
A ROMAN PEDIMENT

THE MEMBERS OF CONGRESS took their new seats only steps away from the Pennsylvania State House, in a nearly new building meant to serve as the Philadelphia County Courthouse. Hoping to make the city so appealing that the federal government would never leave, Pennsylvania had moved the court out and renovated. The first floor was now the U.S. House chamber, the second floor the U.S. Senate chamber. Congress convened there on December 6, 1790.

Hamilton had spent the intervening months opening a new treasury office a few blocks away, on Third Street between Chestnut and Walnut. It would soon fill the whole block, with multiple offices and nearly 100 employees on the scene, plus about 120 customs officials at the ports. In this office, he'd written the new report that the House had asked for, on how to pay for the funding and assumption laws, and on December 14, he sent it over.

The report gave the members some totally unsurprising information. By agreeing to fund the Federal Debt and assume the States' Debt in it, thus swelling the obligation, they would soon find themselves facing a staggering deficit: about $830,000. Fortunately, Hamilton said, new import duties, plus an excise on American whiskey distilled from American grain, would raise $975,000, more than covering the deficit. As always, he showed them the math. It was that simple. The members had nowhere left to hide. The House would finally have to pass an excise on whiskey.

That didn't mean opponents wouldn't seize the opportunity to get back on the record with positions they hoped reflected constituents' passions. Hamilton knew that some dramatic grumblings were bound to occur en route to the destination. During debate, he meant to do everything he could to help the chamber get where it knew it had to be.

But he didn't stop there. He'd decided not to limit his response to Congress's request for a report. When waiting for the body to show up, he'd also written an unsolicited part two, and now, literally the day after giving them news of the looming deficit and the crying need for the excise, he sprung another proposal on them. He wanted Congress to charter an institution that he called the Bank of the United States.

National banking had always been critical to Hamilton's aims. Long before there was a national government, he'd proposed a national-style bank to James Duane; the the concept had brought him and Morris together and launched his career. By now, state banks had been opening. Massachusetts had chartered one, and in 1782, Hamilton himself had started the Bank of New York, which was still in the process of trying to get a charter from that state's legislature. He'd learned a lot about logistics from the institution, much of it set out in the plan for a national bank to be chartered by Congress.

These two big pieces of domestic legislation, the excise and the bank, each innovative, each foundational, began to intertwine as they made rapid progress in Congress. The House, without even opening the tabled banking report, sent it upstairs to the Senate to let a bill originate there while debate on the whiskey excise went on downstairs, and House oratory in opposition to the excise, while predictably hot, proved ineffectual. Had a William Findley been serving in the chamber, he would have discerned the bill's many interlocking features dedicated to ending small-scale growth for ordinary people in rural communities, drawing the most money for the investing class's payoffs from those who could least afford it and putting a big, federal foot on ordinary people of the West. But that kind of analysis took hands-on knowledge of local conditions and technologies. Most members didn't have it.

Anyway, members across the political spectrum were by no means to be instructed by the Democracy or attuned to its issues. Those who did oppose the tax stood on the traditional "damned excise" grounds already raised by Jackson and his crew the previous year, and that posed no problem for Hamilton and his supporters. Such objections were only to excises generally, which had often come with summary police powers such as denial of jury trials, and this one didn't. Even Madison, having privately suggested an excise on whiskey to Hamilton in 1789, and having publicly criticized it in 1790, was supporting the tax as the least worst option. Hamilton himself was going up and down the stairs between the two chambers and hanging around committee rooms, filling members in on distilling statistics and other abstruse data, blandishing upon them every bit of political cover they could ever want for passing a tax they had no practical choice but to pass. Alternatives were few, he reminded them: direct taxes, like land taxes, should be reserved for emergencies. That played. Jackson types, abominating excise on principle, would have been hurt by taxes on land. Further duties on imports would be too burdensome, Hamilton went on, for the merchants who had to pay them, and he reminded the members that merchants made up the group most committed to national authority.

For the excise was a nationalizing force. That was his big point. In the past, the Democracy had been allowed to render uncollectable any tax it didn't like. Hamilton refrained from blaming the state governments for that—something else he was learning—because the states hadn't been lazy or weak, he said, but scared, and his federal officers wouldn't be. The excise would be collected everywhere, because the means to do so now existed.

As a cherry on top, he provided the House with a letter from the Philadelphia College of Physicians, informing the members that drinking distilled spirits had become a ravaging plague of the poor requiring immediate treatment. In his first report, too, Hamilton had called alcohol consumption a "pernicious luxury" that should be reduced for reasons of national health.

This turned out to be an overplay. If people really cut down on whiskey, a whiskey tax would be in trouble, obviously, and to some members, legislation regarding people's personal choices and habits was absurd anyway. What's next, Jackson sputtered: a law banning ketchup?

Still, the excise bill was effectively a done deal in the House. It would pass the chamber 35 to 21 on January 27.

Upstairs in the Senate, the Bank of the United States was getting an easy ride too. Hamilton's idea was to create a financial institution that would be national—chartered by Congress—yet not fully governmental. The twenty-five bank directors would enjoy wide decision-making latitude, though the government could appoint up to five of them, and the treasury reserved a right to audit the books. The bank was to be capitalized at $10 million—far more gold and silver than existed in the entire United States—with a total of 25,000 shares worth $400 each. Eight of the ten million dollars would come from selling shares to investors, with three-quarters of each share to be paid for not in coin but in federal bonds—the type paying 6 percent interest right away—thus shoring up the most attractive bonds' market value. The federal government would profit as a major bank stockholder, buying the remaining $2 million with coin, and because the government didn't have that kind of money, the purchase price of its shares was to be considered a loan from the bank itself, which the United States would pay back in ten equal installments, over ten years, or sooner at its discretion.

The federal government, its Debt, and the bank were thus intricately intertwined. The main branch was to be located right there in the temporary capital—it remained the national mercantile center—and Hamilton didn't outright ban but advised against opening branches in other states, at least not too fast. He wanted to protect state banking. He was personally committed to his bank of New York; other state-chartered institutions would be opening. Too many national bank branches in the states had the potential to undermine state banking via the competitive power of the national bank's paper notes. They were critical to the plan.

The United States would soon start minting gold and silver coin; Hamilton had a separate bill in mind for that. But he didn't want the federal government to follow the old, now-unconstitutional practices of the states and issue a paper currency. Merchants and lenders had never liked government paper because of its tendency to depreciate; a federal currency might tend to rise and fall with confidence in government. Not that Hamilton was as fixated on gold and silver as the merchants were. He considered hard money "dead stock" unless it was used to back fluid commerce and lending. So where Morris had launched the notes of the Bank of North America and Mr. Morris's notes, Hamilton would launch the notes of the Bank of the United States, a U.S.-connected private currency. Having always thought Morris set denominations too high, he wouldn't do the same. His banknotes would be both stable and usable, across state lines, and unlike the state banks', accepted by the federal government for paying the impost, the excise, and any other federal taxes. That would make the notes of the Bank of the United States a highly preferred form of paper.

The Senate majority led by Morris and Schuyler naturally liked the bank plan a lot. The institution would route big commerce and high finance through American government and big commerce and American government through high finance. The investing class would own the shares, deposit the profits, use the notes in deals with one another, accept the notes in interest payments on federal bonds, take loans for private projects, and make loans to the United States for public projects. The Senate gave the Bank of the United States a monopoly charter for twenty years and sent a bill down to the House for perusal, debate, and final passage there. A clerk jogging down the stairs to the House with the banking bill probably didn't pass a clerk jogging up to the Senate with the excise bill, but wheels were turning, and they were turning Hamilton's way.

And yet when the House opened debate on the Senate's bank bill, something new happened.

James Jackson rose, of course, but that wasn't new. He objected in his usual direct and holistic manner to the whole idea of public banking, invoking familiar upscale agrarian values: land wealth is virtue; money, sleaze. Hatred of banking was among the Jackson type's articles of faith.

It was Madison who rose and did something else, something yet again startling, with dire and very long-range consequences. It wasn't so much that he objected to chartering a bank. He wasn't really discussing banking. Instead, he attacked Hamilton's banking proposal and the Senate banking bill for a particular, fundamental violation of principle.

Madison called the Bank of the United States unconstitutional.

A debate on policy thus escalated—instantly—to a constitutional crisis. Instantly and, to Hamilton, absurdly. He saw no constitutional crisis. He couldn't have predicted an objection on this of all grounds. Madison was arguing that the Constitution barred the national government from doing anything not explicitly set out as a federal power in the ratified document: as no power to charter a bank was enumerated, Congress couldn't charter a bank. But in the old Congress, in support of the impost, it was Madison who had shown the way beyond the explicit powers in the Articles of Confederation. At the Constitutional Convention, he'd supported the clause enabling the federal government to do anything "necessary and proper," as the document put it, even if unenumerated, to carrying out the enumerated powers; in The Federalist, he'd defended the doctrine. "No axiom is more clearly established in law or in reason," he'd written, "than that wherever the end is required, the means are authorized."

Madison's inconsistency on the bank was blatant, yet there was method in it. Even on the Morris Continentalist team, he'd voted against chartering the Bank of North America. Many people of his class and region could reel off in their sleep agrarian tropes against money, though some of them were less leery of banking on principle than of banking in northern commercial centers, which threatened their lucrative position as private lenders in the South. Madison was also responding to home-state challenges. Patrick Henry, the Antifederalist Virginia governor, was using his political machine to punish Madison for having helped make the federal government so powerful. In their state's ratifying convention, Henry had inveighed against the Constitution's necessary-and-proper clause: it gave the federal government, he claimed, a tyrannical power to do anything it wanted. Thanks to Henry's animosity, Madison had had no chance of being appointed to the Senate; he'd barely been elected to the House. Now he was out to prove that the Constitution by no means gave the national government the awful power that Henry claimed it did. A power to borrow and tax implied no unenumerated power to charter a bank. He framed that reading as a matter of fundamental American principle.

Some members, though, started passing around allegations that Madison's constitutional challenge to the bank wasn't principled at all, just hardball politics related to the old capital-location issue. He'd been perfectly willing to support the bank if he could get the institution's char-ter cut to ten years. He feared that twenty years of locating the financial center of gravity in Philadelphia would make it hard to get Congress to leave for the Potomac. Robert Morris was believed, credibly enough, to be constantly maneuvering to keep the capital in town, and Madison had supposedly sworn outright in back rooms that if he couldn't get the charter period reduced, he'd go after the institution on constitutional grounds.

It was pretty easy to counter his constitutional position. In the House debate, Hamilton, mainly through Fisher Ames, pointed out that if the issue really wasn't the relative virtue of national banking but the nature of the Constitution, then forming a bank was clearly a necessary and proper means for achieving the enumerated aims of tax collection and borrowing. Hamilton's ally Sedgwick read into the record Madison's remarks in *The Federalist* on the necessity of implied powers. On Febru-ary 8, the Senate's banking bill easily passed the House.

So things were still rolling along. Yet at the very moment of its success, the Hamilton Scheme was reopening the original rift in the American governing elite over federal-government activism, reframed by appeals to the Constitution. Two factions were turning into two national parties, at odds less over policy than over the fundamental meaning of the United States.

That division started to rock Washington's cabinet. When the banking bill came to the president to be signed into law, Jefferson advised him to veto it, not as bad policy but on Madison's basis: unconstitutionality. If Washington agreed, this would be the first-ever use of presidential veto power; it would also make the president the arbiter of constitutionality. On finance, Washington had long been aligned with Hamilton and Morris, despite the Virginia ethos he shared with Jefferson and Madison: he might be expected to sign a national banking bill. But he had some unrelated problems to deal with, and they affected how he handled the possible veto.

For one thing, Washington had reason to suspect that if the Bank of the United States remained in Philadelphia for twenty years, it would draw energy away from his projected capital at the Potomac. For another, Congress's law for siting the capital had established a three-man commission and assigned it to work with him in creating a ten-mile-square federal district somewhere above the lower falls of the Potomac. Washington had taken over, and using the tactics that had made him so rich in land, he selected the site himself and placed it adjacent to his own plantations, well below the falls, contradicting the law and mightily increasing his property's value. He tried to cover himself by exploring, after the fact, the original upstream sites and pretending to consider input from people there, but finally he just asked Congress to change the law to allow retroactively what he'd done. Congress hadn't dealt with it.

Now he let it be known that he might not sign the bank bill unless Congress changed the capital-siting law the way he wanted. He also told both Hamilton and Jefferson that he needed to see written opinions on the bank's constitutionality—but not simultaneously. He tasked Jefferson with writing up the constitutional objections. He presented Hamilton with Jefferson's critique and asked for a response, and Hamilton brought voluminous overkill to demolishing Jefferson's argument point by point. Meanwhile, Senate pro-banking forces, notably Morris and Schuyler, came out publicly against changing the capital-site law on Washington's behalf; privately they let it be known that his signing the bank bill into law might end their opposition. On February 25, 1791, the day Washington signed the banking bill, Hamilton's Senate allies reversed their position on changing the capital-site law. Then the revenue bill with the whiskey excise underwent a very few amendments in the Senate and was sent to the president. On March 3, when Washington signed the first federal tax on an American product into law, the entire Hamilton Scheme became viable.

A staggering achievement. Funding, assumption, and excise, with a national banking hub: in Hamilton's terms, American nationhood realized, the Hamilton Constitution fulfilled. Developed intellectually over the course of ten years, battered and beaten for more than a year in Congress, the Hamilton Scheme was a scheme no more. Hamilton had triumphed. His scheme was a system.

And he was just getting started. Everything he'd achieved so far in making the Money Connection a dynamic force was meant to pave the way for the industrialization of the United States as a great competitor. He was a hero now. Big foreign investors wanted to buy U.S. domestic debt. Hamilton received honorary degrees. His likeness was admired in a wax museum in New York. In this heady mood, he and Tench Coxe moved briskly forward on their project for creating an American factory town from scratch. The factories were to produce mainly textiles, to begin with, but also paper and printed material and someday much more. The project represented an enormous opportunity for the country and a lot of money to be made by the geared-up investing type on whose eagerness the Hamilton Scheme was predicated.

So far, the town existed only on paper. The plan was to build it in real life below the towering falls of the Passaic River in eastern New Jersey. The location was carefully chosen. From the treasury, Hamilton was gaining a sense of national economic conditions and saw northern New Jersey as having strong industrial potential: water power, mineral resources, proximity to both Philadelphia and New York City, and a lot of people in need of work. While the town would be sited not far from two port cities of the North, he also hoped to show the South that industrialization, unlike the bank, could foster national unity and work against sectional division. A manufacturing economy would have benefits and appeal for businesspeople of all regions.

Starting the build would depend on private financial investment, strong government support, and poached talent and industrial theft from Britain, which had made it illegal for factory managers, engineers, and skilled workers to emigrate. Coxe was already on top of the espionage and recruitment. William Duer, no longer Hamilton's assistant, having left the department to avoid a corruption investigation, was serving as investment-money conjurer. Hamilton was in a position to be confident that government would come along.

He had reason for all the headiness. On the Fourth of July 1791, the fifteenth anniversary of the old Congress's passing the Declaration of Independence, the Hamilton Scheme's success was made manifest, even overwhelming, when the initial stock offering in the Bank of the United States opened for business and Philadelphia became the scene of something that few inhabitants, accustomed as they were to intense public action, could ever have imagined. It was a sign of the times that the bank was selling its stock in Carpenters' Hall, on Chestnut Street, which was to serve as its temporary home. This was the artisans' and workmen's gathering place, a building more modest yet more beautifully crafted than the State House. The Continental Congress had met here in 1774 before moving to the more official building. It was from Carpenters' Hall that the working class had launched its takeover of Pennsylvania.

Now the bank, the great hub for Hamilton's system, was lodged here, and a different kind of crowd action ensued. The doors opened. People raced in. Some had gotten to town days before, just for this. On sale, for a down payment, weren't actual shares but subscriptions, documented on paper called "scrip" for short, which gave the buyer a right to purchase the shares. Pandemonium ruled, and an hour later investors had bought out more than the entire legal subscription. The revenues of the federal government were only $4.4 million, but the bank already had its full $10 million: $8 million from investors, $2 million from the U.S. government. Many people got into the building too late and were turned away in a desperate state of ungratified desire, making a fervid secondary market for trading the scrip, which began operations there on the street that day. And that was just the stock sale: the institution itself wouldn't be ready to operate until the end of the year.

The bank would long remain a source of Philadelphia pride. Pennsylvania's dream of keeping the federal city would die in 1799, when the agreed-upon ten-year period was up, but even as a new city started rising from the Potomac swampland, construction began in Philadelphia too. The sole exception to the federal government's departure, the bank was to remain, as Washington and Madison had feared, in a purpose-built edifice on Third Street, with a high, colonnaded, marble façade looking due east toward the main part of the city, the busy docks, the Delaware harbor, the world. The visitor on banking business, leaving the port and walking or riding toward what had once been outskirts, might gaze up the incline ahead and see, before anything else in the recently federal part of town, the high-peaked pediment recalling an Ancient Roman temple. Arriving at ten shallow marble steps, their platform topped by six tall columns recalling an Ancient Greek temple, the visitor would mount the steps, pass between the widely spaced middle columns, and be ushered through a tall central door, portal to the high-toned republic where, in the abomination of desolation prophesied by the book of Daniel, Herman Husband's American Revolution lay in broken pieces, the people weeping in captivity, the Temple of Jerusalem toppled.

PART IV

TO EXTREMES

~

THE END OF PAIN.

The laſt Speech, Dying Words, and Confeſsion of
T. P.

~

17

THE HUSBAND SCHEME

THE OUTCOME OF THE 1787 convention in Philadelphia had shocked Herman Husband into a state of furious disappointment, made all the more painful by the excitement he'd felt, at first, when hearing that a national frame of government was being presented for ratification. He'd been so sure that independent nationhood for the United States was about to bring forth a cosmically transformative explosion. Even when Antifederalists had raised objections to the convention itself—the secrecy of its proceedings, the presence in the chair of a military man—the complaints didn't shake Husband. He saw Washington as the hero of the last battle against the Antichrist and a model of disinterested judgment.

He was home in the Glades when he began reading the ratified Constitution of the United States and saw right away that the Beast so recently on the run had turned, attacked, and chewed up and spit out the Revolution's Millennial spirit. At first he was too aghast to read on. The next day, he studied the whole thing. It was clear. The Constitution imposed a satanic tyranny on the people of the United States.

The proposed new government gave independent power to a solo executive chosen by an unelected body. It gave judicial power to an unelected body appointed by that executive, with the advice and consent of another unelected body, an upper legislative house, which was to check the only elected part of government, the lower legislative house, which was so small, and so subject to the various states' restrictive election laws, that it wasn't representative either. On the one hand, the Constitution severed the confederation of states, "all the sacred ties, oaths, and obligations by which we were united together under our former constitutions."

On the other hand, that unelected upper house was appointed by the state legislatures. The states also selected the presidential electors. They controlled the electoral processes for choosing members of the lower house. They could go their own ways when it came to neglecting their separate citizenries' basic protections, benefits, entitlements, and access to the political process. All "our offices," Husband said, ". . . will beat and abuse the best men, and seize on the inheritance, and rule with the same arbitrary power as heretofore."

Localities, communities, and individuals' freedom were the victims. Husband read Ezekiel 41:7 as clarifying good governmental structure in the image of the Temple restored in the New Jerusalem, built on a big foundation, with side chambers winding upward about the house from lowest to highest, a tapering effect. The new Constitution's structure was the opposite, top-heavy, an anti-scriptural design with two major effects. First, the sharp checks on representation sucked financial and monetary power upward to the national government, eliminating the states' former susceptibilities for providing economic relief, if often grudgingly, in response to popular pressure. Second, far from restraining the existing state governments' domination by small, wealthy, inside groups, the new federalist system gave that domination new national force. The American nationhood emerging from the Philadelphia convention bailed out the investor class, left the free-laboring many at the mercy of money and punitive law, built the institution of slavery into the nation's future, and enabled outright conquest of the confederated western nations and suppression of the citizenry by a national army.

Husband had misplaced his faith. He'd believed in the War of Independence as the last battle to overcome corruption and tyranny. In that belief, in 1776, he'd gone against old comrades in regulation who mistrusted the American governing class and sought fairer treatment from the British. After the war, unlike many of his poor western neighbors, he'd resisted the secessionist mood that made an independent state of Westsylvania seem feasible to some. Husband had seen the West, seen it quite literally, as the center of a redemptive future for a whole, unified United States, the New Jerusalem itself. But now even General Washington, in pursuit of what Husband called sheer pomp, had turned traitor to the people. The Revolution was betrayed by a new, supreme law of the land inspired by "the spirit of the serpent."

This betrayal must be defeated. The true last battle, it had now been revealed, was still to come.

Husband had in the meantime been growing more and more popular in his region. The written record on him, created mainly by the upscale, would remain sparse. The few educated people who set down encounters tended to dismiss him as a weird figure, an embodiment of his character the Philosopher of the Allegheny, living remotely and lost in cryptic biblical theories. Husband didn't seem to mind. Sometimes he made public splashes; sometimes he disappeared; sometimes he masked himself in aliases and characters. If the record made him something of a man of mystery, that wasn't out of keeping with his personality.

Ordinary people saw him differently. It wasn't despite but because of his unassuming dress and prophetic style that they elected him to go up against the corruption of the Bedford courthouse ring of speculators and government insiders. Throughout the 1780s, the supposed madman held administrative offices in Bedford County, from county commissioner to supervisor of highways to overseer of the poor.

Now he renewed his fight on behalf of the Millennium—a fight, now, against the Constitution of the United States—by serving in his state government for the second time. In late 1789, he was elected back to the assembly and took his seat in the State House in Philadelphia, where the Constitution had been written and the state of Pennsylvania had recently ratified the document in a literally bruising contest. He found himself in a minority of one. This assembly was different from those of the late 1770s, when he'd first served; representatives of the upscale dominated. Antifederalists in the body were pushing for constitutional amendments, threatening a do-over on the Constitution if their amend-

ments weren't adopted, and Husband too opposed the ratified Constitution, yet he was at odds with most Antifederalists. Their main concern
was to take back powers for the states. His issue was the Constitution's
anti-democratic nature. He rose and alienated the Antifederalists by arguing that an amendment they were pushing, a minor increase in U.S.
House membership, would do nothing to make the body truly representative. To him, the whole top-heavy constitutional design didn't work for
the people. It shouldn't be tweaked by amendment. It should be replaced
wholesale. He had a design, he announced, for governing the United
States—not a set of amendments but an alternate constitution, as thorough and detailed as the Federalists', based on his vision of the New Jerusalem in North America.

Husband proposed to the assembly following Ezekiel's discussion of the
temple and rebuilding the United States on a broad foundation made up
of the existing thirteen states. Elections and decisions would occur locally,
all the way down to the township level, with no property qualifications
or religious tests for voting or holding office. His scheme was thus highly
localist. But while the foundational states would retain some of their existing powers, overseeing their own counties and townships—there were to
be thirteen hyper-representative, one-chamber legislative bodies—all laws
regarding land ownership were to be nationally, constitutionally, uniform,
Husband explained, and operate across all of the states, equally protecting
all citizens of the nation. Hence the strength of the foundation.

States may only grant titles, for example, to those living on and
working land, not to speculators or absentee landlords. Claiming and
engrossing huge parcels is constitutionally disallowed. Each state is constitutionally responsible for guaranteeing a minimum of wealth, granting
every man 300 acres, his wife an additional 200 in her own name, and
each child 100 at birth. Larger titles may be granted at a state's discretion,
but they're constitutionally limited to 2,000 acres and revert to the public
if purchasers fail to use them.

Related rules, operating across all states, include the abolition of
slavery, a just peace with the original inhabitants, no establishment of
religion. A single paper currency, issued by the national government,

unpegged from gold, thus ending money's volatile relationship to precious metals. Progressive taxes on wealth and income, with the better-off paying proportionally more. Profit-sharing for workers. Freedom of speech and of the press. Public encouragement for science and art. A nationally funded system to ensure older people's security after they retire. A high quality of life, in other words, constitutionally and equally guaranteed to all citizens of the nation across the broad foundation formed by the states' governments.

To ensure that result, a series of national levels rise from the thirteen-state foundation, levels increasingly purified, tapering like Ezekiel's temple, its restoration prophesied in Revelation as a signal of the Millennium. When an elevation of that building, drawn at a scale of five hundred miles to an inch, was overlaid on Husband's map of territory held by the United States—divided geometrically by Husband into prospective new townships, districts, and counties—the temple fit the whole country precisely, the holy inner sanctum the West landing in the center, the prophecy fulfilled. Hence the building's upper floors. The first tier above the foundation ensures proper oversight by dividing the states into four large regions, each governed by a senate appointed by the states' representative legislatures; the number of appointees is apportioned by population. These senates monitor the laws of their member states and veto any that violate the constitutional guarantees of fairness, freedom, and equality. The states retain a right, however, to appeal to the highest and most refined level of government, at the temple roof: the executive body.

This body is appointed by the four regional senates: six appointees each, adding up to the twenty-four elders of Revelation. Having risen through the purifying lower levels of government, the elders are between the ages of fifty and sixty. They're term-limited to ten years, and to further ensure rotation in office, one is retired by lot every other year and replaced by the appropriate regional senate. Holding their personal property communally, making all decisions by majority rule, they hear appeals on senates' vetoes of state laws, appoint judicial systems for the four regions, and manage a slow, planned, natural depreciation of the currency.

Given the special sanctity of the West, a critical job of the executive body is to carry out national expansion—not as a speculation in greed by those with money but as a series of small grants to those who work. The elders buy, not steal, Indian lands, on behalf of the whole country. When enough settlers inhabit an area, the elders make it a new state. When enough new states are formed, the elders create a new region and place it under a new senate. The country grows, while always sustaining the image of the temple: good government.

Such was Herman Husband's plan for the United States, introduced in the Pennsylvania assembly in 1790, to the bafflement, even the barely concealed mirth of both the Federalists and the Antifederalists serving there. The goal, he insisted, was to overcome the ratified Constitution's empowerment of "loaves and fishes": material gain, the rule of Nebuchadnezzar. The people, he said, are still in childhood; they don't yet understand their history. As Daniel shows, the loaves and fishes are the "stinking body of filthy lucre," luxury created on the theft of others' labor, "a prison to all nations," the abomination of desolation. Prophetic references of that kind were common enough in the discourse of working-class proponents of the Democracy and enslaved people seeking freedom. They were enough in themselves to draw snarkiness from the rationalists, Deists, and proponents of liberalizing theologies who dominated both sides of the aisle in the Pennsylvania assembly these days. Anyway, there wasn't going to be any do-over on the U.S. Constitution. Husband's plan was ignored; proposing amendments went on.

There was, however, a do-over on Pennsylvania's democratic constitution of 1776. Even while Husband was presenting his radically egalitarian national constitution to the assembly, a convention formed in the courtroom across the State House hall to write a new state constitution and undo, just as Robert Morris had long wanted, many of the radically egalitarian features inspired by Paine's "Common Sense." James Wilson did the rewrite. He based the new state constitution on the national Constitution to which he'd contributed and whose ratification he'd urged. Paine's single-chamber assembly was replaced by a bicameral legislature: an upper house would now check the lower. The executive was no longer a committee but a solo actor with broad powers, independent of the representative legislature. Judges were no longer elected locally but appointed by the executive, as were county sheriffs. The assembly across the hall, where Husband was sitting, having been elected under the old state constitution, was formally disbanded.

Husband refused to leave. This body had been elected by the people, he insisted.

But he had no support. When the other members left the assembly room, he had no choice but to go home too.

Back in the mountains, he could see America falling further and faster into Daniel's abomination of desolation. Amendments to the U.S. Constitution were ratified and did nothing to alter the Constitution's basic purposes. Slavery might be outlawed in the Northwest Territory, but it wasn't outlawed in the United States. The West, the walled holy city where Husband lived, was being cut up and parceled out by eastern officials in league with speculators. Where Husband's proposed constitution had placed maximums on how much public land anyone could buy, the real federal government set minimums: Congress sold parcels of hundreds of thousands of acres to cronies of government, sometimes outright hucksters. To secure these great public-private land deals, the new federal military force, amplified now, with its jumping-off place, Fort Pitt, not so far from Husband's home, was moving down the Ohio to forts built on the north bank, preparing to launch a war of conquest against the Shawnee, Miami, Delaware, and other confederated nations while removing squatters. To supply the forts, hired men loaded keelboats with milled grain, fodder, ammunition, tar, and horseshoes, made increasingly in factory-type operations, and steered the cargo through the Ohio currents, then poled and hauled the boats back upstream. That kind of work was becoming more and more common. Husband saw the amazing speed at which the small farmers in his region were becoming tenants of large landowners, hired hands of commercial farmers, day laborers in mills and on the rivers.

Poor westerners had one lifeline to some degree of economic independence: artisanal whiskey-making. So in the spring of 1791, when news came of the whiskey excise's passage in Congress, the law brought home—literally home, for Husband—every power of the new government he'd identified as satanic, now deployed for maximum destruction on sacred western ground. Members of the House hadn't analyzed certain particulars of the whiskey excise's action, or cared to. Husband and anybody else living in western Pennsylvania could see right away how the tax gave pragmatic force to the Constitution's overall purpose, at once empowering the investing class and crushing the Democracy. Small distillers knew the excise would force them to a price rise of 7 cents and more while their big competitors lowered prices. They could see that the tax was a cash handout to big whiskey operators and federal bondholders at once, pushing ordinary people into wage labor for the rich. National government was accelerating to industrial speed the corruption that ordinary people in the headwaters region had been resisting all their lives.

Had there been any confusion about the whiskey tax's purpose, it would have been dispelled when Secretary Hamilton appointed, as top tax collector for the five western counties of Pennsylvania, the biggest farmer in the region, General John Neville, an aggressive investor and creditor, well known throughout his new tax survey for many years of monopolizing land and sewing up commerce there. If Husband's biblically influenced descriptions of corruption could seem exaggerated, this appointment put a caricaturish face on the whiskey tax's encouragement of the cartel-like insiderism that Husband condemned as the Beast. Neville had fought both the Shawnee under George Washington and western Pennsylvanians in provincial border skirmishes and been rewarded by Virginia with 500 acres in the region, his first stake in a major land play. After serving in the War of Independence, he built a mansion on a rugged mountaintop not far from the village of Pittsburgh at the Ohio headwaters. Log houses were standard even for comfortable farmers; Neville's home was a frontier showplace with multiple chimneys, mirrors, and fine carpets and curtains.

From there, he operated a 10,000-acre diversified commercial plantation nothing like the subsistence plots owned or rented by most of his neighbors. Neville hired hands, but to grow crops at such scale, he also used a crew of enslaved black laborers, quartering them in outbuildings. Most people in the region weren't rich enough to own people. Some actively opposed the institution. Neville also served as the head of a small group of local entrepreneurs, members of his family, along with others who had pretensions to Neville-like wealth: industrialists, speculators in land and in the Debt, commercial farmers, and merchants who called themselves, bluntly, the Neville Connection and dominated western Pennsylvania's markets and commerce, sending people into landlessness and working for the Connection.

Among his many commercial operations, Neville was an industrial-scale whiskey distiller. Hamilton had thus awarded the job of enforcing the tax in western Pennsylvania to the one man in western Pennsylvania who had the most to gain monetarily from the tax's operations. Neville would not only draw a salary in public funds but also pocket a percentage of what he collected from his competitors. He would get intimate with their operations and finances, and where he found violations, he had the official power, benefiting his market power, to disable the alleged violator's business. And the scarce gold and silver he collected, much of it from people who would never see a federal bond, would be sent to the U.S. Treasury, to be deposited in the bank and flow in the form of interest payments to federal bondholders throughout the country, who included, naturally, Neville himself and the Neville Connection.

Sewing things up. That's what people like the Neville Connection had been doing for generations, what the Democracy had been trying for generations to regulate. But nobody had ever seen a sew-up this big, this perfect, this total. Neville's federal appointment clarified for ordinary westerners the ingenious dynamism of Hamilton's national system.

Madison and Jefferson had been framing a critique of Hamiltonian finance in constitutional terms, a philosophy of American government that would become broadly known as Jeffersonian. The philosophy was based on Madison's notion that the bank violated the Constitution, but it had other features too. Jefferson vocally opposed all government-chartered companies, known as corporations, for creating monopolies that he believed corrupted relationships between commerce and government. Especially egregious to Jefferson, then, were Hamilton's efforts at consolidation, which took monopolization to a national level and gave it new power. Jefferson had come to believe that the federal government was restrained, constitutionally, from pursuing any such action.

The old Antifederalists, having failed to prevent the national government's ratification, were taking the line that the document they'd so recently condemned for giving the federal government tyrannical powers actually disallowed almost every exercise of federal power. A party beginning to call itself Republican, forming behind Jefferson and Madison, opposed the Federalists and the Washington administration on absolutist, constitutionalist grounds. The absolutism was mutual. The Republicans called the Federalist majority a reign of witches. The Federalists called the Republicans democrats and anarchists. In the governing class, things were getting nasty, even zero-sum.

Herman Husband and his followers saw the situation quite differently. The federal destruction of the ordinary people of the West seemed to Husband perfectly consistent with the Constitution. He and Alexander Hamilton shared a view of the United States. It was borne out in the operations of the whiskey tax, exemplified by General Neville's appointment as tax collector. To both Husband and Hamilton, the national government was a combination of financial, military, and judiciary power, connecting political and commercial elites to government for the purposes of imperial growth and the defeat, if necessary by force, of egalitarian economics and finance, most practically and technically via an excise whose mechanisms were calibrated to benefit the biggest players in the industry and crush their small competitors, with revenues earmarked to reward investors in the Public Debt. Hamilton had invented and would defend that system. To Husband, it was the Antichrist.

So unlike the fight between the Federalists and the Republicans, the fight between Hamilton and Husband wasn't to be carried out in seesawing election victories or parliamentary debates or claims on the Constitution. It was a literal fight, the old fight, the fight between the Democracy and concentrations of wealth and power. Now it was occurring at a new, national level, for the highest possible stakes. Hamilton had made his moves against the Democracy. The Democracy would make its moves against him.

Herman Husband's long career as an activist and politician had always been marked by a peculiar tension, first emerging in the days of the North Carolina Regulation and extending into the War of Independence. Through it all, he'd remained a pacifist. He'd never been able to fully work the issue out. In his mid-forties, on the brink of the Battle of Alamance, he'd risked his life trying to arrive at a negotiated solution with the government.

Now he was almost seventy. His life's work was under immediate threat of final defeat. The revolution he'd placed his faith in was betrayed, with ramifications at once constitutional and cosmic. The toughness of his increasingly landless neighbors, their readiness to use the old tactics of regulation, maybe even to defend the West militarily from invasion by the corruption of the East: these moods were taking on new meanings for him. Just as in the War of Independence, natural human tendencies toward violence might be transformed, redeemed—directed, leveraged—on behalf of finally overthrowing satanic tyranny and bringing on good government, globally, in perpetuity.

In sermons, Husband had long reminded his constituents that the body of free laborers, being numerous, has the power to overcome a sinful few: in the last days, he said, citing Daniel, the militias of a laboring, industrious people will prevail over the armies of tyrants who rob the people and live in idleness on their labor. He'd long taken Daniel's militias as symbolic. But now salaried hirelings—by the early 1790s, he meant the Neville Connection and its deputies—were everywhere in the westerners' midst. Like the Jews in the early, virtuous state of their government, western militias could throw off the yoke of tyranny whenever they chose.

The hirelings could be identified. Every person must be on the lookout for them. Good government only awaited the last battle, starting now.

As the whiskey excise began taking effect in General Neville's survey of five counties and Husband's message of resistance began resonating loudly around the region, some people living there, though no friends of the Neville Connection, and no supporters of Hamilton, were by no means as radical as Husband. To these western moderates, the secessionist mood, the Westsylvania movement, and the common cause with Kentuckians and western Virginians against the East looked dangerous enough already; outright resistance to the new federal tax could only make things worse. Secretary Hamilton had made it explicit that the power to collect federal taxes was the sine qua non of national government. If Herman Husband and those he supported and inspired saw a looming conflict with the federal government as the last battle for ultimate stakes, Hamilton and the whole Washington administration could be expected to see things more or less the same way. The government would give no quarter. To western moderates, the West would only suffer further by resorting to radicalism.

In the summer of 1791, these worries began mounting. On one side, Neville's deputies were getting ready to start registering stills throughout the western counties. On the other, the radicals weren't just condemning the whiskey tax; they were condemning any questioning of their radical ideas for defeating the tax and the entire federal finance system that the tax made operational. They had one priority: regional unity. Hirelings had to be rooted out. Compliance with the law might in itself be evidence of treachery. Anybody in the West hoping to achieve moderation on the whiskey-tax issue was finding the middle ground getting narrower and narrower.

18

REASON

ONTO THE NARROWING GROUND between Hamilton and Husband stepped Abraham Alfonse Albert Gallatin. Known as Albert Gallatin, he was thirty, a rationalist and freethinker, highly educated, abstemious in his lifestyle, firm in his convictions, amiable and even shy in his personal manner. In 1791, he was living in Fayette County, Pennsylvania, just west of the mountains, within General Neville's tax survey and not far from Husband's Glades in one direction and the headwaters village of Pittsburgh in the other.

Gallatin hoped for peace, reason, and prosperity. A native speaker of French and a recent speaker of heavily accented English, he'd come to western Pennsylvania, seen by many on the eastern seaboard as a howling wilderness, from the Republic of Geneva, a city-state older and more sophisticated than anyplace in English-speaking America, the site of long conflicts among many traditions. Geneva had heritage in the church of John Calvin, who maintained a surprisingly republican near-theocracy there in the sixteenth century. It also served as an intellectual center for the latest advances in Enlightenment philosophy.

The Gallatin family, an old one in the city, was influential yet less wealthy than others of their type. Albert, born in 1761, was orphaned at nine, taken in by an unmarried friend of his mother and raised in part by his grandparents, who lived out of town in a house on Lake

Geneva. He absorbed his city's Calvinist heritage, its regard for thrift, its skepticism of adornment and pomp. He was also exposed at an early age to a host of revolutionary ideas about liberty, equality, and reason. His grandmother was close friends with Voltaire, the great *philosophe* and skeptic of religion, banned from Paris for shocking ideas, who found a haven in Geneva; as a boy, Albert knew him. Jean-Jacques Rousseau was born in Geneva, and Gallatin became a fan of Rousseau's ideas, which reflected curiosity about the woodland tribes of North Americans, who supposedly lived physically and emotionally closer than Europeans to the forces some Enlightenment thinkers had begun to call Nature. Alexander Hamilton's hero, the great financier Jacques Necker, was not only Gallatin's countryman but also his distant relation. The youngster's head was filled very early with a lot of big ideas.

Yet the Genevan milieu was also hidebound and hierarchical. Gallatin, a reader and dreamer, had little opportunity to stand out. In 1780, when he was nineteen, having graduated from the Academy of Geneva, first in his class in three subjects, he left.

Leaving might not have seemed strange. Choosing the United States as a destination was strange indeed. This was at the height of the War of Independence. The American economy, always straggling, was deeply depressed, American defeat seemingly imminent. Gallatin's plan was oddball enough that at first he didn't even tell his family where he was going but just took ship, with a friend, bound for Boston. Thanks to bad weather, they landed at Cape Ann.

That set a pattern for the veering American youth of Albert Gallatin. During the war and then after it, he knocked about the country in somewhat aimless pursuit of success in business. He hoped at various times to make his pile in arms dealing, in tea selling, in general trade of goods. He traveled way up the rocky coast of Maine to Machias Bay, where he spent a frigid winter cutting wood. Back in Massachusetts, he was hired by Harvard College as a French tutor and served in the militia. He lived in Philadelphia. He lived in Richmond, Virginia. He gained a far wider experience of America than most of his American contemporaries ever would, and he learned to get along with various kinds of Americans who didn't necessarily get along with one another.

He wasn't considered good-looking, but his eyes were piercing, intelligent. Despite his militia experience, he lacked the dash that martial attitude lent certain men, but he was easygoing and friendly, mentally quick, and deeply acculturated in both the ancient European regimes and the most modern ideas. By the mid-1780s, with the war won, Albert Gallatin was considering making a life in the independent United States.

What drew him to western Pennsylvania's backcountry, as with so many others with some money to invest, was land speculation. Some never followed their own investment money westward, but Gallatin, like Washington, did. He even ran into Washington out there. In 1784, he'd been living in Richmond and was starting to consider himself a Virginian; he would soon take an oath of allegiance making him a naturalized citizen of the state. That fall, exploring his way along the Ohio River, he heard that Washington—the general was then on his way back from the Millers Run confrontation—would be at a county surveyor's cabin taking information from locals regarding topography and waterways.

Gallatin entered the crowded cabin and joined the group standing around the seated general. As he listened to Washington's interrogations, it quickly became obvious to him which mountain pass was the best, and not understanding why Washington didn't see it, Gallatin interrupted the general's questions and started to explain.

Washington put down his pen. He looked at the disrupter. The young man fell silent. After a long gaze, Washington turned away and resumed his questioning. But then he stopped, thought a moment, threw down his pen, and addressed Gallatin: "You are right, sir!"

Unlike Washington, Gallatin found he liked the West. In 1785, he inherited some money and moved to the newly created Fayette County, Pennsylvania. One of the most cosmopolitan people in the United States was choosing to live in one of the remotest places in the country. The decision reflected Gallatin's idea of the great opportunity of America: a modest but independent style of life, based on hard work and thrift, available to many more people than had ever enjoyed such privileges in Europe. He built one of the few fancy houses in the region, with nicely landscaped grounds, and named the estate Friendship Hill.

The place wasn't as imposing or well-fitted-out as the Neville spread. But while Gallatin dressed modestly and disapproved of ostentation—he was becoming increasingly abstemious, even at times cheap—in the mountain remoteness of western Pennsylvania, he stood out. By 1787, when the Constitution was written, he'd established himself as a member of the few-and-far-between gentry of western Pennsylvania.

His politics, in keeping with his Enlightenment background, focused on liberty. The Antifederalists seemed to him to share those politics, and Gallatin's trademark combination of learning and amiability got him elected to represent Fayette County at an Antifederalist convention held at Harrisburg, Pennsylvania, in 1788. Yet his thinking about national government was already developing quickly.

It developed partly in a state of grief. In 1789, he married Sophie Allegre, and in 1790, only five months into their marriage, she died. Mourning, needing something constructive to do, he was elected as a Fayette County delegate to the convention for changing the Pennsylvania constitution—the convention held in the courtroom at the State House, when Herman Husband was sitting right across the hall, in what was about to become the last assembly elected under the 1776 constitution. Gallatin opposed changing the constitution and argued against a number of James Wilson's measures. But he wasn't well-known enough to play an important role in the process and was impressed by what he experienced as a fair and rational process.

He found he enjoyed politics. Under the new constitution he'd opposed, he was elected to the lower house of the new, bicameral state assembly. The new upper house met across the hall in the courtroom; the new lower house met in that ground-floor assembly room, so often on loan in recent years, the scene of so much drama. Gallatin took his seat there early in 1790.

Alexander Hamilton was still in New York then, fighting to get his scheme adopted by Congress. In opposition to that effort, Gallatin began proposing to the Pennsylvania assembly a comprehensive approach to public finance at odds with Hamilton's. He was no longer hoping to undo the Constitution. He accepted the existing frame of national government. He also wanted to prevent the Hamilton Scheme from becoming a system.

That was a big ambition. Yet unlike fellow opposition members who made broad oratorical attacks on Hamilton, Gallatin had the technical knowledge to back up his criticism. Calvinist-influenced and personally thrifty, he shared the high agrarians' dislike of public debt, but he took a less absolutist approach than most. His opposition to federal taxes didn't inspire him to the bombastic State Sovereigntism of the James Jackson types. He was a pragmatist.

Like Hamilton, he'd been closely studying public finance theory and practice but had arrived at opposite conclusions.

Gallatin was coming to see the benefits of a unified American nation, but he also saw public debt as a drag on national growth. Taxes earmarked for long-term interest payments to a small group of government bondholders seemed to him to undermine representative, republican institutions and make government accountable to insiders, not voters. Expertise made Albert Gallatin not just another Hamilton opponent but the opposition's own Hamilton. The Anti-Hamilton.

In March 1791, when the federal banking bill and excise tax passed the U.S. Congress and the Hamilton Scheme became a system, Congress was sitting steps away from the Pennsylvania State House where Gallatin was serving in the assembly; Hamilton's treasury office was just blocks away. The federal excise, linchpin of the system, especially got Gallatin's attention. He had personal knowledge of the Neville Connection's sew-up operations around the Ohio headwaters. He could easily see the whiskey tax's deleterious effects on his own hard-pressed western constituents, the business end of the whole national system he'd been criticizing and was now hoping to undo. That summer, with the assembly in recess, Gallatin went home. General Neville had been appointed collector. Fury over the tax's heightening regional corruption and monopolization was brewing among ordinary people throughout the area. Gallatin hoped to engage sympathetically with the opposition.

But he also hoped to calm the tendency toward secessionist violence. He saw short-term possibilities for ameliorating the worst effects of the excise; he saw long-term possibilities for undoing Hamilton's system completely. Going to extremes now, throwing down against the federal government, bringing things to a climax: that would only reduce the chances for realistic improvements over time.

For he was also the Anti-Husband. A man of western Pennsylvania like Husband, Gallatin was unlike Husband in being immune to mystical revelations, ultimates, Apocalypses, Millennialisms. He prized liberty and reason. His differences with Hamilton had a moral dimension—he believed the national finance system fostered elements of tyranny—but they took political and, when it came to public finance, even technical form. His difference with Husband was political, technical, and existential all at once, in some ways just temperamental.

At one point, Gallatin made the differences explicit. Informed of the alternate national constitution that Husband had presented in the old assembly, with its references to Nebuchadnezzar and Ezekiel, he started referring to Husband as "the crazy man of Bedford." The Genevan rationalist was out to make the western situation precisely *less* biblical.

To that end, in July 1791, he attended a meeting at a tavern in the town of Redstone Old Fort, on the southeastern bank of the Monongahela River, not far upstream from Pittsburgh. Certain regionally prominent men—somewhat well-off men, that is—wanted to discuss moderate options for managing what they feared might turn into a regional crisis. Some of the attendees followed the Madison-Jefferson ideology for limiting federal power. Some had old personal and professional beefs with Neville and the Neville Connection. Most, hoping to end the ongoing new-state and secessionist talk, feared that if people reacted violently to the excise, an already tense sectional situation would worsen, maybe to the point of true disaster: military suppression by government.

Alternatives to violence must be found. That was the thrust at

Redstone Old Fort. Given his official role as a member of the assembly, Gallatin served as the meeting's clerk.

William Findley was there too. No longer in the state assembly, he'd recently been elected to the U.S. House of Representatives, taking his seat the day after the president signed the whiskey excise into law. Aligned, like Gallatin, with the emerging Madison-Jefferson party calling itself Republican, highly sympathetic to his poor western constituency, a promoter of deliberative political opposition, Findley intended go hard against the tax in the House while staying away from the rowdy direct action that was starting to trouble his region.

Findley, Gallatin, and the other Redstone Old Fort moderates had a better idea than violent protest. As ratified in 1789, the First Amendment to the U.S. Constitution protected a right to petition the federal government for redress of grievances. The meeting decided to call for delegated county meetings to develop a regional petition from the people of General Neville's survey to the Treasury and Congress. The petition would point out inequities in the excise law and ask for nothing extreme, not the repeal of the law, not even the replacement of General Neville, just some compromise, some fair revisions. This would show the westerners contemplating violence that petitioning was more effective than riot and show Congress and Secretary Hamilton that popular resistance might be avoided by accommodating objections.

In other words: reason. In that spirit, Albert Gallatin, Anti-Hamilton and Anti-Husband, signed the Redstone Old Fort resolutions. He had no idea how risky putting his name to such documents would turn out to be.

19

ENEMIES EVERYWHERE

HAMILTON WAS BUSY THAT summer bringing the triumph of his system to its highest purpose, and things were moving fast. Tench Coxe's agents in British factory towns were stealing secrets and luring managers for the American industrial town to be built on the Passaic. William Duer, pitching investors on providing the cash to make the town a going thing, had identified a set of New York finance men eager to get in on the project's ground floor. Right after the bank scrip sellout in July, Hamilton traveled to New York to help Duer hawk stock in a startup: the Society for Establishing Useful Manufactures, or SUM, which would own and operate the new town. Hamilton had set the company's initial capitalization at $500,000, with another $500,000 to be raised later. Such was Duer's juice that they sold $600,000—an oversell like the bank's—in advance of having a corporate charter, a director, or even a board.

Having gotten the company so quickly financed, Duer personally entered the booming market for stock in the Bank of the United States. The excitement generated on the Fourth of July at Carpenters' Hall in Philadelphia hadn't abated. With the oversubscription, the only way to get the scrip was to buy it from those who had it, and Philadelphia had become the center of wild trading action, with New York and other cities scenes of frantic transaction too, sending the scrip's market value on a quick trip upward. With thousands of dollars said to change hands in a single morning, tens of thousands gained by a single speculator in a month, the rush was spreading beyond the usual investing class. Anyone with collateral was looking to borrow, even at high interest rates, to buy scrip. People with few resources sold furniture, tools, whatever they had just to scrounge what cash they could and buy in. In cities up and down the seaboard, offices and artisan shops alike closed up, and ordinary business came to a halt. Everybody who could seemed to be spending all their time seeking and trading shares.

The bank's long-term profitability wasn't driving this rush. The institution wasn't even yet up and running. Shareholder dividends might be expected to yield about 8 percent—very good, but by no means justifying buying stock at such inflated prices. It was the rising price itself, not the institution's future performance, that made the secondary market, and the rise wasn't only in bank scrip. Federal bonds were accepted for buying scrip; that sent their value shooting up too. New buyers for federal bonds had also emerged among professional European investors—a potentially huge opportunity for U.S. bondsellers.

So when the mighty Duer entered this already soaring market, his characteristic flamboyance in buying both scrip and bonds in astonishing amounts, at high prices, with money borrowed at staggering rates, pumped big blasts of air into an already expanding system. Hamilton was relying on Duer's reputation to hype investment in the factory town, and investors were relying on Duer's track record in buying stock. By mid-August, federal bonds were reaching near face value for the first time since the early days of the war. Bank scrip issued at $25 on July Fourth was selling for more than $300.

Hamilton could see that all this was happening too fast and going too far. His excitable colleague was having a dangerous impact on the whole market for scrip and bonds. This wasn't a boom but a bubble. Any disturbance might shock buyer or lender confidence and start a massive sell-off, bursting the bubble. Then everything would fall: investors, lenders, speculators, the value of federal securities, the bank. To Hamilton, that meant crashing the federal government itself.

He knew the only way to prevent value from suddenly falling far too low and dragging everything else down with it was to slow the rise. On the other hand, any assertive intervention in the market by the Treasury Department might seem to justify the growing criticism—to Hamilton, the ceaseless carping—leveled by Madison and Jefferson against his system. Madison called the stock craze nothing but "a scramble for so much public plunder." "The spirit of gaming," Jefferson lamented, "when once it has seized a subject, is incurable. The tailor who has made thousands in one day, though he has lost them the next, can never again be content with the slow and moderate earnings of his needle." Hamilton had to show political opponents, investors, and the public that his system, though now painfully overheated, had the power to self-regulate, with some mild guidance.

His first step was to publish an article in the Federalist paper the *Gazette of the United States*. He calmly explained that fanatically buying bank scrip would only hurt both individual investors and national credit in the end. The European market was already turning away from U.S. bonds because the price had gone too high. Seeking reasonable profits over time, not astounding fortunes overnight: that was the wisest course.

On the private side, he had to get Duer to cool it. He wrote to warn his partner in SUM in strong terms that the bubble had gotten dangerous, that Duer would be blamed for a crash. Duer wrote back at length, protesting his integrity, hurt feelings, and reliance on Hamilton's trust; meanwhile he redoubled his betting. Hamilton wrote again, this time more personally, even affectionately. But it was too late for Duer to change his personality.

And it was too late to let air out slowly. With no centralizing regulation, the cities' financial markets operated independently. Information lags caused confusion, strangeness. Even while Hamilton was publishing his article and writing to Duer, the market was already turning down, way too fast, because some lenders, especially at the state banks, had woken up and stopped lending for the purpose of buying national bank stock. Loans' drying up overnight triggered a broad desire to sell, but so few people could get money to buy that sale prices began diving to the level dictated by an abruptly cash-strapped market.

On August 15, contacts in New York and Boston were writing to Hamilton to report a sell-off of both bank scrip and federal bonds, with prices crashing. The next day, Philadelphia felt the effects, and it went from there. With so many who had bought too far in now wanting to get all the way out, prices might fall right through the floor. The system was overcorrecting to the point of disaster.

Hamilton decided he had no choice. As treasury secretary, he intervened, launching the full faith and credit of the federal government, never yet tested, into the market.

He wanted to shore up federal bonds: if that worked, bank scrip should stabilize too. The U.S. Treasury, rational speculator of last resort, made a series of bond purchases, ultimately worth between $300,000 and $400,000, via Hamilton's highly favored Bank of New York, where the federal government had deposits. The idea was to make these purchases openly yet quietly: the investing class was to know that a federal program for stabilizing markets was under way; any sense that the government was controlling the market was to be kept muted. To pay for the bonds, Hamilton used the proceeds of the sinking fund that he'd established for paying down the Debt's principal. Just as the agrarians Jackson and Maclay had grimly predicted, the sinking fund was raided in an emergency, but after making the purchases, the fund held a lot of new federal bonds; because the bailout worked, the fund's overall value remained stable. To the Jackson and Maclay type, that was nothing but numerology and black magic, and Madison and Jefferson agreed: a government bailout gave evidence, just in itself, of the rottenness of the system.

As far as Hamilton was concerned, he'd fairly easily swept his system upward to safety before it hit bottom. Speculators got a scare, intense yet short-lived, and there was no crash. A few people went broke—not Duer; he seemed immortal—but the panic quickly subsided, lenders resumed lending, and investors had reason to think that if things got too far out of hand again, Hamilton would step in again. By September, both the bonds' price and the price of bank scrip, having fallen so far and fast, would be back on the rise.

His main push remained: get the model factory town going. Throughout August, even as things were crashing, the secretary stayed focused on SUM, seeking a new round of investors and making public a business prospectus that he and Duer had used privately in the first round. As secretary of the treasury, he kept his name off the prospectus, but he had plans to interconnect SUM's financing, quietly, with both federal bonds and the Bank of the United States. He was also looking for the thing an endeavor like this always needed: monopoly power created by government, making the company a corporation via a state charter.

He had a realistic hope of getting the New Jersey assembly to do that. But now, even as he moved SUM into its next phase, his system sprang another kind of leak. This one needed a different kind of attention.

In September, news arrived from the West. The background was still coming into view for Hamilton, but it was clear that in Pennsylvania's western counties, violent resistance to the whiskey excise was under way.

The view on the ground was clearer. Albert Gallatin, William Findley, and other moderates at the Redstone Old Fort meeting had called for a series of further meetings, delegated, via elections in each county, to advance the writing of a regionally unified petition asking for relief from some particulars of the excise law. One of those meetings, held in August in the small village of Washington, the seat of Washington County, departed sharply from what the moderates had proposed. The men who attended weren't interested in petitioning the government. Herman Husband didn't attend—he lived in Bedford County, for one thing—but his ideas were all over the result.

The meeting was dominated by Hamiltons. The treasury secretary didn't know it yet, but he had a namesake family living in the remote, rugged, steep county, which, though named after George Washington, had become a major site of the Democracy's frustration with the results of the Revolution, frustration that had only grown since 1784, when Washington himself came to evict the Millers Run farmers. Suffering people living around Mingo Creek, not far from a village also named for Washington, and not far from Millers Run, had gotten especially well organized. In a notably tough area, Mingo Creek people were the toughest, and the Hamilton family of Mingo Creek was known for strong leadership.

The most prominent man at the meeting was John Hamilton, forty, a veteran of the War of Independence and the commander of a state militia regiment. He'd had success as a self-made farmer, distiller, and small businessman; many there could no longer expect to achieve that kind of modest prosperity. More typical of the attendees was John's relative Daniel Hamilton, also forty, also with combat experience in the war, with a strong sense of his physical power to intimidate. He'd once owned 240 acres. Soon he'd own only 100. Both he and John could predict how things were going, and they were right. In a few years, all of Daniel's land would be gone.

Another leader on the Mingo Creek scene was Benjamin Parkinson: tall, red-haired, a former justice of the peace both passionate and influential, who still farmed his own land. Then there was David Bradford. He was a fish out of water at the Washington County meeting for being a prominent lawyer with the fanciest house in the village. But he'd always wanted popularity among his poorer neighbors and was eager, even panting, to support their resistant position.

Others attended the meeting too—but most wouldn't be remembered by name. They were tenants and landless day laborers, hoping to end at long last the sewing-up of commerce and resources, going on for years in the region and now accelerating to climactic intolerability thanks to Alexander Hamilton's new national policies.

In that spirit, the Washington County meeting didn't produce a petition. It produced a set of resolutions, addressed not to the federal government but to all the people of western Pennsylvania and putting Herman Husband's ideas about resistance in succinct and practical language. The meeting explicitly attacked not just the excise but Secretary Hamilton's whole system. Husband's fingerprints might be seen especially clearly in the meeting's avoiding the traditional anti-tax oratory of agrarian elites. The resolutions didn't condemn taxation overall or federal taxes or promote the states' right to tax. Instead, they criticized the whiskey tax specifically for being "not in proportion to property." They called instead for a tax on land, with progressive rates: local land monopolizers should pay more. They called for organizing all the people of the Neville survey, identifying eastern hirelings and giving them no quarter, shunning and otherwise making life difficult for anyone who collaborated with or even tolerated government.

Hence General Neville's dramatic report to the treasury office. One of the deputy tax collectors, riding at night on a lonely track in the woods, had been waylaid by a group of about fifteen local men, faces blackened, carrying muskets, rifles, and clubs; some wore women's clothes. They stripped the collector, tarred and feathered him, took his horse, and left him to find his way home. He did get home, and he swore out a complaint naming the attackers he'd recognized, who included the prominent local Hamilton, John, and the increasingly landless Daniel. The Mingo Creek radicals were already carrying out the Washington County resolutions, which they'd written, for how to treat anyone who signed up to betray the region on behalf of the whiskey tax.

To the Hamilton in Philadelphia, this news was by no means unexpected. General Neville had already reported both the moderate Redstone Old Fort meeting and the radical Washington County meeting, whose resolutions were now taking effect, giving names of attendees of both; the department was maintaining a file. News of the attack had been brought to Philadelphia by the victim himself, who now gave a deposition. Resistance to the tax was pretty much what Hamilton had been expecting. He was confident that he had the means for dealing with it.

He had a lot of enemies. Among them, it now seemed, were people named Hamilton, operating in the West with their friends in defiance of his system. Others were the prominent Republican party leaders Madison and Jefferson, operating in government in Philadelphia, and their followers in the federal and state governments and the increasingly vicious Republican press. One was William Findley, the old western Pennsylvania opponent of Robert Morris, now serving in the House and aligned with the Jeffersonian opposition, and it was known that Findley had attended a meeting at Redstone Old Fort objecting to the excise tax. So had Albert Gallatin, the western Pennsylvanian Jeffersonian who spoke in the Pennsylvania assembly against Hamilton's system. The secretary was trying to get a sense of connections prevailing among any and all of these people.

SUM was meanwhile moving fast. Hamilton gave the prospectus to New Jersey's governor, William Paterson, and the governor took it straight to his state's legislature and proposed the special legislation that would make the company a corporation, with a perpetual monopoly on controlling water power below the Passaic Falls and tax-exempt status for a prescribed period. Hamilton was invited to the assembly to pitch the project. Some members had already bought stock in SUM; the governor was made a stockholder too. An act to incorporate the company sailed through the body. SUM named the town Paterson, New Jersey, after the governor.

Hamilton further extended his official position unofficially on SUM's behalf. For a new financing round, he connected the board to the board of the Bank of New York, privately promising the state bank's directors that if they extended loans to SUM on favorable terms, as treasury secretary he would ensure that the bank continued to serve as a depository of federal money. By rolling the Bank of the United States, the Bank of New York, and the U.S. Treasury into a unified force behind SUM's monopoly, he meant, as with the factory town itself, to build a model for American public-private efforts.

Things got exciting. The stockholders elected William Duer executive director. Paterson wasn't to be some one-factory town but a complex of interrelated industries, with purpose-built worker housing, more like a factory city, ultimately making everything from textiles to shoes to pottery to ribbons to iron and more. Hamilton had put in the prospectus that building the machines would require aggressive violations of protective British laws—a policy President Washington endorsed, at least tacitly. Men had been snuck out of Britain to serve as mill managers at Paterson; one housed at Treasury Department expense claimed to have not just committed to memory the Arkwright water-powered weaving machine's specs but actually improved them.

SUM also hired Pierre L'Enfant, an ambitious immigrant from France who had served during the war with Hamilton on Washington's staff; lately, he'd been working with Washington on an advanced design for federal city in the Potomac swamps. As master engineer and architect for Paterson, L'Enfant planned a complicated canal system for powering newfangled machines in three initial factories: a cotton carding mill, a print shop, and a spinning-and-weaving facility.

And yet the city, even when fully built, would be only a one-off, high-fidelity prototype—impressive, but needing widespread replication. To get industrialization realized throughout the country, the ultimate purpose of the finance system, Hamilton had to get Congress to legislate a full-scale national industrial policy.

He was ready for that. Back in 1789, the House had asked, along with the report on public credit, for a report on making the United States no longer dependent on other nations for military supplies. Hamilton had taken that request as a brief for proposing a comprehensive national industrial plan. He'd waited to introduce it until his financial system was in place.

Now, in December 1791, he presented Congress with his second grand report. Capstone to his entire legislative agenda, like the first report it was less a report than an instruction manual, including draft legislation, whose passage was to be the crowning glory, the nation-making triumph, of the Hamilton Scheme.

20

TOO BIG TO FAIL

HAMILTON'S SECOND GRAND REPORT never got anywhere.

The plan was not only characteristically ambitious but also looked novel. As with the report on public credit, the secretary was by no means merely informing Congress of conditions. For the nation to evolve into an empire like Britain's, he was asking the body to take a direct, legislative role in managing not just its own finances this time, but private commerce too, really the entire American economy, with him at the apex of decision-making. He proposed giving special privileges to certain American businesses in early stages. He wanted to encourage domestic manufacturing through protective tariffs on foreign goods, thus driving up the price of imports, with revenues earmarked for giving federal subsidies to select American industries and awarding federal premiums to successful businesses. He wanted to pursue publicly what Tench Coxe had been pursuing privately, for SUM: copping designs for the machinery driving the factory revolution in Britain. He wanted federal support for interstate physical infrastructure.

When the report was submitted, in November 1791, the plan looked too hot to handle, and debate in the House was postponed. In fact, the tariff aspect was nothing novel. When the U.S. Congress passed the federal impost in 1789, it was already a tariff: along with the 5 percent on all imports, certain products were called out for special duties in order to protect certain U.S. industries. The rest of the report, though, was startling, and unlike the finance plan, it didn't speak to a powerfully organized lobby's self-interest or respond to a national crisis.

As 1792 began, the House continued to postpone debate. Privately, Madison and Jefferson were raising what by now were the usual constitutional issues: Hamilton's plan, they said, amounted to centrally planning the nation's economy, even its infrastructure, across state lines; the Constitution didn't empower Congress to do anything like it. Soon, however, it became clear that postponement of debate might be indefinite. National manufacturing wouldn't be attacked but left to die.

To Hamilton, this refusal by Congress to advance his finance system to its ultimate national purpose did represent an attack—yet another attack carried out against his system by a growing numbers of enemies. And even as he suffered this failure, the first of his career, another glitch in his system demanded immediate attention yet again. Duer was at the center of another financial crisis. It was as if the moneyman would never learn.

The speculation buzz had by now become a mass addiction rocking the seaport cities. The Northwest Territory's opening to white settlement, supposedly now to be secured by federal military action, inspired a multitude of startup canal and toll-road companies. Like SUM, they were chartered as corporations by owners' friends in state legislatures—Philip Schuyler started two—and financed by offering shares to the public, and the public was pouncing on the shares. As with the bank, this craze was democratized. People hoped for passive income from dividends, naturally, but the companies were oversubscribed so quickly that they had to turn people away by the thousands, so even greater excitement was generated by gambling on the shares' rising price in a hot market enabled by too-easy borrowing. While few of the schemes for canals, roads, and bridges were likely to turn out winners or even survive, and while founders, stock buyers, and lenders were running on high-grade optimism, even manifestly doomed companies might create overnight fortunes for those who sold out at the right time. Knots of people on street corners opined freely about various companies' stock, and about 3 percent bonds, the 6 percents

TOO BIG TO FAIL 281

and deferred sixes, and the bank scrip, and the mood was just as fervent at more elegant levels of the investing community. Hence in part Duer's easy sale of first-round SUM shares.

Early in 1792, Duer formed a company of his own. This wasn't a transportation company—not that he hadn't invested in some of those too. To a fascinated fan base, his enterprises' sheer proliferation lent him superhuman qualities. He'd registered a company in Paris to sell deeds to land down the Ohio River, which the company didn't entirely own, to émigrés to the United States. A lot of French families ended up stranded in the far woodland, vulnerable to Shawnee attack; some had to rebuy their land just to stay, while others fled east, but Duer made money. He was also making progress in his effort to buy from the French government as much of the U.S. obligation to France as he could, meanwhile trying to get hold of more of the scrip of the Bank of the United States, plus a lot of the stock of the Bank of New York, and while he took loans from both of those banks to buy their stocks, he was also shorting Bank of New York stock—betting against its rise—while telling a partner he had inside information that it would go up.

When Henry Knox put him in charge of military supply for the ramp-up of the war of conquest into the Northwest Territory, Duer diverted a congressional appropriation, advanced to him by the treasury and intended for supplying troops, into personal purchases of a lot of federal bonds and bank scrip for both himself and Knox. They expected to pay the money back out of their profits, but Duer did almost nothing about supply. Knox became anxious and then desperate, the issue troubled Washington's cabinet, and troops were left vulnerable, but Duer rolled on, the most successful financier who ever lived, as far as the public was concerned.

His new enterprise, which he called the Six Percent Club, promised to double investments in six months. The idea was to get his hands on literally all of the best of the federal bonds, those paying 6 percent immediate interest, and sell them in bulk at huge profit margins to European investors. State banks and individual backers were eager to extend high-interest loans to that end, and when his buy-up of bonds and the banks' stock sent prices of every type of security shooting up, Duer kept buying at the rising prices, sending prices further up. Having made legal contracts to buy, he went on borrowing, at whatever rate banks and other lenders were charging. People were so eager to lend that they started pressing small amounts on him in the shops and on the streets of New York. He needed the money, so he took the loans. It didn't seem to occur to anyone that if he needed money so badly, they shouldn't lend it. Even the "noted bawd, Mrs. McCarty" was lending to Duer, reports had it, and why not? Interest on loans in some cases was heading toward 1 percent per day.

And somewhere in there—nobody could ever say exactly where—he stopped making any sense at all.

Hamilton was flatly disgusted. Thanks, yet again, to William Duer, the bubble hadn't just revived but was expanding even more quickly and painfully than before, threatening the market for both commercial stocks and government bonds, and the danger was greater this time. Experienced European investors would easily foresee the inevitable crash. Far from paying premiums to buy Duer's 6 percent bonds, they'd await utter deflation and snap up American debt at rock-bottom prices. Hamilton would be blamed for the crash.

Blamed not only by the usual critics Madison and Jefferson and their developing party but also by the class that had supported the Hamilton Scheme and was critical to the system's success: investors in the Federal Debt, whose wealth would be wiped out overnight by a crash that, in the shortsightedness of their greed, many of them were even now bringing about. In March 1792, with his industrialization plan languishing in the House, Hamilton saw his finance system begin falling too.

In New York City, certain investors had noticed an opportunity in Duer's madness. It was the smallest of worlds; they and Duer had known one another for years, and now they formed a group to take him down. Easily leveraging their mark's insatiability, they offered to sell him stock in both the Bank of the United States and the Bank of New York, as well as federal bonds. So delighted was Duer to buy that he somehow contracted to buy more stock in the Bank of New York than its total capitalization.

What he didn't know: his rivals had meanwhile gotten their hands on most of the gold and silver, the hard money, in the state of New York. Now they withdrew that money, all at once, from the state banks where they'd been keeping it. Almost overnight, the banks couldn't cash their own notes or anyone else's. They certainly couldn't make new loans; just to get money, they had to start calling in existing loans. Duer found himself drowning in stocks and bonds he'd legally contracted to buy at wildly inflated prices, drowning in revolving interest payments he'd agreed to pay creditors, drowning in loans called in. Gasping, he made protestations of high confidence, but he had no realistic hope of saving himself, and the market, having followed him upward, was going down with him.

Hamilton would never publicly admit that this time, his great creation was threatened with utter ruin. To regain and maintain stability required a massive calming effort, and that required a massive public denial of how bad things were, but he knew that, far worse than in '91, here was a banking failure, a depositor and investor panic, and a market crash all in one. It wasn't bound to destroy only one man, his lamentably overoptimistic old friend William Duer, though it was bound to do that. The Bank of the United States, the Bank of New York, the other state banks, and the American economy as a whole were under threat of immediate collapse.

So again he intervened, this time not just decisively and adroitly but with aggressive creativity, seeking outright overkill. Time pressure was intense. Communications hadn't caught up with the scale and speed of the approach to finance that Duer was pioneering; the crisis was becoming day-to-day, even minute-to-minute. To order a new round of bond purchases for the sinking fund, and this time to buy above the diving market rate, Hamilton needed the approval of the rest of the fund's board, but it was a Sunday, so he went ahead anyway and then asked for retroactive approval. He got it, more or less tacitly, but he wanted approval for making further purchases, and that caused a political snarl just when Hamilton needed speed.

Thomas Jefferson, the cabinet member most at odds with Hamilton, served on the board, as did Edmund Randolph, whom Hamilton had come to see as a Jefferson puppet, though Jefferson saw Randolph as a straddler; Vice President John Adams was on the board too. Jefferson and Randolph, withholding approval, were there in Philadelphia; Adams, in Philadelphia too, sent over his approval in writing, but the other member, John Jay, a Hamilton ally and the Supreme Court's chief justice, was in New York on the circuit and hard to reach. As board approval to buy bonds became a Federalist versus Republican standoff, the clock on the whole economy was ticking. To Jefferson, a crash would bear out everything he'd been saying about Hamilton's system. He and Randolph ran the clock, insisting on waiting for Jay's opinion regarding some abstruse terminology in the sinking-fund authorization. Days later, still waiting for Jay, Randolph fulfilled Jefferson's view of him by changing his vote. Hamilton went ahead with the purchases, but it was under Jefferson's protest.

Hamilton didn't stop coming up with ideas. He persuaded an otherwise reluctant Bank of New York to calm the public by agreeing to continue to lend, if at a high rate of interest: in the unlikely event that the bank ended up in trouble, Hamilton promised, the U.S. Treasury would make it at least partially whole. He used the federal customs service to suck nourishing coin into an arid system: the Treasury Department ordered customs officials to make duties from importers payable in forty-five days, considerably shortening the normal revenue schedule. And he made an announcement of good cheer. There was no call for panic, he said. The Netherlands had just extended major credit to the United States. The banks were still open. The treasury was solvent. Especially important: federal taxes were being collected.

Part of that was true. Port duties were coming in—now faster than usual—and eastern distillers were paying the whiskey excise. But just when reliable revenue was needed, the excise had become nearly impossible to collect in the West—not just in western Pennsylvania but everywhere across the Appalachians. The western parts of Pennsylvania, Maryland, Virginia, and North Carolina seemed to be getting unified in using physical force to obstruct execution of the law. In Kentucky, newly made a state, the tax system couldn't get going at all. The treasury office had reports, again from General Neville's survey, of new incidents of violence against deputies. Hamilton had sworn in 1791 that the new federal government, unlike the states and the old Congress, would have the power to require tax payment. Now, when his system needed all possible income and credibility, he wasn't succeeding.

Not all of the anti-excise protest was violent. The office had also received petitions from western moderates objecting to aspects of the tax and asking for revisions; some newspaper articles were taking the same position. To Hamilton, however, these efforts had potentially a more deleterious effect than physical attacks. They might persuade the public and members of Congress to loosen the excise. In the midst of his busiest and most aggressive efforts to save his overall system from collapse, he had to turn some of his ferociously geared-up attention to taking on the western moderates' anti-excise petitions and articles.

In a new report to the House, he laid the foundation for tightening the rules and cracking down on violent uprisers and peaceful petitioners alike. He cast every kind of excise complaint as outright defiance. He dismissed allegations that the tax placed special burdens on the West. He cited his own study of the economic conditions of the country, ruling out reports by poor people—they were biased, he said, by inveterate grievance—to show that even with the current hit to the financial system, the situation in upscale commercial sectors could be described as booming. Exports were way up, with more and more U.S.-flagged ships at sea loaded with American grain and other raw materials. Wheat prices were up too. Land values stayed on the rise. The West might be a veritable paradise, he insisted, if aggrieved locals weren't dead set against his system. Anyway, an excise, he reminded the House, is just a pass-along. If westerners felt they had to convert grain, a non-taxed article, into a taxable one, whiskey, in order to sell it, then westerners were complaining about paying for their own drinking, and if people in the West drank more whiskey than others, maybe they should cut down.

He also doubted any scarcity of hard money in the West, but—here was the crucial point—since scarcity of money might be invoked in objecting to any tax, the real reason for invoking it couldn't be to ask for redress. Clearly the purpose of petitions and articles criticizing the excise, Hamilton told Congress, was to bring about the dissolution of the federal government.

That became his line on all objections to the tax. If Albert Gallatin, William Findley, and the other Redstone Old Fort moderates were relying on the constitutional protections that distinguished legal petitioning from illegal acts of violence, Hamilton wasn't buying it. The Redstone Old Fort meeting called for county meetings to write petitions; the Washington County meeting wrote resolutions inspiring violence. He saw in both cases a justification for asserting the sovereignty and power of the U.S. government and stifling his system's enemies everywhere: his namesakes in far-off Mingo Creek and his political opponents here in Philadelphia.

Meanwhile, thanks to the ongoing financial crisis, he'd begun personally directing all operations of high finance in the United States. He reached out to the Bank of New York, the other state banks, and the Bank of the United States and asked them, first, not to call in their loans, and, second, to extend credit, both to one another and to hurting clients, as far as possible wherever it was needed. Even as private lenders independent of the federal government, he reminded them, banks were part of an all-important national system.

The other thing he had to do was put down William Duer. The treasury now sued the ruined man for repayment of $238,000—a discrepancy Duer had left on the books before leaving the department, though Hamilton had ignored it until now—and the federal district court in New York immediately pursued the matter. Duer wrote piteously to Hamilton to get him off the hook. Hamilton responded in tones of regretful affection, but he was saving a system, not the Hamilton-on-the-flip-side who had come so close to taking down that system. Duer, desperate to escape the wrath of a rowdy crowd of lower-level lenders and investors now, thanks to him, as broke as he was, fled to the jail in Manhattan and turned himself in. The people outside shouted, threw rocks at his cell window, and finally rioted in an attempt to haul him out and lynch him. The most successful American investor of his day would die in prison in 1799. Not present at the riot, yet hit at least as hard as the lower-rung players, were some big merchants and financiers who started taking another look at the Jeffersonians' criticism of Hamilton's system.

But the second bailout succeeded. While many players big and small went bust, the system itself didn't fail, because Hamilton, a fount of rapid invention, had come up with so many ways to prop it up.

That was the problem. He was fed up with having to draw on reserves of creative innovation just to make his system function. He was aghast at the absence of any realistic distinction between respectable stock dealers and imprudent gamblers with no principle but personal gain. He'd expected better judgment, at least, from the people whose rampant self-interest he would never have any choice but to encourage in the service of great American nationhood.

In May, however, the system at least looked stable, and Hamilton sent the House a revised whiskey excise bill. He did change the rules—exactly contrary to the petitioners' requests. Having taken suggestions from large-scale distillers and federal inspectors, the secretary announced through allies in the House, he'd determined that it was time to tighten things up. Deputies would no longer go to farms to register stills: a central excise office was to be opened in each county; distillers would do the traveling and register stills at the offices. Failure to do so would forfeit the still and incur a fine, now raised to $250; nonpayment of tax, too, was to be a lien on the still. Where the earlier law had exempted the smallest stills, those with under 40-gallon capacity, not from the tax but from registration, Hamilton removed the exemption. He did make one reform that, he told Congress, represented a concession to small distillers. They could buy a monthly license to distill, at 10 cents per gallon on the still's capacity; there was a concomitant prohibition against distilling beyond the licensing period. In debate, some members expressed satisfaction that this measure would make the tax easier to pay.

Not William Findley. He hadn't been in the House when the first excise bill was debated, but he was here now. In the Pennsylvania as-

sembly and the Pennsylvania ratifying convention, he'd been one of the
loudest voices against Hamilton's allies Morris and Wilson; recently, at
the Redstone Old Fort meeting, he'd sought ways to moderate his constituents' most extreme attitudes. Now the new member from the Ohio
headwaters rose in House debate and turned his Irish-accented, western-
artisan lawyerliness directly on Hamilton and the tightened excise bill.
Unlike many of his colleagues, Findley could see that Hamilton's single
supposed concession to small distillers would do nothing to encourage
competition. The revised bill only made compliance more difficult for
poorer farmers and penalties for noncompliance harsher. He argued for
lowering the amount of the tax. He got a one-cent reduction.

That was by no means enough, he was sure, to induce his constituents to step down their resistance, but he was more persuasive regarding
another feature of the tax. In the minds of his constituents, Findley explained to the House, the original law's most egregious provision was the
prosecution of alleged violators in federal court in Philadelphia, over the
mountains, many days' hard journey away from home. Ordinary people
believed that one of the oldest liberties, relied on by rich and poor alike,
was trial by a jury of one's peers, which meant trial in one's region. Officials' carrying an alleged offender away to be indicted and tried in a
strange place left a farm and business unattended, caused unnecessary
family hardship, and inflicted punishment in advance of a judgment.

A House majority took Findley's point. The members passed a provision enabling federal courts to travel and sit in the regions where excise offenders were summoned. Issues already in the federal court docket
couldn't be changed, and there were administrative matters for the attorney general to cope with; the liberalized trial provision wouldn't take
effect before the June 1794 docket. But it represented a notable victory for
Findley, who further distinguished himself by objecting to allies' reading
Hamilton's rationales into the record. Rising again and again to declare
the practice out of order, he insisted that only members of the House and
those with local knowledge should be providing information. Reports
from what he condemned as the secretary's closet—the term recalled

secret decision-making by kings—were based on opinions of unelected bureaucrats and highly interested parties such as General Neville and represented an executive-branch intrusion on the House, a violation of the separation of powers.

A majority agreed with him on that one too. Reading Hamilton's explanations was banned. A working-class leader of the western Democracy thus endeared himself to the upscale Jeffersonians becoming known as Republicans, and while Hamilton got most of his tightened-up excise measures passed, he also took note of Findley's combining a now-familiar Jeffersonian hyper-constitutionalism with a hard-nosed western approach to operations, economic conditions, points of law. Then there was the westerner Albert Gallatin, speaking against the financial system over in the Pennsylvania assembly: the Republican opposition would soon be looking to run him for the U.S. Senate. Both Findley and Gallatin, Hamilton knew, had attended anti-excise meetings.

Other projects meanwhile were fizzling. SUM had the immediate problem of its director Duer's being in jail; soon it turned out that the director had embezzled the company nearly dry. The architect and engineer L'Enfant, a perfectionist artiste, having expanded his role to controlling the whole design of the town, made resource-draining demands and yet took a lot of time off. Some of the British factory experts, brought over at great expense, turned out to be pretty shady too. The company would take years to go under all the way, but everybody lost their money. The city meant to model American industry became just another memory of a failed startup in a startup boom, a short-term thrill of investor greed heading for a fall.

Hamilton's manufacturing report, too, stopped languishing in the House and died. Congress imposed some of the tariffs as a kind of one-off legislation, but the bounties and subsidies—critical to the plan, more important to Hamilton than tariffs—weren't seriously debated. Republicans defined the right to give bounties to companies as sacred to the states, and Madison presumed any federal manufacturing scheme would involve the kind of cronyism he'd identified in SUM, but he never even got to mount his critique, because the House refused to treat the report as a comprehensive plan.

Hamilton found himself under personal attack too. Only five years earlier, the Democracy's advance had inspired leaders from across the spectrum to protect the pursuit of wealth, and for all of their disagreements, delegates in Philadelphia found common cause enough to form a national government, but now, with legislative adoption of the Hamilton Scheme that the Constitution was manifestly designed to enable, the original division between Continentalists and State Sovereigntists had flared so angrily that, as the Federalist and Republican parties, they'd gotten enmeshed in an escalating rhetorical conflict over the legitimacy not just of Hamilton's system but of one another's existence. Disagreements over what might seem matters of policy—virtues and drawbacks of national banking and taxes, proper degrees of national-government activism—had become a fight over the essential purposes and values of the United States of America. With the survival of the nation supposedly at stake, any compromise looked like capitulation. All was fair.

So a move was on by the Madison faction in Congress, with the backroom support of Jefferson in the administration, to conduct an investigation of the treasury that would remove Hamilton from office for misconduct or, more likely and just as good, destroy his reputation in the process of failing to prove anything. They saw hope in some treasury irregularities that Madison's and Jefferson's Virginia colleague James Monroe, a young member of the Senate, had turned up. In the end the irregularities were only that. There was no corruption; the books balanced. What had aroused Monroe's attention turned out to be a private payoff to a blackmailing husband of a woman Hamilton was having an affair with, and just to quell unfair suspicions of his public conduct Hamilton was forced to suffer the private indignity of confessing the affair to his enemy Monroe, and thus, via Monroe, to his higher-up enemies Jefferson and Madison. Now they had that to hold over him.

It had been a short, hard ride from the triumph of passing the Hamilton Scheme and opening the bank to the grind of defending his system from attack by political opponents and the unenlightened self-interest of his own kind while defending himself from false accusation. But Congress had passed the more restrictive excise bill, and Washington had signed it into law. Hamilton would bring the western situation "to," as he put it, "an issue."

21

UPRISING, CRACKDOWN

IN 1792, THOMAS PAINE was getting more and more excited about advancing to global scale the radically democratic institutions he'd put on paper in "Common Sense" and seen put into practice in the 1776 Pennsylvania constitution. By now he'd been out of the United States for five years. Europe, where he lived, was undergoing a rapidly accelerating conflict over what Paine saw as the emancipation of labor and all of humankind. The old forces of oppression were to be overcome by a new birth of freedom. Liberty for all would be fostered by a universal right of citizenship, supported, in Paine's developing thinking, by the kind of national government administration that would later be called a welfare state. Though he opposed merchant-crony Continentalism, he thought big projects and big markets would bring widespread benefits to ordinary people. He'd challenged some of the most basic precepts of the Democracy, whose aims he still pursued, when arguing that the paper currency favored by working people undermined their cash flow, and when identifying national advantages in a public debt. Even when unpaid by Robert Morris, he'd criticized the democratic Pennsylvania assembly's withdrawing the charter for Morris's bank: to Paine, the poor were, if anything, underbanked. He'd even come to think Pennsylvania's government did need an upper house. But he still saw the American explosion of 1776 as the first in a chain of radically democratic explosions everywhere.

He'd also spent the late '80s having models built from his design for an iron bridge. Stymied in his plan to span the Harlem River, and then in a plan to span the Schuylkill, he'd seen a chance of raising enough money in England to build a bridge prototype there; hence his return to Europe in 1787. He expected to be back in the United States in a few months, but soon he was channel-hopping between France and England, where political matters were starting to come to a head, both for him and for the regimes. The action seemed to be in the Old World.

In Paris in 1788, he spent time with Jefferson, then serving as the Congress's minister to France. The federal government wasn't yet established, so the American divisions that would emerge in the 1790s weren't set. Both Jefferson and Paine supported the idea of a national constitution for the United States, and Jefferson, a fellow inventor, was impressed by Paine's bridge design. In London later that same year, Paine became a man-about-radical-town. Revered for his role in the American Revolution, in his fifties now, he advised the workers who were building a revolutionary labor movement via an organization that would become famous as the London Corresponding Society. He befriended a fellow self-taught working-class intellectual, young William Blake, an artisan printer and engraver and visionary poet and painter. He dined and talked politics, philosophy, and writing with Mary Wollstonecraft, the feminist, and William Godwin, the utilitarian-anarchist, who would soon be her husband. He met with Edmund Burke, a member of Parliament who had supported the American Revolution.

The explosion came in 1789. To the world's astonishment and Paine's joy, the public stormed the Paris state-prison citadel known as the Bastille, and King Louis XVI tacitly and unhappily began yielding to what would develop into a reform government and a constitutional monarchy. While members of the nobility and the upper bourgeoisie were its first major exponents, the French Revolution was soon linking constitutionally ordained degrees of political equality seen nowhere before—except, for a time, in Pennsylvania—to demolishing old presumptions about the origins and nature of authority. Glittering orders of arbitrary oppression that had prevailed for thousands of years seemed to be tumbling down.

To Paine, it all flowed from the glory days of the American Revolution. He wasn't the only one. When the Bastille fell, the Marquis de
Lafayette, who had served under Washington in the War of Independence, sent its key to Paine in London for delivery to the president of the
United States as a symbol of shared revolutionary purposes. Paine sent
his old friend not just the key but a celebratory note. "The principles of
America," Paine told Washington, "opened the Bastille."

Washington had at first been impressed by the French Revolution,
if worried about what direction it might take. By now, though, everything
he, Hamilton, and many others in the governing elite feared and loathed
about the American movement known as the Democracy seemed to be
sweeping through France with greater frenzy than it ever had in America,
and Paine's total immersion was already known to Washington. Gouverneur Morris, carrying out diplomatic missions abroad, and living it up
especially in Paris, had seen Paine in both London and Paris and told
Washington that the writer was "inflated to the eyes" with revolutionary schemes, probably "a little mad." In those meetings, Morris bluntly
advised Paine to back off, for his own good. Paine couldn't imagine such
advice coming indirectly from Washington. He just as bluntly called
Morris a reactionary and advised him not to exaggerate the violence in
France.

In 1790, at Lisson Green, northwest of London, Paine unveiled a
hundred-foot-long iron model of his bridge. He charged admission to see
it, and many people paid. At the same time, he, Wollstonecraft, and
Blake broke with Burke, who had decided that the French Revolution
was going way too far. Launching a powerful new political ethos—it was
to be called conservatism—Burke praised the American Revolution for
moderation on social and economic equality and lamented in outraged
detail the sufferings of Queen Marie Antoinette at the horrid moment,
which Burke made up, when the dirty-booted crowd penetrated the sanctity of her very bedchamber and plunged bayonets through the very bed
from which, nearly naked, the young queen had to flee. Burke later said
he wept whenever he reread that passage.

In an essay collection published in London in 1791, Paine took Burke on. The essays derided the conservative's prose, politics, personality; the collection's title, *Rights of Man*, was drawn from a declaration by the National Assembly, France's revolutionary government, then meeting to write a constitution. When Paine's essays, passionately defending revolutionary France as a world-changing shift in human consciousness, were taken up by British labor radicals, the scandalized British government did what it could to intimidate booksellers, but *Rights of Man* had strong sales; Part Two sold two hundred thousand copies in one year. The same year, Wollstonecraft's *A Vindication of the Rights of Woman* became the first statement of feminist radicalism published in Britain. Aaron Burr, a recently elected U.S. senator from New York, called it "a work of genius," but for the most part, outside Godwin-Paine circles, Wollstonecraft and her book were belittled and rebuked.

Both sales and scandal fed Paine's exultation. This was his time. The French revolutionary moment was turning hyper-democratic: not just anti-monarchy but anti-aristocracy, anti-entrenched-hierarchy of all kinds, with national citizenship making all people equal before the law. *Rights of Man* was exciting workers in the industrializing north of England, labor organizers in Scotland, and radical book groups throughout the British Isles, inspiring strikes and riots. British police were shadowing Paine. Cartoonists caricatured him as "Mad Tom." He was burned in effigy.

In the spring of 1791, *Rights of Man* was published in Philadelphia. And right there at the bookseller's, on a full page following the title page, blazed forth an honor that couldn't have been less welcome to its recipient. Paine had dedicated his defense of revolutionary France and attack on British government to his inspiration and comrade-in-arms, the president of the United States, George Washington.

This was a significant diplomatic embarrassment. Washington had been working overtime to maintain delicate relations with Britain, which was on the verge of war with France. In receptions and meetings with British diplomats in Philadelphia, U.S. officials started falling all over themselves disassociating Washington from Britain's public enemy number one and denouncing *Rights of Man*. Vice President John Adams put his hand on his chest and assured a British official, "I detest that book and its tendency from the bottom of my heart." He meant it.

Then the last straw. In late 1791, Washington received a large gift from Paine: *Rights of Man*, fifty copies. With them came a cover letter, in which, along with boasting about sales, Paine reminded Washington that the worldwide egalitarian revolution now beginning in France came straight out of what he called their shared ardor of 1776. By then, the book had become one of the hottest topics in the contest within the American governing elite. The Republican opposition, eager to cast the Federalists as pro-monarchy, had taken up the French revolutionary cause, despite the aristocratic modes that marked most of their lifestyles, demanding U.S. support for egalitarian France in any war with tyrannical Britain, denouncing Washington's neutrality policy as pro-British monarchism, and quoting *Rights of Man*: If that great exponent of the American revolutionary spirit Thomas Paine was backing France and attacking Britain, then any other position could only be a sellout of the American Revolution itself.

Washington took a long time to respond to Paine's gift, but in May 1792, around the time he signed Hamilton's tightened-up excise bill, he sent a belated thank-you note, deploying his command of remote, irreproachable courtesy to signal, between men who had known each other so long, a permanent, nonnegotiable brush-off:

Philadelphia, May 6, 1792

Dear Sir,

To my friends, and those who know my occupations, I am sure
no apology is necessary for keeping their letters so much longer
unanswered than my inclination would lead me to do. I shall therefore
offer no excuse for not having sooner acknowledged the receipt of
your letter of the 21st of July. My thanks, however, for the token of

your remembrance, in the fifty copies of the "Rights of Man" are offered with no less cordiality than they would have been had I answered your letter in the first moment of receiving it.

. . . Let it suffice, therefore, at this time to say that I rejoice in the information of your personal prosperity—and as no one can feel a greater interest in the happiness of mankind than I do, that it is the first wish of my heart that the enlightened policy of the present age may diffuse to all men those blessings to which they are entitled— and lay the foundation of happiness for future generations. With great esteem I am—Dear Sir, Your most Obedt. Servt.,

Go. Washington

P.S. Since writing the foregoing I have received your letter of the 13th of February with twelve copies of your new work which accompanied it—and for which you must accept my additional thanks.

Go. W——n

For during Washington's silence, it had occurred to Paine to send copies of volume two as well.

The author had meanwhile been courting serious danger. The month Washington wrote, Prime Minister William Pitt issued a proclamation against seditious writing, and the day it was issued, Paine was charged with seditious libel for *Rights of Man*. Yet his trial was postponed until December. The government didn't want to prosecute him; that might only trigger further unrest. He was being given time to get himself out of the country.

Paine didn't see it. That summer, as labor agitation grew in Britain, he resisted pressure to flee, but the government wasn't going to wait forever. In June, people in Edinburgh rioted during the King's Birthday celebration. If Paine gave them no choice, officials would go ahead and prosecute him. Later, some would say it was William Blake who tipped him off to imminent arrest; anyway, on September 13, 1792, Paine took the night coach to Dover. Customs and border officials detained him at first, but they soon got the word from higher-ups, and he sailed through the looking glass.

The author of "Common Sense" and *Rights of Man* arrived in France to a hero's welcome. Even as he was found guilty in absentia of sedition in Britain, he was ushered into a seat representing Calais in the National Convention. He didn't speak French. But the constitution under discussion at the Convention was to be modeled not on the United States Constitution but on the democratic Pennsylvania constitution of 1776, pilot program for his plan of national government. The presence of a revolutionary American celebrity in a European revolutionary nation gave a glow to the Convention's proceedings. The proceedings gave a glow to Paine.

Liberty, equality, fraternity. Yesterday, America. Today, France. To-morrow, the world.

While Thomas Paine was taking the goals of the American movement called the Democracy to what he saw as world-changing heights in Europe, Alexander Hamilton was deciding that the situation in the American West must be brought to an issue, and the Mingo Creek radicals of western Pennsylvania, inheritors of the Democracy's role in the American Revolution, were deciding the same thing. Now both sides started escalating so fast that it would never be possible to know who incited whom more.

One way Hamilton escalated was via his revised excise law, which Congress passed on May 8, 1792, tightening enforcement. But he made a further move, ingeniously designed to hurt and infuriate small whiskey producers, specifically those living in General Neville's survey, which Congress never got a good look at.

This one had to do with army supply at the Ohio headwaters and new forts down the river. After a tremendous victory by the western woodland confederation over U.S. troops in the Northwest Territory, Washington had finally succeeded in pressuring Congress to create the regular army that he and Hamilton had been pushing for since 1783; soldiers and other personnel were now massed on the Ohio in far greater strength than ever before, training for re-invasion. Many were garrisoned at a new Pittsburgh installation, Fort Fayette, still under construction, with members of the Neville Connection appointed as project managers. The army needed steady supply on a big scale, so federal money was suddenly flooding western Pennsylvania. Almost overnight, that is, local whiskey makers found they had, in the U.S. Army, the handiest, biggest, most reliable customer imaginable.

Hamilton took that customer away from the small-batch producers. Creating an army commissary office, he decreed that it buy in bulk, which only big producers could achieve, and he shifted responsibility for delivery from the army to the seller, thus limiting sellers to those with major transport to spare. He nailed that system all the way down by giving the local people he knew further federal appointments. The commissary at Fort Fayette was to be run by a Neville brother-in-law. The quartermaster was to be the Neville son-in-law who was contracting with Knox to complete Fort Fayette. Now the Neville Connection was not only the region's biggest whiskey seller, and not only the region's whiskey-tax collector, but also, via the military, the region's biggest whiskey buyer, with a government-enabled monopoly at both ends of the transaction. With the federal sew-up getting tighter, the reaction of the tough, angry people of the region was predictable.

But the people were escalating anyway. Benjamin Parkinson, the Hamilton family, and the other Mingo Creek radicals had gone beyond physically attacking individual collectors. They still did that, but in line with the radical Washington County resolutions, in as early as 1792 they started an organization that would end up many hundreds strong. They called it the Mingo Creek Association, and through it, they put Herman Husband's ideas about regional unity into operation.

Headquartered at Mingo Creek Church, a small log structure where the four westernmost counties converged, the association began by attaching itself to the state-sanctioned militia battalion commanded by John Hamilton, who had taken part in attacks on collectors. Every mem-

ber of the association served in his battalion so the association gave itself
a set of sub-associations, each corresponding with one of the battalion
companies, each of which was using its musters not just to drill and elect
officers but also to elect the association's leadership; company captains
received and distributed copies of the association's resolutions, speeches,
and endorsements for public office. Had a John Hamilton or other officer objected to this transformation of the government-sanctioned militia into a movement opposing government—John didn't, he actually led
it—that officer would be voted out of command by his men. The official
militia in Washington County thus became the Mingo Creek Association's military arm.

Or the Mingo Creek Association became the political arm of the
militia. Either way, the organizing strategy quickly spread to other counties in the Neville tax survey. It was the Committee of Privates moment
all over again—when in 1776, the armed working class, enabled by James
Cannon and Thomas Young, organizing itself via militia units in which
it was obligated to serve, overturned the government of Pennsylvania and
cleared the way for American independence. Back then, Pennsylvania
had depended on the militia for defense against the ruling British enemy.
According to the Mingo Creek Association, the West's ruling enemy was
the new national government of the United States.

The association extended itself even beyond the military. It instituted
a kind of independent regional government. The new state constitution,
as revised by James Wilson, had ended popular elections for local judges;
with the new solo governor appointing judges, the creditor class had
been finding debt cases easier to win. The Mingo Creek Association
now decreed that no citizen living in John Hamilton's militia district
was to bring suit in county court against any other citizen in that district
without first applying to the association for mediation by judges chosen
in popular local elections outside the normal political process. Given
the association's identity with the militia, and the assaults for which the
group was known, lawsuits for debt collection in Washington County
court dropped way off. This system, too, was replicated in the other
counties.

The association also imposed social rules. For large-scale distillers to exploit the advantages Hamilton was giving them, they had to comply with the tax law. The Mingo Creek men were out to ensure that nobody in the region felt free to do that, or to sign up as one of Neville's deputies, or to consort with anybody who did. The goal wasn't just to get Neville himself to resign his office but to banish from the region the longtime sewers-up of commerce and the state and federal authorities that enabled them. The goal wasn't resisting government but becoming government.

To that end, in the summer of 1792, an anonymous ad in the *Pittsburgh Gazette* called a delegated convention to meet in Pittsburgh. The call didn't come from regionally prominent men seeking moderation, and the convention wasn't going to be like the Redstone Old Fort meeting. Though anonymous, the call came from the Mingo Creek Association, per the radical Washington County resolutions, so sending delegates from every county was pretty much mandatory.

William Findley could see what this meant. Western moderates like him—he'd been fighting the tax via legitimate process, in the House—were getting squeezed. Anyone who attended the upcoming convention was in danger of implicating himself in a federal crime. Anyone selected as a delegate who refused to attend was in danger of implicating himself as a collaborator with the federal enemy. Findley, ever hardheaded and realistic, made the most careful calculation he could and managed to stay away from the Pittsburgh convention.

Albert Gallatin didn't make a calculation. Still hoping to persuade his neighbors and constituents to refrain from violence, seek compromise, and undo Hamiltonianism over a longer term, the Genevan was elected to the Pittsburgh convention, which met in a tavern crowded with nearly forty delegates in late August 1792. Gallatin served as secretary. That decision would come back to haunt him more than once. Moderation wasn't on the table here. A list of demands notable for radicalism was adopted, with Husband's ideas and the Mingo Creek mood prevailing, and this time the demands weren't coming out of Washington County alone but from the whole multicounty Neville survey. They included repealing the whiskey excise and replacing it with a progressive tax on wealth; and the resignation of General Neville, who couldn't, the document said, be replaced, because nobody would take the job now. The convention created committees of correspondence to resist and reform government, uniting the whole region in the militia-structured, ad hoc governing system, and it resolved to support any action taken against any resident of the region who aided federal officials: a declaration of war against anyone locally connected to or even compliant with officialdom.

Hamilton had attacked the moderates' petitions for being anti-government. The radicals were demanding moderates' loyalty in attacking government.

As secretary to the convention, Gallatin signed the resolutions. He'd lost the middle ground. He still believed he could find it again, but two days later, thirty armed men, faces painted a variety of colors, rode up to the house of one William Faulkner, a tavern owner leasing space to General Neville for registering stills. Faulkner had been waylaid and detained only days before the radical convention by men including Benjamin Parkinson and Daniel Hamilton. Daniel had grabbed Faulkner by the hair and war-whooped in his face; Parkinson, Hamilton, and the others had cautioned him that an organization hundreds of men strong wouldn't tolerate his allowing Neville to open a tax office in his tavern. They'd let him leave, but Faulkner hadn't listened. Now the convention had expressed support for any action taken against Faulkner's ilk.

The men arriving on horseback aimed their guns at his tavern's wooden sign. It featured a representation of George Washington's head. They fired. The president's painted features were splintered by the blasts. That made a point. Faulkner was out, so they battered the door of the house until it split. Invading, they spilled the beds onto the floor and went everywhere, including the attached tavern, where they threatened to smash up the bar. Some said they'd shave Faulkner's head and tar-and-feather him. Some said they'd take a limb, some that they'd kill him. One man called for burning the house: it was at a distance from others; it wouldn't start a town fire. Another argued that just for safety, the house should be torn down, not burned. In the end, the crowd broke everything and rode away, and when Faulkner came home, he gave in. The next day, as directed, he published in the *Gazette* his decision not to allow an excise office on his property.

He was by no means the last to do so. Mingo Creek's regional take-over was rolling on. David Bradford, the upscale Washington County lawyer, always eager for the people's approval, treated the Faulkner attackers to drinks and dinner.

When news of the attack came to Hamilton in Philadelphia in mid-September, he'd been wondering whether, in the event that "the plot should thicken," as he put it, and the use of military force in the West "appear unavoidable," it might be a good idea to have President Washington go personally to what Hamilton envisioned as a scene of commotion. News of a real commotion made western Pennsylvania the scene.

He'd considered western North Carolina as a site for military crack-down: no tax was collected there at all. Collection was so weak every-where in the West that to pay regular interest on bonds, meet expenses for the invasion of the Northwest Territory, and keep up government opera-tions, Hamilton had been forced to adopt two new measures: borrowing from the bank; and getting Congress to pass new excises on snuff and sugar, further import duties, and a tax on pleasure carriages. These taxes tended to hit eastern merchants and creditors, so some Federalists had started expressing concerns about excessive federal taxation. The single whiskey excise had been intended in part to obviate such complexities. Collecting it was imperative to maintaining the credibility of Hamilton's system. But Edmund Randolph, now serving in the cabinet as attorney general, found no evidence justifying a federal prosecution in North Carolina, let alone a military expedition.

Anyway, decisive action at the Ohio headwaters, Hamilton now urged Washington, would send the best message to the rest of the West, the whole country, indeed the world. It was a national embarrassment that recalcitrance and violence against the federal government were occurring in the state where the federal government sat. Too, the army presence at Fort Fayette made the region especially convenient for suppression.

Washington substantially agreed. He remained perennially frustrated by the West. The Indian problem continued to blend with squatting and settler unrest to make the region a constant personal business headache, and as always with him, personal and national matters were inextricable. If the West wasn't soon gotten under control, the land bubble would burst, hurting all investors and stymieing national expansion. He was fed up enough to be considering selling his western lands, but they wouldn't bring a fraction of what they'd bring with the region secured and canals, roads, and governmental authority linking West to East. The British, allied with the the woodland confederation resisting the United States in the Northwest Territory, were still holding forts on the Great Lakes in U.S. territory, even engaging in a military buildup at Fort Detroit. Spain was negotiating with Creeks and Cherokees in the South. Any permanent disaffection of people around the Ohio headwaters might finally cut Philadelphia off from all of the vast and valuable U.S. lands beyond.

Given these worries, Washington found anti-tax petitioning and newspaper opinion at least as disturbing as the violence against tax collectors. He was committed to using force to put down outright unrest, but he also wanted indictments against people who had attended meetings and signed resolutions. Britain, partly in response to Paine's influence on labor activism, was moving toward banning what it called seditious meetings. Washington authorized Hamilton to push Attorney General Randolph to indict, in particular, the attendees of the radical Pittsburgh convention. Hamilton had a report that Albert Gallatin had not only attended the Pittsburgh meeting but also signed its resolutions, and he took Washington's indictment idea straight to Randolph. He also gave the attorney general a draft of a proclamation he'd whipped up, in which President Washington warned the people of the headwaters not to hold any more meetings and explicitly threatened use of federal troops if order weren't restored. Hamilton and Washington agreed privately that if this proclamation failed to restore order—knowing what they knew, there was no way to imagine it wouldn't have the opposite effect—then what Washington euphemistically called "ulterior arrangements" could be made.

But Randolph crossed out the warning about holding meetings and the threat of force. He said it seemed almost deliberately inflammatory and reminded Hamilton that assembling to express grievances is "among the rights of citizens." Hamilton went right back to Washington to urge him that issuing a proclamation means resolving to act on it. But Washington didn't need coaching. In a private response, he expressed no doubt that the proclamation would indeed fail and military action be taken, but he cautioned the secretary that all other measures had to fail first. He also believed eastern citizen militias should be used, not regulars stationed at Fort Fayette. If the professional army were deployed against the citizenry, Washington could imagine the opposition's claiming that it had been created for that purpose. The army would also have its hands more than full reinvading the Northwest Territory. Cracking down on Americans in the West would require raising militias in the East.

In late December 1793, a little more than a year since he'd been welcomed into a seat in the National Convention, Thomas Paine was taken down to the cold, wet basement of Luxembourg Prison, formerly Luxembourg Palace, and placed in a ten-by-eight-foot cell. The charges against him were that as a citizen of Britain, which was now at war with France, he had allied himself with counterrevolutionary elements. As Paine sat in the cell considering his situation, he knew he was facing, at best, deportation to Britain, where he'd been convicted of sedition and could be hanged, and more likely a summary death sentence, to be carried out a block or so from his prison in the presence of what had become a crowd cheering ritual execution after ritual execution.

It was true that he'd started criticizing the Revolution. He'd begun by tolerating and even excusing the violence—this was, after all, a revolution, like the American one—but as the mood turned outright grisly, Paine argued on the Convention floor, through his translator, for sparing the lives of Marie Antoinette and Louis. The Revolution had ended kings. Regicide would suggest kings still existed. In keeping with the new spirit of equality, the better thing would be to ship the former royals off to the United States, which had never had monarchs, and let Louis take up some useful work there as plain old Mr. Capet. Execution, Paine argued, would only demean the Revolution as a bloodbath. He didn't see that Robespierre and Marat, architects of what the government would soon call the Terror, had a bloodbath in plan.

Louis and the queen were beheaded, via the new, quick, humane method known as "guillotine," their heads brandished before the crowds, and dissent from such practices became evidence in itself of treason and collaboration, counterrevolutionary. Day after day, member after member of the Convention was placed on the list for arrest while crowds in the galleries called for a purge. The public executions began. Staying mostly out of the Convention, trying to lower his profile, Paine considered flee-ing to America. But Britain and France were at war: if a British ship caught him on the way, he'd be hauled back as a convicted fugitive. By fall, the executions seemed constant.

And now the worst had happened. He was locked in Luxembourg Prison's basement, branded counterrevolutionary, probably slated for the guillotine.

He had hope, even confidence. He could escape if he acted fast, for unlike so many who had fallen victim to the Terror, he had a spe-cial status that would make it impossible for the French government to continue to detain him, let alone kill him. He was an American citizen. Gouverneur Morris was even now serving as Washington's minister in Paris. Paine asked for paper and ink and wrote for help. He was sure Mor-ris would respond quickly.

Morris responded almost immediately. Writing to François Deforgues, the foreign minister of France, he set out the Washington administration's official understanding of Thomas Paine's career to date and officially clari-fied its relationship to him. As far as he knew, Morris said, Paine was born not in the Atlantic colonies but in England. It was true that he'd become a citizen of the United States, but having gained celebrity there through his revolutionary writings, he'd since been adopted as a citizen of France and elected to the Convention. His behavior and status were therefore out of Morris's jurisdiction. He asked for a reason for the imprisonment— just so he could brief his superiors—and Deforgues replied that France considered Paine its citizen, subject to French law. Morris forwarded that response to Paine in prison without comment.

Paine couldn't believe it. He and Morris had at times wrangled, at times collaborated; Paine had laughed off Morris's warnings about revolutionary violence. But as an official of the United States, Morris couldn't, Paine thought, mean to see him executed by France. Terrified now, he wrote again. He explained to Morris that the exchange made it seem that the United States consented to Deforgues's view of his case.

He hadn't seen that Robespierre and Marat had a bloodbath in mind. He didn't see that the United States did consent to Deforgues's view of his case. Listening for footsteps that might signal his removal to the place of public execution, the prisoner waited for a response to his plea, but as 1794 began, and the rituals of the Terror mounted outside, and no help came, he finally got it—got all of it, all at once. He was marked for death by the two revolutions he'd inspired.

22

BIBLICAL

IN APRIL 1794, PRESIDENT Washington received a petition regarding the plight of the West and threatening to gain settlers access to the Mississippi with or without the federal government. It came from the Democratic Society of Washington County, Pennsylvania, and seemed to the president to clarify connections between what he considered the disastrous effects of the French Revolution and the escalating unrest in the West, especially the western counties of Pennsylvania. The people of the Ohio headwaters, this petition made clear to Washington, a people with which he was already familiar, had come under the sway of local opposition politicians with French Revolution sympathies.

Francophilia had indeed gotten fervent everywhere. With the Republicans now an openly opposition party of the kind Washington despised, Jefferson had resigned his cabinet position at the end of 1793 to lead that opposition: Randolph took over as secretary of state; William Bradford, thirty-nine, a Pennsylvania lawyer, joined the cabinet to replace Randolph as attorney general. A cult developed around Edmond Charles Genet, a young emissary to the United States from revolutionary France. A fad for forming political clubs swept the seaboard cities and sometimes parts of the countryside, clubs in opposition to Federalist policies and in sympathy with Genet and the French Revolution.

Washington hated the clubs above all. Mainly gentlemen's organizations, though admitting some artisans and even mechanics, they offered members a place to sniff and smoke, debate issues, organize support for opposition candidates, and write speeches and letters-to-editors celebrating *liberté, égalité, fraternité*. Friends of Albert Gallatin started such a club in Philadelphia, but there was one as far from the capital as Kentucky. Sometimes the members even celebrated the crowd-and-government violence in France; when Louis and the queen were beheaded, certain titillated U.S. intellectuals wrote approving op-eds. Most of the clubs didn't use the word "democratic" in their names, but some did. For some upscale Republicans "democrat" was becoming a defiant term of self-identification. It seemed to mingle a traditional agrarian oratory of protection for the common man with moods of the French Revolution. In 1793, the streets of Philadelphia saw waves of opposition protest so rowdy that some believed, or later said they believed, that, had yellow fever not shut the city down that summer, the government might have fallen.

Washington assailed the clubs as "self-created" by designing politicians. To him, the only legitimate expressions of dissent from majority policy were scheduled elections and the occasional, more or less spontaneous protest against a particular law. Permanent organizations broadly opposed to policies advanced by a representative legislature seemed "absurd . . . arrogant . . . pernicious to the peace of society," he wrote to a niece's husband: the seeds of party politics. There was no right of association in the constitutional amendments. Tolerating these clubs could only lead to violence against government.

This petition he'd received from the Washington County Democratic Society told the president that his predictions were being borne out. A few designing opposition politicians were clearly filling the people's heads with wild ideas about social and economic equality—the chief danger republican governments faced. The people in this case were the perpetually recalcitrant and disaffected settlers of western Pennsylvania, people like the Millers Run crew, no doubt especially open to demagoguery; hence, no doubt, the growing violence against government there. Washington sent the petition to Secretary of State Randolph, grimly calling it "the fruit" of the craze for self-created opposition societies. He also asked the cabinet for advice on how best to respond. Hamilton suggested that William Bradford, the new attorney general, explore filing criminal charges against the petitioners.

Around the headwaters, things looked not only different from but more or less the reverse of what the president was presuming. The Washington County Democratic Society, an imitation of the city clubs, had only a handful of members and had met only once, so far, just to write the petition; it would have one or two more meetings in total. A founder was David Bradford, the lawyer from the town of Washington who had attended the radical Washington County meeting dominated by the Hamiltons of Mingo Creek, signed the resolutions calling for regionwide resistance, and treated the attackers of Faulkner's tavern to drinks and dinner. He'd long hoped to benefit by allying with regulatory actions by crowds.

It wasn't Bradford's little group but the big Mingo Creek Association and its sister organizations that were committing the region to rejection of all federal and state authority. Not an occasional gentlemen's club but a full-scale working-class operation, the Mingo Creek Association met regularly and numbered many hundreds of men, many of them landless laborers, all of them armed, organized, and networked via the militia system. Prominent men weren't leading a susceptible people; the people were ordering the prominent to lend their support to a popular resistance or face violent consequences. Showing that support was what David Bradford had been doing when founding his barely existent Democratic Society. To the western moderates still trying to lie low and keep the peace, the lawyer seemed at once overexcited and worried by his role as a supposed leader of the people.

The moderates themselves were frankly terrified. The Faulkner attack had been only a beginning. Anyone in western Pennsylvania collecting or even in compliance with the excise was having stillhouses burned, stills shot full of holes, gristmills torn down. Barn burning was the worst: stored crops, precious tools, machines, and animals themselves could be destroyed, and fires spread, doing terrible damage. In notes left by an anonymous new folk hero named Tom the Tinker, victims were ordered to publicly renounce the whiskey tax in the *Gazette*, and they did. Liberty poles were rising, symbolic of trees where committees of correspondence had organized in the 1770s to resist Great Britain. At a muster and militia election, an effigy of General John Neville was hoisted and lit on fire. During a ride with his wife and young granddaughter, the real general beat off a physical assault by a solo attacker. He fortified his mansion, kept candles burning all night, armed his enslaved workers, and drilled them in defensive maneuvers.

At the treasury office in Philadelphia, Hamilton was gaining detailed intelligence on the real impact of the Mingo Creek Association. He debriefed collectors who had been attacked and took depositions from others at the headwaters; he knew what the association was doing. Soon both he and Washington would know the name Herman Husband.

But there was no percentage for Hamilton in clarifying for Washington the glaring distinctions between the Washington County Democratic Society, whose handful of local gentry had written one petition, and the Mingo Creek Association, an ad hoc replicant government in opposition to the national and state governments. Hamilton wanted to eradicate the Democracy and discredit the Republican opposition at once, to blur differences between the hardest core of real insurgents and the French faddism of the clubs and opposition oratory of the Republican party on the other. He observed no distinction between the moderate meeting at Redstone Old Fort and the attacks on excise collectors. He wanted to arrest Herman Husband, "the Pennsylvania madman," who opposed the Constitution of the United States for its Hamiltonian basis. He wanted to arrest Albert Gallatin and William Findley, opposition-party politicians with a western constituency, who cast the Constitution's basis as Jeffersonian and accused Hamilton of violating it.

He'd announced an intention to retire from the treasury in June. In May, however, with the investigation into his conduct over—despite the Jeffersonians' best efforts, there was zero evidence of corruption—Hamilton told Washington that he would remain in the cabinet after all, and in the spring of 1794, working with Attorney General William Bradford—no relation to the Washington County lawyer David Bradford—he put into operation a plan for bringing the western conflict to an issue.

The plan began with a seemingly simple step. Given Washington's private warning about military operation as a last resort, and his own musings about scenes of commotion where a military operation might appear, as he put it, to be necessary, Hamilton had an idea that on the surface seemed elementary. Attorney General Bradford was to send the federal marshal for Pennsylvania out to the headwaters to serve summonses to those on General Neville's list who had failed to register their stills. Hamilton officially described the summonsing as a means of testing the effectiveness of the normal process of federal law, but as the plan would have made clear to anyone examining it, his purpose wasn't to develop prosecutions. The summonses required defendants to appear in federal court in August; courts were closed then. Bradford noted privately that anyone who received a warrant and agreed to register a still on the spot wouldn't be charged at all.

What Hamilton and Bradford knew: it was nearly impossible that anyone in Washington County especially, but also throughout the Neville survey, would agree to register a still. Pan-regional opposition to the execution of federal law was thoroughly organized and locked down. Neville had reported that the whole region was hair-trigger for armed uprising. Everyone familiar with the situation knew it wouldn't take much to set things off.

To that end, Hamilton and Bradford's plan involved a special feature. William Findley had insisted, in House debate, that of all the whiskey tax's outrages, defendants' being taken out of their region and tried in Philadelphia infuriated the people the most. A law addressing that complaint, enabling local trials, was therefore scheduled to take effect on June 5. In May, at Attorney General Bradford's behest, the U.S. attorney for the district rushed the excise summonses into the May docket, making them deliverable under the old law requiring defendants' removal to

Philadelphia. The summonses would deliver what Hamilton had learned from Findley was the nastiest sting.

The effect of that escalation on an armed, organized regional resistance, just as eager to escalate as the government, was easy to predict. An uprising was overwhelmingly likely, and under a recently passed federal militia law, a president responding to an uprising during a congressional recess was empowered to call out a military force on his own discretion—no need for Congress's approval, only a certification from a justice of the Supreme Court. Hamilton and Bradford timed the operation to coincide with Congress's recess. They could count on the judicial certification: James Wilson was serving on the court.

The plan went into effect in mid-June, when the federal marshal David Lenox left Philadelphia and rode westward, tasked with delivering summonses for tax noncompliance to a list of people mainly in the Neville survey. On the morning of July 14, having served a few writs east of the mountains and even some in the West with no trouble, he arrived at Neville's mountaintop mansion, now a fortified citadel, and rode out, the hated Neville riding along, to start delivering summonses in Washington County. The idea was to begin with the Mingo Creek area, known as the hardest core of the resistance.

Word traveled fast through supersensitive networks. Predictably, everyone receiving a summons responded with nothing but loud contempt, and soon Neville and Lenox were followed by a posse of thirty or forty men. The posse made its fateful move while the officials were on a farm delivering what quickly became the last summons of the day and the final step in the summonsing phase of Hamilton and Bradford's plan. The Mingo Creek Association and the U.S. Treasury Department had been in a race to light the fuse. The outcome was a tie.

When Neville and Lenox bolted from that farm on horseback ahead of rifle shots fired from the road, it was July 14, 1794. When Alexander Hamilton resigned his cabinet position in January 1795, the intervening six and a half months had seen the headwaters region transformed into a different country, even a different world. The militia arrested the federal marshal, Lenox, and carried out two military operations against Neville's citadel, both involving shootout battles: one against just Neville; the other against the U.S. Army, when troops from Fort Fayette came to defend him. The rebels fought in military order. No face painting, no garish costumes: those days were over. In the second battle, a rebel captain was killed, a veteran of the War of Independence, and setting the house on fire, the militia left only the slave quarters unharmed; nothing was left of Neville's mansion on the hill but a smoking hulk. The U.S. Postal Service was waylaid, the mail seized and opened for evidence of locals' collaboration with government. Committees met and formally banished from the region many members of the Neville Connection, who packed up and left for the East. Marshal Lenox escaped, and under cover of a late-night thunderstorm, fled with General Neville by boat down the Ohio to Virginia. At meetings run by Benjamin Parkinson and the Hamilton family, all well-off people remaining in the region were publicly required to swear allegiance to the people, endorse all actions taken by the people so far, and provide both wholehearted support and leadership in any further actions.

David Bradford, the Washington County lawyer, went all the way, got himself up in a homemade paramilitary outfit with plumes and feathers and a big hat, and promised to lead the insurrection to victory. Some called him a Robespierre of the West, but others could tell, just by looking into his eyes, that he lived in terror of being shot by the men he supposedly led. After an armed muster mainly of landless laborers and foreclosed farmers and artisans on Braddock's Field, outside Pittsburgh— the site, almost forty years earlier, of a Shawnee and French victory over the British General Braddock—more than a thousand men marched on the town with the stated intention of burning it to the ground as a New Sodom, capital of the Neville Connection; Bradford, supposedly a leader, wore his hat and outfit. Some of the moderates, desperate now, made a hurried deal with the soldiers at Fort Fayette to stand down, and Pittsburghers made a public show of obeisance to their poor rural neighbors, serving them food and whiskey en masse. That kept the town standing, though many a barn burned that night.

By late summer, the insurgent West had a flag representing the five

western counties of Pennsylvania. In August, it flew above a grand congress of the West, held on a high bluff overlooking the Monongahela
River and attended by well-armed delegates, elected by western counties
not only in Pennsylvania but also in Virginia and Maryland, in correspondence with people in Kentucky. Some at the congress expected to
defend the whole West from a military invasion by the East.

Hamilton had meanwhile been bringing his white-heat mode to its
peak. He stayed all summer at the busy Philadelphia center of a massive logistical plan for a military expedition, not just to scare and capture insurrectionists but to shock and awe the whole citizenry of western
Pennsylvania, occupy the region, and make clear to the whole West,
to the rest of the country, and to the world that the United States was
in charge and his system was working. Washington gave Henry Knox,
secretary at war, permission to take off some time he'd asked for, and the
treasury secretary became de facto acting secretary at war, regardless of
his confirmation by the Senate. Crossing every *t* and dotting every *i*,
Hamilton would enforce his system personally.

Just as in his dreams of commotion, the president of the United
States himself, in the first exercise of the constitutional role of commander in chief, was to lead troops against American citizens. Washington had already told Hamilton that the army stationed in Pittsburgh and
down the Ohio would be too busy with the invasion of the Northwest
Territory for this operation; anyway, opposition members would claim
the army had been created to suppress the citizenry. The president would
lead a militia force, federalized under the constitutional provision that
Hamilton had always viewed as putting teeth in his financial scheme.
In collaboration with the governors of Virginia, Maryland, New Jersey,
and Pennsylvania, Hamilton raised about 12,000 troops and sweated the
multitude of administrative issues for supplying and moving west more
than the number of men who had won the Battle of Yorktown in 1781.
The officers were revved-up, rich youngsters who had missed the War of
Independence and saw a chance for easy glory in a quick trip over the

mountains to put down insurgents they called a bunch of drunken white Indians. The rank and file, drawn from the poor and out-of-work segments of eastern society, were recruited by the officers for their dragoon and other companies. Under the new militia law, Washington could call out this gigantic force without congressional authorization, but the administration did need certification by a Supreme Court justice, and James Wilson readily provided it.

During the buildup, Edmund Randolph became the cabinet's odd man out. He called Wilson a tame crony judge rubber-stamping an executive-branch overreach. He argued that ordinary state law enforcement hadn't even been tried. He proposed sending a team of state and federal commissioners west to negotiate with the rebels and return the region to stability peacefully. But Washington, Hamilton, and Bradford were committed to military intervention. The secretary of state had no valence.

The insurrectionists of the West, for their part, were still meeting in the grand congress on the Monongahela, a long congress and now a busy armed camp. Marksmen with battle experience in the War of Independence, as revved-up as the eastern militia officers, talked about defending the narrow mountain passes and steep, forbidding valleys that gave entrance to their land. A cumbersome hireling army of decadent urban officers and dregs-of-the-city soldiery wouldn't know where they were or what had hit them. Westerners would establish themselves by force as an independent people, building a different kind of American society, with no sewing up of commerce, no monopolizing of land and resources, no subservience to eastern corruption.

For both sides, this was it. By early September 1794, the situation around the Ohio headwaters had gotten as biblical as Herman Husband had prophesied and Albert Gallatin had tried to prevent.

Now both of those men arrived at the Monongahela riverbank. There, for the first time, they met.

Gallatin was out of office. Having moved ahead in the Republican party and the Pennsylvania assembly, he'd been appointed by the assembly to the U.S. Senate late the year before and been expelled only months afterward by the Federalist majority, on the grounds of ineligibility by foreign birth. Debate on the question had been intense, and before being expelled he'd gone ahead and introduced a series of measures urging the Senate to demand detailed reports from Treasury Secretary Hamilton on everything from the exact status of the foreign and domestic parts of the Debt to the expenditures of each branch of government, with receipts. His idea was to increase the oversight power of Congress. While a majority expelled Gallatin, a majority also adopted his oversight measures, to Hamilton's annoyance and near-total noncompliance.

Gallatin then left Philadelphia. He'd recently remarried—his wife, Hannah Nicholson, came from a Republican-connected political family in New York City—and he wanted to prepare his house and grounds for her arrival and resume his projects there. But he arrived in the West just in time to see, in the violent transformation of his adopted region, the final collapse of his efforts on behalf of reason.

Now, on the bank of the Monongahela, Gallatin addressed the grand congress. Yet again, he advised moderation, a position that had long since become tantamount to treason. Gallatin sensed he might not be any more popular with the insurrectionists on the riverbank than he was with Hamilton in Philadelphia. He was nevertheless called upon, as a prominent and educated man of the region, an opponent of Hamilton, and a sympathizer with the people, to help the riverbank congress work out a set of resolutions.

Away from the main action, he therefore sat down with Herman Husband. The Anti-Husband would confer with the man known as the Philosopher of the Allegheny, the Old Quaker, Tuscape Death, and in Gallatin's characterization, the crazy man of Bedford.

Husband had been facing, yet again, his fundamental inner conflict. The prophesied last battle is literally a battle. There can't be a literal battle without violence, and the violence Husband's neighbors had been carrying out against the whiskey excise since late 1791 seemed, on the one hand, the final blow against the corruption of money and government that had kept the laboring majority down for generations, a fulfillment of the consciousness of Christ, of the inner light, and of the prophets' words, in that sense the true American Revolution, bringing about the Millennium on Earth. Just as with the American Revolution, literal non-violence couldn't entirely rule Herman Husband—not at this scale, the scale of spiritual warfare.

On the other hand, the violence in the region amounted to sheer terrorism. Law-abiding people and political moderates lived in a state of personal fear for their safety. Husband himself had preached that such people were eastern hirelings of satanic forces. He'd believed that the understandably violent tendencies of the laboring people he'd always known could be directed, channeled, and leveraged for the cause of the Millennium. But just as at the Battle of Alamance thirty years ago, he knew that an invasion by eastern authorities against the people of the West would be a lot harder to repel than many of the rebellion's leaders imagined. His dilemma over violence and justice, at once spiritual and practical, simply couldn't be resolved.

So as in the run-up to Alamance, with higher stakes now, the aged Husband made a difficult turn. He came down from the mountain. He joined the grand congress of the West on the Monongahela bank. He hoped to arrive at a solution short of military contest with the federal government.

Gallatin naturally hoped to arrive at a compromise too, so he and Husband, better aligned than either of them might have expected, started groping toward some way of advising the people to stand down and avoid a crackdown, while also persuading the Washington administration to hear and address the people's grievances. The mystic and the rationalist weren't alone during this odd encounter. As if things weren't awkward enough, they were joined by two other regionally prominent men, also chosen by the people to propose resolutions for moderation or defiance. One was David Bradford, who had been wearing his costume and promising the people victory. If he turned against his supposed followers now, he'd be the first to feel their rage. In this meeting, he argued for declaring war against the United States.

The fourth man, also prominent in the region, also trusted to a degree by the rebels, was Hugh Henry Brackenridge, a Pittsburgh lawyer who wrote the first book ever published west of the Appalachians, a comic novel. When addressing groups, Brackenridge sometimes broke into impromptu stand-up routines. He had a long-standing beef with the Neville family. He'd published articles criticizing the whiskey tax. His eyes, gazing from a distance while popping like a bird's, could make him look at once terrified and amused, and at this point, he really was. He'd been trying for over a year to moderate local unrest without getting attacked by the rebels himself; it was partly thanks to him that Pittsburgh was still standing. Knowing that the rebels questioned the depth of his support, and that they were opening the U.S. mail, he'd recently written a defiant letter to the treasury that he knew the government could only read as seditious. He knew that had been ill-advised. He was just trying to stay alive, tamp down violence, and hope for the best.

Having lived in the region since 1781, Brackenridge had met the other three men in the meeting before. He found Herman Husband's prophesying endlessly hilarious and mistrusted David Bradford. While he admired Albert Gallatin's presence of mind under pressure from the riverbank crowd, Brackenridge's own favored strategy was to assure the people that he supported any and everything they did, get them laughing at his impressions of government figures, and redirect the action away from violence as far as possible. Now, in the group of four, Gallatin argued that the people saw through such expressions of fake support. Despite the high risk of reprisal from both the rebels and the government, he urged honesty as the best policy. To Brackenridge, who had been at the thousand-man muster on Braddock's Field and the rebel march against Pittsburgh, this honesty idea made Gallatin seem as crazy as Husband. Hoping to lighten the mood by getting laughs from Bradford, he started drawing Husband out on his theories of the Book of Daniel and the New Jerusalem. Bradford wasn't laughing. Gallatin thought the only person who seemed to find the comedian funny, in this almost unbearably high-stress situation, was the comedian himself.

But suddenly there seemed to be a chance for a peaceful solution. William Findley, arriving unexpectedly from his home nearby, announced that a commission of state and federal officials, having traveled fast from Philadelphia, wasn't far behind him. Just as Edmund Randolph had urged in the cabinet, the commissioners were to present the grand congress with a process for coming to terms with the president of the United States and avoiding a federal military invasion of the region. This unexpected development seemed to offer hope.

It wasn't serious. The group of four didn't know it—nor did Randolph—but no matter what happened now, Washington and Hamilton were going to bring federal troops. The proposed negotiations were intended to fail.

This had become a favored administration ploy. A similar inevitable failure was even now ending some sham negotiations with the confederation of woodland nations north of the Ohio River. In that conflict, doves in Congress had been bought off by a seeming attempt at U.S. compromise; General Anthony Wayne, under cover of a seeming last resort, would soon move to conquer that territory, and Washington and Hamilton were applying the same kind of political cover to suppressing western Pennsylvanians. Negotiating with the rebels would buy time for the military buildup, create the last-resort feeling that made an expedition easier to justify, and allow Attorney General Bradford himself—he was serving as one of the commissioners arriving at the headwaters—to gather intelligence on the region's military preparedness, which he soon did, sending his observations to Washington by express rider, unofficially, to prevent Randolph from catching the real purport of the commission. Hamilton meanwhile wrote from Philadelphia to his old comrade Henry Lee, now the governor of Virginia, who would command the planned expedition, to tell Lee to postdate his orders from Washington for raising a militia. The military buildup must seem to begin only after the commissioners' negotiations had failed.

Well into September, however, Gallatin, Brackenridge, and Husband took the lead, with David Bradford an ever-defiant wild card, in a series of meetings to consider the federal commissioners' positions and present them to the people. The commissioners made clear that there was to be no discussion of the whiskey tax or any other western problem. The president's message was quite simple: a terrible military crackdown on the whole region would occur unless the whole people of the five western counties made a public expression of total loyalty and submission to the government. When that threat was communicated to the grand congress, the response was not what moderates had feared. It had been a long stalemate. Some who had once been committed to rebellion had begun hoping for a way out. The commissioners offered a blanket amnesty for everybody in the region in exchange for a region-wide referendum in which free adult men signed a loyalty oath. If enough men signed, the military expedition would be halted. If not enough signed, and the army did have to march, anyone who had signed the oath would be under the amnesty and exempt from arrest.

Fair enough. The grand congress of the West voted to make that deal with federal authority. With hope that a long regional crisis was now over, westerners fulfilled the conditions. In late September, the referendum was held throughout western Pennsylvania, at polling places set up for the purpose. The process was tense. Some still rejected any accommodation of government, but most signed the oath. With even the fiery Benjamin Parkinson now urging submission, the Mingo Creek Association's hold on the region had clearly been broken by the commissioners' deal.

It didn't matter. The negotiations had given Hamilton time to raise the troops, and by early October they were marching in two great wings, one up from Virginia, led by Henry Lee, the other from Philadelphia and led by Washington himself, who rode in a carriage most of the time to favor a back injury, getting out to ride his white horse when crowds gathered. With Knox still on leave, Hamilton had prevailed upon Washington to give him administrative leadership of the operation.

In the face of this oncoming force, David Bradford, the Robespierre of the West, took off and was never seen in the region again. Others fled too, but many, having signed the oath, were protected by the agreed-upon amnesty and stayed. William Findley meanwhile made a last-ditch attempt to turn back the federal force. During the riverbank congress, he'd mostly stayed home, but when Washington and Hamilton brought together the army's wings at Carlisle, in the central part of Pennsylvania,

Findley traveled to Carlisle, had meetings with Washington and Hamilton, and tried to clarify for the president the submissive mood of the western people.

He got nothing but skepticism. Washington spoke almost not at all; Hamilton, who seemed to Findley more in charge than the president, asked curt questions that only showed unwillingness to even consider standing down, no matter the answers. Aware of how much Hamilton despised his opposition in the House, and struck by the rowdy mood of the thousands of troops at Carlisle, Findley learned from one of the officers that his own name was on a long list of suspects to be arrested when the army arrived in the West. He decided to move on for Philadelphia.

Hatred for the rebels was rampant in the East, especially in the cities. Francophile turmoil was already passé. Shocked by the news of the Terror, the public was having a moment of new patriotism. Hamilton had published a series of newspaper articles under the common pen name "Tully"—short for the Roman orator Catullus—scoffing at western settlers' complaints and rousing the eastern public to the defense of the nation's borders against low-life ruffians. The Republican opposition in Congress and the press, recently so loud in anti-administration oratory, made little complaint about a military action against American citizens. There was no political percentage in objecting. Both Jefferson and Madison remained notably quiet.

Its wings having joined at Carlisle, the huge army moved westward as one, climbing the mountains with great difficulty to Bedford, near Herman Husband's farm in the Glades. There Washington turned back for Philadelphia, and Hamilton and Lee took full charge of the operation. As the president traveled eastward in his carriage across Maryland through scenes of his youth, he took his usual notes regarding recent improvements and future development potential. The army meanwhile came down out of the mountains, plundering supplies from terrified families as it advanced on the headwaters, with the young officers disappointed to find that there would be no fight, only submission. As the loyalty referendum had made clear, a rebellion was no longer going on. Having been terrorized by the rebels, many people had a desperate hope for peace and a fear of terrorism now by government. Former rebels, moderates, and victims alike believed signing the oath exempted them from violence by dragoons.

They were wrong. Hamilton and Lee had two objectives: indiscriminate large-scale detentions and interrogations, designed to subdue the whole people of the five counties; and charging examples of rebel leadership for transport back over the mountains and trial for sedition. To carry out the first objective, the army came down on the region with door-kicking, late-night mass arrests without warrants. Dragoons hauled men from their beds into the snow while families watched. The arrestees were marched barefoot to impromptu detention centers, where many were held for long periods, without being charged, in conditions of deliberate privation at times verging on torture. That included many men supposedly under the amnesty.

Achieving the second objective—holding people for trial—was harder, but evidence wasn't the issue; making examples was, and Hamilton and Washington had a list. Even John Hamilton had argued for moderation in the end; as Alexander Hamilton reported to Washington, there might not be much evidence against him, but the man was otherwise "a very fit subject" as an example. Arraignments were carried out by a federal judge brought along for the ride, but Washington's orders, written by Hamilton, expressly subordinated civil authority to military authority in an impromptu process defined as battlefield arrest, which supposedly obviated the requirement for due process. As Hamilton put it to the receding Washington in a letter from the West, anyone may arrest a traitor.

Hamilton had another goal: implicate William Findley and Albert Gallatin as insurrectionist leaders. Both had signed petitions; Gallatin had signed the radical resolutions of the Pittsburgh meeting. By now, Findley was in Philadelphia, having failed to convince the president to turn the army back. Gallatin, having helped convince the people to end the rebellion, realizing the army was coming anyway and that his name might be on a list for arrest, had left with his wife for New York, her hometown. With the headwaters under occupation, Hamilton started bringing in people he believed might give evidence against Gallatin and Findley.

John Powers, a local moderate, was hosting Henry Lee's headquarters at his house on the Monongahela. One day, he found himself summoned to one of Hamilton's temporary headquarters and, hoping to be of service, appeared promptly. Hamilton asked him about the role Albert Gallatin had played in the rebellion. Powers had no information to give. Hamilton asked whether Powers's memory might be improved by taking an hour or so in another room. Powers was thrust at bayonet point into a room where he sat amid a group of silent detainees guarded by an armed soldier. The prisoners seemed to him utterly cowed.

When he was ushered back into the office, Hamilton asked whether he'd remembered anything. Powers said he hadn't. The questioning had been a test, Hamilton announced: in fact, he already had the evidence he needed on Gallatin; refusing to help showed rebel sympathy. Powers was taken to the lockup at Fort Fayette. He offered to post bail. The offer was declined. He demanded to know the charge against him. He got no answer. Never charged, Powers was left in jail until after Hamilton had left the area.

Nobody would bite. Hamilton finally had to give up on hanging Findley and Gallatin. In late November, with the examples selected for prosecution scheduled to be marched over the icy Alleghenies to Philadelphia, and soldiers going house-to-house to get signatures on a new round of loyalty oaths, the secretary of the treasury left the Neville tax survey under military occupation and headed back to the capital.

Thomas Paine, still in prison in Paris and awaiting death by guillotine, had been forced to see the horrible truth. Gouverneur Morris's leaving him to his fate had ripped away, all at once, Paine's long-standing belief that he and Washington had shared the ardor of 1776 and been friends. The president had consigned him to the guillotine. But he was so sick— by now he had a massive abscess in his side—that he thought he might escape that fate by dying in the cell. Robespierre meanwhile completed

Paine's execution order. Every night, when groups of inmates were re-moved from prison, never to return, Paine assumed he, too, wouldn't see morning.

He now shared his cell with three others. Their door, like others, had chalk marks noting the number of people inside to be taken to the guillotine. But their particular door had been accidentally hung so that it swung, unlike the others, out into the hall, and the mark had been made when the door was standing open, flat against the outer wall. When the door was closed and locked, the number was on the inside. Every night, the inmates heard what Paine called the destroying angel approach their door, then pass on. In October 1794, he'd been locked up for ten months with no idea how long dumb luck might last.

Herman Husband was in prison too. After the congress on the Monongahela, he'd gone home to the Glades, and by the time the fed-eral army marched westward, treasury reports and depositions from tax collectors had identified him as the top rebel leader, making him the first name on Hamilton and Washington's list for arrest. As soon as the army arrived at Bedford, Hamilton and Lee dispatched dragoons. They seized Husband and one of his allies even before the army began its descent from the mountains to the headwaters. In the end, he'd argued for a peaceful solution, but he had no delusions. Having once admired Wash-ington as the leader of the last battle against the Antichrist, he'd come to see the president as a traitor, his army as a horn of the Beast. Held at first in the Bedford County jail, Husband wrote to Emy to assure her that his spirit remained light, even ecstatic. Then he was taken on the long trip, on foot, over the cold and rugged mountains. Charged with sedition and locked for months in the Philadelphia city jail, Husband could do nothing but await the arrival of the others charged.

They were marched into town in December, bedraggled, limping, ill, having been forced to walk and sleep exposed for thirty days in mud and snow. The city celebrated the return of its militia with pealing church bells and booming salutes. President Washington emerged from his house and watched, with what seemed to observers a look of inexpressible plea-sure, the regiments ride past. He'd received other good news: General

Wayne had defeated the woodland confederation and taken control of
the Northwest Territory. On two fronts, military action had secured U.S.
sovereignty in the West. Washington was able to tell his western land
agent a month later that the value of some of his western holdings was up
50 percent. The prisoners were paraded through streets of jeering crowds
and then locked with Husband in the city jail.

The Terror in France meanwhile came to an end after a seven-month
run. Robespierre went to the guillotine; James Monroe, Madison's and
Jefferson's ally, replaced Gouverneur Morris as minister to France. In
November 1794, Monroe went to the Luxembourg Prison, arranged for
Thomas Paine's release, and brought out a prisoner so starved and sick
that he seemed close to the end.

The American government had called him not American. The great
man who had depended on him in 1776 wouldn't acknowledge him as a
fellow citizen. Paine's health slowly improved as his hatred swelled, and
in 1796, still in Paris, he published an open letter to Washington, at pamphlet length, calling him a cold-blooded "hermaphroditic" personality
whose administration had betrayed the spirit of the Revolution.

It ended this way:

> And as to you, sir, treacherous in private friendship (for so you have
> been to me, and that in the day of danger) and a hypocrite in public
> life, the world will be puzzled to decide whether you are an apostate
> or an impostor; whether you have abandoned good principles, or
> whether you ever had any?

In 1802, officially welcomed back to the United States by President
Thomas Jefferson, Paine thought he might have an influence on Jefferson's administration: it had been established in opposition to Washington's policy and Hamilton's system. But Jefferson, finding Paine too hot to
handle—the author's latest book, *The Age of Reason*, assailed taking the
Bible literally—kept a pointed distance from him on policy. While Paine
never stopped writing, taking political positions, and trying to get money
out of Congress, the once-inveterate optimist of human potential lived

often drunk, bitterly lonely, and largely forgotten, sometimes in New Rochelle, New York, sometimes in Greenwich Village in Manhattan. When he died, in 1809 at seventy-two, a handful of people attended his funeral. None of them was among his comrades of 1776.

Herman Husband was tried in Philadelphia in early 1795, for sedition, but despite his sermons, and despite topping the Treasury Department list of leaders, there was no real evidence that he'd engaged in insurrectionary activity; evidence showed instead that he'd helped bring about the rebel stand-down. There was hardly any evidence against any of the chosen examples. Juries convicted only three men, none of them leaders, and Washington pardoned them. Military suppression of the citizenry and occupation of the whole people of the region had been the operation's primary purpose, not making cases. Acquitted and released, Husband was left to make his way home.

He'd caught pneumonia during his long stay in jail. In a tavern just west of Philadelphia, attended by Emy and his eldest son, John, Herman Husband died, not by execution but by imprisonment. He was seventy-one. If Emy and John buried him in a family plot on the property at the Glades, the grave is unmarked.

Alexander Hamilton, taking great satisfaction in the results of the western operation, left Washington's cabinet in January 1795. He'd succeeded against powerful opposition in fulfilling his ambitions and altering, via legislative implementation of the Hamilton Scheme, as enabled by the Hamilton Constitution, the fundamental nature of the American economy. Yet the ultimate purpose of his system—rapid national transformation of the country into a manufacturing empire—remained stymied, and he would now have to suffer, from outside government, his enemies' rise to national power on a platform of destroying his system.

The Democracy, though, had been truly demolished at last.

PART V

A SCHEME
SUPERSEDED?

23

ALBERT OPTIMISTE

IN SEPTEMBER 1814, AT the age of fifty-two, Albert Gallatin left his job as secretary of the treasury of the United States.

For twenty years, he'd been a leader in the Republican party, at first in the opposition and then during a long period when the party held a majority. For thirteen of those years, he'd served the office founded by the man who'd hoped to have him hanged. Now Hamilton had been dead for ten years, Washington fifteen. Jefferson had served two terms as president, and Madison, having served as Jefferson's secretary of state and succeeded him as president, was a year into his second term. William Findley was still in the House, a lion of the majority now.

Things had changed, putting it mildly. Much of that change had been driven by Gallatin's guiding American public finance and the American economy through a series of transformative phases that sent the country in directions that neither he nor anybody else could have predicted when it all began. Only looking back from 1814 was it clear that the first phase of that great effort had begun twenty years earlier, in the fall of 1794.

That's when Gallatin learned to his surprise that he'd been elected to the U.S. House of Representatives. He hadn't sought the seat. He was even then preparing to flee the region to escape arrest by the oncoming federal military. His home wasn't in the district that had elected him. Yet Republican party operatives had put his name in nomination, and while the win was narrow, it was a small beginning of something big, because the choice seemed to be based on his having taken a clearer position against the western insurrection than the lawyer, writer, and funnyman Brackenridge, who sought the office. Gallatin's opposing Federalist Party authoritarianism while advising compliance with the law gave him appeal for burned-out western voters who had come to feel terrorized both by the rebels and by the U.S. government and were hoping for some tranquility.

Such was voter confidence in the Genevan émigré that he was also returned to the state assembly—the office for which he'd actually stood. That was a strange situation. But it didn't cause any immediate conflict: the U.S. House wasn't scheduled to reconvene until the end of 1795.

So it was in the State House in Philadelphia, as a member of the Pennsylvania assembly, that Albert Gallatin took his first public stand as an aspiring national leader of the Republican party. It was January 1795—a precarious moment for him. His region was under military occupation. Trials of those marched over the mountains were going on in town. Federalist power and popularity were strong. And the immediate issue before the state assembly was the legitimacy of the very election that had returned him to office. Since the western country had been in a state of insurrection, Federalist members said, how valid could its elections have been? One of them made a long speech in the assembly, reviewing the rebellion blow by blow, with the strong implication that Gallatin had been elected because he'd supported violence against government.

When that speech was over, Gallatin rose. While he regretted the necessity, he told the chair, he had no choice but to put his own review of the entire insurrection on the record. Then, possibly startling members of both parties, he made the counterintuitive move that launched his ascent in the party.

He acknowledged having signed the most radical list of resolutions— those of Pittsburgh in 1792, which had reflected a hard-line position against the federal government. Instead of dodging the issue, he expressed regret, calling the act his only political crime.

Thus he isolated it. And he wasn't just talking about himself. He went on, retelling the story of the recent insurrection as the basis for a new discourse on equality in America.

Other Republicans had stayed quiet on the insurrection. Hamilton's anti-western propaganda had been overwhelmingly effective; with Federalists associating the rebellion with the French Revolution, Republicans too denounced the rebellion and disassociated themselves from the Terror. Jefferson might fantasize aloud about the salutary effects of frequent rebellions, but neither he nor Madison made any public statement about the real rebellion, or Hamilton's role in inciting it, or even the flagrantly unconstitutional manner in which a whole region of the United States had been suppressed.

Gallatin addressed the subject head-on. Those resolutions he'd signed, he told the assembly, regrettable but probably not even illegal, represented not just an outlier in his own career: they were a blip in the overall action. The people of the West had for the most part done little more than petition and peaceably assemble. Things had gotten badly out of hand, he didn't deny that—but no organized, regional movement ever existed, he assured the members, to prevent execution of federal law. Some bad-apple local roughnecks played a part. Local demagogues encouraged some unfortunate incidents. But the real problem came down to the Federalist administration's misreading as sedition what was in essence nothing but the people exercising their rights. Accidents, misconceptions, and governmental cruelty: a perfect storm.

Parts of that story were easy to tell. Describing the administration's responses to holding meetings as authoritarian overkill didn't pose Gallatin's logical and narrative powers any challenges. But to put across the overwhelmingly peaceable nature of the people, and the absence of any organized movement, he had to frame the petitions, which had been influenced by upscale moderates like him and sent to Philadelphia, as more reflective of the wishes of the people than the radical resolutions addressed not to government but to the region's inhabitants and demanding defiance of government. He made the Mingo Creek Association's taking over the militia and instituting its own government go away by not mentioning the association at all. He pointed instead to a few upscale men, the David Bradford type who, for reasons of personal ambition, he said, fomented trouble from the top down among a people who remained, for the most part, innocent of any thought of mobilizing from the bottom up.

So he openly called for leniency for those arrested, and at the end of the speech he turned a common Federalist trope back on the Federalists by comparing the administration's crackdown to the recent violent excesses of revolutionary France. When he sat down, he'd made radicalism on the part of free-laboring Americans into a chimera of elites, whose overreaction had been the cause of the trouble.

Hamilton had always seen the Democracy as the critical force to be overcome. To him, the western rebellion and its suppression constituted the final throwdown in a fundamental American class conflict of long standing. Husband had seen the situation the same way, and in that throwdown, Hamilton had beaten, indeed killed, Husband. Gallatin's story, however, washing the Democracy out of public memory, made both Hamilton and Husband examples of the style in American politics later to be called paranoid. The hero of the Gallatin story remained the independent, pioneering, western-settling, liberty-loving, smallholding American farmer, whose exceptional natural virtue and reasonableness, though sorely tried by Hamiltonian abuses, had shone through. Even when the rebels seized Federal Marshal Lenox, Gallatin reminded the assembly, they'd treated him humanely. Would a mob in England, France, Holland, or any other part of Europe have done the same?

The speech, his first to be published, was widely read. Its success was based on his defending the people while erasing their cause. For Gallatin, militant demands for radical social change, to the extent that they existed at all, never had and never would play any significant role in the United States. From Philadelphia he wrote to his wife—she was in New York—and mentioned attending Herman Husband's sedition trial. He'd once called Husband the crazy man of Bedford. Then, near the Monongahela, they'd sat together in tortuous negotiations. Now he told his wife he knew nothing of the man. He seemed to mean it.

In early 1795, Gallatin the Anti-Husband laid out the ground in the state assembly. At the end of the year, steps away from the assembly in the U.S. House of Representatives, Gallatin the Anti-Hamilton got busy. In this phase, he began the work that would define his future in politics and the future of his party in government. He would oppose the Federalist finance system and push for replacing it with a new system, drawn along lines becoming known as Jeffersonian.

While the Senate remained with the Federalists, the Republicans had gained a narrow majority in the House. Gallatin's first move as a member was to try to get the chamber to put a hard brake on what he saw as gross financial excesses luxuriated in by the Federalist administration over the past eight years, to the disgust of his thrifty, Calvinist-influenced spirit and the detriment, in his view, of the country. Hamilton, he thought, had been allowed to operate as an unopposable prime minister. Expenditure of public funds by the executive branch had been subject to no legislative oversight. That process was at once tyrannically unrepresentative and bad policy.

As a freshman member, he might have been expected to move slowly, but the reserved style was personal, not political. Gallatin rose in debate and urged the chamber to restrict all federal spending. Because that effort made him a thorn in the side of Oliver Wolcott, the Hamilton acolyte now serving as secretary of the treasury, and because both Hamilton and Jefferson were out of office, it might have seemed as if the old zero-sum difference was now being carried on by proxy form via Wolcott and Gallatin. But rigid Jeffersonianism represented yet another extreme Gallatin wasn't attracted to. Though adhering to the principle that the states must be free to pursue their own policies and projects, he believed national commercial growth would depend on an interstate infrastructure of canals, roads, and bridges, planned and encouraged to an important degree by the federal government. Nor was he sentimentally agrarian. He thought the United States needed an industrial policy, also encouraged by the federal government, though not along the Hamiltonian lines of granting federal subsidies and bounties. If he was to achieve his long-range aims, the on-going conflict between the promoters of the federal government and the defenders of the states must not be allowed to remain in a condition of zero-sum standoff. For the betterment of the people, the states, and the nation, that conflict must be negotiated.

Negotiated constitutionally. That was the thing.

For as he made his first moves in the House against the entrenched Hamiltonian process of unexamined federal expenditure, Gallatin was developing his own reading of the national founding document of 1787, and it differed from everybody else's. Federalists had embraced the Consti-tution for enabling Hamilton's system and stifling the states. Republicans had begun by rejecting the Constitution for enabling Hamilton's system and stifling the states, but now they embraced it for supposedly hobbling federal power and protecting states' rights above all. Gallatin embraced the Constitution as something else again. In his origin story of national government, the Articles of Confederation had simply been too weak to serve certain underlying, unifying, nationalizing American impulses that had been there all along. The Constitution was meant to foster the nation as a unified sovereign power inherently republican, federal, and national all at once, tending by ingenious design to promote reasonable degrees of democracy, equality, and social mobility, pervasively through-out the country, even while protecting autonomy for states, localities, and individuals . . .

He meant it, this celebration. That, too, made him different. The *Federalist* authors had sung the Constitution's praises, but in real life Hamilton had remained irritated that the states existed at all; Madison had at that point been disappointed by the absence of a federal veto on state laws. At the other extreme, Jefferson was claiming that the Consti-tution reserved literally all domestic policy for each state and allowed the national government literally no power beyond foreign policy. Gallatin opposed extremes. To him, the relationship between the states and the national government was symbiotic precisely because it involved conflict. Anything but a series of bad political compromises, his Constitution represented a set of brilliantly engineered tensions powering both national growth and individual liberty.

He was first to believe, that is—in that sense, he authored—what would one day be widely taught as the exceptional genius of an American system dedicated to what would one day be called the American Dream. The dream was Gallatin's. A foreigner, a Francophone easily mistaken for a despised Roman Catholic, never connected to an American family with dynastic ambitions, he'd come to maturity experiencing the thrill of living in a society open to individuals' freedom to advance on merit measured by performance, not prior social status. That's what he meant by equality. He also expected an equality of rights to mean, over time, the emergence of an equality of means—a rough equality—with more or less everybody more or less living in a broad social and economic middle.

That's why he liked Pennsylvania. Unlike in New York and some other states, he said, no one family had a lot of influence there, at least outside Philadelphia, which made his state, and especially his part of it, a model for the country's westward future: no politically significant commercial aristocracy thrived in western Pennsylvania, no disaffected, dependent, wage-laboring class; he, a poor man, was nevertheless a success. He personally exemplified an exceptional American openness to contributions from all social classes and exceptional encouragement of upward mobility. In no other country on Earth would his story even be possible.

Such was Gallatin's assessment of the economic condition of the United States and the nature of American constitutional law. Such was Gallatin's American Dream.

In normal waking consciousness, he'd been privately educated to high sophistication through deep family background in some of the most refined circles of Europe. By no means poor, he belonged to the small class of nicely landed gentry in an otherwise downtrodden region of the United States. He'd seen right up close the Neville family's vise-grip on commerce, wealth, and governing power in his own region. He'd seen the plight of the truly poor, getting poorer, a growing wage-laboring class that included landless workers and tenants as well as the smallholders crushed by revolving debt and threats of foreclosure, laboring only to serve wealthy creditors and bosses. Rising socially and economically was by no means impossible, of course, in normal waking consciousness. William Findley had begun as a weaver and become a lawyer and then a member of Congress. Herman Husband's family had come to America in indentured servitude.

It was Gallatin who didn't fit the dream he insisted he personally embodied. He nevertheless proceeded on the conviction, which he was adept at demonstrating logically, narratively, and oratorically, that he and his adopted home in the West exemplified the best of the new American nation, whose inherent conflicts might be constitutionally mediated. That was the cause he was taking up in the House, when he began trying to pull the treasury up short. The cause gave him confidence.

He would need it. Gallatin's finance ideas weren't going to get far in the 1790s.

The Federalists still had the majority in the Senate, and while Treasury Secretary Oliver Wolcott was weak, the administration as a whole remained strong. It was true that President Washington had by this time become exhausted, forgetful, and petulant and that Hamilton and Knox were out of office, William Bradford dead, and the second-string crew filling those cabinet slots operated to a degree under an outside aegis. As the former top cabinet member, Hamilton had it in mind to run a shadow executive branch remotely. The new cabinet members may have been less obedient than he might have wished, but they did take down Edmund Randolph, the last of Washington's original appointees, contriving to paint the loyal attorney general as having leaked information to France during the western insurrection. The Federalists, despite some weaknesses, retained a lot of power.

It was when the president sought Senate ratification for a major treaty, which John Jay had negotiated for ending U.S. tensions with

Britain, that Gallatin got his chance to make a splash as an opposition leader. The Treaty of Amity, Commerce, and Navigation between His Britannic Majesty and the United States of America, better known as the Jay Treaty, settled issues left over from the Revolution, including British evacuation of forts on U.S. soil, and created a mutual favored-nation trading status, with the United States agreeing to abide by Britain's anti-French navigation restrictions. To the Republicans, still rampantly anti-British, the treaty seemed to give Britain everything it wanted and get the United States almost nothing. Washington played into fears of Federalist tyranny by keeping the treaty's contents secret as long as he could. When the Senate did ratify it, crowds formed in protest. In New York, Hamilton was pelted with rocks when trying to speak to protestors. Both parties wound up accusing the other, as they always did now, of acting unconstitutionally.

Gallatin acted instead on his positive constitutional interpretation. Focusing on money issues, he argued in debate that the House had the power to withhold funds necessary to carrying out a treaty's provisions, even when ratified by the Senate; otherwise, treaty-making would be just another way for the executive branch to get around Congress's constitutionally exclusive control over public money. Though blunt in his interpretation, Gallatin avoided the mean-spirited zingers that had become de rigueur in these debates. He could engage in pointed sarcasm with the best of them, but he felt that both the Federalists and his own party overindulged in public scurrility and ad hominem attack. Also he was a terrible speaker—or thought he was. Now he simply urged the House to request certain papers from the executive regarding the treaty-making process. It was the chamber's constitutional duty, he said, to assess the public costs of fulfilling the treaty.

Some Federalists saw Gallatin's position as a ploy for getting around the president's constitutionally exclusive power to reach agreements with foreign nations and the Senate's constitutionally exclusive power to ratify treaties. But because the House was to a degree bipartisan in wanting to protect and even enlarge its powers against those of the Senate and the presidency, and some Federalist members agreed that the chamber should review the paperwork and only then, at its discretion, vote for or against appropriations, Gallatin was appointed to a committee to take a request for papers to President Washington.

Gallatin and Washington hadn't met since 1784, in the land office near the Ohio. But by now the president knew who Gallatin was and what he represented and declined to hand the papers over, on the advice of his cabinet, citing executive privilege. Washington and the cabinet had first invoked the concept in 1792, when Congress had asked for paperwork related to the defeat of U.S. troops in the Northwest Territory. Washington had agreed, in that case, to provide the paperwork, but he'd framed the decision as his prerogative. Now he acted on the prerogative in declining the request. That set a precedent.

In the end, Gallatin had to acquiesce anyway in funding the Jay Treaty. An East-West division on the issue prevailed among Republicans. His western constituents liked the treaty, which finally got the British out of western forts on U.S. territory and dovetailed with an agreement with Spain to open the Mississippi permanently. Gallatin triangulated: he voted against treaty funding but fostered conditions that made funding easier to pass, which it did, by three votes. The maneuvering pushed him forward in the party as a pragmatic politician, even a broker.

Jefferson, for one, was excited about Gallatin's arguments regarding House fiscal oversight, even enchanted, he told Madison, by the brilliance. To him, a French accent and an origin in the sanctuary city of the *philosophe* Voltaire recommended the Genevan highly. Jefferson told Madison that Gallatin's arguments on treaty funding ought to be added to a new edition of *The Federalist* as the only existing rational discussion of Congress's fiscal oversight powers.

Madison was impressed too, mainly by Gallatin's teaching abilities. Nobody had ever understood Hamilton's system well enough, Madison thought, to explain it clearly and mount a cogent critique. Gallatin was thus instructing his fellow Republicans as much as obstructing the Federalist majority. The real problem with funding a public debt, he explained to the House, was less moral, as in traditional agrarian thinking, than practical. When nobody has to pay for big projects in real time, nobody feels the pain of payment. That makes the long-range ill effects of deficit spending and excessive expenditure seem to disappear, but they don't. Dispelling the delusion would require, Gallatin said, abolishing the Hamiltonian relationship of government to the investing class, which made the Debt a long-term project for generating private profits and getting the government seemingly easy money.

This was the problem with the sinking fund, too, he said. While Gallatin at times indulged in the Maclay-Jackson traditions of calling the fund a flat-out fraud, the main issue to him was that it perpetuated a delusion: that nations can pay off their debts without running a surplus. For Gallatin, the only way a nation can pay off a debt is to do what households do: spend less than they take in and apply the surplus not just to servicing interest payments but also to reducing the principal, steadily, over time. He therefore urged the House to rule out going any further into debt and advised getting the existing bonds paid down, on various realistic schedules, as quickly as possible.

To create the necessary surplus, he wanted to reduce all federal spending drastically, and that meant he had to get his Republican colleagues to bite a bullet. Hating excises and other domestic taxes, they wanted to draw federal revenue only from taxing foreign imports and charging foreign merchant ships using U.S. ports—the customs and tonnage duties. But the only real way to reduce the deficit, Gallatin insisted, and pay off the Debt while covering government operating expenses with money on hand, was to raise domestic taxes—temporarily—to create more public revenue than tariffs could bring in. Taxation would force government to seek relief of pain by reducing expenditure. An ethos of government frugality would ensue. With the Debt paid off, domestic taxes could be reduced or eliminated; via external taxes, the country could then afford public spending on national growth, on bridges and canals, on supporting manufacturing, all of which Gallatin saw as necessary not, as Hamilton did, to imperial competition abroad but to national comfort and happiness at home. For now, he favored using the constitutional direct-taxing power to tax land; he remained skeptical of excises.

These discussions were taking place in a highly theoretical context.

The Federalists weren't about to support undoing Hamilton's system; and Gallatin's Republican colleagues, including Madison, remained skeptical of raising taxes even temporarily.

Still, in one area, Gallatin could at least dent the Hamilton approach to public spending. He went after the biggest item in the federal budget: military appropriations. They'd been growing fast, with new forts going up in the West, garrisoned by new cadres of troops, and a big coastal naval project with installations and fleets. Gallatin urged the House to go the other way. He wanted to stop funding the military at all, for now. He didn't castigate a standing army in the usual hyper-republican way, as a threat to liberty; the country just couldn't afford one at the moment, and there was no military threat. The Jay Treaty had resolved issues with Britain. Anthony Wayne's invasion of the Northwest had subdued the confederated woodland nations and removed them westward. Naval expansion to defend against European invasion seemed especially pointless. Closing the military down would represent a short-term sacrifice and a minor risk, Gallatin admitted, and should be temporary, but the payoff would more than balance the risk. All federal revenues should be dedicated to essential operations and to applying a surplus gained by strict spending reductions to paying down the Debt.

This idea of a total military shutdown was another nonstarter, of course, and Gallatin knew it. His real goal was congressional control over appropriations, and on that score, he succeeded in permanently altering relations between the executive and legislative branches. Under Hamilton, the treasury had gotten used to sending over lump-sum requests for money with only the vaguest and most general rationales, all funds stirred together to make it impossible for the House to assess any item's real importance. Gallatin had intensified Hamilton's ire when, during his brief time in the Senate, he'd objected to these broad, unaccountable appropriations. Now he called for making Wolcott's treasury accountable to the House, line by line, for every item in its military requisitions. Do the work, he urged the members, put in the hours, study the invoices. Do the constitutionally mandated job of the House.

Again a bipartisan majority in the chamber was eager to assert the chamber's power. But how to do it—a House with no experience of exercising financial oversight? Gallatin proposed an idea borrowed from the Pennsylvania assembly: a committee to oversee and work closely with the Treasury Department on military appropriations. In response, the House formed what would become known as the Committee on Ways and Means. Though not officially listed as a standing committee until 1802, it would go on standing for more than two centuries. Gallatin was appointed to serve on it, and to Treasury Secretary Wolcott's indignation, the committee did begin demanding detailed military budgets, including evidence for expenditures.

Congress was actually functioning as a fiscal check on executive power. Gallatin hoped to expand Ways and Means's purview beyond military matters. To him, this struggle between branches of government was the very genius of the Constitution.

Then, in 1796, came a quake that shook the whole partisan landscape.

President Washington announced that he wouldn't serve a third term. That decision threw the parties into new degrees of turmoil and gave Gallatin and his ideas about the national economy and American equality new leverage, both in the Republican party and in the federal government.

24

THE JESUIT

LOOKING BACK FROM 1814, when Gallatin left the treasury, Washington's decision to leave the presidency didn't look so dire: by then four men had held the office. But because there was no U.S. presidency before Washington, no realistic projection existed for his departure, no practical thought of a transition. While presidential election procedures were clearly set out in the Constitution, the reality, when it came, pulled the last restraint off a partisan war that had been itching to break out.

Washington, fed up from the beginning, had considered retiring after only one term. On the other hand, he had no regard for term limits by law or tradition. "I confess, I differ widely myself from Mr. Jefferson and you," he wrote to the Marquis de Lafayette in 1788, "as to the necessity or expediency of rotation" in the office of the presidency. The issue of term-limiting the president "was fairly discussed in the Convention, and to my full convictions . . . I can see no propriety in precluding ourselves from the services of any man, who on some great emergency shall be deemed universally most capable of serving the public." He probably could have won further terms, though probably suffering dwindling majorities, until he died in office. When announcing his departure, he had no intention of starting a two-term tradition.

He was just done, and for the Republicans, his announced exit gave them their first chance to take over. Gallatin published a book in support of Thomas Jefferson's 1796 presidential candidacy. Rivaling Hamilton's reports to Congress for detail and research, it set out, for the public, everything and more that Gallatin had been saying in the House with regard to the flaws of the Federalist finance system. He didn't rally the base by attacking Hamilton for personal corruption. Restraint and focus made his criticisms land all the harder. He revived an old Madisonian idea and presented calculations that proved, he said, that Hamilton had made the Debt bigger than it would have been if Congress had waited to complete the final-settlement process before starting the assumption process. He also showed that the Debt was growing. Both Hamilton and his successor, Wolcott, had worked with Robert Morris's old partner, Thomas Willing, head of the Bank of the United States, to arrange a series of bank loans to Congress, covering the costs of suppressing western Pennsylvania and keeping up interest payments on federal bonds. To make interest payments on the bank loan, Wolcott floated new rounds of bonds—borrowing money from investors to pay interest on money borrowed from the bank and thus, to Gallatin, corrupting both the bank and the Debt. If the Debt was a driving wheel, it was driving the country into serving the Debt. Sooner or later, he believed, the country would be running on fumes.

Few voters could be expected to read the book closely. Its abstruse wonkiness, like Hamilton's, came complete with tables and charts, and it didn't attack the federal government on the basis of states' rights or throw Republicans the rectitudinous red meat of strict constitutionalism. Still, the book made clear that the Republicans were campaigning almost solely on an economically informed critique of Hamilton's system, and while they didn't take over in the 1796 election, they got close. With Jefferson coming in second, the opposition party's inspirational leader was now presiding over the Senate as vice president and doing everything he could to oppose the newly elected president, Washington's former vice president, John Adams, once Jefferson's friend, by now his mutually infuriated enemy. The Federalists had regained a narrow majority in the House and still held the Senate, but their situation was dicey. Adams, nominally party leader thanks to his election as president, had always harbored somewhat Republican-aligned suspicions of a funded public debt and was scandalized by speculation in it. He and Hamilton, the other party leader, hated each other both personally and politically; during the election, Hamilton had secretly tried to get electors to move Charles Pinckney of South Carolina ahead of Adams, and Adams knew it. The new president also had to deal with men in his cabinet, left over from Washington's, who answered more to Hamilton than to him. Loathing the opposition led by Jefferson as much as he loathed the Hamiltonians, he was becoming his own party.

In this improvisatory, up-for-grabs period for an angrily divided governing class, Gallatin gained greater fame—to the Adams administration, greater infamy—by pushing congressional oversight. He'd become a party builder, moving the Republicans ahead of the Federalists in interstate and local organizing. He was so busy in Philadelphia that he rarely went home, yet he was repeatedly reelected. By 1798, Wolcott was sure Gallatin wasn't trying to oversee the treasury but shatter it with bombardments of demands for minutiae. The majority's position was that, contra Gallatin's complaints, the country was doing well. The Debt, though going up thanks to federal borrowing from the bank, was well supported by taxes, making U.S. credit comparatively good at home and abroad. The whiskey tax could still be hard to collect, less because of open defiance now than moonshining, but the later excises that Hamilton had imposed were in effect, and prosperity in the West was improving thanks to a deal with Spain to open the Mississippi permanently to U.S. navigation. The military suppression of Pennsylvania had made western secession no longer a risk. The conquest of the Northwest Territory was leading to public land sales and new settlement. Kentucky and Vermont had been admitted as states. From the Federalist point of view, any criticism looked like destructive hectoring.

Albert Gallatin thus became the Republican most openly hated by the Federalists. He made an easier target than Madison, too august to touch, or the thorny Findley too ready with brushbacks. His unprepossessing looks, accented speaking, and shy manner combined with his blunt, informed criticisms, his thrift, even parsimoniousness, and his dogged pursuit of change inspired Federalists to label the Republicans "Gallatin & Co.": even the likes of the great Madison, they meant, served as front man for a vagrant, devious French-speaker who sounded like what one called "a wandering Israelite" and was known to have engaged in sedition during the western insurrection. In the Adams household, the president kept a special place in his crowded spleen for Gallatin. The First Lady, Abigail Adams, condemning the émigré as "subtle . . . artful and designing," used one of the worst epithets her New England spirit could muster: *The Jesuit.*

In 1798, the Federalists made two interlocking moves that put Gallatin in peril—physical as well as political—for the first time since the insurrection. The first involved a sudden military buildup that accelerated to astonishing scale in the course of months. Again, France was at issue, having undergone yet another shift. In 1797, Napoleon Bonaparte, a military leader with dictatorial ambitions, revived the nation's long-standing aims of conquest, leading armies to victory in Europe and its colonies. Casting the Jay Treaty with Britain as an attack on France, the French government turned privateers loose on U.S. ships. The Federalists, especially the merchant shipping class, reacted by calling for arming U.S. frigates, building new military sloops, raising huge numbers of troops, and other expensive, warlike acts just short of declaring war.

Gallatin had warned Congress about the Jay Treaty's potential to incite France; now he suspected the Federalists of arousing war fever just to obstruct legislative oversight and continue growing the Debt. He argued in the House for diplomacy, not war, pointing out that the last thing the United States could afford at the moment was to build, man, arm, and maintain warships, as President Adams now said he wanted, at a cost of $850,000 per year. These objections, along with his accent and foreign birth, made Gallatin easy to excoriate as a French-allied seditionist who had infiltrated government.

Anti-French feeling, quickly growing rampant, inspired the Federalists to take a series of positions that Gallatin drew further allegations

of subversion for opposing. The formerly enslaved black population of
the nearby Caribbean island that the French called St. Domingue and
its indigenous inhabitants had called Haiti, having risen up and taken
control of much of the island, were fighting off both French and British forces. During the Washington administration, the Federalists had
supported the white planters with arms and money; now the party saw
commercial and geopolitical opportunity in allying with an independent
Haiti. That position was opposed by many Republicans, especially those
in the South, who lived in fear that an invasion by a free, black Haiti
would coordinate with uprisings by the enslaved in the United States.
Gallatin's position was anti-slavery; he also never enslaved anyone. He
wanted the United States to stay out of France's colonial conflict, and
his party organizing depended on connecting North and South. Speaking in the House against allying with the black freedom movement, he
predicted that an independent Haiti could live only by plunder, hurting
U.S. commerce in the Caribbean. That position gave the Federalists further excuses for branding him a French operative, and the French were
in fact bragging about interfering in U.S. elections to aid the Republican
opposition, slowing diplomacy, demanding loans and flat-out bribes in
exchange for stopping attacks on American shipping. In reaction, U.S.
crowds burned Foreign Minister Talleyrand of France in effigy and attacked Americans who seemed French-aligned. The Federalists thus
found it easy to push laws through the House creating a navy separate
from the army, expanding the naval budget tenfold in one year, quadru-
pling the army's infantry regiments, and sextupling the cavalry. Gallatin
opposed those measures too. To pay for them, Treasury Secretary Wolcott issued $7 million in new bonds and proposed new federal taxes on
land and houses, apportioned among the states by population count—
the first-ever attempt to exercise the Constitution's direct-taxation power.
By then, the Debt, foreign and domestic, had reached almost $84 million,
and while Wolcott had set out a plan for paying down the entire thing by
1824, the government kept taking on new obligations. Gallatin strongly
supported a pay-as-you-go policy and more or less favored direct taxation

as a means, but in this case he voted against it. He saw Wolcott's tax as unfair to modest homeowners, likely to be squandered on a pointless and damaging war, not enough anyway to fund the military buildup or enable paying down the Debt. The Federalist majority passed the bill and cast further aspersions on Gallatin's loyalty.

A Calvinist labeled Jewish and Catholic, a Swiss labeled French, a patriot labeled a traitor, Gallatin managed to remain politically assertive, personally unassuming, no-drama. The insults got to him, and some fellow Republicans, for their part, found him too moderate, but he insisted that blending moderation with firmness would always be his motto. He hoped to steer himself and his party through what were becoming storms of partisan unreason with as much of his trademark calm as possible.

Now Hamilton reemerged. Stepping out of back-channel cabinet leadership, Federalist organizing, and publishing anonymous articles, martial fervor reignited by having suppressed western Pennsylvania, he personally designed an entirely new U.S. army; he even designed its uniforms. This huge force, the kind of army he'd always dreamed of leading, was to be officially commanded by Washington, drawn out of retirement, but administered day-to-day by Hamilton. He had in mind not only making war on France but also conquering two strategically and commercially critical Spanish North American holdings, Florida and the port of New Orleans. He was looking at invading South America too.

President Adams took a dim view of foreign adventuring and hated Hamilton. The new army was also bringing the beloved Washington back to public consciousness; that made the current president look even weaker by comparison. Adams started throwing up obstacles to Hamilton's every military effort, and this open rift between top party leaders took the form of a wrangle over army logistics, climaxing over status. On a list of officers to command the new army, Hamilton made himself Washington's number two. But other Revolutionary veterans, now called on to resume officer roles, outranked Hamilton; their feelings had to be considered. When Adams said he wanted Hamilton lower on the list, Adams's cabinet made Hamilton number two anyway, so Adams left the officer commissions on his desk and went home to Quincy, Massachusetts, pretending he'd forgotten to sign them. There, making his own list, he put Hamilton below Knox and sent the list back to Philadelphia. When that list came out, Hamilton refused to serve in such a capacity, and Washington found himself subjected to appeals from Hamilton allies to correct the situation. Irritated, the former president threatened to walk off the job. That would have humiliated Adams, but Adams felt so humiliated anyway that he finally did the one thing that only he, as president, could do. He made peace with France.

There went the foreign war. There went Hamilton's huge new army and plans for conquest. Hamilton made plans to get back at Adams.

All that money for a war that had never even happened. That's how Gallatin looked at it: an assault on his view of how American government was supposed to work. On the positive side, for him: the Federalists had cast themselves for the voting public as squabbling warmongers. That might give the Republicans an edge.

The other extreme the Federalists went to, in tandem with the military buildup, placed not just Gallatin's policies but the man himself in danger. So committed had the Federalists become to the military buildup and fear of secret French influence in U.S. government that in 1798, the majority passed a series of laws, which Adams signed as war acts, providing for rolling back naturalization; expelling any enemy's nationals during a time of war; and deporting, at the order of the president, any noncitizen deemed even potentially dangerous. Washington, though he supported these measures, thought they didn't go far enough. More and more convinced that public opposition to Federalist policy could be explained only by foreign infiltration of government, he was getting concerned about secret controls exercised by the Illuminati.

The new laws, known as the Alien and Sedition Acts, put Albert Gallatin right in the bull's-eye. Federalist newspapers, bringing back the radical Pittsburgh resolutions of 1792, reminded the public that the Genevan had actively obstructed a measure of the federal government—illegal under the Sedition Act. Massachusetts proposed an amendment to the Constitution to remove from Congress, right now, anyone who hadn't been a citizen for thirteen years when elected, a number inspired by the fact that Gallatin, naturalized in Virginia in 1785, would have just missed the cut. While in the end expulsion wasn't enforced, Secretary of State Timothy Pickering, with President Adams's at least tacit endorsement, scanned opposition papers and prosecuted writers, editors, and publishers. Opposition to the acts was cast as subversive in itself.

Still, Gallatin openly opposed the Alien and Sedition Acts, and while he kept his tone down, he also expressed immense offense at the torrent of personal and political abuse he suffered as a result. At one point, he was burned in effigy. He knew he might be literally attacked. When other Republican leaders left town to wait out the craze, Gallatin stayed and argued. As the crisis mounted, he and Jefferson developed an opposition partnership: Gallatin in the House, Jefferson presiding over the Senate.

But Jefferson and Madison went to extremes of their own. In reaction to the Alien and Sedition Acts, they anonymously drafted resolutions, presented by Kentucky and Virginia, respectively, asserting a constitutional right of the states to set aside federal laws that the states deemed unconstitutional. While Gallatin avoided criticizing his allies' position, he'd never read the Constitution in the absolutist, states-oriented way that Jefferson did in the Kentucky resolutions, or even in the more nuanced way that Madison did in the Virginia resolutions. Hamilton, reacting to the resolutions, dreamed of leading his army into Virginia and putting that state "to the test." Gallatin saw all such apocalyptic tendencies—Federalist militarism, xenophobia, and absolutism, states thinking they could cancel federal laws—as tending toward national division, even civil war. Over Federalist jeers and boos, he presented his western constituents' petitions to the House, not for nullifying the Alien and Sedition Acts, as Jefferson and Madison would have it, but for repealing them by normal legislative process.

He did lose his temper in debate, once. He actually shouted. But what he wanted was to see the Federalists beaten electorally and, with the ascendancy of the Republicans, the national government to start restraining itself. Amid escalating chaos, he believed that if his party could only prevail in the 1800 election and set the country on a proper financial and economic course, reason would prevail and the long national crisis abate.

He had reason for hope. By now, the Federalists had clearly gone too far; the electorate had lost confidence in what had so recently been the party of the great Washington. Thanks in part to Gallatin's own organizing, especially in conjunction with his wife's family in New York City, the Republicans were becoming something of a fully interstate political party: canvassing, strategy, a certain amount of top-down and bottom-up structure.

In 1800, Jefferson ran for president again, campaigning this time against militarism and the Alien and Sedition Acts as well as against Hamilton's system. Gallatin wrote a new book, again covering his views of proper public finance, a slicker and punchier effort this time, more of a campaign book; he also linked Jeffersonian policies, associated with Virginia and the slave-power South, to popular feelings in Pennsylvania and New York against Federalist autocracy. Through his father-in-law, Gallatin had become connected to Aaron Burr, the New York lawyer and member of the U.S. Senate who had praised the feminist Mary Wollstonecraft in 1791. In '94, Burr had argued eloquently in the Senate against Gallatin's expulsion and was now developing an innovative organizational approach to opposing the powerful influence of Hamilton in their shared city and state. Gallatin and Burr leveraged their connections, both in the state and nationally, to get Jefferson and Burr on the Republican ballot as presidential candidates. The plan was for Jefferson to get the most electoral votes, Burr second most, with Burr replacing Jefferson as vice president and creating a solid Republican executive branch linking South to North.

Gallatin fervently hoped the election might also usher in a Republican legislative majority. To him, this election looked like the last, best

hope for stilling the turmoil and setting the country on a rational economic course.

In the electoral contest of 1800, turmoil only intensified. Both parties knew the contest could have only one of three results. There might
be an electoral transfer of power from one party to the other, lawfully
ending the founding Federalist mandate. There might be an electoral
defeat of the opposition, lawfully continuing the Federalists in power.
And there might be unlawful prevention of the opposition's seizing power
or the Federalists retaining power, a coup carried out by one side or the
other or attempted by both, in violation of the constitutional electoral
system. Partisan majorities in state legislatures, sure the other side was
seeking the dissolution of the rule of law, felt a duty to tweak their states'
electoral processes, ad hoc, to assure preferred slates of presidential electors. Elections to the sixteen legislatures that chose the electors thus
became critical to the presidential election.

The Republicans seemed pretty unified, thanks to the organizing and
electioneering of Burr, Gallatin, and others. But among the Federalists,
conflict was ripping things up. Hamilton published a fourteen-thousand-
word, fifty-four-page memo reviewing in almost incredible day-to-day
detail what he characterized as Adams's personal eccentricity, mental
inconsistency, poor character, and utter incompetence for high office.
This was in part a response to Adams's fulminating, when finally firing
key Hamiltonian cabinet members, that if he lost this election he'd go
home to Quincy and document Hamilton's evils in voluminous detail.
The party seemed to be falling apart.

Because each state could choose its own election day, the countrywide voting process for presidential electors began in April and lasted
into October. The chosen electors wouldn't meet in their states' capitals
and conduct the final vote until December 3; their tallies wouldn't be
opened in the nation's capital and certified by the vice president until
February 11. And by then, the nation's capital would be someplace new.
This unpredictable and decisive election was unfolding even as the federal government's ten-year stay in Philadelphia drew to a close. The big

move was on, to a place now officially named Washington, District of Columbia, carved out of Chesapeake Bay regions of Virginia and Maryland and placed under the control of the federal government. The place had been named not only for the first president but also for a female personification of what Europeans called the New World, whose discovery, in the European mind, by Christopher Columbus was thus recentered conceptually in the national capital of the United States.

On November 1, 1800, with the public voting finally over, and the states' electors' choice not yet made, President Adams, the incumbent candidate, moved into the unfinished President's Palace, as the official residence was called, in Washington, D.C. His opponent, Jefferson, was already in town, staying in a boardinghouse and taking in as much information as he could, day to day and hour by hour, on electoral outcomes around the country. On November 17, Congress convened in the unfinished Capitol Building.

Gallatin didn't get there until January 10 and hated the capital, if not on sight, then pretty quickly. The new location seemed not just remote but displacing, a scrubby wetland far from anything like civilization and by no means yet a city. Having left his family in Pennsylvania for now, always intent on saving money, he moved into one of the nine or ten boardinghouses that had sprung up on the hill around the Capitol Building to serve the legislators. There was nowhere else to stay, so the places were overpriced, and with virtually no nearby amenities, there was nowhere to go and nothing to do but sit around the houses smoking, chewing, spitting, talking politics. Two big official buildings, the President's Palace and the Capitol Building, loomed from what looked like wilderness at what seemed a random distance from each other, both still under construction by enslaved laborers. Ramshackle communities were grouped about the whole acreage. Streams and an open sewer ran through muddy ground. In this unencouraging place, the 1800 election was to be certified and the country's course determined.

The election's final certification process—the vice president's tallying electors' votes, state-by-state, in a joint session of Congress, and announcing the winner, per the constitutionally mandated process—

was held on the morning of February 11, 1801, right after a blizzard, in the Senate chamber of the unfinished Capitol Building. It was widely believed that the results wouldn't favor Adams. Jefferson was presiding over a tallying process that many in attendance expected to award him the presidency.

But as the votes were reported, the Georgia tally seemed to have a problem. Georgia's electors' votes favored Jefferson and Burr over Adams, yet the document strayed from the constitutionally mandated form, and if it wasn't certified, a chance existed that neither Jefferson nor Burr would gain the majority required for victory, sending the election to the House for another election, among the top five: Jefferson, Burr, Adams, probably Charles Pinckney of South Carolina, probably John Jay of New York.

Jefferson went ahead and certified the faulty Georgia document for him and Burr. Nobody objected. Adams was thus barely defeated.

His party as a whole, though, went down. Organizing by Gallatin, Burr, and others paid off. The Republicans gained a big majority in the House and a nice edge in the Senate.

But now they faced a new problem. The plan for Burr to win the vice presidency failed: in the elector tally, Jefferson and Burr got 73 votes each. Many had seen this coming. Fearing that one Federalist might vote for Burr, just to beat Jefferson, both Burr's and Jefferson's people had done some electoral maneuvering, like Hamilton's in 1788, to prevent a tie. They'd probably canceled each other out. The election was going to the House after all.

Early that afternoon, the chamber went into session, and a contest commenced between two members of the same party, with the outcome again impossible to predict. Each state delegation got one vote, determined by the majority within each state's caucus; the winner of the election had to have nine votes, a majority of the sixteen states. The election was held. Jefferson got eight votes, Burr six, with two states deadlocked: not a majority of the sixteen. Another ballot, with again no winner. Another. No winner, and twelve ballots later, it was dark outside, cold inside and out, and there was no president-elect.

The real action went on unofficially between ballots. The Republican-majority House wasn't yet sworn in, so the chamber was in lame-duck session, still with a majority of Federalists. They were pursuing means of threatening the validity of the whole larger election, or picking and controlling the supposedly less objectionable of the two Republicans. The Republicans, too, had ploys. Despite the holdover Federalist majority, they controlled more state caucuses; still, every state but Delaware now had multiple representatives, not all from the same party, and because Republicans, too, had mutual disagreements and mistrust, partisan competition and potential trades and deals rived each caucus. After a dinner break, the balloting resumed. It returned the same result, and balloting went on that way, at a slower pace to accommodate the between-ballot action, until three in the morning, and then it went on for days. Between ballots, members slept on the cold floor of the big, drafty structure in the middle of a nowhere that was supposed to be the capital city of a well-functioning national government, supposedly entering its mature phase by following constitutionally mandated procedures, carefully crafted, for deliberative resolution of conflict.

Gallatin, though a Burr friend and ally, was working day and night as floor manager to galvanize support for Jefferson. Even Hamilton, seeing Burr as a monster, was working back-channel on behalf of his former cabinet rival. Some Federalists, ignoring Gallatin and going straight to the candidates, offered support to Burr, others to Jefferson, in exchange for a promise to leave Hamilton's finance system in place. Some Federalists considered never breaking the tie and calling a new national election. As crowds of warring supporters gathered outside the new Capitol, some states readied their militias to march on Washington in the event of a Jefferson defeat; Jefferson envisioned such an event leading to a new convention to "repair," as he thought of it, the Constitution. He met with President Adams and told him that any Federalist "usurpation" would be resisted by force.

Such was the process by which Gallatin's hopes for a new national direction were realized, against what he called "the most wicked and absurd attempt ever tried by the Federalists." On February 17, on the thirty-sixth ballot, brokering gained the election for Jefferson. The president-elect thought it was only the threat of armed force that had backed the Federalists down. The country avoided civil war. A party organizationally on the rise defeated a party entering a long, bitter collapse. What would be celebrated as a peaceful transfer of power occurred on inauguration day, March 4, 1801, when Adams left for Quincy at 4:00 a.m. to avoid seeing anyone.

Looking back from 1814, when Gallatin left his job as secretary, it would be easy to remember the particular thrill of that first Republican victory. The popular vote had played an unusually important role, especially in New York, in choosing the mix of electors that had defeated Adams, and because some states' property qualifications had been somewhat eased in order to achieve that effect, Gallatin and others cast the outcome as a victory for the Republican ideal of the American common man, an ethos becoming known as American democracy. To the Jeffersonians, a second American Revolution—the real one—ending the reign of witches and establishing values that the Republican party deemed essential to the country's nature, made 1800 the most important year in American history.

25

TRIUMVIRATE

THE YEAR 1800 was important for Robert Morris too. He got out of prison.

In his sixties, he'd jumped into the 1790s startup frenzy and launched two canal companies, a steam-engine concern, an iron-rolling mill, and the biggest real-estate trust ever seen. He built a huge new mansion, designed by L'Enfant, a characteristically over-the-top money pit taking up a whole block on the western edge of Philadelphia, and he was busy with projects from the China trade to the development of Washington, D.C., where he bought literally thousands of building lots and contracted to put up ten houses a year for seven years.

The past master of risk was managing all that by his usual means: selling shares in his companies and heavy borrowing. That was easy. Starting in 1790, Morris had quickly become the owner of more undeveloped land than possibly any other American: in North Carolina, in New York, in Georgia, in Kentucky, in Pennsylvania. The land bubble was enabling him to borrow enormous amounts of money against an enormous speculative value in an enormous amount of land, in order to buy enormous amounts more, when in 1797, amid the war frenzy and other turmoil, the land bubble burst, and he couldn't raise any money at all, or pay interest on his loans or mortgages, or pay installments on the lots he'd bought in the new capital, or finish one of the buildings he was contractually obligated to build. All of his ventures and companies collapsed; all of his investments went into foreclosure. Sued by a staggering multitude of people at once, he left his family in town and fled to his country estate up the Schuylkill, armed up, and locked himself in, calling the place Castle Defiance. His creditors gathered on the lawn, built cooking fires, and bivouacked. They kept him under siege for forty days. When at last they attacked the house with axes and crowbars, he held them off with gunfire.

But he knew he was done. He sent word to the county sheriff to come escort him safely away. Robert Morris, the financial wizard without whom the Revolution would have been lost, the visionary of a great American nationhood founded on the Money Connection, was locked up for debt in Philadelphia's Prune Street Prison.

He wasn't alone in such troubles. The year Morris was jailed, his old ally Supreme Court Justice James Wilson died destitute at fifty-six. The legal brain of the Constitutional Convention, the certifier of the military suppression of western Pennsylvania, Wilson, too, hadn't been able to stop speculating in western land on borrowed money. Riding circuit in the South to escape northern creditors didn't work. He served two terms in debtors' prison before coming down with the malaria that ended his life in a tavern in North Carolina. There was no public memorial. James Wilson had become a national embarrassment.

Two years later, in the watershed election year of 1800, the last of the great Federalist majorities passed the nation's first bankruptcy act, designed in part to get Robert Morris out of prison, and three and a half years after going in, he came out. Five years after that, he died and was buried without public ceremony.

In 1801, with Jefferson the president and a Republican majority in the House, Treasury Secretary Gallatin began the phase that, while he couldn't have known it then, would last thirteen years, see four presidential terms, and launch the post-founding period in American life. That the creator of the office he now held had tried to have him hanged was an especially glaring indication of the change brought about by the 1800 election. In more practical terms, the man who had established himself as the Federalists' fiercest opponent on finance, budget, and economics now held the national executive office dealing with finance, budget, and economics. To bring into the cabinet a man so hated by the Federalists, Jefferson had to resort to a recess appointment and await true confirmation until the new Republican majority was seated.

That majority was raring to enshrine in law the happy moment when their man Gallatin consigned the Hamilton Scheme to the dustbin of history. When the new boss showed up at the Treasury Department—a new, two-story brick building on Fifteenth Street and Pennsylvania Avenue, near the President's Palace—he had a clear brief from his boss. He was to write a report detailing all of the errors, failures, blunders, and frauds committed by Hamilton when creating the system.

By now the department employed 1,285 people: 707 in customs at ports and 500 in internal revenue, supervised from Washington by 78 subordinates of the secretary, all dedicated to maintaining the governmental lifeblood flow of money from the people to the treasury, and from the treasury to the executive departments that carried out the laws, per appropriations by Congress. That was accomplished via constant, urgent communications, coordinating complex operations in piles of handwritten, hand-copied letters carried ceaselessly to and from various tax districts and ports by systems of express riders on the gallop. Any cessation in that gigantic effort would bring the federal government to a halt.

Gallatin jumped on top of the perpetual-motion machine. Long days were now spent reading and writing stacks of mail and delegating even more mail to his deputies and staffers. Running that operation on an hour-by-hour basis against a ruthless clock, he also began tracking the minutiae of its intricately interconnected subsystems. Thanks to Hamilton's projects, a lot of economic information was coming in from all over the country. Gallatin got a three-dimensional, hands-on look at Hamilton's creation, for the first time, in all of its stupendous detail.

Jefferson's idea of dismantling Hamilton's system was simple and three-part: repeal all internal taxes; fire all Federalist appointees and employees of the treasury and replace them with Republicans; pay off the Debt as cheaply as possible in a year or two or three. The bank's twenty-year charter wouldn't expire until 1811. That heinous violation of republican virtue couldn't be shuttered yet. All other parts of the machine should be taken down right away.

Gallatin started this phase of his career by disappointing the president. The problem, he informed Jefferson, was that he'd found the Hamilton system perfect. He didn't mean wonderful; he meant remarkably complete. Every part of the machine depended on every other part. You couldn't throw a monkey wrench into its guts and watch it stutter to a satisfying halt: the halt would be in the flow of cash to the government; government itself would be dismantled. Decades later, Hamilton's son John would say that an aged Gallatin told him, "Hamilton did nothing wrong," which the son framed as an endorsement of his father's system. Given Gallatin's uncompromising assaults on that system during the Adams administration, and given his plans for running national finance in 1801, that wasn't the most credible interpretation. Still, it was clear to Gallatin that Hamilton's system was ingeniously well integrated and couldn't be overturned overnight.

Firing everybody at the treasury, for example, would amount to eradicating all experience with operations. Blanket firings and hirings like that also fostered a partisan spoils system, where every time a new party takes power, important positions get handed out to supporters more or less regardless of competence. Gallatin opposed such systems as horribly inefficient. Absent a bureaucracy enjoying some degree of permanence, there was no way to run not just the treasury but the country's executive function as a whole. Jefferson would just have to accept certain facts. National finance had to exist, and it had to operate systematically.

Jefferson already knew that. The facts were, in a way, obvious. Yet he reacted emotionally to the persistence of Hamilton's system. It mortified him to acknowledge reliance on mechanisms he'd been condemning as a demonic violation of all that America was supposed to mean.

Gallatin stayed calm and optimistic. His real goal had never been to upturn everything in some histrionic act of creative destruction pleasing to Republican politicians. His goal was to achieve Jefferson's and the Republicans' best aims: reduce national government expense and indebtedness over time, thus putting the country in a position to afford things like infrastructure and an industrial policy without resort to debt financing, corporate cronyism, and deficit spending. All that could be achieved, Gallatin was sure. It would take hard work, discipline, thrift, patience. He had that, and now he had his hands on the nuts and bolts. He began executing his own, pragmatic version of a Jeffersonian finance policy.

He began with taxation. Reducing and even eliminating domestic taxation was a laudable goal, he thought, but the country couldn't yet afford to do that. Better to maintain the current excises for now, including the whiskey tax. That's what he recommended to Congress.

Jefferson had spoken to the exact contrary in his inauguration address. The Republican majority was hot to end domestic taxation. Congress rejected Gallatin's recommendation, and it didn't just repeal all excises. It abolished the service within the Treasury Department devoted to internal revenue.

Gallatin felt he could cope. Tax repeal didn't have to ruin things. He could make up for the loss of revenue by reducing expenditure. Military spending remained his chief target anyway; given tax repeal, he urged Congress to reduce the military budget even further than he'd already proposed. He also relied on his congressional majority to scrutinize and trim appropriations with special strictness. Here Congress agreed. Gallatin also felt he had the cooperation of his fellow cabinet appointees, who had come down on the antiwar side during the Adams administration: Madison as secretary of state; Henry Dearborn, of New Hampshire, as secretary at war; and Robert Smith, of Pennsylvania, as secretary of the navy, an office created amid the war fever of 1798. None looked likely to push for the kind of freewheeling military expenditures that blow budgets.

The big issue, of course, remained the Debt. Animosity toward it had become nearly a single-issue force in Republican politics. Jefferson's idea was to get rid of it all very quickly.

Gallatin, too, maintained a clear vision of a debt-free United States.

Not this year, though, or next, or anytime soon. The Debt, foreign and domestic combined, now stood at nearly $81 million; Oliver Wolcott had reduced it from the nearly $84 million of 1796. Gallatin's most realistic assessment was that with extreme patience and discipline, it could be fully paid off in less than a generation. That wasn't much sooner than Wolcott's target, but Gallatin thought that he, unlike Wolcott, could do it. Although that time span was far longer than Jefferson wanted, it was nevertheless ambitious. Gallatin knew he would have no choice but to dedicate a lot of annual government revenue just to servicing the huge interest obligation. Chipping away at the principal would be tough.

Still, he calculated, if $73 million of the total federal revenue per year could be earmarked for paying both interest and principal, in sixteen years the Debt brought to life by Morris and fostered by Hamilton could be ushered off the national stage by Gallatin. Reaching that goal, while avoiding the kind of taxes, other than customs duties, that had always been earmarked for funding the Debt, which Jeffersonian ideology now made politically infeasible, created a tiny eye in a tiny needle; to thread it, Gallatin would have to rely heavily on the customs at the ports and revenue from federal postal services. Other federal spending would have to be kept very tight.

The plan was workable, though, because he saw an opportunity for taking in further revenue by increasing sales of public land. Jefferson had always had a nationally expansive idea, which he sometimes called an empire of liberty: the westward spread of the small and middling American freeholder. Given the potential for war between France and Spain, and for Britain's seizing territory west of the Mississippi, the United States needed to populate and strengthen its western regions, partly by further removing the woodland nations into ever smaller areas reserved by treaty and policy for their use. Like other land speculators, Gallatin had his own acreages in the Northwest Territory. The idea of western expansion aligned with the Gallatin dream of American democracy: the virtues of his western Pennsylvania home, rolling farther westward.

Now he launched from the treasury a comprehensive assessment of all federal lands and earmarked sales for help in paying down the Debt.

In keeping with Jeffersonian ideological preference for small and middling farms, the new land system sharply reduced the Federalist administrations' minimums on grant sizes. The Anti-Hamilton, Gallatin would
not abuse government power by setting high minimums, selling only to
the rich and well-connected. Nor would the Anti-Husband impose low
maximums, put ceilings on ownership, bring about equality of means by
federal policy. Avoiding government control at either extreme should encourage, in Gallatin's view, the proper mix, with a preponderance tending toward the middle of the curve, resulting in a fairly even distribution
of property.

Happily, one piece of the Debt could be gotten rid of right away. The
government retained the obligation to the Bank of the United States
that Gallatin had criticized in his campaign books as corrupting. To extinguish it, he made a neat move—high-finance Jeffersonian-style. The
federal government had already sold some of its bank shares in the bank.
Gallatin sold all of the remaining shares to Alexander Baring, a British
banker, charging Baring a premium and applying the proceeds to paying
off the bank. As a result, the government no longer owned shares in or
maintained a financial obligation to its chartered corporation. So much
for that chunk of the Debt.

He had a long way to go with the rest, and bringing about a long-
range, multipart plan relied on political outcomes beyond his control.
The Republican party would have to hold both branches of government
for multiple presidential terms, and in Jefferson's first that by no means
looked inevitable. The Federalists, in the opposition now and fighting
hard, resisted Gallatin's plans and continued to question his patriotism
by calling attention to his foreign birth. Still, with Jefferson as president
and Madison as secretary of state, Gallatin was the third leg of a very
popular and powerful governing combination. Some writers would later
call the combination a triumvirate, associating it with the beginnings of
tyranny in ancient Rome. It wasn't dictatorial in that way. But given a
cooperative Republican majority in Congress, and given Jefferson's continuing popularity with the electorate, the trio was strong enough to get
a lot done.

Something else Gallatin's plan required: almost never leaving his desk. In those early years of cabinet service, when he was learning, operating, and changing the public-finance system of the United States, he sent his family back to Pennsylvania and sometimes to New York City and stayed in Washington right through the sticky, buggy summers when Congress was in recess and he was virtually alone in the swampland, smoking cigars and working. He got out of touch with western Pennsylvania. He continued to hate the capital, but that's where the job was. Innate abstemiousness helped. Amid personal day-to-day discomfort and loneliness, he would get the job done.

Such was Albert Gallatin's system, well under way by 1802, for realistically achieving the Jeffersonian goal of moving the country away from Hamilton's system. The goal was to get the country in a position to afford the great things that, until the country was in such a position, would just have to wait.

Things didn't wait, and the first thing that didn't was war, in Republican orthodoxy the great killer of fiscal discipline and promoter of tyrannical powers. Now the Republicans held power, and when the Pasha of Tripoli, on the North African coast of the Mediterranean Sea, declared war on the United States, Jefferson and the Republican-majority Congress made a priority of deploying ships that Gallatin had already argued against building in the first place. The country couldn't yet afford war, he told Jefferson. According to his calculations, it was about eight years too early.

Smith, the secretary of the navy, was getting excited about building up the fleet, and there was no military element Gallatin had less regard for than the naval. Jefferson tended to agree: navies meant imperial adventuring overseas; both men remained committed to the idea that the United States wouldn't start a foreign war. To Jefferson, a defensive navy was legitimate, though, and he'd ordered the building of gunboats for that purpose. To Gallatin, even gunboats looked like useless extravagance, a mere show of strength at a high cost, and he was realizing that Smith had an interest. The secretary's brother, Samuel Smith, was a Maryland shipper and diversified commercial operator with a lot of influence within the party. He'd considered serving as secretary himself but had gotten his younger brother to do it. Happy to see new ships built and outfitted for war, the Smiths had the clout to persuade some war-averse fellow Republicans to go along.

Then Secretary Smith made a unilateral decision to send a frigate to blockade the Barbary Coast. The move challenged Gallatin's persistent effort to remain firm but calm. There was literally no money to cover the expense of such an operation under the current official naval appropriations, and those appropriations' low levels reflected far more important goals: avoiding domestic taxation and, most important of all, paying the Debt down to zero on schedule. Gallatin sent Jefferson urgent pleas to countermand Smith's orders.

Jefferson came up with a way around the problem. Maybe just make the expense of the blockade a kind of debt, he suggested. That didn't seem super-Jeffersonian, but one way or another, Gallatin realized, Smith's frigate was at sea, the blockade was happening, and it was on him to accept the political facts and find the ways and means of accommodating them: that was the job. Things got even more challenging when officers and crew were captured. In response, Jefferson got Congress to increase naval appropriations to $750,000. With domestic taxes ruled out, Gallatin had to sit at his desk and pound out ways to pay for that too. Smith started asking for various amounts, here and there, with no discipline or clarity, claiming they were critically important and promising to pay the money back out of later years' appropriations. Gallatin put his head down and kept grinding.

It was a scramble, but he found all the money and balanced the books. Increasing taxes on imports, he earmarked them for the war effort. He raised tonnage duty on foreign ships using U.S. ports by 10 percent. He kept his long-range Debt-paydown schedule in place and avoided asking for domestic taxes. That was success. Yet the Tripoli escapade turned out to be only the first in a series of opportunities and problems that led to unexpected political decisions that might as well have been designed to undermine all of his careful fiscal planning. The next one came soon, and it was far bigger than Tripoli.

The issue involved Gallatin's only important predecessor. In 1803, Hamilton was still a Federalist party organizer and strategist and a constant attacker of the Jefferson administration in his newspaper, the *New York Post*, which he'd founded for that purpose; articles focused on allegations of Republican incompetence, with occasional discussions of supposedly scandalous goings-on in Jefferson's personal life. Now Hamilton learned that Napoleon had acquired from Spain a big chunk of the vast region west of the Mississippi, the section known as Louisiana. Having always wanted U.S. possession of both the strategic and commercial hotspot the port of New Orleans and the coastal buffer Florida, he relished apprising Madison of this news, which might represent a serious threat to national security. Hamilton started talking about it that way in the *Post*. Negotiating for a purchase from France was one way to go, he said, but he saw war with France as, yet again, the easiest path to U.S. security, probably inevitable anyway. At least invade both New Orleans and Florida and negotiate from a position of strength.

He called again for military buildup. "If the President would adopt this course," Hamilton wrote, "he might yet retrieve his character; induce the best part of the community to look favorably on his political career, exalt himself in the eyes of Europe, save the country, and secure a permanent fame. But for this, alas! Jefferson is not destined!"

Jefferson hoped to avoid war with France. He was willing to negotiate a deal that would sustain U.S. sovereignty even if France did end up holding the land west of the Mississippi. But then word came that Britain and France were going to war with each other again, and France badly needed money. Napoleon was offering to sell to the United States some or all of the Louisiana territory he'd just acquired.

This was surprising. The offer gave the United States a once-in-a-lifetime chance to acquire, for $15 million, both the port of New Orleans and exclusive control of the Mississippi River that flowed toward it. Negotiators led by James Monroe offered France $11.5 million for New Orleans and river control. The French stuck at the $15 million they'd decided they needed to fund a war, but they made that the price of buying not just New Orleans, plus river control, but the entire vast territory to the west, with only $11.5 million payable in cash, the rest to come from wiping out U.S. claims on France left over from the buildup to war in 1798. Quite a deal.

Hamilton, his war on France yet again stymied, said in the *Post* that the great landmass might not offer much; the goal should be to get hold of New Orleans no matter what. Spain would soon want the western land back, he believed, so the United States should buy it now, then trade it to Spain for Florida, a far more strategic prize, to Hamilton, than all of that western territory, which he saw as more or less valueless to the United States.

Jefferson had meanwhile plunged into a constitutionalist identity crisis. He and Madison had built their party's ideology around strict limitations on power. The thing he was about to do—and he was about to do it—far exceeded powers constitutionally granted the president, in his view. Anything not explicitly enumerated was prohibited, and there was no enumerated power of the presidency, or of the federal government as a whole, to buy land from foreign governments. "The general government," he said, "has no powers but such as the Constitution gives it. It has not given it power of holding foreign territory, and still less of incorporating it into the Union." Tossing and turning in the existential quandary, Jefferson could hardly bear the inconsistency.

So he came up with a solution. He proposed that the Constitution be amended to allow the purchase, specifically, of the Louisiana territory. He sat down and wrote a draft of the amendment, which included a detailed plan for administering the region. The plan largely ignored the port of New Orleans and focused almost entirely on the great western landmass as a good place to remove the woodland Indians.

Gallatin did his best to talk his boss off this ledge. He found both the degree of upset and the granularity of the proposed amendment overwrought. He and Jefferson had long been excited about the potential of the region across the Mississippi, if not for immediate settlement, then for freeing up space for white settlement east of the river by Indian removal west of the river. Even before Napoleon's offer, Jefferson had sent Captains Meriwether Lewis and William Clark to explore all the way to the Pacific, assuring Spain and France that the expedition was solely for scientific purposes. The presidency was well within its powers in making the Louisiana deal, Gallatin assured Jefferson, with no need for something as over-the-top as a constitutional amendment, which would have to go through a long ratification process anyway. The United States enjoyed all the powers of nations, including making treaties to extend their territories. That treaty-making power was in the hands of the presidency, with the advice and consent of the Senate.

The real question Gallatin had to face regarding the deal with France wasn't constitutional but practical. He had reason to see what became known as the Louisiana Purchase as a body slam to his entire fiscal approach. It was to be the biggest land deal ever made. Federal budgeting was already strained by Smith's indulgences in the Mediterranean. Paying down the Debt on schedule remained the highest-priority and longest-range goal not only of Gallatin but also of Jefferson and Congress. Given Jefferson's and Congress's equally firm commitment to avoiding domestic taxes, Gallatin had been keeping budgets stringent. Now he had to come up with $11.5 million out of thin air, without resorting to domestic taxes.

He refused to be overwhelmed. Like everything else, the purchase would just have to be figured out, and the only way he could figure it out was through new debt financing. To Jefferson, debt financing was a noxiously Hamiltonian plan, and Gallatin decided the best way to handle this particular loan would be to get involved with British banks, a situation that, had it been predicted when Jefferson was running for president only three years earlier, neither he nor his supporters would have believed possible. The president writhed with mixed feelings. Gallatin went ahead and set up a deal that would enable the purchase in the absence of domestic taxation.

Aided by the Amsterdam banking house Hope and Company, logistics depended on cooperation between the government of France, as the seller, and British bankers, including Baring, as the underwriters—despite the fact that the situation driving the purchase was impending war between France and Britain. Gallatin had the U.S. Treasury issue a new round of bonds, the first ever introduced solely on the international market, and used them to pay France somewhat more than the $11.5 million cash part of the purchase price. By agreement, the British bankers then bought those bonds from France, but at a discount, so France got its target price. The bonds' price began rising in the market, so the British bankers got a profit from U.S. assets they'd bought cheap. And Europe got the Napoleonic Wars.

Gallatin didn't love the discount on U.S. bonds. It didn't reflect his positive view of U.S. credit. Still, the deal doubled the geographical size of the nation's jurisdiction at about 4 cents per acre, with no new taxes. Hamilton pointed out in the *Post* that as there had been no choice but to do the one thing the Jefferson administration had ever done to serve the country, no brilliant leadership was involved in making the purchase. The ironic fact remained that the government was able to finance the deal only because Hamilton himself had put U.S. credit on a sound-enough basis abroad, via policies that Jefferson had vehemently opposed.

Almost all other Federalists went the other way. Taking up the critique that Jeffersonians had once leveled against them, the minority condemned the purchase as an unconstitutional executive overreach. Jefferson was so worked up over what he'd done that the critiques stung, but by the time the deal had taken full effect, Hamilton's had ceased. In July 1804, the author of the Hamilton Scheme succumbed to wounds from a ball fired by Aaron Burr in a pistol duel over a supposed personal insult purportedly made by Burr during the New York governor's race in 1802.

Gallatin could take satisfaction in the Louisiana deal as quite anti-Hamiltonian. It was true that the purchase had generated a new addition to the Debt, but with thrift and discipline always in mind, he took an inventive approach to paying the interest, even while sticking with the original sixteen-year paydown schedule for the enlarged principal. He got Congress to increase the annual appropriation earmarked for paying both interest and principal, and to raise the money for that, he leveraged new benefits of the purchase itself. A lot of foreign goods were coming through the new U.S. port of New Orleans; Gallatin raised tariffs. Another source of revenue would be new land sales in the new U.S. region west of the Mississippi.

Curveballs had been thrown. Discipline had prevailed. Having navigated both Tripoli and the Louisiana Purchase, with Debt paydown still on schedule and no domestic taxes, Gallatin was fostering the dynamic national growth he'd always wanted to see, along lines as reasonably Jeffersonian as possible, while running the day-to-day operations of the treasury and sacrificing his own comfort and happiness to living in a painfully inhospitable capital. Thanks to his dedication and ingenuity, by 1805 the new system could be said to be more or less working. Exports were rising. Revenues from customs, tonnage, and land sales were strong. The Mississippi could be permanently relied on. The Debt was on a credible track for extinction. The federal government was actually operating on a surplus; it would reach $18 million by 1808. The question now was what to do with it.

It was time, Gallatin and Jefferson agreed, to begin reaching for long-term national goals. The point of fiscal discipline had never been to cripple national government but to nurse it to what they saw as economic health. Having to service a rising public debt kept the country too ill, in their view, for projects to flourish; with the Debt heading to zero and tight spending fostering the surplus, health had been regained. In 1804, having increased the power of the executive branch beyond anything his two predecessors could have imagined and reelected by a far wider margin than that of 1800, Jefferson acknowledged and even asserted a startling shift in policy. In his second inaugural address, he announced that U.S. public finance was approaching what he depicted as a kind of golden age. Day-to-day government expenses were being met. The Debt was being not only reliably serviced but also steadily reduced. The surplus was going up. All that came not from tyrannical Hamiltonian big government but from its opposite: reductions in the size, scope, and force of government, thus proving almost miraculously the essential truths of the Republican philosophy of the Constitution.

So he ran up the flagpole both a federal infrastructure policy and a federal industrial policy. To critics, that was the kind of thing he'd campaigned against in 1800. But both Jefferson and Madison, once so passionate about constitutional restrictions on unenumerated power, no longer saw national initiatives as attacks on the meaning of America itself, and Gallatin had never taken such a restrictive view of the Constitution anyway. The president's seeming reversal of governing philosophy might have confused supporters and enemies alike, and was characteristically mercurial, yet Jefferson had always agreed with Gallatin that national growth was good. The issue was affordability. A national infrastructure seemed critical to American unity and prosperity. Gallatin was eager to run with Jeffersonian nation-building.

By now, the region long called Ohio had been carved out of the Northwest Territory and admitted as a new state. Gallatin had gotten a measure for a federal interstate highway into the law that created it: the Cumberland Road, to originate in Cumberland, Maryland, run past Gallatin's house in western Pennsylvania, connect the Potomac with the Ohio, and save maybe $200,000 per year in trucking costs. Ultimately he hoped to create a network of roads and waterways interconnecting the whole country, North to South, East to West. He planned to advise Congress on writing a comprehensive infrastructure bill.

Jefferson, however, having made the big announcement, again began fretting over the constitutional issues. If some of his supporters and enemies were confused by his change of direction, so was he. Federal management of interstate projects would clearly interfere with the sovereignty of the states involved. Again he thought a constitutional amendment might be needed to let him do legally what he'd ruled out as illegal when the other party was in power. He also thought such projects could legitimately be paid for only by apportioning the necessary funding among the states involved, based on their populations. To Gallatin, that would be a terribly disunifying approach. He argued this point hard with Jefferson. Federal costs should be a matter of federal policy, he said, determined by the federal legislature, as advised by the federal executive regarding how best to spend a federal surplus for the improvement of the whole nation.

A road might benefit states beyond the state where it ran. Benefits and downsides should be fought out on the floor of Congress. That was how the United States would best arrive at a just and balanced national infrastructure law.

This argument between Gallatin and Jefferson wasn't resolved. It was interrupted. In 1807, just as the Senate was asking Gallatin, at Jefferson's behest, for a report on roads, canals, and transportation, foreign affairs pushed the United States into a new crisis, and in response, Jefferson made yet another move that Gallatin couldn't have seen coming.

As usual, a single incident blew up a preexisting turmoil. Financed by the sale of Louisiana, the Napoleonic Wars were under way. Because Britain wanted the U.S. merchant fleet to trade only through British ports, the Royal Navy had started blockading other European harbors to keep American shipping out. Deserters from British ships joined U.S. merchant ships; the Royal Navy pressed U.S. sailors into British service. France meanwhile attacked U.S. ships that complied with British demands. Elements of the American public were already crying for war against France and Britain when, in June 1807, off the coast of Virginia, crewmen from the British warship *Leopard* boarded the American frigate *Chesapeake*, seized four deserters from the Royal Navy, and took them to Halifax, Nova Scotia, where one man, a British citizen, was hanged. The other three, American citizens, were sentenced to five hundred lashes, an astonishing punishment, though the men's release was negotiated and they avoided it.

Jefferson immediately banned British ships from American waters. Clearly far more than that would have to be done to defend U.S. sovereignty from European powers. Congress probably had no choice but to make war. Fighting the Pasha had been expensive enough. This would be a fight with the British Empire.

Gallatin was in Philadelphia on his way to New York when news reached him of the *Leopard* incident. The situation looked disastrous for all his plans. He rushed back to the capital and began his usual patient, diligent scrambling.

26

ALBERT AGONISTES

SECRETARY OF THE NAVY Smith was already hot to send warships. Declaring war on both Britain and France was under discussion in the cabinet. Gallatin calculated the cost of war just against Britain—there was no way to afford waging war on both empires—at about $18 million per year and was considering, naturally, burning through the surplus, borrowing from the Bank of the United States, and imposing domestic taxation. That would ruin all his plans. Yet war looked truly necessary. It was his job to pay for it.

Jefferson, however, began envisioning a course somewhere between accepting ongoing national humiliation at the hands of the European powers, especially Britain, and making outright war. Commercial, not military warfare would better fulfill the Republican ideological principle that the United States should persist, internationally, in a state of benign disentanglement. The president therefore proposed, with Madison's advice and support, what Congress passed at the end of the year: the Embargo Act of 1807.

With a series of additions that Jefferson and Congress made in 1808, the act banned all American ships from engaging in any foreign trade at all—permanently—meaning at first no imports but soon no exports either. The idea was to punish both Britain and France by preventing them from buying U.S. goods or selling their own goods in the United

States; to show all European powers that they needed America more than it needed them; and to obviate war.

The law was conceived and passed over Gallatin's strenuous objections. To him, an embargo didn't obviate the economic disaster of war, and European powers didn't, actually, need the United States more than it needed them. He could easily predict both the diplomatic futility and the economic disaster for the United States ensuing from total stoppage of American exports, which had been on the rise and stimulated the economy, and of customs and tonnage duties, from which, in the absence of domestic taxes, the federal government derived most of its revenue. Nor was this one of those challenges to his plans to which he could apply time and effort to figuring out ways over, under, around, and through. Even actual war itself, Gallatin advised Jefferson, would be less permanently destructive of America's economy and public finance than embargo.

His predictions were correct. Wave after wave of bad effects rolled through the country and set regions at odds. As dock work and all other labor related to foreign trade ceased, New England merchants especially were making no money, further alienating the region's Federalists from the administration. Mass unemployment sparked mass protests. The British no longer had to impress U.S. sailors: U.S. sailors were looking for jobs with the Royal Navy. Aggressive smuggling boomed, and it was up to Gallatin and the treasury to prevent it, but arresting and charging smugglers required such constant policing by the customs service that Gallatin had to ask for help from the army and the navy. The Great Lakes and the Maine coast saw shootouts between soldiers in gunboats and smugglers in light craft.

Most important, to Gallatin: principle was being violated. He tried to tell Jefferson. To have any chance of effective enforcement, the treasury would need arbitrary powers of warrantless search and seizure— tyrannical violations recalling British colonial policy in the 1760s. The embargo's targets were supposed to be European powers, but nothing required heavier-handed federal-government intervention in the day-to-day economic life of American citizens.

Jefferson had gotten the constitutional yips over buying Louisiana.

He seemed immune to Gallatin's constitutional arguments for ending the Embargo Act.

Gallatin remained hopeful nevertheless. In April 1808, he forwarded to Congress his Report on Roads and Canals, which the body had asked him for the year before. The report laid out the nation's first major interstate infrastructure program. Its close attention to local interests and effects was intended to push back against the sectional strife emerging from straitened conditions caused by the embargo. The goal was literal, physical unification. Going well beyond improvements already authorized, Gallatin's proposals included a road stretching from Maine to Georgia and a multitude of canals, some connecting the Hudson River with the Great Lakes; some through Cape Cod, the Delmarva Peninsula, and the Great Dismal Swamp; some connecting seaports such as Charleston with the interior. The plan had a whopping cost of $20 million, but the sum was payable over ten years, simply by new appropriations from the surplus, at $2 million per year. In no way would it slow the Debt paydown or require any domestic taxes. Here was federal infrastructure, Jeffersonian-style.

On the one hand, the report excited states and localities with the prospect of a flow of federal money for turnpikes, canals, bridges. That didn't mean they saw elegance in the comprehensive program Gallatin proposed; they saw what would later be called pork. On the other hand, the mood in Congress had changed since the body authorized the Cumberland Road. The strong federal-budget surpluses needed to pay for a national infrastructure seemed threatened by the effects of the embargo that Congress itself had passed. Proposing to spend $20 million in federal funds made the secretary once seen as cheap look wildly extravagant. Also sparking resistance was Gallatin's insistence that the federal government, not the states, should be handling all funding. The infrastructure report died in committee.

The embargo was meanwhile having an even more disastrous effect on both the ordinary economy and public finance than Gallatin had first feared—and he'd thought he'd feared the worst. Stoppage of trade had virtually no impact on the policies of Britain or France, but its impact on the United States was clear. As Gallatin began making fiscal projections for 1809, he saw that federal revenues were disappearing on him. If he stayed on track with all of his long-range plans for the Debt and other issues, the treasury, though functioning now, would go broke within a year.

Shortly before Jefferson left office early in 1809, the Embargo Act was repealed. During his eight years, the first Republican president had veered in many directions. Sometimes he'd seemed to ignore the basics of the philosophy of government he'd helped invent. Sometimes he'd seemed to double down on rigid but impractical Republican-constitutionalist principles. Gallatin, wending his way, had found means to encourage fiscally thriving nationhood, but the embargo had placed key elements of the nation's economic life beyond his administrative control. As the embargo had shown, in the absence of domestic taxes, the United States was fully dependent on international trade. That condition made the country far more beholden, far less benignly unentangled, than Republican ideology wanted to know. And Congress had failed to act on his infrastructure proposals.

If Jefferson tended to veer, Madison, taking office in 1809, was hard to read at all on national finance, on support for Gallatin's efforts, and on presidential leadership generally. Gallatin had hoped to take Madison's place as secretary of state, and Madison had endorsed the idea at first. But then he told Gallatin that Smith, the naval secretary Gallatin considered incompetent at best, would take over the treasury. Gallatin cracked that he couldn't do both jobs at once, so Madison made Smith secretary of state—a disastrous choice, in Gallatin's view—and asked Gallatin to stay at the treasury. Gallatin did. Madison, though the prime author of the theory of the U.S. Constitution strictly limiting the power of the federal government, now supported, if in a very general way, the idea of a national infrastructure. The new president even seemed to favor the kind of industrialization policy he'd rejected on constitutional grounds when Hamilton had proposed it.

Yet it remained by no means clear to Gallatin how Madison's other policies, which were supported by Republicans in Congress, aligned in any practical way with nation-building. Though the Embargo Act had been repealed, Congress now passed and Madison signed the Non-Intercourse Act, which targeted only Britain and France with an embargo and left the other powers alone. The new act was just as hard to enforce and, to Gallatin, just as ineffectual. Smuggling continued. New England was still in especially deep trouble. Exports plummeted, reducing American commercial income and causing further employment problems, which reduced the American public's buying power and thus dented imports too, which meant reducing all-important federal-government revenue drawn from customs.

Nor did any of these measures for avoiding outright war mean outright war couldn't break out any time—and have to be paid for. That suspense alone had a huge impact on Gallatin's budgets. Congress kept passing appropriations for military buildup; gunboats kept being built. Gallatin could support war, if he had to, just as a logical consequence of conflict. Wars at least had end points. But the majority in Congress feared both war and submission to foreign powers, so what Gallatin saw as the least optimal situation remained indefinitely in place: an expensive military buildup combined with an ineffectual harassment of European powers, economically disastrous for the United States.

At the end of 1809, he reported to Congress a deficit of $1.3 million—the first deficit of his time in the office. And that was just the difference between normal operating expenses and revenue, with nothing dedicated to paying down the Debt's principal. He put Congress on notice that if its military expansion, including the building of gunboats, which seemed especially exorbitant to him, continued on course, the deficit might grow to about $3 million in the next year. While extinguishing the Debt of course remained job one, Gallatin reminded Congress that, should there be an actual war, there would be no choice but to spend everything necessary to win it.

Further borrowing, he announced, was therefore necessary to military preparedness. Early in 1810, he presented the means. He recommended taking a loan from the bank to meet operating costs, including paying interest and principal on the Debt. In May, the law passed, but because it stood at a pretty grim remove from Gallatin's thoroughgoing critiques, in the 1790s, of Hamilton's system, he had to take not just the usual criticism from the opposition but grumbling in his own party. He remained hopeful, though, because he kept pursuing the larger goals. Despite the failure of his canals-and-roads proposal, later that year he presented his Report on the Subject of Manufactures, urging Congress to create a $20 million program to support manufacturing startups. His rationale involved a silver lining of the embargo, which he didn't emphasize. Things had actually been going somewhat better than he'd predicted. The loan from the bank was helping pay down the Debt's principal; customs and tonnage revenue were having a comeback too. And the ban on imports had operated as a kind of chaotic, backdoor form of protectionism, encouraging U.S. businesses to manufacture more goods. Gallatin intended to build on that development with an active, organized federal effort. Taking an approach notably different from Hamilton's outright subsidy-and-reward, he instead proposed instituting the first federal loan program.

Congress rejected this report too. For delivering bad news in 1809, and even for delivering better news in 1810, Gallatin was now getting a lot of intensely articulated criticism from sectors of his party. They took bad news as a sign that he wasn't running the treasury properly, good news as a sign that he'd been exaggerating problems to get them to reduce military spending.

These criticisms reflected fateful shifts in Republican party politics. The Federalists continued their criticisms too, of course, but it was his fellow cabinet member Smith, now secretary of state, who had become Gallatin's real nemesis, along with Smith's brother, Samuel, who now represented Maryland in the Senate. The Smith brothers and Gallatin really just wanted each other out of the way. They saw him as unfairly trimming naval appropriations more harshly than anything else. He saw their commitment to naval budgets as corrupt: they made a lot of their money in transatlantic shipping. He therefore maneuvered an ongoing investigation into reviewing certain expenditures made during Smith's tenure as secretary of the navy. The brothers, outraged by the implicit accusation, planned to drive Gallatin out of office and out of the party.

Another Republican enemy, allied with the Smith brothers, was one William Duane, who operated in Pennsylvania, Gallatin's own state. A far fiercer Jeffersonian than Jefferson himself, Duane was the powerful editor of the hyper-Republican newspaper *The Philadelphia Aurora*. When first taking office, Gallatin had infuriated him by refusing to respond to a list that Duane had made of treasury staffers who should be fired for Federalist loyalties; Duane tried to turn Jefferson against Gallatin and get his own people patronage jobs, over Gallatin's objections. Gallatin looked down on Duane as a crude hack, and while Duane could indeed be crude, it was partly the rowdy style of his working-class roots and constituency that Gallatin seemed to find distasteful, even hard to process. Now Duane's paper had started calling Gallatin a devious secret president dragging Madison down.

Duane and the Smiths were joined in assailing Gallatin by William Giles, a powerful Republican from Virginia, long in the House, now in the Senate. He and Gallatin had once been allied in opposition to the Alien and Sedition Acts, but recently Giles had tried to block the possibility of Gallatin's becoming secretary of state.

The biggest shift in the party, however, was driven by a crew of younger men, mainly southern, active in their states' politics, recently or soon to arrive in Congress, and representing a true postwar generation— not old enough to have fought in the War of Independence, in some cases not old enough to remember it. They included Henry Clay, of Kentucky, born in 1777; and John C. Calhoun, of South Carolina, born in 1783. While not inclined to join forces with party regulars like Giles, they were demanding a full-on war with Britain to salvage what they construed as the violated honor of the United States, and combining the most knee-jerk Republicanism—no taxes, no Debt, no national banking, the national government totally out of all domestic policy—with excitement about glory and conquest, they had no regard for financial punctilio coming from wet-blanket party elder Albert Gallatin.

By 1810, these divisions in the party had hardened along lines that posed real problems for Gallatin's hopes for the country. Aside from the ongoing possibility of war's breaking out—the suspense had prevailed for three years—the main issue now was the fate of the Bank of the United States. On March 4, 1811, the twenty-year congressional charter granted in 1791 would run out, and for a certain breed of lockstep Republican, that would be a glorious day. The last vestige of the Hamiltonian reign of witches, that illegal, un-American institution terminally unfair to states and state banking, might finally be laid to rest.

For Gallatin, though, the bank had become a critically important fiscal tool. He'd been relying on its intended purposes: federal borrowing, federal transactions throughout the country via stable banknotes, and federal deposits. Before taking office, he'd criticized abuses he'd identified in aspects of the government's relationship to the bank. Yet as early as his first year in office, he and Thomas Willing, Robert Morris's old partner, the bank's director, were coordinating federal money operations via the national finance hub, just as Oliver Wolcott had. More recently, he'd come to see federal borrowing from the bank, when necessary, as more reliable and less expensive than issuing securities and trying to get investors to buy them. During the Jefferson administration, when the boss had fulminated against the bank as deadly to the basic principles of the Constitution, Gallatin replied with bland technical descriptions of the operational benefits. Against Jefferson's exasperated better judgment, he'd even gotten permission to open a branch in New Orleans. While that fulfilled Jefferson's worst fears of creeping federal financial presence, to Gallatin it connected the Atlantic Ocean with the Gulf of Mexico via public finance: national banking as a unifying force. During Madison's 1808 election bid, Gallatin had kept the idea of renewing the bank charter muted. Now, in 1810, he began arguing for it.

Madison, of course, had originated the condemnation of the bank as unconstitutional. Back in 1792, he and the other Republicans had hung an entire ideology on that position. Yet as president, he was implying, though only implying, that he would support renewing the charter. At the end of 1810, Gallatin formally urged Congress to renew, and his allies in the House wrote a bill to that effect, with changes to the bank's structure proposed by Gallatin: a doubling of total capitalization to $20 million and somewhat greater involvement by the federal government in ownership and management. At first, support for renewal looked strong in the House. The Senate was considering the question too.

In January 1811, however, opposition came, and refractions in the Republican party played into a passionate renewal of the oldest American constitutional debate. For many Republicans, both veterans and newcomers, an anti-national-bank stance remained a matter of party identification. This preference for financial decentralization was at once ideological and interested: state-chartered banks, from Massachusetts to Virginia, were benefiting the state legislatures. State-finance forces saw a chance of knocking out their biggest competitor by refusing to renew the bank charter.

But some Republicans could see the benefit of national banking. The Federalists still did too. They mocked Gallatin for inconsistency on his party's supposedly sacred principles. The fight came down to votes held in both chambers on motions by anti-bank forces to postpone, indefinitely, a renewal of the bank's charter—meaning never renew it. On January 24, 1811, when the House voted, Gallatin had all of the Federalists, ironically enough, and a chunk of the Republican majority, but not a good enough chunk. The bank charter lost in the House by one vote, thanks to opponents in his party.

The Senate meanwhile debated a similar motion, with the argument against renewal led by Henry Clay. He'd come to the chamber in 1806, at twenty-nine, three months before he was eligible for the seat; he would soon move to the House, becoming the youngest speaker so far and, over the course of a long career, turning the speakership into one of the most powerful forces in American politics. Clay made his first splash in national government in the Senate's bank debate. He passionately revived the old Madison line that Madison had now given up and called the bank charter manifestly unconstitutional. Gallatin's long-standing enemy Senator Smith added objections, at great length, on supposedly practical grounds that would have been irrelevant if the constitutional issue played, arguing for the virtues of the state banks of Maryland, in which he had interests. Senator Giles, for his part, claimed the bank exposed the United States to British political influence.

On February 20, the Senate vote tied. The bank's last chance of survival therefore came down to Madison's vice president, George Clinton: his vote would break the tie. But Clinton was one of Hamilton's oldest nemeses, going back to the 1780s fight in New York over the federal impost. He was an enemy of Madison now too, having lost the presidency to him. Clinton voted not to recharter.

The Bank of the United States, first connection between Alexander Hamilton and Robert Morris, hub for Hamilton's system, and lately also for Gallatin's, ceased operations. The branches closed or were taken over by state banks. The bank's stock, along with the classical-style building in Philadelphia, was bought by the richest man in America, Stephen Girard; he'd already become the institution's major investor. A naturalized American born in France and living in Philadelphia, with a past in seafaring, slaving, smuggling, and arms dealing in Haiti and elsewhere, Girard was now a diversified merchant and financier, but because upscale Philadelphians saw him as foreign and disreputable, the state wouldn't grant him a corporate banking charter. He opened his new operation in the old building as a private, unincorporated institution: the Bank of Stephen Girard.

Gallatin took the bank's closure as a sign. He wrote to Madison resigning his office. His letter criticized the president for weak support on the bank issue and called out Smith's poor performance as secretary of state. Madison responded by replacing Smith with James Monroe; that was a victory for Gallatin, and he withdrew his resignation, but after years of absorbing surprise blows, and turning many of them to account, years of patiently holding his own and the country's course, years of living unhappily in Washington and staying optimistic in the face of opposition, he knew he'd become enmeshed in an irresolvable conflict with strong forces in his own party. Smith's removal couldn't fix that.

The Clay men in Congress now felt themselves on a roll. They'd shut down the bank. It was time to pressure Madison to get a war going. Gallatin dug in, making a bid for fiscally responsible preparations for the war they were pushing. Madison had asked for 10,000 troops. Late in 1811, Gallatin told Congress that even without raising those troops, the country faced a deficit of more than $1 million, not for this year—trade had eased; duties and tonnage had been collected—but for 1812. A new loan would thus be needed. But not from the bank, since, thanks to Congress, the bank no longer existed. This loan could only take the old form of a new bond issue, pitched to investors. Getting them to buy would require offering a sweet deal: 8 percent interest.

He also announced that as of today, despite everything, he'd cut the principal of the Debt down to nearly half its size in 1800. That proved, he told Congress, that even with the new 8 percent bond issue he was proposing, ten years of peace and continued discipline would see the whole of the Debt extinguished, fulfilling the original Republican domestic mandate and his main reason for being in office. If, on the other hand, Congress really wanted to go to war, extinguishing the Debt would require the return of domestic taxation, by excise.

Congress rejected this report with umbrage. The Clay crew castigated Gallatin for trying to quash a war by making it seem as if the country couldn't afford it. At the same time they charged him with using the necessity of war as an excuse for pushing a return to Hamiltonianism in the form of domestic taxation, contradicting his earlier promises. Republican oratory got vicious. Senator Giles called the Treasury Department "decrepit" and mocked "the financial fame of the gentleman at the head of that department." He blamed Jefferson and Madison for pandering to Gallatin: "All the measures which have dishonored the nation . . . are, in a great degree, attributable to the indisposition of the late and the present administration to press on the Treasury Department, and to disturb the popularity and repose of the gentleman at the head of it." When it came to Gallatin's success in paying down the Debt, Giles even reversed the most hallowed Jeffersonian position. Who cared about a big reduction of the Debt? Giles asked. Did that really affect anyone's life?

In the House, Gallatin's fellow westerner William Findley, a veteran party leader these days, expressed his disappointment that excises had been brought up at all. The Republican press evinced horror that all

Secretary Gallatin seemed to be able to come up with were measures identical to Hamilton's.

Gallatin denied flip-flopping on taxation. There was no doubt that an 8 percent loan departed from the fiscally tight positions he'd taken when in the minority during the quasi-war with France, but in his first year as secretary he'd advised retaining excises, to no avail. Nobody remembered that. William Duane would soon publish an article with the headline: "The Rat—in the Treasury!"

Senate Republicans now presented a bill for raising 25,000 troops—more than twice Madison's proposed number—and framed the measure as a challenge to Gallatin's fabled financial abilities. If he was really so good, Giles said, Gallatin would get back to the drawing board and find a way—a Republican way this time, with no 8 percent bonds, no new taxes—to pay for his country's army. Head down, still grinding, war looming, Gallatin came right back to Congress in March 1812 with a proposal for an alternative bond issue, with sales revenues dedicated to funding a war: $11 million, but this time legally capped at 6 percent, to be paid off in twelve years. It would soon turn out that he was asking for far too little, but the amount looked unacceptably extravagant to members who were eager to fight a war and also to believe there must be some way to do so without new debt or new taxes. Given the manifest absence of such a way, Congress had no real choice but to approve the new bond issue, but a huge reaction came from the New England Federalists. They were dead-set against fighting a war at all. When the bonds were issued, almost no purchases were made by New England investors—effectively a boycott to make war fiscally impossible. Some leaders in the region were flirting with outright secession.

It wasn't just New England investors: sales everywhere were slow. Given the likelihood of war with Britain, which the bonds were supposed to pay for, investors thought a twelve-year payoff looked risky; given the absence of domestic taxes for paying the interest, the bonds looked unreliable; given the absence of national banknotes, the interest would have to be paid in hard money, which the treasury was clearly low on. Gallatin asked Congress to raise taxes on imports, and Congress did, but given all the international tension, imports were dwindling. Soon he would start issuing series of a new kind of federal security, known as treasury notes, paying 5.4 percent and accepted for paying federal taxes and debts, with principal to be paid back in a year. All of this borrowing was adding to the total principal of the Debt, reversing Gallatin's long, hard process of bringing it down. And still there wasn't nearly enough money to fight a war.

Such was the financial condition of the country on June 18, 1812, when the United States declared the war against Britain that Gallatin and Congress had been fighting so hard over how to pay for. This was the national government's first declaration of war: President Washington's war of conquest against the western confederation hadn't been declared; Jefferson's war on Tripoli had been fought under a congressional authorization for a police action. The cause of the declaration was officially said to be the ongoing impressment of American merchant sailors to service on British ships. But many Americans were also persuaded by Clay and his crew that taking the province of Quebec—"only a matter of marching," Clay said—would expand the country at little cost. Gallatin remained firm in his conviction that there wasn't enough money in the treasury, enough competence in the cabinet, and enough leadership in the presidency to win a war with Britain. Both William Eustis, secretary at war, and Paul Hamilton, the new secretary of the navy, were in over their heads. It would fall to Gallatin and Monroe to administer the whole effort.

Days after the declaration of war, Gallatin finally demanded what he'd long warned Congress he would have no choice but to demand in such an event. Without domestic taxation, operating expenses wouldn't be met, and the war would be lost. He proposed excises on, among other things, whiskey. Congress put off debate.

The United States failed in its attempt to take Quebec; instead, it surrendered Detroit to the British. In Washington, the British burned the building now officially called the Executive Mansion. Exports and imports dropped from 948,000 tons in 1811 to 60,000 tons by 1814. Hard money's scarcity put the country in a kind of depression, yet inflation reached nearly 30 percent in 1813 and 1814. The country fragmented fiscally, making war hard to carry on. The national bank's closure had launched a startup craze for state banks, which were proliferating so wildly—more than forty would soon operate in Pennsylvania alone—and issuing such a variety of competing notes, in amounts so far beyond their hard money reserves, that the notes lost value quickly, especially as holders got farther from the issuing institution. Transactions across state lines involved tortuous processes and heavy rake-offs and often became literally impossible. The U.S. Treasury, lacking any central place to hold federal funds, had no choice but to scatter its money all over the country in a defined list of state banks—nearly a hundred by 1814. That was good for the listed banks, terrible for federal military operations. Obstacles to moving money around the country made supply sluggish at best. Soldiers weren't getting paid. The federal armory at Springfield, Massachusetts, site of the Shaysites Rebellion of 1786, was forced to shut down.

It was clear to Gallatin that the only realistic way to raise enough money to pursue this war was to scuttle his long-range pay-down program for the Debt—his number one brief for so long, so painstakingly pursued—and borrow heavily. But the government's ability to borrow was badly hampered. The state banks, with capitalizations nowhere near the size of the old national bank's, couldn't lend the sums needed, and tied, legally and fiscally, to their legislatures, they placed parochial conditions on the federal loans they did make, demanding that the money be dedicated to the military defense of their own states and cities. That was no way to fight a war.

But the real problem was the old one: poor credit. State and private banks alike couldn't see how the federal government would pay a loan's interest and principal. Paltry federal revenue kept getting thrown into the gaping maw of wartime operating expenses. For the same reason, international banking houses weren't much help. Unsurprisingly U.S.

credit in foreign markets, recently well-established, had become suspect. By March 1813, Gallatin saw that the treasury wouldn't have enough money to get through the month. With nowhere else to turn, he looked to the American investing class and issued another $16 million in federal bonds. To attract certain buyers, Gallatin could choose, at his discretion, to sell the bonds below face value, but Washington, D.C., was in the process of being burned. The Treasury Building went up in literal flames. Even at a discount, he sold only $6 million of $16 million.

So in the end, it all came down to the most exclusive subset of what Robert Morris had once dubbed the Money Connection. Out of options, Gallatin made contact with the three richest men in America—next-generation rich, beyond the wildest dreams of Morris—and succumbed to their conditions for buying the rest of the bonds in bulk. They were Girard, the French-born Philadelphia banker and financier who had bought the defunct national bank's residue and building; John Jacob Astor, of New York City, born in Germany, a monopolist in the western fur trade; and David Parish, also German-born, a land speculator and financier. This private-equity trio formed a syndicate, involving a few other high rollers, for purchasing the remaining $10 million, at 88 percent of face value, though the real price was more like 42 percent because they paid for the bonds in depreciated state bank notes, which Gallatin accepted at face value, a discount matching, in the syndicate's eyes, the risk they were taking. Then they sold the bonds in smaller batches and at less advantageous prices to buyers whose confidence was bolstered by the involvement of the big players. The treasury took in desperately needed funds. The syndicate invented American investment banking.

To accomplish that feat, Gallatin had to give Girard, especially, an unofficial inside position in U.S. finance and economic policymaking. The investor demanded a flow of federal deposits into his non-chartered Girard bank. State-chartered banks that bought federal bonds had been promised exclusivity in receiving federal deposits, but Girard insisted that Gallatin extend to him the federal-relationship status enjoyed by the competitor banks in Philadelphia that had been trying to put him out of business, and Gallatin complied. The government was also pressured into a tacit agreement, via heavy lobbying by Girard, Parish, and Astor, that Madison and Congress re-create and charter a national bank, this time with the financiers' direct administrative input, a goal that would soon be accomplished. Thus the syndicate interlinked the smallest possible number of private investors, operating at the pinnacle of their enterprise and accountable to no electorate, with the fiscal policies of the presidency and Congress.

And still there was never enough money to fight the war and run the federal government. At the end of 1813, Congress did pass the domestic taxes that it had put off passing when Gallatin proposed them the year before, and added more: federal excises on domestic whiskey, domestically refined sugar, and carriages, plus transaction taxes on auctions. Exercising the cumbersome direct-taxing power that Hamilton had avoided using and Wolcott had briefly attempted, Congress sought revenue from levies on slaves, land, and houses, apportioning the amounts among the states, by population.

No reliable system existed for collecting any of it. In Jefferson's first term, Congress had abolished the treasury's internal revenue service. Because war impeded imports, customs revenue, too, was deeply suppressed. The U.S. Treasury just didn't have enough silver and gold to make all of its interest payments. In November 1814, the Madison administration defaulted on the Public Debt of the United States.

By then, Albert Gallatin was gone. His optimism and patience had long since turned into a kind of burned-out doggedness. In pursuit of reason, he'd taken endless knocks from a legislature and a party that had chosen to ignore and even deride his hard work, his warnings, his advice. With the declaration of war, he'd lost control over public events and public money, and the worst of his predictions had come true.

Instead of formally resigning, he asked Madison to appoint him to the commission traveling to Russia to negotiate with Britain for an end to the war. The idea was that he might be back. But he wouldn't be. Everything had changed. There was no longer any Hamilton, or any Husband, and at fifty-three the Anti-Hamilton and Anti-Husband began what would develop into a long series of further careers.

＊   ＊   ＊

When Gallatin first took office, in 1801, the Debt stood at nearly $81 million. In 1805, Jefferson was pointing to the dawn of a golden age, with a financial surplus and zero public indebtedness clearly in view: the American economy, he predicted, would soon be free of big-government finance, and therefore capable of developing the nation. By 1812, after more than a decade of draining work, continually challenged by one unforeseen executive and congressional decision after another, Gallatin had whittled the Debt down to about $45 million, with a realistic opportunity for extinguishing it all in ten more years.

The age wasn't golden. Nor was it an age—more like two years. Well before 1812, actions taken by two presidents and the Republican-led Congress undermined Gallatin's programs. The war brought that process to a climax. Gallatin left office with the federal government operating at a deficit of more than $17 million and the Debt at $127 million, about a threefold growth in only two years from the steep reduction he'd achieved in a decade of constant effort and over a third more than the total when Jefferson took office. The aftermath of the War of 1812 offered no path for resurrecting his nuanced version of a Jeffersonian America. There was the ongoing financial and economic crisis. There was the gigantic Debt. There were the taxes—many more than had prevailed before the Republicans took over on a rigid anti-tax platform. The situation really looked like a version of Hamiltonianism that, because it couldn't be politically acknowledged as such, was weaker and less stable than the original.

Hamiltonian banking was back too—with a vengeance. That was partly at the insistence of the Girard syndicate, but the war had clarified for many politicians the essential role of national banking in national government. During House debates over chartering a new bank, Henry Clay, now serving as speaker, took part—the first time a speaker did so. He announced that national banking was constitutional after all; John C. Calhoun, an ally of the anti-bank cadre of 1811, sponsored a bill for chartering an institution to be called the Second Bank of the United States. In his last year as president, Madison, having broken with Ham-

ilton a quarter-century earlier when extrapolating from national banking's supposed illegality a constitutional reading that would ring down
the ages, signed the Second Bank into law. It opened in January 1817 in
Philadelphia, a block west of Girard's. Its operations were conceived and
designed largely by Girard, Parish, and Astor, as well as by Alexander Dallas, a Pennsylvania statesman who had brokered relations between Girard
and Gallatin and now served as Madison's treasury secretary. With $35
million in capitalization, more than three times that of the old bank, and
ultimately twenty-five branches, the Second Bank interconnected high
finance and national government far more thoroughly than the first.

Gone almost totally missing, in the long fog of international events
and economic turmoil, was Gallatin's Jeffersonian version of federal support for infrastructure and manufacturing. The Cumberland Road did
get to Wheeling, Virginia, on the Ohio, but when Gallatin left office, no
interstate network of roads and canals was under way, no manufacturing policy had passed Congress. On his final day as president, Madison
vetoed an infrastructure bill sponsored by Calhoun and based in large
part on Gallatin's old report. The lame-duck president's rationale for the
veto was the old Jefferson idea that federal involvement would take a
constitutional amendment.

Gallatin, looking back from his 1814 exit on a career that, beginning in 1795, had played such a big part in what had become a chaotic
situation, put the best face on things. Through the decades to come, he
would go on looking back that way. He meant it, and he wasn't alone.
The proposition that everything might have worked out if not for the
embargo, or if not for the war, would have struck Hamilton, for one, as
tantamount to saying everything might have worked if not for the need to
govern, but many Americans would go on believing in Jefferson's philosophy of government as the great antidote to Hamiltonianism. In Gallatin's
American Dream—it's a dream about a particular definition of American equality—the enterprises of an inherently decent, thrifty, modestly
property-owning citizenry thrive because intrusions by the national government are kept out of their lives, thus rendering null and void the
great concentrations of wealth that depend on connections between

monopolies and too-active government. Hence an all-American brand of moderate democracy, deriving its energy from tension between the federal government and the states and proceeding from no ultimates, no extremes, no demands for guarantees of equal rights, entitlements, and opportunity via national citizenship—no national welfare state—but no crippling the federal government either. In the Gallatin dream, people living in such encouraging circumstances won't even crave excess, neither excessive luxury nor excessive equality. They'll be more like Albert Gallatin.

In normal waking consciousness, Gallatin arranged for the federal government to make a deal with the new generation of American oligarchs that made up the Girard syndicate. Those men, more commercially and financially sophisticated than any Morris, Schuyler, or Washington, presaged the titans of commerce and finance, freewheeling on whole new levels, who would arise in the late nineteenth century through connections to government and monopolize that period's astonishing escalations of speed, power, glister, grift. Gallatin could blur that class of person out of significance as easily as he could blur out the significance of the old Democracy. An organized oligarchy of monopolists in the national government had no more place in his America than an organized movement to emancipate labor via a national welfare state. He'd felt the threat to his personal safety posed by the Mingo Creek Association. He'd known Herman Husband, though he told his wife he hadn't. When he made a deal to give a private-equity syndicate control of national finance, he'd been friends with John Jacob Astor for years. However real the extremes, reality couldn't dent the dream of reason.

As for the War of 1812, it was settled in 1814, and not in Russia after all, but in France, by the Treaty of Ghent. The woodland nations lost further ground, but between Britain and the United States the war could be scored a draw, aside from demolishing the U.S. economy, and exposing Jeffersonian systems as even less sustainable than the Hamiltonian system that Gallatin had dedicated his career to undoing. It took a while for news of peace to arrive in the United States. With the conflict already concluded on paper, the last real battle was fought at New Orleans, and the American victory there, in January 1815, made a national hero of Major General Andrew Jackson, another youngish member of the Republican party with biggish ideas about banking, government, and American democracy. The founding of the United States in the fight over the Hamilton Scheme was over.

EPILOGUE

From the Jackson Era to the New Deal to the Great White Way

ON THURSDAY, MAY 17, 1923, on the south patio of the Treasury Building in Washington, D.C., dignitaries and other onlookers enjoyed the sunny spring weather while watching a gigantic bronze statue of Alexander Hamilton, standing on a high pedestal, receive its unveiling and dedication. As sculpted by James Earl Frazier, Hamilton posed in his glorious prime, open-coated, bareheaded, and swashbuckling, the romantic hero bursting with the Hamilton Scheme, quadriceps in tight breeches visibly surging with energy, the man if not literally larger than life, then acting that way. The statue's model was the bodybuilder Charles Atlas. Born Angelo Siciliano, he would later be known to generations of comic-book readers for a quick muscling-up program, advertised on back pages to what he called "97-pound weaklings" hoping to punch out beach bullies, but in the 1920s and '30s, Charles Atlas was in demand as a Founding Father model. He stood twice for statues of George Washington.

President Warren Harding gave the statue's dedication address, praising the founding treasury secretary's great legacy, but the most important Hamiltonian attending the dedication was Andrew Mellon, age sixty-eight. Serving under Harding, whose administration had become the most ostentatiously corrupt to that point, Mellon would soon begin serving under President Calvin Coolidge, whose administration, business-friendly and anti-labor, would see the start of an unprecedented stock-market rise. Mellon and the organized financiers he represented framed that boom as a trend toward a massive growth of wealth for both businesses and individuals, an irreversible trend, it was said, as long as business remained unfettered by federal regulation, taxation of companies remained low, federal borrowing was restricted, and the books balanced. Many Americans were already starting to revel in a sense that a new model for the economy would make everybody rich beyond their wildest dreams, with no possible downturn.

Throughout the ensuing decade, which came to be known as "the Roaring Twenties" for wild displays of new wealth, poverty stalked big parts of the country, especially the western farming regions hit by crashing agricultural prices. But Treasury Secretary Mellon wasn't just a cabinet official. He was the country's biggest private financier, born rich, the owner of many interconnected corporations and a leader in banking and investing. He opposed federal support for suffering farmers, focused on exciting sectors of the economy, and went on to serve in the administration of President Herbert Hoover.

He was also a big Alexander Hamilton fan—hence his role in the statue's dedication ceremony. Dubbed by the press the most important secretary of the treasury since Hamilton, he reveled in the comparison, and while the statue's donor was anonymous, it was rumored that Mellon's money and clout were behind its creation. What drove the fandom was less Hamilton's specific policies than the founding consolidation of American wealth and American political power. As far as Andrew Mellon and his kind were concerned, Alexander Hamilton was being enshrined that sunny day as a founding father not just for the Twenties, as the decade started roaring, but for all time.

*   *   *

It hadn't always been that way, and it wouldn't stay that way. By the 1920s, Hamilton's career as the preferred founder-of-the-moment had already had some ups and downs. After 1923, it would have some more.

Making political claims on the founders began when some of the founders were still alive. Albert Gallatin, who lived to be eighty-eight, was never in the running, though he served in the treasury three times as long as Hamilton and oversaw national finance during the rapid expansions of the Jefferson and Madison administrations. Gallatin had other achievements too. After leading the U.S. side in the negotiations for the Treaty of Ghent, in company with his young critic Henry Clay and John Quincy Adams, a son of his old enemy John Adams, Gallatin came home in September 1815, and when Madison asked him to resume running the treasury, he declined. He worked on getting Congress to charter the Second Bank of the United States; he discussed joining John Jacob Astor in business. But when Madison asked him to serve as the U.S. ambassador to France, Gallatin accepted with pleasure and moved his family to Paris, where they lived happily until 1823. He was nominated for the vice presidency in 1824, though he withdrew before the campaign; in 1826 and '27, after living for a time back in western Pennsylvania, he served as ambassador to Britain.

The next year, the Gallatins moved permanently to New York City. Long connected to the city and state's Republican party, in 1829 Gallatin founded an institution known as the National Bank in New York City, with a consortium led by Astor; in 1831, he and another group founded New York University. Meanwhile, he became a linguist. With the help of a Cherokee leader named John Ridge, Gallatin delved into the vocabulary and grammar of North American languages and published two books, *A Table of Indian Languages of the United States* and *Synopsis of the Indian Tribes of North America*. He went on to study the peoples of the Southwest. He came to the conclusion that the ancestors of both North and South American tribes had originally migrated from Asia. In 1843, he co-founded the American Ethnological Society, the first organization of its kind in the United States; the same year, he became the ninth president of the New-York Historical Society. By then, he was the last surviving member of Jefferson's cabinet.

Gallatin died in 1849 and was buried in the Trinity Church graveyard, at the corner of Broadway and Wall Street. Alexander Hamilton had been buried there for forty-five years. Their stones are about 160 paces apart.

It was during Gallatin's post-cabinet career that other founders, most notably Hamilton and Jefferson, started playing politically charged roles in the national memory. By the 1820s, the Republican Party, having held both the presidency and often a strong majority in Congress for more than a quarter of a century, was unrecognizable as the opposition group that had developed around Madison's break with Hamilton over the bank more than a generation earlier. The well-known expression "the Era of Good Feelings," introduced by a Federalist Party columnist in 1817—and synonymous with about two years of James Monroe's presidency—reflected the fact that the country effectively had one party now, the Republicans. And yet a largely Hamiltonian approach to the economy—the approach the Republican Party had been created to attack—prevailed nationally.

The whole point of the good feelings was to integrate Hamilton's and Jefferson's legacies. Those young hotheads led by Henry Clay, who had given Gallatin such trouble in the early teens, weren't young now, and their heads had cooled. Following his narrow 1824 presidential victory—another election that went to the House—John Quincy Adams, the New England presidential scion, hereditarily anti-slavery and opposed to what was called the "slave power," appointed as secretary of state the Kentuckian Clay, who enslaved people while condemning the institution, and they advanced an assertive federal legislative agenda intended to accelerate what observers would later call "the market revolution": a commercial and investment boom, ushering in just the kind of federally supported economic nationhood that Hamilton had been trying to foster.

Clay promoted this policy as "the American System." With Congress admitting new western states carved out of the territories, American agriculture was growing fast. Enabled by new technologies, manufacturing took off too. Both expansions were encouraged by assertive federal policies: funding interest payments on the Debt, partly by earmarking revenue drawn from sales of public land in the expanding West; the Second Bank's serving as a national economic hub; federal support for domestic manufacturing; and a federally supported buildout of interstate canals, roads, and bridges, based largely on Gallatin's failed report of 1808. The American System also depended on what had begun as the federal impost and was now called the tariff: a tax on a wide range of imported products. At 38 percent by 1828, the tariff was set high because it was designed not only to support government operations and the Debt, while keeping domestic taxes low, but also to give a big competitive price advantage to domestically manufactured goods.

As a youngster, Clay had slammed the first bank as a Hamiltonian violation of the Constitution. Now he paired Hamilton with Jefferson as what he called dual founding "master minds" of the American economy and promoted the protective tariff as a meeting of those minds.

Not everybody in the party felt that way about the founding period. Some still believed that all things Hamilton had to be destroyed. As differences over the American System started fragmenting the party, the various factions draped their arguments in oratorical deference to the great, departed founding generation's fights. Ironies abounded. It was Andrew Jackson and his followers who took up what had once been the rigidly Jeffersonian position against the bank, but Jefferson himself lived long enough to say, in 1824, "I feel much alarmed at the prospect of seeing General Jackson President. He is one of the most unfit men I know of for such a place." Gallatin said, "[Jackson] entertains, I believe, very sincere but very erroneous and most dangerous opinions on the subject of military and executive power."

Jackson criticized Jefferson, in turn, for never fully adopting and running with the old fundamentalisms. Performatively aggressive, evincing not a bit of Jefferson's philosophical, self-questioning reluctance about using presidential power, Jackson was eager to use all of that power and more to put a stake through the bank's heart and get rid of the whole of the Debt, right away, this time for real. To him, it was long past time to take Hamiltonian federal corruptions down hard.

His presidency, beginning in 1829, also had a peculiar relationship to the long-forgotten hopes of the founding-era Democracy. A backcountry westerner, born in an actual log cabin, Jackson was the first person with that kind of background to gain such high standing in official U.S. politics. In fact a rich landowner and slave driver, big in the cotton industry, with a Nashville estate known as the Hermitage, he hadn't been born to such success; he cast the spirit of American democracy as a national capacity for enabling anyone to rise to great heights socially, economically, and politically while retaining the rough style of a commoner.

So he courted the ordinary farmer and worker by opposing what he called "the monied aristocracy." It was an electioneering style that had begun earlier in the century. The approach wasn't that of 1776 Pennsylvania, empowering ordinary and poor men as a hands-on political class. There was no thought of fostering citizens' committees to oversee economic policy, no sending poor citizens to office or asserting legal protections for labor, nothing to do with Paine's and Husband's ideas about a right of national citizenship. Democracy came haphazardly, in the various states, where competing political groups wanted to organize electoral blocs via favors and loyalties, under strong-arm bosses, in vote-early-vote-often political machines. Universal white male suffrage's becoming law in the states had an effect, maybe not causal but at least concomitant, of further restricting the already strictly limited suffrage in the states of free people of color. Some women of property had been allowed to vote in New Jersey. They lost that right in 1807.

Hence Andrew Jackson's pitch to the common-man voter. Exclusion of others was part and parcel of the new democratic idea. Blending the agrarian, states'-rights rhetoric of a James Jackson, the absolutist constitutionalism of 1790s Madison and Jefferson, and the tendency of some in the old Democracy to mistrust all banking, contra Paine, and all centralized financial controls, contra Husband, Jackson went up against federal banking, federal debt, and domestic taxation on behalf of what he framed as the ordinary American by explicitly attacking the founding legacy of Alexander Hamilton.

To that end, he enlisted the aid of James Hamilton. Fourth son of the founding treasury secretary, sixteen when his father died and forty-four when Jackson became president, James Hamilton was a lawyer who served as Jackson's acting secretary of state before being appointed a U.S. attorney in New York in 1829. The next year, he wrote Jackson a long memo taking up the early position of Madison and Jefferson on the bank as an unconstitutional threat to liberty. Later, he framed that attack, somewhat mysteriously, as an attempt to do justice to his father's true legacy.

Jackson ran with the memo, publicly condemning the bank, accurately enough, as a monopoly; he also called it an avenue for foreign control over U.S. finance, a payoff for its stockholders at the expense of ordinary farmers and workers, and a corrupting influence on government. Refusing to make federal deposits in the bank, he undermined its stability. When the institution's charter again came due, in 1836, he vetoed a recharter. So much for the Second Bank of the United States.

The Debt, too, was finally extinguished before the end of Jackson's second term, and not through any patient, Gallatinian whittling-down but by full-scale presidential blockage of federal spending measures, combined with sales of western and southern public land, whose value was shooting up in yet another bubble. When Clay and others objected to what seemed Jackson's scorched-earth methods, the old divisions of the 1790s were back with a vengeance.

But there was a new division, too, this one over the institution of racial slavery. In the ensuing thirty years, it would become the decisive division. It played in surprising ways into new political claims on the legacies of Hamilton and Jefferson.

During Jackson's presidency, the enslavers' position hardened faster than the anti-slavery position. John Calhoun, Jackson's vice president, became the leading proponent of an influential theory of slavery in which, far from a necessary evil, the institution was a positive good. In this view, the enslavement of black people consolidated southern whites across all social and economic classes and made them one superior people, in contrast to a perpetually menial black class, and thus eliminated class warfare among southern whites. The administration also had another way of consolidating white people in a shared supremacy. In 1830, Congress debated Jackson's comprehensive plan of wholesale depopulation of what he called "a few thousand savages." The Indian Removal Act passed 28–19 in the Senate, 102–97 in the House. Over the next twenty years, the federal government would force more than fifty thousand people to leave their homes and move to designated areas thousands of miles westward.

Such was the origin of a new political entity. Reorganized out of a wing of the Republican Party, emerging in support of the Jackson presidency, it called itself the Democratic Party. Anti-national-banking, anti-Debt, pro-slavery, and pro–Indian Removal, the party put a simplified image of the late Jefferson on its marquee and made a simplified image of the late Hamilton its enemy.

For the actual "common man" of the pre–Civil War nineteenth century— that great majority, the small-farming and laboring white Americans on whose behalf the old Democracy had once made radical efforts—the facts of life differed starkly from glorifications made by the Democratic Party when holding up Jefferson as an inspiration. Politicians and writers, then and later, called the ordinary American a yeoman pioneer of Jeffersonian temperament and associated him with various competing political narratives, from the virtues of "free soil" expansion into new states, where slavery was prohibited, to a ruggedly individualistic libertarianism, in which people were said to thrive best when operating independently of government interference. Those images had little to do with the realities of life for laboring people.

Movements did form, as early as Jefferson's administrations, to assert the rights of western farmers—yet another advance celebrated as a key factor in the spread of American democracy. But despite white men's growing access to the vote, the hired hands, day laborers, and tenants on those farms, a mix of recent immigrants and members of the old landless class, continued to lack the nationally enforced legal protections and economic support that the old Democracy had fought for and failed to achieve, a lack also shaping the experience of the rapidly growing number of American factory workers. The rise of mechanized industry in the United States, critical to the market revolution, did not resemble the cooperative manufacturing put in practice in Philadelphia by the social radicals of the 1770s. The American factory ran much as Hamilton had imagined: production powered by long days of hard manual labor carried out by women, children, and poor men, some skilled at certain crafts, others simply providing the physical strength for running machines, all employed, or not, at the will of their employers.

Some later observers, viewing the nineteenth-century market revolution as a new flourishing of individual freedom, would hold up as an example the pencil factory owned and operated by the father of the writer Henry David Thoreau. While the Thoreau pencil did dominate its all-important industry, workers in that shop would get few mentions: in this brand of Jeffersonianism, all the glory went to the entrepreneur. Often mentioned, by contrast, both later and at the time, were workers in the famous textile mills of Lowell, Massachusetts. At first almost all young women, they were closely observed because they represented a great shift, controversial at first, from farm to factory and rural to urban, which would take more than another century to complete. Many observers praised the Lowell situation for combining control over the women's workdays with control over their meals, housing, education, and brief downtimes, thus assuring their moral upkeep. In 1861, the visiting English novelist Anthony Trollope called the mills a "commercial utopia."

Two-fifths of that labor force was made up of children under sixteen. The workday was thirteen hours in summer, sunrise to sunset in winter. Exhaustion and malnutrition kept workers' health poor. In northern factories in general, wages were already declining by the 1830s, in keeping with Hamilton's hopeful long-range projections: the lowest-paid women made $1.25 per day for a six-day week of sixteen-hour days—about $40.00

in 2024. Factory towns and manufacturing sections of cities were increasingly run-down, polluted, crowded.

Such was the industrializing North. For free laborers in the agricultural South, Calhoun's theory of black slavery as a white class unifier was given the lie by rigid stratification between rich and poor white people, even more pronounced in the South than elsewhere and encouraged, not ameliorated, by the rapid growth and spread of slavery in the booming "Cotton Kingdom." The monoculture depended on factory-organized systems of the ever-expanding field and barn labor of enslaved black people, putting white laborers out of work and making them vagabonds, subject to arrest for crimes that included so much as even socializing with a black person. Jackson's efforts against the bank and the Debt, made in the name of the honest laborer, led to the Specie Circular Act of 1836, which demanded good old "hard money," gold and silver, for rent and sale of public land, triggering the usual waves of foreclosure and hitting white southerners especially hard, with food scarcity rampant.

Extreme inequality thus pervaded the country. When the Civil War began, the top 2 percent of the U.S. population owned 40 percent of U.S. land; the poorest had what would later be called "net worths" of about a hundred dollars, with roughly a third of the total population living day-to-day with nothing more than some clothes and very occasional coin. Stories told then and later of the role of free labor in the rapid geographical and economic growth of the United States made little place for the daily physical and mental labor of the great majority of free people, impoverished despite their hard work in driving that growth, slow hour after slow hour, long day after long day, with no legal protections regarding conditions or hours, no legal floor or ceiling to employees' ages, no hope of rest or retirement, the only alternative to toil a sudden bout of unemployment that would make everything far worse.

In 1834, during Andrew Jackson's first term, workers on a Chesapeake and Ohio Canal construction site at Williamsport, Maryland, went on strike. How the company and the federal government responded to that action said a lot about the founding legacies of Jefferson and Hamilton when put to political purposes.

A group of Irish immigrant workers was demanding that the Chesapeake and Ohio Canal remain, in later labor parlance, a closed shop. The goal was to disallow new hirings of other Irish immigrant groups, in part because outsiders might be willing to work for lower wages; the organizers were also demanding decent working conditions, including a promised three meals a day, long denied. Calling a strike to force ownership to comply with their demands, they prevented, by force of arms, other groups' efforts to work anyway.

Violence among worker groups broke out. Construction stopped. The canal company, a state-chartered monopoly, maintained a cadre of spies and thugs to keep the workers in line and treated the local militia as its own police force. Rumbles among workers were followed by armed skirmishes between workers and the militia. One man was beaten to death. Citizens in the region were in a state of alarm.

But then the various worker groups met, negotiated, and arrived at a signed agreement, among themselves, to keep the peace. That didn't help. The canal company's finances had been crashing anyway, with creditors calling in large loans. The president of the company, John Eaton, was planning a big layoff and expected a lot of further worker trouble. Fortunately for him, he was President Jackson's former secretary of war and a close crony. In late January, Eaton asked Jackson to deploy a cadre of federal troops to occupy the whole line of the canal's construction and break any strike that might arise. With no federal crime even alleged, the Democratic majority in Congress authorized the president's order to move two companies of regulars to the site and maintain them there for months to intimidate labor organizers and suppress labor action.

Andrew Jackson thus became the first president to use the national military to break a strike. Along with Indian Removal and the promotion of slavery, using a national force to crack down on industrial labor organizing on behalf of corporate monopoly, launched the party that called itself Democratic and held up Jefferson, in opposition to Hamilton, as its founding inspiration.

*   *   *

In the 1860s, the Democratic Party was challenged by a new party, formed behind Abraham Lincoln in opposition to the expansion of slavery, and it, too, claimed Jefferson, not Hamilton, as its spiritual founder. The party named itself after Jefferson's: the Republicans. Like the Democratic Party, the new Republican Party framed its constituency as the common man: the small farmer and the free laborer.

So here, too, the old Democracy might have seemed revived and empowered. In 1861, Lincoln made a speech calling the claims of labor superior to those of capital and saying they should get higher consideration. That sounded like the radical line Thomas Young had urged back in the 1760s and '70s—if anyone had remembered it—when demanding that government privilege labor over wealth legislatively. In the 1776 Pennsylvania constitution, Young had wanted a legal cap placed on property ownership. Herman Husband's constitution had imposed similar restrictions in the service of equal rights and a high quality of life for working people.

But Lincoln's labor philosophy really combined the Gallatinian dream of the free, westering farmer with the Hamiltonian need to operate a consolidated national system in the Henry Clay mode. In that same speech, almost in the same breath, Lincoln's free laborer saves enough money to become an owner, hires new free laborers, and the virtuous cycle goes on: it's all good; there's no call to contemplate any national policy protecting labor from wealth by law. In that context, the Homestead Act of 1862 made millions of western acres available, virtually free, to small farmers. The policy dovetailed all too easily with Indian Removal—after the Civil War, U.S. policy for handling the Sioux, President Ulysses S. Grant and General William Tecumseh Sherman agreed, was extermination—but homesteading did echo Husband's system for ensuring land to every citizen by right. Here again, though, the thrust was Gallatinian encouragement, not a right of the citizen. There was to be no overhaul of American economic and political structures to equalize opportunity universally and restrain wealth.

Karl Marx nevertheless harbored hope for Lincoln as a radical. The inventor of a new critique of capital, an activist for a global revolution by labor, a close observer from London of the American Civil War, Marx wrote to the president to congratulate him on the U.S. victory and rope both the victory and Lincoln himself into a dialectical historical process of revolution. The end of racial slavery in the United States, creating an expanded, biracial, free-laboring proletariat, would lead as if inevitably, Marx believed, to those further steps by which the proletariat everywhere in the world would seize the economic engines and the majority would rule at last. Lincoln had his minister to Britain, Charles Francis Adams, a son of John Quincy Adams, write Marx an all-too-polite brush-off.

Lincoln made his most powerful emotional claim on the founding spirit of Jefferson during his greatest effort: at once building on and healing the Civil War. In his famous 1863 speech at the U.S. soldier cemetery in Gettysburg, Pennsylvania, he engaged in a brilliant rhetorical twist, associating the Declaration of Independence's preamble, as drafted in 1776 by Jefferson, with what the war had made a U.S. anti-slavery position now taken on morally absolute grounds; "All hail Jefferson," Lincoln said elsewhere. He thus transformed the great southern slaveholding philosopher of limiting the power of national government and upholding that of the states—the philosopher, too, of a supposedly ancient Saxon right of secession, which had justified American independence—into the founding philosopher of secession's defeat and the advancement of the federal government's power, via the post–Civil War constitutional amendments, at the direct expense of the states.

Lincoln's great creative act in rewriting the Declaration's preamble established Jefferson in the public mind as the author of equality enforced constitutionally and legislatively by the national government. Jefferson could not have abided that outcome. But he remained the founding man.

All that time, Hamilton remained semi-hidden in plain sight. Where Jefferson's penchant for lengthy written philosophizing made the Virgin-

ian a founding representative, however fancifully, of various sets of high
ideals, Hamilton, an actual practitioner of economic policy, had devised
the nuts and bolts that were often put into use, sometimes uncredited
and sometimes combined, if uneasily, with other policy mechanisms.

The scorched-earth anti-Hamiltonianism of Andrew Jackson and
James Hamilton never worked. The bank was closed in 1836; a new financial panic broke out only a year later, and after Jackson's presidency,
the American banking system amounted in large part to a combination
of proliferating state banks taking over private-sector finance. At the
outbreak of the Civil War, the federal government felt a crying need for
the more efficient public-private banking that aids warfare through easy
public borrowing and movement of federal money. In response, Lincoln's
treasury secretary, Salmon P. Chase, didn't reinvent the Hamiltonian
wheel, national banking. He blended Hamiltonian and Gallatinian measures and took innovative measures of his own, raising the tariff on foreign goods even higher; reviving national debt by issuing federal bonds
to war investors, mainly domestic; and issuing, for the first time since the
1776 Continental currency, a federal paper money, printed in green and
known as the greenback, and making it legal tender, requiring creditors
to accept greenbacks in payment of debts, a provision well-aligned with
fiscal ideas of the old Democracy that nobody, including Chase, remembered. With the National Banking Act of 1863, the United States also
reestablished not one but a number of national banks, which accepted
federal deposits and issued uniform notes.

In 1861, as a wartime measure, Congress passed its first tax on income. Beginning as a flat 3 percent levy on annual incomes over $800,
the tax was soon revised with progressive rates. In 1872, it was set aside
by the Supreme Court as unconstitutional, but in 1909, a constitutional
amendment would make it legal.

Some of these measures, such as a government paper currency, went
against Hamilton. Others were Hamiltonian. Yet it wasn't until well after
the Civil War that Hamilton himself was explicitly welcomed back into
the foreground as the great American founding model for public finance.

In the late nineteenth century, an industrial and infrastructure boom—Hamilton had envisioned it a century earlier—was taking forms he couldn't have envisioned. Steam engines, railroads, steel mills, coal mines, big agriculture, oil wells, and banks were inter- and intra-linked with inside-deal government contracts and policies, encouraging monopolistic practices. By the turn of the twentieth century, J. P. Morgan, America's biggest banker, was running a barely fettered Money Connection on a scale Robert Morris couldn't have imagined.

Morgan held no official position. He was the leader of a cadre of dedicated monopolists, notably the upwardly mobile western Pennsylvanians Andrew Carnegie and Henry Clay Frick, who sometimes collaborated, sometimes competed. To eliminate smaller players and consolidate economic power, they put together huge consolidations that became General Electric, U.S. Steel, and others. And they saw Hamilton, not Jefferson, as the American founder whose legacy they were carrying to new heights. On the site where the insurrectionists of 1794 had mustered and threatened to burn Pittsburgh, Carnegie built his first steel mill. With monopoly conjuring vast fortunes overnight, Morris- and Duer-like showiness flourished at a new scale. Gigantic summer homes in Newport, Rhode Island, and mansions in New York, Chicago, and other cities were full of finishes, furnishings, and whole libraries brought home from Europe in literal boatloads, plus fake Medieval and Renaissance decorative touches added by American craftsmen to glorify the new industries that made all the new money.

But poverty was flourishing everywhere too, locking black, white, and immigrant Americans alike in crowded urban neighborhoods and on failing subsistence farms to live through daily cycles of misery. The dominance of unfettered monopoly sparked efforts at reform, and in that context, it emerged that monopolists weren't the only claimants on the legacy of the founding treasury secretary. A famous opponent of monopoly also made Hamilton, not Jefferson, his hero.

In 1902, the Republican President Teddy Roosevelt took on J. P. Morgan, bringing a federal lawsuit to break up his most massive corporate conglomeration, invoking the Sherman Anti-Trust Act, passed by Congress in 1890 in hopes of restraining monopolization's rampancy. When he looked to the American founding period for inspiration, Roosevelt saw Jefferson as a hand-wringing coward and Hamilton as "the most brilliant statesman who ever lived."

That might have seemed contradictory. Jefferson had criticized monopoly; Hamilton had sought monopoly for his factory town on the Passaic and encouraged industry consolidation when sewing up distilling in western Pennsylvania. But Roosevelt associated his power to bust trusts with the founding treasury secretary's consolidating economic policy in the federal government. After he succeeded in breaking up Morgan's biggest company, the man who would go down in history as the great trustbuster made a deal to put one of Morgan's top men on a new federal regulatory board and leave the plutocrat's other companies alone.

Another Hamilton revivalist was the Democratic President Woodrow Wilson. He did succeed in restraining Morgan: Wilson's Supreme Court appointee Louis Brandeis ruled against a huge Morgan railroad merger. A historian before he was a politician, Wilson wrote a five-volume history of the United States, where in the integrationist mode established by Henry Clay, he framed Jefferson as the anti-monopolist philosopher and Hamilton as the creator of federal administration: both good.

And in 1913, Wilson signed into law the Federal Reserve Act, yet again revising national banking. The act established a system at once newly consolidated and newly dispersed: a central Federal Reserve Board and a number of regional Federal Reserve Banks. The institution had the power to print currency, ultimately to address inflation by influencing both interest rates and the supply of available credit. Some in Congress wanted a totally dispersed banking system. Wilson and others wanted centralization. The law seemed to many to accomplish both. As early as 1909, the progressive writer Herbert Croly, thinking like Henry Clay, was identifying a new blend of the thinking of the two great founding enemies, calling the philosophy becoming known as liberalism "Jeffersonian ends by Hamiltonian means."

Still, it was revived public admiration for Alexander Hamilton, not Thomas Jefferson, that President Coolidge's treasury secretary Andrew Mellon was taking all the way, that Thursday in May 1923, at the statue's dedication on the south patio of the Treasury Building. Whatever the real Hamilton might have thought, given his own hard experience, about a stock market soaring on the certainty that investor exuberance would keep driving values up and a crash could never come, the muscular energy of Charles Atlas's body and the intellectual energy of Hamilton's face put the founding treasury secretary's image, anyway, all-in on Mellon's policies. As the crowd watched, and news photographers snapped, the current treasury secretary solemnly bent to lay a wreath at the foot of the pedestal.

It was a victory wreath. An embronzed idol of sheer enterprise loomed over Andrew Mellon as he made Hamilton, not in the flesh but bigger and better than flesh, the perpetual founder of a perpetual-motion machine that was about to make everybody in America perpetually rich.

Of course it didn't work out. In 1938, fifteen years after the Hamilton statue's dedication, Jefferson's profile was stamped on the nickel. The next year, ground broke in Washington's Tidal Basin for a domed pseudo-classical memorial to Jefferson and all his works. A whole Jefferson building, parallel to Lincoln's: that threw Hamilton's stand-alone statue at the treasury into the shade. Federal funding for Jefferson studies in academia was taking off too. And virtually every department of the executive branch had resources dedicated to connecting its own operations to Jefferson's founding legacy.

President Franklin Delano Roosevelt, in an intuitive, culture-changing masterstroke, made Thomas Jefferson the face of his collection of radical economic policies known as the New Deal. New Dealers endowed a revolution in labor policy with Jefferson's founding principles, as invented by Lincoln, of liberty and equality secured by national citizenship. And it worked.

Not that the nineteenth and early twentieth centuries hadn't seen action on behalf of both equal rights and economic equality, also linked to Lincoln's public reverence for Jefferson. After the Civil War, the Radical Republicans amended the Constitution to establish a nationally protected right of male citizens of the United States to vote. That right, denied black citizens in the South for at least a century after the amendment passed, was nevertheless constitutionally revolutionary: no individual right to vote, federally protected against state election laws, had existed before. At the end of the century, too, William Jennings Bryan, a Democratic Party ally of what had become known as Populism, one of the most influential men in America, inveighed against the regressiveness of hardmoney policies—"you shall not crucify mankind on a Cross of Gold"— and supported demands for breaking up monopolies and nationalizing major industries. The period saw labor organizing by groups ranging from the Industrial Workers of the World to the Congress of Industrial Organizations to the Farmer-Labor Party. All of those progressive efforts claimed Jefferson as a founding spirit.

But it was in 1929 and 1930, after the stock-market crash—not just Andrew Mellon but many others had refused to see it coming—that FDR, then governor of New York, used both legislative and executive power in a way never seen before to ameliorate the awful effects of the ensuing Great Depression on ordinary people in his state. In 1932, he was nominated for the presidency against a concerted "Stop Roosevelt" effort led by the Democratic National Committee. Defeating President Hoover in the general election amid the grimmest economic situation the country had experienced since industrialization began, the new president brought to Washington his New York advisor Frances Perkins and made her secretary of labor, the fourth person to serve in the office and the first woman in any presidential cabinet. In 1911, as a young woman, she'd personally witnessed the Triangle Shirtwaist Factory fire, where, thanks to the country's history of near-utter lack of regulation of labor and manufacturing, most of the workers, mostly women and girls, burned to death or jumped from eighth-, ninth-, and tenth-floor windows and were smashed to death on the New York City sidewalk. Perkins later said that the New Deal was born that day.

FDR put Jefferson's face on a long series of new federal services and entitlements made synonymous with nationhood and citizenship. Perkins worked closely with Congress to make the Democratic Party, for the first time, a legislatively active pro-labor force and the federal government a mechanism for ensuring the welfare of the whole citizenry. Centering people's day-to-day lives in federal policy, the New Deal created agencies dedicated to regulation in the oldest sense—obstructing monopoly, restraining the power of wealth—and recast citizenship in a set of rights, entitlements, and protections secured by public promises, obligating the national government in a kind of contract meant to hold up through ensuing generations.

Making Jefferson the patron founder of these novel uses of federal power reflected the program's audacity. Like Lincoln, FDR felt a need to frame what was in fact revolutionary as a fulfillment of recognized founding principles. Though never a big reader, in 1925 he'd written a book review—his only one—of Claude Bowers's *Jefferson and Hamilton: The Struggle for Democracy in America*. From that breathlessly pro-Jefferson, anti-Hamilton chronicle, he learned to see Jefferson as the honest founding fighter for salt-of-the-earth democracy, Hamilton as the deceptive founding monarchist, and to see himself as a Jefferson for the new age. Like William Jennings Bryan, like the IWW, like others who pursued the long-forgotten Democracy's goals for the country, he lacked any real founding models for the revolution he was bringing about. Like them, he roped in Jefferson, who would have recoiled.

FDR's policies really brought about the fulfillment of Herman Husband's biblical prophecies and Thomas Paine's rationalist essays: a national government guaranteeing ordinary basics to all citizens, by right, and limiting wealth's ability to dominate ordinary people. Perkins's most famous contribution, the Social Security Administration, requiring employer and employee contributions to retirement savings, was one of a host of national economic programs that effectively rewrote the founding purpose of national government along lines that had gotten Husband's proposed national constitution laughed out of serious discussion in the 1780s. FDR and his congresses took the country off the gold standard. During World War II, they controlled prices and managed inflation nationwide. They made a federal commitment to enabling widespread homeownership by law, created employment for millions, upheld a right to collective bargaining for labor, and created the Federal Deposit Insurance Corporation to protect ordinary people's savings. FDR's and Perkins's successors, who brought in Medicare, Medicaid, and federal labor, civil rights, and other laws to enforce equality and protection, succeeded to a world-changing extent.

In his 1941 State of the Union address, FDR framed those policies, shrewdly enough, in conservative terms—according to which government exists to secure individual freedom—not in progressive terms, with government providing a mass entitlement. Not four rights *to* but four freedoms *of* and *from*: freedom of speech, of worship, from hunger, from fear. Such were the basics that the national government, in FDR's vision, had the fundamental responsibility to provide all citizens. Thomas Paine had such ideas in the 1790s, but when FDR invoked Paine in that speech he referred only to Paine's "These are the times that try men's souls," urging U.S. support for Allied forces in World War II. Paine's ideas for a pro-labor, pro-welfare national government, the national government that FDR himself was even then creating, remained absent from FDR's pitch, and, more important, from his consciousness.

He'd heard of Paine, at least. The closest FDR ever got to seeing the name Herman Husband, whose ideas he was also fulfilling, might have been in the name of Admiral Husband Edward Kimmel, commander at Pearl Harbor, Hawaii, when that naval base was attacked by Japan. The admiral, who was busted down to a two-star after the attack, testified forthrightly before Congress in the ensuing investigation, and retired in 1942, was directly descended from Herman Husband on both sides of his family.

If the glaring contradictions in forcing Jefferson to serve as the face of a nationally pervasive federal government, consolidating public welfare and economic planning in a host of massive bureaucracies, had been the kind of thing that bothered FDR, he couldn't have revolutionized the country, but some of his supporters did try to reconcile facts with history. Repeating Croly's "Jeffersonian aims by Hamiltonian means," they gave the New Deal a feeling of Henry Clayish founding American compromise. By now, though, nobody was talking about Hamilton anyway.

On the contrary. Albert Gallatin came back. In 1947, as a result of the FDR administration's Jefferson obsession, which continued into President Truman's terms, Gallatin got his own gigantic bronze statue outside the Treasury Building, shoving Hamilton out of the way and taking over as the founding spirit of the country's finances. City planning had already shifted the south patio, where Hamilton still stood, out of focus. The grand front of the building was now at the north plaza, and Democrats had wanted for some time to counter the Mellon Hamilton by putting a Gallatin statue there. In the long New Deal, they got their chance. While Charles Atlas had moved on to bigger and better things, the bronze Gallatin defied biographical reality by being just as dashing as the bronze Hamilton. The Genevan would lord it over the Treasury, with Hamilton hanging around in back, at least into the twenty-first century.

A political benefit to the Democratic party of all the twentieth-century invocations of Jefferson, from William Jennings Bryan's speeches through FDR's presidency, was to keep progressive reform connected to the white South. Though revolutionized in certain critical ways, before 1948 the party continued in perhaps the most critical way in a state of total reaction on racial equality. Progressives on the issue in the party got nowhere legislatively; the Republicans, as the party of Lincoln, retained the support of many black voters through the 1950s. Some forms of economic progressivism and farmer and labor populism remained interconnected with white supremacism. Woodrow Wilson's efforts against monopoly power had been inextricable from his outright racism. The southern wing of the party aggressively upheld the system of violence and exclusion known as racial segregation, wrapping it in a story of the defeated Confederacy as a glorious and tragically lost cause. New Deal programs, administered through the states, remained unevenly distributed on the basis of race. Social Security didn't apply, at first, to domestic and agricultural workers, the two classes of labor employing the majority of southern black people. Reverence for Thomas Jefferson helped unify the white South with the white North in Democratic Party politics.

For many people growing up under the influence of the post–World War II U.S. History Survey, however, such ironies and complications remained opaque. There seemed plenty of reason to revere Jefferson, more or less reflexively, as the apostle of an inherently American belief in equality set out in the Declaration's preamble, without knowing much about him, or the real circumstances of the Declaration's adoption, or his life as an owner of people.

And Alexander Hamilton? There was no reason to think about him at all. Schoolchildren visited the Jefferson Memorial, jingled Jefferson-profile coins in their pockets at the corner store, knew the big faces carved out of Mount Rushmore. President John F. Kennedy made much of Jefferson; Hamilton didn't figure at Camelot. When President Lyndon Johnson and his Congresses extended the New Deal's programs to include black Americans in the welfare state and ensure voting rights, via laws pushing the power of the national government even further against those of the states, that effort, too, was given the now-requisite imprimatur of Jefferson. In 1963, when the civil rights leader Martin Luther King, Jr., was in jail in Birmingham, Alabama, for nonviolent civil disobedience in protesting racial segregation, he wrote a public letter to the white liberals who had been asserting their support for racial equality by advising him to slow down, moderate his tactics, not risk backlash. Noting that no moral imperative had ever been achieved that way, King held up four great models for his uncompromising position: the Apostle Paul, Martin Luther, Abraham Lincoln, and Thomas Jefferson. King quoted the Declaration's preamble as the founding American principle: "all men are created equal."

Who knew even one quote from Alexander Hamilton, of all people? To the extent that he was remembered at all, he was associated with bankers and moneymen, at worst a regressive Hooverite, at best a nebbishy bean counter who figured in an especially boring but mercifully brief section of the survey, and while gaining some interest from dying in a duel, was certainly no visionary. The glow of an inspiring national journey did not emanate from the man still hanging around the treasury's back door.

*   *   *

Then it was Hamilton's time again.

For one thing, by the 1950s the Jefferson industry was saturated. Hamilton, "the forgotten founder," offered career opportunities. Over decades of upheaval in U.S. politics, he came back. He came back slowly. But this time very surely.

On the early side of the comeback process, Broadus Mitchell, a socialist, civil rights activist, and historian, wrote a sober, highly detailed biography of Hamilton, in two thick volumes published in 1957 and 1962, which made a strong case for the founding treasury secretary's brilliance and importance. In 1979, the conservative activist and historian Forrest McDonald—he'd worked for the nomination of the 1964 Republican presidential candidate Senator Barry Goldwater—published a tight, in-depth, often insightful, just as often quirky one-volume Hamilton biography.

Both authors' barely qualified admiration for their subject might have seemed counterintuitive. Mitchell was an inheritor of the American labor activism whose parentage in the founding-era Democracy Hamilton had made every effort to crush. Thanks in part to Hamilton's success, that movement and Hamilton's relationship to it remained unknown to Mitchell; for a socialist biographer, it was Hamilton's assertion of state power in centralizing economics that played. As for McDonald, his candidate Goldwater was a states'-rights, strict-constructionist, small-government, anti-D.C. man, in full-on opposition to the federal centralization that Hamilton invented and fostered. For a conservative biographer, Hamilton's pro-business and investor-class orientation was the hook. Both biographies got a lot of attention.

Also under way, during that twenty-year period and beyond it, was a new public knocking of Jefferson. As an enslaver on a big scale and a proponent, at times, of an extreme states'-rights position taken up in the 1950s and '60s by opponents of civil rights legislation, Jefferson came in for so much criticism from the late 1960s through the 1990s that Conor Cruise O'Brien, the Irish diplomat and student of U.S. history, writing in

The Atlantic in 1996, could call for his permanent ouster from the founding pantheon. In 1974, the biographer Fawn Brodie outraged the aging
academic Jefferson establishment by writing speculatively, though by no
means unsympathetically, on Jefferson's sexual relationship with one of
the people he enslaved, Sally Hemings. "A mockery of history," sputtered
the Jefferson-industry leader Dumas Malone in response to Brodie's book
Thomas Jefferson: An Intimate History, but in 1997, the historian and
legal scholar Annette Gordon-Reed, having pursued the primary record
in punctilious detail, made a highly persuasive case in her book *Thomas
Jefferson and Sally Hemings: An American Controversy* for the Jefferson-
Hemings relationship, confirmed by DNA evidence in 1998. Where
Gordon-Reed went on to pursue both Jefferson and Hemings-family studies in depth, becoming perhaps the best-known Jefferson scholar of her
generation, to many others the man who had once figured as the founding American champion of equality was all the way out.

Hamilton came all the way in. In the 1990s and 2000s, he was celebrated as the founding father of an anti-libertarian Republican Party
ethos welding conservatism to the pursuit of U.S. national greatness. In
1997, David Brooks and William Kristol published a major piece in *The
Wall Street Journal* pushing back against anti-government conservatism and
proposing that federal support for domestic infrastructure and an assertive
foreign policy were fully in keeping with conservative values; they made
Hamilton one of their inspirational figures. In 1999, Richard Brookhiser,
an editor at the legacy conservative magazine *National Review*, published a
crisp, popular Hamilton biography, framing his subject as the forgotten architect of modern America; in 2004, he curated a major Hamilton exhibit
to the same effect at the New-York Historical Society. As the founding
figure of Wall Street and big business, Hamilton was thriving.

Getting that idea around to a broader public was given a decisive
cultural and financial push by an organization created in 1994 by the
Wall Street financiers Richard Gilder, of the right-wing Manhattan Institute and the Club for Growth, and Lewis Lehrman, a former economic
advisor to the Republican president Ronald Reagan. Forming the Gilder
Lehrman Institute of American History, they filled its board with histo-

rians and business leaders from across the conservative-liberal spectrum and made donations to scholarly U.S. history journals and other history nonprofits, organized summer seminars, gave awards to high school history teachers, and founded charter schools with a U.S. history focus. The Hamilton revival became one of its major projects.

Unlike in Mellon's day, the Gilder Lehrman Institute framed the Hamilton legacy in the politically appealing terms of Hamilton's supposed abolitionism, thus equating rigorous pursuit of capital with opposition to slavery. In 2003, the institute also brought about what critics at the time called a philanthropic takeover of the New-York Historical Society, shifting the institution's focus to national history; the Brookhiser Hamilton exhibit ran there the next year. The institute provided support for a 2007 PBS "American Experience" documentary on Hamilton's life and legacy. In 2010, another film, *Rediscovering Alexander Hamilton*, aired on PBS with funding from the Gilder Foundation—Richard Gilder's own institution—featuring Brookhiser as writer and on-air host and directed by Michael Pack, who would be confirmed by the Senate in 2019 as President Donald Trump's CEO of the U.S. Agency for Global Media.

Given all that, the Hamilton revival of the 1990s and the early 2000s might have seemed a pure product of the Republican mainstream of the moment, as the party sought to soften the edges of its racial politics and align its pro–Wall Street ethos with ideas about bootstrapping upward mobility. In fact, though, fascination with Hamilton, by no means limited to the right, was pulling important people across party and political divides. In 2004, Ron Chernow published a bestselling Hamilton biography positioning Hamilton as both an early exponent of the American immigrant experience and, in Chernow's words, an "uncompromising abolitionist." The book won the first Washington Prize, funded by the Gilder Lehrman Institute; received virtually no criticism from liberal scholarly establishments; and was eagerly taken up not only by the public but also by influential people in both major parties who found in Hamilton a founding-era inspiration for a bipartisan approach to finance and economic policy. Born-again 1990s Hamiltonians included some of the most influential Democratic Party operatives.

It made sense. Beginning during the presidency of Jimmy Carter, Democratic leadership had been abandoning the labor-friendly, welfare-state legislative agendas of the New Deal and the Great Society. The new idea was to adopt an employer-aligned, globalist, high-finance, deregulatory approach that would, it was projected, ultimately benefit all Americans, while appealing to the white working class that had left the party in droves, thus reviving Democratic electoral victories. In 1995, when the Goldman Sachs financier Robert Rubin began serving the Democratic president William Jefferson Clinton as treasury secretary, during a period of relative economic stability and prosperity, the administration adopted what was known as a "third way": reducing the national debt, balancing the federal budget, deregulating banking and finance, and moving people off welfare rolls while expanding tax credits for workers and selected programs in the service of opportunity. The plan was to shake up seemingly hidebound liberal ideas and foster dynamism while not forgetting those referred to as "left behind": fallers-through-the-cracks of a system otherwise presumed to provide, when working properly, the greatest good for the greatest number.

Hamilton was drafted to serve as the founding-period guide to the third way. After leaving office, Rubin launched an effort called the Hamilton Project with others at Brookings, a liberal think tank. Its aim was to develop pragmatic ideas about economics and finance inspired by the Hamilton legacy, to "create new opportunities for middle class affluence, bolster economic security, and spur more enduring growth." Admiration for Hamilton drew the Clinton-Rubin approach together with that of Henry Paulson, the Republican president George W. Bush's third and most important treasury secretary, who made a point at his swearing-in ceremony in 2006 of noting that his late father had been a Hamilton fan. The new story taken up on all sides, and largely gained from uncritical absorption of Chernow's biography, emphasized the hero's birth far from what many Americans tend to see as the great scenes of action and advantage. As a classic outsider, Hamilton thus served as a shining reflection of exceptional American openness to anyone willing to work hard, play by the rules, and overcome prejudice. Pursuing that path, the story ran, the hero rose so high that he was able to institute governmental systems dedicated to helping others replicate his own upward mobility. That fantastical construction of his aims was blended with actual disadvantages in his upbringing to eradicate his birth in a central economic site of a great empire and his instant embrace by some of the most powerful people in revolutionary America. Rebronzed this time as a victim, this Hamilton had to struggle to overcome a bigoted "how could anything good come out of Nazareth" mindset, relying on nothing but his own ambition and work ethic in an America that, however unfortunately biased at first, nevertheless fundamentally encourages, in the end, success in just such struggles.

Evidence for this Hamilton as the scrappy immigrant, subject to the universal scorn of insiders, forced thereby to overcome exceptional disadvantage, was impossible to come by. Many of his contemporaries hated Hamilton and his policies, of course, and Jefferson, in a 1792 letter to Washington, did emphasize Hamilton's coming from elsewhere: "a man whose history," Jefferson wrote, "from the moment at which history can stoop to notice him, is a tissue of machinations against the liberty of the country which has not only received and given him bread, but heaped its honors on his head." But it was opposition to Hamilton's views and policies that triggered Jefferson's prejudice; prejudice didn't trigger the opposition. He liked Gallatin, who really was an immigrant.

Only John Adams cooperated with the new Hamilton narrative. His pungent characterization of Hamilton as "the bastard brat of a Scotch peddler" was made emblematic, in both Chernow's book and the Gilder Lehrman Institute's educational materials, of a disdain for Hamilton supposedly felt by the entrenched American establishment of the period. In real life, Adams hated Hamilton enough to say worse things than that. He called him "the Scotch Creolian Boy": a Creole educated in Scotland by what Adams claimed were kilt-wearing, bagpipe-playing oatmeal eaters, the most nauseating mix of backgrounds Adams could imagine. Hamilton's not being Creole and having never been to Scotland wasn't going to stop Adams from winding himself up with his pen. According to him, Hamilton also had an overabundance of semen that "he could not find whores enough to draw off."

Most of that was written years after Hamilton's death and appeared only in some private letters and one newspaper article that never ran. Nobody during Hamilton's career would have taken such invective seriously, especially coming from Adams, who made equally absurd assertions about everyone he hated. Yet Hamilton fans of the 1990s and 2000s positioned Adams's views as typical and even, ironically, to some degree based on fact. To David Brooks, in a long 2004 article in *The New York Times Magazine*, one of the great things about Hamilton was that he "came from nothing." To the Brookings Institution's Hamilton Project, Hamilton's supposed alien status and impoverished background made him the first great exponent of what the project called elemental American traditions of opportunity and upward mobility. When Chernow said Hamilton hadn't grown up in the slave-owning squirearchy of a Jefferson or "cosseted" on the New England farm of an Adams, he avoided mentioning the founders who grew up no more cosseted than Hamilton. Here, then, was the Hamilton for our time: a self-made, center-right Republican, New-Democrat, Wall-Street abolitionist founding American.

In 2008, amid the revived bipartisan Hamilton enthusiasm in policy circles, Barack Obama won the presidency. He put the Hamilton enthusiasm into decisive action, with decisive effects.

Two years earlier, Obama had made a landmark speech at an event hosted by Brookings's Hamilton Project, in which he put forth the long-standing "third way" Clinton-Rubin approach to economic policy, criticizing what he cast as the anti-business extremes of the New Deal and the Great Society. The speech was well received by the audience of consultants, policy advisors, and bankers it praised. Then, elected president amid the worst financial crisis since the stock market crash of 1929, with the venerable investment bank Lehman Brothers declaring bankruptcy, Obama entered the fray even before taking office. He and his people worked with Secretary Paulson of the outgoing Bush administration to craft a transitional fix for what was becoming a potential takedown of the whole U.S. financial system.

Many liberal Democrats hadn't paid close attention to candidate Obama's perfectly up-front admiration for Wall Street leaders—really to any of his announced policies. Some now expected a new FDR moment, a revolutionary overhaul of the interconnected Wall Street and banking system. But Obama, true to his stated principles, ushered back into his administration the Clinton-era Rubinites and their students. Peter Orszag, formerly a director of the Hamilton Project, now Obama's director of the Office of Management and Budget, had a portrait of Hamilton brought over from the National Gallery and hung in his office. Jason Furman, having been director of the Hamilton Project and economic policy director to the Obama campaign, became deputy director at the National Economic Council under Lawrence Summers, formerly Rubin's deputy at the treasury, and worked on the administration's 2009 stimulus package, the American Recovery and Reinvestment Act. This Mellon-reminiscent idolatry of the first treasury secretary gained un-Mellonish buzz from being put to the service of the first black U.S. president, a real outsider who really did play a historical role by making it to the top.

The country now felt the effects of policymakers' Hamilton adulation. Obama and his secretary of the treasury, Timothy Geithner, were presented with the rare opportunity of a great Hamiltonian test: the ongoing crash of a modern banking and investing system more complex than anything their hero had known. Directly inspired by Hamilton's creative efforts during the near-disasters of 1792 and 1793, Geithner replicated those feats on a huge scale in the heroically draining, minute-to-minute, all-nighter series of big moves, creative twists, and hairbreadth escapes described with panache in *Stress Test*, a book he published in 2014, where he called Hamilton "the original mister bailout." The pressing goal was to restabilize the heavily concentrated get-rich-quick banking and corporate system, whose irresponsibility had created the collapse that now threatened it, and which had produced Geithner himself, along with Orszag, Rubin, Paulson, and others who had come to government

424   EPILOGUE

service from high positions in the finance industry and would return
there when their service was complete. The goal was met.

Everyone in policy circles knew that national waves of home foreclosures and evictions were now inevitable. Given Obama's third-way ethos,
a centrist plan known as the Toxic Assets Recovery Program (TARP)
earmarked $100 million for citizens' relief from the onrushing disaster—
very little, compared with the billions spent on bailing out Wall Street,
which the federal government would recoup through Geithner's efforts.
But not nothing, either. The money might have helped.

Almost none of it got to the people it was intended for. The massive
foreclosure disaster that long outlived Obama and Geithner's bank and
corporate bailout would have looked painfully familiar to the families
who became Regulators, Shaysites, and Whiskey Rebels, whose movements Hamilton set out to quell at all costs; and to the hundreds of
thousands made homeless and impoverished under the Hamilton fan
Mellon's policies in the Great Depression. Reaction to just such policies
had brought FDR to power and launched the New Deal and then the
Great Society, efforts that, while far from perfect, took approaches that
Obama brought forty years of Democratic Party policy to fruition by
spurning in a crisis.

The country's banking and finance system got back on track and
was soon chugging along. Banking and corporate leadership loudly celebrated. About twenty million people were forced out of their homes,
lives upended.

In 2011, the widespread protest movement Occupy Wall Street opposed that entire approach to finance and economics. Making demands
nearly identical to those made in American traditions of dissent reaching
back even before the North Carolina Regulation of the 1760s, Occupy
called out the corruption in connecting high-finance institutions and
other big corporations to government. It demanded major programs for
ameliorating inequality. Its tactics, too, were old, though not in fact riot-
ous: literal occupation and civil disobedience, most famously in Zuccotti
Park in Manhattan, near the U.S. Stock Exchange on Wall and Broad
Streets. Like Obama, FDR, Lincoln, and everyone else, Occupy looked

to the U.S. founding for inspiration—for those American values, supposedly essential, that might guide and publicly justify its cause.

But the movement had no access to its antecedents in the eighteenth-century Democracy. The early movement's central importance to the national founding had been erased as early as Albert Gallatin's first published speech. Occupy couldn't invoke Herman Husband as an early author of a revolutionary economic vision, or Thomas Paine as a welfare-state theorist, or tell stories of James Cannon and Thomas Young and Christopher Marshall and the militia privates who brought about the revolutionary democracy of 1776, or William Findley's and Robert Whitehill's using the power of the people to disable that Wall Street precursor Robert Morris's bank. Robbed of connection to the Regulators, the Shaysites, and the Whiskey Rebels, those founding-era Americans who rose up against government policies that favored what Occupy assailed as "the one percent," the movement identified its foundational Americanism in the Boston of Samuel Adams, who supported the anti-democratic Massachusetts constitution and called for the Shaysites' execution. Occupy also repeatedly cited "We the People," Gouverneur Morris's opening to the nation-making document explicitly intended to shut down democratic finance, the phrase that the founding radical Robert Whitehill castigated, in the day, for not referring to the people of the United States at all.

But suppose Occupy had been in a position to embrace the true founding history of dissent from ingrained economic inequality? Would it have wanted to embrace that history? The Shaysites and Whiskey Rebels fought not for the United States government but against it. Husband's politics of equality and good government were grounded in an evangelical moral and spiritual absolutism born of revelation, a mode associated today mainly with the right, an embarrassment to many modern liberals and leftists alike. Paine, the devotee of reason, was unable to analyze his own situation clearly enough to avoid ending up a victim of both the French Terror and the U.S. government. His French Revolution period, Husband's struggle with the problem of violence: these stories raise questions not easily sloganized on banners, and both men's careers ended not in triumph but in defeat.

*   *   *

While realism about history may always present quandaries for a dissenting politics, no such quandaries troubled administration politics in the aftermath of the crisis, when bankers celebrated and Obama and Geithner celebrated too. In 2013, on Geithner's departure from office, Obama made him a parting gift of a printing plate for the front of the ten-dollar bill, where Hamilton's face appears. The president's note read "Hamilton would be proud."

So while it was a big surprise, putting it mildly, when a young actor, playwright, composer, and theater director appeared in 2009 at a White House "Evening of Poetry, Music, and the Spoken Word," before President and Mrs. Obama and an audience of invited guests, and started rapping the first chapter of Chernow's Hamilton biography, the instantaneous creation of a phenomenon that was to dominate popular culture and liberal political discourse for at least the next decade came not from its unpredictability, which was indeed total, but from its being, for that room, so astonishingly on-the-nose. The paroxysms of delight the performance sent the presidential couple into might in retrospect seem almost too pat a payoff for the Gilder Lehrman Institute's quest to position Hamilton as the founding visionary of racial equality and the nation-making benefits of hegemony for Wall Street corporations, too absolute a confirmation of the Democratic Party's rejection of the New Deal and the Great Society, too joyous a celebration of the policies that had drawn Clinton, Bush, and Obama together and would soon, in the supposed Hamilton fandom of Treasury Secretary Steven Mnuchin, link them all to the presidency of Trump.

Hamilton: An American Musical, the full-scale show that ensued from Lin-Manuel Miranda's race-reversing hip-hop White House performance of 2009, was first produced at the Public Theater in New York City, then transferred to Broadway, and would appear in American city after American city and around the world at least into the 2020s. The play had exactly the political effects that might have been expected. The Gilder Lehrman Institute took the musical's record-breaking commercial success not just as a thrilling cultural event—exciting new audiences about U.S. history, vindicating Hamilton fandom, a patriotic pageant with a racially liberating claim on the country, a fresh work of art—but as an opportunity far greater than that. *Hamilton: An American Musical* served as the premise for a massive educational effort, advancing the institute's long-standing claim on the country's foundational purposes across multiple media platforms, institutions, and communities.

The spread of the Twitter hashtag #eduham—education via the Hamilton musical—was only one indicator. Gilder Lehrman published Hamilton-centric curricula adopted by grateful teachers throughout the country. The material framed Hamilton as the man who, as the musical put it, got ahead by working harder than others and "being a lot smarter / by being a self-starter." The institute launched a program to bring underserved schoolchildren, rarely charitably enrolled in trips to hot-ticket Broadway shows, to learn the play's lessons about hard work and self-starting, in America, where you can get always ahead that way, regardless of decks stacked against you.

Many historians of the U.S. founding period went eagerly along with this heady dose of buzz for their field, previously sometimes called boring. In 2016, an interview with Lin-Manuel Miranda was the featured attraction of the plenary session at the annual conference of the venerable Society for Historians of the Early American Revolution—though because of his busy schedule, Miranda could only attend remotely. The original cast album meanwhile reached millions who would never see the show live. With Trump in the presidency, the music wasn't so much telling as brilliantly enacting an optimistically liberal counterstory of the country's history, meaning, and civics. It rendered Trump's racist cult of hectic personality a grotesque anomaly, the racial progress represented by his predecessor a recoverable norm. The album's Obamaist kaleidoscope of positive American themes included the resourcefulness of immigrants, not just Chernow's Hamilton now but also the Marquis de Lafayette; the abolition of slavery, via Chernow's fervent "manumissionist abolitionists"; and the inclusion of women, with a trio of feisty and funny Schuyler Sisters, who now have no brothers. All that and more, embodied musically in a founding America that seems to have transcended racism because it's representationally race-reversed.

Shortly before what would become the fateful Election Day of 2016, yet another PBS documentary, this one on both Hamilton himself and *Hamilton: An American Musical*, featured celebrities newly excited by the musical about the country's founding history. Some historian talking heads appeared too. The leading Hamilton scholar Joanne B. Freeman gave the proceedings a rare moment of bracing realism, noting that some in the day considered Hamilton "an annoying, arrogant asshole"; she was bleeped. But the documentary's biggest star was Obama himself, filmed in a mutually admiring Oval Office conversation with Miranda himself.

At one point in the program, the talk-show host Jimmy Fallon expressed his sense that Miranda had done the historical Hamilton, in a sense, a massive favor by recovering him from centuries of obscurity and misunderstanding, an act for which the forgotten founder would no doubt be grateful. And it's true that a generation earlier, nobody would have thought for a moment of using a quote from Alexander Hamilton in aspirational rhetoric; thanks solely to the musical, during the Trump administration a flurry of magazine articles, op-eds, tweets, and speeches by Democratic members of the House quoted Hamilton again and again in opposition to Trump and in favor of American democracy. That required precision-trimming from his writings the bluntly anti-democratic tendency in more or less everything he wrote.

If he really could have contemplated it in advance, would the real Alexander Hamilton have been happy to know he'd enjoy such ubiquity in the early years of the second decade of the twenty-first century? He couldn't have contemplated it in advance, so the question may be absurd. Still, it can be gratifying for the living to fantasize about renown after death. It's not unfair to imagine him doing that.

Hamilton's romance with immortality, inspired by Jacques Necker, made him long for the lasting fame of the crusading, nation-making finance officer and hold public opinion in such low regard that, had he imagined any centuries-later burst of popular adulation, especially for qualities so far removed from what he considered his life's work, he might have taken it as an insult. The fan-fiction Alexander of the 2010s brought the second-wave Hamilton revival, which had begun in the 1950s and climaxed in the Obama administration, so far over the top that it left the man himself far behind. Manic celebration of his image by the whole liberal culture, pop and intelligentsia alike, made him the forgotten founder yet again.

Forgotten but not gone. A walking-dead kind of permanency. That's a legacy few daydream about.

Other forgotten people and forces critical to the American founding include Robert Morris, and the Democracy, and the class war's role in establishing the country, and Albert Gallatin's optimistic real-time revisions of the history he was living through. Those huge blank spaces in public conceptions of the period support a perpetual recycling of two marquee figures, Hamilton and Jefferson, sometimes blending them, sometimes making them clash, always dissociating them from the realities of their careers. The effect, evidently necessary, is to forget the conflicts over money and power that really created the United States of America, even as that creation has been, is now, and may ever be obsessively celebrated and criticized.

NOTES

As a narrative, *The Hamilton Scheme* proceeds largely by assertion. The interpretations on which I've built the narrative and to which it's led me are supported here with references to the primary and secondary records that inspire and shape the underlying argument. Regarding the two interviews cited, any errors are mine. For expanded notes, see www.hamiltonscheme.com.

1. MEET ALEXANDER HAMILTON

13 *a remote speck:* "[Fryday September 20th. 1776.]," *Founders Online*, National Archives, founders.archives.gov/documents/Adams/01-03-02-0016-0196.

13 *more important than all of the Atlantic thirteen put together:* Holton, *Liberty Is Sweet*, 28. Chernow, 7, cites Benjamin Franklin to the same effect, though Chernow and most other Hamilton biographers emphasize the Caribbean islands' not being on the "mainland" (Michael Newton, *Alexander Hamilton: The Formative Years*, Chapter 5 title) or the "continent" (Mitchell, *Alexander Hamilton: Youth to Maturity*, Chapter 3 title) and St. Croix as remote from New York (ibid., 35). Even when describing the intensity of labor and production in St. Croix, Chernow calls the region "languorous" (29).

13 *leaves of the tea plant . . . British Isles ritual:* Rappaport, 24–42.

13 *nice, hot cup might be enhanced by sweetening:* For the economics of the tea-sugar connection: "The Tea Habit and the Dramatic Increase in British Sugar Consumption in the 17th and 18th Centuries," https://chocolateclass.wordpress.com/2018/03/07/the-tea-habit-and-the-dramatic-increase-in-british-sugar-consumption-in-the-17th-and-18th-centuries/.

13 *cones of sugar . . . the Caribbean, also at great scale:* Williams, 10–15, demonstrates European sugar production's dependence on racial slavery well before Columbus sailed. For development of the Caribbean sugar industry: Dunn, Chapters 6–8. For the cones: Budinger, livesandlegaciesblog.org/2018/12/13/all-about-sugar-cones/.

13 *sugar moved a lot of people:* For the influx especially of Scottish "sojourners": "The Plantation System of the British West Indies."

14 *coffee from Java . . . rum:* For coffee, Pendergrast, 7–8. For cocoa's broadening appeal, Tigner. Richardson, 750–52, notes a sharp rise in British sugar consumption

after 1750, a year roughly coinciding with James Hamilton's arrival in St. Kitts. For sugar products' relationship to mercantile activity among the Atlantic and Caribbean colonies: Holton, *Liberty Is Sweet*, 28.

14 *more and more money exporting*: Richardson's historiography argues for a tight interrelationship among Caribbean sugar production, the growth of slavery, and the growth of British manufacturing, 1748–1776.

14 *boom depended on the arrival*: Richardson, 741–42; Dunn, Chapter 7. Linebaugh and Rediker, 123–27, describe work routines on Barbados sugar plantations.

14 *a tenth of the population was white*: McDonald, 9; Hubbard, 74–75.

14 *sell to Britain and buy British*: An effect of the Navigation Acts of 1651, 1660, and 1696. See "Charles II, 1660."

15 *existential challenges too*: The ensuing depiction is inspired by Dunn, xxii–xxiii and Chapters 8 and 9.

15 *James Hamilton, Jr.*: Ascertaining a birth year for James Jr., is complicated by controversies over Alexander's birth year discussed below.

15 *Out-of-wedlock families . . . without stigma*: Mitchell, *Alexander Hamilton: Youth to Maturity*, 11; Michael Newton, *Alexander Hamilton: The Formative Years*, 17–18.

15 *in 1754, Rachel gave birth*: A recent departure from the long-standing contest among Hamilton biographers over 1755 and 1757, the birth year 1754 is the conclusion of Michael Newton, *Discovering Hamilton*, 4–8, based on exhaustive and to me persuasive research citing primary data filed in the Rigsarkivet (Danish National Archive), endorsed by the Hamilton biographer Richard Brookhiser, for one: twitter.com/RBrook hiser/status/1613225923796471808.

15 *placed fewer restrictions*: On St. Eustatius as a free port, see Kandle, 50–53, and de Bruin. For St. Croix: "Christiansted National Historic Site."

15–16 *the Hamiltons conformed . . . he soon killed himself*: My account of the family's struggles and Rachel's enterprise and resilience is distilled from detail shared by the cited Hamilton biographies. The impression of Hamilton's childhood as squalid, popularized by Miranda's song "Alexander Hamilton," based on Chernow's "squalid," 5, doesn't track with Chernow's own description of relative comfort and cheer (22, 24) or with descriptions by other biographers. See expanded notes at www.hamiltonscheme .com.

16 *David Beekman and Nicholas Cruger*: Brookhiser, *Alexander Hamilton*, 18–19, and Mitchell, *Alexander Hamilton: Youth to Maturity*, 22–24, provide detail on the more important partner, Cruger. For the Cruger family's mercantile and political activities in New York, see Mason.

16–17 *a few big companies . . . all imports from the Caribbean*: For deep background on the East India Company's monopoly, see Bogart, arguing that the monopoly became stable only in the mid-eighteenth century, dovetailing with Holton's discussion, *Liberty Is Sweet*, 30–31, of British merchants' antimonopoly agitation around the same time. For Atlantic trade monopolies, see Zahediah, 145–46.

17 *day-to-day buying and selling*: The ensuing depiction of mercantile life is inspired by Ferguson, 5–7, and Price, 278–82.

17 *Hamilton showed the qualities*: Cited biographies cover Hamilton's effectiveness at Beekman and Cruger more or less as related here.

18 *Rising to merchant status wouldn't have been impossible*: I draw this conclusion from the widely accepted facts that Hamilton's talent and diligence were well recognized and that a number of people showed themselves willing to give financial support to his progress.

18 *he sailed for Boston*: Michael Newton, *Alexander Hamilton: The Formative Years*, 60–61, convincingly settles a long-standing dispute over Hamilton's first port of call.

18 *the most useful part of his education*: John Church Hamilton, 6.

18 *out-of-wedlock birth*: As noted in Chapters 2 and 7, Robert Morris, one of the most powerful men in Revolutionary America, was also born out of wedlock; as discussed in the Epilogue, John Adams's frequently cited "bastard brat" crack didn't reflect any widespread American rejection of Hamilton based on circumstances of his birth.

18 *wherewithal to go to school*: Flexner, *Young Hamilton*, 53–54, makes this point.

18 *changing his birthdate to 1757*: The motivation I suggest for the age change tracks with outright assertions by some biographers who adopt the 1755 birth: see Miller, 8, and Chernow, 48.

19 *King's College*: On the school as a merchant enterprise: Eric Foner, *Columbia and Slavery*, 4–5, and Wilder, 66–68. Chernow, 53, emphasizes Hamilton's ease in making college friends.

19 *political pamphlets . . . New York City was where they landed*: The cited biographies cover Hamilton's involvement with the protests and military action. For orotundity and snark: "The Farmer Refuted, &c., [23 February] 1775," *Founders Online*, National Archives, founders.archives.gov/documents/Hamilton/01-01-02-0057.

19–20 *General George Washington . . . Virginia operator*: In Chapters 2 and 3 of *Autumn of the Black Snake*, I cover Washington's pre–Continental Army business career in detail, with sources including Ferling, *The Ascent of George Washington*, Clary, and Knollenberg.

20 *"land-jobber"*: Simcoe, 40–41.

21 *de facto chief*: Flexner, *Young Hamilton*, 143, notes that while Hamilton became in Washington's words "the most principle and confidential aide," he wasn't the official chief.

21 *engaged to marry up*: "Marrying up" as a male accomplishment is evinced by Goñi's study of the London marriage market.

21 *His in-laws-to-be*: The Schuyler story ensuing here, with details on home and business activities, as well as is Philip Schuyler's business and military activities before and during the War of Independence, is drawn from a talk given by Ian Mumpton, Site Interpreter at the Schuyler Mansion in Albany, New York, based on research by the site staff at the Schulyer Mansion State Historic Site, with details confirmed and expanded in my interview with Ian Mumpton on March 21, 2002.

21 *ordered home on a leave*: That the situation came as a surprise to Schuyler had been the conclusion of Schulyer Mansion site staff; their recent research suggests he may have been in touch with Van Rensselaer prior to the leave (interview with Ian Mumpton, March 21, 2002).

21 *Five months after their wedding*: About one in three brides in the northeastern colonies went to the altar pregnant (ibid.).

21–22 *Hamilton . . . owned and dealt in people*: Noted by writers for many years: see Miller, 122, footnote, citing Nathan Schachner's *Alexander Hamilton* (Appleton-Century Company, 1946); and DuRoss, sharply qualifying Hamilton's anti-slavery stance. For the most recent and decisive scholarship, see Serfilippi.

22 *"be left with only their old men, women and children"*: "To George Washington from Major General Philip Schuyler, 4 February 1779," *Founders Online*, National Archives, founders.archives.gov/documents/Washington/03-19-02-0126.

23 *"destruction and devastation of their settlements"*: "From George Washington to Major

General John Sullivan, 31 May 1779," *Founders Online*, National Archives, founders
.archives.gov/documents/Washington/03-20-02-0661.

23 *Claimed personally by men who had officially ordered it destroyed a land*: Interview with
Ian Mumpton, March 21, 2002.

23 *approval of New York high society*: Schuyler's affection for and support of Hamilton are
emphasized especially by Brookhiser, *Alexander Hamilton*, 48, and Mitchell, *Alexander Hamilton: Youth to Maturity*, 207–208.

23 *Handsome and unusually trim . . . attitude*: For looks and mien: Brookhiser, *Alexander Hamilton*, 1 and 45. McDonald, 5–6, links the gallantry, drive, and impatience to what
he sees as a Romantic type—"That was Hamilton, start to finish" (6)—and gives examples of hauteur and short temper (20). For a sample of Hamilton's youthful ventings:
"From Alexander Hamilton to Lieutenant Colonel John Laurens, 8 January [1780],"
Founders Online, National Archives, founders.archives.gov/documents/Hamilton/01
-02-02-0568.

23 *worried his father-in-law*: Brookhiser, *Alexander Hamilton*, 49; Chernow, 152.

23 *being at odds with his mighty boss*: McDonald, 17, calls Hamilton's time on the staff one
of "frustration and disillusionment." All cited biographers discuss the desire for command and the tension with Washington.

24 *intricate relationships between government and money*: "The Continentalist No. I [12
July 1781]," *Founders Online*, National Archives, founders.archives.gov/documents
/Hamilton/01-02-02-1179; "The Continentalist No. II [19 July 1781]," *Founders Online*,
National Archives, founders.archives.gov/documents/Hamilton/01-02-02-1181; "The
Continentalist No. III [9 August 1781]," *Founders Online*, National Archives, founders
.archives.gov/documents/Hamilton/01-02-02-1186; "The Continentalist No. V [18
April 1782]," *Founders Online*, National Archives, founders.archives.gov/documents
/Hamilton/01-03-02-0015; "The Continentalist No. VI [4 July 1782]," *Founders Online*,
National Archives, founders.archives.gov/fdocuments/Hamilton/01-03-02-0031.

24 *writings on economics*: Most biographers mention Hume, Walpole, Necker, and other
influences. I follow McDonald, 84–85, in emphasizing Hamilton's involvement with
Necker, who, as Brookhiser notes, *Alexander Hamilton: American*, 81, endowed the
finance role with godlike proportions.

25 *Continentalist*: Hamilton's term, made famous in the essays of that title cited above;
I use it in place of "nationalists" and "conservatives," used by both Kohn, *Eagle and
Sword*, and Ferguson, with connotations not ideally appropriate to the politics of the
period.

25 *catastrophe*: "From Alexander Hamilton to Robert Morris [30 April 1781]," *Founders
Online*, National Archives, founders.archives.gov/documents/Hamilton/01-02-02-1167.

26 *State Sovereigntists*: Ferguson, whom I follow closely on public-finance struggles, never
provides a consistent term. Virginians like Henry and Lee are often mentioned in
this context, contributing to a misconception that states-rights moods were largely
southern; oratory of Rhode Islander David Howell (Chapter 7 herein) and arguments
by Elbridge Gerry of Massachusetts (Chapter 12 herein) reflect the sectional pervasiveness of the conflict.

26 *small-minded . . . even timidly*: See the contained tone of the letters to James Duane,
cited below, and outright fulminations to Henry Laurens: "From Alexander Hamilton
to Lieutenant Colonel John Laurens [30 June 1780]," *Founders Online*, National Archives, founders.archives.gov/documents/Hamilton/01-02-02-0742; "From Alexander
Hamilton to George Clinton, 13 February 1778," *Founders Online*, National Archives,
founders.archives.gov/documents/Hamilton/01-01-02-0365.

26 *comprehensive, detailed scheme*: The scheme may be derived from the "Continentalist" essays, cited above; the first letter to Duane, cited below; and "From Alexander Hamilton to—— [December–March 1779–1780]," *Founders Online*, National Archives, founders.archives.gov/documents/Hamilton/01-02-02-0559-0002, whose recipient is believed to be Schuyler.

27 *sent Duane his scheme*: "From Alexander Hamilton to James Duane [3 September 1780]," *Founders Online*, National Archives, founders.archives.gov/documents/Hamilton/01-02 -02-0838.

27 *Duane cautioned Hamilton politely*: Duane's response is lost; its contents and tone may be deduced from Hamilton's response: "From Alexander Hamilton to James Duane, 18 October 1780," *Founders Online*, National Archives, founders.archives.gov/documents /Hamilton/01-02-02-0912.

27 *to extinguish the states*: As discussed in Chapter 12, Hamilton made his true preference public in 1787.

28 *That was according to Hamilton*: "From Alexander Hamilton to Philip Schuyler, 18 February 1781," *Founders Online*, National Archives, founders.archives.gov/documents /Hamilton/01-02-02-1089.

28 *disparaged his generalship too*: "From Alexander Hamilton to Robert R. Livingston, 7 August 1777," *Founders Online*, National Archives, founders.archives.gov/documents /Hamilton/01-01-02-0247.

28 *advised Hamilton to patch things up*: "To Alexander Hamilton from Philip Schuyler, 25 February 1781," *Founders Online*, National Archives, founders.archives.gov/documents /Hamilton/01-02-02-1110.

28 *wheedling an increasingly irritated Washington*: "From Alexander Hamilton to George Washington [27 April 1781]," *Founders Online*, National Archives, founders.archives .gov/documents/Hamilton/01-02-02-1163; "To Alexander Hamilton from George Washington, 27 April 1781," *Founders Online*, National Archives, founders.archives.gov /documents/Hamilton/01-02-02-1164; "From Alexander Hamilton to George Washington [2 May 1781]," *Founders Online*, National Archives, founders.archives.gov/documents /Hamilton/01-02-02-1169.

28 *Hamilton's only mentor . . . barely rated a footnote*: The financier's central importance to the war effort is made clear by Bouton, "Tying Up the Revolution" and *Taming Democracy*, fully supported by Ferguson's Chapters 3, 6, and 7. Rappleye, too, argues passim for the crucial importance of Morris to the American Revolution, as does Ver Steeg. Many Hamilton biographers give Morris little note; Syrett and Cooke, the editors of Hamilton's papers, outright deny any Morris influence on Hamilton ("Introductory Note: Report Relative to a Provision for the Support of Public Credit [January 9, 1790]," *Founders Online*, National Archives, founders.archives.gov/documents/Hamil ton/01-06-02-0076-0001.) Ensuing chapters herein largely follow Ferguson in showing that while Hamilton's ideas were drawn, as Syrett and Cooke argue, from a variety of sources, had formed prior to the Morris relationship, and differed from Morris's, the critical fact of Morris's mentorship in linking high finance to the peculiar politics of American government can be denied only via the elision practiced by some of Hamilton's biographers.

2. FOUNDING FATCAT
29 *Gregarious . . . the richest man*: Distilling descriptions of the mature Morris in Rappleye, 2, 22–33; and Bouton, *Taming Democracy*, 70. On Morris's importance to the emergence of the United States, and to Hamilton, see the final note to Chapter 1 herein.

29 *untoward events*: The ensuing account of Morris's early life and rise in commerce distills that of Rappleye, Chapter 1.

29 *Liverpool merchants*: "Liverpool, England."

30 *the port was the colonies' busiest*: Rappleye, 9.

30–31 *more than sixty piers . . . tear-jerking ballads*: The depiction is inspired by ibid., 4–15.

31 *The city*: My description is influenced by Rappleye, 8–9, and Soderlund's section "Philadelphia as Cornerstone." For the Schuykill fishing club, see Pirro.

31 *by no means either utopian or fully Quaker*: In *Declaration*, 55–58, I provide a concise
discussion, based largely on Newcombe, of the successful effort spearheaded in the
1750s by Benjamin Franklin to overcome strict Quaker domination in official Pennsylvania politics.

31 *enslaved Africans . . . merchants eagerly took part*: Nash, *The Urban Crucible*, 109–10.
See Gigantino for the comparatively small number of people held by most owners.

31 *slave auction went on at the London Coffee House*: Widely discussed; see, for example,
"London Coffee House Historical Marker."

31 *miserable living and employment conditions*: Rappleye, 9. For details of the ill effects on
labor, specifically in Philadelphia, of the post–Seven Years' War depression, see Nash,
The Urban Crucible, 250–53 and 254–56. For the city's poverty, see Susan E. Klepp's
"Malthusian Miseries and the Working Poor in Philadelphia" and Karin Wulf's "Gen-
der and the Political Economy of Poor Relief in Colonial Philadelphia," in Billy G.
Smith, *Down and Out in Early America*, also cited by Bouton, "Tying Up the Revolution," 270–72.

32 *"hard money"*: A term widely used throughout the eighteenth and nineteenth centuries for what economists call "specie," or money in the form of coin. The distinction
between hard and paper money is made without need for explanation, for example, in
a 1765 letter objecting to the Stamp Tax: "To Benjamin Franklin from 'A Merchant in
Philadelphia' [Charles Thomson], 19 June 1765," *Founders Online*, National Archives,
founders.archives.gov/documents/Franklin/01-12-02-0088.

32 *Spanish silver dollar*: "The History of U.S. Circulating Coins"; "Spanish Milled Dollar."

32 *paper instruments*: For a concise and informative overview of the history of paper
money, see Cleveland. For the importance of paper money in the British Atlantic
colonies, see Ferguson, Chapter 1, and Bouton, *Taming Democracy*, 16–21, both citing
Brock, among others.

32 *rife with uncertainty*: Rappleye, 12–14.

33 *Willing and Morris*: The ensuing sketch of Morris's rise follows Rappleye, 22–25.

34 *in an awkward position*: The ensuing account of Morris's reluctant entry into politics
follows Rappleye, Chapter 2.

34 *a clubman*: Ryan K. Smith's characterization, 277.

34 *calling himself an American*: Rappleye, 28.

34 *stopped importing British goods*: Innumerable works trace the larger development of
the imperial tensions that began reaching the critical phase with the trade-law violation; I've benefited especially from Jensen, *The Founding of a Nation*. For Robert Morris's conflicted entrance into the politics of resistance, I follow Rappleye, Chapters
3–5.

35 *tobacco consumption, mainly by nose*: The high likelihood of ongoing tobacco smoking and, even more likely, sniffing during meetings of eighteenth-century deliberative
bodies is a conclusion drawn from my interview with Karie Diethorn, Chief Curator,
Independence National Historical Park, and Deborah Miller, Museum Curator, Independence National Historical Park, on May 11, 2022.

35 *especially well with . . . George Washington*: Rappleye, 30; and noting, 90, that Morris and Washington had first met in 1773.

35 *a negotiated reconciliation*: The sway of the reconciliationist position after the outbreak of war in April 1775, both in the Congress and in some of the states, once taken as given, seems to me underrated and even elided by recent historians across various divides who seek to identify a unified American purpose in breaking from Britain and thus tend to frame the military outbreaks of spring 1775 as leading inevitably to the legal and military bid for independence of July 1776. See expanded notes at www .hamiltonscheme.com.

35 *John Dickinson*: In *Declaration*, 51–75, I present a detailed narrative of Dickinson's progress through the Pennsylvania political battles, relying mainly on Flower, New-combe, and Jacobson and linking Dickinson's reconciliationism with early and un-compromising patriot leadership.

36 *Unsettling working-class agitation*: See Chapter 6.

36 *Morris kept doing*: The account of Morris's rise as an arms dealer distills Rappleye, 36–47.

36 *"as free as the air"*: Ibid., 52, quoting Morris. Ferguson, 72–74, explores the overall absence of ethical considerations regarding public funds and interests in Morris's and other merchants' ideology of free markets.

37 *he'd rightly predicted would be immense profits*: Ibid., 68–69, quoting Morris.

37 *his own gain was the country's gain*: Ibid., 70, and Rappleye, 69, both quoting Morris.

37 *Morris joined the committee*: The account of Morris's increasing control over politics and commerce distills Rappleye, 45–52.

38 *events, which even Morris found impossible to track*: See Chapter 6.

38 *That August*: An August signing is now widely accepted; see for example "Declaration of Independence."

38 *bolder and more profitable*: The account of Morris's expanding commercial and political dominance after July 2, 1776, blends Rappleye, Chapters 4 and 5, with Ferguson, 75–81.

39 *So novel was the free trade . . . deals, side pots, skims*: The passage is inspired by and drawn from a wealth of complicated detail in Ferguson, 78–93.

39 *Willing stayed in the occupied city*: Rappleye, 124.

39–40 *The Lee brothers . . . Silas Deane*: "The Deane Affair" and the Lees' involvement are widely discussed. The brief sketch here distills much detail in Ferguson, 81–93.

40 *documents leaked to the press*: As noted in Chapter 8, the leaker was Thomas Paine.

40 *pilfering budgets . . . medical supplies for personal profit*: Ferguson, 98–103.

40 *He'd done business and even held office in London*: Ibid., 90, 93.

41 *difference between virtue and Mammon*: Ibid., 145.

41 *On Laurens's lands, enslaved black people*: "Henry Laurens."

41 *return to the Pennsylvania assembly*: The results are related in Chapter 8.

41 *build his wealth to staggering scale*: For detail, see Rappleye, 204–10.

41 *Continental currency*: For a detailed history of the Continental dollar and an argument that it was not a "fiat currency" but a zero-interest bearer bond, see Grubb.

41 *superintendent of finance*: The ensuing account of Morris's position, his conditions for accepting it, and its pervasive power is drawn from Ferguson, 117–24, and Rappleye, 233–35.

42 *consolidated federal measures*: Carp, 391, argues that in 1780–81, in "reaction to eco-nomic chaos and military defeat," broad support for a nationalistic approach prevailed among army officers and state legislators. That point is also made by Ferguson, 111, yet Carp disputes Ferguson's emphasis on the role of Morris and the merchants in the

drive toward nationhood, pointing to merchants' objections to certain decisions that Morris made in 1781 (386, n. 67), discussed in Chapter 7 herein.

42 *had been called "prime"*: Before acceptance as a title, the term was used disparagingly, from at least as early as 1715, to suggest a power grab; Robert Walpole was first referred to as "Prime Minister" when resuming his office as First Lord of the Treasury and Chancellor of Exchequer in 1721. See Jeffery.

43 *depressing everyday economies*: For a thorough examination of wartime depression's worsening into the 1780s, see Bouton, *Taming Democracy*, Chapter 4.

43 *His vision of dynamic American growth*: Inspired by Ferguson, 121, 140, 144, 146.

44 *the Money Connection*: Rappleye, 239, quoting Morris.

3. EXCHANGING EYE-ROLLS

45 *Hamilton gave himself credit*: "From Alexander Hamilton to Robert Morris [30 April 1781]," *Founders Online*, National Archives, founders.archives.gov/documents /Hamilton/01-02-02-1167.

45 *he'd tried to show Duane . . . centralized banking*: "From Alexander Hamilton to James Duane [3 September 1780]," *Founders Online*, National Archives, founders.archives .gov/documents/Hamilton/01-02-02-0838.

45 *book-learning on finance was becoming better known*: McDonald, 40.

45 *His own name had come up*: "To George Washington from John Sullivan, 29 January 1781," *Founders Online*, National Archives, founders.archives.gov/documents /Washington/99-01-02-04696.

46 *Office of Finance on Front Street*: Toogood, 47, n. 17.

46 *came from somebody Morris knew*: The initial correspondence suggests that Morris and Hamilton didn't know each other well before May 1781; given many mutual connections within a small circle and Hamilton's duties on Washington's staff, it's impossible to imagine they were strangers.

46 *a performance*: "To Alexander Hamilton from Robert Morris, 26 May 1781," *Founders Online*, National Archives, founders.archives.gov/documents/Hamilton/01-02-02 -1176.

46 *the Bank of England*: The early purposes of the Bank of England and their connections to the British financial revolution are very readably discussed in Kynaston's Prologue. For a full-scale interpretation of critical relationships among warfare, high finance, taxation, and British institutional growth in the eighteenth century, with some reference to the bank, see Brewer, passim.

46 *corporation*: The eighteenth-century corporate system differed from the modern U.S. arrangement in which a state issues a corporate charter under a general incorporation law not dependent on passing case-by-case legislation. The old system created a direct monopolistic link between a government and a specially chartered company, privileging the chartered entity while obstructing and even outright prohibiting competition. Eighteenth- and early nineteenth-century objections to corporations as corruptions of government, discussed later in this book, refer specifically to that arrangement. In the United States, general incorporation began state by state in New York in 1811 and became common in the 1830s.

46 *high-denomination notes*: Kynaston, 2–3, shows that the capacity to issue well-backed notes was fully worked into the Bank of England's founding purposes; by 1732, the bank was printing notes in sets by denomination, instead of filling in their values against specie by hand: see "Early Banknotes." Scott Reynolds Nelson, xv, says that much of the bank's profit came from "discounting" checks drawn on others: cashing them for a cut.

47 *capitalization . . . deeply informed detail*: McDonald, 41, noting what he sees as certain flaws in the proposal: "Glimpses of the mature Hamilton lace the document."

47 *he got back to Hamilton*: See Morris's letter to Hamilton, cited above.

47–48 *a bank plan of his own . . . charter, to the federal government*: The bank-plan sketch here is drawn from Ferguson, 123, 135–38; and Rappleye, 239.

48 *The bank charter did pass the Congress*: Rappleye, 237, with some detail on the vote count. Sommer, 1019–20, notes the extremely unrestrictive nature of the granted charter and the highly influential nature of the bank's structure on later state banking.

49 *capitalization wasn't nearly enough*: See Morris's letter to Hamilton, cited above.

49 *When they next connected*: "To Alexander Hamilton from Robert Morris, 2 May 1782," *Founders Online*, National Archives, founders.archives.gov/documents/Hamilton/01 -03-02-0019. A first face-to-face meeting is undocumented, as far as I can tell.

49 *gone on hocking Washington*: "From Alexander Hamilton to George Washington [27 April 1781]," *Founders Online*, National Archives, founders.archives.gov/documents /Hamilton/01-02-02-1163; "From Alexander Hamilton to George Washington [2 May 1781]," *Founders Online*, National Archives, founders.archives.gov/documents /Hamilton/01-02-02-1169.

49 *further pleading on the spot*: Mitchell, *Alexander Hamilton: The Revolutionary Years*, 275, citing Marquis de Lafayette's memory.

49 *light-infantry brigade . . . finally checked the glory box*: All of the biographers have more detail on Hamilton's action at Yorktown.

49 *sniffy letter*: "From Alexander Hamilton to George Washington [1 March 1782]," *Founders Online*, National Archives, founders.archives.gov/documents/Hamilton/01 -03-02-0006.

49 *more or less estranged*: On the record, at least, silence prevails after March 1, 1782, and before Hamilton's ice-breaking letter of February 13, 1783, discussed in Chapter 7.

49 *a series of newspaper essays*: Two of the "Continentalist" essays cited in Chapter 1 appeared during this period: "The Continentalist No. V [18 April 1782]," *Founders Online*, National Archives, founders.archives.gov/documents/Hamilton/01-03-02-0015; and "The Continentalist No. VI [4 July 1782]," *Founders Online*, National Archives, founders.archives.gov/documents/Hamilton/01-03-02-0031.

49 *didn't want to be a lawyer*: McDonald, 50–51.

50 *invited him into public life for the first time*: I think most Hamilton biographers underrate this turning point. McDonald does note that the job represented "Hamilton's first venture into public life" (43), but only Mitchell, *Alexander Hamilton: Youth to Maturity*, calls Hamilton's relationship to Morris an "apprenticeship" (262), and none gives close attention to the development of that relationship in the ensuing months or the urgency that the failed effort to collect requisitions lent the next steps in Hamilton's career.

50 *"Mr. Morris's notes"*: Ferguson, 136, 138–39.

50 *cracking down on the states for money*: The account of the early failure of the state-oriented war-finance system, and Morris's attempt to collect requisitions in hard money, follows Ferguson, 129–30 and 140–42. For detail on all of the states' and colonies' own taxation systems, see Einhorn, also detailing the war-requisition system's involvement in the conflicted relationship of the states and the Congress (124–31); noting that all taxes dedicated to the war effort were state taxes (20–21); and saying "only three states raised more than half their quotas from 1781 through 1788" (26, citing Roger H. Brown).

51 *a percentage of the total quota*: "To Alexander Hamilton from Robert Morris, 4

June 1782," *Founders Online*, National Archives, founders.archives.gov/documents
/Hamilton/01-03-02-0025.

51 *nobody would have taken the job*: Hamilton at first declined, on that basis. "From Alexander Hamilton to Robert Morris, 18 May 1782," *Founders Online*, National Archives, founders.archives.gov/documents/Hamilton/01-03-02-0023.

51 *the plan could only fail*: Per Roger H. Brown, passim, it was the failure first of the requisition system and then of the federal impost (see Chapter 7 herein) that brought about nationalization in 1787. I think in 1782 Morris saw the requisition system's inevitable and even desirable failure as an inducement for passing the impost and saw the impost as a "wedge" (Ferguson, 146) for transforming the Congress into a national government—the plan that failed, opening a door for the 1787 convention.

51 *small-denomination paper currencies*: The widespread misconception that government currencies issued during the colonial and founding periods were at best useless and at worst toxic is a long-range effect of Morris's recoil from them, with antidemocratic connotations brought out in later chapters. For the clearest account of the economic benefits to Atlantic colonial economies of government-issued paper currencies, see Bouton, *Taming Democracy*, 16–21, citing among others Ferguson's more detailed Chapter 1, which draws in part on Brock, passim.

51 *"This Bill . . . the CONVENTION"*: "1776 Maryland $1/9 One-Ninth of a Dollar Colonial Currency Note—August 14th, 1776."

52 *liked to view his state as first among equals*: "First among equals": McDonald, 87, in discussing Clinton's "Empire State" concept.

53 *the superintendent and his employee exchanged eye-rolls . . . "epitome of the follies"*: As Ferguson puts it: "Morris had nothing but scorn for the constitutional mode of raising revenue by requisitions" (140). See "From Alexander Hamilton to Robert Morris, 13 July 1782," *Founders Online*, National Archives, founders.archives.gov/documents /Hamilton/01-03-02-0034; "From Alexander Hamilton to Robert Morris, 22 July 1782," *Founders Online*, National Archives, founders.archives.gov/documents/Hamilton/01-03 -02-0039; "From Alexander Hamilton to Robert Morris, 13 August 1782," *Founders Online*, National Archives, founders.archives.gov/documents/Hamilton/01-03-02-0057 -0001; and "To Alexander Hamilton from Robert Morris, 28 August 1782," *Founders Online*, National Archives, founders.archives.gov/documents/Hamilton/01-03-02-0065, with Morris's "the epitome of the follies that prevail."

54 *a mechanism for building Continentalism on the Money Connection*: Ferguson, 120–24, argues that "Morris's plan of action anticipated the major features of the later Federalist programs" (124); hence again Morris's critical importance to Hamilton.

53 *Hamilton began learning*: See McDonald, 41, taking Hamilton's first letter to Morris to task for not yet comprehending the specific nature and structure of the U.S. war debt; and Ferguson, 124, noting Morris's early insight into the unifying power specifically for the United States of specifically a domestic rather than a foreign debt, supported by interstate tax collection.

54 *the Public Debt of the United States*: Ferguson, 35–69 and Chapter 12, informs this chapter, as does Bouton, *Taming Democracy*, Chapter 3, and "Tying Up the Revolution," Chapters 3 and 4. Where Ferguson and some others use an easily confused terminology—"certificate" for one type of instrument, "Loan Office certificate" for another—I've simplified by using "bond" (not an eighteenth-century term) for any government-issued, interest-bearing loan instrument; "chits" for the supply-impressment and army-pay IOUs; and "currency" for the Continental paper discontinued in 1779.

4. IN WHICH WE ARE INTRODUCED TO THE PUBLIC DEBT
OF THE UNITED STATES

55 *nothing but a big problem*: A vague impression widespread in popular summations features a Hamilton forced to wrestle down a supposedly too-large public debt that he supposedly first encountered only on becoming treasury secretary ("In his new post as Secretary of the Treasury, Alexander Hamilton inherited the old problem of the huge war debt": "Hamilton and the National Debt," George Washington, sheb falls-georgewashington.weebly.com/hamilton-and-the-national-debt.html. "The paramount problem facing Hamilton was a huge national debt": "Alexander Hamilton's Financial Program," Digital History, www.digitalhistory.uh.edu/disp_textbook.cfm ?smtid=2&psid=2973.) Of Hamilton's biographers, Miller, McDonald, and Mitchell, *Alexander Hamilton: The National Adventure*, seem to me to be the most realistic on this issue.

55 *public borrowing enabled governments*: The ensuing sketch is based on a now-standard view of the growth of the British Empire via debt financing supported by extensive and reliable tax collection, as argued closely by Brewer, passim, and especially Chapter 3. As early as 1756, Robert Morris was involved in a pilot program on the British model when he and others launched the first American sale of interest-bearing government bonds, with proceeds dedicated to financing Pennsylvania's trade with indigenous nations. See Rappleye, 15, noting, "It was a mercantile world, but Morris and his partner were practicing capitalism."

56 *Robert Morris knew the story intimately . . . Congress would have to borrow*: Distilling Ferguson, 26–35.

56 *foreign sources yielded little money*: Ibid., 40–44.

57 *about $63 million by 1790*: Sylla, 60, n. 1.

57 *Lending money as a business venture*: Bouton, "Tying Up the Revolution," 86–87.

57–59 *the Congress issued for sale . . . $2.5 million in federal bonds*: My depiction of what became the blue-chip tier of the debt closely follows Ferguson, 35–39.

57 *paper money it began printing in 1775*: Ibid., 26–35, tracking the currency's issue and early depreciation.

57 *Lenders preferred paper money*: Ibid., 15, noting that lenders' preference hadn't caused major conflicts when colonial currencies were well-managed—in merchants' terms—for stability; the mercantile "hard money" obsession began with the Revolution, in reaction to the Congress's lack of power to tax and manage its paper and the increasingly democratic control over the states' fiscal policies, explored in Chapters 6 and 9–11 herein.

58 *secret French grant*: Ferguson, 36; Rappleye, 109–10.

58 *"bills of exchange"*: Ferguson, 36.

58 *Anyone in the know*: Ibid., 37.

58 *accepting its own weak Continental currency*: Bouton, "Tying Up the Revolution," 136, with the thousand-dollar-bond-discount example closely paraphrased here.

59 *the Congress rethought its offer*: Ferguson, 39.

59 *infiltrated the upscale sector of the economy*: Ibid., 39–40, 53–54.

59 *stopped even printing its currency*: Ibid., 46–47.

60 *Secondary markets*: Ibid., 251–54, referring to "brisk" trading, with "transfers . . . continuous from the moment securities were issued," continuing through the 1780s, leading to the transfer of most of the bonds to secondary holders, and mounting to a "frenzy" by the beginning of the 1790s. McDonald, 152–54, outlines the opposed strategies of speculators.

60   *small but very busy trading class:* Ferguson, 284, estimates that in 1790 there were
only about fifteen to twenty thousand holders of public securities. Wright, 164, using
more precise tools, and arguing that by the late nineteenth century the debt hadn't
in fact remained in the hands of an elite few, roughly concurs with Ferguson regarding the number of early holders, arriving at 21,500 entities in 1795, including individuals, businesses, and towns, and concludes that one such entity out of every 212
people was a federal bondholder after assumption of the state debt—slightly lower
than half of 1 percent—with the largest few players holding "most of the debt by
value" (though Wright emphasizes dispersal of smaller holdings across socioeconomic
groups); Wright also argues persuasively for a wide regional dispersal, thus supporting
Ferguson's idea that in Morris's and Hamilton's vision, funding a public debt would
tend to unify the country. To me, Ferguson's statement "the mass of the population
certainly had no stake in the funding program" therefore holds up. For conflicts between Wright and certain other writers on the founding debt, see expanded notes at
www.hamiltonscheme.com.

60   *The most preferred bonds . . . were hard to get:* Ibid., 254, 255.

60   *emotional turmoil:* While the anxiety of public creditors became flagrant when Morris began poking at it in the 1782–1783 fight over the impost (see Chapter 7), it was
evident earlier. Ferguson, 115, n. 14, cites a Connecticut federal-bondholder petition;
Hamilton and Schuyler attended a similar 1781 convention of antsy New York federal
bondholders, as noted in Chapter 7 herein.

61–62   *sheer impressment . . . pennies on the dollar:* Ibid., 57–64, detailing the history of a
"mass expropriation" effected by the impressment system.

62   *as much as $95 million:* Ibid., 63.

62   *whom the IOUs obligated:* Ibid., 60 and 62, emphasizing this part of the debt's "merged"
and "mingled" state-federal nature.

63   *securitized and financialized even this:* Ibid., 252–53.

63   *army-pay paper did bear interest:* Ibid., 50–51, and noting, 252, that in secondary markets, with bonds often hard to get, army-pay paper became "the speculators' best
game."

63   *about $40 million . . . at least $20 million:* "Report Relative to a Provision for the Support of Public Credit [9 January 1790]," *Founders Online,* National Archives, founders
.archives.gov/documents/Hamilton/01-06-02-0076-0002-0001.

63   *consolidation of a small group of rich Americans:* Ibid., 143, calling the public debt central to the strategy of national centralization. Bouton, "Tying Up the Revolution,"
calls this phenomenon "The Centrality of the Public Debt."

64   *creditors wanted regular interest coming in for generations:* As Chapter 4 and later chapters make clear, the bondholders feared not just repudiation of the Debt but also fast
payoff at reduced value.

65   *interstate federal collection power . . . further federal lawmaking:* The strategy is discussed in Chapter 7.

65   *transforming the existing Congress step by step:* This is Ferguson's main theme. Roger H.
Brown, 6–7 and passim, argues with close attention to fiscal detail that those who became known as Federalists were not initially in favor of creating a whole new system,
nor even pulled that way in 1786 by the Shaysites Rebellion (discussed in Chapter 11
herein) but began considering the extreme measure that became the Constitutional
Convention only after a) the failure of state taxation for requisitions and b) the final
failure of the federal impost (discussed in Chapters 7 and 8 herein). I frame that idea
in Ferguson's terms: only when the impost failed as a replacement of the requisition

system and a transformative wedge (see below) for nationalizing the Congress did an outright overturning of the Articles and the Congress become the goal.

65 *notion that the Federal Debt was already too big*: "To John Jay from Robert Morris, 4 July 1781," *Founders Online*, National Archives, founders.archives.gov/documents/Jay/01 -02-02-0206.

65 *assume all of the states' separate obligations*: Ferguson, 144–45, notes that Morris's ultimate goal, stymied during his tenure, was to consolidate the mass of all of the varying debt instruments as a responsibility of the Congress.

66 *The first federal tax was thus to be a wedge*: Ibid., 146. Miller, 88, also calls the tax a wedge (yet sees its revenues as earmarked for the foreign debt, contra all other sources). But Einhorn, 136–37, casts the "wedge" concept as a rhetorical chimera invoked by David Howell when arguing against the impost (see Chapter 7 herein), a view that seems in keeping with her assertion, contra Ferguson, that pro-impost people outside the group Ferguson calls Nationalists "only wanted the impost," not a national transformation (119–20); and her dissent, 155–56, from "historians generally"—which must mean chiefly Ferguson and Roger H. Brown—that the impost was intended to centralize the country. See expanded notes: www.hamiltonscheme.com.

66 *"The political existence"*: Ibid., 146.

5. MAN IN BLACK

69 *Herman Husband*: Some of Husband's most important work is in the John Irwin Scull Archive; the Mary Elinor Lazenby Collection holds an important batch of correspondence and records. With the cited published primary sources, the major secondary sources are Mark Haddon Jones's unpublished dissertation, for many years the only full-length scholarly work; Stewart, the first biographer since Jones, and Harvey, perhaps the most original current scholarship, exploring the spiritual dynamics central to Husband's life and vision within a radically dissenting religious tradition going back to seventeenth-century Britain. Important essays and chapters on Husband include Holt, "The New Jerusalem"; Ekirch; Fennell, Chapter 6; Bloch, Chapters 3, 6, and 7; and Troxler, especially Chapters 3 and 4.

69 *variations on a birth name*: "Hermon Husbands," John Badollet's journal entry, in Hunter, 173; "Harmon Husband"; "Hermon Husband's Continuation of the Impartial Relation"; "Herman Husbands, Regulator"; Husband sometimes signed his name "Harmon": see the Regulator Papers photocopies, No. 5., in the Mary Elinor Lazenby Collection (Box 1, Folder 2).

69 *Lycurgus*: Husband, "XIV Sermons on the Characters of Jacob's Fourteen Sons," originally published under the pseudonym. Other aliases are discussed in later chapters.

69 *Isaac Newton . . . of Daniel and Revelation*: See Isaac Newton.

69–70 *naturalist . . . surveying and mapmaking skills*: See Chapter 6.

70 *Husband was born in 1724*: The ensuing account of Husband's forebears, early life, and moral and spiritual development is drawn largely from Mark Haddon Jones, Chapter 1; Stewart, Chapter 1; with reference to Husband, "Some Remarks on Religion," in Boyd, 198–246, and the Manuscript Sermon, John Irwin Scull Archive. Harvey, Chapter 1, places the Husband family's rise amid upheavals in early capitalism and various forms of religious and political dissent.

71 *Great Awakening*: My sketch of Awakening theology and practice follows Heimert, Chapters 1–4, in dissenting from fire-and-brimstone stereotypes of eighteenth-century American evangelical Christianity and linking the commitment to inner spiritual experience both to egalitarianism and to the American Revolution. Eric Foner, *Tom*

444 NOTES

Paine and Revolutionary America, 111, supports the link between revolutionary and Millennial thought; Nash, *The Unknown American Revolution*, 6–15, gives many examples; Bloch, 10–31, is clear and illuminating on the role of Millennialism in the pre-Revolution Atlantic colonies.

71–72 rule of Christ . . . at first in America: Heimert, 395–400, explores how an America-focused theology connected with and morphed into the broader American revolutionary mood. In later chapters herein, Husband becomes a particularly intense example of a phenomenon that Heimert shows to be widespread and critical to the Revolution, though in tension with revolutionary elites' liberal Enlightenment values.

72 movement aiming to undo combinations of wealth and government: My understanding of the movement's importance, dimensions, tactics, and background has been shaped by the cited works of Young and Nobles, Countryman, Holton, Nash, Lemisch (*Jack Tar in the Streets*), Eric Foner (*Tom Paine and Revolutionary America*), Bouton, Thompson, and Hill. On the American version climaxing in 1794—a key arc of this book's narrative—Elkins and McKitrick, 473, take what they call the popular movement seriously, though limiting discussion to the reaction to the excise in western Pennsylvania.

72 American conflicts . . . went back to Britain: Scholarship on the survival and development of British modes of agitation in the Atlantic colonies includes Barbara Clark Smith; Lemisch, *Jack Tar in the Streets*; Linebaugh and Rediker, especially Chapter 7; Nash, *The Urban Crucible*, especially Chapter 4; Stock, 19–22; Alfred Young, "English Plebian Culture and Eighteenth-Century America," in Jacob and Jacob; and all of the essays in Pencak, Dennis, and Newman (see especially the dual introductions; Thomas J. Humphrey, "Crowd and Court: Rough Music and Popular Justice in Colonial New York"; Brendan McConville, "The Rise of Rough Music: Reflections on an Ancient New Custom in Eighteenth-Century New Jersey"; and Roger D. Abrahams, "White Indians in Penn's City: The Loyal Sons of St. Tammany").

72 went back to Britain: The ensuing look at the movement's British roots, moods, inspirations, and religious sects is influenced by Hill (*The World Turned Upside Down*, passim, especially Chapter 7; and "Radical Pirates?" in Jacob and Jacob); Thompson (*Whigs and Hunters*, passim; *Customs in Common*, passim; and *The Making of the English Working Class*, 22–25); Nash (*The Urban Crucible*, 42); Linebaugh and Rediker (17–20 and Chapter 4); and Robert Malcolmson ("Workers Combinations in Eighteenth-Century England" in Jacob and Jacob).

72 Fifth Monarchy Men: Harvey argues, Chapter 7, that Husband's vision and thought best be understood within the Fifth Monarchist theology.

73 "subtle selfish councils . . . without excuse": For the whole Digger statement, see Winstanley, 75–95.

73 Levellers: "1647: The Putney Debates." For commentary, see Wootton, 285–317. Thompson, *The Making of the English Working Class*, 22–25, clarifies the role of the debates as a foundation for the English working class. Barbara Clark Smith, *The Freedoms We Lost*, 8–9, discusses the elite nature of the elected House of Commons; Nash, *The Urban Crucible*, 343, discusses the American folk tradition of a Cromwell-era democratic working-class movement.

73 conditioned on owning a certain amount of property: The fact is irrefutable; certain scholarship has therefore tried to make it irrelevant, mainly with reference to a 1955 study, now debunked, by Robert E. Brown, concluding that in Massachusetts, and by implication throughout eighteenth-century America, virtually all white male adults could vote legally and that those who couldn't vote legally voted anyway. See expanded notes at www.hamiltonscheme.com.

74 *other than white men:* Scholars who explore important connections between the movement on behalf of free labor and movements on behalf of other oppressed people in the Atlantic imperial world include Holton, especially *Liberty Is Sweet,* and Linebaugh and Rediker.

74 *by women themselves:* Holton, *Liberty Is Sweet,* 300, citing Barbara Clark Smith, "Food Rioters and the American Revolution."

74 *pirate crews included women:* Linebaugh and Rediker, 167.

74 *white seamen and dockworkers . . . resist and escape:* Ibid., 220–21.

74 *Equiano . . . slavery of another kind:* Ibid., 245, presenting Equiano as personifying a general sympathy among various oppressed classes. Exploring the source material leaves me unsure whether Equiano, in having this perception of the oppression of white sailors, was representative or extraordinary. See expanded notes at www .hamiltonscheme.com.

74 *led largely, on the record, by white men:* As ensuing chapters show, in the primary and secondary records for uprisings and other resistance featured in this book, the roles for women and free and enslaved black men were rare and muted. See expanded notes at www.hamiltonscheme.com.

75 *calls for abolishing slavery . . . sexual pleasure:* on slavery, see Nash, *The Urban Crucible,* Chapter 8, especially on James Davenport; on greed as the major vice, see Heimert, Chapter 1, going back to the 1730s.

75 *new-light Presbyterians . . . Society of Friends:* Mark Haddon Jones, 38–47; Stewart, 24–27.

75 *Quaker Meeting had largely shed the histrionic style:* Troxler, 72; Mark Haddon Jones, 87–88. Mark Haddon Jones, 53–54, sees evangelical converts to the Society of Friends feeding the Quakers' growing abolitionism, which wasn't full-fledged until 1772.

75 *Quakers . . . greater equality of women:* Troxler, 73, notes the prevalence as early as the 1750s of women preaching in Quakerism and certain Baptist sects. For an Anglo-American tradition of women as visionaries and preachers, see Linebaugh and Rediker, 88–93.

76 *the backcountry of North Carolina:* For much more detail on Husband's progress from the eastern shore to the backcountry and his land purchases and holdings, see Mark Haddon Jones, Chapters 3 and 4; and Stewart, 31–37.

76 *never enslaved anybody:* Probably. Mark Haddon Jones, 101, and Harvey, 65, assert that Husband had no slaves, Jones noting that Husband accepted none from his father's estate and that Quakerism was at that moment becoming abolitionist. Yet Ekirch, 637, says Husband may have owned one person, citing "a 1771 list of government expenses incurred during the Regulator campaign" that "refers to 'Husband's Negro'" (n. 15). Harvey, 65, n. 3, identifies the recipient and notes an ambiguity, finding it unlikely that Husband was the owner. See expanded notes at www.hamiltonscheme.com.

76 *manifestation of the biblical land of Canaan:* Mark Haddon Jones, 77.

76 *conflict with the Quaker Meeting:* Mark Haddon Jones, Ibid. 84–90, reads the incident in the light of Husband's insistence on freedom of conscience. Stewart, 37–40, sees it as a major turning point, with mixed motivations. Troxler, 68–73, associating Husband's moves against Wright with loyalty to a patriarchal order, speculates that "Husband may have been uneasy" with women's relative equality and freedom in the Meeting. While Husband certainly was in many ways traditionally patriarchal, I don't think other parts of the record support the speculation. See expanded notes at www.hamiltonscheme.com.

77 *the right to voice revelations:* Troxler, 72, though critical, notes that Husband may have

been asserting "the claims of individual conscience over the authority of the religious group" and that he was already viewed in the Meeting as reviving an old "ranting" style that the Society of Friends no longer tolerated (also discussed by Mark Haddon Jones, 87–88). For roots of Husband's religious and political dissent in older British levelling traditions discussed above, see Kars, Chapter 6, and Harvey, Chapter 7.

77 *the situation of free labor*: The ensuing broad-stroke overview reflects the influence of Middleton and Lombard, Stock, Nash, Fennell, Bouton, and Billy G. Smith, contra the major "consensus" historians Gordon Wood, Bernard Bailyn, and David Hackett Fischer (see Billy G. Smith, xiii). On the high rate of unfree white laborers in the early-arriving colonial population and difficulties faced on becoming free, see Gary Nash, "Poverty and Politics in Early America," in Billy G. Smith. I include in the working class the large number of at-risk owners of small-scale subsistence farms and shops. See Chapter 6 herein for parallel conditions of port-city workers.

77 *land was held in huge parcels*: Stock, 23–24. Middleton and Lombard, 133, note that as early as 1660, land in the Chesapeake region was nearly unavailable and that 25 percent of former indentured laborers were already working as tenants or day laborers, with only 6 percent able to hire workers themselves. The enormous holdings of the New York manorial system are widely discussed; for an interesting dissent from the widely accepted class-war basis of New York's 1760s tenant riots, see Sung Bok Kim, discussed in the expanded notes at www.hamiltonscheme.com.

77 *"Babylonish"*: Husband, "Sermon to the Bucks and Hinds of America."

78 *stymied by revolving debts*: Middleton and Lombard, 213, clarifying that from as early as the 1660s deep indebtedness was a persistent problem for small operators even in relatively prosperous tidewater Virginia. Bouton, *Taming Democracy*, 94–103, zooms in on debt's crushing effect on small operators in rural Pennsylvania in the late 1770s and '80s. For North Carolina regulators' awareness of predatory lending, see Troxler, 35–36.

78 *12 percent per month*: Bouton, *Taming Democracy*, 80, regarding 1780s Pennsylvania.

78 *tenants . . . or making them vagrants*: The sketch of American tenancy's worsening situation and the plight of the landless is drawn from Bouton, *Taming Democracy*, 14–16; Stock, 23–29; Middleton and Lombard, 220–33; and Nash, "Poverty and Politics in Early America," and Philip Morgan, "Slaves and Poverty," both in Billy G. Smith.

78 *the chief designer as the Beast*: Husband, "Sermon to the Bucks and Hinds."

78 *extreme political inequality*: For a discussion of colonial voter qualifications, see *conditioned on owning a certain amount of property*, above. For representative imbalances favoring port cities and certain counties and sluggishness on erecting counties, see Klein and Hoogenboom, 53, and Lincoln, 44–51, regarding Pennsylvania.

79 *Law existed to enforce the inequality . . . passed down in rich families as assets*: Mark Haddon Jones, 96–101, focusing on the administrative operations of rural North Carolina, calls that province's system the most regressive and corrupt in the colonies. Einhorn calls Virginia's administration "hopelessly corrupt" in the seventeenth century and details fee-collecting sinecures and sheriffs' "rapacity" in the eighteenth (34–35). Massachusetts, less prolifically corrupt and fairer in granting tax exemptions, routinely awarded lucrative salaried and fee-collecting positions to insiders, along with grants of land for public service: Osgood, 97–99.

79 *what ordinary people meant by corruption*: See, for example, "The Leveller," passim; and Murray, 50, tracing the problem all the way back to ancient Rome. As Kars notes, 121–22, Murray was a direct influence on Husband; see the dedication to "A Sermon to the Bucks and Hinds of America," ii, and the title page, where Husband calls the

pamphlet an imitation of Murray's "Sermons to Asses." Husband's "Issachar" interpretation, discussed later in this chapter, may be an extrapolation of an interpretation of Murray's.

80 *white people stole land . . . settlers in poverty*: See Husband's letter to Granville, transcribed in full in Ekirch, 637–44. Holt, "The New Jerusalem," 21, notes Husband's racism in viewing Africans as "more foreign by one half" than indigenous Americans (Ekirch, 643).

80 *Great Indian Trading Path and the Great Wagon Road*: Stewart, 33.

80 *prevented them from getting clear title*: Mark Haddon Jones, 62.

80 *written to Lord Granville*: Ekirch, 637–44.

80 *"However trifling"*: Ibid., 643.

81–82 *sexual attraction . . . "I shall not say all I can say"*: Husband explores his ideas about sex and marriage in detail in "XIV Sermons," 37–47. Other writers on Husband seem not to make anything of the passage.

82 *Emy . . . ready to make a stand*: Emy sometimes signed her name "Emey"; see the Regulator Papers photocopies, No. 16, in the Mary Elinor Lazenby Collection (Box 1, Folder 2). Some writers have called her Emmy and Amy. For her evident education, see Badollet's journal entry in Hunter, 173. Kars provides the family background given here, 118, and quotes a later exchange between Emy and a juryman, 181, showing her readiness to accept a fight against authority.

82 *good government*: Husband, Manuscript Sermon, John Irwin Scull Archive, 66.

83 *"prize worth all the kingdoms of Europe"*: Whittenburg, 647–50, also cited by Harvey, 97, who connects it to Ezekiel.

83 *"Nothing is more hurtful to the common wealth"*: Harvey, 117–88, connects the idea to Nehemiah.

83 *"rather than exert themselves"*: Ibid., 118–19, on the Issachar reference. "Neutrals," and "despicable slaves": Husband, "XIV Sermons . . .," 18–19.

83–84 *regulation . . . regulators*: While applied most often to the North Carolina Regulation, Bouton, *Taming Democracy*, 218, and Barbara Clark Smith, *The Freedoms We Lost*, 52–53, clarify the terms' deeper roots. Events of 1760s North Carolina ensuing here are highly simplified in part by placing Husband at the center. Kars and Troxler are major sources for the big story; Troxler, 56, calls Husband a "crystallizer." Mark Haddon Jones, Chapter 6, and Stewart, Chapter 3, provide detail on phases of Husband's involvement glossed over here. See Harvey, 117–25, on Husband's "liberation theology" in the regulation.

84 *Joseph advises Pharaoh*: Husband, "Proposals to Amend and Perfect the Policy of the Government," 20–21; for exegesis, see Harvey, 155–56.

84 *clinging to gold and silver*: Husband's theories against a gold standard are further developed in Chapter 8.

85 *Husband remained a pacifist*: This despite his wholehearted endorsement of the War of Independence. See Chapter 22 for the development of Husband's pacifism dilemma.

85 *riot was flat-out violence*: Sources on traditional crowd actions, often violent, include Rudé; Countryman; Thompson, *Customs in Common*; Hoerder, especially Chapter 1; and the essays in Pencak, Dennis, and Newman, and Billy G. Smith. Barbara Clark Smith, *The Freedoms We Lost*, 18–46, explores the high degree to which "the mob" in colonial America, by no means operating extralegally, lived in tension with legitimate execution of the law, a tension that the Revolution depended on and struggled to manage.

85–87 *Husband made clear . . . Occupying the town for two days*: Highlights in this account of Husband's role in the regulation are drawn from far more thorough accounts by Mark Haddon Jones, Chapter 4, and Stewart, Chapter 3, including Husband's conflicts with the assembly and the regulators, with reference to other sources cited below. On the violence issue, Jones says "Husband was torn" (163).

85   *He could publish pamphlets*: The most thoroughgoing expression of the regulators' complaints and their view of unfolding events is probably Husband's "An Impartial Relation of the First Rise and Cause of the Recent Differences in Public Affairs in North Carolina," in Boyd, 250–332, and "A Continuation of the Impartial Relation of the First Rise and Cause &c.," in Henderson.

85   *"Should we now"*: "An Impartial Relation of the First Rise and Causes of the Recent Differences in the Province of North Carolina," in Boyd, 247–333.

86   *Emy, at home, was to organize*: For a glimpse of Emy's role in November 1771, see the Regulator Papers, No. 16, in the Mary Elinor Lazenby Collection (Box 1, Folder 2).

86   *Serving in the assembly was what really changed*: Mark Haddon Jones, 142, notes the division between Husband's efforts at moderating regulator violence and the escalation that occurred when he entered the assembly.

86   *His style alone*: The song quoted below gives the sense.

86   *jury refused to indict him*: Troxler, 110.

86   *regulators massed*: Kars, 120.

86   *"would have thought Harmon"*: The lines are quoted by Mark Haddon Jones, 131, et al.; Troxler, 57, notes that the speaker is meant to be an official, a regulator target bemoaning Husband's effectiveness. On Howell: "Rednap Howell"; Troxler, 30.

87   *didn't want fame*: Mark Haddon Jones, 142.

87–88   *Lord William Tryon . . . regulators had signed loyalty oaths*: For much detail left out of sketch of the buildup, the climax, and the denouement, see Kars, Chapters 10–12; and Troxler, Chapters 8 and 9, with special nuance regarding the role of Tryon.

88   *self-described patriots*: Troxler, 142, calls the upscale North Carolina revolutionaries "oligarchs."

88   *in the county of Alamance, Husband*: The ensuing account of the end of the regulation, through Husband's and his family's flight, is drawn mainly from Mark Haddon Jones, 178–83.

6. NOTHING COMMONSENSICAL

90   *"the Democracy"*: Perhaps the most striking example of the locution occurred at the Constitutional Convention: see Chapter 12. The word "democracy" could mean a number of things in eighteenth-century usage, usually negative, recalling attempts at social and economic "levelling" by workers in seventeenth-century England and generally deplored by even by the most radically Whiggish American elites. But not always negative. Some who strongly condemned any attack on property rights, seen as under threat by egalitarian agitation, prided themselves on having democracy in their representative legislatures (see Henry). They meant not representation of the majority of the people but robust representation of the propertied, with majority and plurality rule in procedural bodies from which most people remained excluded, in their minds properly (see "From Alexander Hamilton to Gouverneur Morris, 19 May 1777," *Founders Online*, National Archives, founders.archives.gov/documents/Hamilton/01-01-02-0162). Contrary to some assertions, the founders only sometimes used "democracy" to belittle case-by-case referendum voting, by comparison with their preferred mode, representative lawmaking. Far more often they used it to mean inappropriate representation of, pandering to, and action by the less and unpropertied (see Holton, *Forced Founders*,

Chapter 7). There was no natural connection anyway between plebiscite and broad access to participation: before 1786, Rhode Island, which did employ referenda, was notably undemocratic regarding who got to participate. Yet in 1782 David Howell boasted of that situation as "pure and unmixed Democracy" (Head, 70) and even claimed that it represented the common people. See expanded notes at www.hamiltonscheme.com.

91 *Thomas Paine*: His background, marriages, connection with Franklin, arrival in North America, and early activities in Philadelphia are covered in a host of standard biographies; I've relied largely on Fruchtman, Chapters 2 and 3; Eric Foner, *Tom Paine and Revolutionary America*, Chapters 1 and 2; and Hawke, *Paine*, Chapters 2 and 3.

93 *the crew of radical outsiders*: Eric Foner, *Tom Paine and Revolutionary America*, Chapter 4, throws a wider net around the group than I do here; Hawke, *In the Midst of a Revolution*, 26, 33–35, 131–42; Nash, *The Urban Crucible*, 378–79.

93 *Thomas Young*: His story as sketched here is drawn mainly from Maier, "Reason and Revolution," and Hawke, "Dr. Thomas Young," both relying on and expanding Edes. Nash, *The Urban Crucible*, 355–65, exploring Young's role in Boston organizing. On tenant riots, see Thomas Humphrey, "Poverty and Politics in the Hudson River Valley," in Billy G. Smith.

93 *Boston Sons of Liberty*: Multiple upscale Boston groups operated against British elements in government: see Maier, *From Resistance to Revolution*, passim. Hoerder calls the Boston Sons in particular a "middle class dining club after 1768" (139) and emphasizes its nonartisan standing throughout its existence.

94 *James Cannon*: The sketch is drawn from Eric Foner, *Tom Paine and Revolutionary America*, 115; Rosswurm, 94, 102; Ryerson, 112–15; Nash, *The Urban Crucible*, 381; and Hawke, *In the Midst of a Revolution*, 105, 170, noting Cannon's abilities and relatively low profile.

94 *Timothy Matlack*: Better known as the first copyist of the Declaration, Matlack is placed in the radical group by Eric Foner, *Tom Paine and Revolutionary America*, 109–11; and Hawke, *In the Midst of a Revolution*, 103–104.

94 *Christopher Marshall*: Hawke, 103; Eric Foner, *Tom Paine and Revolutionary America*, 109–11; and Marshall's Diary in the Christopher Marshall Papers, passim. For pharmacy as a less-than-reputable business, see Kremers and Urdang, 155–62. Marshall's expulsion from the Meeting is discussed in Tolles, 79–80. On his faith and universalism: Marshall's Diary, entries for September 5, 1775, and March 18, 1776, Christopher Marshall Papers.

94 *Benjamin Rush*: Of the Philadelphia radicals, Rush has received the most attention, after Paine, thanks in part to friendships with George Washington, Thomas Jefferson, and John Adams, which began during the period discussed here and drew him away from the radicals after July 1776 (see Chapter 8), and in part to his becoming a prominent advocate for both public health and social reform, including abolition of slavery. Fried is the most recent Rush biographer; along with other matters, his Chapters 12 through 15 show Rush as a leader in the radical group. More specifically, I follow Hawke, *In the Midst of a Revolution*, 104; Fruchtman, 60–62; Eric Foner, *Tom Paine and Revolutionary America*, 109–15, 119; Nash, *The Urban Crucible*, 308, 321.

94 *drinking a lot of coffee*: Extrapolated from Hawke, *In the Midst of a Revolution*, 23, 98, 125, 180.

94 *Bettering House*: Nash, *The Urban Crucible*, 327–32, Eric Foner, *Tom Paine and Revolutionary America*, 46–47.

95 *American Manufactory*: See Nash, *The Urban Crucible*, 336–37, for the company's institutional structure.

95 *bettering the Bettering House*: Ibid., 337.

95   *school of working-class politics*: Because Marshall's diary entries on meetings at the fac-
     tory tail off when radicals start leading the City Committee, I think the factory was
     the first headquarters for radical planning.
95   *ad hoc governing bodies*: Ryerson, Chapters 3–5, tracks all iterations of the Philadelphia
     groups that began as the Committee of Forty-Three, became the Sixty-Six, then the
     First One Hundred, then the Second One Hundred; also operating were the more
     conservative provincial Committee of Safety (a function of the assembly) and Phila-
     delphia county committees. Ryerson at times uses "city committee" for the Second
     One Hundred. I've simplified much further here.
95   *artisans and laborers marched*: Nash, *The Urban Crucible*, 377.
95   *committees' social composition began going downscale*: Ibid., 374–82; Ryerson, Chapters
     3–5.
96   *reconciliationist position*: Discussed in Chapter 2.
96   *Committee of Privates*: Eric Foner, *Tom Paine and Revolutionary America*, 62–66, notes
     that while upper and middling artisan interest was motivated to enter the commit-
     tees in 1774, laboring interest was motivated via the militia in 1775–76, and reviews
     terminology for artisans, mechanics, and other groups, 28–38. Rosswurm explores the
     militia's call for radical democracy (Chapter 2) and discusses the explosion of radical-
     ism leading up to the May 1 election (Chapter 3). For the Privates' and artisans' focus
     on expanding suffrage and removing the property qualification, see Nash, *The Urban
     Crucible*, 380, a work I closely paraphrase on the Committee of Privates as a school of
     labor politics and a folk echo of the New Model Army (379). Hawke, *In the Midst of a
     Revolution*, takes a characteristically dimmer view of the Privates (147–50), describing
     Cannon's and Young's organizing as manufacturing aggrievement in young men who,
     if left alone, would have been having "the time of their lives" (149) in militia service.
97   *the Adams-Lee group*: Jensen, *The Founding of a Nation*, 477, noting that fellow del-
     egates called the group the "Lee-Adams junto." Wills discusses Lee's relationship with
     Samuel Adams, 7–10, 22–26.
97   *despised the Democracy*: Nash, *The Urban Crucible*, 360–62, tracking Samuel Adams's
     leadership in quelling class conflict in Boston. Samuel's attitude about the Shaysites
     (see Chapter 11 herein) shows his idea of a unified New England as contrary to the
     democratic radicalism of 1776 Pennsylvania. John's attitude about economic levelling,
     clear in much of his writing, is emphatically expressed later in this chapter. The Lees
     and their ally in Virginia's legislature, Patrick Henry, too, were committed above all to
     a defense of property that the Philadelphia radicals seemed to threaten.
97–98 *strange-bedfellow meetings . . . bloodless military coup*: My account distills the co-
     ordination between independents in the Congress and radicals outside and the re-
     action in the assembly, which I recount in detail in *Declaration*, based on a variety
     of scholarly and primary sources, including Marshall's Diary, Christopher Marshall
     Papers; John Adams; Wills; Maier; Hawke; and Foner. See the expanded notes at www
     .hamiltonscheme.com.
98   *On July 2, Dickinson and Morris*: The abstention of Dickinson and Morris is widely
     known—a version was dramatized in the HBO series *John Adams*—without the con-
     text provided here.
99   *the radicals of Pennsylvania wrote a state constitution*: "Constitution of Pennsylvania—
     September 28, 1776." For the electoral processes of delegating the convention, see
     Hawke, *In the Midst of a Revolution*, 171–77; Ryerson, 228–40; Rosswurm, 101–102; and
     Owen, Chapter 1. For the convention itself, Selsam, 146–59; Owen, Chapter 1; and
     Bouton, *Taming Democracy*, 51–57.

99   *Benjamin Franklin . . . paying much attention:* Selsam, 149, quoting Alexander Graydon's memoirs. Owen notes that Franklin was "preoccupied: by Congressional duties" (40).

99   *Writing the new Pennsylvania constitution was led:* Eyewitnesses and scholars agree that Cannon played the major role, with Young's help: see Ryerson, 241; Hawke, *In the Midst of a Revolution,* 186–88; Selsam, Chapters 4 and 5; and Eric Foner, *Tom Paine and Revolutionary America,* 131, noting Paine's influence, which is also noted by Hawke, 184; and John Adams, *Autobiography,* Part One, Sheet 23. (For conflicts within the radical group regarding the drafting, see Chapter 8 herein.) The document's radical features are discussed by Selsam, Chapter 5; and Bouton, *Taming Democracy,* 51–57. Owen, Chapter 1, reads the democratic revolution as unrelated to class consciousness, given the well-off status of many popular leaders (13), in keeping with his larger thesis that the radicalism of 1776 furthered ideas of political community that had flourished in colonial Pennsylvania (see expanded notes at www.hamiltonscheme.com).

100   *"Common Sense":* Paine, "Common Sense," Part Three. Few of the many popular readings of the famous pamphlet focus on its radically democratic plan for a national government. Regarding the pamphlet's name: Eric Foner, *Tom Paine and Revolutionary America,* 74–75. On the American-republican sense of the British constitution: Everdell, 151–55. Thompson, *The Making of the English Working Class,* 92, writing mainly on *Rights of Man,* calls Paine's departure from classic Whig constitutionalist ideology "shocking." Rush's involvement is discussed by Fried, 125–27; and Fruchtman, 60–62.

101   *radical program . . . piloted in Pennsylvania:* Hawke, *In the Midst of a Revolution,* 184; Eric Foner, *Tom Paine and Revolutionary America,* 131–32.

101   *gave ordinary Pennsylvanians power:* The most thoroughgoing study of the constitutionally localized diffusion of power is Owen, passim, but especially 40–50.

101   *cap how much property:* Selsam, 149. Walter Isaacson, in *Benjamin Franklin: An American Life* (Simon and Schuster, 2004) fancifully ascribes the proposed measure to Franklin; Eric Foner, *Tom Paine and Revolutionary America,* 133, credibly associates it with Cannon and Young.

101   *the first government anywhere in Europe and its colonies:* Nash, *The Unknown American Revolution,* 193: "the most advanced democracy in the world."

101   *"Good God!":* According to Rush, and widely quoted. "To John Adams from Benjamin Rush, 12 October 1779," *Founders Online,* National Archives, founders.archives.gov /documents/Adams/06-08-02-0138.

102   *Husband had ridden away:* For much more detail on Husband's progress from North Carolina to the Glades to the state assembly, see Mark Haddon Jones, Chapters 5 and 6; and Stewart, 74–92.

103   *eight hundred books and pamphlets:* Troxler, 58.

103   *Husband explored:* Husband, letter to Governor Mifflin, John Irwin Scull Archive, describing explorations and gear.

103   *A political ring, tied to eastern officialdom:* Mark Haddon Jones, Chapter 6; Stewart, 83–85.

103   *regulators . . . had stayed loyal:* Troxler, 140–43.

103   *petitions and articles . . . same Millennial spirit:* Husband, the Manuscript Sermon, John Irwin Scull Archive.

104   *bring about what he'd wanted from the regulation:* Mark Haddon Jones, 219.

104   *General Washington leading the army prophesied to win the last battle:* Mark Haddon Jones, 219, notes Husband's view of the Revolution as a new chance for good government,

as well as his sense that even the democratic revolution in Pennsylvania hadn't gone far enough, and notes (4), that Millenarian hopes for the Revolution were by no means limited to Husband, citing Heimert, among others. In "Sermon to the Bucks and Hinds," Husband notes his admiration for Washington as a disinterested moral leader.

104   *most dynamic commercial economy . . . most democratic government*: Paraphrasing Rappleye, 177–78.

104   *committees, outside the assembly, with ongoing regulatory powers*: Owen, passim, is the major source on the citizen-committee nature of the state's radical democracy.

105   *economic matters in 1778 Pennsylvania*: Rappleye, 180; Stewart, 93; Mark Haddon Jones, 247–78.

105   *Food prices were quintupling in a year*: Rappleye, 180.

105   *Each side blamed the other*: Stewart 93. Rappleye, 180, fully adopts the Morris point of view, blaming farmers, not merchants, for withholding staples, and dismisses popular objections to merchant practices as foolish displays of "righteous indignation." Contrary to many writers' focus on withholding flour, Bezanson, 18–19, claims the more relevant product would have been wheat.

105   *issue a small-denomination paper currency*: Rappleye 180; Stewart, 93.

105   *talk . . . of fixing prices by law*: Mark Haddon Jones, 248.

105   *should be as free as the air*: Eric Foner, *Tom Paine and Revolutionary America*, 170, and Nash, *The Unknown American Revolution*, 316, quote 1779 essays by the merchant Pelatiah Webster making moral claims on what merchants called free trade; Foner, 170, also quotes Christopher Marshall criticizing the Morris-Webster notion that ungoverned trade will always regulate itself.

106   *off the hard-money standard*: Husband's plan for a paper-money system was printed in Lancaster in 1778; that document is lost, but the plan is documented in Husband, "Proposals to Amend" and "A Dialogue between an Assembly-Man and a Convention Man." Its ideas are explored by Mark Haddon Jones, 249–53; Stewart, 93–94; and Holt, "The New Jerusalem," 19–20. Harvey, 156–60, is original in connecting Husband's ideas not only to Keynesian economics but also to Modern Monetary Theory.

106   *balsam of life to a nation*: "Proposals to Amend", 29.

106   *"Money . . . should be taxed"*: Ibid., 22.

107   *back to his state assembly*: Rappleye, 178.

107–10   *When Morris reentered . . . merchants and investors held off the Democracy*: These few paragraphs drastically simplify the remarkable concatenations of economic and political action in Pennsylvania, 1778–1780. Sources influencing my account, with separate and sometimes opposing angles, include Alexander; C. Page Smith, "The Attack on Fort Wilson"; Bezanson; Nash, *The Unknown American Revolution*, Chapter 7; Brunhouse, passim; Owen, Chapter 2; Eric Foner, *Tom Paine and Revolutionary America*, Chapter 5; Rappleye, 178–97; Bouton, "Tying Up the Revolution," 68–70.

107   *a city full of nervous suspicion*: Brunhouse, 50, 73; Owen, 58.

107   *"the rapid progress of luxury"*: Bouton, "Tying Up the Revolution," 66, quoting John Jay's reporting from Paris.

107   *weren't serving army tours of duty*: Rosswurm, 207.

107   *General Benedict Arnold*: Eric Foner, *Tom Paine and Revolutionary America*, 163.

108   *The tensions started becoming unbearable . . . further restricting monopoly*: My sketch of the rising conflict is influenced by Rappleye, 180–90.

108   *refusing to accept paper money*: Eric Foner, *Tom Paine and Revolutionary America*, 162.

108   *The fight was getting physical*: Ibid., 165–66.

108   *more evidence of chicanery against other merchants*: Rappleye, 183–86; Brunhouse, 71–72.

109   *Others opposing price controls:* Owen, 72–73, noting that the price-control situation "highlighted tensions inherent in the committee system."

109   *firewood prices were beyond reach:* Rosswurm, 207.

109   *"disaffected persons":* All sources quote a militia proclamation to this effect, relying on letters sent by observers from Philadelphia. Beyond the brief quote (or paraphrase), little of the exact content is known; the purport is clear. Eric Foner, *Tom Paine and Revolutionary America,* 164, and C. Page Smith, "The Attack on Fort Wilson," passim, associate the militia attack not only with prices and apparent British loyalism but also with the political fight over the state constitution.

109   *Fort Wilson:* All of my cited sources on 1790–80 Philadelphia give accounts of the fight in more or less detail, noting discrepancies in the eyewitness accounts.

109   *Joseph Reed:* Eric Foner, *Tom Paine and Revolutionary America,* notes Reed's upscale background and belief in free trade, 174; C. Page Smith, "The Attack on Fort Wilson," quotes Benedict Arnold's condemning Reed after the Fort Wilson affair for having fomented a mob that he couldn't control, 185.

110   *black man:* Rappleye, 193, quoting an eyewitness using the term "boy."

110   *Morris was swept out of office:* See Brunhouse, Chapters 4–6, for the ongoing ups and downs between the democrats and the merchants in the assembly, glimpsed in Chapter 10 herein. Rosswurm, 7–8, calls Fort Wilson both a failure and a success of the radical new approach to government.

110   *pardoned all of the attackers . . . while the majority around them went hungry:* Nash, *The Unknown American Revolution,* 319.

111   *legislatures remained lame . . . "detestable tribe":* Ferguson 64, 111–12, and 115, with "detestable tribe."

112   *leery:* Mark Haddon Jones, 253–54, noting that Husband's colleagues didn't disdain him for his monetary radicalism: in Lancaster, Husband was often entertained at the home of Christopher Marshall, the universalist radical, who advised him to put the paper-money plan aside.

112   *after only one session:* Stewart, 94, noting that Husband seems not to have stood for reelection.

112   *The Glades region was suffering deepening poverty:* Mark Haddon Jones, 265–66.

112   *Husband's hopes stayed high:* Stewart, 100, saying "high hopes"; Mark Haddon Jones, 255.

7. NEVER WASTE A CRISIS

113   *they had to act fast:* Ferguson, 148.

114   *proposed federal impost:* The ensuing account of the first segment of the federal impost's arc under the Articles of Confederation is drawn largely from Ferguson, 116–17 and 146–70. The critical importance of the whole arc to the journey toward the Constitutional Convention and the development of Hamilton's programs is demonstrated—in differing and sometimes conflicting ways—by Ferguson, Johnson, Roger H. Brown, and Einhorn.

114   *They would just pass the tax on:* Einhorn, 118–20.

114   *The fight . . . was going to get rough:* In 1781, Morris thought the impost would sail through (Ferguson, 148), for reasons Einhorn details, 118–19; what Ferguson calls the "emergency" of the prospect of peace caused the roughness.

114   *a strong team of supporters:* I think Morris's leadership, from the finance office, of some of the best-known delegates to the Congress who would become Federalists is widely underrated. Ferguson, however, calls Morris their "presiding genius," 109, and refers to the group, passim, as "Nationalists," meaning they formed the core of those who

would push for national government in 1787. McDonald, 44, calls the group "Robert Morris and his circle."

114 *Gouverneur Morris . . . pronounced "governeer":* Notable modern biographies include William Howard Adams; and Brookhiser, *Gentleman Revolutionary*, with the pronunciation according to Abigail Adams's phonetic spelling (xiii; 222, n. 2); also see the title, with "Governeer," of B.B. Ellis's engraving from "Gouverneur Morris," National Portrait Gallery, npg.si.edu/object/npg_NPG.75.67.

115 *James Wilson:* A standard narrative biography is C. Page Smith, *James Wilson*. I've especially benefited from the constitutional Wilson symposium in Barnett, Holton's references in *Unruly Americans*, and Mikhail.

115 *James Madison:* For biography, I rely on Ketcham. While I focus on Madison as a day-to-day political actor, for nuance on his thought I've benefited from Rakove, as well as from a number of discussions of Madison in Elkins and McKitrick. Ferguson, 109, places Madison in the Morris group in the Congress; all cited Hamilton biographers discuss Hamilton's efforts with Madison in trying to get the impost passed.

115 *Virginians . . . role as private lenders:* Scott Reynolds Nelson, 19.

116–19 *He'd first pushed the federal-impost idea . . . Unanimity was fractured:* My account of the early struggle to pass the impost and its progress and failure in 1783 is largely drawn from Ferguson, 148–55.

116 *Morris did what he could to underreport and hide the money:* Ferguson, 147.

116 *the subject of slavery came up:* See Einhorn, 120–45, for much detail on the role of slavery in debates on apportionment and "the absurdity of Article 8" (124) of the Articles of Confederation.

117 *Imported goods crossing from Rhode Island:* Einhorn, 119.

119 *demanding that Rhode Island's delegates:* Georgia, too, was included in the demand: Head, 70.

119 *a permanent measure and a wedge for further taxes:* Einhorn, 136–37, reduces this to bluster, contra Ferguson, 146.

119 *"yoke of tyranny fixed on all the states, and the chains riveted":* Ferguson, 153.

119 *led in part by Morris's enemies in the Lee family:* Head, 72.

119 *"that great friend to sovereign authority . . . powers to the American sovereign":* Ferguson, 154, quoting Gouverneur Morris in a letter to General Nathanael Greene of December 24, 1781; also quoted, at greater length, with reference to absolute monarchy, in Gouverneur Morris, *Diary and Letters*, Vol. 1, 15.

119 *Washington . . . was a strong Continentalist:* For Washington's thoughts on the federal impost, see for example "From George Washington to Benjamin Harrison, Sr., 4 March 1783," *Founders Online*, National Archives, founders.archives.gov/documents/Washington/99-01-02-10768.

119 *"War is more likely than peace":* "To George Washington from Robert Morris, 16 October 1782," *Founders Online*, National Archives, founders.archives.gov/documents/Washington/99-01-02-09743. William Howard Adams, 136, says Gouverneur drafted the letter.

120 *the New York legislature had elected him:* All of the cited biographers have more detail on Hamilton's progress through November 1781.

120 *the overall quality of these delegates was uneven at best:* Brookhiser, *Alexander Hamilton*, 52, says "erratic."

121 *Madison . . . unenumerated powers:* See Elkins and McKitrick, Chapter 3, and Ketcham, 87, 113, 117. In contradiction of many standard readings, Banning sees Madison

as never by any means well-aligned with the Morris group, making later divisions less than surprising.

121   *"neither wrong nor forbidden"*: Jensen, "The Idea of a National Government," 374.

121   *"open the purses of the people"*: Bouton, *Taming Democracy*, 73.

121   *his passion was at odds with his reason*: "From Alexander Hamilton to George Washington, 25 March 1783," *Founders Online*, National Archives, founders.archives.gov /documents/Hamilton/01-03-02-0194.

122   *three officers had a petition*: For the petition and other relevant documents, see Hamilton's committee report of April 24, 1783, in *Journals of the American Congress*. My account of the incidents that would become known as the Newburgh Crisis, in the context of the drive to pass the impost and earmark its proceeds for federal bondholders, draws mainly on Kohn, *Eagle and Sword*, Chapter 2, and "The Inside History of the Newburgh Conspiracy"; Ferguson, 155–67; Flexner, *Young Hamilton*, Chapters 42–44; and Bouton, "Tying Up the Revolution," 141–51; Paul David Nelson; and Head, the only monograph on the crisis, with a thesis that interests me, literally, as it was evidently inspired by the author's dissent from my discussion of the crisis in *The Whiskey Rebellion* (see Manwaring) and thus presumably from Kohn's, Ferguson's, and Flexner's interpretations, which Head draws together under the rubric "traditional accounts" (159, 182); he frames his work as correcting theirs. It seems to me that regarding my subject—the goals and actions of the Morris team—Head doesn't subject those accounts to much substantial revision, just frames them differently. See expanded notes at www.hamiltonscheme.com.

122   *Washington himself . . . vetted it*: Flexner, *George Washington in the American Revolution*, 486, demonstrates Washington's knowledge of the petition's contents and style, quoting the letter to the Virginia delegate; Knox's involvement in the petition is explored in detail by Head, 58–63. I find it hard to imagine the commander's not having also endorsed, if possibly tacitly, the assertive tactics of the petition's presentation.

122   *Robert Morris, with a surge of hope*: Ferguson, 157. For detail on the delight of others on the Morris team, from Madison to Gouverneur Morris, see Head, 80–81.

123   *brought their petition to his office*: Kohn, *Eagle and Sword* 21; Ferguson, 157.

123   *550 veterans in command of almost 10,000 enlisted men*: Kohn, *Eagle and Sword*, 19.

124   *pushing concerns about a military coup*: Ibid., 22; Ferguson, 157–58.

124   *"Every engine is at work here"*: Ferguson 158.

124   *explicitly brought up mutiny*: Kohn, *Eagle and Sword*, 22.

124   *the young New York delegate rose again and again*: "Continental Congress Remarks on Raising Funds for the United States [27 January 1783]," *Founders Online*, National Archives, founders.archives.gov/documents/Hamilton/01-03-02-0147; "Continental Congress Remarks on the Collection of Funds by Officers of the United States [28 January 1783]," *Founders Online*, National Archives, founders.archives.gov/documents/Hamilton /01-03-02-0148; "Continental Congress Remarks on Plans for Paying the Public Debt [29 January 1783]," *Founders Online*, National Archives, founders.archives.gov/documents /Hamilton/01-03-02-0149; "Continental Congress Remarks on Appropriating the Impost Exclusively to the Army [19 February 1783]," *Founders Online*, National Archives, founders.archives.gov/documents/Hamilton/01-03-02-0161. See Head, 97–106, for detail on the nature of the larger debate in the Congress.

125   *"imprudent and injurious"*: Miller, 90, et al.

125   *disrespected General Gates*: Kohn, *Eagle and Sword*, 26; Head, 162.

125   *Hamilton wrote to Governor Clinton*: Flexner, *Young Hamilton*, 404; Head, 104.

125 *if the officer class demanded a federal tax*: Ferguson, 158; Head, 107–108.

125 *after the generals had taken the post*: Head, 107.

125 *resigning as superintendent*: Ferguson, 160, calls that move "the big guns," emphasizing the drama of the publication.

126 *divine what Washington was really thinking*: Head, 116.

126 *Hamilton wrote to Washington*: "To George Washington from Alexander Hamilton, 13 February 1783," *Founders Online*, National Archives, founders.archives.gov/documents /Washington/99-01-02-10638. Head, 113–14, says this letter has been misunderstood by other writers on the Newburgh Crisis and cites them in note 26 (I'm one), listing what he suggests are various misinterpretations but not connecting each writer to a particular one. For my point of view on Head's interpretation, see expanded notes at www.hamiltonscheme.com.

126 *polite, even fawning coaching*: Ferguson, 159: "endeavored to coach."

127 *Washington was in that sense the real author*: I think this idea is underrated in most accounts of the crisis.

127 *he also wanted federal taxes passed*: Washington's explicit commitment to a federal taxing power for the purposes of what he called "justice to the Public Creditors" begins as early as the revived correspondence with Hamilton discussed below, as borne out in later chapters.

127 *the Morris team might be blowing its best chance*: "To Alexander Hamilton from George Washington, 16 April 1783," *Founders Online*, National Archives, founders.archives .gov/documents/Hamilton/01-03-02-0213.

128 *dispatched one of the three petitioning officers . . . Knox said no*: Kohn, *Eagle and Sword*, 24–25, 27–28, with detail on the transactions.

128 *disgruntled officers then got word from Philadelphia*: Regarding a March 9 meeting between Colonel Walter Stewart and a group of officers that included Gates, Kohn, *Eagle and Sword*, speculates and argues that Stewart carried a message from Morris to Gates offering support for mutiny (29). The argument and cited evidence remain persuasive to me, yet Head's dissent from the speculation, 128–29, leads me to question my having followed Kohn so wholeheartedly on this question. On the other hand, I think Head misstates what he calls "traditional accounts" of this moment (161): see expanded notes at www.hamiltonscheme.com.

128 *the general asked Hamilton to make urgently clear*: "To Alexander Hamilton from George Washington, 12 March 1783," *Founders Online*, National Archives, founders .archives.gov/documents/Hamilton/01-03-02-0179.

128 *he showed up after all*: The ensuing scene is widely retailed in Washington biographies. For a thorough analysis of the speech, see Head, 144–53.

129 *suggested that he write to the Congress himself*: Head, 109–10.

129 *he advised the Congress . . . The Congress complied*: Ferguson, 163–64. As with Washington's sponsorship, effectively, of the officers' petition and mode of presenting it, I think the Congress's compliance with what was now Washington's direct demand, effectively, for officer-pay resolution, with an invocation of a continuing danger of mutiny, has been underrated in most accounts of the crisis. Bouton, "Tying Up the Revolution," 147–53, inspires my idea that the Morris team's activities in the crisis led to a durable nationalist success—though its benefits were deferred.

129 *A deal . . . written up in a committee by Hamilton*: "Continental Congress Report on Half Pay to the Army, 21 March 1783," *Founders Online*, National Archives, founders .archives.gov/documents/Hamilton/01-03-02-0189. Ferguson, 164, explains the options and conditions; Bouton, "Tying Up the Revolution," 152, presents the numbers.

130 *watchdogging the payoff situation*: Holton, *Unruly Americans*, 208. See Chapter 11 for a major example.

130 *Society of the Cincinnati*: I follow Cutterham, 22–36, on the society's founding, rituals, and controversies.

131 *the Cincinnati an irritating embarrassment*: Ibid., 28.

131 *inducting upscale noncombatants*: Ibid., 33.

131 *Hamilton hoped . . . an officially certified military arm*: Ibid., 34–35.

131 *strengthening his reconnection to Washington*: To trace the relationship's revival, see "To Alexander Hamilton from George Washington, 12 March 1783," *Founders Online*, National Archives, founders.archives.gov/documents/Hamilton/01-03-02-0179; "From Alexander Hamilton to George Washington, 17 March 1783," *Founders Online*, National Archives, founders.archives.gov/documents/Hamilton/01-03-02-0182, with Hamilton's crossed-out confession of having desired, however briefly, to produce a threat of coup; "From Alexander Hamilton to George Washington [24 March 1783]," *Founders Online*, National Archives, founders.archives.gov/documents/Hamilton/01 -03-02-0191; "From Alexander Hamilton to George Washington, 25 March 1783," *Founders Online*, National Archives, founders.archives.gov/documents/Hamilton/01 -03-02-0194; "To Alexander Hamilton from George Washington, 31 March 1783," *Founders Online*, National Archives, founders.archives.gov/documents/Hamilton /01-03-02-0197; "To Alexander Hamilton from George Washington, 4 April 1783," *Founders Online*, National Archives, founders.archives.gov/documents/Hamilton /01-03-02-0202, with Washington's warnings about playing with an army; "From Alexander Hamilton to George Washington [8 April 1783]," *Founders Online*, National Archives, founders.archives.gov/documents/Hamilton/01-03-02-0204, with Hamilton's most complete confession; "From Alexander Hamilton to George Washington [15 April 1783]," *Founders Online*, National Archives, founders.archives.gov /documents/Hamilton/01-03-02-0209; "To Alexander Hamilton from George Washington, 16 April 1783," *Founders Online*, National Archives, founders.archives.gov /documents/Hamilton/01-03-02-0213, with Washington's qualification of his remarks of April 4; and "To Alexander Hamilton from George Washington, 22 April 1783," *Founders Online*, National Archives, founders.archives.gov/documents/Hamilton/01 -03-02-0217.

8. PEACETIME

133 *nothing like a true federal impost . . . Hamilton voted against it*: Ferguson, 166–67.

133 *"perverse sister"*: Calvin H. Johnson, 8, quoting Madison.

133 *"a little detestable corner of the continent"*: Ibid., quoting Noah Webster.

134 *his own state became the holdout*: For much detail on Clinton's issues and New York's rejection of the new effort at an amendment, see "The Proposed Impost of 1783 (and Hamilton's Famous New York Assembly Speech)."

134–35 *centralized military establishment . . . The delegates refused even to debate*: My account of the failed effort at passing a peacetime army resolution follows Kohn, *Eagle and Sword*, Chapter 3. See "Washington's Sentiments on a Peace Establishment, 1 May 1783," *Founders Online*, National Archives, founders.archives.gov/documents /Washington/99-01-02-11202; and "Continental Congress Report on a Military Peace Establishment [18 June 1783]," *Founders Online*, National Archives, founders.archives .gov/documents/Hamilton/01-03-02-0252.

134 *militias . . . appropriate armed force*: Kohn, *Eagle and Sword*, 2–6, 81–83.

134 *militias' poor performance*: See, for example, "George Washington to Samuel Hun-

tington, 20 August 1780," *Founders Online*, National Archives, founders.archives.gov /documents/Hamilton/01-02-02-0817.

135   *the Congress faced a mutiny*: The ensuing account is drawn mainly from Rappleye, 361–64, and Mitchell, *Alexander Hamilton: Youth to Maturity*, 315–22.

135   *Common soldiers had received only $200–$300*: Ferguson, 169–71.

136   *paid three months' salary . . . 50 percent markdowns*: Rappleye, 356–57, emphasizing Morris's personal sacrifice and commitment; Ferguson, 170, emphasizing Morris's dilatoriness and "dickering."

137   *wrote a blazing set of resolutions*: Mitchell, *Alexander Hamilton: Youth to Maturity*, 323–25.

137   *Madison . . . was in the Virginia assembly*: Ferguson, 171.

137   *Gouverneur Morris . . . partner and agent*: William Howard Adams, 140–41.

137   *Illinois-Wabash Company*: Wilson's involvement is widely noted in legal scholarship thanks to his landmark arguments on the company's behalf regarding ex-post-facto law. See, for example, Mikhail, also with reference to the size of Wilson's Illinois-Wabash claims, 92.

137   *He still wanted to push New York to reverse its refusal*: See Chapter 11.

137   *stopped even trying to run the finance office*: Ferguson, 224.

137   *stepped down on June 26, 1784*: Rappleye, 366.

138   *declined to stand*: Flexner, *Young Hamilton*, 434; Miller, 100.

138   *"It is to be hoped . . . correct our errors"*: "From Alexander Hamilton to John Jay [25 July 1783]," *Founders Online*, National Archives, founders.archives.gov/documents /Hamilton/01-03-02-0270.

9. THE NEW JERUSALEM

139   *"popular frenzy"*: "John Lansing's Version [18 June 1787]," *Founders Online*, National Archives, founders.archives.gov/documents/Hamilton/01-04-02-0098-0005.

139–140   *Rush . . . "mobocracy"*: "To John Adams from Benjamin Rush, 22 January 1789," *Founders Online*, National Archives, founders.archives.gov/documents/Adams/06-19 -02-0264.

140   *Marshall . . . Young and Cannon*: For the internecine conflicts, see Ryerson, 239–40.

140   *Cannon . . . died in early 1782*: "James Cannon: 1740–1782."

140   *Young*: Maier, "Reason and Revolution," 235.

140   *Matlack*: "Timothy Matlack: c. 1730–1829."

141   *The American Crisis*: Paine, *The American Crisis*. My account of its composition is cobbled together from Paine's two conflicting accounts, cited in Conner's analysis.

142   *filing a newspaper story*: Paine, "Retreat Across the Delaware."

142   *classified information . . . excoriate not only Deane but also both Morrises*: Fruchtman, 113–23.

143   *served on a Philadelphia price-control investigation committee*: Ibid., 122.

143   *Morris wrote to Paine . . . Continentalists' writer-for-hire*: Ibid., 138–39, 146–50; Conway, 181–82.

143   *He hadn't, like Rush, deradicalized*: I think the segment of Paine's career discussed in Chapters 21 and 22 makes this clear.

144   *against the attack on Fort Wilson*: Paine, "To the Printer of the Pennsylvania Packet."

144   *write, even anonymously, anything he disagreed with*: Fruchtman, 139.

144   *the two spent time relaxing . . . Paine's only coat*: Ibid., 152–53; Eveleigh. For the loan of the coat, see "Letter from Flemmington [sic], N. J., May 16, 1788, to John Coltman, Leicester, England," in the Hall Manuscripts.

144   *Paine rode beside him at the head*: I think I first saw this story, asserted as fact with no source cited, in Craig Nelson's *Thomas Paine: Enlightenment, Revolution, and the Birth of Modern Nations* (Viking Penguin, 2006); I repeated it as fact, regrettably, in *Founding Finance*. Since then, the only earlier example I've been able to find—so far, anyway—appears in John Keane's *Tom Paine: A Political Life* (Little, Brown and Company, 1995), with a note citing Flexner, *George Washington and the American Revolution*, on related matters but not on that. If a primary source does support the account put forth by Keane, Nelson, and me, none of us has cited it.

144   *"begin the world again"*: Paine, "Common Sense."

144   *all-iron structures might be used to span wide rivers*: For Paine's development on bridge-building, see Delony; for the ultimate design, see Sweeney.

145   *a more natural highway*: Husband's letter to Governor Mifflin, John Irwin Scull Archive. The collection of roads known as the Lincoln Highway was officially opened coast-to-coast in 1913; its Pennsylvania portion, now U.S. Route 30, follows routes Husband began exploring in the 1770s. In her somewhat fanciful *Herman Husband: A Story of His Life* (Old Neighborhoods Press, 1940), Mary Elinor Lazenby, 134, instead associates Husband's surveying not with the Lincoln Highway but with the Pennsylvania Turnpike, which opened the year she published. That project was notable for employing drilled and blasted tunnels, precisely to avoid the high mountain passes that Husband was studying and mapping, and which, in 1793, he pressed Governor Mifflin to consider feasible for road building.

145–146   *the New Jerusalem . . . the Millennium on Earth*: My account of the vision draws mainly on Husband's varying versions in "Proposal to Amend and Perfect," "XIV Sermons on the Characters of Jacob's Fourteen Sons," and "Sermon to the Bucks and Hinds," with contemporary reporting from Schöpf, 292–96, and Badollet's journal entry in Hunter, 173. For exegesis of those and other sermons, see especially Holt, "The New Jerusalem," and Harvey.

146   *his life changed again . . . back to the Hudson Bay*: For the travels: Schöpf, 292–96.

147   *"Hutrim Hutrim" . . . the "Philosopher of the Allegheny"*: Schöpf, 292–96; Badollet's entry in Hunter, 174.

147   *visitors to his prosperous, 4,000-acre farm and busy sawmill*: Schöpf, 292–94; Badollet's entry in Hunter, 173–75; Mark Haddon Jones, 288–91.

147   *the Pennsylvania madman*: "Gallatin to Jefferson, April 23, 1805," in Gallatin, *Writings*, vol. 1, 229. See Online Library of Liberty, https://oll.libertyfund.org/title/adams -the-writings-of-albert-gallatin-vol-1.

147   *well-educated and practical as Emy Husband*: Badollet's entry in Hunter, 173.

147   *stood for elected office again*: See Chapter 17.

10. WASHINGTON'S COUNTY

149–50   *north and west of the Ohio River . . . April 1784*: I discuss the cession and the creation of the territory in more detail in *Autumn of the Black Snake*, 91–95 and 104–105, drawing on Ritcheson, Hutchinson, Lynd, Onuf, and Hinderaker.

150   *grants of land to startup companies*: Ibid., 108–10, 239–40, drawing mainly on Sword and Calloway.

150   *nations, including the Shawnee, Miami, Delaware*: Ibid., passim.

151   *thirty-year depression*: Bouton, *Taming Democracy*, 91–92.

151   *things were even worse after the Revolution*: Ibid., 91; Slaughter, 65–69.

151   *work as tenants and day laborers*: Fennell, 73–74.

151   *far fewer and much richer*: Slaughter, 67; Fennell, 39–43.

151–152   *deal with Spain . . . vicious savages*: Slaughter, 30.
152   *what was to stop western settlers*: Ibid., Chapter 2, with an important discussion of a host of other western new-state and independence movements and tracing steps in their development toward outright secessionism.
153   *"white Indians"*: Baldwin, 192.
153   *Filth . . . "abandoned wretches" . . . "scum" . . . "dirty"*: Slaughter, 64. In dealing with the Whiskey Rebellion, Hamilton biographers and certain scholars have tended to more or less concur, though few have gone as far as McDonald, 297: "uncouth, lazy, brutal, wasteful, and contentious [quoting Michel de Crevecour]; "no better than carnivorous animals of a superior kind."
153   *feats of violence . . . Scots-Irish*: Many historians, founder biographers, and other writers present the trans-Appalachian culture as uniquely rough, wild, and intransigent, based in part on ethnic determinism regarding Scots-Irish culture. See, for example, Cooke, "The Whiskey Rebellion: A Re-Evaluation," and Jim Webb's *Born Fighting: How The Scots-Irish Shaped America* (Crown, 2005). Yet the Whiskey Rebellion, often cited as a prime example of supposedly hardwired cultural tendencies, had many notably uncompromising leaders and participants who were not Scots-Irish. See expanded notes at www.hamiltonscheme.com. For an extraordinarily deep and informed exploration of white settlement of the region before the Revolution, see McClure, Vol. 1, Parts One and Two.
154   *60,000 choice acres across the Appalachians*: Slaughter, 82.
154   *confident that he knew the people*: Ibid., 78–79.
155–57   *in early September 1784 . . . fined the general on the spot*: My account of Washington's concerns and his confrontation at Millers Run closely follows Slaughter, 83–85. For the progress of the western trip and the outcome of the confrontation, I follow Flexner, *George Washington and the New Nation*, 59, also cited by Slaughter; Flexner calls the story of the fine for swearing a local tradition. Both scholars cite Washington's diaries of the trip: "[Diary entry: September 1784]," *Founders Online*, National Archives, founders.archives.gov/documents/Washington/01-04-02-0001-0001; "[Diary entry: 15 September 1784]," *Founders Online*, National Archives, founders.archives .gov/documents/Washington/01-04-02-0001-0001-0014; "[Diary entry: 18 September 1784]," *Founders Online*, National Archives, founders.archives.gov/documents /Washington/01-04-02-0001-0001-0017; "[October 1784]," *Founders Online*, National Archives, founders.archives.gov/documents/Washington/01-04-02-0001-0002; "[Diary entry: 20 September 1784]," *Founders Online*, National Archives, founders.archives .gov/documents/Washington/01-04-02-0001-0001-0019. For Washington and the Potomac Canal project, see Achenbach, passim.
158   *the real nature of the problem was confirmed*: Slaughter, 85.
158   *Robert Whitehill*: Bouton, *Taming Democracy*, 133, 143, 185. Crist's biography is lively but not politically illuminating.
158   *William Findley*: For a capsule biography, see Slaughter, 254, n. 2.
158   *terrible foreclosure crisis*: Bouton, *Taming Democracy*, 89–94.
159   *Morris group had been making headway*: Brunhouse, Chapters 5 and 6, shows rapid seesawing, session by session, between radicals and the merchant interest in the assembly.
159   *withdraw the bank charter*: Bouton, *Taming Democracy*, 134–35; Brunhouse, 173–75.
160   *yammering, unlearned demagogue*: Findley is the original of both Traddle the Weaver and Teague O'Regan in his political enemy Hugh Henry Brackenridge's poem "On the Popularity of _____," which makes Findley a "mechanical" type out of *A Midsummer Night's Dream* and pillories him as stupid, pandering, and cowardly; Traddle

shows up again in Volume One of Brackenridge's three-volume novel *Modern Chivalry* (Claude Newlin, ed., Hafner Publishing Company, 1968).

160 *Wilson himself had borrowed $100,000*: Morgan, 477.

160 *Findley . . . what were known as corporations*: For anticorporatism in the bank fight, see Bouton, *Taming Democracy*, 110–13, and "Tying Up the Revolution," 192–200; and Sommer, with a thorough exploration of Findley's views, plus a connection to Frank Capra and *It's a Wonderful Life.*

161 *Morris and Wilson vigorously defended*: For far more detail on the fight, see Rappleye, Chapter 16, bringing in other participants, including another western radical, John Smilie.

161 *angel from heaven . . . a fallen one*: Crist, 23.

161 *Thomas Paine entered . . . castigating their former spokesman*: Fruchtman, 164–76.

161 *bridge fully made of iron*: Ibid., 161–63.

161 *an algorithm with universal application*: Sweeney.

162 *Morris accused . . . Whitehill reminded him*: Bouton, "Tying Up the Revolution," 202–203.

162 *immediate target the speculative value of Pennsylvania's bonds*: Bouton, *Taming Democracy*, 114–18; Brunhouse, 170–73.

162 *more like 20 percent*: Holton, *Unruly Americans*, 37, quoting Benjamin Rush.

163 *enthusiastic public support*: Bouton, *Taming Democracy*, 118.

163 *let down the radicals . . . let down the investing class*: Ibid., 136.

163 *Alarm was resounding*: Roger H. Brown, 171–73. Ferguson, 242–44, shows democratic finance inspiring many originally opposed to Morris's plans to revise their views.

163 *Rhode Island . . . passed a big paper-money emission*: Ferguson 243–45.

11. TO ANNIHILATE ALL DEBTS

164 *a convention . . . at Annapolis*: All cited Hamilton biographers discuss their subject's disappointment at Annapolis and role in calling for a convention in Philadelphia; Mitchell, *Alexander Hamilton: Youth to Maturity* has the most detail.

164 *The Congress . . . wouldn't even seriously debate a federal taxing power*: Roger H. Brown, 28.

165 *Hamilton used his pen to eviscerate . . . Cooler heads prevailed*: Mitchell, *Alexander Hamilton: Youth to Maturity*, 362.

165 *shutting down the state's debt courts . . . taxation without representation*: Major sources for my sketch of the Shaysites Rebellion are the modern standards Szatmary and Richards; I follow the latter, especially, for both the rebellion's background in the regulation tradition discussed in Chapter 5 herein and the moral and ideological basis regarding representation (see Richards, 67).

165 *higher property qualifications*: Richards, 67–73, discussing the Adams-led gentry's writing the 1780 state constitution in the context of recoil from the democratic approach of Pennsylvania and western reaction.

165 *took an intolerable form . . . drama of the Debt*: Ibid., 74–77, making a direct link between the Berkshires people's moral objections to the constitution's regressiveness and the struggle against their government's pursuing the aims of the bondholding class. Ferguson, 246, says "the main object of [Shaysite] attack was the . . . debt-funding program."

166 *Massachusetts's bonds had long since crashed . . . pay off the whole principal*: Ferguson, 245–46.

166 *many were sunk in the usual revolving debt*: See Chapter 10 herein.

166–167   *To the Berkshires people . . . join the rebellion*: For much more detail on progress from protest to rebellion and outright warfare, see Richards and Szatmary.

167   *"annihilate all debts public and private"*: "To George Washington from Henry Knox, 23 October 1786," *Founders Online*, National Archives, founders.archives.gov/documents /Washington/04-04-02-0274; "To George Washington from Henry Knox, 17 December 1786," *Founders Online*, National Archives, founders.archives.gov/documents /Washington/04-04-02-0396.

167   *Daniel Shays*: See Richards and Szatmary for much more information on Shays and other leaders. Richards, 73, discusses fantasies about Shays's goals; Szatmary, 54, notes that Shays was not destitute. Hamilton, rallying support for the national Constitution in "Federalist Six," dismisses any moral underpinning to the Shaysites Rebellion by ascribing the incident to the supposed ambition of "SHAYS" himself: *"a desperate debtor"* [emphasis his]. That characterization has been misread as expressing sympathy for Shays (Chernow, 225); in context, "desperate" has the traditional outlaw connotation.

167   *"The moment is, indeed, important"*: "From George Washington to Henry Knox, 3 February 1787," *Founders Online*, National Archives, founders.archives.gov/documents /Washington/04-05-02-0006.

168   *skeleton military crew*: Kohn, *Eagle and Sword*, 60–72.

168   *pretend it was sending them . . . no federal force was sent*: Coakley, 5.

168   *armed uprising, this one in Exeter*: Richards, 78–79.

168   *Society of the Cincinnati . . . sacred by government*: Cutterham, 138–39, also quoting Mercy Warren on the visible elation.

169   *Knox wrote to Washington*: Cutterham, 139.

169   *suspended its program*: Ferguson, 248–49.

169   *Samuel Adams . . . called for the death penalty*: Pencak, 70, 64.

169   *a convention that called on all settlers to unify*: Slaughter, 54.

170   *Widespread fear among the well-off did bode well*: Ferguson, 249.

170   *agreement, as Hamilton saw it, amounted to rejection*: Calvin H. Johnson, 1496.

170   *"If these states are not united . . . which would attend its dissolution?"*: "New York Assembly. Remarks on an Act Granting to Congress Certain Imposts and Duties [15 February 1787]," *Founders Online*, National Archives, founders.archives.gov/documents /Hamilton/01-04-02-0030.

171   *the confederation died*: Calvin H. Johnson, 1496, calls the final failure of the impost in New York "the nearest cause" of the adoption of the Constitution.

171   *The impost . . . "begat convention"*: "New York Ratifying Convention. Notes for Second Speech of July 17 [17 July 1788]," *Founders Online*, National Archives, founders .archives.gov/documents/Hamilton/01-05-02-0012-0073.

171   *"That a thorough reform"*: "From George Washington to James Madison, 31 March 1787," *Founders Online*, National Archives, founders.archives.gov/documents/Washington /04-05-02-0111.

171   *"Were an energetic and judicious system"*: "To George Washington from Henry Knox, 19 March 1787," *Founders Online*, National Archives, founders.archives.gov/documents /Washington/04-05-02-0095.

12. THE HAMILTON CONSTITUTION

175   *Nathaniel Gorham*: See Beeman, 99, on Gorham's chairmanship.

176   *first to doff his coat*: The conclusion that delegates would be unlikely to shed outerwear is drawn from my interview with Karie Diethorn and Deborah Miller, May 11, 2023.

176 *caucus secretly and at length*: Beeman, Chapter 3.
176 *delegates would have been shocked . . . Yates and John Lansing*: Beeman, 57.
177 *"Our chief danger" . . . "imbecilities" of the existing system*: Farrand, 24–27.
177 *near the shut and guarded door*: Beeman, 80, discusses the likely arrangement of delegations and provides a seating chart, 81. Current curators at National Independence Park suggest that any specific arrangement remains speculative (interview with Karie Diethorn and Deborah Miller, May 11, 2023).
178 *started scribbling notes*: The ensuing presentation of Hamilton's thinking is extrapolated from "Alexander Hamilton's Notes [18 June 1787]," *Founders Online*, National Archives, founders.archives.gov/documents/Hamilton/01-04-02-0098-0002.
179 *his own proposals . . . strike down state laws*: For delegates' notes on Hamilton's speech, see Farrand, 282–311.
180 *silence . . . adjourn for the day*: Beeman, 169, citing Farrand.
181 *fostering a state of balance*: The influence on the convention's outcomes of the Massachusetts constitution and of John Adams's thought regarding republics is widely noted. For Adams on balanced government, see Elkins and McKitrick, among many others; for Adams and republicanism, I've especially benefited from Everdell, Chapter 8.
181–182 *didn't like the idea . . . "tone it as high as possible"*: Farrand, 424.
182 *Gerry confessed . . "the levelling spirit"*: Farrand, 48.
183 *Washington . . . "justice to the Public Creditors"*: "From George Washington to Robert Morris, 8 March 1783," *Founders Online*, National Archives, founders.archives.gov/documents/Washington/99-01-02-10796; "From George Washington to Thomas Jefferson, 31 August 1788," *Founders Online*, National Archives, founders.archives.gov/documents/Washington/04-06-02-0440.
183 *"in all cases whatsoever"*: "From James Madison to George Washington, 16 April 1787," *Founders Online*, National Archives, founders.archives.gov/documents/Madison/01-09-02-0208.
183 *"improper and wicked project[s]"*: "The Federalist Number 10 [22 November], 1787," *Founders Online*, National Archives, founders.archives.gov/documents/Madison/01-10-02-0178.
184 *But the states had militias*: The ensuing account of debates over the federal military power distills Farrand, 385–95. For the role of colonial and revolutionary militia in fantasy and reality, see Carrol and Baxter, Introduction; and Shy.
184 *reduce the states to mere drill sergeants*: Farrand, 385.
185 *no longer a confederation but a nation*: George Mason's argument in the Virginia ratification debates. See *The Debates in the Several State Conventions*, Vol. 3, 29.
185 *can't be taxed without their consent*: The June 9 debates (Farrand, 180–91) represent an early exploration of connections between taxation and representation in a federal system. See June 12 and June 13 (Farrand, 589–97) for the first substantive discussion of representation in the context of what the delegates called "direct taxation" (also see *"direct taxation"* below).
185 *slavery . . . they didn't feel like talking about*: Einhorn, 118: "The 'founding fathers' hated discussions about slavery"; and 117–19, on the impost as a way around confronting slavery in the context of taxation. Beeman, 205, says "there was no way to avoid" the issue once representation was introduced.
185 *Gouverneur Morris . . . spoke up passionately*: Farrand, Vol. II, 221–22. Beeman, 214–15, associates Morris's unhappiness about including the slave population with solely pragmatic considerations. While the speech does note those considerations, it seems to me

to offer a rare hint of a moral dimension. For much more on Morris's highly active role at the convention, see Rasmussen, Chapters 2 and 3.

186   *The real slavery questions therefore had to do . . . duty on the trade would never be levied*: Beeman, 318–29. For Madison's successful effort in the first U.S. Congress to block a duty on the importation of enslaved people, see Einhorn, 153.

186   *extradited by the free state . . . easily overcome*: Beeman, 329–30.

187   *refused to sign*: Ibid., 362–64.

187   *Gouverneur Morris went the other way*: McDonald, 107, on Hamilton's role in changing Morris's mind.

187   *"I do not well see"*: "To George Washington from Henry Knox, 14 August 1787," *Founders Online*, National Archives, founders.archives.gov/documents/Washington/04-05 -02-0269.

188   *Gerry got off a bitter crack*: Farrand, 201.

188   *Hamilton proposed . . . counting only free inhabitants*: Beeman, 155.

188–189   *older compromise . . . three-fifths*: For pre-convention discussions of the three-fifths concept, see Einhorn, 139–44.

189   *James Wilson had urged direct election*: Beeman, 129–33, noting Wilson's antidemocratic nature. For more on Wilson's motivations, see expanded notes at www.hamiltonscheme .com.

190   *envision judges setting aside . . . laws*: For an illuminating discussion of Hamilton's advancement of judicial review in Federalist 78, see Hoffer, 118–21.

190   *"direct taxation"*: Both the original process of direct taxation and the term itself were highly problematic. Einhorn, 158–60, notes that the framers weren't of one mind about the logistics and never successfully defined the term. See expanded notes at www.hamiltonscheme.com.

192   *Gouverneur Morris serving as copy lead*: Beeman, 246. See Rasmussen, passim, for a thorough exploration of Morris's role in writing the document.

193   *"reflection and choice"*: "The Federalist Papers: No. 1."

193   *passions and interests*: McDonald, 111, explores the roots of Hamilton's idea that the irreducible power of passion and interest should be channeled for the public good.

193   *The Federalist . . . no impact on ratification*: McDonald, 114.

193   *outnumbered the Federalists 46 to 19*: Ibid., 114.

193   *New York City would secede*: McDonald, 115, possibly influenced by Clinton Rossiter, *Alexander Hamilton and the Constitution* (Harcourt, Brace, World, 1964), asserts this rumor as fact, though the primary-record citations don't seem to me to provide strong evidence for it. For a detailed historiography of Hamilton's role in ratification, see Brooks, dissenting from a picture of Hamilton as a persuasive factor; a thorough review of the complexities of the New York debates and the Antifederalists' strategies, see Maier, *Ratification*, Chapters 11–13.

193   *cadre led by Morris and Wilson . . . had been advancing*: Brunhouse, Chapter 6, tracks the rise of the anti-state-constitution-pro-U.S.-Constitution faction.

195   *Whitehill*: "The Pennsylvania Assembly, Friday, 28 September 1787."

194   *Wilson made a pro-ratifying-convention speech*: Wilson.

194   *denying it a quorum . . . force them into the chamber*: "The Controversy Surrounding the Calling of the Pennsylvania Convention."

13. TA-DA!

195   *without George Washington*: Elkins and McKitrick, 33–34.

196   *Hamilton contacted certain electors . . . more scattered than expected*: My account fol-

lows Miller, 220–21. For the intensity of Hamilton's anxiety, see "From Alexander Hamilton to James Wilson [25 January 1789]," *Founders Online*, National Archives, founders.archives.gov/documents/Hamilton/01-05-02-0075. In 1800, Hamilton didn't only admit his actions of 1788 but also cited them as proof of Adams's unfitness for office: "Letter from Alexander Hamilton, Concerning the Public Conduct and Character of John Adams, Esq. President of the United States [24 October 1800]," *Founders Online*, National Archives, founders.archives.gov/documents/Hamilton/01-25-02-0110 -0002.

196   *stung, infuriated*: "From John Adams to Benjamin Rush, 17 May 1789," *Founders Online*, National Archives, founders.archives.gov/documents/Adams/06-19-02-0322.

196–197 *ask him to serve as head of finance . . . Senate confirmed Alexander Hamilton's appointment*: For detail on the process for creating the office and confirming the appointment, see Mitchell, *Alexander Hamilton: The National Adventure*, 15–23; and McDonald, 132–33. For a major chunk of the debate itself, see *Annals of the Congress of the United States*, Vol. 1, 615–31. Elkins and McKitrick, 137, note Madison's support for a strong Treasury.

196   *the equivalent, to Hamilton, of prime minister*: McDonald, 126, also makes this point about Hamilton's view of himself and Washington.

198   *imposed a duty on all foreign imports*: Elkins and McKitrick, 65–69, covering the relevant House debates, clarify that the adopted measure wasn't in fact the 1783 impost but a tariff, in that it protected some domestic products by adding extra duties to specified imports; Einhorn, 149–54, discusses the issue as well. For more, see Chapter 15 herein.

198   *national customs system*: All of Hamilton's cited biographers provide more detail.

198   *thirty-nine full-time employees, the most*: Mitchell, *Alexander Hamilton: The National Adventure*, 358.

198   *questionnaires*: McDonald, 139–40.

198   *final settlement*: Ibid., 144–45, has the most succinct explanation.

199   *$40,414,085.94*: "Report Relative to a Provision for the Support of Public Credit [9 January 1790]," *Founders Online*, National Archives, founders.archives.gov/documents /Hamilton/01-06-02-0076-0002-0001.

199   *a blunt petition*: *Annals of Congress*, Vol. I, 337–39.

200   *a report on the status of the public credit*: Ibid., 395–96.

200   *Businesspeople consulted*: The draft excise bill shows the strong influence of people with advanced technical and commercial knowledge of the distilling industry in particular. "Report Relative to a Provision for the Support of Public Credit [9 January 1790]," *Founders Online*, National Archives, founders.archives.gov/documents/Hamilton/01-06 -02-0076-0002-0001.

200   *Schuyler helped with the math*: Mitchell, *Alexander Hamilton: The National Adventure*, 39–40.

200   *Hamilton wrote to Madison*: "From Alexander Hamilton to James Madison [12 October 1789]," *Founders Online*, National Archives, founders.archives.gov/documents /Hamilton/01-05-02-0224.

200   *Madison responded*: "To Alexander Hamilton from James Madison, 19 November 1789," *Founders Online*, National Archives, founders.archives.gov/documents/Hamilton/01 -05-02-0325.

201   *single out British ships . . . how the world really worked*: Widely discussed. For especially clear detail, see Elkins and McKittrick, 65–75, 125.

201   *William Constable . . . Andrew Craigie*: Ferguson, 258–72, provides much detail on

the complicated operations of Constable, Craigie, and others in their circle. Capsule biographies: Meredith; Connors.

201 *taverns, coffeehouses, homes, and offices*: Maclay, 177–78; Mitchell, *Alexander Hamilton: The National Adventure*, 44–45. Brookhiser, *Alexander Hamilton*, 86: "all New York began to hum with speculation, in both senses of the word."

202 *bills called indents*: Ferguson, 223–25, 270–71.

202 *driven by borrowing*: McDonald, 153–55; Mitchell, *Alexander Hamilton: The National Adventure*, 157–59.

203 *in this market, the outsider was doomed*: Mitchell, 160, quoting the speculator Craigie.

203 *"From your situation"*: "To Alexander Hamilton from Henry Lee [16 November 1789]," *Founders Online*, National Archives, founders.archives.gov/documents/Hamilton/01 -05-02-0313.

203 *"I am sure"*: "From Alexander Hamilton to Henry Lee [1 December 1789]," *Founders Online*, National Archives, founders.archives.gov/documents/Hamilton/01-06-02 -0001.

204 *Schuyler . . . held the equivalent*: McDonald, 137–38.

204 *Constable . . . sent indent prices shooting up*: Ferguson, 271; McDonald, 156.

204 *channel, direct, and leverage . . . longest-term strategy*: McDonald, 156–57: "Their greed could be harnessed, but only in the short run."

205 *William Duer*: For a full-scale biography, see Robert Francis Jones. I've benefited especially from Scott Reynolds Nelson, Chapters 1 and 2.

206 *proposed to come over to Federal Hall*: Mitchell, *Alexander Hamilton: The National Adventure*, 43–44.

206 *A kind of prime minister . . . the permanent U.S. capital*: Maclay, 177–79; for "Hamiltonople," 222.

206 *But what was it?*: "Report Relative to a Provision for the Support of Public Credit [9 January 1790], with enclosures," *Founders Online*, National Archives, https://founders .archives.gov/documents/Hamilton/01-06-02-0076-0002-0001.

207 *three major elements*: Most discussions of the report frame its program as having two major elements: funding and assumption, with internal taxation a necessary corollary. (For example: "Once assumption of state debts was agreed upon, a method of repaying them inevitably followed"; Slaughter, 95.) For reasons sketched in the text here and developed in Chapter 15, I see the excise measure as central to a three-part plan, in some ways even first among equals, with assumption serving to justify its adoption: see Chapter 15 and expanded notes at www.hamiltonscheme.com.

207 *sustain investor profits over ensuing decades*: For granular detail on Hamilton's proposed means, including creating an investor annuity fund of the kind called a "tontine," see Jennings, Swanson, and Trout, 110–15; and Dunbar, 37–45. Swanson and Trout, "Alexander Hamilton's Secret Sinking Fund," 112, notes that Hamilton's initial plan was to sustain the existing debt, in its new form, not permanently but for "only thirty-four years."

207 *average rate of around 4 percent*: Writers explain Hamilton's proposed interest-rate plan in surprisingly varied ways. Some seem to focus on the final bills sent to the president, which reflected changes discussed later in this chapter. My description simplifies that of McDonald, 169, with reference to Jennings, Swanson, and Trout, 111; and Swanson and Trout, "Alexander Hamilton's Secret Sinking Fund," 111, and "Alexander Hamilton, Conversion, and Debt Reduction," passim, arguing that Hamilton valued the principal too, at a somewhat reduced value.

208 *sinking fund . . . encouraged public confidence*: Swanson and Trout, "Alexander Hamil-

ton, 'the Celebrated Mr. Neckar,' and Public Credit," 428, and "Alexander Hamilton's Secret Sinking Fund," 110.

208 *Constable and Craigie . . . betting on it*: Ferguson, 271–72.

209 *just one tax on just one product*: See Einhorn, 187–88, on the excise as a way around using the cumbersome, state-apportioned direct-taxing power. For more on how a whiskey excise in particular aided Hamilton's biggest plans, see Chapter 15 herein.

210 *He included his excise bill in the main body*: "Report Relative to a Provision for the Support of Public Credit [9 January 1790]," *Founders Online*, National Archives, founders .archives.gov/documents/Hamilton/01-06-02-0076-0002-0001."

14. BREAKUP

211–214 *Taking the field for Hamilton . . . The minority, stymied again, let go of its latest ploy*: Highlights presented here of debate on the scheme's first component, the funding plan, are drawn mainly from Mitchell, *Alexander Hamilton: The National Adventure*, 57–68, the most detailed secondary account, with further reference to *Annals of Congress* and other sources noted below. Mitchell and McDonald differ on the dates of certain occurrences; Mitchell seems to me to be well-supported by *Annals*, Vol. 1, starting on 511 and proceeding steadily, with only a few breaks for other business, well into *Annals*, Vol. 2.

211 *having to speak through them*: Mitchell, *Alexander Hamilton: The National Adventure*, 65–66 and 73, makes clear the extent of Hamilton's backroom coaching.

212–213 *closed their windows . . . arms outstretched*: Fisher Ames to Thomas Dwight, July 25, 1790, Ames, 87; Stevenson, 479, n. 111, quoting a newspaper report.

213–214 *rescued, he insisted, only by discrimination . . . made no sense*: Ferguson, 297–300, clarifies the issues in the discrimination debate.

215 *drastic reversal*: Ferguson, 297–98. For Hamilton's prior awareness: "From Alexander Hamilton to Edward Carrington, 26 May 1792," *Founders Online*, National Archives, founders.archives.gov/documents/Hamilton/01-11-02-0349, quoted by Elkins and McKitrick, 137. Many have speculated as to Madison's motives for the switch; few take his finance proposals seriously as policy. See, for example, McDonald, 178–79; Mitchell, *Alexander Hamilton: The National Adventure*, 63–64; and Elkins and McKitrick, 136–42.

215 *re-bellow*: Fisher Ames to Timothy Dwight, July 25, 1790, Ames, 87.

215 *sniffles and blown noses*: Miller, 241.

215 *Maclay . . . Lecturing Madison*: Ferguson, 299–300.

216 *thought twice about taking the job*: "From Alexander Hamilton to Edward Carrington, 26 May 1792," *Founders Online*, National Archives, founders.archives.gov/documents /Hamilton/01-11-02-0349.

216 *Should the States' Debt be assumed in the Federal Debt?*: The ensuing highlights of the debate over assumption are drawn mainly from Mitchell, *Alexander Hamilton: The National Adventure*, 68–79, checked against *Annals of Congress*, with other sources cited below. For the sub rosa maneuvers and connections to and disconnections from the capital-site issue, I follow the analysis of Cooke, "The Compromise of 1790," both for the likely machinations and for dissent from the familiar story of Jefferson's brokering a deal.

217 *Madison was demanding*: Mitchell, *Alexander Hamilton: The National Adventure*, 69–71; Ferguson, 314–15.

217 *postpone assumption*: Ferguson, 310–11.

217 *no state . . . could lose or gain*: Writers differ on the relationship between funding and

assumption on the one hand and final settlement on the other. I follow Ferguson, 307–308, presenting the processes as, in Hamilton's view, separate and Madison as drawing them together, possibly disingenuously and at least erroneously. But Elkins and McKitrick, 120, despite frequently citing Ferguson, describe Hamilton as bringing final settlement together with the assumption plan. See expanded notes at www .hamiltonscheme.com.

217–218   *divisions in the House . . . Pennsylvania now looked like the swing state*: The delegations' divisions are covered by Mitchell, 68–79. For much detail on Pennsylvania's role, see Bauman, with "swing state" (202).

218   *Philadelphia lobby . . . didn't like the proposed reduction*: "To Alexander Hamilton from Tench Coxe, 5[–9] March 1790," *Founders Online*, National Archives, founders .archives .gov/documents/Hamilton/01-06-02-01.

218   *"Avarice often disappoints itself"*: Cooke, 527.

219   *Morris . . . falls of the Delaware*: McDonald, 183.

219   *Washington . . . Potomac estuary*: For Washington's involvement with Alexandria, Virginia, in the context of the canal project, see Achenbach, especially 34–37, 122–23.

219   *Madison . . . a commercial center*: McDonald, 175; for details, see Littlefield.

219   *backroom capital deal with Virginian*: Ibid., 528, n. 16.

219   *nobody would want to move*: Ibid., 528, n. 17; Elkins and McKitrick, 134.

219   *boats left the New York docks*: Maclay, 179.

220   *opposition's hyperrepublican sensibilities*: Maclay, 189, for example.

220   *assumption lost, 32 to 29*: Mitchell, 74–75, with the Sedgwick-Madison dispute and Madison's remarks on excise.

220   *Madison had suggested an excise*: "To Alexander Hamilton from James Madison, 19 November 1789," *Founders Online*, National Archives, founders.archives.gov/documents /Hamilton/01-05-02-0325.

221   *scholars in future generations couldn't fully agree*: See, for example, Bowling, debating Cooke, with Cooke's rebuttal; and Baumann. The most honest assessment may come from editors of Jefferson's *Papers*: "The atmosphere of bargaining and intrigue is impenetrable." "Editorial Note: Opinions on the Constitutionality of the Residence Bill," *Founders Online*, National Archives, founders.archives.gov/documents/Jefferson /01-17-02-0018-0001.

221   *Thomas Jefferson's arrival*: My discussion of Jefferson's three accounts of the bargain ("X. Jefferson's Account of the Bargain on the Assumption and Residence Bills [1792?]," *Founders Online*, National Archives, founders.archives.gov/documents/Jefferson/01-17 -02-0018-0012; "From Thomas Jefferson to George Washington, 9 September 1792," *Founders Online*, National Archives, founders.archives.gov/documents/Jefferson/01-24 -02-0330; "Thomas Jefferson's Explanations of the Three Volumes Bound in Marbled Paper [the so-called 'Anas'], 4 February 1818," *Founders Online*, National Archives, founders.archives.gov/documents/Jefferson/03-12-02-0343-0002), as repeated in some of the scholarly accounts cited here and popularized by Joseph Ellis's bestselling *Founding Brothers* (Vintage, 2002), follows Cooke, "The Compromise of 1790," especially 525 and 534–36—but see Bowling's objections to Cooke, with Cooke's rebuttal. Mitchell, *Alexander Hamilton: The National Adventure*, 82–83, notes that retellings of Jefferson's version, limited to the bargain itself, largely elide the hostility with which Jefferson reported it.

222   *William Maclay . . . could only imagine Hamilton*: Maclay, 331—though the senator had also taken pleasure in what he saw as Hamilton's being "uneasy" about the fate of the funding plan (211).

222 *that summer's hidden moves*: Fisher Ames admitted privately to engaging in what he called "intrigue" in the cause of assumption. See Ames to George Richards Minot, June 23, 1790, Ames 81.

222 *Hamilton and his allies come to the conclusion*: Given the emphasis of Mitchell, *Alexander Hamilton: The National Adventure*, 65–66 and 73, on Hamilton's direct involvement in caucusing, and given Hamilton's style overall, it's impossible to imagine him not in the room when the tactics of what Ames calls "intrigue" were determined.

222 *Senate . . . shove assumption back into*: Cooke, "The Compromise of 1790," 540–41.

223 *a bill that's exactly Hamilton's*: Annals of Congress, Vol. 2, 1552.

223 *excise's origins*: For detail on excise's controversial history in Britain, see Slaughter, Chapters 1 and 6.

223 *attack Fitzsimon's revenue bill on traditional anti-excise grounds*: The Annals of Congress, not a daily record taken in real time but a later compilation of the writings of congressionally approved reporters, goes silent on the funding debates—mysteriously, to me—precisely during the period when what Fisher Ames called an intrigue was operating, though not necessarily as an effect of the intrigue. My presumption is that the proposed excise measure was subject to the style of criticism it received in 1791: see Chapter 15.

223 *vote the bill down in committee*: The Annals of Congress, Vol. 2, 1644. Slaughter, 95–96, points to the tactical purpose of the negative result, quoting Ames to Richard Minot, June 23, 1790, Ames.

223 *a site in Pennsylvania . . . permanent capital*: Cooke, "The Compromise of 1790," 531.

224 *sends Tench Coxe to talk to Pennsylvania senator Maclay*: Ibid., 532, n. 40.

224 *"boyish, giddy"*: Maclay, 332.

224 *"constrain[s] his indignation . . . this business"*: Ibid., 313.

224 *Morris and Philip Schuyler . . . threaten to tank assumption*: McDonald, 185.

224 *On the sod . . . meet at the flat, grassy Battery*: Maclay, 314–15.

225 *concluded their backroom negotiations . . . Fitzsimons nailed down the transaction*: Cooke, "The Compromise of 1790," 539.

225 *Hamilton addressed the various sides' money issues*: Ibid., 525; McDonald, 185–87, 193; Swanson and Trout, "Hamilton's Hidden Sinking Fund," 111–12.

15. INDUSTRY AND RYE

228 *justice to the public creditors . . . would have been for nothing*: "From George Washington to Thomas Jefferson, 31 August 1788," *Founders Online*, National Archives, founders .archives.gov/documents/Washington/04-06-02-0440.

229 *families were turning their rye into spirits*: The ensuing discussion of the development of American artisanal distilling relies heavily on Fennell, Chapters 2 and 7.

230 *The important customer was eastern*: Baldwin, 25.

230 *eight bushels of milled rye*: The calculation is extrapolated from Baldwin, 26, footnote.

230 *whiskey was a people's currency . . . micro-industrialization*: Ibid., 56, 238–40.

231 *ultimate purpose of the financial scheme*: I align with some of Hamilton's biographers on this issue, especially Mitchell, *Alexander Hamilton: The National Adventure* (143); and McDonald (232). But see John R. Nelson (1, n. 2) on conflicts between the finance plan and the manufacturing plan, quoting William Appleman Williams to challenge the idea that to Hamilton the two were integrated.

231 *seize this world-changing moment—the factory moment*: Miller, 283; Mitchell, *Alexander Hamilton: The National Adventure*, 145.

231 *machines, techniques, and expertise from Britain*: Miller, 301, notes that it was illegal in

Britain for managers, engineers, and skilled workers to emigrate. Coxe, a manufacturing enthusiast, had already been engaged in industrial spying. See Mitchell, *Alexander
Hamilton: The National Adventure*, 187–88.

231 *startups to build connective infrastructure:* See Chapter 20.

232 *"competent numbers of European workmen":* "Alexander Hamilton's Final Version of
the Report on the Subject of Manufactures [5 December 1791]," *Founders Online*, National Archives, founders.archives.gov/documents/Hamilton/01-10-02-0001-0007.

232 *fourteen-hour days, six days a week:* Widely given as the standard during the U.S. Industrial Revolution.

232 *"many of them of a very tender age":* "Alexander Hamilton's Final Version of the Report on the Subject of Manufactures [5 December 1791]," *Founders Online*, National
Archives, founders.archives.gov/documents/Hamilton/01-10-02-0001-0007. Samuel
Slater's Rhode Island factory system, of which Hamilton was aware, began with almost
all child workers, some as young as seven.

232 *"would not force the introduction":* "From George Washington to Lafayette, 29 January 1789," *Founders Online*, National Archives, founders.archives.gov/documents
/Washington/05-01-02-0198.

233 *advertising that he was now hiring whole families:* Turgeon.

233 *working in increasingly mechanized industries:* Miller, 287–89, is the biographer most
explicitly focused on widespread factory employment as critical to Hamilton's vision
of the U.S. future—but I think it's obvious that implicit in all praise of Hamilton as
the author of modern America is that his view of the proper relationship of labor to
ownership is pretty much as I've described it. See Orszag, however, associating Hamilton's support for employee ownership in the American cod fishery with a supposed
endorsement of employee ownership in general, an association that seems wishfully
strained to me.

233 *"bought up the grain" . . . "three or four times":* Fennell, 230.

234 *elimination from the British Isles:* Fennell, 231–34. Slaughter, 148–49, calls Fennell's discussion of the tax's mechanisms an unprovable allegation of "conspiracy" to centralize
the industry and drive small farmers "into economic despondency." But Hamilton's effort, requiring no conspiracy, was consistent with his cogently articulated plans for national industrialization, which he believed would have pervasive benefits for all classes.

234 *his target . . . was about 9 cents per gallon:* The ensuing presentation of the tax's operations with reference to distilling operations closely follows and drastically simplifies
both Fennell, 235–36, and the excise bill in Hamilton's first report, cited in Chapter 13
herein. Hamilton's framing the excise as a luxury tax passed on to consumers appears
both in that report and in his response to petitions in 1792 discussed in Chapter 20.

235 *"to about three fifths of a cent per gallon":* Fennell, 241, quoting Albert Gallatin.

236 *Internal revenue officers would show up unannounced:* The ensuing description is based
on the extraordinarily detailed operating-procedures manual Hamilton sent customs
and excise collectors: "Enclosure: Explanations and Instructions Concerning the Act
[26 May 1791]," *Founders Online*, National Archives, founders.archives.gov/documents
/Hamilton/01-08-02-0340-0002.

236 *The skeleton army:* For Hamilton's thoughts on using the federal military for enforcement purposes, see Chapter 21.

16. SIX GREEK COLUMNS AND A ROMAN PEDIMENT

238 *serve as the Philadelphia County Courthouse:* "Congress Hall."

238 *new treasury office:* "Secretary of the Treasury's Office Site."

238   *100 employees on the scene, plus about 120 customs officials*: For a detailed account of the growth of the department over time, see Mitchell, *Alexander Hamilton: The National Adventure*, 357–59.

238   *The report gave the members*: "Final Version: First Report on the Further Provision Necessary for Establishing Public Credit [13 December 1790]," *Founders Online*, National Archives, founders.archives.gov/documents/Hamilton/01-07-02-0227-0003.

239   *the Bank of the United States*: "Final Version of the Second Report on the Further Provision Necessary for Establishing Public Credit (Report on a National Bank), 13 December 1790," *Founders Online*, National Archives, founders.archives.gov /documents/.

239   *Massachusetts had chartered one*: "A History of Boston's Oldest Bank."

239   *Bank of New York*: All of the cited Hamilton biographers have more detail on the state bank. For obstructions to the charter: Mitchell, *Alexander Hamilton: The National Adventure*, 86.

239   *opposition to the excise, while predictably hot*: See Slaughter, 98–100, on both the House and Senate debates.

240   *Madison . . . was supporting the tax*: Mitchell, *Alexander Hamilton: The National Adventure*, 116.

240   *this one didn't . . . means to do so now existed*: These points are made in the report, cited above; Hamilton's personal lobbying is attested to by Maclay, 407.

241   *If people really cut down on whiskey*: Krom and Krom, 95, discussing the college's letter, note the irony. Mitchell, *Alexander Hamilton: The National Adventure*, 112–13, buys fully into the health angle; Hamilton's more recent biographers, too, seemingly oblivious to detailed scholarship by Slaughter, Bouton, Holt, and especially Fennell, read the whiskey excise the way Hamilton wanted it read.

241   *a law banning ketchup*: Slaughter, 100–101. "Ketchup" then referred to a condiment including mushrooms and so might theoretically be accidentally made with poisonous varieties.

241   *pass the chamber 35 to 21*: Krom and Krom, 97.

241   *Hamilton's idea was to create a financial institution . . . or sooner at its discretion*: This sketch of the plan is drawn from part two of Hamilton's report, cited above, with reference to McDonald 193–94, slightly simplifying section 24; and Miller, 260–62.

241   *opening branches in other states*: Mitchell, *The National Adventure*, 91, suggests Hamilton favored "probably, one per state" and wanted to start slowly; Miller, 275, notes Hamilton's leeriness of the national branches that the directors' latitude soon had them creating.

242   *"dead stock"*: See part two of Hamilton's report, cited above.

242   *Morris set denominations too high*: "From Alexander Hamilton to Robert Morris, 21 September 1782," *Founders Online*, National Archives, founders.archives.gov/documents /Hamilton/01-03-02-0080.

242   *monopoly charter for twenty years*: Mitchell, *Alexander Hamilton: The National Adventure*, 93.

243   *Jackson rose, of course*: Ibid., 94.

243   *called the Bank of the United States unconstitutional*: Most writers on the first Congress discuss this moment and its ramifications.

243   *in The Federalist, he'd defended*: "The Federalist: No. 44."

243   *lucrative position as private lenders*: Scott Reynolds Nelson, 19.

243   *Patrick Henry . . . punish Madison*: Ketcham, 275–78.

244   *against the Constitution's necessary-and-proper clause*: Henry.

244   *Madison's constitutional challenge . . . hardball politics:* McDonald, 200–203, presenting the allegations as fact; and 203, noting Morris's machinations.
244   *easy to counter:* The argument is widely covered; see for example, McDonald, 201–202.
245   *Jefferson advised him to veto it:* Ibid., 202.
245–246   *selected the site himself . . . allies reversed their position:* My account of Washington's and Hamilton's maneuvering is drawn from McDonald, 202–10, whose citations in this case seem to me to support his conclusion. The conflicting written opinions on constitutionality are widely discussed.
246   *a hero now:* Miller, 278–79.
246–247   *The factories were to produce . . . people in need of work:* All cited biographers discuss the model town in more or less the same terms. Miller, 299–301, is succinct.
247   *industrialization . . . could foster national unity:* Ibid., 293–94, citing the "Report on Manufactures," notes Hamilton's contention that while the bank did tend to cut out the South and favor the North, industrialization would tend to soften the sectional conflict. For Hamilton's regrets about the negative impact on the South of the too-speedy bank sellout: "From Alexander Hamilton to James Brown, John Graham, and George Pickett, 27 August 1791," *Founders Online,* National Archives, founders .archives.gov/documents/Hamilton/01-09-02-0097.
247   *Coxe was already on top:* For Coxe's involvement, see Cooke, "Tench Coxe, Alexander Hamilton, and the Encouragement of American Manufactures." For Duer's involvement, see Chapters 19 and 20 herein.
247   *Duer . . . avoid a corruption investigation:* Robert Francis Jones, 130–33; Scott Reynolds Nelson, 11.
247   *Bank of the United States opened for business:* The scene is drawn from multiple well-known accounts; see, for example, McDonald, 223; and Miller, 268–69. Most writers dive straight from the sellout into the panics of 1791 and '92; Hamilton, though he was keenly aware of the dangers of excessive exuberance, had reason to see the bank as, in Wright's terms, "a smashing success" (149).
247   *"scrip":* Hamilton often called it "script." For how it worked: Sylla, Wright, and Cowen, 67.
248   *purpose-built edifice:* The building was completed in 1796.

17. THE HUSBAND SCHEME

251   *Washington as the hero . . . imposed a satanic tyranny:* For the admiration of Washington (as well as of Benjamin Franklin) and Husband's experience of reading the Constitution: Husband, "Sermon to the Bucks and Hinds of America," 25–28. Husband's political development before and after publication of the Constitution is traced especially closely by Fennell, 198–200.
251   *The proposed new government:* My overview of the critique of the Constitution is extrapolated from Husband, "Sermon to the Bucks and Hinds of America," "XIV Sermons on the Characters of Jacob's Fourteen Sons," and "A Dialogue Between an Assembly-Man and a Convention Man," with attention to interpretations by Fennell; Harvey; Holt, "The New Jerusalem"; Mark Haddon Jones; and Stewart.
252   *"our offices . . . same arbitrary power as heretofore":* Husband, "XIV Sermons," 12.
252   *Ezekiel 41:7 . . . tapering effect:* Husband, "Sermon to the Bucks and Hinds," 14.
253   *sheer pomp:* Mark Haddon Jones, 312.
253   *"the spirit of the serpent":* Husband, "Sermon to the Bucks and Hinds," 15.
253   *educated people who set down encounters:* Schöpf, 292–96; Badollet's journal entry in Hunter, 173; and Albert Gallatin's remarks, mentioned in later chapters herein.
253   *administrative offices . . . back to the assembly:* Stewart, 116.

254 *an amendment they were pushing*: Ibid., 117.
254 *an alternate constitution*: The ensuing account of Husband's scheme of national government, presented in the Pennsylvania assembly in February 1790 (Jones, 117), is extrapolated from Husband, "Sermon to the Bucks and Hinds," "XIV Sermons," and "A Dialogue Between an Assembly-Man and a Convention Man," with attention to the interpretations by Fennell; Holt, "The New Jerusalem"; Mark Haddon Jones; Stewart; and Harvey, whose exegesis of the relevant pamphlets is the most detailed. That the national design was as thoroughgoing as the Federalists' is Fennell's observation, 213.
256 *barely concealed mirth*: Stewart, 117.
256 *"stinking body"* . . . *the abomination*: Husband, "XIV Sermons," 32–33, also discussed by Harvey, 188–89.
256–257 *a convention formed . . . he had no choice*: Stewart, 120–21. For a wealth of background on the state's shifting politics, 1786–1790: Brunhouse, Chapter 7.
257 *Congress sold . . . to cronies of government*: In *Autumn of the Black Snake*, 108–110, I discuss the big land deals that launched settlements at Marietta and Cincinnati and their connection to the development of the army and the war of conquest, with reference to scholarship by Sword and Calloway. "outright hucksters": see William Duer's activities in the business, discussed in Chapter 20 herein.
257 *becoming . . . day laborers in mills*: For detail on growing landlessness in the 1790s headwaters region, see Fennell, 38–40, 179–80.
258 *could see . . . how the tax gave pragmatic force*: Fennell, 232, notes that western distillers, especially immigrants with experience of the British whisky excises, had an understanding of how excises worked even more refined than Hamilton's.
258–259 *General John Neville . . . the Neville Connection*: My sources for Neville's background and family include the Craig-Neville Papers; Baldwin; McClure; and Brackenridge. For the commercial dominance of the Neville Connection, see Baldwin, 47–48; and Fennell, Chapters 2 and 4.
260 *A party beginning to call itself Republican*: Historians often use the term "Democratic-Republican," rarely used at the time.
261–262 *militias of a laboring, industrious people . . . message of resistance began resonating*: Husband, "XIV Sermons," 21–31. See Harvey, 194–95, for the militia as an electoral, not a military force. The switch to an endorsement of violent uprising at this late point in Husband's career is characteristically enigmatic. Fennell, 192–94, presents evidence for the major significance of his influence on what was to become a violent, secessionist uprising; also note Hamilton's and Washington's urgency about his arrest in the 1794 crackdown, with Husband the first person apprehended, discussed in Chapter 22 herein. See expanded notes at www.hamiltonscheme.com.
262 *In the summer of 1791*: See Chapter 18.

18. REASON
263 *Albert Gallatin*: The ensuing overview of Gallatin's early life in Geneva, emigration to the United States, and travels during and after the Revolution is distilled from accounts by his biographers, in substantial agreement on events: Walters, Chapters 1 and 2; May, Chapter 1; Dungan, Chapters 1 and 2; Stevens, Chapter 1; Henry Adams, *The Life of Albert Gallatin*, Book One. All have details on their subject's personal and entrepreneurial projects not discussed here.
265 *wasn't considered good-looking, but his eyes were piercing*: May, 10–11, 103–104.
265 *He even ran into Washington*: Henry Adams, *The Life of Albert Gallatin*, 42–44, dovetails the third-person account with Washington's 1783 travel diary, which hadn't been

published when Adams wrote, in order to determine the day of the occurrence: September 24, 1784.

265 *consider himself a Virginian . . . oath of allegiance:* Ibid., 44–46.

265 *moved to the newly created Fayette County:* All cited biographers have more information on the many complications that brought Gallatin to Fayette County. Henry Adams, *The Life of Albert Gallatin,* 46, explores the process by which he settled not in Virginia but in nearby Pennsylvania.

266 *Antifederalists seemed to him to share:* Gallatin's brief stint as an opponent of the Constitution is covered most thoroughly by Stevens, 34–42, and Walters, *Albert Gallatin,* 30–34. Henry Adams, *The Life of Albert Gallatin,* 57–59, includes the resolutions of the Harrisburg convention.

266 *Sophie Allegre:* All cited Gallatin biographers have more information.

266 *Gallatin opposed changing the constitution:* See Walters, *Albert Gallatin,* 34–41, for the most thorough discussion of Gallatin at the convention.

273 *and was impressed:* Henry Adams, *The Life of Albert Gallatin,* 61–62, quoting Gallatin.

267 *public finance at odds with Hamilton's:* Dungan, 45; May, 30–35; Walters, *Albert Gallatin,* 44–46.

267 *prevent the Hamilton Scheme from becoming a system:* Henry Adams, *The Life of Albert Gallatin,* 65, notes Gallatin's opposition to the whole system; Gallatin's ambition to undo it is borne out in later chapters herein.

267 *The federal excise . . . got Gallatin's attention:* All cited biographers discuss Gallatin's focus on the excise; each handles his involvement with the resistance differently. See notes to Chapters 21 and 22.

268 *meeting at a tavern in the town of Redstone Old Fort:* Brackenridge, Vol. 1, 108–17, describes the meeting, as does Findley, 43. The town soon changed its name to the modern one: Brownsville.

269 *Findley . . . the U.S. House:* He was elected in March 1791.

19. ENEMIES EVERYWHERE

270 *Duer . . . New York finance men:* Robert Francis Jones, 159.

270 *Hamilton traveled to New York:* Cooke, "Tench Coxe, Alexander Hamilton, and the Encouragement of American Manufactures," 384.

270 *SUM:* Historians use this abbreviation, often with periods between the letters, and sometimes the acronym SEUM; the company's founders called it "the Manufacturing Society" (McDonald, 331). A prospectus dated "August, 1791" was in use privately in July (ibid., 385): "Prospectus of the Society for Establishing Useful Manufactures [August 1791]," *Founders Online,* National Archives, founders.archives.gov/documents /Hamilton/01-09-02-0114.

270 *sold $600,000:* Miller, 301.

270 *Duer personally entered the booming market:* Duer's driving up the bank stock price in 1791 is widely covered, though often blurred with his even more ambitious efforts of '92 (see Chapter 20). For '91, I've benefited especially from Miller, 269–71.

270–271 *wild trading action . . . soaring market:* All writers on Hamilton and most writers on early U.S. finance discuss the panic of '91, sometimes as a kind of "mini-panic" teaser for '92. My account, including numerical values, is drawn mainly from Miller, 268–71; McDonald, 223; and Sylla, Wright, and Cowen, 71–73.

272 *"scramble for so much public plunder":* "From James Madison to Thomas Jefferson, 10 July 1791," *Founders Online,* National Archives, founders.archives.gov/documents /Madison/01-14-02-0034.

272 *"The spirit of gaming"*: "From Thomas Jefferson to Edward Rutledge, 25 August 1791," *Founders Online*, National Archives, founders.archives.gov/documents/Jefferson/01-22-02-0071.

272 *publish an article*: Miller, 270.

272 *wrote to warn his partner*: The first letter has been lost, but its contents and tone can be roughly deduced from Duer's response and Hamilton's second letter: "To Alexander Hamilton from William Duer [16 August 1791]," *Founders Online*, National Archives, founders.archives.gov/documents/Hamilton/01-26-02-0002-0299; "From Alexander Hamilton to William Duer, 17 August 1791," *Founders Online*, National Archives, founders.archives.gov/documents/Hamilton/01-09-02-0055.

272 *redoubled his betting*: Miller, 271.

272 *financial markets operated independently . . . confusion, strangeness*: I don't think any writer has tracked causes and effects with perfect chronology. The selloff is generally said to have begun on August 11. Hamilton published on the 13th—still warning *against* imprudent buying. On August 15, correspondents were sending him news of a big downturn, but that day he was already moving into the market (see the next note). His second letter to Duer on the 17th refers to a bubble seemingly still only about to burst—and the attitude he takes there is calmer than that in the first letter, possibly tactically.

273 *he intervened*: The ensuing account of the bailout is drawn largely from Miller, 271; and Sylla, Wright, and Cowen, 71–73.

273 *between $300,000 and $400,000*: Sylla, Wright, and Cowen, 71.

273 *openly yet quietly*: Ibid., 71–72, with more detail on Hamilton's use of pricing for the bond purchases.

274 *making public a business prospectus*: Cooke, "Tench Coxe, Alexander Hamilton, and the Encouragement of American Manufactures" 385. For the prosectus, see *SUM*, above.

275 *the Hamilton family of Mingo Creek*: See Fennell, 49–50, on John Hamilton, and 168–69, on Daniel. Daniel's tendency for physical intimidation and the leading role of Benjamin Parkinson are described in the deposition of William Faulkner, in the Whiskey Rebellion Collection.

275 *David Bradford*: Slaughter, 267, n. 18; McClure, 605–10. Brackenridge, though by no means unbiased, presents Bradford as unstable, ambitious, and pandering.

275 *In that spirit, the Washington County meeting*: For the resolutions, see editors' note 6: "From Alexander Hamilton to George Washington, 5 August 1794," *Founders Online*, National Archives, founders.archives.gov/documents/Hamilton/01-17-02-0017.

276 *dramatic report to the treasury office*: John Neville to George Clymer, September 15, 1791, in the Oliver Wolcott Jr. Papers—probably a cover note for a more formal communication. (The note's front page, with the description the attackers' garb, wasn't microfilmed and must be seen in the original.)

276 *Neville had already reported*: For the Washington County meeting, John Neville to George Clymer, September 9, 1791, in the Oliver Wolcott Jr. Papers. Hamilton's knowledge of the Redstone Old Fort and its attendees and his close monitoring of protest activities are borne out in his report to Washington: "From Alexander Hamilton to George Washington, 5 August 1794," *Founders Online*, National Archives, founders.archives.gov/documents/Hamilton/01-17-02-0017.-0017.

277 *get a sense of connections prevailing*: Hamilton's growing interest in connecting his political opponents to the western unrest is borne out in later chapters.

277 *gave the prospectus . . . named the town Paterson*: Miller, 300–301. For Paterson's having stock: Roberts, 24.

277 *perpetual monopoly*: Miller, 300, footnote, notes that Hamilton intended SUM's monopoly not to cut out other players but to model how to pursue such ventures.

277 *connected the board to the board*: Ibid., 301–302.

277 *interrelated industries*: Miller, 300; Mitchell, *Alexander Hamilton: The National Adventure*, 184.

277 *a policy President Washington endorsed*: "To Thomas Jefferson from George Washington, 13 February 1789," *Founders Online*, National Archives, founders.archives.gov /documents/Jefferson/01-14-02-0308."

277 *snuck out of Britain . . . committed to memory*: Cooke, "Tench Coxe, Alexander Hamilton, and the Encouragement of American Manufactures," 381.

278 *Pierre L'Enfant*: For L'Enfant and SUM: Miller, 309. For the story of L'Enfant and the creation of Washington, D.C.: Berg. For L'Enfant's failed career in Philadelphia after his troubles with the capital design: Ryan K. Smith.

278 *his second grand report*: See Chapter 20.

20. TOO BIG TO FAIL

279 *second grand report never got anywhere*: Irwin argues that aspects of the plan succeeded yet also notes that the features most important to Hamilton weren't adopted and that "Hamilton was not indifferent to the fate of the report" (801), contra John R. Nelson (994), who sees Hamilton as less committed to this report than to others.

279 *The plan . . . looked novel*: Mitchell, *Alexander Hamilton: The National Adventure*, 142.

279 *direct, legislative role in managing . . . private commerce*: "Alexander Hamilton's Final Version of the Report on the Subject of Manufactures [5 December 1791]," *Founders Online*, National Archives, founders.archives.gov/documents/Hamilton/01-10-02 -0001-0007. See discussions by Mitchell, *Alexander Hamilton: The National Adventure*, 142–53, emphasizing the report's unique nature; Miller, 285–94; McDonald, 233–36; Irwin; and John R. Nelson.

279 *tariff aspect was nothing novel*: Einhorn, 149.

280 *Privately, Madison and Jefferson*: Irwin, 804–805.

280 *canal and toll-road companies . . . Philip Schuyler*: Miller, 303.

280 *people on street corners opined*: Miller, 269.

281 *land down the Ohio River*: Robert Francis Jones, 142–51, gives a detailed yet all too forgiving account of Duer's involvement with the Scioto Company and the Gallipolis settlement. In *Autumn of the Black Snake*, I focus on the settlement's ongoing plight, citing Gaff and Sword.

281 *buy from the French government*: See Veru for earlier efforts to gain that debt, in which Duer tried to involve Hamilton.

281 *get hold of more of the scrip . . . information that it would go up*: Mitchell, *Alexander Hamilton: The National Adventure*, 171.

281 *purchases . . . for both himself and Knox*: I give details in *Autumn of the Black Snake*, citing Sword, 148–51.

281 *Six Percent Club*: The ensuing account of Duer's popularity and operations, the efforts of the rival speculators, and Duer's fall is drawn from Miller, 304–307; McDonald, 245–46; Scott Reynolds Nelson, 26–31; and Mitchell, *Alexander Hamilton: The National Adventure*, 169–74.

282 *pressing small amounts . . . "Mrs. McCarty"*: Robert Francis Jones, 176. Miller, 304, presents this money as investing, others as lending; it was both, with no chance of return either way.

282 *1 percent per day*: Scott Reynolds Nelson, 29.

282   *Hamilton was flatly disgusted:* See *stock dealers and imprudent gamblers,* below.

282   *European investors . . . await utter deflation:* Scott Reynolds Nelson, 29–30.

282   *In New York City, certain investors had noticed an opportunity:* The ensuing account of the crash, panic, and bailout is drawn from Miller, 305–308; McDonald, 247–49; Scott Reynolds Nelson, 29–31; Mitchell, *Alexander Hamilton: The National Adventure,* 174–79; and Sylla, Wright, and Cowen, 75–84.

282   *formed a group to take him down:* The group was led by Livingstons: Mitchell, *Alexander Hamilton: The National Adventure,* 178. For detail on the operation, see ibid., 304–305; and McDonald, 246.

283   *he went ahead anyway and then asked for retroactive approval:* Mitchell, *Alexander Hamilton: The National Adventure,* 176.

283–284   *making further purchases . . . under Jefferson's protest:* McDonald, 248–49; Sylla, Wright, and Cowen, 78–79.

284   *Jefferson saw Randolph:* Gutzman, 472.

284   *reluctant Bank of New York:* Sylla, Wright, and Cowen, 74.

284   *payable in forty-five days:* Miller, 305.

284   *announcement of good cheer:* Ibid., 305; McDonald, 248.

284   *impossible to collect in the West:* Slaughter, 117–19, with detail on the difficulties, and also asserting that no evidence exists of a widespread independence movement, a conclusion that seems to me to be contradicted by succeeding events.

285   *new incidents of violence:* John Neville to George Clymer, November 11, 1791, in the Oliver Wolcott Jr. Papers; Slaughter, 113.

285   *Exports were way up . . . Land values stayed on the rise:* Miller, 279. For a dissenting view, see Francis, Chapter 4.

285–286   *new report to the House . . . dissolution of the federal government:* My account of Hamilton's thinking is based on "A Report on the Difficulties in the Execution of the Act Laying Duties on Distilled Spirits [5 March 1792]," *Founders Online,* National Archives, founders.archives.gov/documents/Hamilton/01-11-02-0079.

286   *He saw in both cases a justification:* Hamilton's August 1794 report to Washington makes this clear. "From Alexander Hamilton to George Washington, [5 August] 1794," *Founders Online,* National Archives, founders.archives.gov/documents/Hamilton/01 -17-02-0017.

286   *stifling his system's enemies everywhere:* Borne out in Chapters 21 and 22.

286   *directing all operations of high finance:* McDonald, 248; Sylla, Wright, and Cowen, 79–81; Mitchell, *Alexander Hamilton: The National Adventure,* 176.

286–287   *put down William Duer . . . finally rioted:* My account of Duer's fall is drawn largely from Miller, 306; and Scott Reynolds Nelson, 1.

287   *taking another look at the Jeffersonians' criticism:* Scott Reynolds Nelson, 30–31.

287   *respectable stock dealers and imprudent gamblers:* "From Alexander Hamilton to Philip Livingston, 2 April 1792," *Founders Online,* National Archives, founders.archives.gov /documents/Hamilton/01-11-02-0182.

287   *revised whiskey excise bill:* "An Act Concerning the Duties on Spirits Distilled within the United States, May 8, 1792," *The Public Statutes at Large of the United States of America,* Vol. 1, 267–71. Debate on April 30, 1792, in *Annals of Congress,* Vol. 3, shows that some members thought the bill made the tax easier to pay.

287   *Not William Findley:* Findley, 273–76, covers his own positions in the House debate and his sense that Hamilton began harboring animosity toward him.

289   *had attended anti-excise meetings:* Hamilton's August 1794 report to Washington makes clear that the Treasury had detailed intelligence on meeting attendees and

mentions Gallatin by name. "To George Washington from Alexander Hamilton, 5 August 1794," *Founders Online*, National Archives, founders.archives.gov/documents /Washington/05-16-02-0357.

289 *embezzled the company nearly dry*: Widely covered; see, for example, Miller, 308.

289 *L'Enfant . . . pretty shady*: Mitchell, *Alexander Hamilton: The National Adventure*, 186, 194; Cooke, "Tench Coxe, Alexander Hamilton, and the Encouragement of American Manufactures," 390.

289 *would take years to go under*: For details, see ibid., 389–92; and Mitchell, *Alexander Hamilton: The National Adventure*, 184–98.

289 *tariffs as a kind of one-off*: Irwin, 808–13.

289 *bounties and subsidies . . . more important*: Ibid., 811–12.

289 *weren't seriously debated*: Ibid.,806–808, on the fisheries debate, with Hamilton's exasperation with Madison (808).

290 *Hamilton was having an affair*: The investigation and the affair are covered by all cited biographers—and beyond.

291 *the grind*: Elkins and McKitrick, 282, see Hamilton's "creative phase" approaching "its eclipse" with the 1792 bailout.

291 *"to," as he put it, "an issue"*: "From Alexander Hamilton to Edward Carrington, 25 July 1792," *Founders Online*, National Archives, founders.archives.gov/documents /Hamilton/01-12-02-0076.

21. UPRISING, CRACKDOWN

292 *welfare state*: See Paine, *Rights of Man*, Vol. 2, and "Agrarian Justice'; and Thompson, *The Making of the English Working Class*, 94–95.

292 *Pennsylvania's government did need an upper house*: Fruchtman, 176.

293 *models built from his design*: Delony.

293 *Stymied in his plan . . . return to Europe in 1787*: Fruchtman, 177–79.

293 *spent time with Jefferson*: Ibid., 182, 188–90.

293 *London Corresponding Society*: Thompson, *The Making of the English Working Class*, 20–22, 102.

293 *befriended . . . William Blake*: McDevitt.

293 *Mary Wollstonecraft . . . William Godwin*: On Paine's relationship with the former, see Larkin, 396; with the latter, Paul, Chapter 3.

293 *Edmund Burke*: For Paine and Burke before the rift: Fruchtman, 186.

294 *sent its key . . . "opened the Bastille"*: "George Washington from Thomas Paine, 1 May 1790," *Founders Online*, National Archives, founders.archives.gov/documents /Washington/05-05-02-0238.

294 *Washington had at first been impressed*: "From George Washington to Gouverneur Morris, 13 October 1789," *Founders Online*, National Archives, founders.archives.gov /documents/Washington/05-04-02-0125.

294 *the governing elite feared and loathed*: Widely covered; see, for example, Elkins and McKitrick, 354–85.

294 *"inflated to the eyes" . . . "a little mad"*: Gouverneur Morris, *Diary and Letters*, Vol. 1, 429 and 403.

294 *advised Paine to back off*: Ibid., 515.

294 *iron model of his bridge*: Sweeney.

294 *Burke . . . Marie Antoinette*: Burke, *Reflections on the Revolution in France*, 68–69. For Burke's weeping and scholars' and contemporaries' skepticism regarding veracity, see Mieszkowski, n. 3.

295   derided the conservative's prose, politics, personality: Paine, Rights of Man, Vol. 1.
295   scandalized British government did what it could: Conway, 364.
295   200,000 copies in one year: Elkins and McKitrick, 326.
295   Rights of Woman . . . "a work of genius": Isenberg, 83.
295   Rights of Man was exciting workers: Thompson, The Making of the English Working Class, 87–101 and Chapter 5.
295   inspiring strikes and riots: Ibid., 105–106.
295   "Mad Tom": See the caption to Cruikshank's engraving, Fruchtman, illustration insert.
295   burned in effigy: Thompson, 104; and O'Gorman.
295   Paine had dedicated his defense: For background on Jefferson's involvement in an unauthorized introduction, see Fruchtman, 229–30.
296   "I detest that book": Conway, 315.
296   fifty copies . . . cover letter: "To George Washington from Thomas Paine, 21 July 1791," Founders Online, National Archives, founders.archives.gov/documents/Washington /05-08-02-0253.
296   The Republican opposition . . . French revolutionary cause: Elkins and McKitrick, 354–85.
296   belated thank-you note: In full: "From George Washington to Thomas Paine, 6 May 1792," Founders Online, National Archives, founders.archives.gov/documents /Washington/05-10-02-0225.
297   Pitt issued a proclamation: Fruchtman, 263–64.
297   time to get himself out of the country: McDevitt.
297   people in Edinburgh rioted: For detail, see Meikle.
297   Blake who tipped him off: McDevitt.
297–298   September 13, 1792 . . . got the word: Ibid.
298   representing Calais: Conway, 368.
298   modeled on the democratic Pennsylvania constitution: Fruchtman, 281.
298   victory by the western woodland confederation: In Autumn of the Black Snake, I provide details, with sources including Calloway, Sword, and Gaff.
299   Hamilton took that customer away . . . further federal appointments: For changes in army buying and the Neville-connected appointments: Fennell, 249–54. Construction of the blockhouse at Fort Fayette, behind schedule and over budget, can be traced in the increasingly tense tone of letters from Henry Knox, as Secretary at War, to Isaac Craig, the Neville son-in-law contracted to manage the project, in the Craig-Neville Papers and the Isaac Craig Papers.
299   They called it the Mingo Creek Association: The association was known by a number of names; I simplify by sticking to one. The ensuing account covers the organization's activities beginning in 1792 and continuing into '94, closely following McClure, 580–96, with detail from William Faulkner's deposition, in the Whiskey Rebellion Collection.
301   Genevan was elected to the Pittsburgh convention: Both Slaughter and Fennell cast the convention as relatively moderate, but the presence of Mingo Creek delegates, the nature of the resolutions (see McClure, 575–76; and Hamilton's report of August 5, 1794, cited in notes to Chapter 20 herein), and the ensuing Faulkner attack suggest otherwise. See expanded notes at www.hamiltonscheme.com.
302   thirty armed men: The account of the attack is drawn from depositions of Margaret Faulkner, Margaret Campbell, and others, in the Whiskey Rebellion Collection.
303   "the plot should thicken" . . . scene of commotion: "From Alexander Hamilton to John

Jay, 3 September 1792," *Founders Online*, National Archives, founders.archives.gov /documents/Hamilton/01-12-02-0242.

303 *considered western North Carolina*: See Hamilton's letter to Carrington, cited in notes to Chapter 20.

303 *borrowing from the bank . . . new excises* : For the loans: Francis, Chapter 4. For the carriage tax in particular: Einhorn, 160, with reference to the Supreme Court's 1796 decision that it wasn't a direct tax, thus avoiding the "absurd" effects of trying to apportion it constitutionally among the states by population.

303 *no evidence justifying a federal prosecution*: Slaughter, 119.

303 *decisive action . . . Hamilton now urged Washington*: Ibid., 119–21.

304 *business headache . . . national matters*: Ibid., 88–89. An example of Washington's expressions of personal exasperation over his land situation: "From George Washington to John Canon, 7 September 1791," *Founders Online*, National Archives, founders .archives.gov/documents/Washington/05-08-02-0353.

304 *at Fort Detroit. Spain was negotiating*: In *Autumn of the Black Snake*, I give detail on the British at Detroit, with citations including Simcoe, Sword, and Kohn. For Spain: Slaughter, 160.

304 *banning what it called seditious meetings*: For the notorious 1795 "Gagging Acts," see Bugg, Chapter 5.

304 *indict . . . radical Pittsburgh convention*: "To Alexander Hamilton from George Washington, 7 September 1792," *Founders Online*, National Archives, founders.archives.gov /documents/Hamilton/01-12-02-0257.

304 *a draft of a proclamation*: "Proclamation, 15 September 1792," *Founders Online*, National Archives, founders.archives.gov/documents/Washington/05-11-02-0058.

305 *"ulterior arrangements" . . . In a private response*: "From George Washington to Alexander Hamilton, 17 September 1792," *Founders Online*, National Archives, founders .archives.gov/documents/Washington/05-11-02-0060.

305 *"among the rights of citizens"*: "To Alexander Hamilton from Edmund Randolph, 8 September 1792," *Founders Online*, National Archives, founders.archives.gov/documents /Hamilton/01-12-02-0261.

305 *Paine was taken down*: Paine, *Writings*, 212, describes the basement room in a letter to Monroe late in his imprisonment. As he notes, 395, he sometimes shared a room with other prisoners; it seems likely he was moved during his imprisonment, possibly more than once.

305 *sparing the lives of Marie Antoinette and Louis*: Fruchtman, 294–95.

306 *considered fleeing to America*: Ibid., 314.

306–307 *wrote for help . . . consented to Deforgues's view*: The account is drawn from Paine, *The Age of Reason*, Vol. 3 (Part One, Epilogue and Part Two, Preface), and *Writings*, Chapter 21 (Editor's Introduction), with explication by Fruchtman, 320–24 and 484, n. 15; and Hawke, 294–99.

22. BIBLICAL

308 *Democratic Society of Washington County*: See Editor's Note 1, "Edmund Randolph to Alexander Hamilton, Henry Knox, and William Bradford, 14 April 1794," *Founders Online*, National Archives, founders.archives.gov/documents/Hamilton/01-16-02-0206. A full copy is in the Rawle Family Papers; the cabinet circular of April 17, 1794, regarding how to handle the petition is in the Tench Coxe Letters, National Archives. The group was also known as the Society of [John] Hamilton's District.

308 *opposition party . . . political clubs*: Elkins and McKitrick, 451–61. As with the Republican party of the period, historians commonly call the clubs "Democratic-Republican," but as Philip Foner's list shows, fewer than half used that name. Most sources see the phenomenon as largely urban, with some spread into the country, but Owen, 135, notes the clubs' efficacy getting backcountry issues, especially, addressed.

308 *Mainly gentlemen's organizations*: Elkins and McKitrick, 457–58.

309 *wrote approving op-eds*: Ibid., 356.

309 *"democratic"*: See ibid., for the novelty, rarity, and Francophilia of the usage.

309 *1793 . . . government might have fallen*: "John Adams to Thomas Jefferson, 30 June 1813," *Founders Online*, National Archives, founders.archives.gov/documents/Jefferson /03-06-02-0216.

309 *"self-created"*: "From George Washington to the U.S. Senate and House of Representatives, 19 November 1794," *Founders Online*, National Archives, founders.archives.gov /documents/Washington/05-17-02-0125.

309 *"absurd . . . arrogant . . . pernicious to the peace of society"*: "From George Washington to Burgess Ball, 25 September 1794," *Founders Online*, National Archives, founders .archives.gov/documents/Washington/05-16-02-0492.

309 *no right of association*: This is Elkins's and McKitrick's point, 455.

309 *"the fruit"*: See the Editors' Note cited in *petition . . .* above.

310 *an imitation of the city clubs*: My description follows McClure, 593–96 and notes to Chapter 20, on the comparatively immense vigor and significance of the Mingo Creek Association. Owen, by contrast, doesn't focus on concerted Mingo Creek–connected action until the attack on Neville's, 139, emphasizing the Bradford petition's "eloquence" in seeking redress of western grievances (135). See the expanded notes at www.hamiltonscheme.com.

310 *at once overexcited and worried*: Brackenridge, 55, 63.

310 *Anyone in western Pennsylvania . . . in compliance*: I cover this period in detail in *The Whiskey Rebellion*, with reference to Brackenridge; Findley; Slaughter; Fennell; Baldwin; Bouton, "Tying Up the Revolution"; McClure; et al.

311 *was gaining detailed intelligence*: The lists for arrest discussed in Chapter 21 bear this out.

311 *an intention to retire . . . he would remain*: "From Alexander Hamilton to George Washington, 21 June 1793," *Founders Online*, National Archives, founders.archives .gov/documents/Hamilton/01-15-02-0012; "From Alexander Hamilton to George Washington, 27 May 1794," *Founders Online*, National Archives, founders.archives .gov/documents/Hamilton/01-16-02-0380.

312 *The plan began with a seemingly simple step*: My account of the summonsing effort is drawn mainly from Slaughter, 177–78, and Baldwin, 113–14. Findley, 73–76, was the first to publicly accuse Hamilton of abusing the judicial process, specifically by intervening in the writ-filing process in order to incite a reaction that would justify a region-wide military suppression, calling the plan "a refinement in cruelty" (76); his argument is supported by scholarship. See Slaughter, 182, citing primary evidence to show that Bradford knew the dates were in error and said the purpose wasn't arrest and prosecution; and 267, n. 14, pointing out that all of Hamilton's statements to that point make Findley's charge "plausible, indeed likely." Hamilton's biographers and some other Hamiltonians ignore the issue or read it differently.

313–315 *Neville and Lenox bolted . . . defend the whole West from a military invasion*: This sketch of what became known as the Whiskey Rebellion presents highlights; in *The*

Whiskey Rebellion, I provide day-to-day detail, drawn from the Craig-Neville Papers, the Isaac Craig Papers, the Olver Wolcott Jr. Papers, *American State Papers* ("Claims," Volume 1), Findley, Brackenridge, and other primary sources, with reference to secondary work by Baldwin, Bouton, Slaughter, Fennell, Holt, and others.

315 *white-heat mode to its peak*: See ibid., where I present much more detail on the administration's ensuing activities, with reference to *American State Papers*, cabinet correspondence, and the primary and secondary writers cited above.

315 *The officers were revved-up*: The best source for the nature and activities of the invading army is Slaughter, Chapter 13.

316 *Randolph became the cabinet's odd man out*: "To George Washington from Edmund Randolph, 5 August 1794," *Founders Online*, National Archives, founders.archives.gov /documents/Washington/05-16-02-0362.

316 *grand congress on the Monongahela*: Brackenridge, Chapter 10, reports in detail on the scene at the long congress and the impulse to armed secession.

316 *Gallatin was out of office*: All cited Gallatin biographers provide more detail on his expulsion from the Senate.

317 *introduced a series of measures*: Walters, *Albert Gallatin*, 63–64.

317 *addressed the grand congress*: Brackenridge, 90.

318 *He came down from the mountain*: Husband's turnabout here, like his turn toward inspiring the region to resist, remains characteristically enigmatic.

318 *The mystic and the rationalist weren't alone*: See Brackenridge, 93–95, for the meeting of four, including Gallatin's saying of Brackenridge "he laughs all by himself"; and 138, with Gallatin's view of Brackenridge's tactics.

319 *announced that a commission*: In *The Whiskey Rebellion*, I provide detail on the commissioners' formation, travels, purposes, and activities in the West, based largely on reports, logs, and correspondence in the John William Wallace Collection, the Jasper Yeates Papers, and the Whiskey Rebellion Collection. Holt, "The Whiskey Rebellion of 1794," 11, bluntly calls the ensuing negotiations "sham"; Kohn, *Eagle and Sword*, 163–68, describes the process as buying time for the military buildup and connects it to the similar negotiations with the Native confederation, which I explore in depth in *Autumn of the Black Snake*.

320 *tell Lee to postdate his orders*: "From Alexander Hamilton to Henry Lee, 25 August 1794," *Founders Online*, National Archives, founders.archives.gov/documents /Hamilton/01-17-02-0111

320 *meetings to consider the federal commissioners' positions*: Brackenridge, 97–124, with much detail on the tense back-and-forth among the committee of four, the commissioners, and the western congress.

321 *they were marching in two great wings*: Slaughter, Chapter 13, provides much important detail, glossed over here, regarding the march.

321 *the referendum was held*: Brackenridge, 16–17, on the changed mood of the region, with the submission of Parkinson and others; Findley, who rarely agrees with Brackenridge, concurs. Kohn, 172, quotes one of the commissioners to the effect that the commission had cut off "the heads of the hydra."

321 *prevailed upon Washington*: "From Alexander Hamilton to George Washington, 19 September 1794," *Founders Online*, National Archives, founders.archives.gov/documents /Hamilton/01-17-02-0217.

322 *Findley . . . meetings with Washington and Hamilton*: Findley, 169–87; on Hamilton's wanting grounds for charging him, see also 142–43.

322 *"Tully"*: For example: "Tully No. I [23 August 1794]," *Founders Online*, National Archives, founders.archives.gov/documents/Hamilton/01-17-02-0102.

322 *the president . . . took his usual notes*: "October [1794]," *Founders Online*, National Archives, founders.archives.gov/documents/Washington/01-06-02-0003-0003.

323 *detentions and interrogations . . . mass arrests*: In *The Whiskey Rebellion*, I cover these events in detail, with reference to Findley, Brackenridge, Lee's orders, Hamilton's and Washington's correspondence, and other sources.

323 *"a very fit subject"*: "To George Washington from Alexander Hamilton, 11 November 1794," *Founders Online*, National Archives, founders.archives.gov/documents/Washington/05-17-02-0110.

323 *anyone may arrest a traitor*: "From Alexander Hamilton to George Washington, 8 November 1794," *Founders Online*, National Archives, founders.archives.gov/documents/Hamilton/01-17-02-0344.

323 *Gallatin . . . left with his wife for New York*: May, 55.

324 *John Powers*: Findley, 228–30. For more on the effort to charge Gallatin and Findley: Walters, *Albert Gallatin*, 87–88.

324 *The president had consigned him to the guillotine*: Paine, Writings, Vol. 3, Chapters 21 and 22.

324–325 *Robespierre meanwhile . . . approach their door, then pass on*: The account is from Paine, *Writings*, 394–96, relating what Paine thought happened: he was so ill that he may have been informed of it later. Thanks to Thomas Carlyle's crediting the story in his book *The French Revolution* (James Fraser, 1837), its veracity was questioned and debated in the London *Atheneum* in 1894 (*Writings*, 396, n. 1). While Paine locates the room in the basement, it seems not to have been his first room.

325 *Husband . . . the first name*: Husband's central importance had been clarified in September by the tax collector Benjamin Wells, among others, in depositions: Tench Coxe to William Rawle, October 1, 1794, Tench Coxe Letters, also cited by Fennell, 193, n. 2 (the depositions themselves have been lost). Mark Haddon Jones, 360, says Husband was taken to Philadelphia with Washington commanding, but correspondence concerning him suggests otherwise: "To George Washington from Alexander Hamilton, 25 October 1794," *Founders Online*, National Archives, founders.archives.gov/documents/Washington/05-17-02-0075; "From George Washington to Alexander Hamilton, 26 October 1794," *Founders Online*, National Archives, founders.archives.gov/documents/Washington/05-17-02-0077.

325 *forced to walk and sleep exposed for thirty days*: Holt, "The Whiskey Rebellion of 1794," 73.

325 *inexpressible pleasure*: Slaughter, 219.

326 *value . . . up 50 percent*: "From George Washington to Charles Morgan, 17 January 1795," *Founders Online*, National Archives, founders.archives.gov/documents/Washington/05-17-02-0269. On this issue, I follow Slaughter, 224, citing further primary evidence.

326 *Monroe . . starved and sick*: Fruchtman, 331.

326 *"And as to you, sir"*: "To George Washington from Thomas Paine, 30 July 1796," *Founders Online*, National Archives, founders.archives.gov/documents/Washington/05-20-02-0329.

326 *Jefferson . . . distance from him on policy*: See the Editor's Note, "From Thomas Jefferson to Thomas Paine, 19 June 1792," *Founders Online*, National Archives, founders.archives.gov/documents/Jefferson/01-20-02-0076-0014. I think the editor takes a too-sweepingly-negative view of Paine, but it does seem significant that Jefferson "allowed

all of Paine's various letters to go unanswered" from 1792 to 1800, as does Jefferson's cited letter, personally friendly yet firmly dismissive on policy: "From Thomas Jefferson to Thomas Paine, 18 March 1801," *Founders Online*, National Archives, founders .archives.gov/documents/Jefferson/01-33-02-0302.

327   *a handful of people attended his funeral:* Fruchtman, 433.

327   *Husband was tried in Philadelphia:* For detail on the trials, see Holt, "The Whiskey Rebellion of 1794," 74–81. For Husband's death: Mark Haddon Jones, 363.

327   *taking great satisfaction:* "From Alexander Hamilton to Angelica Church, 8 December 1794," *Founders Online*, National Archives, founders.archives.gov/documents /Hamilton/01-17-02-0407.

23. ALBERT OPTIMISTE

331   *elected to the U.S. House of Representatives:* Henry Adams, *The Life of Albert Gallatin*, 102–103.

332   *took his first public stand:* "A Representative from the County of Fayette, in the House of Representatives of the General Assembly of Pennsylvania . . . ," oll.libertyfund.org /title/adams-the-writings-of-albert-gallatin-vol-3#lf1358-03_head_002.

333   *neither he nor Madison made any public statement:* Jefferson's privately expressed view, like Gallatin's public argument, was that there hadn't been any organized insurrection. See "From Thomas Jefferson to James Monroe, 26 May 1795," *Founders Online*, National Archives, founders.archives.gov/documents/Jefferson/01-28-02-0275.

335   *he knew nothing of the man:* Mark Haddon Jones, 262.

335   *Republicans had gained a narrow majority:* Walters, *Albert Gallatin*, 91.

335   *restrict all federal spending:* Balinky, 11; May, 66.

336   *constitutionally. That was the thing:* The ensuing reading of Gallatin's constitutionalism is inspired by Rothman, 126–35.

337   *why he liked Pennsylvania . . . a poor man:* Henry Adams, *The Life of Albert Gallatin*, 107.

338   *administration as a whole remained strong . . . take down Edmund Randolph:* The post-Hamilton-Jefferson-Knox cabinet is widely covered. For Hamilton's backstage involvement, see, for example, McDonald, 314–19; and Mitchell, *Alexander Hamilton: The National Adventure*, 356. For the Randolph story: Mitchell, 328–29; and Randolph.

339   *Hamilton was pelted:* May, 61.

339   *House had the power to withhold funds:* Ibid., 70. For detail on the House treaty debates, see Stevens, 111–25; and Walters, *Albert Gallatin*, 103–104.

339   *avoided the mean-spirited zingers:* Ibid., 73, 81–82.

339   *terrible speaker:* Ibid., 73.

340   *executive privilege:* For the 1792 background: "To George Washington from Henry Knox, 30 March 1792," *Founders Online*, National Archives, founders.archives.gov/documents /Washington/05-10-02-0104"; "Memoranda of Consultations with the President [11 March–9 April 1792]," *Founders Online*, National Archives, founders.archives.gov /documents/Jefferson/01-23-02-0219.

340   *western constituents liked the treaty . . . pushed him forward in the party:* May, 71–72.

340   *even enchanted . . . new edition of* The Federalist: Ibid., 70.

340   *Madison . . . Gallatin's teaching abilities:* Ibid., 73–74.

340   *problem with funding a public debt:* Ibid., 66–67.

341   *sinking fund . . . perpetuated a delusion:* Balinky, 44–45.

341   *raise domestic taxes . . . skeptical of excises:* Balinky, 51–53; May, 76.

342 *didn't castigate a standing army*: May, 67.
343 *Committee on Ways and Means*: Ibid., 68; Balinky, 11; Walters, *Albert Gallatin*, 92–93.

24. THE JESUIT
344 *Washington . . . no regard for term limits*: Peabody, 441–43.
344 *"I confess, I differ widely"*: Ibid., 442.
344 *Gallatin published a book*: Gallatin, *A Sketch of the Finances of the United States*. For the critiques of Hamilton, see Sections Two and Three. For a more detailed explication: Walters, *Albert Gallatin*, 95–98.
345 *series of bank loans to Congress*: May, 66–67; and for detail, Francis, Chapter 4, including a skeptical reading of Hamilton's final fiscal report to Congress.
345–346 *Adams, nominally party leader . . . his own party*: President Adams's struggles with both the Republicans and his party are widely covered; I've benefited especially from Ferling, *Adams vs. Jefferson*, Chapters 7 and 8.
346 *Wolcott . . . bombardments of demands for minutiae*: "To Alexander Hamilton from Oliver Wolcott, Junior, 5 April 1798," *Founders Online*, National Archives, founders .archives.gov/documents/Hamilton/01-21-02-0231.
346 *contra Gallatin's complaints, the country was doing well*: For a dissenting modern view, see Francis, Chapter 4.
347 *"Gallatin & Co." . . . "wandering Israelite"*: Walters, *Albert Gallatin*, 103–105.
347 *The Jesuit*: May, 79.
347 *sudden military buildup*: The actions of France and the United States, the military buildup, and the war fever are widely covered. My sketch, leaving out signal events like the XYZ Affair and the passage of five successively named armies, is largely drawn from a wealth of detail in Kohn, *Eagle and Sword*, 204–14 and Chapter 10; and Walters, *Albert Gallatin*, 108–13.
347 *$850,000 per year*: Walters, 108.
348 *Haiti . . . commerce in the Caribbean*: Hickey, 368.
348 *Federalists thus found it easy to push laws*: Ibid., 214.
348 *Wolcott issued $7 million . . . plan for paying down the entire thing*: Edling, 104.
348–349 *new federal taxes . . . voted against it*: May, 82–83.
348 *the Debt . . . had reached almost $84 million*: Edling, 104.
349 *Republicans . . . found him too moderate*: Ibid., 80–81.
349 *Hamilton reemerged*: My ensuing sketch of what become known as the Quasi War, Hamilton's involvement in what became known as the New Army, and Adams's struggles are influenced especially by Kohn, *Eagle and Sword*, Chapters 10–12; see his footnote, 29, for the army's names, citing "From Thomas Jefferson to James Madison, 5 February 1799," *Founders Online*, National Archives, founders.archives.gov/documents /Jefferson/01-31-02-0005. For a contrary point of view, see Coleman. For my take on Coleman's dissent, see expanded notes at www.hamiltonscheme.com.
349–350 *Adams started throwing up obstacles . . . made peace with France*: The squabbles ending the Quasi-War are detailed by Kohn, *Eagle and Sword*, 230–38.
350 *the majority passed a series of laws*: The Alien and Sedition Acts are widely covered. For Gallatin as a target: May, 80–84; Walters, *Albert Gallatin*, 119.
350 *Washington . . . the Illuminati*: See Editor's Note 1, "To George Washington from G. W. Snyder, 22 August 1798," *Founders Online*, National Archives, founders.archives.gov /documents/Washington/06-02-02-0435, quoted by Smelser, 331–33.
350 *Gallatin right in the bull's-eye*: May, 80–84; Walters, *Albert Gallatin*, 119.
351 *Pickering . . . scanned opposition papers*: Farber, 325.

486 NOTES

351   *burned in effigy*: Walters, *Albert Gallatin*, 118.
351   *Jefferson . . . opposition partnership*: May, 80.
351   *resolutions, presented by Kentucky and Virginia*: The Virginia and Kentucky Resolutions are widely covered. For Gallatin's only expressed opinion on them, see Henry Adams, *The Life of Albert Gallatin*, 155, quoting Gallatin on Madison's "justifying the resolutions as well as he could." For differences between the resolutions, especially in Jefferson's first draft, see Koch and Ammon, 157.
351   *"to the test"*: "From Alexander Hamilton to Theodore Sedgwick, 2 February 1799," *Founders Online*, National Archives, founders.archives.gov/documents/Hamilton/01 -22-02-0267.
351   *He did lose his temper*: Walters, *Albert Gallatin*, 116.
352   *a new book*: Gallatin, *Views of the Public Debt, Receipts and Expenditures of the United States*.
352   *connected to Aaron Burr*: May, 89–91; Walters, *Albert Gallatin*, 128–29. Ferling, *Adams vs. Jefferson*, 127–28, notes an irony, given how few Americans were city-dwellers, in New York City's becoming the key battleground.
353   *the electoral contest of 1800*: Widely covered. My account benefits especially from Ferling, *Adams vs. Jefferson*, and Freeman and Neem.
353   *felt a duty to tweak*: See Freeman and Neem, 1973–74; Ferling, *Adams vs. Jefferson*, 131–32.
353   *the organizing and electioneering of Burr*: Ferling, 129–31; Freeman and Neem, 1975–78; Wilentz, 86–87.
353   *fourteen-thousand-word, fifty-four-page memo*: "Letter from Alexander Hamilton, Concerning the Public Conduct and Character of John Adams, Esq. President of the United States [24 October 1800]," *Founders Online*, National Archives, founders .archives.gov/documents/Hamilton/01-25-02-0110-0002.
354   *hated the capital*: Henry Adams, *The Life of Albert Gallatin*, 187–90.
355   *the Georgia tally*: Ferling, *Adams vs. Jefferson*, 186–87.
355   *Many had seen this coming . . . electoral maneuvering*: Ibid., 187; Walters, *Albert Gallatin*, 130.
355   *the chamber went into session, and a contest commenced*: The ensuing account of the House election is drawn largely from detailed discussions by Ferling, *Adams vs. Jefferson*, 187–96; and Freeman and Neem, 1986–99.
356   *floor manager . . . ignoring Gallatin*: Walters, *Albert Gallatin*, 134.
356   *readied their militias . . . "usurpation"*: Ferling, *Adams vs. Jefferson*, 188–89.
356   *a new convention to "repair"*: Freeman and Neem, 1988.
356   *"the most wicked and absurd attempt ever tried by the Federalists"*: Henry Adams, *The Life of Albert Gallatin*, 194.
357   *brokering gained the election*: For details, see Ferling, *Adams vs. Jefferson*, 192–95; and Walters, *Albert Gallatin*, 136–37.
357   *Jefferson . . . thought it was only the threat of armed force*: Freeman and Neem, 1988.

25. TRIUMVIRATE
358–359   *startup frenzy . . . Prune Street Prison*: My sketch of Morris's later career and flight from creditors is drawn in large part from Rappleye, Chapter 20.
358   *two canal companies*: Sullivan; and Ringwalt, 57–59, also cited in "Robert Morris (financier)," Wikipedia.
358   *steam-engine concern, an iron-rolling mill*: Widely asserted—see, for example, "Robert Morris," Descendants of the Signers of the Declaration of Independence, www .dsdi1776.com/signer/robert-morris/—but weakly sourced.

NOTES 487

358 *biggest real-estate trust:* For Morris's partnership with John Nicholson and James Greenleaf, see Rappleye, 496–501. Sakolski, 38, calls it the biggest such trust ever formed in the United States aside from the post–Civil War railroad trusts.

358 *contracted to put up ten houses a year: Journal of the 64th Council of the City of Washington,* Vol. 64 (1867), 300, also cited in "Robert Morris (financier)," Wikipedia.

359 *James Wilson died destitute:* Mosvick.

359 *passed the nation's first bankruptcy act:* Rappleye, 512.

360 *resort to a recess appointment:* Bell.

360 *new, two-story brick building:* May, 102.

360 *failures, blunders, and fraudss . . . "Hamilton did nothing wrong":* James Hamilton, 23, quoting Gallatin; squinting through an unpersuasive total recall of dialogue has led me to the reading here. For more on James Hamilton, see the Epilogue herein.

360 *the department employed 1,285 people:* Walters, *Albert Gallatin,* 147–48.

361 *Blanket firings and hirings:* Henry Adams, *The Life of Albert Gallatin,* 205–207; May, 116–18; Heinlein, 65–66.

361 *It mortified him:* "From Thomas Jefferson to Pierre Samuel Du Pont de Nemours, 18 January 1802," *Founders Online,* National Archives, founders.archives.gov/documents /Jefferson/01-36-02-0242.

361 *His real goal had never been to upturn:* For Gallatin's rejection of out-party-style rejectionism, see Leonard J. Sadosky's "How the Jeffersonians Learned to Love the State," 153, in Freeman and Neem.

362 *maintain the current excises . . . internal revenue:* Balinky, 60–64; May, 105–106.

362 *scrutinize and trim appropriations:* Walters, *Albert Gallatin,* 150–51.

363 *$81 million; Oliver Wolcott had reduced it:* Edling, 104, arguing that reduction of the original debt was in fact much deeper: the aggregate debt had been swelled by the military buildup.

363 *fully paid off in less than a generation . . . if $73 million:* Walters, *Albert Gallatin,* 149.

363–364 *sales of public land . . . grant sizes:* Ibid., 179–80; May, 125–29.

364 *sold all of the remaining shares:* Lane, 605.

364 *a triumvirate:* Henry Adams, *The Life of Albert Gallatin,* 199; Stevens, 174.

365 *stayed in Washington . . . smoking cigars:* Walters, *Albert Gallatin,* 221–22; for the smoking, see May, 104.

365 *Smith . . . building up the fleet:* Walters, *Albert Gallatin,* 148.

366 *Gallatin sent Jefferson urgent pleas . . . blockade a kind of debt:* Ibid., 154.

366 *he found all the money:* Ibid., 155–56.

367 *Hamilton . . . "Jefferson is not destined!":* For Hamilton's passing the news to Madison, focus on New Orleans and Florida, and published opinions regarding the Purchase, see "Hamilton on the Louisiana Purchase," 268–72.

367 *Napoleon had acquired from Spain:* The politics and logistics of the Louisiana Purchase are widely covered. My account, with Gallatin at the center, is drawn largely from ibid.; Walters, *Albert Gallatin,* 156–58; May, 129–33; and Rothman.

368 *Hamilton . . . great landmass might not offer much:* "Hamilton on the Louisiana Purchase," 276.

368 *constitutionalist identity crisis:* Henry Adams, *The Life of Albert Gallatin,* 239–42.

368 *"The general government":* "From Thomas Jefferson to John Dickinson, 9 August 1803," *Founders Online,* National Archives, founders.archives.gov/documents/Jefferson/01-41 -02-0127.

368 *proposed that the Constitution be amended:* "I. Draft Amendment, on or before 9 July 1803," *Founders Online,* National Archives, founders.archives.gov/documents/Jefferson /01-40-02-0523-0002.

369   *The presidency was well within its powers:* Rothman, 130–31; May, 130–31.
369   *a deal that would enable the purchase:* My account is drawn from May, 131–33; Walters, *Albert Gallatin,* 157–59; and "Exhibitions: The Louisiana Purchase."
370   *Gallatin didn't love the discount:* May, 132; Walters, *Albert Gallatin,* 158.
370   *no brilliant leadership was involved:* "Hamilton on the Louisiana Purchase," 274.
370   *only because Hamilton himself had put U.S. credit:* Miller, 562.
370   *inventive approach to paying the interest:* Ibid., 158–59; May, 132–33.
371   *more or less working . . . $18 million:* Balinky, no wholehearted admirer of Jeffersonian policy, calls 1802–1808 a "golden age" of Republican finance, all the more impressive because of the cost of the Louisiana Purchase (90–91), yet also notes, 116, that it all depended on a boom in foreign trade; for the surplus of 1808, see 160.
371–372   *a kind of golden age . . . industrial policy:* "Second Inaugural Address, 4 March 1805," *Founders Online,* National Archives, founders.archives.gov/documents/Jefferson /99-01-02-1302.
372   *a federal interstate highway:* Walters, *Albert Gallatin,* 178.
372   *the Cumberland Road:* Ibid., 185–86.
372   *fretting over the constitutional issues . . . costs should be a matter of federal policy:* Ibid., 187.
373   *seized four deserters:* The *Leopard* incident is widely covered. Henry Adams, *The Life of Albert Gallatin,* writing in 1879 and emphasizing the national humiliation, asserts that the incident would "probably be familiar to every school-boy in the United States for generations to come" (357).
373   *on his way to New York:* Walters, *Albert Gallatin,* 199, says Gallatin was in Philadelphia on treasury business; May, 159, that he was there on his way to New York; Henry Adams, *The Life of Albert Gallatin,* 266, that he was already in New York.

26. ALBERT AGONISTES
374   *Smith was already hot to send warships:* May, 160.
374   *afford waging war on both empires:* Balinky, 132–33.
374   *$18 million per year:* Walters, *Albert Gallatin,* 200.
374   *war looked truly necessary:* May, 160.
374   *the Embargo Act:* Very widely covered. For an exploration of the act's sectionally divisive effects, see Benjamin Carp's "Jefferson's Embargo: National Intent and Sectional Effects," in Freeman and Neem. See Mannix for a dissent from the intensive involvement of Jefferson asserted by, for example, Henry Adams, *The Life of Albert Gallatin,* and Balinky.
375   *actual war itself, Gallatin advised Jefferson:* May, 165.
375   *Wave after wave of bad effects:* Also widely covered. My sketch is influenced largely by the Benjamin Carp chapter in Freeman and Neem, cited above; Balinky, 167–68; Walters, *Albert Gallatin,* Chapter 16; May, 167–70.
375   *treasury would need arbitrary powers:* May, 170.
376   *Report on Roads and Canals:* Ibid., 135–38; Henry Adams, *The Life of Albert Gallatin,* 262–63; Walters, *Albert Gallatin,* 186–88.
376   *what would later be called pork:* For detail, see Larson, 173–75, calling Gallatin's plan "elegant."
376   *the mood in Congress had changed:* May, 136–37.
377   *federal revenues were disappearing:* Ibid., 181–82.
377   *Gallatin had hoped to take Madison's place:* Ibid., 176–77.
377   *he couldn't do both jobs at once:* Dungan, 86.

378   Non-Intercourse Act . . . just as ineffectual: Ibid., 90.
378   deficit of $1.3 million: Walters, Albert Gallatin, 234.
378   taking a loan from the bank . . . In May, the law passed: Stevens, 211–12.
379   Report on the Subject of Manufactures: Walters, Albert Gallatin, 238–39; May, 194–98.
379   Smith brothers and Gallatin . . . maneuvered an ongoing investigation: May, 183–85.
380   William Duane: Ibid., 120–22; Stevens, 308. For Duane's list of officers to be fired:
       Henry Adams, The Life of Albert Gallatin, 205.
380   William Giles . . . Alien and Sedition Acts: May, 176.
380   block the possibility of Gallatin's becoming secretary of state: Walters, Albert Gallatin, 214.
380   Henry Clay . . . John C. Calhoun: Both men's later careers are, of course, widely cov-
       ered. While Calhoun arrived in the House in March 1811, just missing the bank re-
       charter debate, his alliance with the anti-recharter cadre lends irony to his leading
       role in forming the Second Bank, discussed later in the chapter. For more on this
       group in the states and Congress in the 1810s, see Walters, Albert Gallatin, 247–49; for
       Clay's lack of sympathy with Giles, see Henry Adams, The Life of Albert Gallatin, 320.
381   he and Thomas Willing . . . open a branch in New Orleans: Walters, Albert Gallatin, 175.
381   renewing the bank charter: All cited Gallatin biographers cover the bank fight in both
       the House and the Senate in more or less the terms presented in the ensuing discus-
       sion. The best narrative: Henry Adams, The Life of Albert Gallatin, 318–21. The closest
       look at state banking interests: May, 185–91.
381   Madison . . . support renewing the charter: May, 188. For a thorough exploration of
       Madison's role, see Leonard J. Sadosky, "How the Jeffersonians Came to Love the
       State," 162–66, in Freeman and Neem.
383   Stephen Girard: For a biography and overview of the private bank, see Kenneth L.
       Brown. For the state's refusal to charter: May, 216.
383   resigning his office: Henry Adams, The Life of Albert Gallatin, 323–25.
384   in 1811, Gallatin told Congress: Ibid., 332–34; Walters, Albert Gallatin, 249–50.
384   rejected this report with umbrage: Walters, 250–52.
384   "financial fame of the gentleman": Henry Adams, The Life of Albert Gallatin, 234–35.
384   Who cared about a big reduction of the Debt?: May, 201.
384   Findley . . . expressed his disappointment: Henry Adams, The Life of Albert Gallatin, 338.
385   "The Rat—in the Treasury!": Walters, Albert Gallatin, 251.
385   raising 25,000 troops . . . If he was really so good: Henry Adams, The Life of Albert Galla-
       tin, 334–35.
385   he was asking for far too little: Ibid., 338.
385   Congress no real choice but to approve: Walters, Albert Gallatin, 252.
385   from the New England Federalists . . . sales everywhere were slow: Ibid., 253–54.
386   treasury notes: May, 205–206.
386   "only a matter of marching": Ibid., 209–10.
386   in over their heads . . . fall to Gallatin and Monroe: Walters, Albert Gallatin, 255–56.
386   He proposed excises: May, 205.
387   Exports and imports dropped . . . inflation reached nearly 30 percent: "The War of 1812:
       Economic Performance Index." For a wealth of detail on the war's economic impact,
       see Morales, especially Chapter 8.
387   state banks, which were proliferating wildly: Henry Adams, The Life of Albert Gallatin,
       353.
387   more than forty would soon operate in Pennsylvania alone: Kenneth L. Brown, "Stephen
       Girard, Promoter of the Second Bank of the United States," 126.
387   nearly a hundred by 1814: Austin, 7.

387   *The federal armory . . . shut down:* Van Sickle, 2.
387   *only realistic way to raise enough money:* The ensuing account of the problems facing Gallatin and his successors in financing the war, and the tactics for addressing them, closely follows Cowen.
388   *wouldn't have enough money to get through the month:* Henry Adams, *The Life of Albert Gallatin,* 354.
388   *succumbed to their conditions for buying the rest of the bonds:* My drastically simplified account of the $16 million deal is drawn largely from Stevens, 268–69; Kenneth L. Brown, "Stephen Girard's Bank," 38–42; and Donald R. Adams, 104–15.
388   *invented American investment banking:* Adams, 114–15.
388   *extend to him the federal-relationship status:* Kenneth L. Brown, "Stephen Girard's Bank," 43–44.
389   *re-create and charter a national bank:* Kenneth L. Brown, "Stephen Girard, Promoter of the Second Bank," 125–31.
389   *did pass the domestic taxes . . . direct-taxing power:* Einhorn, 196.
389   *defaulted on the Public Debt:* Van Sickle, 2.
389   *asked Madison to appoint him:* Walters, *Albert Gallatin,* 263–64.
390   *the Debt at $127 million:* Ibid., 3. Gallatin's biographers tend to finesse this fact, pointing instead to debt reduction before 1812. See, for example, Walters, *Albert Gallatin,* 268–69. May's subtitle, "How Albert Gallatin Saved the New Nation from Debt," takes the tendency all the way.
390   *Hamiltonian banking was back:* For the political process, see Walters, "The Origin of the Second Bank of the United States."
390   *called the Second Bank of the United States:* For political detail regarding its formation, see Walters, "The Origins of the Second Bank of the United States."
391   *Madison vetoed an infrastructure bill:* Madison, "Veto Message on the Internal Improvements Bill."

EPILOGUE

395–429   Much of the epilogue tracks with widely known events covered in standard U.S. history surveys. For the less obvious elements, I've referred to the cited Gallatin biographies for Gallatin's post-cabinet career; "Americans," at the National Museum of the American Indian, for emphasis on the critical involvement of Congress in the Indian Removal Act; Atack, for the persistence of tenancy and day labor in nineteenth-century American agriculture; Black, for Charles Atlas's background; Gilbert, for Andrew Mellon as a Hamilton fan; Lemisch, for the role of Gilder and Lehrman at the New-York Historical Society; the Mary Elinor Lazenby Collection, for the ancestry of Admiral Kimmel; McCloskey, for the libertarian view of the Thoreau pencil factory; Merritt, for the realities of southern free labor before the Civil War, the effect of the Specie Circular Act, and pre–Civil War inequality generally; Lyra D. Monteiro, for "Race-Conscious Casting and the Erasure of the Black Past in 'Hamilton'," in Potter and Russo; Richard B. Morris, for President Jackson as a strikebreaker; Peterson, for FDR's Jeffersonianism; Slonimsky, for James Hamilton; Stoller, for J. P. Morgan as a Hamiltonian, Teddy Roosevelt as other than antimonopoly, Brandeis's restraining Morgan, and Obama's meeting with the Hamilton Project; Wilentz, for the rise of democracy in the states; Wills, for Lincoln at Gettysburg. For further discussion and more detailed citation, see www.hamiltonscheme.com.

SOURCES

ARCHIVES

Christopher Marshall Papers, Historical Society of Pennsylvania
Craig-Neville Papers, Detre Library and Archives, Heinz History Center
Isaac Craig Papers, Carnegie Library, Pittsburgh
Jasper Yeates Papers, Historical Society of Pennsylvania
John Irwin Scull Archive, Detre Library and Archives, Heinz History Center
John William Wallace Collection, Historical Society of Pennsylvania
Mary Elinor Lazenby Collection, Archives and Special Collections, University of Pittsburgh Library
Oliver Wolcott Jr. Papers, Historical Society of Connecticut Museum and Library
Rawle Family Papers, Historical Society of Pennsylvania
Tench Coxe Letters, Records of the Internal Revenue Service, National Archives
Whiskey Rebellion Collection, Library of Congress

INTERVIEWS

Diethorn, Karie, Chief Curator, Independence National Historical Park, and Deborah Miller, Museum Curator, Independence National Historical Park, interview, May 11, 2022.
Mumpton, Ian, Site Interpreter, Schuyler Mansion State Historic Site, interview, March 21, 2002.

PUBLISHED WORKS

Achenbach, Joel. *The Grand Idea: George Washington's Potomac and the Race to the West.* Simon and Schuster, 2004.
Adams, Donald R. "The Beginning of Investment Banking in the United States." *Pennsylvania History: A Journal of Mid-Atlantic Studies* 45:2 (April 1978).
Adams, Henry. *The Life of Albert Gallatin.* J. B. Lippincott, 1879.
Adams, John. *Autobiography.* Adams Family Papers, Massachusetts Historical Society. www .masshist.org/digitaladams/archive/autobio.
Adams, William Howard. *Gouverneur Morris: An Independent Life.* Yale University Press, 2003.

Alexander, J. K. "The Fort Wilson Incident of 1779: A Case Study of the Revolutionary Crowd." *The William and Mary Quarterly* 31:4 (October 1974).

American State Papers, "Claims," Vol. 1. Library of Congress, memory.loc.gov/ammem/amlaw/lwsp.html.

"Americans." Exhibit of the National Museum of the American Indian.

Ames, Fisher. *Works of Fisher Ames*. Edited by Seth Ames. Little, Brown and Company, 1854.

Annals of the Congress of the United States. Gales and Seaton, 1834.

Atack, Jeremy. "Tenants and Yeomen in the Nineteenth Century." *Agricultural History* 62:3, Quantitative Studies in Agrarian History (Summer 1988).

Austin, D. A. "Has the U.S. Government Ever 'Defaulted'?" Congressional Research Service, December 8, 2016.

Bailey, Kenneth P. *The Ohio Company of Virginia and the Westward Movement, 1748–1792: A Chapter in the History of the Colonial Frontier*. Arthur H. Clark, 1939.

Baldwin, Leland. *Whiskey Rebels*. University of Pittsburgh Press, 1939.

Balinky, Alexander. *Albert Gallatin: Fiscal Theories and Policies*. Rutgers University Press, 1958.

Banning, Lance. "James Madison and the Nationalists." *The William and Mary Quarterly*, 3rd Series., 40:2. (April 1983).

Baumann, Roland M. "'Heads I Win, Tails You Lose': The Public Creditors and the Assumption Issue in Pennsylvania, 1790–1802." *Pennsylvania History: A Journal of Mid-Atlantic Studies* 44:3 (July 1977).

Beeman, Richard. *Plain, Honest Men: The Making of the American Constitution*. Random House, 2010.

Bell, J. L. "The Birth of the Recess Appointment." *Boston 1775* (blog), January 26, 2013. boston1775.blogspot.com/2013/01/the-birth-of-recess-appointment.html.

Berg, Scott W. *Grand Avenues: The Story of Pierre Charles L'Enfant, the French Visionary Who Designed Washington, D.C.* Vintage Books, 2009.

Bezanson, Anne. "Inflation and Controls, Pennsylvania, 1774–1779." *The Journal of Economic History* 8, Supplement: The Tasks of Economic History (1948).

Black, Jonathan. "Charles Atlas: Muscle Man." *Smithsonian Magazine*, August 2009.

Bloch, Ruth H. *Visionary Republic: Millennial Themes in American Thought, 1756–1800*. Cambridge University Press, 1985.

Bogart, Dan. "The East Indian Monopoly and the Transition from Limited Access in England, 1600–1813." *National Bureau of Economic Research*, September 2015. www.nber.org/system/files/working_papers/w21536/w21536.pdf.

Bouton, Terry. *Taming Democracy: "The People," the Founders, and the Troubled Ending of the American Revolution*. Oxford University Press, 2007.

_____. "Tying Up the Revolution: Money, Power, and the Regulation in Pennsylvania: 1765–1800." PhD diss., Duke University, 1996.

Bowling, Kenneth R. "Dinner at Jefferson's: A Note on Jacob E. Cooke's 'The Compromise of 1790.'" *The William and Mary Quarterly* 28:4 (October 1971).

Boyd, William Kenneth, ed. *Some Eighteenth Century Tracts Concerning North Carolina*. Edwards and Broughton Company, 1927.

Brackenridge, Hugh Henry. *Incidents of the Insurrection in the Western Parts of Pennsylvania, in the Year 1794*. John McCulloch, 1795.

Brewer, John. *Sinews of Power: War, Money, and the English State, 1688–1783*. Harvard University Press, 1990.

Brock, Leslie V. *The Currency of the American Colonies, 1700–1764: A Study in Colonial Finance and Imperial Relations*. Arno Press, 1975.

Brodie, Fawn M. *Thomas Jefferson: An Intimate History*. W. W. Norton and Company, 1974.

Brookhiser, Richard. *Alexander Hamilton, American*. 1999; Free Press, 2011.

_____. *Gentleman Revolutionary: Gouverneur Morris, the Rake Who Wrote the Constitution*. Free Press, 2004.

Brooks, Robin. "Alexander Hamilton, Melancton Smith, and Ratification of the Constitution in New York." *The William and Mary Quarterly*, Series 3, Vol. 24 (1967).

Brown, Kenneth L. "Stephen Girard, Promoter of the Second Bank of the United States." *The Journal of Economic History* 2:2 (November 1942).

_____. "Stephen Girard's Bank." *The Pennsylvania Magazine of History and Biography* 66:1 (January 1942).

Brown, Roger H. *Redeeming the Republic: Federalists, Taxation, and the Origins of the Constitution.* Johns Hopkins University Press, 1993.

Brunhouse, Robert L. *The Counter-Revolution in Pennsylvania, 1776–1790.* Pennsylvania Historical Commission, 1908.

Budinger, Meghan. "All About Sugar Cones." *Lives and Legacies* (blog), Historic Kenmore and George Washington's Ferry Farm, December 13, 2008. livesandlegaciesblog.org/2018/12/13/all-about-sugar-cones/.

Bugg, John. *Five Long Winters: The Trials of British Romanticism.* Stanford University Press, 2014.

Burke, Edmund. *Reflections on the French Revolution.* E.P. Dutton & Co., 1910.

Calloway, Colin G. *The Victory with No Name.* Oxford University Press, 2014.

Carp, E. Wayne. "The Origins of the Nationalist Movement of 1780–1783: Congressional Administration and the Continental Army." *The Pennsylvania Magazine of History and Biography* 107:3 (July 1983).

Carrol, John M., and Colin F. Baxter. *The American Military Tradition: From Colonial Times to the Present.* Rowman and Littlefield, 2006.

"Charles II, 1660: An Act for the Encouraging and Increasing of Shipping and Navigation." In *Statutes of the Realm*, Vol. 5, *1628–80.* Edited by John Raithby (s.n., 1819). British History Online, www.british-history.ac.uk/statutes-realm/vol5/pp246-250.

Chernow, Ron. *Alexander Hamilton.* Penguin Books, 2004.

"Christiansted National Historic Site." National Park Service. Updated October 31, 2022. npshistory.com/publications/chri/index.htm.

Clary, David A. *George Washington's First War: His Early Military Adventures.* Simon and Schuster, 2011.

Cleveland, Don. "A History of Printed Money." International Bank Note Society, July 20, 2008. www.theibns.org/joomla/index.php option=com_content&view=article&id=251%3Aa-history-of-printed-money&catid=1%3Aarticles&Itemid=129.

Coakley, Robert W. *The Role of Federal Military Forces in Domestic Disorders, 1789–1878.* Center of Military History, U.S. Army, 1988.

Coleman, Aaron N. "A Second Bounaparty? A Reexamination of Alexander Hamilton during the Franco-American Crisis, 1796–1801." *Journal of the Early Republic* 28:2 (Summer 2008).

"Congress Hall." National Park Service. www.nps.gov/inde/learn/historyculture/places-congresshall.htm.

Conner, Jett. "The American Crisis Before Crossing the Delaware?" *Journal of the American Revolution*, February 25, 2015.

Connors, Anthony J. "Andrew Craigie: Brief Life of a Patriot and Scoundrel: 1754–1819." *Harvard Magazine*, November–December 2011. www.harvardmagazine.com/2011/11/andrew-craigie.

"Constitution of Pennsylvania—September 28, 1776." Text available at the Avalon Project, Lillian Goldman Law Library, Yale Law School. avalon.law.yale.edu/18th_century/pa08.asp.

"The Controversy Surrounding the Calling of the Pennsylvania Convention." Center for the Study of the American Constitution, University of Wisconsin, Madison. csac.history.wisc.edu/states-and-ratification/pennsylvania-2/pennsylvania-convention.

Conway, Moncure Daniel. *The Life of Thomas Paine, with a History of His Literary, Political and Religious Career in America, France, and England.* G. P. Putnam's Sons, 1893.

Cooke, Jacob E. "The Compromise of 1790." *The William and Mary Quarterly* 27:4 (October 1970).

_____. "Tench Coxe, Alexander Hamilton, and the Encouragement of American Manufactures." *The William and Mary Quarterly* 32:3 (July 1975).

_____. "The Whiskey Rebellion: A Re-Evaluation." *Pennsylvania History: A Journal of Mid-Atlantic Studies* 30:3 (July 1963).

Countryman, Edward. *The American Revolution*. Hill and Wang, 1985.

Cowen, David. "Financing the War of 1812." Lecture Cowen, given at the Museum of American Finance, August 20, 2014. C-SPAN. www.c-span.org/video/?320973-1/financing-war -1812.

Crist, Robert G. *Robert Whitehill and the Struggle for Civil Rights*. Lemoyne Trust Co., 1958.

Cutterham, Tom. *Gentlemen Revolutionaries: Power and Justice in the New American Republic*. Princeton University Press, 2017.

The Debates in the Several State Conventions, On the Adoption of the Federal Constitution, as Recommended by the General Convention at Philadelphia, in 1787. Edited by Jonathan Elliott. Printed for the editor, 1836.

de Bruin, Willem. "How a Small Dutch Island Lay at the Cradle of the United States of America." Translated by Louise Snape. The Low Countries: High Road to Culture in Flanders and the Netherlands, August 29, 2019. www.the-low-countries.com/article/how-a-small-dutch -island-lay-at-the-cradle-of-the-united-states-of-america/.

"Declaration of Independence (1776)." Milestone Documents, National Archives. www.archives .gov/milestone-documents/declaration-of-independence.

Delony, Eric. "Tom Paine's Bridge." *Invention and Technology*, Spring 2000. www.inventionandtech .com/content/tom-paine%E2%80%99s-bridge-1.

Dunbar, Charles. "Some Precedents Followed by Alexander Hamilton." *The Quarterly Journal of Economics* 3:1 (October 1888).

Dungan, Nicholas. *Gallatin: America's Swiss Founding Father*. New York University Press, 2010.

Dunn, Richard S. *Sugar and Slaves: The Rise of the Planter Class in the English West Indies*. University of North Carolina Press, 1972.

DuRoss, Michelle. "Somewhere in Between: Alexander Hamilton and Slavery." *The Early America Review* 15, no. 1 (Winter/Spring 2011). Varsity Tutors. www.varsitytutors.com/earlyamerica /early-america-review/volume-15/hamilton-and-slavery.

"Early Banknotes." Bank of England Museum. Updated January 31, 2023. www.bankofengland.co .uk/museum/online-collections/banknotes/early-banknotes.

Edes, Henry H. "A Memoir of Dr. Thomas Young, 1731–1777." Colonial Society of Massachusetts, *Publications*, 11 (1910).

Edling, Max. *A Hercules in the Cradle*. University of Chicago Press, 2014.

Egnal, Marc. *A Mighty Empire: The Origins of the American Revolution*. Cornell University Press, 1988.

Einhorn, Robin L. *American Taxation, American Slavery*. University of Chicago Press, 2006.

Ekirch, A. Roger. "A New Government of Liberty: Hermon Husband's Vision of Backcountry North Carolina, 1755." *The William and Mary Quarterly* 34:4 (October 1977).

Elkins, Stanley M., and Eric McKitrick. *The Age of Federalism: The Early American Republic, 1788– 1800*. Oxford University Press, 1994.

Eveleigh, Doug. "George Washington, Scientist." *Chemical and Engineering News*, September 24, 2014. cen.acs.org/articles/92/i38/George-Washington-Scientist.html.

Everdell, William. *The End of Kings*. University of Chicago Press, 1983.

"Exhibitions: The Louisiana Purchase." The Baring Archive. baringarchive.org.uk/exhibition/ the-louisiana-purchase/.

Farber, Alan J. "Reflections on the Sedition Act of 1798." *American Bar Association Journal* 62:3 (March 1976).

Farrand, Max, ed. *The Records of the Federal Convention of 1787*. Yale University Press, 1911.

"The Federalist Papers: No. 1." The Avalon Project, Lillian Goldman Law Library, Yale Law School. avalon.law.yale.edu/18th_century/fed01.asp.

"The Federalist Papers: No. 44." The Avalon Project, Lillian Goldman Law Library, Yale Law School. avalon.law.yale.edu/18th_century/fed44.asp.

Fennell, Dorothy. *From Rebelliousness to Insurrection: A Social History of the Whiskey Rebellion, 1765–1802.* PhD diss., University of Pittsburgh, 1982.

Ferguson, E. J. *The Power of the Purse: A History of American Public Finance, 1776–1790.* Omohundro Institute of Early American History, 1961.

Ferling, John E. *Adams vs. Jefferson: The Tumultuous Election of 1800.* Oxford University Press, 2005.

_____. *The Ascent of George Washington: The Hidden Political Genius of an American Icon.* Blooms-bury Press, 2009.

Findley, William. *History of the Insurrection in the Four Western Counties of Pennsylvania.* Samuel Harrison Smith, 1796.

Flexner, James. *George Washington and the New Nation 1783–1793.* Little, Brown and Company, 1970.

_____. *George Washington in the American Revolution, 1775–1783.* Little, Brown and Company, 1968.

_____. *The Young Hamilton.* Fordham University Press, 1997.

Flower, Milton E. *John Dickinson: Conservative Revolutionary.* University of Virginia Press, 1983.

Foner, Eric. "Columbia and Slavery: A Preliminary Report." Columbia University and Slavery, 2017. columbiaandslavery.columbia.edu/content/dam/cuandslavery/about/Eric-Foner-Preliminary-Report.pdf.

_____. *Tom Paine and Revolutionary America.* Oxford University Press, 1976.

Foner, Philip, ed. *The Democratic-Republican Societies, 1790–1800: A Documentary Sourcebook of Constitutions, Declarations, Addresses, Resolutions, and Toasts.* Greenwood Press, 1976.

Founders Online: Correspondence and Other Writings of Seven Major Shapers of the United States. National Archives, founders.archives.gov.

Francis, Joe. [Untitled book.] Harvard University Press [in press].

Freeman, Joanne. "The Election of 1800: A Study in the Logic of Political Change." *Yale Law Journal* 108:8 (June 1999).

Freeman, Joanne, and Johann Neem, eds. *Jeffersonians in Power: The Rhetoric of Opposition Meets the Realities of Governing.* University of Virginia Press, 2019.

Fried, Stephen. *Rush: Revolution, Madness, and Benjamin Rush, the Visionary Doctor Who Became a Founding Father.* Crown, 2019.

Fruchtman, Jack. *Thomas Paine: Apostle of Freedom.* Basic Books, 1996.

Gaff, Alan D. *Bayonets in the Wilderness: Anthony Wayne's Legion in the Old Northwest.* University of Oklahoma Press, 2004.

Gallatin, Albert. *A Sketch of the Finances of the United States.* William A. Davis, 1796.

_____. *Views of the Public Debt, Receipts and Expenditures of the United States.* M. L. and W. A. Davis, 1800.

_____. *The Writings of Albert Gallatin.* 3 vols. Edited by Henry Adams. J. B. Lippincott, 1879; reprint Peter Smith, 1943. Text available at Online Library of Liberty, oll.libertyfund.org/title/adams-the-writings-of-albert-gallatin-3-vols.

Gigantino, James. "Slavery and the Slave Trade." *The Encyclopedia of Greater Philadelphia*, 2012. philadelphiaencyclopedia.org/essays/slavery-and-the-slave-trade.

Gilbert, Clinton W. "Andrew W. Mellon, Secretary of the Treasury." *Current History* 34:4 (July 1931).

Goñi, Marc. "The London Season Marriage Mart: Matching Technology and Sorting." Universitat Pompeu Fabra, 2017. www.eief.it/files/2012/06/goni-i-trafach.pdf.

"Gouverneur Morris." Engraving by B. B. Ellis, after Eugène Du Simitière. National Portrait Gallery, https://npg.si.edu/object/npg_NPG.75.67.

Grubb, Farley. "The Continental Dollar: How the American Revolution Was Financed with Paper Money." National Bureau of Economic Research, October 2013. www.nber.org/system/files/working_papers/w19577/w19577.pdf.

Gutzman, Kevin. "Edmund Randolph and Virginia Constitutionalism." *The Review of Politics* 66:3 (Summer 2004).

The Hall Manuscripts. Moncure Conway, ed. Thomas Paine Historical Association. thomaspaine .org/pages/resources/the-hall-manuscripts-ed-by-moncure-conway.html.

Hamilton, James. *Reminiscences of James Hamilton.* Charles Scribner and Company, 1869.

Hamilton, John Church. *The Life of Alexander Hamilton.* Halstead and Voorhis, 1834.

"Hamilton on the Louisiana Purchase: A Newly Identified Editorial from the *New-York Evening Post.*" *The William and Mary Quarterly* 12:2, Alexander Hamilton: 1755–1804 (April 1955).

"Harmon Husband." Historical Marker Database. www.hmdb.org/m.asp?m=21568.

Harvey, Doug. *Conscience as a Historical Force: The Liberation Theology of Herman Husband.* Routledge, 2024.

Hawke, David Freeman. "Dr. Thomas Young—Eternal Fisher in Troubled Waters: Notes for a Biography." *New-York Historical Society Quarterly* 64:1 (January 1970).

_____. *In the Midst of a Revolution.* University of Pennsylvania Press, 1961.

_____. *Paine.* Harper and Row, 1974.

Head, David. *A Crisis of Peace: George Washington, the Newburgh Conspiracy, and the Fate of the American Revolution.* Pegasus Books, 2019.

Heimert, Alan. *Religion and the American Mind: From the Great Awakening to the Revolution.* Harvard University Press, 1966.

Heinlein, Jay C. "Albert Gallatin: A Pioneer in Public Administration." *The William and Mary Quarterly* 7:1 (January 1950).

Henderson, Archibald, ed. "Hermon Husband's Continuation (1770) of the Impartial Relation." *North Carolina Historical Review* 18:1 (January 1941).

"Henry Laurens." Charles Pinckney National Historic Site, National Park Service. Updated August 19, 2022. www.nps.gov/chpi/learn/historyculture/henry-laurens.htm.

"Herman Husbands, Regulator." North Carolina Periodical Index. digital.lib.ecu.edu/ncpi/ view/14149.

"Hermon Husband's Continuation of the Impartial Relation." *The North Carolina Historical Review* 18:1 (January 1941).

Hickey, Donald R. "America's Response to the Slave Revolt in Haiti, 1791–1806." *Journal of the Early Republic* 2:4 (Winter 1982).

Hill, Christopher. *The World Turned Upside Down: Radical Ideas During the English Revolution.* Penguin Books, 1984.

Hinderaker, Eric. *Elusive Empires: Constructing Colonialism in the Ohio Valley, 1673–1800.* Cambridge University Press, 2010.

"A History of Boston's Oldest Bank." *Bulletin of the Business Historical Society,* 11:6 (December 1937).

"The History of U.S. Circulating Coins." U.S. Mint. Updated October 27, 2023. www.usmint.gov /learn/history/us-circulating-coins.

Hoerder, Dirk. *Crowd Action in Revolutionary Massachusetts, 1765–1780.* Academic Press, 1977.

Hoffer, Charles Peter. *Rutgers v. Waddington: Alexander Hamilton, the End of the War for Independence, and the Origins of Judicial Review.* University Press of Kansas, 2016.

Hogeland, William. *Autumn of the Black Snake: George Washington, Mad Anthony Wayne, and the Invasion That Opened the West.* Farrar, Straus and Giroux, 2018.

_____. *Declaration: The Nine Tumultuous Weeks When America Became Independent, May 1–July 4, 1776.* Simon and Schuster, 2010.

_____. *The Whiskey Rebellion: George Washington, Alexander Hamilton, and the Frontier Rebels Who Challenged America's Newfound Sovereignty.* Scribner, 2006.

Holt, Wythe. "The New Jerusalem: Herman Husband's Egalitarian Alternative to the United States Constitution." Alabama Law Scholarly Commons, 2010. papers.ssrn.com/sol3/papers .cfm?abstract_id=1547202.

_____. "The Whiskey Rebellion of 1794: A Democratic Working-Class Insurrection." Paper presented at the Georgia Workshop in Early American History and Culture, 2004. Text available at web.archive.org/web/20110925091324/http://www.uga.edu/colonialseminar/whiskeyrebellion-6.pdf.

Holton, Woody. *Forced Founders: Indians, Debtors, Slaves, and the Making of the American Revolution in Virginia.* Omohundro Institute of Early American History and Culture and the University of North Carolina Press, 1999.

_____. *Liberty Is Sweet: The Hidden History of the American Revolution.* Simon and Schuster, 2021.

_____. *Unruly Americans and the Origins of the Constitution.* Hill and Wang, 2007.

Hubbard, Vincent K. *A History of St Kitts: The Sweet Trade.* Macmillan Caribbean, 2002.

Hunter, William A. "John Badollet's 'Journal of the Time I Spent in Stony Creek Glades,' 1793–1794." *The Pennsylvania Magazine of History and Biography* 104:2 (April 1980).

Husband, Herman. "XIV Sermons on the Characters of Jacob's Fourteen Sons." Spotswood, 1789.

_____. "A Dialogue Between an Assembly-Man and a Convention Man." Printed for the author, William Spotswood, s.d.

_____. "Proposals to Amend and Perfect the Policy of the Government." s.n., 1782.

_____. "Sermon to the Bucks and Hinds of America." Printed for the author, 1787.

_____. "Some Remarks on Religion, with the Author's Experience Pursuant Thereof, for the Consideration of All People, Being the Real Truth of What Happened, Simply Delivered, without Help of School-Words or Dress of Learning." William Bradford, 1761.

_____. "To the Inhabitants of North Carolina." *"Shew Yourselves to be Freemen": Herman Husband and the North Carolina Regulators, 1769.* History Matters, George Mason University, his torymatters.gmu.edu/d/6233/#:~:text=To%20the%20INHABITANTS%20of%20the,to%20the%20Apprehension%20of%20it.

Hutchinson, William Thomas. "The Bounty Lands of the Revolution in Ohio." PhD diss., University of Chicago, 1927.

Irwin, Douglas A. "The Aftermath of Hamilton's 'Report on Manufactures." *The Journal of Economic History* 64:3 (September 2004).

Isenberg, Nancy. *Fallen Founder: The Life Aaron Burr.* Viking, 2007.

Jacob, Margaret, and James Jacob, eds. *The Origins of Anglo-American Radicalism.* Allen and Unwin, 1983.

Jacobson, David L. *John Dickinson and the Revolution in Pennsylvania, 1764–1776.* University of California Press, 1965.

James, Alfred P. *The Ohio Company: Its Inner History.* University of Pittsburgh Press, 1959.

"James Cannon: 1740–1782." Penn People, University of Pennsylvania Libraries. archives.upenn.edu/exhibits/penn-people/biography/james-cannon.

"James Wilson's Speech in the State House Yard." Center for the Study of the American Constitution, University of Wisconsin, Madison. archive.csac.history.wisc.edu/17_James_Wilson_Speech_in_the_State_House_Yard.pdf.

Jeffery, Connie. "300 Years of Leadership and Innovation: Sir Robert Walpole, Britain's First 'Prime Minister.'" The History of Parliament, September 14, 2021. thehistoryofparliament.wordpress.com/2021/09/14/300-years-of-leadership-and-innovation-celebrating-robert-walpole-with-the-history-of-parliament-online.

Jennings, Robert M., Donald F. Swanson, and Andrew P. Trout. "Alexander Hamilton's Tontine Proposal." *The William and Mary Quarterly* 45:1 (January 1988).

Jensen, Merrill. *The Founding of a Nation: A History of the American Revolution, 1763–1776.* Hackett Publishing Company, 1968.

_____. "The Idea of a National Government During the American Revolution." *Political Science Quarterly* 58:3 (September 1943).

Johnson, Calvin H. "'Impost Begat Convention': Albany and New York Confront the Ratification of the Constitution." *Albany Law Review,* 2016/2017.

Jones, Mark Haddon. "Herman Husband: Millenarian, Carolina Regulator, and Whiskey Rebel." PhD diss., Northern Illinois University, 1982.

Jones, Robert Francis. *The King of the Alley: William Duer, Politician, Entrepreneur, and Speculator, 1768–1799.* American Philosophical Society, 1992.

Journal of the 64th Council of the City of Washington, 1866–7. Jos. L. Pearson, Printer, 1867.

Journals of the American Congress from 1774–1778. Way and Gideon, 1823.

Kandle, Patricia Lynn. "St. Eustatius: Acculturation in a Dutch Caribbean Colony." MA thesis, College of William and Mary, 1985. scholarworks.wm.edu/cgi/viewcontent.cgi?article=4844&context=etd.

Kars, Marjoleine. *Breaking Loose Together: The Regulator Rebellion in Pre-Revolutionary North Carolina.* University of North Carolina Press, 2002.

Ketcham, Ralph. *James Madison: A Biography.* University of Virginia Press, 1990.

Klein, Philip S., and Ari Hoogenboom. *A History of Pennsylvania.* McGraw Hill, 1973.

Knollenberg, Bernhard. *George Washington: The Virginia Period, 1732–1775.* Duke University Press, 1964.

Koch, Adrienne, and Harry Ammon. "The Virginia and Kentucky Resolutions: An Episode in Jefferson's and Madison's Defense of Civil Liberties." *The William and Mary Quarterly* 5:2 (April 1948).

Kohn, Richard. *Eagle and Sword: The Federalists and the Creation of the Military Establishment in America, 1783–1802.* Free Press, 1975.

———. "The Inside History of the Newburgh Conspiracy: America and the Coup d'Etat." *The William and Mary Quarterly* 27:2 (April 1970).

Kremers, Edward, and George Urdang. *Kremers and Urdang's History of Pharmacy.* Edited by Glenn Sonnedecker. Lippincott, 1976.

Krom, Cynthia L., and Stephanie Krom. "The Whiskey Tax of 1791 and the Consequent Insurrection: A Wicked and Happy Tumult." *Accounting Historians Journal* 40:2 (December 2013).

Kynaston, David. *Till Time's Last Sand: A History of the Bank of England, 1694–2013.* Bloomsbury Press, 2017.

Lane, Carl. "For 'A Positive Profit': The Federal Investment in the First Bank of the United States, 1792–1802." *The William and Mary Quarterly* 54:3 (July 1997).

Larkin, Edward. "The Private Life of Radicalism." *American Literary History* 26:2 (Summer 2014).

Larson, Lauritz. "'Bind the Republic Together': The National Union and the Struggle for a System of Internal Improvements." *The Journal of American History* 74:2 (September 1987).

Lemisch, Jesse. "Are Gilder and Lehrman Tilting American History to the Right? A Case in Point." History News Network, https://historynewsnetwork.org/article/8420.

———. "Jack Tar in the Streets: Merchant Seamen in the Politics of Revolutionary America." *The William and Mary Quarterly* 25:3 (July 1968).

"The Leveller: Or, the Principles and Maxims Concerning Government and Religion, Which Are Asserted by Those That Are Commonly Called Levellers." Printed for Thomas Brewster, the Three Bibles, 1659.

Lincoln, Charles H. *The Revolutionary Movement in Pennsylvania.* University of Pennsylvania, 1901.

Linebaugh, Peter, and Marcus Rediker. *The Many-Headed Hydra: Sailors, Slaves, Commoners, and the Hidden History of the Revolutionary Atlantic.* 2nd ed. Beacon Press, 2013.

Littlefield, Douglas. "The Potomac Company: A Misadventure in Financing an Early American Internal Improvement Project." *The Business History Review* 58:4 (Winter 1984).

"Liverpool, England: 'The European Capital of the Slave Trade.'" *Kreol International Magazine*, January 20, 2017. kreolmagazine.com/culture/history-and-culture/liverpool-england-the-european-capital-of-the-slave-trade-liverpools-ships-transported-1-5-million-slaves-in-the-18th-and-19th-centuries.

"London Coffee House Historical Marker." ExplorePAHistory.com. explorepahistory.com/hmarker .php?markerId=1-A-21.

Lynd, Staughton. "The Compromise of 1787." *Political Science Quarterly* 81:2 (June 1966).

Maclay, William. *Journal of William Maclay: United States Senator from Pennsylvania, 1789–1791.* D. Appleton and Company, 1890.

Madison, James. "Veto Message on the Internal Improvements Bill," March 3, 1817. Text available at Miller Center, University of Virginia. millercenter.org/the-presidency/presidential -speeches/march-3-1817-veto-message-internal-improvements-bill.

Maier, Pauline. *From Resistance to Revolution: Colonial Radicals and the Development of American Opposition to Britain, 1765–1776.* Alfred A. Knopf, 1972.

_____. *Ratification: The People Debate the Constitution, 1787–1788.* Simon and Schuster, 2010.

_____. "Reason and Revolution: The Radicalism of Dr. Thomas Young." *American Quarterly* 28:2, Special Issue: An American Enlightenment (Summer 1976).

Mannix, Richard. "Gallatin, Jefferson, and the Embargo of 1808." *Diplomatic History* 3:2 (Spring 1979).

Manwaring, Kurt. "George Washington and the Newburgh Conspiracy." From the Desk: Learning by Study and Faith, March 10, 2020. www.fromthedesk.org/10-questions-with-david-head/.

Mason, R. Paul. "Neglected Histories: The Cruger Family and the Roots of American Independence." *Journal of the American Revolution.* allthingsliberty.com/2017/04/neglected-histories -cruger-family-roots-american-independence.

May, Gregory. *Jefferson's Treasure: How Albert Gallatin Saved the New Nation from Debt.* Regnery History, 2018.

McCloskey, Dierdre Nansen. "Slavery Did Not Make America Rich." *Reason,* August/September 2018.

McClure, James Patrick. "The Ends of the American Earth: Pittsburgh and Upper Ohio Valley, to 1795." PhD diss., University of Michigan, 1983.

McDevitt, Niall. "Revolting Romantics." *History Today,* April 14, 2021. www.historytoday.com /miscellanies/revolting-romantics.

McDonald, Forrest. *Alexander Hamilton: A Biography.* W. W. Norton and Company, 1979.

Meikle, Henry W. "The King's Birthday Riot in Edinburgh, June, 1792." *The Scottish Historical Review* 7:25 (October 1909).

Meredith, Mark. "William Kerin Constable (1751–1803)." House Histree, July 26, 2021. househis tree.com/people/william-kerin-constable.

Merritt, Keri Leigh. *Masterless Men: Poor Whites and Slavery in the Antebellum South.* Cambridge University Press, 2017.

Middleton, Richard, and Anne Lombard. *Colonial America: A History to 1776.* 4th ed. Wiley-Blackwell, 2011.

Mieszkowski, Jan. "Shelley's Wars, Burke's Revolutions." *Partial Answers: Journal of Literature and the History of Ideas* 20:1 (January 2022). muse.jhu.edu/article/843022.

Mikhail, John. "James Wilson, Early American Land Companies, and the Original Meaning of 'Ex Post Facto Law.'" *The Georgetown Journal of Law and Policy* 17:1 (2019).

Miller, John. *Alexander Hamilton: Portrait in Paradox.* Barnes and Noble Books, 1959.

Miranda, Lin-Manuel. "Alexander Hamilton." *Hamilton: An American Musical (Original Broadway Cast Recording).* Atlantic Records, 2015.

Mitchell, Broadus. *Alexander Hamilton: The National Adventure, 1785–1804.* Macmillan, 1962.

_____. *Alexander Hamilton: The Revolutionary Years.* Thomas Y. Crowell Company, 1970.

_____. *Alexander Hamilton: Youth to Maturity, 1755–1788.* Macmillan, 1957.

Morgan, H. Wayne. "The Origins and Establishment of the First Bank of the United States." *The Business History Review* 30:4 (December 1956).

Morris, Gouverneur. *The Diary and Letters of Gouverneur Morris.* Edited by Anne Cary Morris. Charles Scribner's Sons, 1888.

Morris, Richard B. "Andrew Jackson, Strikebreaker." *The American Historical Review* 55:1 (October 1949).

Mosvick, Nicholas. "Forgotten Founders: James Wilson, Craftsman of the Constitution." *Constitution Daily Blog* (blog), National Constitution Center, July 13, 2020. constitutioncenter.org /blog/forgotten-founders-james-wilson-craftsman-of-the-constitution.

Murray, James. *Sermons to Asses, to Doctors in Divinity, to Lords Spiritual, and to Ministers of State.* William Hone, 1819.

Nash, Gary B. *The Unknown American Revolution: The Unruly Birth of Democracy and the Struggle to Create America.* Penguin Books, 2006.

_____. *The Urban Crucible: The Northern Seaports and the Origins of the American Revolution.* Harvard University Press, 1979.

Nelson, John R. "Alexander Hamilton and American Manufacturing: A Reexamination." *The Journal of American History* 65:4 (March 1979).

Nelson, Paul David. "Horatio Gates at Newburgh, 1783: A Misunderstood Role." *The William and Mary Quarterly* 29:1 (January 1972).

Nelson, Scott Reynolds. *A Nation of Deadbeats: An Uncommon History of America's Financial Disasters.*

Newcombe, Benjamin H. *Franklin and Galloway: A Political Partnership.* Yale University Press, 1972.

Newton, Isaac. *Observations upon the Prophecies of Daniel, and the Apocalypse of St. John.* J. Darby and T. Browne, 1733.

Newton, Michael E. *Alexander Hamilton: The Formative Years.* Eleftheria Publishing, 2015.

_____. *Discovering Hamilton: New Discoveries in the Lives of Alexander Hamilton, His Family, Friends, and Colleagues.* Eleftheria Publishing, 2019.

O'Gorman, Frank. "The Paine Burnings of 1792–1793." *Past and Present* 193:1 (November 2006).

Onuf, Peter S. *Statehood and Union: A History of the Northwest Ordinance.* Notre Dame Press, 1987.

Orszag, Peter R. "Alexander Hamilton Loved Employee Ownership. So Should We." *Bloomberg,* February 22, 2017. www.bloomberg.com/view/articles/2017-02-22/alexander-hamilton-loved -employee-ownership-so-should-we#xj4y7vzkg.

Osgood, Herbert L. "New England Colonial Finance." *Political Science Quarterly* 19:1 (March 1904).

Owen, Kenneth. *Political Community in Revolutionary Pennsylvania, 1774–1800.* Oxford University Press, 2018.

Paine, Thomas. *The Age of Reason: The Definitive Text.* Michigan Legal Publishing, 2014.

_____. *Agrarian Justice.* Benjamin Franklin Bache, 1797. Text available at Thomas Piketty, École des hautes études Sciences Sociale. piketty.pse.ens.fr/files/Paine1795.pdf.

_____. *The American Crisis, 1776–83.* Text available at American History: From the Revolution to Reconstruction and Beyond. www.let.rug.nl/usa/documents/1776-1785/thomas-paine -american-crisis/index.php.

_____. *Common Sense.* R. Bell, 1776. Text available at Online Library of Liberty. oll.libertyfund .org/page/1776-paine-common-sense-pamphlet.

_____. "Retreat Across the Delaware." *The Pennsylvania Journal,* January 29, 1777. Text available at Thomas Paine National Historical Association. www.thomaspaine.org/works/works-removed -from-the-paine-canon/retreat-across-the-delaware.html.

_____. *Rights of Man.* J. Johnson, 1791–92. Text available at American History: From the Revolution to Reconstruction and Beyond. www.let.rug.nl/usa/documents/1786-1800/thomas-paine -the-rights-of-man/text.php.

_____. "To the Printer of the Pennsylvania Packet." *Pennsylvania Packet,* October 16, 1779. Text available at Thomas Paine National Historical Association. www.thomaspaine.org/works /recently-discovered/to-the-printer-of-the-pennsylvania-packet.html.

_____. *Writings,* Vol. 3. Edited by Moncure Daniel Conway. G. P. Putnam's Sons, 1894.

Paul, C. Kegan. *William Godwin: His Friends and Contemporaries*, Vol. 1. Henry S. King and Company, 1876.

Peabody, Bruce G. "George Washington, Presidential Term Limits, and the Problem of Reluctant Political Leadership." *Presidential Studies Quarterly* 31:3 (September 2001).

Pencak, William. "Samuel Adams and Shays's Rebellion." *The New England Quarterly* 62:1 (March 1989).

Pencak, William, Matthew Dennis, and Simon P. Newman. *Riot and Revelry in Early America*. Pennsylvania State University Press, 2002.

Pendergrast, Mark. *Uncommon Grounds: The History of Coffee and How It Transformed Our World*. Basic Books, 2010.

"The Pennsylvania Assembly, Friday, 28 September 1787." Text available at Center for the Study of the American Constitution, University of Wisconsin, Madison. csac.history.wisc.edu/wp-content/uploads/sites/281/2017/07/pennsylvania_assembly_28sept.pdf.

Peterson, Merrill. *The Jefferson Image in the American Mind*. Rev. ed. University of Virginia Press, 1998.

Philyaw, L. Scott. *Virginia's Western Visions: Political and Cultural Expansion on an Early American Frontier*. University of Tennessee Press, 2004.

Pirro, J. F. "The (Somewhat) Secret History of the Oldest Social Club in America." *Main Line Today*, August 29, 2016, mainlinetoday.com/life-style/the-somewhat-secret-history-of-the-oldest-social-club-in-america.

"The Plantation System of the British West Indies." The San Lauretia Project, University of Glasgow. runaways.gla.ac.uk/minecraft/index.php/the-plantation-system-of-the-british-west-indies/.

Potter, Claire, and Renee Romano, eds. *Historians on Hamilton: How a Blockbuster Musical Is Restaging America's Past*. Rutgers University Press, 2018.

Price, Jacob M. "What Did Merchants Do? Reflections on British Overseas Trade, 1660–1790." *The Journal of Economic History* 49:2 (June 1989).

"The Proposed Impost of 1783 (and Alexander Hamilton's Famous New York Assembly Speech)." *Statutes and Stories* (blog), September 16, 2021. www.statutesandstories.com/blog_html/the-proposed-impost-of-1783-and-hamiltons-famous-new-york-assembly-speech.

The Public Statutes at Large of the United States of America, Vol. 1. Richard Peters, ed. Charles C. Little and James Brown, 1845.

"The Putney Debates" (October 28, 1647). In Sir William Clarke, *Puritanism and Liberty, Being the Army Debates (1647–9) from the Clarke Manuscripts with Supplementary Documents*, ed. A. S. P. Woodhouse, part 1 (University of Chicago Press, 1951). Text available at Online Library of Liberty. oll.libertyfund.org/page/1647-the-putney-debates.

Rakove, Jack. *James Madison and the Creation of the American Republic*. Pearson, 2006.

Randolph, Edmund. *A Vindication of Edmund Randolph, Written by Himself and Published in 1795*. C. H. Wynne, 1855.

Rappaport, Erika. *A Thirst for Empire: How Tea Shaped the Modern World*. Princeton University Press, 2019.

Rappleye, Charles. *Robert Morris: Financier of the American Revolution*. Simon and Schuster, 2011.

Rasmussen, Dennis C. *The Constitution's Penman: Gouverneur Morris and the Creation of America's Basic Charter*. University Press of Kansas, 2023.

"Rednap Howell." *North Carolina Regulator Movement* (blog). regulatormovement.wordpress.com/rednap-howell.

Richards, Leonard. *Shays's Rebellion: The American Revolution's Final Battle*. University of Pennsylvania Press, 2003.

Richardson, David. "The Slave Trade, Sugar, and British Economic Growth, 1748–1776." *The Journal of Interdisciplinary History* 17:4 (Spring 1987).

Ringwalt, J. Luther. *Development of Transportation Systems in the United States*. Published for the author, 1888.

Ritcheson, C. R. "The Earl of Shelbourne and Peace with America, 1782–1783: Vision and Reality." *The International History Review* 5:3 (August 1983).

"Robert Morris." Descendants of the Signers of the Declaration of Independence, 2008. www .dsdi1776.com/signer/robert-morris.

Roberts, Russell. "Hamilton's Great Experiment: The Society for Establishing Useful Manufactures." *Financial History*, Issue 65 (1999).

Rosswurm, Steven. *Arms, Country, and Class: The Philadelphia Militia and the Lower Sort During the American Revolution.* Rutgers University Press, 1989.

Rothman, Rozann. "Political Method in the Federal System: Albert Gallatin's Contribution." *Publius* 1:2 (Winter 1972).

Rudé, George F. E. *The Crowd in History: A Study of Popular Disturbances in France and England, 1730–1848.* Lawrence and Wishart, 1981.

Ryerson, Richard Alan. *The Revolution Is Now Begun: The Radical Committees of Philadelphia, 1765–1776.* University of Pennsylvania Press, 1978.

Sakolski, A. M. *The Great American Land Bubble: The Amazing Story of Land-Grabbing, Speculations, and Booms from Colonial Days to the Present Time.* Johnson, 1966.

Schöpf, Johann David. *Travels in the Confederation, 1783–1784.* Translated and edited by Alfred James Morrison. William J. Campbell, 1911.

"Secretary of the Treasury's Office Site." The Historical Marker Database. www.hmdb.org/m .asp?m=106745.

Selsam, Paul J. *The Pennsylvania Constitution of 1776: A Study in Revolutionary Democracy.* University of Pennsylvania Press, 1936.

Serfilippi, Jessie. "As Odious and Immoral a Thing: Alexander Hamilton's Hidden History as an Enslaver." Schuyler Mansion State Historic Site, 2020.

"1776 Maryland $1/9 One-Ninth of a Dollar Colonial Currency Note—August 14th, 1776." Pristine Auction. www.pristineauction.com/a1305116-1776-Maryland-19-One-Ninth-of-a-Dollar -Colonial-Currency-Note-August-14th-1776.

Shy, John W. *A People Numerous and Armed: Reflections on the Military Struggle for American Independence.* University of Michigan Press, 1990.

Simcoe, John. *Remarks on the Travels of Marquis de Chastellux in North America.* G. and T. Wilkie, 1787.

Slaughter, Thomas P. *The Whiskey Rebellion: Frontier Epilogue to the American Revolution.* Oxford University Press, 1988.

Slonimsky, Nora. "James A. Hamilton: Mousetraps, Memory and a Forgotten Secretary of State." *NYPL Blog* (blog), New York Public Library, December 22, 2012. www.nypl.org/blog/2012/12 /22/hamilton-mousetraps-memory-and-forgotten-secretary-state.

Smelser, Marshall. "George Washington and the Alien and Sedition Acts." *The American Historical Review* 59:2 (January 1954).

Smith, Barbara Clark. "Food Rioters and the American Revolution." *The William and Mary Quarterly* 51:1 (January 1994).

_____. *The Freedoms We Lost: Consent and Resistance in Revolutionary America.* New Press, 2010.

Smith, Billy G. ed. *Down and Out in Early America.* Pennsylvania State University Press, 2010.

_____. *The Lower Sort: Philadelphia's Laboring People, 1750–1800.* Cornell University Press, 1990.

Smith, C. Page. "The Attack on Fort Wilson." *The Pennsylvania Magazine of History and Biography* 78:2 (April 1954).

_____. *James Wilson: Founding Father, 1742–1798.* Omohundro Institute of Early American History and Culture and the University of North Carolina Press, 1956.

Smith, Ryan K. "The 'Mad' Engineer: L'Enfant in Early National Philadelphia." *The Pennsylvania Magazine of History and Biography* 138:3 (July 2014).

Soderlund, Jean R. "Colonial Era." *The Encyclopedia of Greater Philadelphia*, 2017. philadelphia encyclopedia.org/time-periods/colonial-philadelphia.

Sommer, Joseph H. "The Birth of the American Business Corporation: Of Banks, Corporate Governance, and Social Responsibility." *Buffalo Law Review* 49:3 (Fall 2001).

"Spanish Milled Dollar." *Columbia Gazette*. www.columbiagazette.com/smd.htm.

"Speech of Patrick Henry (June 7, 1788)." American History: From the Revolution to Reconstruction and Beyond. www.let.rug.nl/usa/documents/1786-1800/the-anti-federalist-papers/speech -of-patrick-henry-(june-7-1788).php.

Stevens, John Austin. *Albert Gallatin*. Houghton Mifflin and Company, 1884.

Stevenson, Dru. "Revisiting the Original Congressional Debates About the Second Amendment." *Missouri Law Review* 88:2, Article 9 (Spring 2023).

Stewart, Bruce E. *Redemption from Tyranny: Herman Husband's American Revolution*. University of Virginia Press, 2020.

Stock, Catherine McNicol. *Rural Radicals: Righteous Rage in the American Grain*. Cornell University Press, 2017.

Stoller, Matt. *Goliath: The 100-Year War Between Monopoly Power and Democracy*. Simon and Schuster, 2020.

Sullivan, Nancy. "The Delaware and Schuylkill Canal Navigation." Historical Society of Montgomery County, August 31, 2017. hsmcpa.org/index.php/component/k2/item/41-the-delaware -and-schuylkill-canal-navigation.

Sung Bok Kim. "Impact of Class Relations and Warfare in the American Revolution: The New York Experience." *Journal of American History* 69:2 (1982).

Swanson, Donald F., and Andrew P. Trout. "Alexander Hamilton, 'the Celebrated Mr. Neckar,' and Public Credit." *The William and Mary Quarterly* 47:3 (July 1990).

_____. "Alexander Hamilton, Conversion, and Debt Reduction." *Explorations in Economic History* 29:4 (October 1992).

_____. "Alexander Hamilton's Hidden Sinking Fund." *The William and Mary Quarterly* 49:1 (January 1992).

Sweeney, Patrick. "Tom Paine's Bridge." Republican Socialists, 2017. www.republicansocialists.org .uk/tom-paine.php.

Sword, Wiley. *President Washington's Indian War: The Struggle for the Old Northwest, 1790–1795*. University of Oklahoma Press, 1993.

Sylla, Richard. "Financial Foundations: Public Credit, the National Bank, and Securities Markets." In Douglas Irwin and Richard Sylla, eds. *Founding Choices: American Economic Policy in the 1790s*. University of Chicago Press, 2010. Text available at National Bureau of Economic Research, www.nber.org/system/files/chapters/c11737/c11737.pdf.

Sylla, Richard, Robert E. Wright, and David J. Cowen. "Alexander Hamilton, Central Banker: Crisis Management During the U.S. Financial Panic of 1792." *The Business History Review* 83:1 (Spring 2009).

Szatmary, David P. *Shays' Rebellion: The Making of an Agrarian Insurrection*. University of Massachusetts Press, 1980.

"The Tea Habit and the Dramatic Increase in British Sugar Consumption in the 17th and 18th Centuries." *Chocolate Class: Multimedia Essays on Chocolate, Culture, and the Politics of Food*, chocolateclass.wordpress.com/2018/03/07/the-tea-habit-and-the-dramatic-increase-in-british -sugar-consumption-in-the-17th-and-18th-centuries/.

Thompson, E. P. *Customs in Common: Studies in Traditional Popular Culture*. New Press, 1993.

_____. *The Making of the English Working Class*. Vintage, 1966.

_____. *Whigs and Hunters: The Origin of the Black Act*. Pantheon Books, 1975.

Tigner, Amy. "Chocolate in Seventeenth-Century England, Part I." The Recipes Project, September 1, 2013. recipes.hypotheses.org/711.

"Timothy Matlack: c. 1730–1829." Penn People, University of Pennsylvania Libraries. archives .upenn.edu/exhibits/penn-people/biography/timothy-matlack.

Tolles, Frederick B. *Meeting House and Counting House: The Quaker Merchants of Colonial Phila-*

delphia, 1682–1763. 1948. Reprint; Omohundro Institute of Early American History and Culture and the University of North Carolina Press, 2011.

Toogood, Anna Coxe. *Historic Resource Study, Independence Mall: The 18th Century Development, Block One, Chestnut to Market, Fifth to Sixth Streets.* Independence National Historic Park Publications, 2001.

Troxler, Carole Watterson. *Farming Dissenters: The Regulator Movement in Piedmont North Carolina.* North Carolina Office of Archives and History, 2011.

Turgeon, Julia. "Industrialization and the Need for Child Labor." EnCompass: A Digital Archive of Rhode Island History. library.providence.edu/encompass/rhode-island-and-the-industrial-revolution/primary-sources/child-laborers/.

Van Sickle, Eugene. "Financing the War of 1812." Bandy Heritage Center, Dalton State College. www.bandyheritagecenter.org/Content/Uploads/Bandy%20Heritage%20Center/files/1812/Financing%20the%20War%20of%201812.pdf.

Ver Steeg, Clarence L. *Robert Morris: Revolutionary Financier.* Printed for the American Historical Association by the University of Pennsylvania Press, 1954.

Veru, Peter Theodore. "The French Bonds: The Little-Known Bidding War for France's Holdings in American Debt, 1786–1790." *Financial History Review* 28:2 (August 2021).

Walters, Raymond. *Albert Gallatin: Jeffersonian Financier and Diplomat.* University of Pittsburgh Press, 1957.

———. "The Origins of the Second Bank of the United States." *Journal of Political Economy* 53:1 (June 1945).

"The War of 1812: Economic Performance Index." 5 Minute Economist, 2016. 5minuteeconomist .com/history/1812-1815-the-war-of-1812.html.

Whittenburg, James P. "'The Common Farmer (Number 2)': Herman Husband's Plan for Peace between the United States and the Indians, 1792." *The William and Mary Quarterly* 34:4 (October 1977).

Wilder, Craig Steven. *Ebony and Ivy: Race, Slavery, and the Troubled History of America's Universities.* Bloomsbury Press, 2014.

Wilentz, Sean. *The Rise of American Democracy: Jefferson to Lincoln.* W. W. Norton, 2006.

Williams, Ian. *Rum: A Social and Sociable History of the Real Spirit of 1776.* Bold Type Books, 2006.

Wills, Garry. *Inventing America: Jefferson's Declaration of Independence.* Vintage Books, 1979.

———. *Lincoln at Gettysburg: The Words That Remade America.* Simon and Schuster, 1992.

Winstanley, Gerrard. *The Law of Freedom and Other Writings.* Cambridge University Press, 1983.

Wootton, David, ed. *Divine Right and Democracy: An Anthology of Political Writing in Stuart England.* Hackett Publishing Company, 2003.

Wright, Robert E. *One Nation Under Debt: Hamilton, Jefferson, and the History of What We Owe.* McGraw Hill, 2008.

Young, Alfred, and Gregory Nobles. *Whose American Revolution Was It? Historians Interpret the Founding.* NYU Press, 2011.

Zahedieh, Nuala. "Making Mercantilism Work: London Merchants and Atlantic Trade in the Seventeenth Century." *Transactions of the Royal Historical Society,* Vol. 9 (1999).

ACKNOWLEDGMENTS

Thanks to Alex Star for invaluable depth in reading and judgment in editing, and to Ian Van Wye and everybody at Farrar, Straus and Giroux whose seemingly endless reserves of imagination, diligence, and patience have made this book what it is.

Thanks to Eric Lupfer for encouragement and guidance, yet again, from conception through fruition.

Thanks to Daniel Bergner for, among other things, humor and support in navigating the storm summed up for me in the words *Hamilton: An American Musical*. What a funny and inspiring irony that without the phenomenal impact of that show—I acknowledge my gratitude to it, too—I never would have written this book.

Thanks, as always, and forever, to my family.

Thanks to: Doug Harvey for sharing his transcript, far more thorough and careful than mine, of Herman Husband's handwritten work; Karie Diethorn and Deborah Miller for insights into probable goings-on in eighteenth-century deliberative bodies; Ian Mumpton for insights into the Schuylers' world; John Bell for sources on the pronunciation of "Gouverneur" and, with David Hurwitz, an on-the-fly historiography of Paine on Evacuation Day; Katherine Patterson and Anna Plumlee for sending me after primary sources on Paine and George Washington's coat; Claire Potter and Renee Russo for including me among historians writing on *Hamilton* the play; Robert Sullivan for making me a source on Hamilton the person (and thereby getting me on Page Six); the staffs of the archives and libraries I cite, most recently the Detre Library and Archives at the Heinz History Center and the Archives and Special Collections of the University of Pittsburgh Library; and literally everybody who worked in the New York Public Library's Milstein Division in the 2000s.

Alexander Hamilton and Herman Husband: Hail and farewell, my brothers. We'll always have the summer of '03.

And thanks especially to my earlier books' readers—not the world's largest readership, maybe, but surely the world's most discerning. Only you will know how fully I've built this book on twenty years of storytelling. Without your hearing, the telling wouldn't exist.

INDEX

abolition movement, 94
Adams, Abigail, 347
Adams, Charles Francis, 407
Adams, John, 97–98, 140, 284, 296,
    421; Alien and Sedition Acts under,
    350–51; election to presidency,
    345–46; hatred of Hamilton, A.,
    349–50; Massachusetts constitution
    written by, 165; reaction to
    Pennsylvania constitution, 101–102;
    as vice-presidential candidate, 195
Adams, John Quincy, 397–98, 407
Adams, Samuel, 93, 97–98, 124, 425,
    450n
Age of Reason, The (Paine), 326
agrarian class: in anti-corporatism
    movement, 161; on Public Debt,
    208; as State Sovereigntists, 214–15
agriculture, in U.S.: diversified farms,
    233; subsistence farming, 7; tenant
    families on farms/plantations, 7, 22
Alien and Sedition Acts, U.S.,
    350–51, 380
American Atlantic colonies: resistance
    to colonial trade acts in, 87–88;
    riots in, 85; voting rights in, 79;
    see also American Revolution;

independence movement; War of
    Independence
American Crisis, The (Paine), 141–43
American Ethnological Society, 397
Americanism, 425
American Philosophical Society, 31
American Recovery and Reinvestment
    Act, U.S. (2009), 423
American Revolution: big commerce
    linked with, 39; early foundations
    of, 19; Great Awakening and, 72;
    Husband, H., on, 104; as moral
    response, 100, 165; Paine on, 144;
    protests against Stamp Act, 34;
    War of Independence and, 22;
    working people as foundation of, 90
American West: Bank of North
    America and, 159; confederation
    of Native nations in, 150;
    Continentalists and, 150; East-
    West divide and, 153; enslaved
    persons in, 155; exploration of,
    369; Gallatin in, 265–66; land
    claims in, 152; land grants in, 150;
    land squatters in, 155–59, 163;
    Millers Run, 155–56, 158–59;
    Northwest Territory, 150; paper

American West (*cont.*)
currency in, 159; public perception
of westerners, 153; Seceders
in, 156; Seven Years' War, 156;
startup companies for, 150; State
Sovereigntists and, 150, 163;
Washington, G., land claims in,
148–49, 152, 157; Westsylvania,
153–54, 157; white expansion in,
150
Ames, Fisher, 197, 211, 214–15, 244
Annapolis, Maryland, congressional
convention in, 164–65
anti-corporatism movement,
160–61
Antifederalists, 192–93, 243–44, 474n;
on amendments to Constitution,
253–54; Gallatin and, 266;
Husband, H., and, 254; on
presidency, 195–96
anti-slavery beliefs: of Hamilton,
A., 7, 22, 41, 419; of Husband, H.,
80; of Morris, G., 114; of Paine,
92–93
army pay, 63, 122, 128; federal pension
and, 129; Public Debt and, 129;
raise in amount, 135–36
army pay certificates, 208
Arnold, Benedict, 107–108
Articles of Confederation, 19, 453n;
amendments of, 171; bank charters
under, 48; Continentalists on the
weaknesses of, 157; federal tax and,
116; Gallatin on weaknesses of,
336; Hamilton, A., on weaknesses
of, 182; imposts under, 133; Morris,
R., on weaknesses of, 182; review of,
164–65; three-fifths compromise in,
189–90
asceticism, 81
Astor, John-Jacob, 388–89, 392, 397
Atlantic world, 8, 77; *see also*
American Atlantic colonies
Atlas, Charles, 395, 411, 415, 490n

Baltimore, Maryland, 39
banking systems, banks and:
centralized, 45; congressional
power over, 48; decentralization of,
382; under Federal Reserve Act,
410; Jackson, J., criticism of, 243;
in Massachusetts, 239; Morris,
R., support of, 245–46; under
National Banking Act of 1863, 408;
nationalization of, 239; Paine as
advocate for, 161–62; Schuyler, P.,
support of, 245–46; Senate support
for, 242–43; solvency of, 282–84;
State Sovereigntists and, 48; in
U.S., 48–49; *see also specific banks*
Bank of England, 46–47, 57, 438n
Bank of New York, 239; Duer and,
282–83; Hamilton, A., and, 239,
241, 273, 277, 284; paper scrip
market and, 273; SUM and, 277;
threat of collapse for, 283
Bank of North America: American
West and, 159; charter
removal, 159, 161–62, 175, 194,
292; Congress and, 50, 138;
Continentalism supported by, 54;
initial capitalization of, 47, 49;
Madison opposition to, 243; Morris,
G., and, 115; Morris, R., and,
159–60; Pennsylvania charter of,
138; Public Debt and, 65; recharter
of, 193; state currency and, 52; War
of Independence and, 52; Wilson, J.,
and, 159–60, 193
Bank of Stephen Girard, 383
Bank of the United States, 241, 364;
closure of, 383; constitutionality of,
243–44; Duer and, 282–83; Gallatin
and, 381–82; Madison's opposition
to, 243–44; in Philadelphia, 245,
248; public infrastructure projects
funded by, 242; scrip for, 281; threat
of collapse, 283; Willing and, 48,
345, 381

bankruptcy acts, establishment of, 359
Baring, Alexander, 364
Battle of Alamance, 88, 91, 102, 110, 261
Battle of Concord, 35
Battle of Fort Wilson, 112, 194
Battle of Lexington, 35
Battle of Saratoga, 107
Battle of Yorktown, 49, 59, 315
Beekman, David, 16
Beekman and Cruger, 16–18
Berkshires farmers, 166–67
Bettering House, 95
Blake, William, 293–94, 297
Bonaparte, Napoleon, 347, 373
bonds: Continental currency and, 57–59, 208; interest-bearing government bonds, 55–56; interest payments on, 207; interest rates for, 201–202; for Louisiana Territory purchase, 370; in Massachusetts, 166; in Pennsylvania, 162–63; war bonds, 57–59
Book of Daniel, 69–70, 76, 82, 146
Book of Ezekiel, 82–83, 146, 252
Book of Genesis, 83
Book of Matthew, 82
Book of Nehemiah, 83
Book of Revelation, 71, 78
Boudinot, Elias, 211–12
Bowers, Claude, 413
Brackenridge, Hugh Henry, 318–20
Braddock, Edward, 20
Bradford, David, 303, 310, 312, 314, 318, 320–21
Bradford, William, 308, 310, 312, 338
Brandeis, Louis (Justice), 410, 490n
Bretton Woods System, 10
Britain: Bank of England, 46–47; cession of western lands to U.S., 149; Civil War in, 72; excises in, 210; House of Commons, 178; House of Lords in, 178; labor agitation in, 84; *Leopard* maritime

conflict, 373; Lord of Treasury in, 42; Magna Carta in, 73; reduction of national debt, 208; religious sects in, 72–75, 97, 99; treaty-in-principle with U.S., 120, 122; Treaty of Amity, Commerce, and Navigation, 338–40, 342; U.S declaration of war with, 374; U.S. Embargo Act of 1807 and, 374–78; War of 1812 and, 386–88, 390, 392, 397; see also British Empire
British East India Company, 17, 432n
British Empire: in Caribbean region, 13–15; public debt philosophy of, 55
Brodie, Fawn, 418
Brookhiser, Richard, 418
Brooks, David, 418
Bryan, William Jennings, 412–13, 415
Burke, Aedanus, 213–14
Burke, Edmund, 293, 295–96
Burr, Aaron, 295, 352
Bush, George W., 420

Calhoun, John C., 380, 390, 489n; white supremacist theory of slavery, 401–402, 404
Calvin, John, 263
Calvinism: for Gallatin, 263–64; Great Awakening and, 71–72, 74, 81; Husband, H., and, 71
Cannon, James, 9, 94–96, 100, 139, 300, 425
Caribbean region: British colonies in, 13–15; British East India Company and, 17; forced exports to Britain, 14; rebellion in Haiti, 348; see also *specific islands*
Carlyle, Thomas, 483n
Carnegie, Andrew, 409
Carpenter, Mary, 22
Carter, Jimmy, 420
Catullus, 322

Charles I (king), 72
Chase, Salmon, 408
Chernow, Ron, 419
Cherokee Nation, 304
child labor, 232
China, New York trade with, 201
Clark, William, 369
Clay, Henry, 380, 382, 390, 397,
    398–99, 410, 489n
Clinton, George, 26, 170, 383; as
    Antifederalist, 193; as State
    Sovereigntist, 52, 117
Clinton, William Jefferson, 420
colonial trade acts, 87–88
Committee of Privates, 96, 98, 109,
    300
"Common Sense" (Paine), 100–101,
    111, 140, 143, 256, 292
Congress, U.S., 9; Articles of
    Confederation and, 19; assumption
    of state debt, 65–66, 216; Bank
    of North America and, 50, 138;
    British constitution as inspiration
    for, 179; as check on executive
    power, 343; Committee on Ways
    and Means, 343; 1800 presidential
    election decided by, 355–57;
    evacuation from Philadelphia,
    136; Federalist majority in,
    197–98, 211–12; lawmaking
    power of, 25–26; military policy
    consolidation in, 183–84; move
    to Princeton, 144; mutiny against,
    137; non-importation boycott and,
    37; Paine on representative system,
    188; power to establish banks, 48;
    Reconciliationists in, 97; relocation
    of, 164; Republican Party majority
    in, 335; state representation issues
    for, 187–88; see also Continental
    Congress; specific members of
    Congress
Congress of Industrial Organizations,
    412

Constable William, 201, 204
Constitution, U.S.: amendments
    to, 257; Antifederalists and,
    253–54; debating of, 187; direct
    taxation in, 190–91; executive
    branch created by, 190; financial
    institutions established through,
    191; Fourteenth Amendment, 10;
    government structure in, 251–52;
    Hamiltonian, 5; in Hamilton
    Scheme, 175–94, 246; judicial
    branch created by, 190; Louisiana
    Territory purchase and, 368;
    monetary institutions established
    through, 191; paper currency in,
    191; preamble, 192; redrafting
    of, 187; slavery in, 186; state-
    by-state ratification of, 192–94;
    state population counts and,
    186–88; structural components
    of, 190; three-fifths compromise
    in, 189–90; see also Articles of
    Confederation
Constitutional Convention of 1787,
    251
Continental Army: army pay
    grievances, 63, 122, 128;
    disbanding of, 122–23, 168;
    Hamilton, A., in, 20; military
    takeover threats by, 123–24;
    as public creditor of U.S., 122;
    public debt to, 122–23; retreat of,
    141; state debt and, 61–62; under
    Washington, G., 19–20, 36–37
Continental Congress: under Articles
    of Confederation, 19; Articles of
    Confederation amendments in,
    175–76; formation of republic in,
    181–82; Morris, R., as delegate, 35,
    104; in Philadelphia, 34–35; secret
    caucus at, 176; State Sovereigntists
    at, 176–77; War of Independence
    and, 56–59; Washington, G., as
    delegate, 35

Continental currency, 41, 202, 437n; depreciation of, 58; federal bonds and, 208; war bonds and, 57–59; War of Independence and, 57–59
Continentalists, Continentalism and, 25, 90, 434n; American West and, 150; Bank of North America and, 54; centralization of governance as foundation for, 130; centralized banking system and, 45; on consolidated government, 64; expansion of, 54; failure of, 133; Hamilton, A., and, 66; incremental pace of, 26; merchant-crony, 282
Coolidge, Calvin, 396
corporations, 438n; anti-corporatism movement, 160–61; banks as, 46; monopolies by, 260
Coxe, Tench, 223–24, 231, 246–47, 270
Craigie, Andrew, 201, 204
Creek Nation, 304
Croly, Herbert, 410
Cromwell, Oliver, 73–74, 96–97
Cruger, Nicholas, 16
currencies: Continental, 41, 202, 437n; the Democracy and, 105; depreciation of, 106; gold and silver coins as, 32, 51, 64; hard money, 32, 46; Spanish silver dollar, 32; state, 52; whiskey as, 230; see also bonds; paper currency; paper scrip

Dallas, Alexander, 391
Deane, Silas, 40–41, 142
Dearborn, Henry, 362
debt courts, 165
debt trials, 165
Declaration of Independence: adoption of, 175; Dickinson and, 38; Jefferson drafting of, 99; passage of, 98–99; social radicals and, 403

Deforgues, François, 306–307
Delaware Nation, 9, 20; in Northwest Territory, 150, 257
democracy, democracies and: binary approaches to, 7–8; oligarchy compared to, 4
the Democracy, 448n; American independence and, 91; American revolution and, 90; Hamilton, A., eradication of, 311; paper currency issued under, 105; suppression of, 111
Democratic Party, establishment of, 402
Dickinson, John, 35–36, 96, 437n; Declaration of Independence and, 38
Diggers, 72–73, 75
direct elections, 189–90
direct taxation policies, 190–91, 348–49, 464n
distilling industry: boom, 229–31; costs and margins in, 230; Federalists and, 228; industrial approach to, 233–34; landless laborers and, 230; markets for, 230; micro-industrialization of, 230–31; national enforcement system for, 236; by Neville, 259; as people's currency, 230; registration requirements for, 235; tax rates for, 234–35
Duane, James, 27–28, 45, 53, 239
Duane, William, 380
Duer, William, 205, 247; bank stocks and, 282–83; Knox and, 281; public infrastructure projects and, 281; public response to, 286–87; repayment claims against, 286; Six Percent Club, 281–82; SUM and, 270, 277, 289
duties, see import duties; tonnage duties

Eaton, John, 405
1800 presidential election: Burr and,
    352–53; certification process for,
    354–55; congressional vote on,
    355–57; electors during, 355;
    Jefferson and, 352–57
elections: Adams, J., 345–46;
    congressional, 120, 331; direct,
    189–90; 1800 presidential election,
    352–57; for Gallatin, 332; 1796
    presidential election, 345–46
electoral systems: direct, 189–90
Emancipation Proclamation, 10
Embargo Act of 1807, U.S., 374, 488n;
    economic effects of, 375–76; repeal
    of, 377–78
enslaved persons: in American West,
    155; Hamilton, A., and ownership
    of, 7; Jefferson and ownership of, 7;
    in Philadelphia, 31; in rice
    production, 41; Schuyler, P., as
    owner of, 21–22; white responses
    to, 9
Equal Rights Party, 10
Equiano, Olaudah, 74, 445n
Eustis, William, 386
excise taxes: compliance with, 262; in
    Britain, 210; Findley's opposition
    to, 384–85; Madison's criticism
    of, 240; national response to, 240;
    Neville and, 258–59, 261–62;
    protests against, 285; unpopularity
    of, 210, 240; see also whiskey,
    excise on
executive branch, under U.S.
    Constitution: Congress as check
    on power of, 343; creation of,
    190, 192; see also presidency, U.S.;
    specific presidents

Fallon, Jimmy, 428
Familist sect, 72, 75
Farmer-Labor Party, 412

farms, farming and: diversified, 233;
    subsistence, 7
Faulkner, William, 302–303
federal debt, See Public Debt
Federalist Papers, The (Madison and
    Hamilton, A.), 193, 243–44, 336,
    340
Federalist Party: anti-French
    sentiment within, 347–48, 350;
    Gallatin targeted by, 332, 346–47,
    364; on Jay Treaty, 339–40; Senate
    majority for, 335, 338
Federalists, 192, 442n, 453n; in
    Congress, 197–98; in Pennsylvania,
    218; Republican Party as opposition
    to, 260; skeptical, 217; on whiskey
    production, 228; see also
    Antifederalists
Federal Reserve Act, U.S. (1913), 410
federal taxation, 113; under
    Articles of Confederation, 116–17;
    bondholders paid through, 117–18;
    funding of public creditors through,
    127; imposts and, 184; Morris, R.,
    support for, 171; for Public Debt,
    64–66; state-apportionment model,
    116–17; tax collectors for, 125
federal taxation policies, 209
Fifth Monarchy Men, 72
final settlement, 198–99
Findley, William, 9, 158–60, 162,
    193–94, 239, 269, 286; accusation
    as insurrectionist leader, 323; arrest
    of, 311; election to Congress, 331;
    opponent of Morris, R., 276,
    425; opposition to excises, 384–85;
    opposition to whiskey excise,
    287–88, 301, 312, 319–22;
    Redstone Old Fort meetings
    and, 274
Fitzsimons, Thomas, 126, 197, 211–12,
    218, 223, 469n
Fort Lee, evacuation of, 141
Fort Pitt, 236, 257

Fourteenth Amendment, U.S.
Constitution, 10
France: Bonaparte rule in, 347; French
Revolution in, 293, 294, 306–309,
322, 324–26; funding of American
War of Independence, 56, 58;
Gallatin appointment as U.S.
ambassador to, 397; Jay Treaty as
attack on, 347; Napoleonic Wars,
373; new patriotism in, 322; Paine
jailed in, 324, 326; rebellion in
Haiti, 348; revolution in, 293–94;
the Terror in, 306, 322, 326; U.S
declaration of war with, 374; U.S.
Embargo Act of 1807 and, 374–78
Franklin, Benjamin, 31, 33, 58, 99,
121; at Continental Congress, 176;
Society of Honest Whigs and, 92
Frazier, James Earl, 395
Freeman, Joanne B., 428
French Revolution, 293; Gallatin's
response to, 332–33; Marat and,
306–307; Robespierre and, 306,
324–25; the Terror and, 306, 322;
U.S. public sympathy for, 308–309;
Washington, G., attitude toward,
294
French Revolution, The (Carlyle), 483n
Frick, Henry Clay, 409

Gallatin, Albert, 6, 8, 286, 415,
425; accusation as insurrectionist
leader, 323; and Alien and
Sedition Acts, 350; American
Dream of, 337; in American West,
265–66; Antifederalism and,
266; apology for signing radical
resolutions, 332–33; appointment
as U.S. ambassador to France, 397;
approach to fiscal responsibility,
341; arrests of, 311; attitude toward
Hamilton's system, 361; Bank of
the United States and, 381–82;

calls for congressional oversight,
346; as Calvinist, 263–64; on
direct taxation policies, 348–49;
early life of, 263–64; election to
Pennsylvania state assembly, 332;
emigration to U.S., 264; Federalist
Party targeting of, 332, 346–47,
364; fiscal projections of, 377;
founding of New York University, 397; Husband, H., compared
to, 268, 335; import taxes under,
385–86; infrastructure projects,
372–73, 376; Jefferson and, 340,
345–46; Madison and, 340;
marriages of, 266, 317; on military
appropriations, 343, 366, 378;
opposition to Alien and Sedition
Acts, 380; Public Debt under, 390;
Redstone Old Fort meetings and,
269, 274; in Republican Party,
316–17, 332; tariffs on foreign
goods under, 371; on taxation,
341–42; in Treasury Department,
360–62; and U.S. Constitution,
336; War of 1812 and, 386–88, 390;
Washington, G., and, 340–41; on
whiskey excise, 267–68
Gates, Horatio, 124–25, 128
Gazette of the United States, 272
Geithner, Timothy, 423
Genet, Edmond Charles, 308
Gerry, Elbridge, 26, 182–84, 187,
197
Gilder, Richard, 418–19
Giles, William, 380, 384
Girard, Stephen, 383, 388–89
Godwin, William, 293
gold and silver coins: as currency, 32,
51; U.S. Public Debt and, 64
gold mining, 242
gold standard, abandonment of, 112
Goldwater, Barry, 417
Gordon-Reed, Annette, 418
Gorham, Nathaniel, 175

government bonds, see bonds
Grant, Ulysses S., 406
Granville, Lord, 80–81
Great Awakening, 74, 81, 443n;
American Revolution and, 72;
Calvinism and, 71–72; Husband,
H., and, 71
Great Britain, see Britain; British
Empire
Great Society, 10
Greene, Nathanael, 125, 140
Griswold v. Connecticut, 10

Haiti (St. Domingue), rebellion in,
348
Hamilton, Alexander: Adams, J.,
hatred of, 349–50; in antislavery
movement, 22; apprenticeship
at Beekman and Cruger, 16–18;
approach to democracy, 7–8; Bank
of North America and, 47, 49;
birthplace of, 13; as colonial citizen
of British Empire, 13; consolidation
of public and private finance,
7–8; departure from Continental
Congress, 137; on domestic public
debt, 60; early life, 15–16; election
to Congress, 120; on eradication
of state governments, 179; The
Federalist Papers, 193, 243–44,
336, 340; Hume as influence on,
24; Husband, H., and, 260–61;
Jefferson as political opponent of,
7; Madison as political opponent
of, 8, 124–26, 214–16; marriage of,
21–23; Morris, R., as mentor to,
6, 28, 44, 120–21; move to New
York, 18–19; Necker as influence
on, 24, 55; New York Post, 367;
ownership of enslaved persons, 7;
political goals of, 7–8; political
legacy of, 5, 396; on Public Debt,
65–66, 200; public perception of,

4–5; relationship with Washington,
G., 20–21, 27–28; report on public
credit, 279; on Republicanism,
181–82; retirement from Treasury
Department, 311–12; revenue plan
for, 210; revival of public profile,
410–11, 416–21; statues of, 395–96;
support of Continentalism, 129,
164; taxation policies, 200–201,
209; trade career for, 17–18; on
U.S. capital location, 206; Walpole,
R., as influence on, 24, 55, 208,
212; Washington and, 126–27;
see also Bank of North America;
specific topics
Hamilton, Daniel, 275, 302, 310
Hamilton, Elizabeth (née Schuyler),
21–23
Hamilton, James (father of A.
Hamilton), 13–14, 431n, 490n
Hamilton, James (son of A.
Hamilton), 401, 408
Hamilton, James, Jr. (brother of A.
Hamilton), 15, 401, 408
Hamilton, John, 275, 299–300, 310,
323
Hamilton, Paul, 386
Hamilton, Rachel, 15–16
Hamilton: An American Musical, 4,
426–28
Hamiltonianism, 301; political struggle
for, 5; U.S. Constitution influenced
by, 5, 175–94
Hamilton Scheme: assumption
element of, 217–18; conceptual
approach to, 3–4; foundations
of, 172; Jackson, J., criticism of,
212–15, 226; Jefferson critique
of, 259–60; Jefferson's attempted
dismantling of, 360–61; legislative
adoption of, 290; Madison critique
of, 259–60; opposition to, 212–14;
political disputes over, 4; purpose
of, 231; state debt in, 218; success

of, 327; U.S. Constitution in,
175–94, 246; *see also specific topics*
Hancock, John, 38–39
Harding, Warren, 395–96
hard money, 32, 46, 106, 436n, 441n,
452n; scarcity of, 285–86
Hemings, Sally, 418
Henry, Patrick, 26; as Antifederalist,
243–44
Holland, funding of American War of
Independence, 56–57
Homestead Act of 1862, U.S., 406
Hoover, Herbert, 396
House of Commons, in Britain, 178
House of Lords, in Britain, 178
House of Representatives, *see*
Congress, U.S.
Howell, David, 26, 118–19, 448n
Howell, Rednap, 87
Hume, David, 24, 229
Husband, Emy, 147, 325
Husband, Herman, 319–20, 425,
443n; aliases and pseudonyms of,
69; on American Revolution, 104;
Antifederalists and, 254; anti-
slavery stance of, 80; arrests of, 86,
311; Battle of Alamance and, 88,
102; Book of Daniel and, 69–70,
76, 82, 146; Book of Ezekiel and,
82–83, 146, 252; Book of Genesis
and, 83; Book of Matthew and, 82;
Book of Nehemiah and, 83; Book of
Revelation and, 71, 78; Calvinism
and, 71; and code of nonviolence,
75; disappearance of, 112; as
enemy of Washington, G., 9–10,
148, 251; on equality for women,
75; folk-hero status of, 86–87; on
freedom of conscience, 75, 80;
Gallatin compared to, 268, 335;
and government based on biblical
principles, 106, 406; Granville and,
80–81; Great Awakening and, 71;
Hamilton, A., and, 70, 260–61;

imprisonment of, 325; marriage
of, 76; on Millennial America,
104, 253; Morris, R., opposition
to, 106–107; New Birth for, 71; on
new government structure, 251–62;
nonviolent principles of, 85, 87–88;
in North Carolina, 76, 80, 151; in
Pennsylvania, 102–103; popularity
of, 253; regulators and, 83–87, 105,
261; response to Constitutional
Convention, 251; return to
Pennsylvania, 102–103; sedition
charges and trial, 327, 334; Society
of Friends and, 75–76, 81, 86; Song
of Songs, 81; visions and prophecies
of, 9–10, 69–70, 145, 147, 317–18;
on War of Independence as
spiritual force for change, 104, 252

import duties (imposts): under
Articles of Confederation, 133;
federal amendment for, 117–19;
federal taxes and, 184; Madison's
opposition to, 116; Morris, G.,
support for, 114–15; Morris, R.,
support for, 116, 119, 126; new,
238–39; passage of, 114, 279–80;
across state lines, 116–17; state
opposition to, 114, 116–19,
133–34; tonnage duties, 201
import taxes, 385–86
imposts, *see* import duties
impressment, 61–62
indents, 202; bondholders and, 207;
funding of, 204; holders of, 207
indentured labor, 77–78
Indian Removal Act, U.S. (1830), 402
industrialization: promotion of, 7; of
whiskey production, 233–34
industrial-scale agriculture, 229
Industrial Workers of the World, 10, 412
infrastructure, *see* public infrastructure
projects

internal taxes, repeal of, 360
IOUs: for Public Debt, 208; for state
    debt, 62

Jackson, Andrew, 393; anti-
    Hamiltonianism of, 408; criticism
    of Jefferson, 399; Democratic Party
    and, 402; Hamilton, J. and, 401,
    408; and Indian Removal Act, 402;
    and industrialization of labor force,
    403; labor strikes and, 404–405;
    opposition to moneyed classes,
    400; populist policies, 400–401;
    presidency of, 400–402; and Public
    Debt, 401; and slavery policies,
    401–402; Specie Circular Act of
    1836, 404; and White male suffrage
    rights, 400
Jackson, James, 212–15, 226, 243
Jay, John, 138, 192–93, 284, 355;
    Treaty of Amity, Commerce, and
    Navigation, 338–40
Jefferson, Thomas, 283–84, 411,
    415–16; attempted dismantling of
    Hamilton Scheme, 360–61; critique
    of Hamilton Scheme, 259–60; in
    1800 presidential election, 352–57;
    Embargo Act of 1807, 374–78;
    Gallatin and, 340, 344, 345–46,
    356–57, 359–73; Hamilton, A.,
    political opponent of, 7; Jackson,
    A., criticism of, 399; Leopard
    maritime conflict, 373; Louisiana
    Territory purchase, 367–68;
    ownership of enslaved persons, 7;
    Paine and, 326–27; and Public Debt
    policy, 362–63, 371; reassessment
    of historical legacy, 417–18; repeal
    of internal taxes, 360; Republican
    Party and, 260, 289; resignation from
    Washington administration, 308;
    response to Alien and Sedition Acts,
    351; return from France, 221; sales of

public land under, 363; as secretary
    of state, 221; support for agrarian
    society, 8; taxation policies, 362;
    and Treasury Department overhaul,
    360–61; on white working class, 8
Jefferson and Hamilton (Bowers), 413
Jeffersonianism, 335
Johnson, Lyndon, 416
judicial branch, under U.S.
    Constitution, 190

Kennedy, John F., 416
Kentucky, as new state, 346
Kickapoo Nation, 150
Kimmel, Edward, 414
King, Martin Luther, Jr., 416
Knox, Henry, 121–22, 127–28, 180,
    315; approach to federal debt,
    129–30; Duer and, 281; as secretary
    of war, 167–68; Washington, G.,
    and, 167–68
Kristol, William, 418

labor: agitation of, 84; in Atlantic
    world, 8; in Caribbean world,
    8; child, 232–33; Congress of
    Industrial Organizations, 412;
    indentured, 77–78; industrialization
    of, 403; Industrial Workers of the
    World, 412; landless laborers, 230;
    organization of, 412; women in
    labor force, 232, 403–404
labor movement, 6; see also white
    working class
labor strikes, 404–405
Lafayette, Marquis de, 294, 344, 427
land bubble, 358
land grants, in American West, 150
landless laborers, whiskey production
    and, 230
landlords, as investors in Public Debt,
    78

land squatters, in American West,
    155–59, 163
land taxes, 276
Lansing, John, 176, 180
Laurens, Henry, 41
Lee, Arthur, 39–41, 124
Lee, Henry, 203, 320–21
Lee, Richard Henry, 26, 97, 98
Lee, William, 39–41
Lehrman, Lewis, 418
L'Enfant, Pierre, 278
Lenox, David, 313–14
Leopard maritime conflict, between
    U.S. and Britain, 373
Levellers sect, 72–75, 97, 99
levelling, 90
Lewis, Meriwether, 369
Lincoln, Abraham, 406, 416
London Corresponding Society, 293
Louisiana Territory: purchase of
    367–70; removal of Native nations
    peoples from, 368–69
Louis XVI (King), 24, 293

Maclay, William, 206, 222
Madison, James: on Bank of the North
    America, 243; on Bank of the
    United States, 243–44; Clinton,
    G., as political enemy of, 26, 383;
    criticism of whiskey excise, 240;
    critique of Hamilton Scheme,
    259–60; discrimination amendment,
    214–16; The Federalist Papers,
    193, 243–44, 336, 340; Gallatin
    and, 340; Hamilton, A., political
    opposition to, 8, 124–26, 214–16;
    Monroe and, 383; Non-Intercourse
    Act and, 378; opposition to Bank of
    North America, 115; opposition to
    imposts, 116; as president, 377–93;
    Republican Party and, 260; response
    to Alien and Sedition Acts, 351;
    Second Bank of the United States

and, 390–91; as secretary of state,
    362; on slavery in U.S. constitution,
    186; succession to presidency, 331;
    on taxation policies, 200–201; war
    pressures on, 383–84
Magna Carta, 73
Malone, Dumas, 418
Marat, Jean-Paul, 306–307
Marie Antoinette (Queen), 294
Marshall, Christopher, 94–95, 100,
    108, 139, 425, 453n
Marx, Karl, 407
Massachusetts: banks in, 239; bond
    trading in, 166; constitutional
    amendments against noncitizens,
    351; repeal of taxes in, 169;
    Shaysites Rebellion in, 167–70,
    182, 184, 220, 425, 450n; state debt
    in, 217–18; state militia in, 167
Matlack, Timothy, 94, 97, 100, 139–40
McDonald, Forrest, 417
Mellon, Andrew, 396, 410–11, 490n
merchant class: as investors in Public
    Debt, 78; in Philadelphia, 30–31
merchant-crony Continentalism, 282
Miami Nation, 20; in Northwest
    Territory, 150, 257
micro-industrialization, of whiskey
    production, 230–31
military appropriations: by Gallatin,
    343, 366, 378; for War of 1812,
    386–88, 390
militias, see state militias
Millers Run, 155–56, 158–59, 309;
    eviction of farmers, 274
Mingo Creek Association, 299–300,
    310–11, 479n; takeover of local
    militia, 334; Treasury Department
    and, 313
Mingo Creek radicals, 274–75, 298–99;
    attack on Faulkner, 302–303, 479n;
    Hamilton family and, 310; military
    response to, 313–21; Whiskey
    Rebellion, 313–21, 460n

Miranda, Lin-Manuel, 426–27
Mitchell, Broadus, 417
Mnuchin, Steven, 426
modern monetary theory, 10
Money Connection: Continentalism
and, 54; Public Debt and, 65
monopolies: by corporations, 260;
Sherman Anti-Trust Act, 409–10;
SUM and, 277
Monroe, James, 290, 326, 367–68,
383, 398
Morgan, J. P., 409, 490n
Morris, Gouverneur, 137, 294, 324;
Bank of North America and, 115;
at Constitutional Convention,
448n; at Continental Congress,
176; revival of Continentalism,
164; on state sovereignty, 187
Morris, Robert, 222, 224, 244, 429,
441n; arrival in colonial America,
29–30; Bank of North America
and, 159–60; in Congress, 35,
41–42, 104, 113; critics of, 40–41,
120–21; on domestic public debt,
60–61; early life of, 29–30; electoral
losses of, 110; end of imprisonment
of, 358; Findley as opponent
of, 276, 425; funding of War of
Independence, 56–57; Hamilton,
A., mentored by, 6, 28, 44, 120–21;
imprisonment for debt, 359;
investigation of, 108–109; as leader
of investing class, 84; on location
of U.S. capital, 219; marriage of,
33; on new American wealth, 44,
50; in Office of Finance, 46, 117,
120; opposition to Husband, H.,
106–107; ownership of undeveloped
land, 358; pacifism of, 85; Paine
and, 143; Pennsylvania state
constitution and, 140; personal
wealth of, 50; as political leader,
37–38; as pro-banking advocate,
245–46; as reconciliationist, 35,

38, 96; rise to power, 29–31; on
role of federal projects, 54; in
Senate, 196, 201, 222, 224–25, 242,
245–46; on state debt, 61; support
for federal tax, 171; support for
Continentalism, 129, 164; support
for imposts, 116, 119, 126; on
U.S. Public Debt, 55–56, 60–61;
Washington, G., and, 143; see also
Bank of North America
Morris, Thomas, 40
Muggletonian sect, 72
Mumpton, Ian, 433n

Napoleonic Wars, 373
National Bank, 397
National Banking Act of 1863, U.S.,
408
national industrialization, see
industrialization
Native nations and tribes:
confederation of, 150; under Indian
Removal Act, 402; removal from
Louisiana Territory, 368–69; see also
specific nations
Necker, Jacques, 197, 208, 229,
264, 428; on governmental role
of finance administrator, 42;
Hamilton, A., influenced by, 24,
55; on public debt, 63
Neville, John, 258–59, 261–62,
311
Nevis, 13–14
New Deal, 10
New Deal policies, 411–12, 414; Social
Security Administration, 413
New England: Shaysites rebellion in,
167, 169–70, 182, 184; unification
of, 450n; see also specific states
New Hampshire: paper currency in,
168; state militia in, 168
New Model Army, 96–97
Newton, Isaac, 69

New York: evacuation of, 144;
  interstate investing in, 201;
  ratification of U.S. Constitution,
  192–93; state-oriented payoff
  policies in, 169; support for U.S.
  capital, 221; trade with China, 201
New York City, as U.S. capital, 206,
  218–19
New-York Historical Society, 398, 418,
  419
New York Post, 367
Nicholson, Hannah, 317
Non-Intercourse Act, U.S., 378
North Carolina: Battle of Alamance,
  88, 91, 102, 110, 261; federal
  compensation for, 225; Great
  Indian Trading Path in, 80; Great
  Wagon Road in, 80; Husband, H.,
  move to, 76, 80, 151; invasion of,
  305, 315–16; proprietorships in,
  87; regulators in, 83–87, 105, 261;
  resistance to colonial trade acts in,
  87–88
Northwest Territory: development of,
  231–32; land sales in, 346; Native
  nations in, 150, 257; opening to
  white settlement, 280; slavery
  outlawed in, 257; surveying teams
  for, 168; U.S. troops in, 298–99; war
  for conquest of, 281; see also Ohio
  Territory

Obama, Barack, 423, 490n
O'Brien, Conor Cruise, 417
Occupy Wall Street Movement, 424–25
Ohio, as new state, 372
Ohio Territory: Fort Pitt, 236; Millers
  Run, 155–56, 158–59, 274
Orszag, Peter, 423

Pack, Michael, 419
Page, John, 197, 212

Paine, Thomas, 9, 91, 139, 414,
  425; The Age of Reason, 326;
  The American Crisis, 141–43; on
  American Revolution, 144; anti-
  slavery beliefs of, 92–93; arrest
  of, 297–98; bridge construction
  projects, 293; Burke, E., and,
  294–95; "Common Sense,"
  100–101, 111, 140, 143, 256, 292;
  French Enlightenment as influence
  on, 92; imprisonment of, 305–306,
  324, 326; Jefferson and, 326–27;
  London Corresponding Society
  and, 293; Morris, R., and, 143;
  opposition to merchant-crony
  Continentalism, 282; on paper
  currencies, 144; in Philadelphia,
  93; philosophical influences of, 92;
  as pro-bank advocate, 161–62; as
  radical, 93; on representative system
  in Congress, 188; Society of Honest
  Whigs and, 92; Washington, G.,
  and, 140–41, 143, 295–96, 326
paper currency: in American
  West, 159; the Democracy and,
  105; national, 254–55; in New
  Hampshire, 168; Paine's opposition
  to, 144; in U.S. Constitution, 191
paper scrip, 247; Bank of New York
  and, 273; economic bubble for,
  271–72; market value for, 270–71;
  sell-offs of, 273
Parish, David, 388–89
Parkinson, Benjamin, 275, 299, 302,
  314, 321
Pasha of Tripoli, 365–66
Paterson, William, 277
Paulson, Henry, 420
Penn, William, 31, 98
Pennsylvania: Adams, J., and, 165;
  Bank of North America chartered
  in, 138; Committee of Privates in,
  96, 98, 109, 300; constitution of,
  101–102, 140, 145, 166, 256, 265,

Pennsylvania (*cont.*)
266, 300; democracy in,
169; democratic government
in, 139–40; Federalists in, 218;
Husband, H., in, 102–103;
issuance of bonds in, 162–63;
Mingo Creek Association in,
299–301; Mingo Creek radicals
in, 274–75, 298; mobocracy
in, 140; Morris, R., in state
legislature, 41–42; ratification
of U.S. Constitution, 193–94;
Reconciliationists in, 96–97;
revision of state constitution,
256, 266, 300; support for imposts,
118; support for U.S. capital,
221; violence against federal
government in, 303–304; war debt
for, 163; *see also* Philadelphia
Perkins, Frances, 412
Philadelphia, Pennsylvania:
Bank of the United States in,
245, 248; British occupation
of, 39; Congress move from,
136; Continental Congress in,
34–35; enslaved persons in, 31;
intellectual institutions in, 31;
merchant class in, 30–31; Morris,
R., in, 30, 97; Quakers and,
31; as temporary capital, 225;
Treasury Department in, 238;
United Company of Philadelphia
for Promoting American
Manufactures, 95; as U.S. capital,
218–19
Philadelphia Aurora, 380
Pickering, Timothy, 351
Pinckney, Charles, 346, 355
Pitt, William, 297
Pittsburgh Gazette, 301
populism, under Jackson, A.,
400–401
Potawatomie Nation, 150
Powers, John, 324

presidency, U.S.: Antifederalists
and, 195–96; term limits for, 344;
Washington, G., and, 195–96;
see also specific presidential elections;
specific presidents
price-fixers, 194
Princeton, New Jersey, 144
Progressive Party, 10
progressive taxes, 255
Public Debt, of U.S.: agrarian class
response to, 208; army-pay issue
as element of, 129; assumption of
state debts, 65–66, 216, 223–24;
Bank of North America and,
65; conceptual approach to, 5;
Continental Army and, 122–23;
domestic element of, 60, 199, 207,
209; federal tax and, 113; federal
taxation approaches to, 64–66;
under Gallatin, 390; gold and
silver coins and, 64; Hamilton, A.,
on, 65–66, 200; interest-bearing
government bonds and, 55–56;
IOUs for, 208; under Jackson,
A., 401; under Jefferson, 362–63,
371; Knox approach to, 129–30;
landlords' role in, 78; loss of
nationalizing power of, 113; under
Madison, 382; merchant class
role in, 78; Money Connection
and, 65; Morris, R., on, 55–56,
60–61; Necker on, 63; as public
obligation, 65; single-payer
structure for, 65; state, 61–63;
state-by-state approach to, 56;
State Sovereigntists and, 48;
valuation of, 207; Walpole, R.,
on, 63
public domain, 143
public finance, consolidation of private
finance and, 7–8
public infrastructure projects: Bank of
the United States loans for, 242;
Duer and, 281; for Gallatin,

372–73, 376; interstate, 229; of
Paine, 293; schemes for, 280–81
public lands: sales of, 363; western
expansion on, 363; see also
Louisiana Territory; Northwest
Territory; Ohio Territory
Publius, see Jay, John
Puritans, 72

Quakers (Society of Friends), 31, 72,
445n; Husband, H., and, 75–76,
81, 86

radicalism, party, 94–95, 100, 108;
leadership in relation to, 4; Paine
and, 93
Randolph, Edmund, 164–65, 187,
283–84, 303, 320; at Continental
Congress, 176–77; in Washington
cabinet, 316
Ranters sect, 72, 75
Reagan, Ronald, 418
rebellions, see riots and rebellions
Reconciliationists, 437n; in Congress,
97; in Pennsylvania, 96–97
Redstone Old Fort resolutions, 269,
274, 276, 288
Reed, Joseph, 109–11
regulators: Battle of Alamance and,
88, 91; Husband, H., and, 83–87,
105, 261
republicanism: Continental Congress
and, 181; Hamilton, A., critique
of, 181–82; on national scale,
181
Republican Party: company bounties
and, 289–90; congressional
majority for, 335; Federalists in
opposition to, 260; formation of,
260, 269; Gallatin in, 316–17;
Jefferson and, 260, 289, 308;
Madison and, 260

Rhode Island: child labor workforce in,
233; democracy in, 163; opposition
to imposts, 118–19, 133
Ridge, John, 397
Rights of Man (Burke, E.), 295–96
riots and rebellions: in American
Atlantic colonies, 85; in Haiti,
348; see also regulators; Shaysites
Rebellion; Whiskey Rebellion
Robespierre, Maximilien, 306, 324–26
Roosevelt, Franklin Delano, 411–14,
490n
Roosevelt, Teddy, 409–10, 490n
Rousseau, Jean-Jacques, 264
Rubin, Robert, 420
Rush, Benjamin, 94, 97, 139–40, 142,
449n

Schuyler, Catherine Van Rensselaer, 21
Schuyler, Philip, 222, 224, 433n; as
Continentalist, 25, 52; federal
taxation policies and, 117–18;
interest in American West, 148–49;
as owner of enslaved persons,
21–22; as pro-banking advocate,
245–46; profiteering during War of
Independence, 22; in Senate, 204;
Six Nations of the Iroquois, 22
Scott, Thomas, 197
scrip, for Bank of the United States,
281; see also paper scrip
Seceders, 156
Second Bank of the United States,
390–91, 397, 399
Securities and Exchange Commission,
10
Sedgwick, Theodore, 211, 220, 244
sedition, 126; Husband, H., charges
and trial of, 327, 334
Senate, U.S.: Federalist Party majority
in, 335, 338; Morris, R., in, 196;
support for centralized banking
system, 242–43

1796 presidential election: Adams, J., electoral win for, 345–46; Federalist Party during, 345–46
Seven Years' War, 20–21, 156
Shawnee Nation, 9, 20; in Northwest Territory, 150, 257; War of Independence and, 112
Shays, Daniel, 167, 182
Shaysites Rebellion, 167–68, 182, 184, 220, 425, 387, 442n, 450n.461n; Society of the Cincinnati and, 169–70
Sherman, William Tecumseh, 406
Sherman Anti-Trust Act, U.S. (1890), 409–10
Siciliano, Angelo, see Atlas, Charles
silver coins, see gold and silver coins
silver mining, 242
Six Nations of the Iroquois, 22
Six Percent Club, 281–82
skeptical Federalists, 217
Slater, Samuel, 233
slavery, slave trade and: abolition of, 254; Calhoun on, 401–402, 404; under Jackson, A., 401–402; merchant class participation in, 31; moral arguments over, 183; in Northwest Territory, 257; state populations and, 186–88; sugar industry and, 14; taxation policies and, 186; white supremacist theory of, 401–402, 404; see also enslaved persons
Smilie, John, 159
Smith, Robert, 362, 365–66, 374
Smith, Samuel, 365–66
Smith, William, 211–12
Society for Establishing Useful Manufactures (SUM), 272; Bank of New York and, 277; Duer and, 270, 277, 289; financing of, 274; as monopoly, 277; success of, 277
Society of Friends, see Quakers
Society of Honest Whigs, 92

Society of the Cincinnati, 138; hereditary membership in, 130–31; Shaysites Rebellion quelled by, 169–70; Washington, G., on, 130–31
Song of Songs, 81
the South, industrialization in, 232; see also slavery
South Carolina, rice production in, 41
Spain: funding of American War of Independence, 56; negotiations with Cherokee Nation, 304; negotiations with Creek Nation, 304; silver dollar currency, 32
Spanish silver dollar, 32
Specie Circular Act of 1836, U.S., 404
Stamp Act, colonial protests against, 34
state constitution: Pennsylvania, 101–102, 140, 145, 166, 265, 266, 300
state currencies, 52
state debt: army-pay papers and, 63; components of, 61; congressional assumption of, 65–66, 216, 223–24; Continental Army and, 61–62; in Hamilton Scheme, 218; impressments and, 61–62; interest as part of, 63; IOUs for, 62; in Massachusetts, 217–18; Morris, R., and, 61; in Virginia, 216–17
state legislatures, states and: Hamilton, A., on eradication of, 179; limitations of authority for, 183; presidential electors selected by, 252; state militias controlled by, 134–35; see also specific states
state militias: in Massachusetts, 167; Mingo Creek Association and, 299–300, 334; in New Hampshire, 168; state legislatures in control of, 134–35
State Sovereigntism, State Sovereigntists and, 90; agrarians and, 214–15; American West and, 150, 163;

attacks on, 177; banking systems and, 48; at Continental Congress, 176–77; definition of, 434n; erosion of, 111; fear of professional armies, 184; federal taxes and, 113; indivisibility of, 181; U.S. Public Debt and, 48, 55; War of Independence and, 26; *see also specific people*

state sovereignty, 187; *see also* state legislatures; *specific topics*

St. Domingue, *see* Haiti

Stone, Michael Jenifer, 213

sugar industry, 13–14

SUM, *see* Society for Establishing Useful Manufactures

Summers, Lawrence, 423

Synopsis of the Indian Tribes of North America (Ridge), 397

Table of Indian Languages of the United States, A (Ridge), 397

TARP, *see* Toxic Assets Recovery Program

taxation policies: consent and, 185; direct, 190–91, 348–49, 464n; federal, 209; federal impost as wedge, 443n; Gallatin on, 341–42; Hamilton, A., on, 200–201, 209; import, 385–86; on income, 408; under Jefferson, 362; for land ownership, 276; Madison, J., on, 200–201; in Massachusetts, 169; in newly formed U.S., 187–88; progressive, 255; for Public Debt, 64–66; repeal of internal taxes, 360; slavery and, 186; in U.S. Constitution, 190–91; for whiskey production, 234–35; *see also* excise taxes; federal taxation

tax collection, tax officers and, 50–51; for federal taxes, 125; by state, 53

taxes: import, 385–86; internal, 360; land, 276; Massachusetts repeal of,

360; Morris, R., support for federal taxes, 171; progressive taxes, 255; whiskey production, 234–35; *see also* excise taxes; federal taxation

the Terror, 306, 322, 326

Thoreau, Henry David, 403

three-fifths compromise, in U.S. Constitution, 189–90

tonnage duties, 201

top-down Continentalism, 135

Toxic Assets Recovery Program (TARP), 424

Treasury Department, U.S.: creation of, 197; final settlement, 198–99; Gallatin at, 360–62; Hamilton, A., and, retirement from, 311–12; under Jefferson, 360–61; Mingo Creek Association and, 313; in Philadelphia, 238

Treaty of Amity, Commerce, and Navigation (Jay Treaty), 338, 342; Federalist response to, 339–40; French response to, 347; funding of, 340

Treaty of Ghent, 392, 397

Trollope, Anthony, 403

Trump, Donald, 419

Tryon, William, 87–88

United Company of Philadelphia for Promoting American Manufactures, 95

United States (U.S.): Alien and Sedition Acts, 350–51; American Recovery and Reinvestment Act, 423; cession of western lands by Britain, 149; creation as consolidated union, 187–88; declaration of war with Britain, 374; declaration of war with France, 374; early banking system in, 48–49; Embargo Act of 1807, 374–78, 488n; Federal Reserve Act,

United States (U.S.) (*cont.*)
410; gold and silver mining in,
242; Homestead Act of 1862, 406;
Indian Removal Act, 402; as major
stockholder for Bank of the United
States, 241; National Banking
Act of 1863, 408; national taxing
power of, 187–88; Non-Intercourse
Act, 378; Sherman Anti-Trust
Act, 409–10; Specie Circular Act
of 1836, 404; treaty-in-principle
with Britain, 120, 122; Treaty of
Amity, Commerce, and Navigation,
338–40, 342; War of 1812, 386–88,
390, 392, 397; *see also* American
Revolution; American West;
Articles of Confederation;
Constitution, U.S.; Public Debt, of
U.S.; War of Independence; *specific
states*; *specific topics*
U.S. Post Office, 314; establishment
of, 208

Vermont, as new state, 346
Vindication of the Rights of Woman, A
(Wollestonecraft), 295
Virginia: federal compensation for,
225; state debt in, 216–17, 225;
support for imposts, 118; water-
navigation issues for, 164
Voltaire, 93, 264, 340
voting rights: in American colonies,
79; for white males, 400

Wabash Nation, 150
Walpole, Horace, 24
Walpole, Robert, 229; Hamilton, A.,
influenced by, 24, 55, 208, 212;
on Public Debt, 63; war bond system,
57
war bonds, Continental currency and,
57–59

War of 1812, 386; aftermath of, 390;
federal revenues for, 387–88; Treaty
of Ghent and, 392, 397
War of Independence, 433n;
American Revolution and, 22;
army-pay papers and, 63, 122;
Bank of New York and, 52; Bank
of North America and, 52; Battle
of Alamance, 88, 91, 102, 110;
Battle of Concord, 35; Battle of
Fort Wilson, 110, 112; Battle of
Lexington, 35; Battle of Saratoga,
107; Battle of Yorktown, 49,
59, 315; Berkshires farmers and,
166–67; Continental Congress role
in, 56–59; Continental currency
during, 57–59; costs of, 59; Dutch
support of, 56–57; French support
of, 56, 107; funding of, 56–59;
Husband, H., on, 104; interstate
nature of, 43; negative economic
effects of, 22; profiteering during,
22; secondary funding markets for,
60, 441n; Shawnee Nation role
in, 112; Spanish support of, 56; as
spiritual force for change, 104, 252;
State Sovereigntists and, 26;
treaty-in-principle with Britain,
120, 122; war bonds for, 57
Washington, D.C., as U.S. capital:
construction of, 248; during 1800
election, 353–54; fire damage
in, 388; negotiations over, 225;
New York state support for, 219;
Pennsylvania support for, 219;
Potomac estuary site, 219
Washington, George: attitude
toward French Revolution, 294;
Continental Army under, 19–20,
36–37; at Continental Congress,
176; as Continentalist, 115;
decision to leave presidency, 344; as
delegate to Continental Congress,
35; Gallatin and, 340; Hamilton,

A., and, 126–27; Husband, H.,
and, 9–10, 148; Knox and, 167–68;
land claims in American West,
148–49, 152, 157; limited military
experience of, 20; Morris, R., and,
143; national banking bill under,
245; Paine and, 140–41, 143,
295–96, 326; Potomac estuary site,
219; relationship with Hamilton,
A., 20–21, 27–28; reputation as
military leader, 142; on Society of
the Cincinnati, 130–31
Washington County Democratic
Society, 308–309, 311
Wayne, Anthony, 320
Westsylvania, 153–54, 157, 253
wheat prices, 285
whiskey, excise on, 209–10, 223, 232,
237–38, 261–62; Findley opposition
to, 287–88, 301, 312, 319–22;
Gallatin on, 267–68; Madison on,
240; repeal of, 301–302; revision of,
287; Whiskey Rebellion, 313–21,
460n
Whiskey Rebellion, 313–21, 460n
White, Mary, 33
Whitehill, Robert, 158–59, 162,
193–94, 425

white supremacy, slavery and, 401–402,
404
Willing, Thomas, 48, 345, 381
Wilson, James, 109, 115, 124, 137;
Bank of North America and,
159–60, 193; at Continental
Congress, 176; court appointment
of, 313; death of, 359; on direct
elections, 189–90; interest
in American West, 148–49;
ratification of U.S. Constitution,
115, 124, 181, 193, 256; revision
of Pennsylvania Constitution, 256,
266, 300
Wilson, Woodrow, 410, 415
Wolcott, Oliver, 335, 338, 342, 348,
363
Wollestonecraft, Mary, 293, 294, 295,
352
women: equality for, 75; in labor force,
232, 403–404
Wright, Rachel, 76–77
Wyandot Nation, 150

Yates, Robert, 176, 180
Young, Thomas, 93–94, 96–97, 100,
139, 300, 406, 425

A Note About the Author

William Hogeland is the author of several books about the founding period, including *Autumn of the Black Snake, Declaration*, and *The Whiskey Rebellion*, as well as the essay collections *Founding Finance* and *Inventing American History*. He has been a contributor to *The New Republic, Boston Review, Lapham's Quarterly*, and other magazines, and he publishes "Hogeland's Bad History" on Substack.